Volume 1: To 1789

Western Civilization
Ideas, Politics, and Society

Tenth Edition

Marvin Perry
Baruch College, City University of New York

Myrna Chase
Baruch College, City University of New York

James R. Jacob
John Jay College of Criminal Justice, City University of New York

Margaret C. Jacob
University of California, Los Angeles

Theodore H. Von Laue
Late of *Clark University*

George W. Bock, *Editorial Associate*

WADSWORTH
CENGAGE Learning™

Australia • Brazil • Japan • Korea • Mexico • Singapore • Spain • United Kingdom • United States

WADSWORTH
CENGAGE Learning

Western Civilization: Ideas, Politics, and Society, Volume 1: To 1789, **Tenth Edition**
Marvin Perry, Myrna Chase, James R. Jacob, Margaret C. Jacob, Theodore H. Von Laue

Senior Publisher: Suzanne Jeans

Acquiring Sponsoring Editor: Brooke Barbier

Editorial Acquisitions Coordinator: Kimberly Taylo

Associate Editor: Adrienne Zicht

Editorial Assistant: Katie Coaster

Senior Media Editor: Lisa Ciccolo

Marketing Manager: Cynthia Barnes

Marketing Coordinator: Lorreen Towle

Marketing Communications Manager: Glenn McGibbon

Senior Content Project Manager: Jane Lee

Senior Art Director: Cate Rickard Barr

Manufacturing Planner: Sandra Milewski

Rights Acquisition Specialist, Image: Jennifer Meyer Dare

Rights Acquisition Specialist, Text: Shalice Shah-Caldwell

Production Service: PreMediaGlobal

Cover Designer: Tony Saizon

Cover Image: *Vincent de Beauvais Reading in His Study,* c. 1475–c. 1500. British Library London, Great Britain/HIP/Art Resource, N.Y.

Compositor: PreMediaGlobal

For product information and technology assistance, contact us at **Cengage Learning Customer & Sales Support, 1-800-354-9706**

For permission to use material from this text or product, submit all requests online at **www.cengage.com/permissions.** Further permissions questions can be emailed to **permissionrequest@cengage.com**

Library of Congress Control Number: 2011935445

Student Edition:

ISBN-13: 978-1-111-83170-7

ISBN-10: 1-111-83170-X

Wadsworth
20 Channel Center Street
Boston, MA 02210
U.S.A.

Cengage Learning is a leading provider of customized learning solutions with office locations around the globe, including Singapore, the United Kingdom, Australia, Mexico, Brazil, and Japan. Locate your local office at: **international.cengage.com/region**

Cengage Learning products are represented in Canada by Nelson Education, Ltd.

For your course and learning solutions, visit **www.cengage.com.**

Purchase any of our products at your local college store or at our preferred online store **www.cengagebrain.com.**

Instructors: Please visit **login.cengage.com** and log in to access instructor-specific resources.

Printed in the United States of America
1 2 3 4 5 6 7 15 14 13 12 11

Contents

Maps

Chronologies

Preface

Western civilization is a grand but tragic drama. The West has forged the instruments of reason that make possible a rational comprehension of physical nature and human culture, conceived the idea of political liberty, and recognized the intrinsic worth of the individual. But the modern West, though it has unraveled nature's mysteries, has been less successful at finding rational solutions to social ills and conflicts between nations. Science, the great achievement of the Western intellect, while improving conditions of life, has also produced weapons of mass destruction. Though the West has pioneered in the protection of human rights, it has also produced totalitarian regimes that have trampled on individual freedom and human dignity. Although the West has demonstrated a commitment to human equality, it has also practiced brutal racism.

Despite the value that Westerners have given to reason and freedom, they have shown a frightening capacity for irrational behavior and a fascination for violence and irrational ideologies, and they have willingly sacrificed liberty for security or national grandeur. The world wars and totalitarian movements of the twentieth century have demonstrated that Western civilization, despite its extraordinary achievements, is fragile and perishable. Yet the West has also shown the capacity to reassert its best values and traditions.

Western Civilization: Ideas, Politics, and Society examines the Western tradition—those unique patterns of thought and systems of values that constitute the Western heritage. While focusing on key ideas and broad themes, the text also provides a balanced treatment of economic, political, and social history for students in Western civilization courses.

The text is written with the conviction that history possesses profound meaning. Without a knowledge of history, men and women cannot fully know themselves, for all human beings have been shaped by institutions and values inherited from the past. Without an awareness of the historical evolution of reason and freedom, the dominant ideals of Western civilization, commitment to these ideals will diminish. Without knowledge of history, the West cannot fully comprehend or adequately cope with the problems that burden its civilization and the world.

In attempting to make sense out of the past, the authors have been careful to avoid superficial generalizations that oversimplify historical events and arrange history into too neat a structure. But they do strive to interpret and to synthesize in order to provide students with a frame of reference with which to comprehend the principal events and eras in Western history.

CHANGES IN THE TENTH EDITION

For the tenth edition, every chapter has been reworked to some extent. The hundreds of carefully selected modifications and additions significantly enhance the text. Some changes deepen the book's conceptual character while others provide useful and illustrative historical detail. In several chapters the concluding essays, which strive for meaning and significance, have been enlarged and improved. We have been particularly careful to strengthen chapters dealing with intellectual history, the text's distinguishing feature. Each chapter continues to contain a profile of a significant historical figure. The most significant addition in the previous edition was the insertion in every chapter of a primary source that illuminates the narrative. These primary sources are retained in the tenth edition, and we have added questions for analysis of the documents. The Geography of Europe essay at the beginning of the book has been updated. In order to strengthen the organization of the book, we have combined two chapters of the previous edition, reducing the total number of chapters from thirty-four to thirty-three.

In Chapter 1, "The Ancient Near East," we introduced Sargon's daughter, Enheduanna, the world's oldest known poet. The sections dealing with Egypt now contain a discussion of Egyptian literature and Rameses II. In Chapter 2, "The Hebrews," we expanded the discussion of Hebrew law and strengthened the concluding section, "The Legacy of the Ancient Jews." Several short insertions strengthen and clarify the narrative in both Chapters 3 and 4—"The Greek City-State" and "Greek Thought." A section on women has been inserted in Chapter 5, "The Hellenistic Age." The most notable changes in Chapter 6, "The Roman Republic," are fuller discussions of the battle of Cannae, the Roman response to the disaster, and the military accomplishments of Julius Caesar. In Chapter 7, "The Roman Empire," we have strengthened the sections on Pax Romana and the problems of the Late Roman Empire. Chapter 8, "Early Christianity," now includes the views of Early Christian theorists towards various sexual concerns. The most noteworthy additions to Chapter 9, "The Heirs of Rome," are expanded discussions of the iconoclast struggle in Byzantium, the Islamic concept of jihad, Muslim acquisition of Greek learning, and the waning of classical culture in the West. In Chapter 10, "The High Middle Ages," more attention is given to the revival of trade and the extermination of the Cathars. Added to Chapter 11, "The Flowering of Medieval Culture," is a profile of Maimonides, medieval Judaism's most outstanding scholar. The treatment of the Black Death in Chapter 12, "The Late Middle Ages," has been expanded and upgraded.

In Chapter 13, "The Renaissance," a section has been added that explores the debt the European Renaissance owed to the Islamic civilization that developed in the Mediterranean beginning in the eighth century and that flourished in cities stretching from Baghdad and Cairo in the Near East to Cordoba in Moorish Spain. Chapter 14, "The Reformation," introduces the most recent thinking on the Reformation, and in particular the role of the major reformers, and continues its coverage into Eastern Europe. Chapter 15, "European Expansion," adds to the discussion of the preconditions within Europe for global overseas expansion in the fifteenth and sixteenth centuries. Chapter 16, "The Rise of Sovereignty," lays more emphasis on institutions of state and continues an emphasis upon the Dutch Republic, traditionally left out of most accounts of the building of the nation-state. Chapter 17, "The Scientific Revolution," supplies new perspectives on alchemy and its contribution to the formation of a new understanding of nature. It addresses the relationship between the new science and the Industrial Revolution that began late in the eighteenth century. Chapter 18, "The Age of Enlightenment," puts more stress on the importance of the book trade for making the new ideas accessible and internationally available and highlights what is now called the Radical Enlightenment.

For this edition we have combined the chapters on the French Revolution and Napoleon into one chapter. The new Chapter 19, "The French Revolution," contains additional material on the Terror in the Vendée; providing examples of the elements of total war in the Napoleonic wars enhances the end piece, "The Meaning of the French Revolution." In Chapter 20, "The Industrial Revolution," the discussion of the major social and economic changes resulting from industrialization and urbanization has been strengthened. A generation of scholarship tracing technological and entrepreneurial change together with the resulting impact on the lives of social and national groups has been incorporated. In Chapter 22, "Revolution and Counterrevolution," we have upgraded the treatment of both the Revolution of 1830 and the revolutions of 1848. Strengthening the section "Religion in a Secular Age" is the most significant change in Chapter 23, "Thought and Culture in the Mid-Nineteenth Century." The treatment of anti-Semitism has been improved in Chapter 24, "The Surge of Nationalism." In Chapter 25, "The Industrial West," we provide expanded treatment of the complex relationship between the advance of industry and the political developments in the major European powers and the United States up to the outbreak of the first World War. In Chapter 26, "Imperialism," we have improved the discussion of the expansionist program of Western states in terms of the impact it would have on their foreign and domestic policies as well as the impact it has had on political developments in the non-Western world. Also improved is the discussion of Freud's theory of human nature in Chapter 27, "Modern Consciousness."

The principal changes in Chapter 28, "World War I," are a telling example of the enthusiasm displayed in Germany when war broke out, a deeper analysis of Germany's last offensive, and some additional material on the problems of the Provisional Government in Russia. In Chapter 29, "An Era of Totalitarianism," we have expanded the treatment of the Russian Civil War and both Stalin's and Hitler's dictatorships. In Chapter 30, "Thought and Culture in an Era of World Wars and Totalitarianism," the section on Existentialism has been restructured and abridged, and a new profile on Albert Camus has been inserted. In Chapter 31, "World War II," several topics have been expanded and deepened, particularly the collapse of France in 1940, Germany's recovery and resilience in the months following its defeat in France in 1944, the Battle of the Bulge, and the Holocaust. Two significant improvements have been inserted in the concluding section, "The Legacy of World War II": new material on the significance of the war for women and a deeper discussion of the impact of the war on Western consciousness. Chapter 32, "Europe After World War II," has been significantly restructured, and greater attention is now given to both the origins and demise of the Cold War. In Chapter 33, "The Troubled Present," the coverage of Europe contains new material on Europe's current economic problems and a new section, "New and Old Threats: Muslim Immigration and the Resurgence of Anti-Semitism." The treatments of the wars in Afghanistan and Iraq and the threat from al Qaeda have been updated. Also added to the chapter are the revolts that rocked the Arab world in 2011.

The text represents the efforts of several authors. Marvin Perry, general editor of the project, wrote Chapters 1–12, 19, 21–24, 27–31, much of the new material in Chapters 32 and 33, and the Epilogue. James R. Jacob is the author of Chapters 13 and 15. Margaret C. Jacob wrote Chapters 14 and 16–18. Myrna Chase is the author of Chapters 20, 25, and 26. The late Theodore H. Von Laue wrote the sections on Russia and the Soviet Union in Chapters 28 and 29 and was largely responsible for Chapters 32 and 33. Since Von Laue's death in 2000, Marvin Perry has reworked the sections on the Russian Revolution in Chapter 28 and the Communist regime in Chapter 29 and Myrna Chase has revised the section on tsarist Russia in Chapter 26. For several editions Marvin Perry and Angela Von Laue have reworked substantially Chapters 32 and 33. I regret that Angela Von Laue, who had added her literary and research skills to the project after her husband's death, opted for a too-early retirement. I missed working with her on the tenth edition. Over the years Marvin Perry and George Bock have edited the manuscript for continuity and clarity.

DISTINCTIVE FEATURES

The text contains several pedagogical features. Chapter outlines and introductions provide comprehensive overviews of key themes and give a sense of direction and coherence to the flow of history. Many chapters contain concluding essays that treat the larger meaning of the material. Facts have been carefully selected to illustrate key relationships and concepts and to avoid overwhelming students with unrelated and disconnected data. Appropriate quotations, many not commonly found in texts, have been integrated into the discussion. Each chapter contains notes and an annotated bibliography. Each chapter also begins with focus questions to aid students' reading of the chapter. A glossary is provided online.

Western Civilization: Ideas, Politics, and Society is available in both one- and two-volume editions, and in a third edition, *From the 1400s*. *From the 1400s* (twenty-two chapters) has been prepared for those instructors whose courses begin with the Renaissance or the Reformation.

Volume I of the two-volume edition covers the period from the first civilizations in the Near East through the Age of Enlightenment in the eighteenth century (eighteen chapters). Volume II covers the period from the growth of national states in the seventeenth century to the contemporary age (nineteen chapters). Because some instructors start the second half of their course with the period prior to the French Revolution, Volume II incorporates the last three chapters of Volume I: "The Rise of Sovereignty," "The Scientific Revolution," and "The Age of Enlightenment." Volume II also contains a comprehensive introduction that surveys the ancient world, the Middle Ages, and the opening centuries of the modern era; the introduction is designed particularly for students who did not take the first half of the course. *From the 1400s* also contains an introduction that covers the ancient world and the Middle Ages.

ANCILLARIES

We are pleased to introduce an expanded ancillary package that will help students in learning and instructors in teaching.

Instructor's Resources

PowerLecture DVD with ExamView® and JoinIn®. An all-in-one multimedia resource for class preparation, presentation, and testing. The Instructor's Resource Manual, prepared by Jennifer Deane, includes instructional objectives, chapter outlines, lecture suggestions, group learning projects, analyzing primary sources, audiovisual bibliographies, suggested readings, and Internet resources. Microsoft® PowerPoint® slides of lecture outlines, as well as images and maps from the text, can be used as offered or customized by importing personal lecture slides or other material; JoinIn PowerPoint slides with clicker content are also provided. An image library contains .jpg images from the text. The test bank, prepared by Stephen Gibson, includes key term identification, multiple-choice, essay, and map questions. ExamView, an easy-to-use assessment and tutorial system, allows instructors to create, deliver, and customize tests in minutes. Instructors can build tests with as many as 250 questions using up to twelve question types. Using the complete word-processing capabilities of ExamView, instructors can enter an unlimited number of new questions or edit existing ones.

Companion Website. This website for instructors features all of the free student assets, plus an Instructor's Resource Manual (instructional objectives, chapter outlines, lecture suggestions, group learning projects, primary source analysis, audiovisual bibliographies, suggested readings, and Internet resources) and PowerPoint presentations (lecture outlines, images and maps, and JoinIn PowerPoint slides with clicker content). In addition, access to HistoryFinder, a searchable online database with thousands of assets, allows instructors to easily create exciting presentations for their classroom by downloading art, photographs, maps, primary sources, and audio/video clips directly into a Microsoft PowerPoint slide.

WebTutor™ on Blackboard® or WebCT®. With the WebTutor text-specific, preformatted content and total flexibility, instructors can easily create and manage their own custom course website. Instructors can provide virtual office hours, post syllabi, set up threaded discussions, track student progress with the quizzing material, and much more. For students, WebTutor offers real-time access to an interactive eBook and a full array of study tools, including animations and videos that bring the book's topics to life, plus chapter outlines, summaries, learning objectives, glossary flashcards (with audio), practice quizzes, and weblinks.

CourseMate. Cengage Learning's History CourseMate brings course concepts to life with interactive learning, study tools, and exam preparation tools that support the printed textbook. Use Engagement Tracker to monitor student engagement in the course and watch student comprehension soar as your class works with the printed textbook and the textbook-specific website. An interactive eBook allows students to take notes, highlight, search, and interact with embedded media (such as quizzes, flashcards, and videos). Access to the History Resource Center, a "virtual reader," provides students with hundreds of primary sources. Learn more at www.cengage.com/coursemate.

Wadsworth Western Civilization Resource Center. Wadsworth's Western Civilization Resource Center gives your students access to a "virtual reader" with hundreds of primary sources including speeches, letters, legal documents and transcripts, poems, maps, simulations, timelines, and additional images that bring history to life, along with interactive assignable exercises. A map feature including Google Earth™ coordinates and exercises will aid in student comprehension of geography and use of maps. Students can compare the traditional textbook map with an aerial view of the location today. It's an ideal resource for study, review, and research. In addition to this map feature, the resource center also provides blank maps for student review and testing.

CourseReader: Western Civilization This application is Cengage Learning's easy, affordable way to build your own online customizable reader. Through a partnership with Gale, *CourseReader: Western Civilization* searches thousands of primary and secondary sources, readings, and audio and video clips from multiple disciplines. Select exactly and only the material you want your students to work with. Each selection can be listened to (using the "Listen" button) to accommodate varied learning styles. Additionally, an instructor can choose to add his or her own notes to readings to direct students' attention or ask them questions about a particular passage. Each primary source is accompanied by an introduction and questions to help students understand the reading. *CourseReader: Western Civilization* is the perfect complement to any class.

Student Resources

Companion Website. This website provides a variety of resources, prepared by Jeffrey Webb, to help you review for class. These study tools include glossary, crossword puzzles, short quizzes, essay questions, critical thinking questions, primary sources links, and weblinks.

WebTutor on Blackboard or WebCT. Web-Tutor offers real-time access to an interactive eBook and a full array of study tools, including animations and videos that bring the book's topics to life, plus chapter outlines, summaries, learning objectives, glossary flashcards (with audio), practice quizzes, and weblinks.

CourseMate. The more you study, the better the results. Make the most of your study time by accessing everything you need to succeed in one place. Read your textbook, take notes, review flashcards, watch videos, and take practice quizzes online with CourseMate. In addition, you can access the History Resource Center, a "virtual reader" that provides you with hundreds of primary sources.

Wadsworth Western Civilization Resource Center. Wadsworth's Western Civilization Resource Center gives you access to a "virtual reader" with hundreds of primary sources including speeches, letters, legal documents and transcripts, poems, maps, simulations, timelines, and additional images that bring history to life, along with interactive assignable exercises. A map feature including Google Earth coordinates and exercises will aid in your comprehension of geography and use of maps. You can compare the traditional textbook map with an aerial view of the location today. It's an ideal resource for study, review, and research. In addition to this map feature, the resource center also provides blank maps for student review and testing.

Rand McNally Historical Atlas of Western Civilization, 2e. This valuable resource features over forty-five maps, including maps that highlight classical Greece and Rome; maps documenting European civilization during the Renaissance; maps that follow events in Germany, Russia, and Italy as they led up to World Wars I and II; maps that show the dissolution of Communism in 1989; maps documenting language and religion in the Western world; and maps describing the unification and industrialization of Europe.

Document Exercise. Prepared by Donna Van Raaphorst, Cuyahoga Community College, *Document Exercise* is a collection of exercises based around primary sources, available in two volumes.

Music of Western Civilization. Available free to adopters, and for a small fee to students, this CD contains a broad sampling of many important musical pieces of Western civilization.

Writing for College History, 1e. Prepared by Robert M. Frakes, Clarion University, this brief handbook for survey courses in American History, Western Civilization/European History, and World Civilization guides students through the various types of writing assignments they encounter in a history class. Providing examples of student writing and candid assessments of student work, this text focuses on the rules and conventions of writing for the college history course.

The History Handbook, 1e. Prepared by Carol Berkin of Baruch College, City University of New York, and Betty Anderson of Boston University, this book teaches students both basic and history-specific study skills such as how to read primary sources, research historical topics, and correctly cite sources. Substantially less expensive than comparable skill-building texts, *The History Handbook* also offers tips for Internet research and evaluating online sources.

Doing History: Research and Writing in the Digital Age, 1e. This book was prepared by Michael J. Galgano, J. Chris Arndt, and Raymond M. Hyser of James Madison University. Whether you're starting down the path as a history major or simply looking for a straightforward and systematic guide to writing a successful paper, you'll find this text to be an indispensible handbook to historical research. This text's "soup to nuts" approach to researching and writing about history addresses every step of the process, from locating your sources and gathering information to writing clearly and making proper use of various citation styles to avoid plagiarism. You'll also learn how to make the most of every tool available to you—especially the technology that helps you conduct the process efficiently and effectively.

The Modern Researcher, 6e. Prepared by Jacques Barzun and Henry F. Graff of Columbia University, this classic introduction to the techniques of research and the art of expression is used widely in history courses but is also appropriate for writing and research methods courses in other departments. Barzun and Graff thoroughly cover every aspect of research, from the selection of a topic through the gathering, analysis, writing, revision, and publication of findings, presenting the process not as a set of rules but through actual cases that put the subtleties of research in a useful context. Part One covers the principles and methods of research; Part Two covers writing, speaking, and getting one's work published.

Acknowledgments

The authors would like to thank the following instructors for their critical reading of sections of the manuscript: Gregory Brown, University of Nevada, Las Vegas; James Carter, Saint Joseph's University; David Flaten, Tompkins Cortland Community College; Stephen Gibson, Allegany College of Maryland; Sylvia Gray, Portland Community College; Ann Kuzdale, Chicago State University; William Landon, Northern Kentucky University; Joseph McMahon, Bridgewater State College; Anne Rodrick, Wofford College; Ronald Schechter, The College of William and Mary; and Jeffrey Webb, Huntington University. Several of their suggestions were incorporated into the final version.

We are grateful to the staff of Cengage Learning who lent their considerable talents to the project. In particular, we would like to thank Associate Editor Adrienne Zicht for her conscientiousness and superb administrative skills, and Jane Lee, Senior Content Project Manager, for her careful supervision. This edition rests substantially on the editorial talents of Freda Alexander, who worked closely with us on earlier editions of the text. Over the years, both Jean Woy, Senior Consulting Editor, who has been affiliated with the text since the first edition published in 1981, and Nancy Blaine, Senior Sponsoring Editor, who has worked with us for ten years, continued to recognize and support what we are trying to do—and for this we remain grateful. Although Nancy Blaine is no longer with Cengage Learning, her replacement, Brooke Barbier, has immediately identified with the project—and for this we are also grateful. In addition, we would like to thank Cate Barr, Senior Art Director, for her creativity and artistic vision in updating the cover and interior design for this edition. Three people not part of the Cengage Learning staff made valuable contributions to the project. A special thanks to Karunakaran Gunasekaran at PreMediaGlobal, who managed the overall production with skill and dedication. Wendy Granger from the Bill Smith Group, the photo researcher, deserves praise for her fine eye and enthusiasm for the project. So, too, does Daniel Nighting, the copy editor, for his careful eye for detail.

Unfortunately, Angela Von Laue, who had assisted me since the death of her husband, Theodore Von Laue, in 2000, has taken a too-early retirement from the book. I miss her literary and research skills. I would like to express my personal gratitude to my good friend George Bock, whose creative insights in previous editions continue to contribute to the text's distinguishing character—a concern for crucial concepts and essential relationships. Our often heated but always fruitful discussions demonstrate to me the intrinsic value of the Socratic dialogue. And, as always, I am grateful to my wife, Phyllis Perry, for her encouragement and computer expertise, which have saved me much time and frustration.

Geography of Europe

The map on the following pages features the continent of Europe and parts of North Africa and the Middle East. Like most maps, it contains a selected combination of physical and political information. The physical part pertains to the natural world—the shapes of landmasses, mountains, and bodies of water—and serves as a kind of background or screen onto which the political information is projected. Categories of political information commonly featured on historical maps include the location and names of important cities and states, the changing borders of countries and empires, and the routes people traveled as they explored, migrated, traded, and fought with one another.

Europe is one of seven continents; the others are Africa, Asia, North America, South America, Australia, and Antarctica. Europe is bounded in the north by the Arctic Sea, in the west by the Atlantic Ocean, in the south by the Mediterranean Sea, and in the southeast by the Black Sea and the Caspian Sea. Off the mainland but traditionally considered a part of Europe are thousands of islands, from those of the United Kingdom, Ireland, and Iceland in the northwest, to Crete, Sicily, and Sardinia in the southeast.

Europe is quite distinctive in shape. The first thing to notice is that there is no natural border between Europe and Asia. The traditional eastern boundary is the Ural River, but looked at from a purely geographic standpoint, Europe might simply be called western Asia. The second thing to notice is how much of Europe is made up of peninsulas. In fact, Europe itself is one gigantic peninsula, with a coastline equal in distance to one and a half times around the equator (37,877 miles).

North Americans are often surprised to discover the small size of the European continent. The geographic area of France, for example, is less than that of Texas; Britain is similar in size to Alabama. The distance from London to Paris is about the same as from New York to Boston, while the distance from Berlin to Moscow is comparable to that of Chicago to Denver.

MAJOR PENINSULAS AND ISLANDS There are six major European peninsulas: the Iberian (comprising Portugal and Spain); the Apennine (Italy); the Balkan (Slovenia, Croatia, Bosnia-Herzegovina, Serbia and Montenegro, Albania, Greece, Bulgaria, and Macedonia); the Anatolian (Turkey); the Scandinavian (Norway, Sweden, and Finland); and the Jutland or Danish peninsula. The islands of Iceland, Ireland, and the United Kingdom lie to the Atlantic west, while to the east lie some of the major islands of the Mediterranean, such as Corsica, Sardinia, Sicily, Crete, and Cyprus.

SEAS, LAKES, AND RIVERS Europe's irregular coastline encloses large areas of water into bays, gulfs, and seas. Moving from west to east in the Mediterranean, we have the Tyrrhenian Sea (between Italy and the islands of Sicily, Sardinia, and Corsica), the Adriatic (between Italy and the nations of the western Balkan peninsula), the Ionian (between Italy and Greece), and the Aegean (between Greece and Turkey). The Baltic Sea is bordered on the east (moving clockwise from the north) by Finland, Russia, Estonia, Latvia, Lithuania, Poland, Germany, and Sweden. It is connected by narrow channels to the North Sea, which lies (moving clockwise from the north) between Norway, Denmark, Germany, the Netherlands, and Belgium in the east and south, to the United Kingdom in the north and west. The English Channel separates England and France; the Bay of Biscay lies between southwestern

France and northern Spain. The Black Sea, on the southern border of Russia and Ukraine, is connected by two straits—the Bosphorous and the Dardanelles—to the Aegean Sea. The Caspian Sea, bordered in the north by Russia and Kazakhstan, is the world's largest saltwater lake and, at 92 feet below sea level, the lowest point in Europe.

Several of Europe's major rivers flow across the Russian plain. At 2,194 miles, the Volga is the longest river in Europe. Linked by canals and other river systems to the Arctic Ocean in the north and the Baltic Sea in the south, the Volga originates west of Moscow and empties into the Caspian Sea after flowing some 2,194 miles. At 1,777 miles, the Danube is Europe's second longest river and the principal waterway in the central part of the continent. It originates in southern Germany and flows through Austria, Slovakia, Hungary, Croatia, Serbia and Montenegro, Bulgaria, Moldova, Ukraine, and Romania, before reaching the Black Sea. The Rhine river comes next, at 766 miles, winding its way from the Swiss Alps to the Netherlands and the North Sea. Other prominent riverways in Europe include the Elbe (678 miles), which originates in the Czech Republic and passes through Germany before it, too, empties into the North Sea, and the Rhône (505 miles), which runs from Switzerland, through France, and into the Mediterranean Sea. The proximity of most areas of the European landmass to the coastline and to major river systems greatly affected the Continent's history.

LAND REGIONS Despite its relatively small size, the European continent presents a wide range of landforms, from rugged mountains to sweeping plains. These can be separated into four major regions: the Northwest Mountains, the Great European Plain, the Central Uplands, and the Alpine Mountain System. The mountains of the Northwest Region cover most of the region, running through northwestern France, Ireland, northern Great Britain, Norway, Sweden, northern Finland, and the northwest corner of Russia. The Great European Plain covers almost all of the European part of the former Soviet Union, extending from the Arctic Ocean to the Caucasus Mountains. This belt stretches westward across Poland, Germany, Belgium, the western portion of France, and southeastern England. The Central Uplands is a belt of high plateaus, hills, and low mountains. It reaches from the central plateau of Portugal, across Spain, the central highlands of France, to the hills and mountains of southern Germany, the Czech Republic, and Slovakia. The Alpine Mountain System is made up of several mountain ranges, including the Pyrenees between Spain and France, the Alps in southeastern France, northern Italy, Switzerland, and western Austria, and the Apennine range in Italy. Also included are the mountain ranges of the Balkan Peninsula, the Carpathian Mountains in Slovakia and Romania, and the Caucasus Mountains between the Black and Caspian Seas.

When studying the map of Europe, it is important to notice the proximity of Central Asia, the Middle East, and North Africa. Interaction with the peoples and cultures of these regions has had a profound impact on the course of European history.

Western Civilization

Ideas, Politics, and Society

Part One

The Ancient World: Foundation of the West

to A.D. 500

3000
B.C.

2000
B.C.

1000
B.C.

500
B.C.

100
B.C.

A.D.
200

Politics and Society

Rise of civilization in Sumer (c. 3200)
Union of Upper and Lower Egypt (c. 2900)
Rise of Minoan civilization (c. 2600)

Rise of Mycenaean civilization (c. 2000)
Hammurabi of Babylon builds an empire
   (1792–1750)

Creation of a unified Hebrew monarchy
   under David (1000–961)
Dark Age in Greece (c. 1100–800)
Hellenic Age (c. 800–323)
Fall of Assyrian empire (612)
Persian conquest of Near East (550–525)
Formation of Roman Republic (509)

Persian Wars (499–479)
Peloponnesian War (431–404)
Conquest of Greek city-states by Philip of
   Macedon (338)
Conquests of Alexander the Great (336–323)
Hellenistic Age (323–330)
Roman conquest of Carthage and
   Hellenistic kingdoms (264–146)

Political violence and civil wars in Rome
   (88–31)
Assassination of Julius Caesar (44)
Octavian takes the title Augustus and
   becomes first Roman emperor (27)
Greco-Roman Age (30 B.C.–c. A.D. 500)
Pax Romana—the height of Roman Empire
   (27 B.C.–A.D. 180)

Military anarchy in Rome (235–285)
Goths defeat Romans at Adrianople (378)
End of Roman Empire in the West (476)

Thought and Culture

Cuneiform writing in Sumer; hieroglyphics
   in Egypt

Epic of Gilgamesh (c. 1900)
Code of Hammurabi (c. 1790)
Amenhotep IV and a movement toward
   monotheism in Egypt (c. 1369–1353)
Moses and the Exodus (1200s)

Homer's *Iliad* and *Odyssey* (700s)
Age of classical prophecy: flowering of
   Hebrew ethical thought (750–430)

Law of the Twelve Tables (c. 450)
Rise of Greek philosophy: Ionians, Pythag-
   oreans, Parmenides (500s and 400s)
Greek dramatists: Aeschylus, Sophocles,
   Euripides, Aristophanes (400s)
Greek philosophers: Socrates, Plato,
   Aristotle (400s and 300s)
Hellenistic philosophies: Epicureanism,
   Stoicism, Skepticism, Cynicism

Roman philosophers during the Republic:
   Lucretius, Cicero (1st cent. B.C.)
Rise and spread of Christianity: Jesus
   (d. A.D. 29); Paul's missionary activity
   (c. 34–64)
Gospel According to Mark (c. 66–70)
Roman historians, poets, and philosophers
   during the Pax Romana: Livy, Tacitus,
   Virgil, Horace, Ovid, Juvenal, Seneca,
   Marcus Aurelius

Church fathers: Jerome, Ambrose,
   Augustine (300s and 400s)

Chapter 1

The Ancient Near East: The First Civilizations

With the body of a lion and the face of a man, the Sphinx watches over Giza as a testament to the divine kingship of the pharaohs. (dgmata/Shutterstock.com.)

Focus Questions

1. What is meant by the term *civilization*? Under what conditions did it emerge?

2. What did Mesopotamian and Egyptian civilizations have in common? How did they differ?

3. In what ways did mythopoeic thought characterize Near Eastern civilization? How does this type of thinking differ from that of science?

4. What elements of Near Eastern civilization were passed on to Western civilization?

Civilization was not inevitable; it was an act of human creativity. The first civilizations emerged about five thousand years ago, in the Near Eastern river valleys of Sumer and Egypt. Before that time stretched the vast ages of prehistory, when our ancestors did not dwell in cities and knew nothing of writing; some 99 percent of human history took place before the creation of civilization. Today, when human beings have the capacity to destroy civilization, we might reflect on humanity's long and painful climb to a civilized state.

PREHISTORY

The period called the **Paleolithic Age,** or Old Stone Age, began with the earliest primitive toolmaking human beings who inhabited East Africa some three million years ago. It ended ten thousand years ago in parts of the Near East when people discovered how to farm. Our Paleolithic ancestors lived as hunters (no doubt also as scavengers) and food gatherers. Because they had not learned how to farm, they did not establish permanent villages. When their food supplies ran short, they abandoned their caves or tentlike structures of branches and searched for new dwelling places.

Human social development was shaped by this three-million-year experience of hunting and food gathering. For survival, groups of families formed bands consisting of around thirty people; members learned how to plan, organize, cooperate, trust, and share. The men hunted for meat, and the women cared for the young, tended the fires, and gathered fruits, nuts, berries, and grain. Hunters assisted one another in tracking and killing game, finding cooperative efforts more successful than individual forays. By sharing their kill and bringing some back to their camp for the rest of the group, they reinforced the social bond. So, too, did women who gathered food for the group. Bands that did not cooperate in the hunt, in food gathering, or in food distribution were unlikely to survive.

Hunting and food gathering also stimulated mental and physical development. Food gatherers had to know which plants were safe to eat and where to find them. Hunting required strength, speed, good eyesight and hearing, and mental

3200 B.C.*	Rise of civilization in Sumer
2900	Union of Upper and Lower Egypt
2686–2181	Old Kingdom: essential forms of Egyptian civilization take shape
2180	Downfall of Akkadian empire
1792–1750	Hammurabi of Babylon brings Akkad and Sumer under his control and fashions a code of laws
1570	Egyptians drive out Hyksos and embark on empire building
1369–1353	Reign of Amenhotep IV: a movement toward monotheism
1200	Fall of Hittite empire
612	Fall of Assyrian empire
604–562	Reign of Nebuchadnezzar: height of Chaldean empire
550–525 B.C.	Persian conquests form a world empire

*Most dates are approximations.

ability. Hunters had to study and analyze the habits of their prey, judge weather conditions, recall the location of dens and watering places, and make better tools and weapons. The physically weak and mentally deficient, unable to track animals and to cope with new problems, did not survive long. Individuals with superior intelligence and physical attributes lived longer and had more opportunities to produce offspring, passing on their characteristics and gradually improving the human species.

Although human progress was very slow during the long centuries of the Paleolithic Age, advances occurred that influenced the future enormously. Paleolithic people developed spoken language and shaped bone, wood, and stone tools that corresponded to ideas in their minds. They preserved their creations and taught other people how to use them. Succeeding generations improved on what they had learned from their ancestors. With these simple but useful tools, Paleolithic human beings dug up roots; peeled the bark off trees; trapped, killed, and skinned animals; made clothing; and fashioned fish nets. They also discovered how to control fire, which allowed them to cook their meat. By killing microbes, fire made meat safer to eat. Fire also provided warmth and protection against predators—lions and leopards, for example—that feared fire. From evidence

discovered in caves, it is certain that Paleolithic people had domesticated fire about 500,000 years ago. Some evidence points to fire use as far back as 1.5 million years.

Like toolmaking and the control of fire, language was a great human achievement. Language enabled individuals to acquire and share with one another knowledge, skills, experiences, and feelings. Thus, language was the decisive factor in the development of culture and its transmission from one generation to the next. Language helped parents teach their children rules of conduct and religious beliefs, as well as how to make tools and light fires.

Most likely, our Paleolithic ancestors developed mythic-religious ideas to explain the mysteries of nature, birth, sickness, and death. They felt that living powers operated within and beyond the world that they experienced, and they sought to establish friendly relations with these powers. To primitive peoples, the elements—sun, rain, wind, thunder, and lightning—were alive. The natural elements were spirits; they could feel and act with a purpose. To appease these forces of nature, hunters and gatherers made offerings to them. Gradually, there emerged shamans, medicine men, and witch doctors, who, through rituals, trances, and chants, seemed able to communicate with these spirits. Paleolithic people also began the practice of burying their dead, sometimes with offerings, which suggests belief in life after death. Corpses were sometimes dusted with red ocher, which represented blood, a source of life. Another belief is revealed in the many small statues of women, made between forty thousand and twenty-five thousand years ago, that have been found by archaeologists in Europe and Asia. Fashioned from ivory, wood, and clay and often marked by huge breasts and distended stomachs, these fertility figurines represent a mother goddess who gave life, food, and protection.

Between thirty thousand and twelve thousand years ago, Paleolithic people sought out the dark and silent interior of caves, which they probably viewed as sanctuaries, and, with only torches for light, they painted remarkably skillful and perceptive pictures of animals on the cave walls. Even prior to civilization, human beings demonstrated artistic talent, an esthetic sense. When these prehistoric artists drew an animal with a spear in its side, they probably believed that this act would make them successful in hunting; when they drew a herd of animals, they probably hoped that this would cause game to be plentiful. This belief that something done to an image of an animal or a person will produce the same effect on the being itself is called *sympathetic magic*. Hunting societies that endured into the modern world still engage in rituals designed to protect the hunter and to ensure a kill.

Some ten thousand years ago, the New Stone Age, or **Neolithic Age**, began in the Near East. During the Neolithic Age, human beings discovered farming, domesticated animals, established villages, polished stone tools, made pottery, and wove cloth. So important were these achievements that they are referred to as the Neolithic Revolution.

Agriculture—the deliberate planting and cultivation of crops—first developed in the hilly regions of the Near East, where rainfall was plentiful and wheat and barley grew abundantly in the wild. People there also began to domesticate the sheep and wild goats that roamed the hills. In other parts of the world, farming and the domestication of animals developed independently.

Agriculture and the domestication of animals revolutionized life. Whereas Paleolithic hunters and food gatherers had been forced to use whatever nature made available to them, Neolithic farmers altered their environment to satisfy human needs. Instead of spending their time searching for grains, roots, and berries, women and children grew crops near their homes; instead of tracking animals over great distances, men could slaughter domesticated goats or sheep nearby. (Later, horses, camels, and donkeys were tamed, providing people with a means of transportation.) Since farmers had to live near their fields and could store food for the future, farming led to the rise of permanent settlements. Villages containing as many as two hundred or three hundred people had occasionally emerged in late Paleolithic times, before the discovery of agriculture. Hunter-gatherers built such villages in areas that had an abundant, stable food supply—near a river or lake well stocked with fish, or in a valley with plenty of wild wheat and barley and herds of gazelles or goats. The development of farming greatly speeded the shift to villages. It is likely that trade also impelled people to gather in village communities. Herdsmen, hunters, and food gatherers living in regions rich in salt (needed for preserving food), volcanic glass (used for mirrors, blades, and spearheads), or hematite (an iron ore that was a source of red coloring for pottery) formed trading settlements, which exchanged raw materials for food.

Villages changed the patterns of life. A food surplus freed some people to devote part of their time to sharpening their skills as basket weavers or toolmakers. The demand for raw materials and the creations of skilled artisans fostered trade, sometimes across long distances, and the formation of trading settlements. An awareness of private property emerged. Hunters had accumulated few possessions, since belongings presented a burden in moving from place to place. Villagers, however, acquired property and were determined to protect it from one another and from outsiders—nomadic herdsmen who might raid the village. Hunting bands were egalitarian; generally, no one member had more possessions or more power than another. In farming villages, a ruling elite emerged that possessed wealth and wielded power.

No doubt farming also affected our emotional development. Human beings who had evolved as hunters and foragers, enjoying considerable leisure, personal freedom, independence, and equality, were now forced to adjust to a different tempo of life—unending toil, stifling routine, and the need to obey the commands of the elites. Scholars ponder the psychological dimensions of this shift from the hunter's way of life to sedentary farming.

In recent years, archaeologists have uncovered several Neolithic villages, the oldest of which was established before 8000 B.C. Among the most famous of these sites are Çatal Hüyük in Anatolia (Turkey), Jericho in Palestine, and Jarmö in eastern Iraq. Scholars disagree on whether these communities were just highly developed villages or the first cities. The traditional view is that cities arose about 3000 B.C. in Sumer, the home of the earliest civilization. Some scholars argue that five thousand years before the Sumerian cities Jericho's two thousand inhabitants had created urban life by engaging in trade and embarking on public works. Jericho's walls were six feet six inches thick at the base and in some places twenty feet high. Their construction required cooperation and a division of labor beyond the capacity of an agricultural village. Similar communities, or primitive cities, spread throughout much of the Near East in late prehistoric times.

Neolithic people made great strides in technology. By shaping and baking clay, they made pottery containers for cooking and for storing food and water. The invention of the potter's wheel enabled them to form bowls and plates more quickly and precisely. Stone tools were sharpened by grinding them on rock. The discoveries of the wheel and the sail improved transportation and promoted trade, and the development of the plow and the ox yoke made tilling the soil easier for farmers.

The Neolithic period also marked the beginning of the use of metals. First used was copper, which was easily fashioned into tools and weapons. Copper implements lasted longer than those made of stone and flint, and they could be recast and reshaped if broken. In time, artisans discovered how to make bronze by combining copper and tin in the proper ratio. Bronze was harder than copper, a characteristic that made a sharper cutting edge possible.

During the Neolithic Age, the food supply became more reliable, village life expanded, and the population increased. Families that acquired wealth gained a higher social status and became village leaders. Religion grew more formal and structured; nature spirits evolved into deities, each with specific powers over nature or human life. Altars were erected in their honor, and ceremonies were conducted by priests, whose power and wealth increased as people gave offerings to the gods. Neolithic society was growing more organized and complex; it was on the threshold of civilization.

THE RISE TO CIVILIZATION

What we call **civilization** arose some five thousand years ago in the Near East (in Mesopotamia and Egypt) and then later in the Far East (in India and China). The first civilizations began in cities, which were larger, more populated, and more complex in their political, economic, and social structure than Neolithic villages. Because the cities depended on the inhabitants of adjacent villages for their food, farming techniques must have been developed sufficiently to produce food surpluses. Increased production provided food for urban inhabitants who engaged in nonagricultural occupations; they became merchants, craftsmen, bureaucrats, and priests.

The invention of writing enabled the first civilizations to preserve, organize, and expand knowledge and to pass it on to future generations; it also allowed government officials and priests to conduct their affairs more efficiently. Moreover, civilized societies possessed organized governments, which issued laws and defined the boundary lines of their states. On a scale much larger than Neolithic communities, the inhabitants erected buildings and monuments, engaged in trade and manufacturing, and used specialized labor for different projects. Religious life grew more organized and complex, and a powerful and wealthy priesthood emerged. These developments—cities, specialization of labor, writing, organized government, monumental architecture, and a complex religious structure—differentiate the first civilizations from prehistoric cultures.

Religion was the central force in these primary civilizations. It provided satisfying explanations for the workings of nature, helped ease the fear of death, and justified traditional rules of morality. Law was considered sacred, a commandment of the gods. Religion united people in the common enterprises needed for survival—for example, the construction and maintenance of irrigation works and the storage of food. Religion also promoted creativity in art, literature, and science. In addition, the power of rulers, regarded as gods or their agents, derived from religion.

The emergence of civilization was a great creative act and not merely the inevitable development of agricultural societies. Many communities had learned how to farm, but only a handful made the leap into civilization. How was it possible for Sumerians and Egyptians, the creators of the earliest civilizations, to make that breakthrough? This question has intrigued and baffled historians, and no single explanation is entirely convincing. Most scholars stress the relationship between civilizations and river valleys. Rivers deposited fertile silt on adjoining fields, provided water for crops, and served as avenues for trade. But environmental factors alone do not adequately explain the emergence of civilization. What cannot be omitted is the human contribution: capacity for thought and cooperative activity.

Both the Tigris and Euphrates rivers in Mesopotamia and the Nile River in Egypt deposited fertile soil when they overflowed their banks. But before these rivers could be of any value in producing crops, swamps around them had to be drained; jungles had to be cleared; and dikes, reservoirs, and canals had to be built—activities that required the cooperation of large numbers of people. Learning to work together for the good of the community was an indispensible requirement for civilization. In the process of constructing and maintaining irrigation networks, people learned to formulate and obey rules and developed administrative, engineering, and mathematical skills. The need to keep records stimulated the invention of writing. These creative responses to the challenges posed by nature spurred the early inhabitants of Sumer and Egypt to make the breakthrough to civilization, thereby altering the course of human destiny. By the time the Hebrews and the Greeks, the spiritual ancestors of Western civilization, appeared on the stage of history, civilizations had been in existence for some two thousand years.

Civilization also had its dark side. Epidemic disease thrived in urban centers, where people lived close together in unsanitary conditions, drinking contaminated water and surrounded by rotting garbage. Slavery was an essential and accepted feature of early civilizations. The authority wielded by rulers and their officials and the habits of discipline acquired by the community's members made possible the construction of irrigation works, but they were also harnessed for destructive conflicts between states. Such warfare, which involved managing large numbers of combatants, was far more lethal than the sporadic and generally disorganized acts of violence that occurred in Neolithic times. A hostile and aggressive attitude toward members of alien groups has plagued human beings since the rise of civilization. Warfare fascinated the people who created the first civilizations: scribes recounted battle after battle, warrior-kings boasted of their military conquests, and military heroes were held in the highest esteem. Cultural historian Lewis Mumford observes:

> *War was not a mere residue of more common primitive forms of aggression. . . . In all its typical aspects, its discipline, its drill, its handling of large masses of men as units, in its destructive assaults en masse, in its heroic sacrifices, its final destructions, exterminations, seizures, enslavements, war was rather the special invention of civilization: its ultimate drama.*[1]*

MESOPOTAMIAN CIVILIZATION

Mesopotamia is the Greek word for "land between the rivers." It was here, in the valleys of the Tigris and Euphrates rivers, that the first civilization began. The first to develop an urban civilization in Mesopotamia (present-day Iraq) were the Sumerians, who colonized the marshlands of the lower Euphrates, which, together with the Tigris, flows into the Persian Gulf. The Sumerians' origin is obscure, although scholars speculate that they migrated from the East, perhaps northern India.

*Numbered source notes appear at the end of each chapter, along with suggested readings.

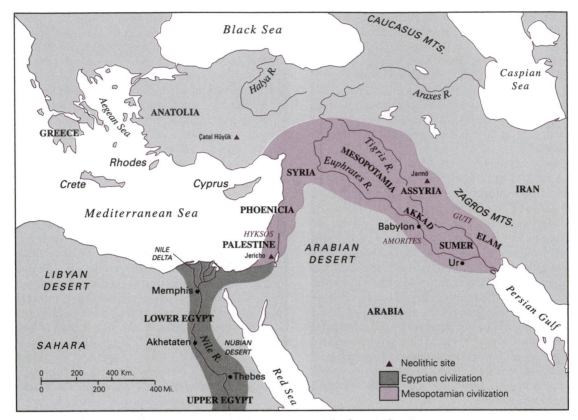

Map 1.1 MESOPOTAMIAN AND EGYPTIAN CIVILIZATIONS The first civilizations emerged in river valleys: Mesopotamia in the valleys of the Tigris and Euphrates rivers, Egypt in the Nile Valley. (Copyright © 2013 Cengage Learning.)

They spoke a language unrelated to the tongues of their Semitic neighbors, who had migrated from Arabia into Mesopotamia and adjacent regions.

Through constant toil and imagination, the Sumerians transformed the swamps into fields of barley and groves of date palms. Around 3000 B.C., their hut settlements gradually evolved into twelve independent city-states, each consisting of a city and its surrounding countryside. Among the impressive achievements of the Sumerians were a system of symbol writing (*cuneiform*), in which pictograms and signs for numbers were engraved with a reed stylus on clay tablets to represent ideas; elaborate brick houses, palaces, and temples; bronze tools and weapons; irrigation works; trade with other peoples; an early form of money; religious and political institutions; schools; religious

and secular literature; varied art forms; codes of law; medicinal drugs; and a lunar calendar.

The history of Mesopotamia is marked by a succession of conquests. To the north of Sumer was a Semitic city* called Akkad. About 2350 B.C., the people of Akkad, led by Sargon the Great, the warrior-king, conquered the Sumerian cities. Sargon built the world's first empire, which extended from the Persian Gulf to the Mediterranean Sea. Establishing a pattern that future despotic rulers would emulate, Sargon stationed garrisons in conquered lands and appointed governors and officials to administer the territories, as well as additional bureaucrats to register and parcel

---

*Semites included Akkadians, Hebrews, Babylonians, Canaanites, Assyrians, and Aramaeans. Hebrew and Arabic are Semitic languages.

SUMERIAN ZIGGURAT. This ziggurat of the moon god, Nanna, which included an impressive temple, dominated the Sumerian city of Ur. (© Charles and Josette Lenars/Corbis.)

out the precious metals, horses, grain, and other commodities exacted from conquered peoples. He also retained a large standing army to quell revolts and to launch new imperialist ventures. The Akkadians adopted Sumerian cultural forms, including cuneiform, and spread them beyond the boundaries of Mesopotamia with their conquests. Mesopotamian religion became a blend of Sumerian and Akkadian elements. Illustrating the confluence of Akkadian and Sumerian culture was Sargon's daughter, Enheduanna, the world's oldest known poet. Serving as high priestess in the Sumerian city of Ur, Enheduanna wrote numerous poems and hymns to temple deities. In one of her hymns to the Sumerian goddess Ianna, she depicts Ianna as a fierce warrior; in a second, Ianna emerges as an overseer of home and children; and in the third surviving hymn, the poetess appeals to Ianna to help her regain her position as temple priestess after it was taken from her by a male enemy.

In succeeding centuries, the Sumerian cities were incorporated into various kingdoms and empires. The Sumerian language, which was replaced by a Semitic tongue, became an obscure language known only to priests, and the Sumerians gradually disappeared as a distinct people. But their cultural achievements endured. Akkadians, Babylonians, Elamites, and others adopted Sumerian religious, legal, literary, and art forms. The Sumerian legacy served as the basis for a Mesopotamian civilization that maintained a distinct style for three thousand years.

Religion: The Basis of Mesopotamian Civilization

Religion lay at the center of Mesopotamian life. Every human activity—political, military, social, legal, literary, artistic—was generally subordinated to an overriding religious purpose. Religion was the Mesopotamians' frame of reference for understanding nature, society, and themselves; it dominated and inspired all other cultural expressions and human activities. Wars between cities, for instance, were interpreted as conflicts between the gods of those cities, and victory ultimately depended on divine favor, not on human effort. **Myths**—narratives about the activities of the gods—explained the origins of the human species. According to the earliest Sumerian myths, the first human beings issued forth from the earth like plant life, or were shaped from clay by divine craftsmen and granted a heart by the goddess Nammu, or were formed from the blood of two gods sacrificed for that purpose.

The Mesopotamians believed that people were given life so that they could execute on earth the will of the gods in heaven. No important decisions were made by kings or priests without first consulting the gods. To discover the wishes of the gods, priests sacrificed animals and then examined their livers; or the priests might find their answers in the stars or in dreams.

The cities of Mesopotamia were sacred communities dedicated to serving divine masters, and people hoped that appeasing the gods would bring security and prosperity to their cities. The Sumerians erected ziggurats—huge multilevel mounds—on which temples were built. The ziggurat in Ur measured 205 feet by 140 feet at the base and was about 70 feet high; staircases connected its levels and led to the top platform, on which stood a majestic temple.

The ziggurat was surrounded by low walls enclosing offices and houses for the priests and shops where potters, weavers, carpenters, and tanners performed their crafts. The temple was the religious and economic heart of the city. A particular city belonged to a god, who was the real owner of the land and the real ruler of the city; often a vast complex of temples was built for the god and the god's family. In the temple, the god was offered shelter, food, clothing, and the homage of dutiful servants. Temple priests collected rents, operated businesses, and received contributions for festivals. Most inhabitants of the city worked for the temple priests as tenant farmers, agricultural laborers, or servants. Anxious to curry favor with the gods and goddesses who watched over the

fields, peasants surrendered part of their crops to the temple. Priests coordinated the city's economic activity, supervising the distribution of land, overseeing the irrigation works, and storing food for emergencies. Temple scribes kept records of expenditures and receipts. By serving as stewards of the city's deities and managing their earthly estates, the priests sustained civilized life.

The gods and goddesses, invisible to human eyes but omnipresent, controlled the entire universe and everything in it. The moon, the sun, the storm, the city, the irrigation works, and the fields—each was directed by a god. Mesopotamians saw gods and demons everywhere in nature. There was a god in the fire and another in the river; evil demons stirred up sandstorms, caused disease, and endangered women in childbirth. To shield themselves from hostile forces, Mesopotamians wore charms and begged their gods for help. Each Mesopotamian offered prayers and sacrifices to a personal god or goddess, who provided protection against evil spirits.

Mesopotamians believed that they were manipulated by divine beings. When misfortune befell them, people attributed it to the gods. Even success was not due to their own efforts but to the intervention of a god who had taken a special interest in them. Compared with the gods, an individual was an insignificant and lowly creature.

Uncertainty and danger filled life in Mesopotamia. Sometimes, the unpredictable waters of the rivers broke through the dikes, flooding fields, ruining crops, and damaging cities. At other times, an insufficient overflow deprived the land of water, causing crops to fail. Great windstorms left the countryside covered with a layer of sand, and heavy thunderstorms turned fields into a sea of mud that made travel impossible. Unlike Egypt, which was protected by vast deserts, Mesopotamia had no natural barriers to invasion. Feeling themselves surrounded by unfathomable and often hostile forces, Mesopotamians lived in an atmosphere of anxiety, which permeated their civilization.

Contributing to this sense of insecurity was the belief that the gods had little love for humanity. They had created a "savage, 'man' shall be his name . . . [who] shall be charged with the service of the gods that they might be at ease."[2] Toward humans the gods behaved capriciously, maliciously, and vindictively, and it was difficult to please them.

What do the gods demand of me? Is it ever possible to please them? To these questions Mesopotamians had no reassuring answers, for the gods' behavior was a mystery to mere human beings.

> *What is good for oneself may be offense to one's god,*
> *What in one's own heart seems despicable may be proper to one's god.*
> *Who can know the will of the gods in heaven?*
> *Who can understand the plans of the underworld gods?*
> *Where have humans learned the way of a god?*
> *He who was alive yesterday is dead today.*[3]

A Mesopotamian man or woman hoped to experience the good life by being obedient to his or her older brother, father, foreman, priest, and king and to a personal deity, who could influence the decisions of the other gods. The rewards for obedience were long life, health, and worldly success. Nevertheless, the feeling persisted that happiness was either transitory or beyond reach—a pessimism that abounded in Mesopotamian literature.

A mood of uncertainty and anxiety, an awareness of the cosmos as unfathomable and mysterious, a feeling of dread about the fragility of human existence and the impermanence of human achievement—these attitudes are as old as the first civilization. The *Epic of Gilgamesh*, the finest work of Mesopotamian literature, masterfully depicts this mood of pessimism and despair. The epic deals with a profound theme: the human protest against death. The death of his close friend causes Gilgamesh to face the reality of his own death. "Despair is in my heart. What my brother is now that shall I be when I am dead. . . . I am afraid of death."[4] Gilgamesh yearns for eternal life, but he learns that when the gods created human beings, they allotted to them only death. "Where is the man who can clamber to heaven? Only the gods live forever . . . but as for us men, our days are numbered, our occupations are a breath of wind."[5]

And in contrast to the Egyptians, the Mesopotamians had little to look forward to after death.

They believed that they would either be confined to a dreary underworld whose rulers would inflict pain on them or be transformed into spirits, flying about and tormenting the living.

Government, Law, and Economy

Kingship, bestowed on a man by the gods, was the central institution in Mesopotamian society. Unlike Egyptian pharaohs, Mesopotamian kings saw themselves not as gods but rather as great men selected by the gods to represent them on earth. Gods governed through the kings, who reported to the gods about conditions in their land (which was the gods' property) and petitioned the gods for advice.

The king administered the laws, which came from the gods. Like everyone else in the land, the king had to obey divine laws. These laws provided Mesopotamians with a measure of security. The principal collection of laws in ancient Mesopotamia was the famous code of Hammurabi (c. 1792– c. 1750 B.C.), the Babylonian ruler. Unearthed by French archaeologists in 1901–1902, the code has provided invaluable insights into Mesopotamian society. The laws were inscribed on a stone slab (*stele*), near the top of which Hammurabi was depicted, standing reverently before the throne of Shamash, the sun god and patron of justice. In typical Mesopotamian fashion, Hammurabi claimed that his code rested on the authority of the gods; to violate it was to contravene the divine order.

The code reveals social status and mores in that area and time. Men were the heads of the family, although efforts were made to protect women and children from mistreatment and poverty. Thus, if a man divorced his wife because she did not bear him a son, he had to provide her with money. Punishments were generally severe— "an eye for an eye and a tooth for a tooth." The code prescribed death for housebreaking, kidnapping, aiding the escape of slaves, receiving stolen goods, and bearing false witness; however, it allowed consideration of extenuating circumstances. Being forgiven by the wronged party could also mitigate the penalty. For example, a wife who committed adultery could be spared execution if pardoned by her husband. Class distinctions were expressed in the code. Penalties varied with the status of both the wrongdoer and the victim. For instance, a person received a harsher punishment for harming a noble than for harming a commoner. Government officials engaging in extortion or bribery were punished severely. The code's many provisions relating to business transactions show the importance of trade to Mesopotamian life.

The economy of Mesopotamian cities depended heavily on foreign and domestic trade. Whereas trade in Egypt was conducted by the state bureaucracy, in Mesopotamia there was greater opportunity for private enterprise. Besides merchants, temple priests engaged in trade because they possessed surplus produce collected as rents from farmers using temple land. Early in Mesopotamian history, merchants were subservient to the king and the temple priests. Over the centuries, however, merchants began to behave as professionals—not just as agents of the palace or temple, but as private entrepreneurs.

Because of trade's importance to the life of the city, governments instituted regulations to prevent fraud. Business transactions had to be recorded in writing, and severe punishments were imposed for dishonesty. A system of weights and measures facilitated trade, and efforts were made to prevent excessive interest rates for loans.

Mesopotamians imported resources not found at home—stone, silver, and timber. In exchange, they exported textiles, fine handicrafts, and (less often because of difficulty in transporting them by donkey) agricultural products. They also imported copper from the Persian Gulf, precious metals from Afghanistan, ivory from Africa and the west coast of India, and cedar and cypress woods, oils, and essences from the Mediterranean coastal areas. Enterprising businessmen set up trading outposts in distant lands, making the Mesopotamians pioneers in international trade.

Writing, Mathematics, Astronomy, and Medicine

The Sumerians established schools, which trained the sons of the upper class in the art of cuneiform writing. Hundreds of tablets on which Sumerian students practiced their lessons have been discovered, testifying to the years of disciplined and demanding work required to master the scribal art. Virtually all scribes were men, but female scribes are at times mentioned in Mesopotamian writings. Noble women in particular were literate.

To assist their pupils, teachers prepared textbooks of word lists and mathematical problems with solutions. In translating Sumerian words into the Akkadian language, they compiled what was probably the world's first dictionary. Students who completed the course of study successfully were employed as archivists, secretaries, or accountants by the temple, the palace, the law courts, or merchants. The Sumerian system of cuneiform writing spread to other parts of the Near East.

The Mesopotamians made some impressive advances in mathematics. They devised multiplication and division tables, including even cubes and cube roots. They determined the area of right-angle triangles and rectangles, divided a circle into 360 degrees, and had some understanding of the principles that centuries later would be developed into the Pythagorean theorem and quadratic equations. But the Babylonians, who made the chief contribution in mathematics, barely advanced to the level of theorizing; they did not formulate general principles or furnish proofs for their mathematical operations.

By carefully observing and accurately recording the positions of planets and constellations of stars, Babylonian sky watchers took the first steps in developing the science of astronomy, and they devised a calendar based on the cycles of the moon. As in mathematics, however, they did not form theories to coordinate and illuminate their data. Believing that the position of the stars and planets revealed the will of the gods, astronomers did not examine the heavens to find what we call cause-and-effect connections between the phenomena. Rather, they sought to discover what the gods wanted. With this knowledge, people could organize their political, social, and moral lives in accordance with divine commands and escape the terrible consequences that they believed resulted from ignoring the gods' wishes. Thus, despite its impressive achievements, Babylonian astronomy remained essentially a mythical interpretation of the universe.

As was consistent with their religious worldview, the Mesopotamians believed that disease was caused by gods or demons. To cure a patient, priest-physicians resorted to magic; through prayers and sacrifices, they attempted to appease the gods and eject the demons from the sick body. Nevertheless, in identifying illnesses and prescribing appropriate remedies, Mesopotamians demonstrated some accurate knowledge of medicine and pharmacology.

EGYPTIAN CIVILIZATION

During the early period of Mesopotamian civilization, the people of another river valley, to the west, put themselves on the path toward civilization. The Egyptians developed their civilization in the fertile valley of the Nile. For good reason, the Greek historian Herodotus called Egypt "the gift of the Nile," for without this mighty river, which flows more than four thousand miles from central Africa northward to the Mediterranean, virtually all of Egypt would be a desert. When the Nile overflowed its banks, as it did reliably and predictably, the floodwaters deposited a layer of fertile black earth, which, when cultivated, provided abundant food to support Egyptian civilization. The Egyptians learned how to control the river—a feat that required cooperative effort and ingenuity, as well as engineering and administrative skills.

Nature favored Egypt in a number of ways. Besides water, fish and fowl, and fertile land, the Nile also provided an excellent transportation link between Upper (southern) and Lower (northern) Egypt. Natural barriers—mountains, deserts, cataracts (rapids) in the Nile, and the Mediterranean—protected Egypt from attack, allowing the inhabitants to enjoy long periods of peace and prosperity. Gold, copper, and stone abounded, along with other natural resources. In addition, the climate of Egypt is dry and salutary. To the Egyptians, nature seemed changeless and beneficent. Hence, unlike Mesopotamians, Egyptians derived a sense of security from their environment.

From the Old Kingdom to the Middle Kingdom

About 2900 B.C., a ruler of Upper Egypt, known as Narmer or Menes, conquered the Nile Delta and Lower Egypt. By 2686 B.C., centralized rule had been firmly established, and great pyramids, tombs for the pharaohs, were being constructed. The pyramids required rigorous central planning to coordinate the tens of thousands of Egyptian laborers drafted to build these immense monuments. During this Pyramid Age, or Old Kingdom (2686–2181 B.C.), royal power reached its height and the essential forms of Egyptian civilization crystallized.

The Egyptians believed the pharaoh to be both a man and a god, the earthly embodiment of the deity Horus; he was an absolute ruler of the land and held his court at the city of Memphis. The Egyptians regarded the pharaoh as a benevolent protector who controlled the floodwaters of the Nile, kept the irrigation works in order, maintained justice in the land, and expressed the will of heaven. They expected that when the pharaoh died and joined his fellow gods, he would still help his living subjects.

In time, the nobles who served as district governors gained in status and wealth and gradually came to undermine the divine king's authority. The nobles' growing power and the enormous expenditure of Egypt's human and material resources on building pyramids led to the decline of the Old Kingdom. From 2181 to 2040 B.C.— a time called the First Intermediate Period—rival families competed for the throne, thus destroying the unity of the kingdom. The civil wars and the collapse of central authority required to maintain the irrigation system cast a pall over the land, as illustrated in this ancient Egyptian poem:

> *The wrongdoer is everywhere....*
> *Plunderers are everywhere....*
> *Nile is in flood, yet none plougheth for*
>   *him....*
> *Laughter hath perished and is no longer*
>   *made.*
> *It is grief that walketh through the land,*
>   *mingled with lamentations....*
> *The storehouse is bare.*[6]

During what is called the Middle Kingdom (2040–1786 B.C.), strong kings reasserted pharaonic rule and reunited the state. The restoration of political stability reinvigorated cultural life and revived economic activity. Pharaohs extended Egyptian control south over the land of Nubia, which became a principal source of gold. A profitable trade was carried on with Palestine, Syria, and Crete.

About 1800 B.C., central authority again weakened. In the era known as the Second Intermediate Period (1786–1570 B.C.), the nobles regained some of their power, the Nubians broke away from Egyptian control, and the Hyksos (a mixture of Semites and Indo-Europeans) invaded Egypt. For centuries, desert and sea had effectively guarded Egypt from foreign invasion, but the Hyksos invaders, using horse and chariot and body armor, ended Egyptian complacency. The Hyksos succeeded in dominating Egypt for about a hundred years. Resentful of foreign rule, the Egyptians became more militant and aggressive; they learned to use the Hyksos' weapons and drove out the invaders in 1570 B.C. The period of empire building known as the New Kingdom (1570–1085 B.C.) then began.

The basic features of Egyptian civilization had been forged during the Old and Middle Kingdoms. The Egyptians looked to the past, believing that the ways of their ancestors were best. For almost three thousand years, Egyptian civilization sought to retain a harmony with the order of nature instituted at creation. Believing that the universe was changeless, the Egyptians did not value change or development—what we call progress—but venerated the institutions, traditions, and authority that embodied permanence.

Religion: The Basis of Egyptian Civilization

Religion was omnipresent in Egyptian life and accounted for the outstanding achievements of Egyptian civilization. Religious beliefs were the basis of Egyptian art, medicine, astronomy, literature, and government. The great pyramids, which took decades to finish and required the labor of thousands of people, were tombs for the pharaohs, man-gods. Magical utterances pervaded

AKHENATON. A bas-relief found in Tell el-Amarna shows Akhenaton and his family sacrificing to Aton, the sun god. (Erich Lessing/Art Resource, N.Y.)

medical practices, for disease was attributed to the gods. Astronomy evolved to determine the correct time to perform religious rites and sacrifices. The earliest examples of literature dealt wholly with religious themes. The pharaoh was a sacrosanct monarch who served as an intermediary between the gods and human beings. Justice was conceived in religious terms, something bestowed by a creator-god. Egyptians appealed to the gods to grant victory in war, provide a bountiful harvest, and protect them from illness and misfortune. The Egyptians developed an ethical code, which they believed the gods had approved. In a number of treatises compiled by high officials, now called

Books of Instruction, Egyptians were urged to tell the truth and to treat others fairly. In one *Book of Instruction* prepared at the end of the second millennium, the author, in a high ethical tone, enjoined Egyptians to express compassion for the poor, widows, and the handicapped.

Egyptian **polytheism** took many forms, including the worship of animals, for the Egyptians believed that gods manifested themselves in animal shapes. Certain gods were conceived by the Egyptians as taking various forms. Thoth, for example, was represented as the moon, a baboon, an ibis, and an ibis-headed man. The god Amon was depicted both in human form and as a ram. To the Egyptians, these different representations were not contradictory, for they did not seek logical consistency in religion. The Egyptians also believed great powers in nature—sky, sun, earth, the Nile—to be gods or the abodes of gods. Thus, the universe was alive with divinities—there were about two thousand gods in the Egyptian pantheon—and human lives were tied to the movements of the sun and the moon and to the rhythm of the seasons. In the heavens the Egyptians found answers to the great problems of human existence. In their temples, Egyptians prayed and dedicated offerings to their gods. During temple rituals, women chanted and played musical instruments.

A crucial feature of Egyptian religion was the afterlife. Through pyramid-tombs, mummification to preserve the dead, and funerary art, the Egyptians showed their yearning for eternity and their desire to overcome death. Mortuary priests recited incantations to ensure the preservation of the dead body and the continuity of existence. Inscribed on the pyramids' interior walls were so-called pyramid texts, written in *hieroglyphics*—a form of picture writing in which figures such as crocodiles, sails, eyes, and so forth represented words or sounds that would be combined to form words. The texts contained fragments from myths, historical annals, and magical lore and provided spells to assist the king in ascending to heaven.

At first, the Egyptians believed that only the pharaoh and the royal family were immortal. In time, the nobility and then the commoners claimed that they, too, could share in the blessings of the "other world." Prayers hitherto reserved for the pharaoh were, for a fee, recited by priests at the burial of commoners. Egyptians believed that

their deceased relatives would intercede with the gods in their behalf. They wrote letters to these spirits, petitioning them for help for such problems as infertility, inheritance of property, and family quarrels. Widows and widowers placed letters in the tomb of a deceased spouse in which they expressed their grief, often with great tenderness. To the Egyptians, the other world contained the same pleasures as those enjoyed on earth—friends, servants, fishing, hunting, paddling a canoe, picnicking with family members, entertainment by musicians and dancers, and good food. However, because earthly existence was not fundamentally unhappy, Egyptians did not yearn for death. Unlike early Christians, they did not reject this world or willingly endure martyrdom in order to enter a higher and better world. The following song, inscribed in a pharaoh's tomb, reveals the Egyptians' relish for life.

Enjoy yourself while you live,
put on fine linen
anoint yourself with wonderful ointments,
multiply all your fine possessions on earth,
follow your heart's command on earth
be joyful and make merry.[7]

Divine Kingship

"What is the king of Upper and Lower Egypt? He is a god by whose dealings one lives, the father and mother of men, alone by himself, without an equal."[8] Divine kingship was the basic institution of Egyptian civilization. Perhaps the requirements of the Egyptian environment helped forge the idea of the pharaoh as a living god because a ruler with supernatural authority, held in favor by the gods, could hold together the large kingdom and draft the mass labor required to maintain the irrigation system. Both the priesthood and a standing army answered to the pharaoh and enhanced his authority.

Through the pharaoh, the gods made known their wishes for the Egyptian people. As kingship was a divine, not a manmade, institution, it was expected to last for eternity. The Egyptians rejoiced in the rule of an all-powerful, all-knowing **god-king** who controlled the Nile, bringing fertility to the land, and could intercede in their behalf with the other deities. Even after death, when the pharaoh joined the other gods in the otherworld, he would still assist his subjects. To the Egyptians, the pharaoh was "the herdsman of everyone without evil in his heart."[9] They believed that divine kingship, which was instituted by a creator-god, was the only acceptable political arrangement, that it was in harmony with the order of the universe, and that it brought stability and authority to the nation.

The power of the pharaoh extended to all sectors of society. Peasants were drafted to serve in labor corps as miners or construction workers. Foreign trade was a state monopoly. The pharaoh authorized commercial ventures—caravan expeditions south to Nubia for ivory, gold, and ebony and sailing expeditions east to Lebanon for timber. Profits from foreign trade enriched the royal treasury. Although private ownership of land was recognized in practice, in theory, all land belonged to the pharaoh. As the supreme overlord, the pharaoh oversaw an army of government officials, who collected taxes, managed construction projects, checked the irrigation works, surveyed the land, kept records, and supervised government warehouses, where grain was stored as insurance against a bad harvest. All Egyptians were subservient to the pharaoh, and there was no conception of political liberty.

Egyptian rulers, like their Mesopotamian counterparts, believed that they had an obligation to render justice. Injustice was seen as an offense against the gods. Most pharaohs took their responsibilities seriously and tried to govern as benevolent protectors of the people as instructed by Egyptian wisdom literature.

> *Be not evil, it is good to be kindly. . . . Do right so long as thou abidest on the earth. Calm the weeper, oppress no widow, expel no man from the possessions of his father. . . . Take heed lest thou punish wrongfully. . . . Slay not a man whose good qualities thou knowest. . . . Exalt not the son of one of high degree more than him that is of lowly birth, but take to thyself a man because of his actions.*[10]

Egyptians derived a sense of security from the concept of divine kingship. It meant that earthly government and society were in harmony with the

STROLL IN THE GARDEN, EIGHTEENTH DYNASTY, C. 1350 B.C. This relief portrays members of the Egyptian royal family ("Stroll in the Garden," relief depicting Tutankhamun and his wife, Ankhesenamun, New Kingdom, c. 1330 B.C. (painted limestone), Egyptian 18th Dynasty (c. 1567–1320 B.C.)/Aegyptisches Museum, SMPK, Berlin/Ancient Art and Architecture Collection Ltd./The Bridgeman Art Library International.)

cosmos, a divine order that provided justice and security. The Egyptians believed that the institution of kingship dated from the creation of the universe, that as part of the rhythm of the universe kingship was necessary and beneficial to human beings.

The pharaoh was seen as ruling in accordance with Ma'at, which means justice, law, right, and truth. The pharaoh embodied Ma'at; his divinity assured that he would correctly determine which actions accorded with Ma'at and which did not. To oppose the pharaoh was to violate the universal and divinely ordained order of Ma'at and to bring disorder to society. Because the Egyptians regarded Ma'at, which had been established with the creation of the universe, as the right order of nature, they believed that its preservation must be the central object of human activity—the guiding norm of the state and the standard by which individuals conducted their lives. Those who did Ma'at and spoke Ma'at would be justly rewarded. Could anything be more reassuring than this belief that divine truth was represented in the person of the pharaoh, who guaranteed and defended the sacred order of the universe?

Science and Mathematics

Like the Mesopotamians, the Egyptians made practical advances in mathematics and science. They demonstrated superb engineering skills in building pyramids. For example, the pyramid of Khufu, still the largest stone building ever constructed, contains 2.3 million stone blocks, each averaging 2.5 tons. The Egyptians fashioned an effective system of mathematics, including geometry for measurements, that enabled them to solve relatively simple problems.

Controlling the floodwaters of the Nile required careful planning. Therefore, it was vital to know when the Nile would begin to overflow. Noting that the Nile flooded after the star Sirius appeared in the sky, the Egyptians developed a calendar by which they could predict the time of the flood. Eventually, they fashioned a calendar of twelve months, each having thirty days. To complete the solar year, they added a separate period of five days after the last month. The Egyptian calendar based on the sun was more accurate than the Babylonian lunar calendar.

In the area of medicine, Egyptian doctors were more capable than their Mesopotamian counterparts. They were able to identify illnesses; they recognized that uncleanliness encouraged contagion; they had some knowledge of anatomy and performed operations—circumcision and perhaps the draining of abscessed teeth. Sick people were instructed to recite an incantation designed to free their body from the demon's hold and to perform a ritual act such as being burned with hot irons. Although the progress of medicine was handicapped by the belief that supernatural forces caused illnesses, nevertheless, there is evidence that some Egyptian doctors examined the body in a scientific way. In a scroll, the Edwin Smith Surgical Papyrus (named after the nineteenth-century American Egyptologist who acquired it), the writer omitted all references to divine intervention in his advice for treating wounds and fractures. He described fractures in a matter-of-fact way and recommended healing them with splints and casts. In another papyrus document (papyrus is a writing material made from the stalks of the papyrus plant), the writer identified the various snakes, analyzed the effects of their bites, and listed treatments, including the use of specific drugs—and he did so with only minimum references to magical incantations.

Egyptian Literature

Generally only a small percentage of the population, the elite, was literate. Egyptian literature took a wide variety of forms: hymns and other religious texts; love poems; tales of adventure, romance, and fantasy; and collections of maxims prepared by elderly sages for the benefit of young rulers.

Containing hymns, litanies and other religious texts, the *Book of the Dead* was written to guide the deceased person safely between this world and the afterlife. In the Judgment Hall, before Osiris and other gods who assisted him in the judgment of souls, deceased individuals proclaimed that they did not commit any of the following sins:

> 2. *I have not robbed with violence.*
> 3. *I have not done violence [to any man].*
> 5. *I have not slain a man or a woman.*
> 11. *I have not uttered evil words.*
> 41. *I have not increased my wealth, except with such things as are [justly] mine own possessions.*[11]

The New Kingdom and the Decline of Egyptian Civilization

The New Kingdom began in 1570 B.C. with the war of liberation against the Hyksos. This war gave rise to an intense militancy, which found expression in empire building. Aggressive pharaohs conquered territory that extended as far east as

Hatchepsut

Hatchepsut, daughter of Thutmose I (1493–1482 B.C.), was an exceptional figure in Egyptian history—a female pharaoh. As the wife of her half brother, Thutmose II, she did not produce a male heir. When Thutmose II died after a three-year reign, his infant son by a secondary wife inherited the throne. But because of his tender years, Hatchepsut served as regent. By the seventh year of the regency, Hatchepsut had assumed the royal title of king of Egypt. Although females were not officially barred from becoming pharaohs, it was an unchallenged tradition that this revered position was reserved for men. To legitimize her rule, Hatchepsut had a sequence of pictures carved on the porch of her mortuary temple that told the story of her divine birth. She was conceived when the god Amon-Re, disguised as Thutmose I, visited her mother's boudoir. Amon indicated that he intended to father a female, who one day would rule Egypt. "Come to me in peace, daughter of my loins, . . . thou art the king who takes possession of the diadem [crown] on the Throne of Horus of the Living, eternally."*

Hatchepsut came to be depicted with male attire and a male body. Apparently, by casting off her female appearance, she aimed to be seen as a king, the equal of all other pharaohs, and not as a queen, who was not regarded as divine. Hatchepsut, says Egyptologist Joyce Tyldesley, "needed to make a sharp and immediately obvious distinction between her former position as queen regent and her new role as pharaoh. The change of dress was a clear sign of her altered state."†

During her twenty-year reign, from about 1479 to 1458, Hatchepsut promoted extensive building projects, including her royal tomb, and trading expeditions, particularly to the land of Punt, in present-day Eritrea and Djibouti. From Punt the Egyptians obtained myrrh and frankincense, precious resins used for making

the Euphrates River. From its subject states, Egypt acquired tribute and slaves. Conquests led to the expansion of the bureaucracy, the creation of a professional army to protect the new territorial acquisitions, and the increased power of priests, whose temples, which grew larger and more lavish, shared in the spoils. Foreign slaves acquired from imperial conquests provided much of the labor for the construction of new shrines and temples. The formation of the empire ended Egyptian isolation and accelerated commercial and cultural intercourse with other peoples. During this period, Egyptian art, for example, showed the influence of foreign forms.

A growing cosmopolitanism was paralleled by a movement toward **monotheism** during the reign of Pharaoh Amenhotep IV (c. 1369–1353 B.C.). Amenhotep sought to replace traditional polytheism with the worship of Aton, a single god of all people, a supreme force in nature represented as the sun disk. Amenhotep took the name Akhenaton ("Servant of Aton") and moved the capital from Thebes to a newly constructed holy city called Akhetaten ("Horizon of Aton," which is near present-day Tell el-Amarna). The city had palaces, administrative centers, and a temple complex honoring Aton. Akhenaton and his wife, Nefertiti, who played a prominent role in his court, dedicated themselves to Aton—the creator of the world, the maintainer of life, and the god of love, justice, and peace. Akhenaton (or Ikhnaton) also ordered his officials to remove the names and images of other gods from temples and monuments. With awe, Akhenaton celebrated Aton's power and magnificence.

> *How manifold are thy works!*
> *They are hidden from man's sight.*
> *O sole god, like whom there is no other.*
> *Thou hast made the earth according to thy desire.*[12]

incense that was burned in temple rituals and perfumes and for the mummification of bodies. It was an arduous journey to Punt; the return of the expeditions with these treasures must have greatly increased the prestige of the female pharaoh.

After Hatchepsut's death, her monuments were mutilated and her name and image deleted in a deliberate attempt to obliterate her memory. The campaign was probably initiated by Thutmose III, but his motivation is not clear. Was he demonstrating hatred for his stepmother, who had relegated him to a subordinate role for so many years? Did he try to erase the memory of Hatchepsut in order to prevent the succession in the future of still another female pharaoh in the belief that such a situation was a grave violation of tradition and Ma'at?

---

*Quoted in Joyce Tyldesley, *Hatchepsut: The Female Pharaoh* (New York: Penguin Books, 1998), 105.

†Ibid., 133.

Akhenaton's monotheism had little impact on the masses of Egyptians, who remained devoted to their traditional gods and ancient beliefs, and was resisted by priests, who resented his changes. The new religion could not survive the death of its founder. Akhenaton's successor, Tutankhamen (1352–1344 B.C.), abandoned the capital at Amarna and returned to Thebes. Tutankhamen was succeeded by an elderly relative, who reigned briefly. In 1340, Horemheb (1340–1315 B.C.), an army commander, seized power and had the monuments to Aton destroyed, along with records and inscriptions bearing Akhenaton's name. The great visionary was vilified as "The Blasphemer."

Historians are not certain why Akhenaton made such a radical break with tradition by propagating the worship of a single god. Was he trying to strike at the priests, whose wealth and prestige had increased considerably with Egypt's conquests? Did the break stem essentially from

the vision of a great prophet? But the most significant historical questions concerning Akhenaton are these: First, was Akhenaton's religion genuine monotheism, which pushed religious thought in a new direction? And second, if this was the case, did it influence the ancient Hebrews who, according to the Old Testament, left Egypt about a century later?

These two questions have aroused controversy among historians. The principal limitation on the monotheistic character of Atonism is that there were really two gods in Akhenaton's religion—Aton and the pharaoh himself, who was still worshiped as a deity. Egyptologist John A. Wilson sheds light on this notion. Because Egyptians could not break with the central idea of their civilization, divine kingship, "one could say that it was the closest approach to monotheism possible within the thought of the day. That would still fall short of making it a belief in and worship of only one god."[13] Regarding the relationship of Atonism to a later Hebrew monotheism, Wilson says, "The mechanism of transmission from the faith of Akhenaton to the monotheism of Moses is not apparent."[14] Moreover, the Hebrews never identified God with the sun or any other object in nature.

Reigning almost 67 years from 1279 B.C. to 1213 B.C., Ramesses II is considered one of Egypt's greatest pharaohs. He campaigned to the south in Nubia, to the west in Libya, and to the east in Canaan and Syria against the Hittite empire. His inconclusive struggles with the Hittites resulted in the signing of a peace treaty, copies of which survive both in hieroglyphics and cuneiform. In order to honor Ramesses II, the Egyptian version of the treaty falsely claims that the Hittites had begged for peace. Ramesses II is most noted for the construction of numerous huge monuments, statues of himself, and temples whose walls contain extravagant glorifications of his person and achievements. Two pairs of colossal statues of Ramesses flank the entrance to a temple at Abu Simbel in Lower Nubia.

Late in the thirteenth century B.C., Libyans, probably seeking to settle in the more fertile land of Egypt, attacked from the west, and the Peoples of the Sea, as unsettled raiders from the Aegean Sea area and Asia Minor were called, launched a series of strikes at Egypt. A weakened Egypt abandoned its empire. In the succeeding centuries, Egypt came under the rule of Libyans, Nubians,

Assyrians, Persians, and finally Greeks, to whom Egypt lost its independence in the fourth century B.C. Egyptian civilization had flourished for nearly two thousand years before it experienced an almost one-thousand-year descent into stagnation, decline, and collapse. During its long history, the Egyptians tried to preserve its ancient forms, revealed to them by their ancestors and representing for all time those unchanging values that they believed to be the way of happiness.

EMPIRE BUILDERS

The rise of an Egyptian empire during the New Kingdom was part of a wider development in Near Eastern history after 1500 B.C.—the emergence of international empires. Empire building led to the intermingling of peoples and cultural traditions and to the extension of civilization well beyond the river valleys.

One reason for the growth of empires was the migration of peoples known as Indo-Europeans. Originally from a wide area ranging from southeastern Europe to the region beyond the Caspian Sea, Indo-Europeans embarked, around 2000 B.C., on a series of migrations, which eventually brought them into Italy, Greece, Asia Minor, Mesopotamia, Persia, and India. From a core Indo-European tongue emerged the Greek, Latin, Germanic, Slavic, Persian, and Sanskrit languages.

Hittites

Several peoples established strong states in the Near East around 1500 B.C.—the Hurrians in northern Mesopotamia, the Kassites in southern Mesopotamia, and, most important, the Hittites in Asia Minor.

Penetrating Asia Minor, Indo-Europeans coalesced with native Hattic-speaking peoples to create the Hittite empire (1450–1200 B.C.). The Hittites ruled Asia Minor and northern Syria, raided Babylon, and challenged Egypt for control of Syria and Palestine.

The Hittites wanted to control the trade routes that ran along the Euphrates River into Syria. In the 1300s, the Hittite empire reached its peak and included much of Asia Minor and northern Syria. The Hittites succeeded because of their

well-trained army. Mass attacks by light, horse-drawn chariots demolished enemy lines, while foot soldiers made effective use of the battle-ax and a short curved sword.

The Hittites borrowed several features of Mesopotamian civilization, including cuneiform, legal principles, and literary and art forms. Hittite religion blended the beliefs and practices of Indo-Europeans, native inhabitants of Asia Minor, and Mesopotamians. The Hittites were probably the first people to develop a substantial iron industry. Initially, they apparently used iron just for ceremonial and ritual objects and not for tools and weapons. However, because iron ore was more readily available than copper or tin (needed for bronze), after 1200 B.C. iron weapons and tools spread throughout the Near East, although bronze implements were still used. Around 1200 B.C., the Hittite empire fell, most likely to Indo-European invaders from the north.

Small Nations

During the twelfth century B.C., a temporary lull in empire building permitted a number of small nations in Syria and Palestine to assert their sovereignty. Three of these peoples—the Phoenicians, the Aramaeans, and the Hebrews*—were originally Semitic desert nomads. The Phoenicians were descendants of the Canaanites, a Semitic people who had settled Palestine about 3000 B.C. The Canaanites who had migrated northwest into what is now Lebanon were called Phoenicians.

Settling in the coastal Mediterranean cities of Tyre, Byblos, Berytus (Beirut), and Sidon, the Phoenicians were naturally drawn to the sea. These daring explorers established towns along the coast of North Africa, on the islands of the western Mediterranean, and in Spain, and they became the greatest sea traders of the ancient world. Phoenician merchants exported lumber, glass, copper and bronze utensils, and the purple dye produced from the murex, a mollusk that was plentiful in the coastal waters. The Phoenicians (or their Canaanite forebears) devised the first alphabet—a monumental contribution to writing. Since all words could be represented by combinations of letters, it saved memorizing thousands of diagrams and aided the Phoenicians in transmitting the cul-

*The Hebrews are discussed in Chapter 2.

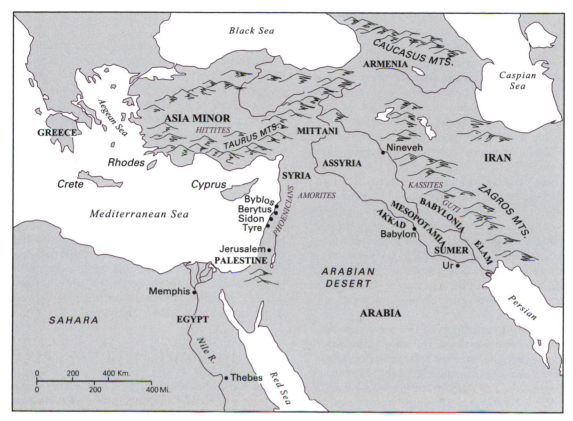

Map 1.2 **KINGDOMS AND PEOPLES OF THE ANCIENT WORLD** In addition to the Sumerians and Egyptians, founders of the first civilizations, other peoples contributed to the development of civilization in the Near East. The Hebrews conceived the idea of the one God, the Phoenicians invented the alphabet, and the Hittites developed a substantial iron industry. (Copyright © 2013 Cengage Learning.)

tural achievements of the Near East to the western Mediterranean. Adapted by the Greeks, who added vowels, the phonetic alphabet became a crucial component of European languages.

The Aramaeans, who settled in Syria, Palestine, and northern Mesopotamia, performed a role similar to that of the Phoenicians. As great caravan traders, they carried both goods and culture to various parts of the Near East. The Hebrews and the Persians, for example, acquired the Phoenician alphabet from the Aramaeans.

Assyria

In the ninth century B.C., empire building resumed with the Assyrians, a Semitic people from the region around the upper Tigris River. The Assyrians carefully planned their military campaigns and excelled in siege weapons—battering rams built on massive wheeled frames—which pulverized city walls that had hitherto resisted attackers. Their soldiers wore armor and wielded iron swords, and charging chariots terrorized the foe's infantry, which generally consisted of farmer-soldiers armed with little more than bows and arrows.

Although they had made forays of expansion in 1200 and 1100 B.C., the Assyrians began their march to "world" empire three centuries later. In the eighth and seventh centuries, the Assyrians became a ruthless fighting machine that stormed through Babylonia, Syria, Palestine, and Egypt. Assyrian kings believed that their gods commanded them to conquer and assisted them in their campaigns. At its height, the Assyrian empire extended from the Iranian plateau in the east to the Egyptian city of Thebes.

How did the Assyrians administer such a vast empire? An Assyrian king, who was the representative and high priest of the god Ashur, governed absolutely. Nobles appointed by the king kept order in the provinces and collected tribute, which they probably used for building palaces, temples, and canals. The Assyrians improved roads, established messenger services, and engaged in large-scale irrigation projects to facilitate effective administration of their conquered lands and promote prosperity. To keep their subjects obedient, the Assyrians resorted to terror and to deportation of troublesome subjects from their home territories. (It is also likely that masses of people were moved around for economic reasons—to replenish a diminishing labor supply.) Assyrian kings boasted of their ruthlessness toward rebellious subjects.

> *13,000 of their warriors I cut down with the sword. Their blood like the water of a stream I caused to run through the squares of their city. The corpses of their soldiers I piled in heaps. . . . [The Babylonian king's] royal bed, his royal couch, the treasure of his palaces, his property, his gods and everything from his palace without number, I carried away. His captive warriors were given to the soldiers of my land like grasshoppers. The city I destroyed, I devastated, I burned with fire.*[15]

Despite an almost all-consuming concern for war, the Assyrians maintained and spread the culture of the past. They copied and edited the literary works of Babylonia, adopted the old Sumerian gods, and used Mesopotamian art forms. The Assyrian king Ashurbanipal (669–626 B.C.) maintained a great library, which contained thousands of clay tablets.

"The king knows that all lands hate us," wrote an official to King Esarhaddon (680–669 B.C.).[16] After a period of wars and revolts weakened Assyria, a coalition of Medes, or Indo-Europeans from Iran, and the Semitic Chaldeans, or Neo-Babylonians, sacked the Assyrian capital of Nineveh in 612 B.C. The conquerors looted and destroyed the city, and the surviving Assyrians fled. Assyrian power was broken.

The Neo-Babylonian Empire

The destruction of the Assyrian empire made possible the rise of a Chaldean empire, which included Babylonia, Assyria, Syria, and Palestine. Under Nebuchadnezzar, who ruled from 604 to 562 B.C., the Chaldean, or Neo-Babylonian, empire reached its height. A talented general and statesman and a brilliant administrator, Nebuchadnezzar had Babylon rebuilt. The new Babylon that arose on the shore of the Euphrates had magnificent processionways that led to palaces and temples. On his palace grounds, Nebuchadnezzar created the famous Hanging Gardens for his Median wife, according to legend. The 350-foot building was a series of vaulted terraces and was surrounded by a moat of flowing water. Trees, shrubs, and flowers decorated each terrace. In the interior, vaulted halls were stocked with vessels, fabrics, ornaments, and wines gathered from different regions of the empire. Here guests reclined on divans and were attended by slaves.

Persia: Unifier of the Near East

After Nebuchadnezzar's death, the Chaldean empire was torn by civil war and threatened by a new power—the Persians, an Indo-European people who had settled in southern Iran. (Iranians today are descendants of the ancient Persians.) Under Cyrus the Great and his son and successor, Cambyses, the Persians conquered all lands between the Nile in Egypt and the Indus River in India. This conquest took twenty-five years, from 550 to 525 B.C. The Near Eastern conception of absolute monarchy justified by religion reached its culminating expression in the person of the Persian king, who, with divine approval, ruled a vast empire, "the four quarters of the earth." Persian kings developed an effective system of administration—based in part on an Assyrian model—which gave stability and a degree of unity to their extensive territories. In so doing, they performed a creative act of statesmanship. The Persian empire was divided into twenty provinces (satrapies), each administered by a governor (satrap) responsible to the emperor. To guard against subversion, the king employed special agents—"the eyes and ears of the emperor"—who supervised

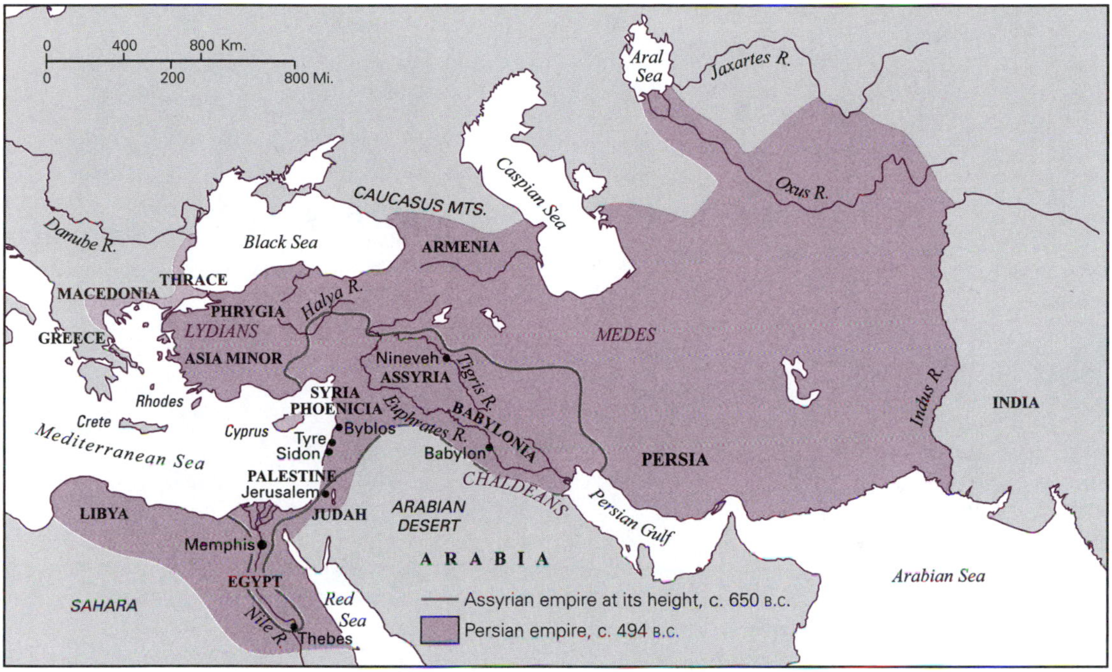

Map 1.3 **THE ASSYRIAN AND PERSIAN EMPIRES** In the last part of the sixth century B.C., the Persians established the greatest empire of the ancient Near East, conquering all the lands between the Nile in Egypt and the Indus River in India. (Copyright © 2013 Cengage Learning.)

the activities of the governors. Persian kings allowed the provincials a large measure of self-rule. They also respected local traditions, particularly in matters of religion, as long as subjects paid their taxes, served in the royal army, and refrained from rebellion; and they deliberately tried to win the goodwill of priests in conquered lands. But they also were brutal, impaling and mutilating opponents.

The empire was bound together by a uniform language, Aramaic (the language of the Aramaeans of Syria), which was used by government officials and merchants. Aramaic was written in letters based on the Phoenician alphabet. By making Aramaic a universal language, the Persians facilitated written and oral communication within the empire. The empire was further unified by an elaborate network of roads, an efficient postal system, a common system of weights and measures, and an empire-wide coinage, based on an invention of the Lydians from western Asia Minor.

Besides providing impressive political and administrative unity and promoting international trade, the Persians fused and perpetuated the various cultural traditions of the Near East. Persian palaces, for example, boasted the terraces of Babylon, the colonnades of Egypt, the winged bulls that decorated Assyrian palace gates, and the craftsmanship of Median goldsmiths.

The political and cultural universalism of the Persian empire had its counterpart in the emergence of an ethically oriented religion, Zoroastrianism. Named for its founder, the Persian prophet Zarathustra (Zoroaster in Greek), who probably lived in the sixth century B.C. (some scholars place him much earlier), this religion taught belief in Ahura Mazda—the Wise Lord— god of light, the embodiment of justice, wisdom, goodness, and immortality. In addition to the Wise Lord, there also existed Ahriman, the spirit of darkness, who was evil and destructive. Ahriman was in conflict with Ahura Mazda. People

PERSEPOLIS, IRAN, C. 500 B.C. The Persian ruler Darius (522–486 B.C.) constructed a thirty-acre earthen terrace almost fifty feet above the plain and built there a complex of palaces, reception halls, a treasury, and barracks for his royal guards. Persepolis became the ceremonial center of the vast Persian empire until it was destroyed by Alexander the Great's soldiers. (© George Holton/Photo Researchers, Inc.)

were free to choose whom they would follow. By choosing Ahura Mazda, they chose good over evil. To serve Ahura Mazda, one had to speak the truth and be good to others; the reward for such behavior was life eternal in paradise, the realm of light and goodness. Followers of the evil spirit could be cast into a realm of darkness and torment. In contrast to the traditional religions of the Near East, Zoroastrianism rejected magic, polytheism, and blood sacrifices and instead stressed ethics.

Persia unified the nations of the Near East into a world-state, headed by a divinely appointed king, and synthesized the region's cultural traditions. Soon it would confront the city-states of Greece, whose political system and cultural orientation differed from that of the Near East.

THE RELIGIOUS ORIENTATION OF THE NEAR EAST

Religion dominated, suffused, and inspired all features of Near Eastern society—law, kingship, art, and science. In the first civilizations, the deepest thoughts of human beings were expressed in the form of religious myths. They were the source of the vitality and creativity of Mesopotamian and Egyptian civilizations. Near Eastern art derived from religion, and science was permeated with it; literature and history dealt with the ways of the gods; and priest-kings or god-kings, their power sanctioned by divine forces, furnished the necessary authority to organize large numbers of people in cooperative ventures. Religion also encouraged and justified wars—including enslavements and massacres—which were seen as conflicts between the gods. Religious beliefs and values served as a powerful social force uniting people into a cohesive community.

A Mythmaking Worldview

A religious or **mythopoeic** (mythmaking) **view** of the world gives Near Eastern civilization its distinctive form and allows us to see it as an organic whole. Mesopotamians and Egyptians inherited from their prehistoric ancestors a great variety of communally produced imagery, rituals, and tales accounting for the origin of the world and human life. Giving free play to their imagination, they altered the old myths and elaborated new ones to resolve questions that today we try to answer with science. Mythmaking was humanity's first way of thinking; it was the earliest attempt to explain the beginnings of the universe and human history, to make nature's mysteries and life's uncertainties comprehensible. Appealing primarily to the imagination and emotions, rather than to reason, mythical thinking, as expressed in language, art, poetry, and social organization, has been a fundamental formative element of human culture.

Originating in sacred rites, ritual dances, feasts, and ceremonies, myths narrated the deeds of gods, who, in some remote past, had brought forth the world and human beings. Holding that human destiny was determined by the gods, Near Eastern people interpreted their experiences through myths. Myths also enabled Mesopotamians and Egyptians to make sense out of nature, to explain the world of phenomena. Through myths, the Near Eastern mind sought to give coherence to the universe, to make it intelligible. Mesopotamian myths, for example, attributed personal misfortune and the catastrophes that afflicted a city to supernatural forces displeased with people's behavior. These myths gave Near Eastern peoples a framework with which to pattern their experiences into a meaningful order, justify their rules of conduct, and help them to overcome the uncertainty of existence.

The civilizations of the ancient Near East were based on a way of thinking fundamentally different from the modern scientific outlook. The difference between scientific and mythical thinking is profound. The scientific mind views physical nature as an *it*—inanimate, impersonal, and governed by universal law. The mythmaking mind of the Near East saw every object in nature as a *thou*—personified, alive, with an individual will. It saw gods or demons manipulating things. The world was enchanted, imbued with mysterious spirits. The sun and stars, the rivers and mountains, the wind and lightning were either gods or the dwelling places of gods. Live agents were the forces behind natural events. An Egyptian or a Mesopotamian experienced natural phenomena—a falling rock, a thunderclap, a rampaging river—as life facing life. If a river flooded the region, destroying crops, it was because it wanted to; the river or the gods desired to punish the people. A drought was caused by the hot breath of the Bull of Heaven. Relief came when the gigantic bird Imdugud devoured the bull and released storm clouds from her wings.

The Egyptians believed that Nut, the sky goddess, gave birth to the sun, a deity who sailed west across the celestial sea before descending into his mother's womb to be reborn again in the morning. For the Egyptians, the rising and setting of the sun were not natural occurrences—a celestial body obeying an impersonal law—but a religious drama.

The scientific mind holds that natural objects obey universal rules; hence, the location of planets, the speed of objects, and the onset of a hurricane can be predicted. The mythmaking mind of the ancient Near East was not troubled by contradictions. It did not seek logical consistency and had no awareness of repetitive laws inherent in nature. Rather, it attributed all occurrences to the actions of gods, whose behavior was often erratic and unpredictable. Shamans employed magic to protect people from evil supernatural forces that surrounded them. The scientific mind appeals to reason—it analyzes nature logically and systematically and searches for general principles that govern phenomena. The mythmaking mind appeals to the imagination and feelings and proclaims a truth that is emotionally satisfying, not one that has been arrived at through intellectual analysis and synthesis. Thus, mythical explanations of nature and human experience made life seem less overwhelming and death less frightening.

Of course, Near Eastern people did engage in rational forms of thought and behavior. They certainly employed reason in building irrigation works, preparing a calendar, and performing mathematical operations. Moreover, in their daily life, men and women were often driven by purely pragmatic concerns. Fields had to be planted, goods sold, and household chores attended to. In dealing with these concerns, people did what had to be done in commonsense ways. They planned and prepared; they weighed actions as either beneficial or harmful and behaved accordingly. However, because rational or logical thought remained subordinate to a mythic-religious orientation, they did not arrive at a *consistently* and *self-consciously* rational method of inquiring into physical nature and human culture.

Thus, Near Eastern civilization reached the first level in the development of science—observing nature, recording data, and improving technology in mining, metallurgy, and architecture. But it did not advance to the level of self-conscious philosophical and scientific thought—that is, logically deduced abstractions, hypotheses, and generalizations. Mesopotamians and Egyptians did not fashion a body of philosophical and scientific ideas that were logically structured, discussed, and debated. They had no awareness of general laws that govern particular events. These later developments were the achievement of Greek philosophy. It gave a "rational interpretation to natural occurrences which had previously been explained by ancient mythologies. . . . With the study of nature set free from the control of mythological fancy, the way was opened for the development of science as an intellectual system."[17]

Near Eastern Achievements

Sumerians and Egyptians demonstrated enormous creativity and intelligence. They built irrigation works and cities, organized governments, charted the course of heavenly bodies, performed mathematical operations, constructed large-scale monuments, engaged in international trade, established bureaucracies and schools, and considerably advanced the level of technology and engineering skills. Without the Sumerian invention of writing—one of the great creative acts in history—what we mean by *civilization* could not have emerged.

Many elements of ancient Near Eastern civilization were passed on to the West. The wheeled vehicle, the plow, coinage, and the phonetic alphabet—all important to the development of civilization—derive from the Near East. In the realm of medicine, the Egyptians knew the value of certain drugs, such as castor oil; they also knew how to use splints and bandages. The innovative divisions that gave 360 degrees to a circle and 60 minutes to an hour originated in Mesopotamia. Egyptian geometry and Babylonian astronomy were utilized by the Greeks and became a part of Western knowledge. The belief that a king's power came from a heavenly source, a key idea in historic Western political thought, also derived from the Near East. In Christian art, too, one finds connections to the Mesopotamian art forms—for example, the Assyrians depicted winged angel-like beings.

Both the Hebrews and the Greeks borrowed Mesopotamian literary themes. For example, some biblical stories—the Flood, the quarrel between Cain and Abel, and the Tower of Babel—stem from Mesopotamian antecedents. A similar link exists between the Greek and the earlier Mesopotamian mythologies.

Thus, many achievements of the Egyptians and the Mesopotamians were inherited and assimilated by both the Greeks and the Hebrews, the principal founders of Western civilization. Even more important for an understanding of the essential meaning of Western civilization are the ways in which the Greeks and Hebrews rejected or transformed elements of the older Near Eastern traditions to create new points of departure for the human mind.

Mythical Thinking

The mythopoeic mind accounts for causation by personifying inanimate substances. To explain through personification is to seek the "who" behind events, to attribute these events to the will of a god (or to an object suffused with divine presence). Thus, if a river did not rise, it was because it refused to do so; either the river or the gods were angry at the people.

The following excerpts from Mesopotamian literature are examples of personification. Whereas we regard table salt as an ordinary mineral, to the Mesopotamians it was alive, a fellow being. In one passage, a person appeals to salt to end his bewitchment. In the second, an afflicted person who believes himself bewitched calls on fire to destroy his enemies.

O Salt

O Salt, created in a clean place,
For food of gods did *Enlil* [father of the Sumerian gods] destine thee.
Without thee no meal is set out in *Ekur,*
Without thee god, king, lord, and prince do not smell incense.
I am so-and-so, the son of so-and-so,
Held captive by enchantment,
Held in fever by bewitchment.

O Salt, break my enchantment! Loose my spell!
Take from me the bewitchment!—And as My Creator
I shall extol thee.

Scorching Fire

Scorching Fire, warlike son of Heaven,
Thou, the fiercest of thy brethren,
Who like Moon and Sun decidest lawsuits—
Judge thou my case, hand down the verdict.
Burn the man and woman who bewitched me;
Burn, O Fire, the man and woman who bewitched me;
Scorch, O Fire, the man and woman who bewitched me;
Burn them, O Fire;
Scorch them, O Fire;
Take hold of them, O Fire;
Consume them, O Fire;
Destroy them, O Fire.

Questions for Analysis

1. How does mythical thinking differ from scientific thinking?
2. When might the ancient Mesopotamians have turned to the gods for help?

Henri Frankfort et al., *Before Philosophy* (Baltimore: Penguin Books, 1949), 143, 147.

NOTES

1. Lewis Mumford, *Transformation of Man* (New York: Harper Torchbooks, 1972), 46–47.
2. Excerpted in James B. Pritchard, ed., *Ancient Near Eastern Texts Relating to the Old Testament,* 3rd ed., with supplement (Princeton, N.J.: Princeton University Press, 1969), 67.
3. Excerpted in James B. Pritchard, ed., *The Ancient Near East: A New Anthology of Texts and Pictures* (Princeton, N.J.: Princeton University Press, 1975), 154.

4. *The Epic of Gilgamesh*, with an introduction by N. K. Sandars (Baltimore: Penguin Books, 1960), 94.

5. Ibid., 69, 104.

6. Excerpted in Adolf Ehrman, ed., *The Ancient Egyptians* (New York: Harper Torchbooks, 1966), 94, 97, 99.

7. Quoted in Eugen Strouhal, *Life of the Ancient Egyptians* (Norman: University of Oklahoma Press, 1992), 41.

8. Quoted in Henri Frankfort, *Ancient Egyptian Religion* (New York: Harper Torchbooks, 1961), 43.

9. Quoted in John A. Wilson, "Egypt," in Henri Frankfort et al., *Before Philosophy* (Baltimore: Penguin Books, 1949), 88.

10. Excerpted in Erhman, *The Ancient Egyptians*, 76–78.

11. E. A. Wallis Budge, *The Book of the Dead* (London: Arkana, 1985), 366–371.

12. Quoted in John A. Wilson, *The Culture of Ancient Egypt* (Chicago: University of Chicago Press, Phoenix Books, 1951), 227.

13. Ibid., 225.

14. Ibid., 226.

15. Quoted in Joan Oates, *Babylon* (London: Thames and Hudson, 1979), 110–111.

16. Quoted in Georges Roux, *Ancient Iraq* (Harmondsworth, England: Penguin Books, 1966), 278.

17. S. Sambursky, *The Physical World of the Greeks* (New York: Collier Books, 1962), 18–19.

SUGGESTED READING

David, Rosalie A., *The Ancient Egyptians* (1982). Focuses on religious beliefs and practices.

Leick, Gwendolyn, *The Babylonians: An Introduction* (2003). An accessible survey.

Moscati, Sabatino, *The Face of the Ancient Orient* (1962). An illuminating survey of the various peoples of the ancient Near East.

Oates, Joan, *Babylon* (1979). A survey of the history of Babylon from its origin to Hellenistic times; includes a discussion of the legacy of Babylon.

Saggs, H. W. F., *Civilization Before Greece and Rome* (1989). Focuses on culture and society.

Sherman, David P. ed., *Ancient Egypt* (1997). Leading scholars explore ancient Egyptian culture.

Snell, Daniel C., *Life in the Ancient Near East* (1997). An excellent synthesis.

Stiebing, William H., Jr., *Ancient Near Eastern History and Culture* (2003). A sound general introduction for students.

Strouhal, Eugen, *Life of the Ancient Egyptians* (1992). Daily life of Egyptians; lavishly illustrated.

Tyldesley, Joyce, *Hatchepsut: The Female Pharaoh* (1996). A biography based largely on archeological evidence.

von Soden, Wolfram, *The Ancient Orient* (1994). A thematic treatment of ancient Mesopotamian civilization.

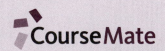

Chapter 2

The Hebrews: A New View of God and the Individual

A sculptured relief from the triumphal Arch of Titus showing Jewish captives bearing the menorah and vessels from the holy temple burned by the Romans at the end of the Jewish revolt, first century A.D. (Vanni/Art Resource, N.Y.)

Focus Questions

1. In what ways did the Hebrew view of God mark a revolutionary break with Near Eastern thought?

2. How did Hebrew religious thought promote the ideas of moral autonomy?

3. What were the distinguishing features of Hebrew law?

4. What were the unique achievements of the Hebrew prophets?

5. Why are the Hebrews regarded as a principal source of the Western tradition?

Ancient Mesopotamia and Egypt, the birthplace of the first civilizations, are not the spiritual ancestors of the West. For the origins of the Western tradition, we must turn to the Hebrews and the Greeks. Both the Greeks and the Hebrews, of course, absorbed elements of the civilizations of Mesopotamia and Egypt, but even more significant is how they transformed this inheritance and shaped worldviews that differed markedly from the outlooks of these first civilizations. As Egyptologist John A. Wilson writes,

> The Children of Israel built a nation and a religion on the rejection of things Egyptian. Not only did they see God as one, but they ascribed to him consistency of concern for man and consistency of justice to man. . . . Like the Greeks, the Hebrews took forms from their great neighbors; like the Greeks, they used those forms for very different purposes.[1]

In this chapter, we examine one source of the Western tradition, the Hebrews, whose conception of God broke with the outlook of the Near East and whose ethical teachings helped fashion the Western idea of humanity and the dignity of the individual.

OUTLINE OF HEBREW HISTORY*

The Hebrews (Israelites or Jews) originated in Mesopotamia and migrated to Canaan, a portion of which was later called Palestine. The Hebrew patriarchs—Abraham, Isaac, and Jacob, so prominently depicted in the Old Testament—were chieftains of seminomadic clans that roamed Palestine and occasionally journeyed to Mesopotamia and Egypt. The early Hebrews absorbed some features of Mesopotamian civilization. For example, there are parallels between biblical law and the Mesopotamian legal tradition. Several biblical stories, including the Garden of Eden and the Flood, derive from Mesopotamian sources.

*Since there is a paucity of references to the early Hebrews in nonbiblical sources, scholars have to rely almost entirely on the Hebrew Bible for reconstructing much of the history of the ancient Israelites. The divergence of scholarly opinion regarding the Bible's accuracy and reliability creates additional uncertainty for the historian.

Chronology 2.1 ❖ The Hebrews

1250 B.C.*	Hebrew Exodus from Egypt
1024–1000	Reign of Saul, Israel's first king
1000–961	Creation of a united monarchy under David
961–922	Reign of Solomon: construction of the first temple
750–430	Age of classical prophecy
722	Kingdom of Israel falls to Assyrians
586	Kingdom of Judah falls to Chaldeans; the temple is destroyed
586–539	Babylonian exile
538	Cyrus of Persia allows exiles to return to Judah
515 B.C.	Second temple is dedicated

*Most dates are approximations.

The biblical account tells us that some Hebrews journeyed from Canaan to Egypt to be herdsmen and farmers, but they eventually became forced laborers for the Egyptians. Fearful of remaining permanent slaves of the pharaoh, the Hebrews yearned for an opportunity to escape. In the early thirteenth century B.C., an extraordinary leader rose among them, called Moses, who came to his people as a messenger of God. Leading the Hebrews in their Exodus from Egypt, Moses transformed them during their wanderings in the wilderness of Sinai into a nation, welded together and uplifted by a belief in Yahweh, the one God.

Arguing that there is no extrabiblical evidence for the Exodus or even for the presence of Jews in Egypt, some scholars dismiss the Exodus as fiction; although numerous Egyptian hieroglyphics detail events at the time, none of them refer specifically to Israelites in Egypt. Certainly, say these scholars, the flight of thousands of foreigners would have attracted notice. Moreover, it is highly unlikely that an escape by a large group of slaves could have succeeded when Egypt was at the peak of its power. The biblical account says that Israelites wandered in the Sinai desert for forty years, but archaeologists, who have excavated a number of sites in the Sinai mentioned in the book of Exodus, have uncovered no traces of Israelite campsites. These scholars, known as biblical minimalists, deny the Exodus from Egypt ever occurred. Other scholars reject this position, holding that there is

evidence of Asiatic slaves toiling in Egypt, some of whom might have been Hebrews. Moreover, assert these scholars, ancient Hebrew scribes would not have concocted and faithfully preserved such an inglorious history of enslavement unless the biblical account contained a core historical truth along with legend, folklore, and mythic imagery.

The Israelite Kingdom

The wandering Israelites returned to Canaan to rejoin other Hebrew tribes that had not migrated to Egypt. The colonization of Canaan, a gradual process, took many generations. Threatened by the Philistines, originally from the islands of the Aegean Sea and the coast of Asia Minor, and from whom the name Palestine derives, the twelve tribes united under the leadership of Saul, a charismatic hero, whom they acclaimed as their first king. Under Saul's successor, David, a gifted warrior and a poet, the Hebrews (or Israelites) broke the back of Philistine power and subdued neighboring peoples.

David's son Solomon erected a royal palace in Jerusalem and beside it a splendid temple honoring God. Under Solomon, Israel experienced a cultural flowering: some magnificent sections of the Old Testament took form, and music flourished. Under Solomon, ancient Israel was at the height of its power and prosperity. However, opposition

33

WALL PAINTING FROM THE SYNAGOGUE OF DURA-EUROPOS, ROMAN SYRIA, EARLY THIRD CENTURY A.D. Although a strict prohibition of the use of images inhibited representational art among the Hebrews, in Hellenistic times scenes from Hebrew history appeared on the walls and floors of Jewish synagogues. Here the prophet Samuel is depicted anointing David as king of Israel. (Art Resource, N.Y.)

to Solomon's tax policies and his favored treatment of the region of Judah in the south led to the division of the kingdom after his death in 922 B.C. The tribes loyal to Solomon's son belonged to the kingdom of Judah, whereas the other tribes organized the northern kingdom of Israel. Both second-rate powers, neither Judah nor Israel could hold on to earlier conquests.

Conquest, Captivity, and Restoration

In 722 B.C., Israel fell to the Assyrians, who deported many Hebrews to other parts of the Assyrian empire. These transported Hebrews—the so-called ten lost tribes—merged with neighboring peoples and lost their identity as the people who had made a covenant with God. By 586 B.C., the Chaldeans had conquered Judah, destroyed Solomon's temple, devastated the land, and deported several thousand Hebrews to Babylon. The prophets Isaiah, Ezekiel, and Jeremiah declared that the destruction of Judah was a punishment that the Hebrews had brought on themselves by violating God's laws. This time was the darkest moment in the history of the Hebrews. Their state was gone, neighboring peoples had overrun their land, and their holy temple was in

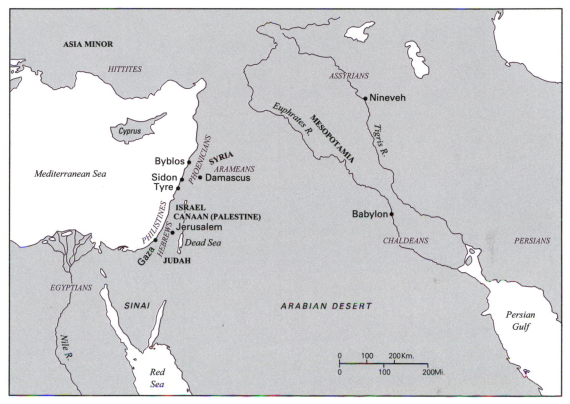

Map 2.1 **Hebrews and Other Peoples of the Ancient Middle East** Despite conquest and exile, the Hebrews survived as a people, retained their faith, and remained devoted to their homeland, which, they believed, God had given them. (Copyright © 2013 Cengage Learning.)

ruins. Thousands had died in battle, had been executed, or had fled to Egypt and other lands, and thousands more were in exile in Babylon. This exile is known as the Babylonian Captivity.

Still, in what is a marvel of history, the Hebrews survived as a people. Although many of the exiles in Babylon assimilated Babylonian ways, some remained faithful to their God Yahweh and the Law of Moses and longed to return to their homeland. Priests struggled to understand the misfortunes that had befallen their people and to prevent the erosion of faith in a foreign environment. They codified ancient traditions, records, and practices, particularly laws, and in the process created the Torah (see below). Thus, their faith enabled them to endure conquest and exile. When the Persians conquered Babylon, King Cyrus, in 538 B.C.,

permitted the exiles to return to Judah, now a Persian province, and to rebuild the temple. The majority of Judeans preferred to remain in prosperous and cosmopolitan Babylon. But some of them did return to Judah, and in 515 B.C. the Hebrews, now commonly called Jews, dedicated the second temple at Jerusalem.

The Hebrew Scriptures

In the following centuries, the Jews would lose their independence to Rome and become a dispersed people. But they never relinquished their commitment to God and his Law as recorded in the Hebrew Scriptures. Called *Tanak* by Jews (and Old Testament by Christians), the

A DEAD SEA SCROLL, JUDEA, SECOND CENTURY B.C. God's law, as recorded in the Holy Scriptures, still remains a unifying force among Jews. Many ancient Hebrew scrolls were found in caves near the west bank of the Dead Sea beginning in the late 1940s. The scroll depicted here contains the earliest existing copy of a complete Hebrew text of the book of the prophet Isaiah. It barely differs from more modern manuscripts. (© John Trevor, Ph.D., courtesy of the Trevor family; photo provided by the Ancient Biblical Manuscript Center, Claremont, Calif.)

Hebrew Scriptures consist of thirty-nine books* by several authors who lived in different centuries. Jews call the first five books of the Old Testament—Genesis, Exodus, Leviticus, Numbers, and Deuteronomy—the Torah (which originally meant "teaching" or "instruction"). Often, the Torah is referred to as the Pentateuch, a Greek word meaning "five books."

*In ancient times, the number of books was usually given as twenty-four. Certain books are now divided into two parts, and the twelve works by the minor prophets are now counted as individual books.

The Hebrew Scriptures represent Jewish oral and written tradition dating from about 1250 to 150 B.C. Compiled by religious devotees, not research historians, they understandably contain factual errors, imprecisions, discrepancies, legends, and folklore. However, there are also passages that offer reliable history, and historians find the Old Testament an indispensable source for studying the ancient Near East. Literary scholars study it for its poetry, legends, and themes, all of which are an integral part of the Western literary tradition. But it is as a work of religious inspiration that the Hebrew Scriptures attain their most profound importance.

The Old Testament is the record of more than a thousand years of ancient Jewish history. Containing Jewish laws, wisdom, hopes, legends, and literary expressions, it describes an ancient people's efforts to comprehend the ways of God. The Old Testament emphasizes and values the human experience; its heroes are not demigods but human beings. It depicts human strength as well as weakness. Some passages exhibit cruelty and unseemly revenge against the enemies of Israel and apostates, while others express the highest ethical values. As set forth in the Hebrew Scriptures, the Hebrew idea of God and his relationship to human beings is one of the foundations of the Western tradition.

GOD: ONE, SOVEREIGN, TRANSCENDENT, GOOD

The Hebrew view of God evolved through the history and experiences of the Hebrew people. In the days of the patriarchs, before the sojourn in Egypt, the Hebrews most likely were not monotheists. They probably devoted themselves to the god of their particular clan and expressed no hatred for the idolatrous beliefs of neighboring peoples. The chief of each clan established a special attachment to the god of his fathers, hoping that the deity would protect and assist the clan.

Some historians say that Moses' religion was not pure monotheism because it did not rule out the existence of other gods. According to this view, not until the prophets, centuries later, did the Hebrews explicitly deny that other gods existed and proclaim that Yahweh stood alone. Other scholars believe that Moses proclaimed a monotheistic idea, that this idea became the central force in the life of the Hebrews at the time of the Exodus from Egypt, and that it continues to be central today. John Bright, an American biblical scholar, suggests a judicious balance. The religion of Moses "did not deny the existence of other gods," says Bright, but it "effectively denied them status as *gods*."[2] The Hebrews could serve only Yahweh and "accorded all power and authority to Him." Consequently, Israel was

forbidden to approach [other deities] as gods. . . . The gods were thus rendered irrelevant, driven from the field. . . . To Israel only the one God was God. . . . The other gods, allowed neither part in creation, nor function in the cosmos, nor power over events. . . . were robbed of all that made them gods and rendered non-entities, in short, were "undeified." Though the full implications of monotheism were centuries in being drawn, in the functional sense Israel believed in but one God from the beginning.[3]

The Hebrew view of the one God marked a profound break with Near Eastern religious thought. The gods of other Near Eastern peoples were not truly free; their power was not without limits. Unlike Yahweh, Near Eastern gods were not eternal but were born or created; they issued from some prior realm. They also were subject to biological conditions, requiring food, drink, sleep, and sexual gratification. Sometimes they became ill or grew old or died. When they behaved wickedly, they had to answer to fate, which demanded punishment as retribution; even the gods were subject to fate's power.

The Hebrews regarded God as *fully sovereign*. He ruled all and was subject to nothing. Yahweh's existence and power did not derive from a preexisting realm, as was the case with the gods of other peoples. The Hebrews believed that no realm of being preceded God in time or surpassed him in power. They saw God as eternal and omnipotent, the source of all in the universe, and having a supreme will. He created and governed the natural world and shaped the moral laws that govern human beings. He was not subservient to fate but determined what happened.

Whereas Near Eastern divinities dwelt within nature, the Hebrew God was transcendent, above nature and not a part of it. Yahweh was not identified with any natural force and did not dwell in a particular place in heaven or on earth. Nature was God's creation but was not itself divine. Therefore, when the Hebrews confronted natural phenomena, they experienced God's magnificent handiwork, not objects with wills of their own. All natural phenomena—rivers, mountains, storms, stars—were divested of any supernatural quality. The stars and planets were creations of Yahweh, not divinities or the abodes of divinities. The Hebrews neither regarded them with awe nor worshiped them. This removal of the gods from nature is a necessary prerequisite for scientific thought.

The Hebrews demythicized nature, but concerned as they were with religion and morality, they did not create theoretical science. As testimony to God's greatness, nature inspired people to sing the praises of the Lord; it invoked worship of God, not scientific curiosity. When Hebrews gazed at the heavens, they did not seek to discover mathematical relationships but admired God's handiwork. The Hebrews did not view nature as a system governed by natural law. Rather, they saw the rising sun, spring rain, summer heat, and winter cold as God intervening in an orderly manner in his creation. The Hebrews, unlike the Greeks, were not philosophers. They were concerned with God's will, not with the human intellect; with the feelings of the heart, not the power of the mind; with righteous behavior, not abstract thought.

Unlike the Greeks, the Hebrews did not speculate about the origins of all things and the operations of nature; they knew that God had created everything. For the Hebrews, God's existence was based on religious conviction, not on rational inquiry; on revelation, not reason. It was the Greeks, not the Hebrews, who originated systematic rational thought. But Christianity, born of Judaism, retained the Hebrew view of a transcendent God and the orderliness of his creation—concepts that could accommodate Greek science.

The Hebrews also did not speculate about God's nature. They knew only that he was *good* and that he made ethical demands on his people. Unlike Near Eastern gods, Yahweh was not driven by lust or motivated by evil but was "merciful and gracious, long-suffering, and abundant in goodness and truth . . . forgiving iniquity and transgression and sin" (Psalm 145:8).[4]* In contrast to pagan gods, who were indifferent to human beings, Yahweh was attentive to human needs.

By asserting that God was *one, sovereign, transcendent*, and *good*, the Hebrews effected a

religious revolution that separated them entirely from the worldview held by the other peoples of the ancient Near East.

THE INDIVIDUAL AND MORAL AUTONOMY

This new conception of God made possible a new awareness of the individual, who was seen as the culmination and centerpiece of God's creation. Created in the image of God, the human being is unique, qualitatively different from the rest of animate nature. Only the human being has the power of volition, the power to make choices. The Hebrews believed that God, who possessed total freedom himself, had bestowed on his people moral freedom—the capacity to choose between good and evil. Thus, in confronting God, the Hebrews developed an awareness of *self*, or *I*; the individual became conscious of his or her own person, moral autonomy, and personal worth.

Fundamental to Hebrew belief was the insistence that God did not create people to be his slaves. The Hebrews regarded God with awe and humility, with respect and fear, but they did not believe that God wanted people to grovel before him; rather, he wanted them to fulfill their moral potential by freely choosing to follow or not to follow God's Law. Thus, in creating men and women in his own image, God made them autonomous and sovereign. In God's plan for the universe, human beings were the highest creation, subordinate only to God. Of all his creations, only they had been given the freedom to choose between righteousness and wickedness, between "life and good, and death and evil" (Deuteronomy 30:15). But having the power to choose freely, men and women must bear the responsibility for their choice.

God demanded that the Hebrews have no other gods and that they make no images "nor any manner of likeness, of anything that is in heaven above, or that is in the earth beneath, . . . thou shalt not bow down unto them nor serve them" (Exodus 20:4–5). Breaking in a revolutionary way with their pagan surroundings, the Hebrews held that the one true God, both omnipotent and invisible, could not be represented in statues or other

---

*The Bible passages in this chapter are quoted from *The Holy Scriptures* (published by the Jewish Publication Society of America).

human creations. The Hebrews believed that the worship of **idols** deprived people of their freedom and dignity; people cannot be fully human if they surrender themselves to a lifeless idol. Hence, the Hebrews had to destroy images and all other forms of idolatry. A crucial element of Near Eastern religion was the use of images—art forms that depicted divinities—but the Hebrews believed that God, the Supreme Being, could not be represented by pictures or sculpture fashioned by human hands. The Hebrews rejected entirely the belief that an image possessed divine powers that could be manipulated for human advantage. Ethical considerations, not myth or magic, were central to Hebrew religious life.

By making God the center of life, Hebrews could become free moral agents; no person, no human institution, no human tradition could claim their souls. Because God alone was the supreme value in the universe, only he was worthy of worship. Thus, to give *ultimate* loyalty to a king or to a general violated God's stern warning against the worship of false gods. The first concern of the Hebrews was supposed to be righteousness, not power, fame, or riches, which were only idols and would impoverish a person spiritually and morally.

There was, however, a condition to freedom. For the Hebrews, people were not free to create their own moral precepts or their own standards of right and wrong. Freedom meant voluntary obedience to commands that originated with God. Evil and suffering were not caused by blind fate, malevolent demons, or arbitrary gods; they resulted from people's disregard of God's commandments. The dilemma is that in possessing freedom of choice, human beings also are free to disobey God, to commit a sin, which leads to suffering and death. Thus, in the Genesis story, Adam and Eve were punished for disobeying God.

For the Hebrews, to know God was not to comprehend him intellectually, define him, or prove his existence; to know God was to be righteous and loving, merciful and just. When men and women loved God, the Hebrews believed, they were uplifted and improved. Gradually, they learned to overcome the worst elements of human nature and to treat other people with respect and compassion. The Jews came to interpret the belief

that man was created in God's image to mean that each human being has a divine spark in him or her, giving every person a unique dignity, which cannot be taken away.

By devotion to God, the Hebrews asserted the dignity and autonomy of human beings. Thus, the Hebrews conceived the idea of moral freedom, that each individual is responsible for his or her own actions. These concepts of human dignity and moral autonomy, which Christianity inherited, are at the core of the Western tradition.

THE COVENANT AND THE LAW

Central to Hebrew religious thought and decisive in Hebrew history was the covenant, God's special agreement with the Hebrew people.

> *And Moses went up unto God, and the Lord called unto him out of the mountain saying: "Thus shalt thou say to the house of Jacob and tell the children of Israel: Ye have seen what I did unto the Egyptians, and how I bore you on eagles' wings, and brought you unto Myself. Now therefore, if ye will hearken unto My voice indeed, and keep My covenant, then ye shall be Mine own treasure from all peoples; for all the earth is Mine; and ye shall be unto Me a kingdom of priests and a holy nation." (Exodus 19:3–6)*

By this act, the Israelites as a nation accepted God's lordship.

The Hebrews came to see themselves as a unique nation, as a "chosen people," for God had given them a special honor, a profound opportunity, and (as they could never forget) an awesome responsibility. The Hebrews did not claim that God had selected them because they were better than other peoples or because they had done anything special to deserve God's election. They believed that God, in a remarkable manner, had rescued them from bondage in Egypt and had selected them to receive the Law so that their nation would set an example of righteous behavior—"a light to the nations," said the prophet Isaiah—and ultimately lead other peoples to acknowledge God, his greatness, and his moral commands.

JUDAEA CAPTA S(ENATUS) C(ONSULTO). With a commander's baton in hand and his foot upon a helmet, a victorious centurion proclaims Rome's victory over Judea, personified weeping at the foot of the palm tree. The destruction of the city of Jerusalem under Titus was complete, but the ethics of Old Testament writing would become part of the foundation of Western civilization. (Courtesy of the American Numismatic Society.)

This divinely assigned responsibility to be the moral teachers of humanity weighed heavily on the Hebrews. They believed that God had revealed his Law—including the moral code known as the Ten Commandments—to the Hebrew people as a whole, and obedience to the Law became the overriding obligation of each Hebrew. The Law of the Torah provided Hebrews with normative guidelines for determining proper behavior. Violating the Law meant breaking the sacred covenant— an act that could lead to national disaster. As the Law originated with the one God, the necessary prerequisite for understanding and obeying it was surrendering belief in other gods forever, since they were barriers to comprehending and carrying out God's universal Law.

Justice was the central theme of Old Testament ethics. The Israelites, liberated from slavery by a righteous and compassionate God, had a moral responsibility to overcome injustice, to care for the poor, the weak, and the oppressed. Because the covenant was made with the entire Hebrew nation, society as a whole had a religious obligation to root out evil and make justice prevail. Duty to God demanded also a duty toward one's neighbor: "Thou shalt surely open thy hand unto thy poor and needy brother, in thy land" (Deuteronomy 15:11). Thus, there were laws to protect the poor, widows, orphans, resident aliens, hired laborers, and slaves. For example, in contrast to ancient Near Eastern law, which regarded slaves as property, biblical legislation emphasized the slave's humanity, although it acknowledged the slave's status as chattel. It called for the punishment of masters who used excessive force against slaves, and it required masters to allow slaves to participate in religious observances and to rest on the Sabbath.

Israelite law incorporated many elements from Near Eastern legal codes and oral traditions. But by making people more important than property, by expressing mercy toward the oppressed, and by rejecting the idea that law should treat the poor and the rich differently, Israelite law demonstrated a greater ethical awareness and a more humane spirit than other legal codes of the Near East.

> *And a stranger shalt thou not wrong, neither shalt thou oppress him; for ye were strangers in the land of Egypt. Ye shall not afflict any widow or fatherless child.* (Exodus 22:20–21)
>
> *If thy brother, a Hebrew man, or a Hebrew woman, be sold unto thee, he shall serve thee six years; and in the seventh year thou shalt let him go free from thee. And when thou lettest him go free from thee, thou shalt not let him go empty; thou shalt furnish him liberally. . . .* (Deuteronomy 15:12–14)
>
> *Thou shalt not curse the deaf, nor put a stumbling-block before the blind, but thou shalt fear thy God: I am the Lord. . . . Thou shalt love thy neighbor as thyself.* (Leviticus 19:14, 18)

While biblical law valued human life and was concerned with human welfare, it also contained provisions that shock us as cruel, for example, ordering the slaughter of the enemy in war, the stoning to death of one's family members who chose to serve other gods, and the execution of homosexuals. It is unknown to what extent these prescriptions were actually carried out, and over the centuries, there arose an oral and interpretive tradition that made the written law less rigid and enabled the Hebrews to adapt to changing cultural conditions.

Hebrew law regulated all aspects of daily life, including family relationships. The father had supreme authority in the family, and this authority extended to his married sons and their wives if they remained in his household. Although polygamy was permitted, monogamy was the general rule; adultery was punishable by death.

As in other Near Eastern societies, the Jews placed women in a subordinate position. The husband was considered his wife's master, and she often addressed him as a servant or subject would speak to a superior. A husband could divorce his wife, but she could not divorce him. Only when there was no male heir could a wife inherit property from her husband or a daughter inherit from her father. Women were not regarded as competent witnesses in court and played a lesser role than men in organized worship.

On the other hand, the Jews also showed respect for women. Wise women and prophetesses such as Judith and Deborah were respected by the community and were consulted by its leaders. Prophets compared God's love for the Hebrews with a husband's love for his wife. Jewish law regarded women as persons, not as property. Even female captives taken in war were not to be abused or humiliated. The law required a husband to respect and support his wife and never to strike her. One of the Ten Commandments called for honoring both father and mother.

THE HEBREW IDEA OF HISTORY

Their idea of God made the Hebrews aware of the crucial importance of historical time. Holidays commemorating specific historical events such as the Exodus from Egypt, the receiving of the Ten Commandments on Mount Sinai, and the destruction of Solomon's temple kept the past alive and vital. Egyptians and Mesopotamians did not

have a similar awareness of the uniqueness of a given event: to them, today's incident merely reproduced events experienced by their ancestors. To the Jews, the Exodus and the covenant at Mount Sinai were singular, nonrepetitive occurrences, decisive in shaping their national history. This historical uniqueness and importance of events derived from the idea of a universal God profoundly involved in human affairs—a God who cares, teaches, and punishes.

The Jews valued the future as well as the past. Regarding human history as a process leading to a goal, they envisioned a great day when God would establish on earth a glorious age of peace, prosperity, happiness, and human brotherhood. This utopian notion has become deeply embedded in Western thought.

The Hebrews saw history as the work of God; it was a divine drama filled with sacred meaning and moral significance. Historical events revealed the clash of human will with God's commands. Through history's specific events, God's presence was disclosed and his purpose made known. When the Hebrews suffered conquest and exile, they interpreted these events as divine retribution for violating the covenant and the Law, sinful acts that brought down the wrath of God upon them. For the Hebrews, history also revealed God's compassion and concern. Thus, the Lord liberated Moses and the Israelites at the Red Sea and appointed prophets to plead for the poor and the oppressed. Because historical events revealed God's attitude toward human beings, these events possessed spiritual meaning and were worth recording, evaluating, and remembering.

THE PROPHETS

Jewish history was marked by the emergence of spiritually inspired individuals called prophets who felt compelled to act as God's messengers. The prophets believed that God had commanded them to speak and had legitimated their words. The prophets cared nothing for money or possessions, feared no one, and preached without invitation. Often emerging in times of social distress and moral confusion, the prophets pleaded for a return to the covenant and the Law. Speaking in God's name, they exhorted the entire nation to make

the prophets were Amos, a shepherd from Judea in the south; his younger contemporary, Hosea, from Israel in the north; Isaiah of Jerusalem; and Jeremiah, who witnessed the siege of Jerusalem by the Chaldeans in the early sixth century B.C.

Social Justice

The flowering of the prophetic movement—the age of classical, or literary, prophecy—began in the eighth century B.C. In attacking oppression, cruelty, greed, and exploitation, the classical prophets added a new dimension to Israel's religious development. These prophets were responding to problems emanating from Israel's changed social structure. The general lack of class distinctions characterizing a tribal society had been altered by the rise of Hebrew kings, the expansion of commerce, and the growth of cities. By the eighth century, there was a significant disparity between the wealthy and the poor. Small farmers in debt to moneylenders faced the loss of their land or even bondage; the poor and their families were often dispossessed and enslaved by the greedy wealthy. To the prophets, these social evils were religious sins that would bring ruin to Israel. Amos, a mid-eighth-century prophet, felt a tremendous compulsion to speak out against these injustices. In the name of God, he denounced the pomp of the heartless rich and the hypocrisy of pious Jews who worshiped God in the prescribed manner but neglected their social obligations to their neighbors, and he demanded that the Hebrews

> Hate the evil and love the good,
> And establish justice in the gate. (Amos 5:15)

For Amos, the pursuit of justice was the most important requirement of the Law. The purpose of worship and ritual was to instill in human beings a passion for justice.

> I hate, I despise your feasts,
> And I will take no delight in your solemn
>   assemblies.
> Yea, though ye offer me burnt-offerings and
>   your meal-offerings,

WALL PAINTING FROM THE SYNAGOGUE IN DURA-EUROPOS, ROMAN SYRIA, EARLY THIRD CENTURY A.D. This painting shows a Hebrew prophet reading from an open scroll. (Art Resource, N.Y.)

God's religious-moral commands central to its existence. Believing that they had been dispatched by God to rescue the disobedient Hebrews from their headlong rush to destruction, the prophets reminded their brethren that because of their moral deterioration, God, who rules history, would inflict swift and terrible punishment on them. The prophets were remarkably courageous people who did not quake before the powerful. Among

Isaiah and Social Justice

The prophets' insistence that rituals were not the essence of the Law and their passion for righteousness are voiced in the Scriptures by Isaiah of Jerusalem, who lived in the mid-eighth century B.C. Scholars agree that Isaiah of Jerusalem did not write all sixty-six chapters that make up the book of Isaiah. Some material appears to have been written by his disciples and interpreters, and Chapters 40 to 55, which were composed two centuries later, are attributed to a person given the name Second Isaiah. The following verses come from Isaiah of Jerusalem.

[11]"What to me is the multitude of your
    sacrifices?
  says the LORD;
I have had enough of burnt offerings of rams
  and the fat of the fed beasts;
I do not delight in the blood of bulls, or of
  lambs, or of he-goats. . . .
[13]Bring no more vain offerings;
  incense is an abomination to me.
New moon and sabbath and the calling of
    assemblies—
  I cannot endure iniquity and solemn
    assembly.
[14]Your new moons and your appointed feasts
    my soul hates;
they have become a burden to me,
  I am weary of bearing them.
[15]When you spread forth your hands,
  I will hide my eyes from you;
even though you make many prayers,

I will not listen;
  your hands are full of blood.
[16]Wash yourselves; make yourselves clean;
  remove the evil of your doings
  from before my eyes;
cease to do evil,
[17] learn to do good;
seek justice,
  correct oppression;
defend the fatherless,
  plead for the widow.
  (Isaiah 1)

Isaiah denounces the rich and the powerful for exploiting the poor.

[13]The LORD has taken his place to contend,
  he stands to judge his people.
[14]The LORD enters into judgment
  with the elders and princes of his people:
"It is you who have devoured the vineyard,
  the spoil of the poor is in your houses.
[15]What do you mean by crushing my people,
  by grinding the face of the poor?"
  says the Lord God of hosts.
  (Isaiah 3)

Question for Analysis

1. Discuss the following statement: For Isaiah, ethical conduct was preferable to ritual acts as a way to worship God.

I will not accept them;
Neither will I regard the peace offerings of
*   your fat beasts.*
Take thou away from Me the noise of thy
*   songs;*
And let Me not hear the melody of the
*   psalteries.*

But let justice well up as waters,
And righteousness as a mighty stream. (Amos
5:21–24)

Justice and righteousness are God's principal concerns and his supreme commandments, said the prophets. God's injunctions, declared Isaiah, were to

Jeremiah

In 597 B.C., the Babylonians, under King Nebuchadnezzar, captured Jerusalem, looted the temple, removed many leading citizens to Babylon, and placed Zedekiah on the throne of David as a puppet ruler. In 589 B.C., Zedekiah, ignoring the warnings of the prophet Jeremiah (born c. 645 B.C.), rebelled against Babylonian rule.

Jeremiah began prophesying when still in his teens, exhorting the Hebrews to avoid the evils of idol worship and mistreatment of their fellows. If the people did not change their ways, he warned, a "foe from the north"—clearly, he meant the Babylonians—would devastate the land and even destroy the temple. After the Babylonian conquest, Jeremiah warned Zedekiah to accept Babylonian dominion. Nebuchadnezzar,

he said, was fulfilling God's purpose. God imposed the Babylonian yoke on Judah to provide the people with an opportunity for true contrition and spiritual renewal. To oppose Babylon was to contravene God's plan and bring down his wrath on Judah. Jeremiah told King Zedekiah: "Why should you and your people die by the sword, by famine, and by pestilence, as the Lord has spoken concerning any nation that will not serve the king of Babylon?" (27:12).

Jeremiah's political advice angered royal officials and popular prophets, who urged a war of liberation. When Zedekiah rebelled, Nebuchadnezzar responded with force. The enemies of Jeremiah demanded his execution as a traitor, and he was left to die in a deep cistern. However, Zedekiah allowed the prophet to be rescued but placed him under court arrest. Shortly

Seek justice, relieve the oppressed,
Judge the fatherless, plead for the widow.
(Isaiah 1:17)

Prophets also denounced people whose principal concern was the accumulation of possessions and wealth. These objects are only transient, said Isaiah, "but the word of God will stand forever" (Isaiah 40:8).

Prophets stressed the direct spiritual-ethical encounter between the individual and God. Their concern was the inner person rather than the outer forms of religious activity. They criticized priests whose commitment to rites and rituals was not supported by a deeper spiritual insight or matched by a zeal for morality in daily life. To the prophets, an ethical sin was far worse than a ritual omission.

The prophets thus helped shape a social conscience that has become part of the Western tradition. This revolutionary social doctrine states that everyone has a God-given right to social justice and fair treatment; that each person has a religious obligation to denounce evil and oppose

the mistreatment of others; and that the community has a moral responsibility to assist the unfortunate. The prophets held out the hope that life on earth could be improved, that poverty and injustice need not be accepted as part of an unalterable natural order, and that the individual was capable of elevating himself or herself morally.

Universalism

Hebrew thought displayed two tendencies: **parochialism** and universalism. Parochial-mindedness stressed the special nature, destiny, and needs of the chosen people—a nation set apart from others—for from among all the nations, God had chosen to give it his Law, the Torah. This narrow, tribal outlook was offset by **universalism,** a concern for all humanity, which found expression in the prophets who envisioned the unity of all people under God. Those prophets told of a great day when God, for whom all people were equally precious, would establish everlasting justice and peace among all nations.

afterward, the Babylonians poured through Jerusalem's breached walls; they burned the city, destroyed the temple, slaughtered nobles, and forcibly removed many people to Babylon. King Zedekiah met a dreadful end. After being forced to watch the execution of his sons, he was blinded and taken in chains to Babylon.

For Jeremiah's support, Nebuchadnezzar ordered his release from prison. Remaining in Jerusalem, the prophet sent out a message of hope to the survivors. God had punished you, he told them, because "your guilt is great, because your sins are so numerous" (30:15). But God, who loved the people of Israel "with an everlasting love" (31:3) and also recognized his abiding commitment to them, will one day "restore the fortunes of my people" (30:3). The exiles will be returned, Jerusalem rebuilt, and the temple restored, he prophesied.

> In that day shall there be a highway out of Egypt to Assyria, and the Assyrian shall come into Egypt, and the Egyptian into Assyria; and the Egyptians shall worship with the Assyrians. In that day shall Israel be the third with Egypt and with Assyria. . . . For that the Lord of hosts hath blessed him saying: "Blessed be Egypt My people and Assyria the work of My hands, and Israel Mine inheritance."
> (Isaiah 19:23–24)

Israel was charged with a sacred mission: to lead in the struggle against idolatry and to set an example of righteous behavior for all humanity.

The prophets were not pacifists, particularly if a war was being waged against the enemies of Yahweh. But some prophets denounced war as obscene and looked forward to its elimination. In a world where virtually everyone glorified the warrior, the prophets of universalism envisioned the day when peace would reign over the earth, when nations

> shall beat their swords into plowshares,
> And their spears into pruning-hooks;
> Nation shall not lift up sword against nation,
> Neither shall they learn war any more.
> (Isaiah 2:4)

These prophets maintained that when people glorify force, they dehumanize their opponents, brutalize themselves, and dishonor God. When violence rules, there can be no love of God and no regard for the individual.

Individualism

The prophets' universalism was accompanied by an equally profound awareness of the individual and his or her worth to God. Before Moses and the later prophets, virtually all religious tradition had been produced communally and anonymously. The prophets, however, spoke as fearless individuals who, by affixing their signatures to their thoughts, fully bore the responsibility of their religious inspiration and conviction. The prophets' emphasis on the individual's responsibility for his or her own actions is a key component of Western thought. In coming to regard God's Law as a *command to conscience, an appeal to the inner person*, the prophets heightened the awareness of the human personality. They enjoined individuals to be introspective, to examine their inner selves—their thoughts and feelings. They indicated that the individual could not know God by merely following edicts and by performing rituals; the individual must experience God. Precisely this *I-Thou* relationship could make the individual fully conscious of self and could deepen and enrich his or her personality. During the Exodus, the Hebrews were a tribal people who obeyed the Law largely out of awe and group compulsion. By the prophets' time, the Jews appeared to be autonomous individuals who heeded the Law because of a deliberate, conscious inner commitment.

The ideals proclaimed by the prophets helped sustain the Jews throughout their long and often painful historical odyssey, and they remain a vital force for Jews today. Incorporated into the teachings of Jesus, these ideals, as part of Christianity, are embedded in the Western tradition.

THE LEGACY OF THE ANCIENT JEWS

For the Jews, monotheism had initiated a process of self-discovery and self-realization unmatched by other peoples of the Near East. The great value that Westerners give to the individual and to human dignity derives in part from the ancient Hebrews, who held that man and woman were created in God's image and possessed free will and a conscience answerable to God. Inherited by Christianity, the prophets' teachings constitute the core principles of Western morality, and their command to the power structure not to abuse their authority but to pursue justice continues to inspire reformers.

Throughout the centuries, the Jewish Bible, with its view of God, human nature, divine punishment, the pursuit of righteousness, and social justice, has played a pivotal and profound role in Jewish life. Moreover, its significance has transcended the Jewish experience; it is also a cornerstone of Western civilization.

Christianity, the essential religion of Western civilization, emerged from ancient Judaism, and the links between the two, including monotheism, moral autonomy, prophetic values, and the Hebrew Scriptures as the Word of God, are numerous and strong. The historical Jesus cannot be understood without examining his Jewish background, and his followers appealed to the Hebrew Scriptures in order to demonstrate the validity of their beliefs. For these reasons, we talk of a Judeo-Christian tradition as an essential component of Western civilization.

The Hebrew vision of a future **messianic age**, a golden age of peace and social justice, is at the root of the Western idea of progress—that people can build a more just society, that there is reason to be hopeful about the future. This way of perceiving the world has greatly influenced modern reform movements. People longing to escape from oppression—African Americans in particular—have found inspiration in the Hebrews' deliverance from bondage in Egypt, the theme of Exodus.

In seeking to comprehend their relationship to God, the writers of the Hebrew scriptures produced a treasury of themes, stories, and models of literary style and craftsmanship that have been a source of inspiration for Western religious thinkers, novelists, poets, and artists to the present day. Historians and archaeologists find the Hebrew Scriptures a valuable resource in their efforts to reconstruct ancient Near Eastern history.

❖ ❖ ❖

NOTES

1. John A. Wilson, "Egypt—the Kingdom of the 'Two Lands,'" in *The World History of the Jewish People*, vol. 1, *At the Dawn of Civilization*, ed. E. A. Speiser (New Brunswick, N.J.: Rutgers University Press, 1964), 267–268.

2. John Bright, *A History of Israel* (Philadelphia: Westminster Press, 1972), 154.

3. Ibid.

4. From *The Holy Scriptures* (Philadelphia: The Jewish Publication Society of America, 1917). The scriptural quotations are used in this chapter with the permission of The Jewish Publication Society of America.

SUGGESTED READING

Anderson, Bernhard, *Understanding the Old Testament*, 2nd ed. (1966). An excellent survey of the Old Testament in its historical setting.

Armstrong, Karen, *A History of God* (1994). Changing views of God from the ancient Hebrews until today.

Boadt, Lawrence, *Reading the Old Testament* (1984). A study of ancient Israel's religious experience by a sympathetic Catholic scholar.

Bright, John, *A History of Israel* (1972). A thoughtful, clearly written survey; one of the best of its kind.

Dever, William G., *Who Were the Israelites and Where Did They Come From?* (2003).

An archeologist explores the controversies regarding biblical accounts of the origins of the Israelites.

Finkelstein, Israel, and Neil Asher Silberman, *The Bible Unearthed: Archeology's New Vision of Ancient Israel and the Origin of Its Sacred Texts* (2001). Challenges several assumptions derived from biblical accounts.

Grant, Michael, *The History of Ancient Israel* (1984). A lucid account.

Heschel, Abraham, *The Prophets*, 2 vols. (1962). A penetrating analysis of the nature of prophetic inspiration.

Metzger, Bruce M., and Michael D. Coogan, eds., *The Oxford Companion to the Bible* (1993). A valuable reference work.

Shanks, Hershel, ed., *Ancient Israel* (1999). The revised and expanded edition contains authoritative essays on various phases of the history of ancient Israel. Highly recommended.

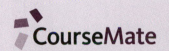

Chapter 3

The Greek City-State: Democratic Politics

The Acropolis of Athens. (Robert Harding World Imagery.)

Focus Questions

1. What were the basic features and limitations of Greek democracy?

2. How did the Greek city-state differ from Near Eastern governments?

3. How did Greek political life demonstrate both the best and the worst features of freedom as well as both the capabilities and the limitations of reason?

4. Why is the Greek political experience crucial to the shaping of the Western tradition?

The Hebrew conception of ethical monotheism, with its stress on human dignity, is one principal source of the Western tradition. The second major source is ancient Greece. Both the Hebrews and the Greeks absorbed the achievements of Near Eastern civilizations, but they also developed their own distinctive viewpoints and styles of thought that set them apart from the Mesopotamians and Egyptians. The great achievements of the Hebrews lay in the sphere of religious-ethical thought; those of the Greeks lay in the development of rational thought. As Greek society evolved, says British historian James Shiel, there

> was a growing reliance on independent reason, a devotion to logical precision, progressing from myth to logos [reason]. Rationalism permeated the whole social and cultural development. . . . Architecture. . . . developed from primitive cultic considerations to sophisticated mathematical norms; sculpture escaped from temple image to a new love of naturalism and proportion; political life proceeded from tyranny to rational experiments in democracy. From practical rules of thumb, geometry moved forward in the direction of the impressive Euclidian synthesis. So too philosophy made its way from "sayings of the wise" to the Aristotelian logic, and made men rely on their own observation and reflection in facing the unexplained vastness of the cosmos.[1]

The Greeks conceived of nature as following general rules, not acting according to the whims of gods or demons. They saw human beings as having a capacity for rational thought, a need for freedom, and a worth as individuals. Although the Greeks never dispensed with the gods, they increasingly stressed the importance of human reason and human decisions. They came to assert that reason is the avenue to knowledge and that people—not the gods—are responsible for their own behavior. In this shift of attention from the gods to human beings, the Greeks broke with the mythmaking orientation of the Near East and created the rational outlook that is a distinctive feature of Western civilization.

Chronology 3.1 ❖ The Greek City-State

1700–1450 B.C.*	Height of Minoan civilization
1400–1230	Height of Mycenaean civilization
1100–800	Dark Age
750–550	Age of Colonization
c. 700	Homer
621	Draco's code of law
594	Solon is elected chief executive
546–527	Under Pisistratus, tyranny replaces oligarchy
507	Cleisthenes broadens democratic institutions
499	Ionians revolt against Persian rule
490	Athenians defeat Persians at battle of Marathon
480	Xerxes of Persia invades Greece; Greek naval victory at Salamis
479	Spartans defeat Persians at Plataea, ending Persian Wars
478–477	Formation of Delian League
431	Start of Peloponnesian War
429	Death of Pericles
413	Athenian defeat at Syracuse
404	Athens surrenders to Sparta, ending Peloponnesian War
399	Execution of Socrates
387	Plato founds a school, the Academy
359	Philip II becomes king of Macedonia
338	Battle of Chaeronea: Greek city-states fall under the dominion of Macedonia
335 B.C.	Aristotle founds a school, the Lyceum

*Some dates are approximations.

EARLY AEGEAN CIVILIZATIONS

Until the latter part of the nineteenth century, historians placed the beginning of Greek, or Hellenic, history in the eighth century B.C. Now it is known that two related civilizations preceded Hellenic Greece: the Minoan and the Mycenaean. Although the ancient Greek poet Homer had spoken of an earlier Greek civilization in his works, historians believed that Homer's epics dealt with myths and legends, not with a historical past. In 1871, however, a successful German businessman, Heinrich Schliemann, began a search for earliest Greece. Having been enthralled by Homer's epics as a youth, Schliemann was convinced that they referred to an actual civilization. In excavating several sites mentioned by Homer, Schliemann discovered tombs, pottery, ornaments, and the remains of palaces of what hitherto had been a lost Greek civilization. The ancient civilization was named after Mycenae, the most important city of the time. Mycenaean civilization pervaded the

Greek mainland and the islands of the Aegean Sea for much of the second millennium B.C.

In 1900, Arthur Evans, a British archaeologist, made an equally extraordinary discovery. Excavating on the island of Crete, southeast of the Greek mainland, he unearthed a civilization even older than that of the Mycenaean Greeks. The Cretans, or Minoans, were not Greeks and did not speak a Greek language, but their influence on mainland Greece was considerable and enduring. Minoan civilization lasted about 1,350 years (2600 to 1250 B.C.) and reached its height during the period from 1700 to 1450 B.C.

The centers of Minoan civilization were magnificent palace complexes whose construction was evidence of the wealth and power of Minoan kings. That the architects of these palaces and the artists who decorated the walls were sensitive to beauty is shown in the ruins uncovered at various Cretan sites. The palaces housed royal families, priests, and government officials and contained workshops that produced decorated silver vessels, daggers, and pottery for local use and for export. Numerous Cretan artifacts have been found in Egypt, Syria, Asia Minor, and Greece, attesting to a substantial export trade.

Judging by the archaeological evidence, the Minoans seemed peaceful. Minoan art did not generally depict military scenes, and Minoan palaces, unlike the Mycenaean ones, had no defensive walls or fortifications. Thus, the Minoans were vulnerable to the warlike Mycenaean Greeks, who invaded and conquered Knossos, the Minoan capital. The Minoans never recovered from this blow, and within two centuries Minoan civilization faded away.

Who were these Mycenaeans? Around 2000 B.C., Greek-speaking tribes moved southward into the Greek peninsula, where, together with the pre-Greek population, they fashioned the Mycenaean civilization. In the Peloponnesus, the Mycenaeans built palaces that were based in part on Cretan models. In these palaces, Mycenaean kings conducted affairs of state, and priests and priestesses performed religious ceremonies; potters, smiths, tailors, and chariot builders practiced their crafts in the numerous workshops, much like their Minoan counterparts. Mycenaean arts and crafts owed a considerable debt to Crete. A script that permitted record keeping probably also came from Crete. The Mycenaeans were traders, too, exchanging goods with the peoples of Egypt, Phoenicia, Sicily, southern Italy, Macedonia, and the western coast of Asia Minor.

At the apex of Mycenaean society was the king, who headed the armed forces, controlled production and trade, and was the highest judicial authority. Assisting the king were aristocrats, who were officers in the army and held key positions in the administration. The priestesses and priests were also in the upper echelons of the society; they supervised sanctuaries and other properties of the gods. Farmers, stockbreeders, and craftsmen constituted the bulk of the free population. At the bottom of the social pyramid were the slaves—mostly foreign prisoners of war.

Mycenaean civilization, which consisted of several small states, each with its own ruling dynasty, reached its height in the period from 1400 to 1230 B.C. Following that, constant warfare between the Mycenaean kingdoms (and perhaps foreign invasions) led to destruction of the palaces and the abrupt disintegration of the Mycenaean civilization about 1100 B.C. But to the later Greek civilization the Mycenaeans left a legacy of religious forms, pottery making, metallurgy, agriculture, language, a warrior culture and code of honor immortalized in the Homeric epics, and myths and legends, which offered themes for Greek drama.

THE RISE OF HELLENIC CIVILIZATION

From 1100 to 800 B.C., the Greek world passed through the Dark Age, an era of transition between a dead Mycenaean civilization and a still unborn Hellenic civilization. The Dark Age saw the migration of Greek tribes from the barren mountainous regions of Greece to more fertile plains, and from the mainland to Aegean islands and the coast of Asia Minor. One group of invaders, the Dorians, penetrated the Peloponnesian peninsula in the south and later founded Sparta. Another group, the Ionians, settled in Attica, where Athens is located, and later crossed to Asia Minor. During this period, the Greeks experienced insecurity, warfare, poverty, and isolation. The bureaucratic system of Mycenaean government had disappeared, extensive trade had ceased, the art of writing had been forgotten, the palace workshops no longer existed, and art had reverted to primitive forms.

After 800 B.C., however, town life revived. Writing again became part of the Greek culture, this time with the more efficient Phoenician script. (Other borrowings from the Near East included artistic imagery and motifs, religious practices, craft skills, and mythological tales that were adapted and transformed by Greek poets.) The population increased dramatically, there was a spectacular rise in the use of metals, and overseas trade expanded. Gradually, Greek cities founded settlements on the islands of the Aegean, along the coast of Asia Minor and the Black Sea, and to the west in Sicily and southern Italy. These colonies, established to relieve overpopulation and land hunger, were independent, self-governing city-states, not possessions of the homeland city-states, although close ties were maintained between the two. During the two hundred years of colonization (750–550 B.C.), trade and industry expanded, the pace of urbanization quickened, and a new class emerged: the merchants, whose wealth derived from goods and money rather than from land. In time, this middle class would challenge the landholding aristocracy.

Homer, Shaper of the Greek Spirit

The poet Homer lived during the eighth century B.C., just after the Dark Age. His great narrative epics, the *Iliad* and the *Odyssey*,* helped shape the Greek spirit and Greek religion. Homer was the earliest molder of the Greek outlook and character. For centuries, Greek youngsters grew up reciting the Homeric epics and admiring the Homeric heroes, who strove for honor and faced suffering and death with courage. Greek thinkers quoted Homer to illustrate moral truths.

In contrast to earlier works of mythology, Homer dealt not just with a hero's actions but also with what the hero thought and felt about his

*Although scholars agree that Homer composed the *Iliad,* some of them hold that the *Odyssey* was probably the work of an unknown poet who lived sometime after Homer; some say that Homer composed both epics, most likely utilizing oral poetic traditions already in circulation, in their earliest forms and that others altered them.

behavior. Homer was a poetic genius who could reveal a human being's deepest thoughts, feelings, and conflicts in a few brilliant lines. His characters, complex in their motives and expressing powerful human emotions—wrath, vengeance, guilt, remorse, compassion, and love—would intrigue and inspire Western writers down to the present.

The *Iliad* deals, in poetic form, with a small segment of the tenth and last year of the Trojan War, which had taken place centuries before Homer's time, during the Mycenaean period. At the very beginning, Homer states his theme.

> *The Wrath of Achilles is my theme, that fatal wrath which, in fulfillment of the will of Zeus, brought the Achaeans [Greeks] so much suffering and sent the gallant souls of many noblemen to Hades, leaving their bodies as carrion for the dogs and passing birds. Let us begin, goddess of song, with the angry parting that took place between Agamemnon King of Men and the great Achilles Son of Peleus.[2]*

The story goes on to reveal the cause and tragic consequences of this wrath. In depriving "the swift and excellent" Achilles of his rightful war-prize (the captive young woman Briseis), King Agamemnon has insulted Achilles' honor and has violated the solemn rule that warrior heroes treat each other with respect. His pride wounded, Achilles refuses to rejoin Agamemnon in battle against Troy and plans to affirm his honor by demonstrating that the Achaeans need his valor and military prowess. Not until many brave men have been slain, including his dearest friend Patroclus, does Achilles set aside his quarrel with Agamemnon and enter the battle.

Homer employs a *particular* event, the quarrel between an arrogant Agamemnon and a revengeful Achilles, to demonstrate a *universal* principle: that "wicked arrogance" and "ruinous wrath" will cause much suffering and death. Homer grasps that there is an internal logic to existence. For Homer, says British classicist H. D. F. Kitto, "actions must have their consequences; ill-judged actions must have uncomfortable results."[3] People, and even the gods, operate within a certain unalterable framework; their deeds are subject to the demands of fate, or necessity. With a poet's intuition, Homer sensed what would become a fundamental attitude

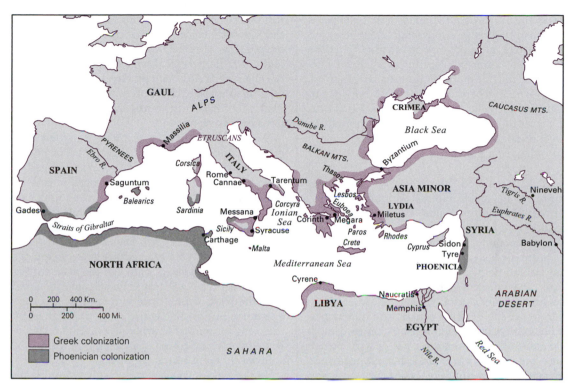

Map 3.1 GREEK COLONIZATION OF THE MEDITERRANEAN BASIN From 750 to 550 B.C., the Greeks colonized the islands of the Aegean, the coasts of Asia Minor and the Black Sea, and, to the west, Sicily and southern Italy. (Copyright © 2013 Cengage Learning.)

of the Greek mind: there is a universal order to things. Later Greeks would formulate Homer's poetic insight in philosophical terms.

Although human life is governed by laws of necessity, the Homeric warrior expresses a passionate desire to assert himself, to demonstrate his worth, to gain the glory that poets would immortalize in their songs—that is, to achieve **aretē**, excellence. In the *Iliad*, Hector, prince of Troy, does battle with Achilles, even though defeat and death seem certain. He fights not because he is a fool rushing madly into a fray nor because he relishes combat, but because he is a prince bound by a code of honor and conscious of his reputation and of his responsibility to his fellow Trojans. In the code of the warrior-aristocrats, cowardice brought unbearable shame, and honor meant more than life itself. When Hector knows that he is going to be slain by Achilles, he expresses this overriding concern with

heroism and glory: "So now I meet my doom. Let me at least sell my life dearly and have a not inglorious end, after some feat of arms that shall come to the ears of generations still unborn."[4]

Heroism, the pursuit of glory and fame, and war's exhilaration are central to the *Iliad*, but Homer is also sensitive to the suffering caused by war. Battlefields littered with dead and maimed warriors fill soldiers with tears, and the grief of widows, orphans, and parents is unremitting.

Homer grasped war's tragic character: it confers honor and dignity on the victorious, but suffering, grief, enslavement, and death on the defeated. And one day, the hero, who had been lauded for his courage and prowess and had brought glory to his family and city, will also perish by the sword. This is his destiny. Homer's insights into life's tragic nature instructed the great Greek dramatists (see Chapter 4) and future Western writers.

In the warrior-aristocrat world of Homer, aretē, was principally interpreted as bravery and skill in battle. Homer's portrayal also bears the embryo of a larger conception of human excellence, one that combines thought with action. A man of true worth, says the wise Phoenix to the stubborn Achilles, is both "a speaker of words and a doer of deeds." In this passage, we find the earliest statement of the Greek educational ideal: the molding of a man who, says classicist Werner Jaeger, "united nobility of action with nobility of mind," who realized "the whole of human potentialities."[5] Thus, in Homer we find the beginnings of Greek humanism—a concern with the individual and his achievements.

To Mesopotamian and Egyptian minds, the gods were primarily responsible for the good or evil that befell human beings. In Homer's work, the gods are still very much involved in human affairs, but Homer also makes the individual a decisive actor in the drama of life. Human actions and human personality are very important. Homer's heroes demonstrate a considerable independence of will. Human beings pay respect to the gods but do not live in perpetual fear of them; they choose their own way, at times even defying the gods. As British classicist C. M. Bowra notes, "the human actors . . . pursue their own aims and deal their own blows; the gods may help or obstruct them, but success or failure remains their own. The gods have the last word, but in the interval men do their utmost and win glory for it."[6] Homer's view of the eternal order of the world and his conception of the individual striving for excellence form the foundations of the Greek outlook.

Greek Religion

During the Dark Age, Greek religion was a mixture of beliefs and cults of gods and goddesses inherited from the Mycenaean past and from an even older Indo-European past imported from Asia Minor and from the early civilizations of the Near East. The Greeks had no prophets or works of scripture like the Hebrews, but Homer's epics and Hesiod's poetry (see profile in next chapter) gave some clarity and structure to Greek religion. They were not intended to have any theological significance, but their treatment of the gods had important religious implications for the Greeks. In time, Homer's epics

formed the basis of the Olympian religion accepted throughout Greece. The principal gods were said to reside on Mount Olympus in northern Greece, and on its highest peak was the palace of Zeus, the chief deity. Although all Greeks recognized the Olympian gods, each city retained local gods and rituals that had been transmitted through generations by folk memory.

Many Greeks found an outlet for their religious feelings in the sacred ceremonies of mystic cults. Devotees of the cult of Dionysus, the god of wine and agricultural fertility, engaged in ecstatic dances and frenzied prayers for abundant harvests. Participants in the Eleusinian cult felt purified and reborn through their rituals and believed in a happy life after death. The Orphic cult, which was popular in the sixth century B.C., taught the unimportance of earthly life and the need to prepare for life after the grave. The Orphics believed that the soul, which once had enjoyed a happy existence in another world, was imprisoned in the body for an unknown fault, and that if the individual controlled his or her bodily desires, the soul would be liberated after death.

In the early stages of Greek history, most people sought to live in accordance with the wishes of the gods. Through prayer, offerings, and ritual purification, they tried to appease the gods and consulted oracles to divine the future. Although religion pervaded daily life, the Greeks had no official body of priests who ruled religious matters and could intervene in politics. Instead, religious ceremonies were conducted by citizens chosen to serve as priests. Nor was there an official creed with established doctrines. Religion was more social than spiritual; that is, it was more a way of expressing attachment to the community than finding inner peace through personal communion with a higher reality. In time, traditional religion would be challenged and undermined by a growing secular and rational spirit.

THE EVOLUTION OF THE CITY-STATE

The Break with Theocratic Politics

From 750 B.C. to the death of Alexander the Great in 323 B.C., Greek society consisted of independent city-states. The city-state based on tribal allegiances was generally the first political association during the early stages of civilization. Moreover, Greece's many mountains, bays, and islands—natural barriers to political unity—favored this type of political arrangement.

The scale of the city-state, or *polis*, was small; most city-states had fewer than 5,000 male citizens. Athens, which was a large city-state, had some 35,000 to 40,000 (some estimates are as high as 55,000) adult male citizens; the rest of its population of 350,000 consisted of women, children, resident aliens, and slaves, none of whom could participate in lawmaking. The citizens of the polis, many of whom were related by blood, knew one another well, and together they engaged in athletic contests and religious rituals. The polis gave individuals a sense of belonging, for its citizens were intimately involved in the political and cultural life of the community.

In the fifth century B.C., at its maturity, the Greeks viewed their polis as the only avenue to the good life—"the only framework within which man could realize his spiritual, moral, and intellectual capacities," in the words of Kitto.[7] The mature polis was a self-governing community that expressed the will of free citizens, not the desires of gods, hereditary kings, or priests. In the **theocracies** of the Near East, religion dominated political activity, and to abide by the mandates of the gods was the ruler's first responsibility. The Greek polis also had begun as a religious institution, in which the citizens sought to maintain an alliance with their deities. But gradually the citizens deemphasized the gods' role in political life and based government not on the magic powers of divine rulers, but on human intelligence as expressed through the community. Seers, purported to have supernatural skills, might offer advice but could not override the rulings of the Assembly. The great innovation introduced by the Greeks into politics and social theory, says classicist Mason Hammond, was "the view that law did not emanate from gods, or divine rulers, but from the human community."[8] The evolution of the Greek polis from a tribal-religious institution to a secular-rational institution was only a part of the general transition of the Greek mind from myth to reason.

The emergence of rational attitudes did not, of course, spell the end of religion, particularly for the peasants, who remained devoted to their ancient cults, gods, and shrines. Greek commanders and statesmen, at times, were not beyond consulting omens and oracles before making decisions, and considerable public revenue went to the construction of temples and the observance of religious festivals. The Greeks were careful to show respect for the gods, for many believed that these deities could aid or harm a city. Paying homage to the god of the city remained a required act of patriotism, to which Greeks unfailingly adhered.

Thus, the religious-mythical tradition never died in Greece but existed side by side with a growing **rationalism**. As Greek rationalism gained influence, traditional religious beliefs and restrictions either were made to comply more with the demands of reason or grew weaker through neglect and disuse. When Athenian **democracy** reached its height in the middle of the fifth century B.C., religion was no longer the dominant factor in politics. For many Athenians, religion had become largely ceremonial, a way of expressing loyalty to the city. They had come to rely on human reason, not divine guidance, in their political and intellectual life.

Greek political life was marred by violent party conflicts, demagoguery, intercity warfare, and the exploitation of weak states by stronger ones. Nevertheless, the Greek political achievement was extraordinary. What made Greek political life different from that of earlier Near Eastern civilizations, and also gave it enduring significance, was the Greeks' gradual realization that community problems are caused by human beings and require human solutions. Thus, the Greeks came to understand law as an achievement of the rational mind rather than as an edict imposed by the gods; law was valued because it expressed the will and needs of the community, not out of fear of the divine. The Greeks also valued free **citizenship**. An absolute king, a tyrant who ruled arbitrarily and by decree and who was above the law, was abhorrent.

The ideals of political freedom are best exemplified by Athens. Before turning to Athens, however, let us examine another Greek city, which followed a different political course.

Sparta: A Garrison State

Situated on the Peloponnesian peninsula, farther inland than most Greek cities, Sparta had been settled by Dorian Greeks. The Greek city-states dealt with overpopulation and the need for new agricultural land by founding colonies. Sparta, however, established only one colony, Tarentum, in southern Italy. Sparta's chief means of expansion was to conquer, in the eighth century B.C., its neighbors on the Peloponnesian peninsula, including Messenia. Instead of selling the Messenians abroad, the traditional Greek way of treating a defeated foe, the Spartans kept them as state serfs, or *helots*. Helots were owned by the state rather than by individual Spartans. Enraged by their enforced servitude, the Messenians, also a Greek people, desperately tried to regain their freedom. After a bloody struggle, the Spartans suppressed the uprising, but the fear of a helot revolt became indelibly stamped on Spartan consciousness.

To maintain their dominion over the Messenians, who outnumbered them ten to one, the Spartans—with extraordinary single-mindedness, discipline, and loyalty—transformed their own society into an armed camp. Agricultural labor was performed by helots; trade and crafts were left to the *perioikoi*, conquered Greeks who were free but were not citizens and had no political rights. The Spartans learned only one craft, soldiering, and were inculcated with only one conception of excellence: fighting bravely for their city.

The Spartans were trained in the arts of war and indoctrinated to serve the state. Military training for Spartan boys began at age seven; they exercised, drilled, competed, and endured physical hardships. Other Greeks admired the Spartans for their courage, obedience to law, and achievement in molding themselves according to an ideal. Spartan soldiers were better trained and disciplined and were more physically fit than other Greeks. But the Spartans were also criticized for having a limited conception of aretē.

Before Sparta converted itself into a military state, its cultural development had paralleled that of the other Greek cities. By isolating itself economically and culturally from the rest of Greece, however, Sparta became a closed provincial town and did not share in the cultural enlightenment that pervaded the Greek world. Sparta paid a heavy price for its militaristic outlook.

By 500 B.C., Sparta had emerged as the leader of the Peloponnesian League, an alliance of southern Greek city-states whose land forces were superior to those of any other combination of Greek cities. Sparta, though, was concerned with protecting its position, not with expansion. Cautious by temperament and always fearful of a helot uprising, Spartans viewed the Peloponnesian League as an instrument for defense rather than aggression.

Athens: The Rise of Democracy

The contrast between the city-states of Athens and Sparta is striking. Whereas Sparta was a land power and exclusively agricultural, Athens, located on the peninsula of Attica near the coast, possessed a great navy and was the commercial leader among the Greeks. Reluctant to send soldiers far from home, where they were needed to control the helots, Sparta's leaders pursued an isolationist foreign policy. The daring and ambitious Athenians, on the other hand, endeavored to extend their hegemony over other Greek cities. Finally, Athenians and Spartans differed in their concept of freedom. To the Spartans, freedom meant preserving the independence of their fatherland; this overriding consideration demanded order, discipline, and regimentation. The Athenians also wanted to protect their city from enemies, but, unlike the Spartans, they valued political freedom and sought the full development and enrichment of the human personality. Thus, while authoritarian Sparta became culturally sterile, Athens, with its relatively free and open society, emerged as the cultural leader of Hellenic civilization.

Greek city-states generally moved through four stages: rule by a king (monarchy), rule by landowning aristocrats (oligarchy), rule by one man who seized power (tyranny), and rule by the people (democracy). During the first stage, monarchy, the king, who derived his power from the gods, commanded the army and judged civil cases.

Oligarchy, the second stage, was instituted in Athens during the eighth century B.C. when aristocrats (*aristocracy* is a Greek word meaning "rule of the best") usurped power from hereditary kings. In the next century, aristocratic regimes experienced a social crisis. There was tension between the land-holding nobles, who dominated the government, and the newly rich and ambitious merchants, who wanted a share in governing Athens.

ZEUS, C. 460 B.C. This bronze statue was found off the Greek coast in 1926. Although his face is still stylized, his athletic body pulsates with life, capturing the essence of Zeus as the omnipotent ruler of the gods. (The Art Archive/National Archeological Museum Athens/ Gianni Dagli Orti.)

Furthermore, peasants who borrowed from the aristocracy, pledging their lands as security, lost their property and even became enslaved for nonpayment of their debts. Merchants and peasants also protested that the law, which was based on oral tradition and administered exclusively by aristocrats, was unjust. The embittered and restless middle and lower classes were granted one concession. In 621 B.C., the aristocrats appointed Draco to draw up a code of law. Although Draco's code let the poor know what the law was and reduced the possibilities of aristocratic judges behaving arbitrarily, penalties were extremely severe (hence the word *draconian*), and the code provided

no relief for the peasants' economic woes. As the poor began to organize and press for the cancellation of their debts and the redistribution of land, Athens was moving toward civil war.

Solon, the Reformer. In 594 B.C., Solon (c. 640–559 B.C.), a traveler and poet with a reputation for wisdom, was elected chief executive. He maintained that the wealthy landowners, through their greed, had disrupted community life and brought Athens to the brink of civil war. Solon initiated a rational approach to the problems of society by deemphasizing the gods' role in human affairs and attributing the city's ills to the specific

DETAIL OF GREEK KYLIX (CUP), C. 490–480 B.C. The frenzied dancing of the Bacchantes, worshippers of the god Dionysius, is depicted by the vase painter Macron. Maenads (mad ones) dressed in fawn skins and carrying the thrysos, a wand made of vine leaves, leap and carouse in ecstatic orgies with satyrs in worship of the god of wine and sexual liberation. (The Metropolitan Museum of Art/Art Resource, N.Y.)

behavior of individuals; he sought practical remedies for these ills; and he held that written law should be in harmony with **Dikē**, the principle of justice that underlies the human community. The concept of a just city, a unifying principle of Solon's reforms, became a formative ideal of Greek political thought. At the same time, he wanted to instill in Athenians of all classes a sense of working for the common good of the city.

Solon aimed at restoring a sick Athenian society to health by restraining the nobles and improving the lot of the poor. To achieve this goal, he canceled debts, freed Athenians enslaved for debt, and brought back to Athens those who had been sold abroad; however, he refused to confiscate and redistribute the nobles' land as the extremists demanded. He permitted all classes of free men, even the poorest, to sit in the Assembly, which elected magistrates and accepted

or rejected legislation proposed by a new Council of Four Hundred. He also opened the highest offices in the state to wealthy commoners, who had previously been excluded from these positions because they lacked noble birth. Thus, Solon undermined the traditional rights of the hereditary aristocracy and initiated the transformation of Athens from an aristocratic oligarchy into a democracy.

Solon also instituted ingenious economic reforms. Recognizing that the poor soil of Attica was not conducive to growing grain, he urged the cultivation of grapes for wine and the growing of olives, whose oil could be exported. To encourage industrial expansion, he ordered that all fathers teach their sons a trade and granted citizenship to foreign craftsmen who were willing to migrate to Athens. These measures and the fine quality of the native reddish-brown clay allowed Athens to become the leading producer and exporter of pottery. Solon's economic policies transformed Athens into a great commercial center. However, Solon's reforms did not eliminate factional disputes among the aristocratic clans or relieve much of the discontent of the poor.

Pisistratus, the Tyrant. In 546 B.C., Pisistratus (c. 605–527 B.C.), an aristocrat, took advantage of the general instability to become a one-man ruler, driving into exile those who had opposed him. Tyranny thus replaced oligarchy. Tyranny occurred frequently in the Greek city-states. Almost always aristocrats themselves, tyrants generally posed as champions of the poor in their struggle against the aristocracy. Pisistratus sought popular support by having conduits constructed to increase the Athenian water supply; like tyrants in other city-states, he gave to peasants land confiscated from exiled aristocrats and granted state loans to small farmers.

Pisistratus' great achievement was the promotion of cultural life. He initiated grand architectural projects, encouraged sculptors and painters, arranged for public recitals of the Homeric epics, and founded festivals, which included dramatic performances. In all these ways, he made culture, formerly the province of the aristocracy, available to commoners. Pisistratus thus launched a policy that eventually led Athens to emerge as the cultural capital of the Greeks.

Cleisthenes, the Democrat. Shortly after Pisistratus' death, a faction headed by Cleisthenes, an aristocrat sympathetic to democracy, assumed leadership. By an ingenious method of redistricting the city, Cleisthenes ended the aristocratic clans' traditional jockeying for the chief state positions, which had caused much divisiveness and bitterness in Athens. Cleisthenes replaced this practice, rooted in tradition and authority, with a new system that was rationally planned to ensure that historic allegiance to tribe or clan would be superseded by loyalty to the city as a whole.

Cleisthenes hoped to make democracy the permanent form of government for Athens. The power to govern Athens, he believed, should rest with male citizens acting as a body and not with aristocratic factions or a tyrant. To safeguard the city against tyranny, he utilized (or perhaps introduced) the practice of **ostracism.** Once a year, Athenians were given the opportunity to inscribe on a fragment of pottery (*ostracon*) the name of anyone who, they felt, endangered the state. An individual against whom six thousand votes were cast was ostracized, that is, forced to leave Athens for ten years.

Cleisthenes firmly secured democratic government in Athens. The Assembly, which Solon had opened to all male citizens, was in the process of becoming the supreme authority in the state. But the period of Athenian greatness lay in the future; the Athenians first had to fight a war of survival against the Persian empire.

ATHENIAN GREATNESS

The Persian Wars

In 499 B.C., the Ionian Greeks of Asia Minor rebelled against their Persian overlord. Sympathetic to the Ionian cause, Athens sent twenty ships to aid the revolt, an act that the Greek historian Herodotus said "was the beginning of trouble not only for Greece, but for the rest of the world as well."[9] Bent on revenge, Darius I, king of Persia, sent a small detachment to Attica. In 490 B.C., on the plains of Marathon, the citizen army of Athens defeated the Persians—for the Athenians, one of the finest moments in their history. Ten years later, Xerxes, Darius' son, organized a huge invasion force—some 250,000 men and more than 500 ships—with the aim of reducing Greece to a Persian province. Setting aside their separatist instincts, many of the city-states united to defend their independence and their liberty. Herodotus viewed the conflict as an ideological clash between Greek freedom and Asian despotism.

The Persians crossed the waters of the Hellespont (Dardanelles) and made their way into northern Greece. Herodotus describes their encounter at the mountain pass of Thermopylae with three hundred Spartans, who were true to their training and ideal of aretē and "resisted to the last with their swords if they had them, and if not, with their hands and teeth, until the Persians, coming on from the front over the ruins of the wall and closing in from behind, finally overwhelmed them."[10] Northern Greece fell to the Persians, who continued south, pillaging and burning a deserted Athens.

When it appeared that the Greeks' spirit had been broken, the Athenian statesman and general Themistocles (c. 527–460 B.C.), demonstrating in military affairs the same rationality that Cleisthenes had shown in political life, lured the Persian fleet into the narrowest entry to the Bay of Salamis. In this cramped space, the Persians were unable to deploy their more numerous ships. Excelling in ramming maneuvers and knowing what was at stake, the Athenian crews picked off the jammed Persian ships in a decisive victory. In 479 B.C., a year after the Athenian naval victory at Salamis, the Spartans defeated the Persians in the land battle of Plataea. The inventive intelligence with which the Greeks planned their military operations and a fierce desire to preserve their freedom—which, the war made them realize, was their distinguishing attribute—enabled them to defeat the greatest military power the Mediterranean world had yet seen.

The Persian Wars were decisive in the history of the West. Had the Greeks been defeated, it is very likely that their cultural and political vitality would have been aborted. The confidence and pride that came with its astonishing victory, however, propelled Athens into a golden age, which became marred by the Athenian urge for dominance in Greece.

The Persian Wars ushered in an era of Athenian imperialism, which had drastic consequences for the future. Immediately after the wars, more than 150 city-states organized a confederation, the Delian League (named after its treasury on the island of Delos), to protect themselves against a renewed confrontation with Persia. Because of its wealth, its powerful fleet, and the restless energy of its citizens, Athens assumed leadership of the Delian League. Largely thanks to the Athenian fleet, the league was able to drive both pirates and Persians from the Aegean Sea.

Although it had been conceived as a voluntary association of independent Greek states seeking protection against Persia, the league gradually came under the domination of Athens. The Athenians, seeing no contradiction between imperialism and democracy, also manipulated the league for their own economic advantage. They believed that their freedom and prosperity required subduing, exploiting, and enslaving others, and they adhered to the principle that strong states had a natural right to dominate weaker ones. They relished the empire that gave them wealth, power, and glory. Moreover, the Athenians claimed that the other city-states benefited from Athenian hegemony. Athens forbade member states to withdraw, crushed revolts, and stationed garrisons on the territory of confederate states. It used both tribute from members and the league's treasury to finance public works in Athens.

Although member states did receive protection, were not overtaxed, and enjoyed increased trade, they resented Athenian domination. As the Persian threat subsided, hatred for Athenian imperialism grew. In converting the Delian League into an instrument of Athenian imperialism, Athens may have lost an opportunity to perform a great creative act—forming a broad voluntary confederation that might have forestalled the intercity warfare that gravely weakened Hellenic civilization.

The Mature Athenian Democracy

Athenian imperialism was one consequence of the Persian Wars; another was the flowering of Athenian democracy and culture. The Athenian state was a direct democracy, in which the citizens themselves, not elected representatives, made the laws. In the Assembly, which was open to all adult male citizens and that met some forty times a year, Athenians debated and voted on key issues of state; they declared war, signed treaties, and spent public funds. All decisions were arrived at after public discussion, in which all citizens had a right to speak. It is likely that on most occasions farmers did not journey into the city to attend a meeting of the Assembly. By the middle of the fifth century B.C., the will of the people, as expressed by a majority vote in the Assembly, was supreme. Rejecting the arbitrary rule of tyrants and domination by a small circle of nobles, the Athenians conceived the idea of **isonomy**—equality of political rights for citizens of the polis, that is, the right to vote, to speak before and submit motions to the Assembly, to hold the highest public positions, and to receive equal treatment before the law.

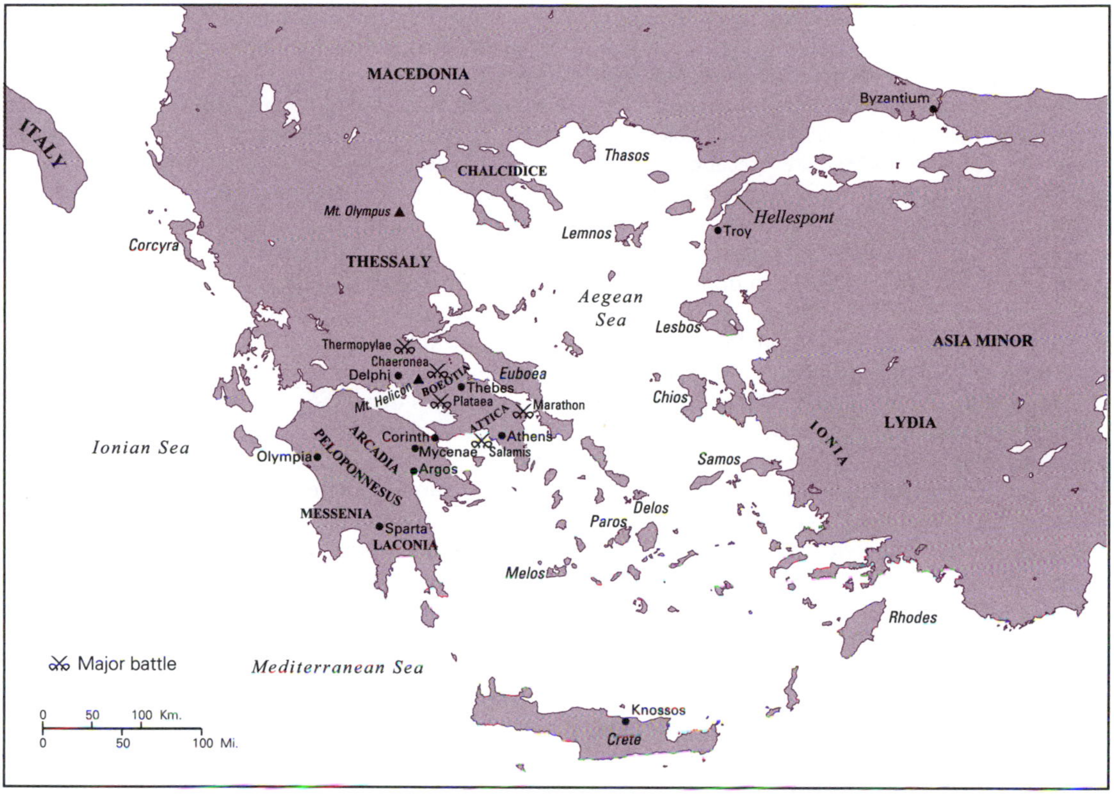

Map 3.2 THE AEGEAN BASIN This map shows major battle sites. Note also the Hellespont, where Xerxes' forces crossed into Greece, and Ionia, the coast of Asia Minor, where Greek philosophy was born. (Copyright © 2013 Cengage Learning.)

The Council of Five Hundred (which had been established by Cleisthenes to replace Solon's Council of Four Hundred) managed the ports, military installations, and other state properties and prepared the agenda for the Assembly. Because its members were chosen annually by lot and could not serve more than twice in a lifetime, the Council could never supersede the Assembly. Chosen at random, its membership could not become a cabal of the most powerful and ambitious citizens. Some 350 magistrates, also chosen by lot, performed administrative tasks: collecting fines, policing the city, repairing streets, inspecting markets, and so forth. Because of the special competence that their posts required, the ten generals who led the army were, for obvious reasons, not chosen by lot but were elected annually by the Assembly.

The introduction of pay for government officials marked a great democratic advance. It meant that an average person could afford to leave his job for a year in order to serve on the Council of Five Hundred, on a commission overseeing the administration of the city, or in the law courts.

Athens has been aptly described as a government of amateurs. There were no professional civil servants, no professional soldiers and sailors, no state judges—all legal cases were decided by juries chosen by lot—and no elected lawmakers. The duties of government were performed by ordinary citizens. Such a system rested on the assumption that the average citizen was capable of participating intelligently in the affairs of state and that he would, in a spirit of civic patriotism, carry out his responsibilities to his city. In fifth-century Athens, excellence was equated with good citizenship—a concern for the good of the community that outweighed personal aspirations. Indeed, to a surprisingly large number of Athenians, politics was an overriding concern, and they devoted considerable time and thought to civic affairs. Those who allowed private matters to take precedence over the needs of the community were denounced as useless people living purposeless lives.

Although Athens was a democracy in form, in practice aristocrats continued to dominate political life for most of the fifth century. Generals came from noble houses, as did the leading voices in the Assembly. This situation was not surprising, for aristocrats took for granted a responsibility to exercise leadership and acquired the education, particularly in public speaking and debate, needed to perform this role. The economic expansion after the Persian Wars produced a wealthy class of tradesmen, who eventually challenged aristocratic dominance in the Assembly during the last third of the fifth century B.C.

Judged by modern standards, Athenian democracy undoubtedly had its limitations and weaknesses. Modern critics point out that resident aliens were almost totally barred from citizenship and therefore from political participation. Slaves, who constituted about one-fourth of the Athenian population, enjoyed none of the freedoms that Athenians considered so precious. The Greeks regarded slavery as a necessary precondition for civilized life; for some to be free and prosperous, they believed, others had to be enslaved. The large number of slaves available for labor, they believed, permitted free citizens to devote themselves to civic affairs and to fight for the city when needed.

Slaves usually did the same work as Athenian citizens: farming, commerce, manufacturing, domestic chores. Some slaves—the three hundred Scythian archers who made up the police force and those sufficiently educated to serve the state as clerks—enjoyed a privileged position. However, slaves, including preadolescent children, who toiled in the mines suffered a grim fate. In Athens, some slaves were Greeks, but most were foreigners. Slaves were generally prisoners of war and captives of pirates. Sometimes they were foreign children sold by their parents or abandoned infants left to die, a not uncommon practice in ancient Greece and Rome. A person finding the infant might eventually sell the child into slavery.

Athenian women were another group denied legal or political rights. Most Greeks, no doubt, agreed with Aristotle, who said: "[T]he male is by nature superior, and the female inferior; and . . . the one rules and the other is ruled."[11] A girl usually was married at fourteen to a man twice her age, and the marriage was arranged by a male relative. The wedding day might be the first time that the young bride saw her future husband. Although either spouse could obtain a divorce, the children remained with the father after the marriage was dissolved. Wives did not dine with their husbands and spent much of their time in the women's quarters.

Athenian women were barred from holding public office and generally could not appear in court without a male representative. They could not act in plays, and, when attending the theater, they sat in the rear, away from the men. Greek women received no formal education, although some young women learned to read and write at home. Training in household skills was considered the only education a woman needed. Since it was believed that a woman could not act independently, she was required to have a guardian—normally her father or husband—who controlled her property and supervised her behavior. Convinced that financial dealings were too difficult for women and that they needed to be protected from strangers, men, not women, did the marketing. When a woman left the house, she was usually accompanied by a male. The Athenian wife was treated as a minor; in effect, she was her husband's ward.

Modern critics also point out the failure of Hellenic Greeks to arrive at a conception of what seventeenth- and eighteenth-century liberal thinkers were to call natural or inalienable rights and what are now generally known as human rights. The Greeks limited rights to members of a particular community; they had no awareness of the modern idea that all individuals possess as a birthright basic rights that government must respect.

Ancient critics, too, attacked Athenian democracy. Having no confidence in the ability of the common people to govern, these aristocratic critics equated democracy with mob rule. In a democracy, they said, the envious, volatile, and incompetent poor tyrannize the rich; make unwise, impetuous decisions; and are easily manipulated by clever demagogues. A political system that gives power to people of limited merit is destined to fail. The Assembly did at times make rash and foolish decisions and was swayed by the oratory of demagogues. For the most part, however, as British historian A. H. M. Jones concludes,

> *the Assembly seems to have kept its head, and very rarely to have broken its rules of procedure. . . . Moreover, the people demanded high standards of its advisors. . . . It was informed advice, and not mere eloquence, that the people expected from rising politicians, and they saw to it that they got it.*[12]

That the Athenians found democracy an indispensable form of government is proved by the paucity of revolts. In the almost two hundred years after Cleisthenes, there were only two attempts to undo the democracy, both made under the stress of the Peloponnesian War and both short-lived.

The flaws in Athenian democracy should not cause us to undervalue its extraordinary achievement. The idea that the state represents a community of free, self-governing citizens remains a crucial principle of Western civilization. Athenian democracy embodied the principle of the legal state—a government based not on force but on laws debated, devised, altered, and obeyed by free citizens.

This idea of the legal state could have arisen only in a society that was aware of and respected the rational mind. In the same way that the Greeks demythicized nature, they also removed myth from the sphere of politics. Holding that government was something that people create to satisfy human needs, the Athenians regarded their leaders neither as gods nor as priests but as men who had demonstrated a capacity for statesmanship. Athens was unique, writes Italian historian Mario Attilio Levi, for Athenians "had the audacity to maintain that human reason is itself the source of legitimacy and therefore of the right to govern and command, in a world in which the only recognized source of legitimacy was the gods."[13]

Both democratic politics and systematic political thought originated in Greece. There people first asked questions about the nature and purpose of the state, rationally analyzed political institutions, speculated about human nature and justice, and discussed the merits of various forms

ATTIC BLACK-FIGURE HYDRIA, C. 510 This hydria, or water jug, shows women drawing water from a fountainhouse. Trips to the fountainhouse provided one of the few opportunities for women to socialize outside the home. (Museum of Fine Arts, Boston/William Francis Warden Fund, 61.195.)

of government. It is to Greece that we ultimately trace the idea of democracy and all that accompanies it: citizenship, constitutions, equality before the law, government by law, reasoned debate, respect for the individual, and confidence in human intelligence.

Nevertheless, there is a fundamental difference between the Greek concept of liberty and our own. We are concerned with protecting the individual from the state, which we often see as a threat to personal freedom and a hindrance to the pursuit of our personal lives. Identifying the good of the individual with the good of the community, the Greeks were not concerned with erecting safeguards against the state; they did not view the state as an alien force to be feared or to be

Pericles on Athenian Greatness

During the Peloponnesian War, Pericles delivered a funeral oration that eloquently expressed the ideals of Athenian society. Reconstructed by Thucydides, the oration is regarded as one of the finest speeches in world history.

"Let me say that our system of government does not copy the institutions of our neighbours. It is more the case of our being a model to others, than of our imitating anyone else. Our constitution is called a democracy because power is in the hands not of a minority but of the whole people. When it is a question of settling private disputes, everyone is equal before the law; when it is a question of putting one person before another in positions of public responsibility, what counts is not membership of a particular class, but the actual ability which the man possesses. No one, so long as he has it in him to be of service to the state, is kept in political obscurity because of poverty. And, just as our political life is free and open, so is our day-to-day life in our relations with each other. We do not get into a state with our next-door neighbour if he enjoys himself in his own way, nor do we give him the kind of black looks which, though they do no real harm, still do hurt people's feelings. We are free and tolerant in our private lives; but in public affairs we keep to the law. This is because it commands our deep respect.

"We give our obedience to those whom we put in positions of authority, and we obey the laws themselves, especially those which are for the protection of the oppressed, and those unwritten laws which it is an acknowledged shame to break.

"And here is another point. When our work is over, we are in a position to enjoy all kinds of recreation for our spirits. There are various kinds of contests [in poetry, drama, music, and athletics] and sacrifices regularly throughout the year; in our own homes we find a beauty and a good taste which delight us every day and which drive away our cares. Then the greatness of our city brings it about that all the good things from all over the world flow in to us, so that to us it seems just as natural to enjoy foreign goods as our own local products. . . .

"Our love of what is beautiful does not lead to extravagance; our love of the things of the mind does not make us soft. We regard wealth as something to be properly used, rather than as something to boast about. As for poverty, no one need be ashamed to admit it: the real shame is in not taking practical measures to escape from it. Here each individual is interested not only in his own affairs but in the affairs of the state as well: even those who are mostly occupied with their own business are extremely well-informed on general politics—this is a peculiarity of ours: we do not say that a man who takes no interest in politics is a man who minds his own business; we say that he has no business here at all. We Athenians, in our own persons, take our decisions on policy or submit them to proper discussions: for we do not think that there is an incompatibility between words and deeds; the worst thing is to rush into action before the consequences have been properly debated."

Questions for Analysis

1. According to Pericles, what are the chief characteristics of a democratic society?
2. Of what was Pericles most proud regarding Athens?

Thucydides, *History of the Peloponnesian War*, trans. Rex Warner (New York: Penguin Books, 1972), 145–147.

protected against. Rather, they saw it as a moral association, a second family, which taught proper conduct and enabled them to fulfill their human potential. Given this orientation, they were not much interested in universal human rights.

Pericles: Symbol of Athenian Democracy

Pericles (c. 495–429 B.C.), a gifted statesman, orator, and military commander, was the central figure in Athenian life during the middle of the fifth century So impressive was his leadership that this period is called the Age of Pericles. During these years, Athenians achieved greatness in politics, drama, sculpture, architecture, and thought.

In the opening stage of the monumental clash with Sparta, the Peloponnesian War (431–404 B.C.), Pericles delivered an oration in honor of the Athenian war casualties (see Primary Source box). The oration, as reconstructed by Thucydides, the great Athenian historian of the fifth century B.C., contains a glowing description of the Athenian democratic ideal, which encompassed both civic and personal freedom.

Throughout the speech, Pericles contrasted the narrow Spartan concept of excellence with the Athenians' humanistic ideal of the full development of the human personality. Unlike Sparta, Athens valued both political freedom and cultural creativity; indeed, as Pericles recognized, freedom released an enormous amount of creative energy, making possible Athens's extraordinary cultural accomplishments. "Our love of what is beautiful does not lead to extravagance, our love of the things of the mind does not make us soft," continued Pericles in praise of Athenian society.[14]

THE DECLINE OF THE CITY-STATES

Although the Greeks shared a common language and culture, they remained divided politically. A determination to preserve city-state sovereignty prevented them from forming a larger political grouping, which might have contained the intercity warfare that ultimately cost the city-state its

vitality and independence. But the creation of a Pan-Hellenic union would have required a radical transformation of the Greek character, which for hundreds of years had regarded the city-state as the only suitable political system.

The Peloponnesian War

Athenian control of the Delian League engendered fear in the Spartans and their allies in the Peloponnesian League. Sparta and the Peloponnesian states decided on war because they felt that a dynamic and imperialistic Athens threatened their independence. At stake for Athens was hegemony over the Delian League, which gave Athens political power and contributed to its economic prosperity. Neither Athens nor Sparta anticipated the catastrophic consequences that the war would have for Greek civilization.

The war began in 431 B.C. and ended in 404 B.C., with a temporary and uneasy interlude of peace from 421 to 414 B.C. Possessing superior land forces, the Peloponnesian League invaded Attica and set fire to the countryside. In 430 B.C., a plague, probably coming from Ethiopia by way of Egypt, ravaged Athens, killing about one-third of the population, including its leader, Pericles (in 429 B.C.). Because of Athenian sea power and Spartan inability to inflict a crushing defeat on Athenian ground troops, the first stage of the war ended in stalemate. In 421 B.C., the war-weary combatants concluded a peace treaty.

What led to the resumption of the war and the eventual defeat of Athens was the Athenian expedition against Sicily and its largest city, Syracuse. Athenians were intoxicated by an imperialist urge to extend the empire in the west and by prospects of riches. Swayed by speeches that stirred the emotions, the Athenian populace, believing disaster to be impossible and forsaking caution and reason, approved the Sicilian venture.

Launched with extravagant expectations, the Sicilian expedition ended in dismal failure. Athens and its allies lost fifty thousand men and two hundred ships in the venture; the expedition also cost Athens all hope of victory in the struggle with Sparta. Fearful that victory in Sicily would increase Athenian manpower and wealth, Sparta in 414 B.C. had again taken up the sword.

WRESTLERS: RELIEF FROM A STATUE BASE, ATHENIAN, LATE SIXTH CENTURY B.C. Physical fitness and athletics were highly prized by the Greeks. Poets sang the praise of Olympic champions, and sculptors captured the beauty of athletic physiques for an admiring public. (Young men wrestling, from a statue base found in the Dipylon Cemetery, Athens, c. 510 B.C. (marble) (see also 60008-9 and 60011), Greek, (6th century B.C.)/National Archaeological Museum, Athens, Greece/The Bridgeman Art Library International.)

Strengthened by financial support from Persia and by the defection of some Athenian allies, Sparta moved to end the war. Finally, with its navy decimated and its food supply dwindling, besieged Athens surrendered in 404 B.C. Sparta dissolved the Delian League, left Athens with only a handful of ships, and forced the city to pull down its long walls—ramparts designed to protect it against siege weapons. But the Spartans refused to massacre Athenian men and enslave the women and children, as some allies had urged.

The Peloponnesian War shattered the spiritual foundations of Hellenic society. During the course of the long war, men became brutalized—cities were sacked and captives murdered—selfish individualism triumphed over civic duty, moderation gave way to extremism, and politics degenerated into civil war.

The deterioration of Greek political life was exemplified by conflicts between oligarchs and democrats. Oligarchs, generally from the wealthier segments of Greek society, wanted to concentrate power in their own hands by depriving the lower classes of political rights. Democrats, generally from the poorer segment of society, sought to preserve the political rights of adult male citizens. Strife between oligarchs and democrats was quite common in the Greek city-states even before the Peloponnesian War. Both sides sought to dominate the Assembly and to manipulate

the courts; both resorted to bribery and at times even assassinated opponents. During the Peloponnesian War, in many cities, including Athens, these party conflicts erupted into savage civil war marked by fanaticism and vengeance. The moral basis of Hellenic society was wrecked. In the words of Thucydides,

Love of power, operating through greed and through personal ambition, was the cause of all these evils. To this must be added the violent fanaticism which came into play once the struggle had broken out. Leaders of parties in professing to serve the public interest . . . were seeking to win the prizes for themselves. In their struggle for ascendancy nothing was barred; terrible indeed were the actions to which they committed themselves, and in taking revenge they went further still. Here they were deterred neither by the claims of justice nor by the interests of the state. . . . Thus neither side had any use for conscientious motives; more interest was shown in those who could produce attractive arguments to justify some disgraceful action. As for the citizens who held moderate views, they were destroyed by both the extreme parties. . . . As the result of these revolutions, there was a general deterioration of character throughout the Greek World.[15]

Athens shared the political problems of the Greek world during the war. Pericles had provided Athenians with effective leadership in the three decades prior to the war; when the Assembly seemed to support unwise policies, he had won it over with sound arguments. After his death in 429 B.C., the quality of leadership deteriorated. Succeeding statesmen were motivated more by personal ambition than by civic devotion; instead of soberly examining issues, they supported policies that would gain them popularity. Without Pericles' wise statesmanship, the Assembly at times acted rashly, as it did in the case of the Sicilian expedition.

Taking advantage of the decline in morale after the failure of this expedition, oligarchs gained control of Athens in 411 B.C.; a body of citizens, known as the Four Hundred, wielded power. Seeking to deprive the lower classes of political influence, the Four Hundred restricted citizenship to four thousand men. But the crews of Athenian ships, loyal to democracy, challenged the authority of the Four Hundred, who were forced to flee.

After the defeat of Athens in 404 B.C., oligarchs again gained control, this time with the support of Sparta. A ruling council of thirty men, the so-called Thirty Tyrants, held power. Led by Critias, an extreme antidemocrat, the Thirty trampled on Athenian rights, confiscating property and condemning many people to death. In the winter of 404–403 B.C., returned exiles led an uprising against the Thirty, who were unseated.

The Fourth Century

The Peloponnesian War was the great crisis of Hellenic history. The golden age of Athenian culture came to an end, and the city-states never fully recovered from their self-inflicted spiritual wounds. The civic loyalty and confidence that had marked the fifth century B.C. waned, and the fourth century was dominated by a new mentality, which the leaders of the Age of Pericles would have abhorred. A concern for private affairs superseded devotion to the general good of the polis. Increasingly, professionals, rather than ordinary citizens, administered the tasks of government, and mercenaries began to replace citizen soldiers.

The political history of the fourth century can be summed up briefly. Athens, the only state that might have united the Greek world, had lost its chance. A culturally sterile, provincial-minded, and heavy-handed Spartan government lacked the talent to govern the Greeks. In many cities, Sparta replaced democratic governments with pro-Spartan oligarchies under the supervision of a Spartan governor. But Spartan hegemony was short-lived; before long, the Greek city-states had thrown off the Spartan yoke. The quarrelsome city-states formed new systems of alliances and persisted in their ruinous conflicts. Some Greek thinkers, recognizing the futility of constant war, argued that peace should be the goal of Greek politics. However, their efforts were in vain.

In addition to wars between city-states, fourth-century Greece experienced a new outbreak of civil wars between rich and poor. Athens largely escaped these ruinous conflicts, but they engulfed many other cities. With good reason, Greek thinkers regarded social discord as the greatest of evils.

While the Greek cities battered one another in fratricidal warfare, a new power was rising in the north—Macedonia. To the Greeks, the Macedonians, a wild mountain people who spoke a Greek dialect and had acquired a sprinkling of Hellenic culture, differed little from other non-Greeks, whom they called barbarians. In 359 B.C., at the age of twenty-three, Philip II (382–336 B.C.) ascended the Macedonian throne. Having spent three years as a hostage in Thebes, Philip had learned the latest military tactics and had witnessed firsthand the weaknesses of the warring Greek states. He converted Macedonia into a first-rate military power and began a drive to become master of the Greeks.

Patient, deceitful, clever, and unscrupulous, Philip gradually extended his power over the Greek city-states. The Greeks did not correctly assess Philip's strength and were slow to organize a coalition against Macedonia, despite the efforts of Demosthenes (c. 384–322 B.C.), the Athenian orator and patriot, who urged the Greeks to unite against this threat to their freedom. In 338 B.C., at Chaeronea, Philip's forces inflicted a decisive defeat on the Greeks, and all of Greece was his. The city-states still existed, but they had

Demosthenes

Debates in the Assembly stimulated the development of oratory as an art form in Athens and other city-states. Demosthenes (384–322 B.C.), the greatest of the Greek orators, earned his reputation through disciplined effort, for he was not a naturally gifted speaker. When he first addressed the Assembly, wrote Plutarch, the second-century biographer, he was "derided for his strange and uncouth style, which was cumbered with long sentences and tortured with formal arguments to a most harsh and disagreeable excess. Besides, he had, it seems, a weakness in his voice, a perplexed and indistinct utterance and a shortness of breath, which by breaking and disjointing his sentences, much obscured the sense and meaning of what he spoke."* But the very determined Demosthenes practiced constantly until he perfected his enunciation and delivery.

Demosthenes' fame rests mainly on his Philippics—speeches delivered over a ten-year period warning Greeks of the threat posed by Philip of Macedon. He urged the city-states of Greece to unite against the common enemy and lamented the deterioration of the Greek character since the heroic struggle against Persia.

And we, the Greek community . . . instead of sending embassies to one another about [the danger] and expressing indignation, are in such a miserable state, so intrenched in separate towns, that to this day we can attempt nothing that interest or necessity requires; we cannot combine, or form any association for succour and alliance; we look unconcernedly on the man's growing power, . . . not caring or striving for the salvation of Greece.†

lost their independence. The world of the small, independent, self-sufficient polis was drawing to a close, and Greek civilization was taking a different shape.

THE DILEMMA OF GREEK POLITICS

Philip's conquest of the city-states points to fundamental weaknesses of Greek politics. Despite the internal crisis and persistent warfare, the Greeks were unable to fashion any other political framework than the polis. The city-state was fast becoming an anachronism, but the Greeks were unable to see that, in a world moving toward larger states and empires, the small city-state could not compete. An unallied city-state, with its small citizen army, could not withstand the powerful military machine that Philip had created. A challenge confronted the city-states: the need to shape some form of political union, a Pan-Hellenic federation, that would end the suicidal internecine warfare, promote economic well-being, and protect the Greek world from hostile states. Because they could not respond creatively to this challenge, the city-states ultimately lost their independence to foreign conquerors.

The waning of civic responsibility among the citizens was another reason for the decline of the city-states. The vitality of the city-state depended on the willingness of its citizens to put aside private concerns for the good of the community. However, although Athens had recovered commercially from the Peloponnesian War, its citizens had suffered a permanent change in character; the abiding devotion to the polis, which had distinguished the Age of Pericles, greatly diminished during the fourth century. The factional strife, the degeneration of politics into personal ambition, the demagoguery, and the fanaticism that Thucydides had described persisted into the fourth century and were aggravated by the economic discontent of the poor. The Periclean ideal of citizenship dissipated as Athenians neglected the community to concentrate on private affairs or sought to derive personal profit

A passionate patriot, Demosthenes warned his fellow citizens that Philip, an autocratic king, wanted to conquer Athens and put an end to Athenian democracy.

> There is nothing which [Philip] strives and plots against so much as our constitution, nothing in the world he is so anxious about, as its destruction. . . . First then you must assume that he is an irreconcilable enemy of our constitution and democracy; secondly, you must be convinced that all his operations and contrivances are designed for the injury of our state.[‡]

Demosthenes negotiated an alliance between Thebes and Athens, but the two were defeated by Philip at Chaeronea in 338 B.C. Demosthenes, who witnessed the battle, delivered a funeral oration for the Greek dead, but the speech is lost. After the death of Alexander the Great in 323 B.C., Demosthenes helped organize Greek resistance to Macedonian rule. The Greeks were defeated the following year, and Antipater, the Macedonian governor of Greece, ordered the execution of Demosthenes and other orators who had urged war. The aging orator and passionate patriot took poison.

Demosthenes' speeches served as a model for subsequent orators, including Cicero, Rome's greatest orator. In modern times, patriots and lovers of freedom have evoked Demosthenes' devotion to his city and its free institutions.

---

[*]Plutarch, *The Lives of Noble Grecians and Romans*, trans. John Dryden, rev. A. H. Clough (New York: Modern Library, n.d.), 1025.

[†]*Demosthenes' Orations,* intro. by John Warrington (London: Dent, Everyman's Library, 1954), Third Philippic, 195–196.

[‡]Ibid., Fourth Philippic, 209.

---

from public office. The decline in civic responsibility could be seen in the hiring of mercenaries to replace citizen soldiers and in the indifference and hesitancy with which the Athenians confronted Philip. The Greeks did not respond to the Macedonian threat as they had earlier rallied to fight off the Persian menace because the quality of citizenship had deteriorated.

Greek political life demonstrated the best and the worst features of freedom. On the one hand, as Pericles boasted, freedom encouraged active citizenship, reasoned debate, and government by law. On the other hand, as Thucydides lamented, freedom could degenerate into factionalism, demagoguery, unbridled self-interest, and civil war. Because monarchy deprives people of freedom and self-rule, the Greeks regarded monarchy as a form of government appropriate for uncivilized barbarians. Nevertheless, their political experience showed that free men in a democracy are susceptible to demagogues, will base political decisions on keyed-up emotions rather than on cool reasoning, and are capable of behaving brutally toward political opponents. Moreover, Greek democracy, which valued freedom, was unable to overcome a weakness that has afflicted despotic rulers: an incautious attitude toward power that causes the state to overreach itself. Such an attitude demonstrated a self-destructive **hubris**, excessive pride or arrogance, that Greek moralists warned against. This is how Thucydides interpreted Athens's disastrous Sicilian expedition during the Peloponnesian War. Driven by a mad passion to possess what was beyond their reach, the Athenians brought ruin to their city.

The Athenians, who saw no conflict between imperialism and democracy, considered it natural for stronger states to dominate weaker ones, an attitude that helped precipitate the destructive Peloponnesian War. A particularly egregious example of this outlook occurred during that war when Athenians decided to invade the island of Melos despite the assurances of the Melians that they represented no threat to Athens. As reported by Thucydides, the Athenian envoys told the Melians that "the strong do what they

69

have the power to do, and the weak accept what they have to accept."[16] When the Melians resisted, the Athenians slaughtered the men, enslaved the women and children, and colonized the territory.

Greek politics also revealed both the capabilities and the limitations of reason. Originally, the polis was conceived as a divine institution in which the citizen had a religious obligation to obey the law. As the rational and secular outlook became more pervasive, the gods lost their authority. When people no longer regarded law as an expression of sacred traditions ordained by the gods but saw it as a merely human contrivance,

respect for the law diminished, weakening the foundations of the society. The results were party conflicts, politicians who scrambled for personal power, and moral uncertainty. Recognizing the danger, conservatives insisted that law must again be conceived as issuing from the gods and that the city must again treat its ancient traditions with reverence. Although the Greeks originated the lofty ideal that human beings could regulate their political life according to reason, their history, marred by intercity warfare and internal violence, demonstrates the extreme difficulties involved in creating and maintaining a rational society.

NOTES

1. James Shiel, ed., *Greek Thought and the Rise of Christianity* (New York: Barnes and Noble, 1968), 5–6.

2. Homer, *The Iliad,* trans. E. V. Rieu (Baltimore: Penguin Books, 1950), 23.

3. H. D. F. Kitto, *The Greeks* (Baltimore: Penguin Books, 1957), 60.

4. Homer, *The Iliad,* 405.

5. Werner Jaeger, *Paideia: The Ideals of Greek Culture,* trans. Gilbert Highet (New York: Oxford University Press, 1945), 1:8.

6. C. M. Bowra, *Homer* (London: Gerald Duckworth, 1972), 72.

7. Kitto, *The Greeks,* 78.

8. Mason Hammond, *The City in the Ancient World* (Cambridge, Mass.: Harvard University Press, 1972), 189.

9. Herodotus, *The Histories,* trans. Aubrey de Sélincourt (Baltimore: Penguin Books, 1954), 350.

10. Ibid., 493.

11. Aristotle, *Politics,* in *Basic Works of Aristotle,* ed. Richard McKeon (New York: Random House, 1941), 1132.

12. A. H. M. Jones, *Athenian Democracy* (Oxford: Basil Blackwell, 1969), 132–133.

13. Mario Attilio Levi, *Political Power in the Ancient World* (New York: Mentor Books, 1968), 122–123.

14. Thucydides, *History of the Peloponnesian War,* trans. Rex Warner (Baltimore: Penguin Books, 1954), 118.

15. Ibid., 210.

16. Ibid., 360.

SUGGESTED READING

Frost, Frank J., *Greek Society* (1987). Social and economic life in ancient Greece.

Hanson, Victor Davis, *A War Like No Other* (2005). A Perceptive analysis of the Peloponnesian War.

Hooper, Finley, *Greek Realities* (1978). A literate and sensitive presentation of Greek society and culture.

Kitto, H. D. F., *The Greeks* (1957). A stimulating survey of Greek life and thought.

Meier, Christian, *Athens: A Portrait of the City in Its Golden Age* (1999). Rich in details and interpretation.

_____, *The Greek Discovery of Politics* (1990). Answers the question, How was it that Greek civilization, unlike all others preceding it, gave birth to democracies?

Ober, Joseph, *The Athenian Revolution* (1996). Thoughtful essays on Greek democracy and political theory.

Stockton, David, *The Classical Athenian Democracy* (1990). The evolution and nature of Greek democracy.

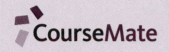

CourseMate

Go to the CourseMate website at **www.cengagebrain.com** for additional study tools and review materials—including audio and video clips—for this chapter.

Chapter 4

Greek Thought:
From Myth to Reason

Theater at Epidaurus, Greece, c. 350 B.C. (Hirmer Verlag Fotoarchiv, München.)

- **Philosophy**
- **Art**
- **Poetry and Drama**
- **History**
- **The Greek Achievement: Reason, Freedom, Humanism**

Focus Questions

1. How did the Pre-Socratic thinkers make the transition from myth to reason?

2. How did the Sophists and Socrates advance the tradition of reason and humanism?

3. Why is Plato's *Republic* considered a milestone in the emergence of political thought?

4. What do Plato and Aristotle have in common? How do they differ?

5. How did Greek drama, art, and historiography contribute to the tradition of reason and humanism?

The Greeks broke with the mythopoeic outlook of the Near East and conceived a new way of viewing nature and human society, which is the basis of the Western scientific and philosophical tradition. After an initial period of mythical thinking, by the fifth century B.C. the Greek mind had gradually applied reason to the physical world and to all human activities. This emphasis on reason marks a turning point for human civilization.

The development of rational thought in Greece was a process, a trend, not a finished achievement. The process began when some thinkers rejected mythical explanations for natural phenomena. The nonphilosophical majority never entirely eliminated the language, attitudes, and beliefs of myth from their lives and thought. For them, the world remained controlled by divine forces, which were appeased through cultic practices. Even in the mature **philosophy** of Plato and Aristotle, mythical modes of thought persisted. What is of immense historical importance, however, is not the degree to which the Greeks successfully integrated the norm of reason, but the fact that they originated this norm, defined it, and consciously applied it to their intellectual and social life.

PHILOSOPHY

The first theoretical philosophers in human history emerged in the sixth century B.C., in the Greek cities of Ionia in Asia Minor. Curious about the essential composition of nature and dissatisfied with earlier creation legends, the Ionians sought physical, rather than mythic-religious, explanations for natural occurrences. In the process, they arrived at a new concept of nature and a new method of inquiry. They maintained that nature was not manipulated by arbitrary and willful gods, nor was it governed by blind chance. The Ionians said that there is an intelligible pattern to nature; that nature contains a hidden structure—principles of order or general laws—that governs phenomena; and that these fundamental rules were ascertainable by the human mind. They implied that the origin, composition, and structure of the world can be investigated rationally and systematically. Thus, in seeking to account for rainbows, earthquakes, and eclipses, the Ionians posited entirely naturalistic explanations that relied on observation, had an awareness of cause and effect, and excluded the gods. This new outlook marks the beginning of scientific thought.

What conditions enabled the Greeks to make this breakthrough? Perhaps their familiarity with Near Eastern achievements in mathematics and science stimulated their ideas. But this influence should not be exaggerated, says Greek scholar John N. Theodorakopoulos, for Egyptians and Mesopotamians "had only mythological systems of belief and a knowledge of practical matters. They did not possess those pure and crystal-clear products of the intellect which we call science and philosophy. Nor did they have any terminology to describe them."[1] Rooted in mythological thinking, the ancient Near East experienced no eruption of theorizing about nature in pristine philosophical and scientific terms as Greece did beginning in the sixth century B.C. Perhaps the poets' conception of human behavior as subject to universal destiny was extended into the philosophers' belief that nature was governed by law. Perhaps the breakthrough was fostered by the Greeks' freedom from a priesthood and rigid religious doctrines that limit thought. Or perhaps Greek speculative thought was an offspring of the city, because if law governed human affairs, providing balance and order, should not the universe also be regulated by principles of order?

The Cosmologists: A Rational Inquiry into Nature

The first Ionian philosophers are called cosmologists because they sought to discover the underlying principles of the universe: how nature came to be the way it was. They held that some single, eternal, and imperishable substance, which underwent various modifications, gave rise to all phenomena in nature.

Ionian philosophy began with Thales (c. 624–548 B.C.) of Miletus, a city in Ionia. He was a contemporary of Solon of Athens and concerned himself with understanding the order of nature. Thales said that water was the basic element, the underlying substratum of nature, and that through some natural process—similar to the formation of ice or steam—water gave rise to everything else in the world.

Thales revolutionized thought because he omitted the gods from his account of the origins of nature and searched for a natural explanation of how all things came to be. He broke with the commonly held belief that earthquakes were caused by Poseidon, god of the sea, and offered instead a naturalistic explanation for these disturbances: that the earth floated on water and when the water experienced turbulent waves, the earth was rocked by earthquakes. Thales was the first person to predict an eclipse of the sun. To do this, he had to dismiss traditional mythical explanations and to grasp a crucial scientific principle—that heavenly objects move in regular patterns, which can be known.

Anaximander (c. 611–547 B.C.), another sixth-century Ionian, rejected Thales' theory that water was the original substance. He rejected any specific substance and suggested that an indefinite, undifferentiated substance, which he called the Boundless, was the source of all things. He believed that from this primary mass, which contained the powers of heat and cold, there gradually emerged a nucleus, the seed of the world. According to Anaximander, the cold and wet condensed to form the earth and its cloud cover, while the hot and dry formed the rings of fire that we see as the moon, the sun, and the stars. The heat from the fire in the sky dried the earth and shrank the seas. From the warm slime on earth arose life, and from the first sea creatures there evolved land animals, including human beings. Anaximander's account of the origins of the universe and nature understandably contained fantastic elements. Nevertheless, by offering a natural explanation for the origin of nature and life and by holding that nature was lawful, it surpassed the creation myths.

Like his fellow Ionians, Anaximenes, who died around 525 B.C., made the transition from myth to reason. He also maintained that a primary substance, air, underlay reality and accounted for nature's orderliness. Air that was rarefied became fire, whereas wind and clouds were formed from condensed air. If the process of condensation continued, it produced water, earth, and eventually stones. Anaximenes also rejected the old belief that a rainbow was the goddess Iris; instead, he saw it as the consequence of the sun's rays falling on dense air.

The Ionians have been called matter philosophers because they held that everything issued from a particular material substance. Other sixth-century B.C. thinkers tried a different approach. Pythagoras (c. 580–507 B.C.) and his followers, who lived in the Greek cities in southern Italy, found the nature of things not in a particular substance but in mathematical relationships. The Pythagoreans discovered that the intervals in the musical scale can be expressed mathematically. Extending this principle of structure and proportion found in sound to the universe at large, they concluded that the cosmos also contained an inherent mathematical order and harmony. Thus, the Pythagoreans shifted the emphasis from matter to form, from the world of sense perception to the logic of mathematics. The Pythagoreans were also religious mystics who believed in the immortality and transmigration of souls. Consequently, they refused to eat animal flesh, fearing that it contained former human souls.

Parmenides (c. 515–450 B.C.), a native of the Greek city of Elea in southern Italy, argued that the fundamental view of the Ionians that the universe underwent change and development over time was utterly mistaken. In developing his position, Parmenides applied to philosophical argument the **logic** used by the Pythagoreans for mathematical thinking. In putting forth the proposition that an argument must be consistent and contain no contradictions, Parmenides became the founder of formal logic.

Despite appearances, asserted Parmenides, reality—the cosmos and all that is within it—is one, eternal, and unchanging. It is made known not through the senses, which are misleading, but through the mind; not through experience, but through reason. Truth could be reached through abstract thought alone. Parmenides' concept of an unchanging reality apprehended by thought alone influenced Plato and is the foundation of **metaphysics**—the branch of philosophy that attempts to define ultimate reality, or Being.

Parmenides' thought also had religious implications. Although he did not refer to True Being as God, he did ascribe to it the attributes of oneness, transcendence, permanence, and perfection. Such a description of Being abounds with religious meaning. Particularly as developed by Plato, the quest for Being would greatly influence

religious thought, including Christian theology, in the ancient world.

Democritus (c. 460–370 B.C.), from the Greek mainland, renewed the Ionians' concern with the world of matter and reaffirmed their confidence in knowledge derived from sense perception—and the senses indicated that change did occur in nature, in contrast to Parmenides' view. But Democritus also retained Parmenides' reverence for reason. His model of the universe consisted of two fundamental realities: empty space and an infinite number of atoms. Eternal, indivisible, and imperceptible, these atoms moved in the void. All things consisted of atoms, and combinations of atoms accounted for all change in nature. In a world of colliding atoms, everything behaved according to mechanical principles. (Of course, Democritus' atomic theory did not derive from any empirical evidence of atoms but was purely speculative.)

Concepts essential to scientific thought thus emerged in embryonic form with Greek philosophers: natural explanations for physical occurrences (Ionians), the mathematical order of nature (Pythagoras), logical proof (Parmenides), and the mechanical structure of the universe (Democritus). By giving to nature a rational, rather than a mythical, foundation and by holding that theories should be grounded in evidence and that one should be able to defend them logically, the early Greek philosophers pushed thought in a new direction. This new approach allowed a critical analysis of theories, whereas myths, accepted unconditionally on faith and authority, did not promote discussion and questioning. Greek thinkers established the crucial principle that a proposition is not considered true unless it can be supported by logic or empirical evidence. For the most part, the early Greek philosophers rejected the old mythical explanations of nature. Nevertheless, when they proclaimed the unity and orderliness of nature and asserted that an ultimate reality underlies the finite world, they were also expressing ideas integral to religious thought.

These early philosophers made possible theoretical thinking and the systematization of knowledge—as distinct from the mere observation and collection of data. The systematization of knowledge extended into several areas. Greek mathematicians, for example, organized

PORCH OF THE MAIDENS, ATTIC SCULPTURE FROM THE ACROPOLIS. The architect has incorporated the human form as a functional element in a rationally organized structure. The balance and harmony of the Porch of the Maidens weds humanity with art. (Vanni/Art Resource, N.Y.)

the Egyptians' practical experience with land measurements into the logical and coherent science of geometry, in which each statement followed logically from given assumptions. They established mathematics as a body of theoretical knowledge, an ordered system based on fundamental premises and necessary connections, and they developed logical procedures for arriving at mathematical proofs. Both Babylonians and Egyptians had performed fairly complex mathematical operations, but unlike the Greeks, they made no attempt to prove underlying mathematical principles—to demonstrate that certain conclusions must flow from certain hypotheses. In another area, Babylonian priests observed the heavens for religious reasons, believing that the stars revealed the wishes of the gods. The Greeks used the data collected by the Babylonians, but

not for a religious purpose; rather, they sought to discover the geometrical laws that govern the motions of heavenly bodies.

A parallel development occurred in medicine. No Near Eastern medical text explicitly attacked magical beliefs and practices. In contrast, Greek doctors, because of the philosophers' work, were able to distinguish between magic and medicine. The school of the Greek physician Hippocrates (c. 460–c. 377 B.C.), located on the island of Cos, off the Asia Minor coast, was influenced by the thought of the early Greek cosmologists. Hippocratic physicians recorded in detail their observations of ill patients, classified symptoms, and predicted the future course of the disease. They also ruled out supernatural and magical explanations and cures. The following tract from the school of Hippocrates on epilepsy, which was considered a sacred disease, illustrates the development of a scientific approach to medicine.

> *I am about to discuss the disease called "sacred." It is not, in my opinion, any more divine or sacred than any other disease, but has a natural cause, and its supposed divine origin is due to men's inexperience, and to their wonder at its peculiar character. Now . . . men continue to believe in its divine origin because they are at a loss to understand it. . . . My own view is that those who first attributed a sacred character to this malady were like the magicians, purifiers, charlatans, and quacks of our own day; men who claim great piety and superior knowledge. Being at a loss, and having no treatment which would help, they concealed and sheltered themselves behind superstition, and called this illness sacred, in order that their utter ignorance might not be manifest.*[2]

The Sophists: A Rational Investigation of Human Society

In their effort to understand the external world, the cosmologists had created the tools of reason. These early Greek thinkers were developing a new and profound awareness of the mind's capacity for theoretical thinking. And equally important, they were establishing the mind's autonomy—its ability to inquire into any subject, relying solely on its own power to think. Greek thinkers then turned away from the world of nature and attempted a rational investigation of people and society, dismissing efforts to explain the social world through inherited beliefs about the gods. The Sophists exemplified this shift in focus. They were professional teachers who wandered from city to city teaching rhetoric, grammar, poetry, gymnastics, mathematics, and music. The Sophists insisted that it was futile to speculate about the first principles of the universe, for such knowledge was beyond the grasp of the human mind. Instead, they urged that individuals improve themselves and their cities by applying reason to the tasks of citizenship and statesmanship. The Western **humanist** tradition owes much to

the Sophists who examined, at times with great insight, political and ethical concerns, cultivated the minds of their students, and invented formal secular education.

The Sophists answered a practical need in Athens, which had been transformed into a wealthy and dynamic imperial state after the Persian Wars. Because the Sophists claimed that they could teach *political* aretē—the skill to formulate the right laws and policies for cities and the art of eloquence and persuasion needed for success in public life—they were sought as tutors by politically ambitious young men, especially in Athens.

Traditionally, the Greeks had drawn a sharp distinction between Greeks, the bearers of an enlightened civilization, and uncivilized and immoderate non-Greeks, whom they called barbarians, and held that some people were slaves by nature. The dramatist Euripides expressed these sentiments: "It is natural for Hellenes to rule barbarians and not . . . for barbarians to rule Hellenes. They are a slave race, Hellenes are free."[3] Some Sophists in the fourth century B.C. arrived at a broader conception of humanity. They asserted that slavery was based on force or chance, that people were not slaves or masters by nature, and indeed that all people, Greek and non-Greek, were fundamentally alike.

The Sophists were philosophical **relativists**—that is, they held that no truth is universally valid. Protagoras, a fifth-century Sophist, said that "man is the measure of all things." By this he meant that good and evil, truth and falsehood, are matters of community and individual judgment; there are no universal standards that fit all people at all times. Human laws and ethical beliefs have evolved according to a particular community's needs; they are simply human contrivances and conventions, not objective truths or standards written into nature. While not based on moral absolutes, hopefully the city's laws derive from the judgment of wise and good men.

In applying reason critically to human affairs, the Sophists challenged the traditional religious and moral values of Athenian society. Some Sophists taught that speculation about the divine was useless. Others went further, asserting that religion was just a human invention to ensure obedience to traditions and laws. Thus, the Sophist

Critias (c. 480–403 B.C.) argued that to deter people from committing "open crimes of violence, . . . a wise and clever man invented fear (of the gods) for mortals, that there might be some means of frightening the wicked, even if they do anything or say or think it in secret. Hence he introduced the Divine (religion), saying that there is a God flourishing with immortal life, . . . who will hear everything said among mortals, and will be able to see all that is done."[4]

The Sophists also applied reason to law, with the same effect: the undermining of traditional authority. The laws of a given city, they asserted, did not derive from the gods; nor were they based on any objective, universal, and timeless standards of justice and good, for such standards did not exist. Each community determined for itself what was good or bad, just or unjust. Beginning with this premise, some Sophists simply urged that laws be changed to meet new circumstances. Some radical Sophists argued that law was merely something made by the most powerful citizens for their own benefit. (Or they said that law was a clever invention of the weak in order to check the strong, who benefited from natural advantages.) This view had dangerous implications: first, law did not need to be obeyed since it rested on no higher principle than might; and second, the strong should do what they have the power to do, and the weak must accept what they cannot resist. Both interpretations were disruptive of community life, for they stressed the selfish interests of the individual over the general welfare of the city.

Some Sophists combined this assault on law with an attack on the ancient Athenian idea of **sophrosyne**—moderation and self-discipline— because it denied human instincts. Instead of moderation, they urged that individuals should maximize pleasure and trample underfoot the traditions that restricted them from fully expressing their desires. As these radical Sophists saw it, the concept of sophrosyne was invented by the weak to enslave nobler natures.

In subjecting traditions to the critique of reason, the radical Sophists triggered an intellectual and spiritual crisis. Their doctrines encouraged loss of respect for authority, disobedience to law, neglect of civic duty, and selfish individualism. These attitudes became widespread during and after the Peloponnesian War, dangerously weakening community bonds.

Socrates: The Rational Individual

In attempting to comprehend nature, the cosmologists had discovered theoretical reason. The Sophists then applied theoretical reason to society. In the process, they created a profound problem for Athens and other city-states: the need to restore the authority of law and a respect for moral values. Conservatives argued that the only way to do so was by renewing allegiance to the sacred traditions that the Sophists had undermined.

Socrates, one of the most extraordinary figures in the history of Western civilization, took a different position. Born in Athens, probably in 469 B.C., about ten years after the Persian Wars, he was executed in 399 B.C., five years after the end of the Peloponnesian War. His life spanned the glory years of Greece, when Athenian culture and democracy were at their height, as well as the tragic years of the lengthy and shattering war with Sparta.

Both the Sophists and Socrates continued the tradition of reason initiated by the cosmologists, but unlike the cosmologists, both felt that knowledge of the individual and society was more important than knowledge of nature. For both, the old mythological traditions, which had served as a foundation for religion and morality, were no longer valid. Socrates and the Sophists endeavored to improve the individual and thought that this could be accomplished through education. Despite these similarities, Socrates' teaching marks a profound break with the Sophist movement.

Socrates attacked the Sophists' relativism, holding that people should regulate their behavior in accordance with universal values. As he saw it, the Sophists taught skills but had no insights into questions that really mattered: What is the purpose of life? What are the values by which man should live? How does man perfect his character? Here the Sophists failed, said Socrates; they taught the ambitious to succeed in politics, but persuasive oratory and clever reasoning do not instruct a man in the art of living. He felt that the Sophists had attacked the old system of beliefs but had not provided the individual with a satisfactory replacement.

Socrates' central concern was the perfection of individual human character, the achievement of moral excellence. Moral values, for Socrates, did not derive either from a transcendent God, as they did for the Hebrews, or from an inherited mythic-religious tradition. They were attained when the individual regulated his life according to objective standards arrived at through rational reflection: that is, when reason became the formative, guiding, and ruling agency of the soul. For Socrates, true education meant the shaping of character according to values discovered through the active use of reason.

Socrates wanted to subject all human beliefs and behavior to the scrutiny of reason and in this way remove ethics from the realm of authority, tradition, dogma, superstition, and myth. He believed that reason was the only proper guide to the most crucial problem of human existence: the question of good and evil. Socrates taught that rational inquiry—a questioning mind—was a priceless tool, allowing one to test opinions, weigh the merit of ideas, and alter beliefs on the basis of knowledge. To Socrates, when people engaged in critical self-examination and strove tirelessly to perfect their nature, they liberated themselves from prevailing opinions and conventions and based their conduct on convictions that they could rationally defend. Socrates believed that people with questioning minds could not be swayed by sophistic eloquence or delude themselves into thinking that they knew something when they really did not.

Socrates' fundamental premise was that wrong thinking resulted in wrongdoing and, conversely, that knowledge of what is right gave one the strength of will to do what is right. Critics, including religious thinkers, have castigated this assumption as naïve, arguing that Socrates credited others with his own extraordinary inner strength and underestimated the immense power of instinct and passions, which drive people, even those who know better, to do what is wrong.

Dialectics.   In urging Athenians to think rationally about the problems of human existence, Socrates offered no systematic ethical theory, no list of ethical precepts. What he did supply was a method of inquiry called **dialectics**, or logical discussion. As Socrates used it, a dialectical exchange between individuals (or with oneself), a *dialogue*, was the essential source of knowledge. It forced people out of their apathy and smugness and

made them aware of their ignorance. It compelled them to examine their thoughts critically; confront illogical, inconsistent, dogmatic, and imprecise assertions; and express their ideas in clearly defined terms.

Dialectics affirmed that the acquisition of knowledge was a creative act. The human mind could not be coerced into knowing; it was not a passive vessel into which a teacher poured knowledge. The dialogue compelled the individual to play an active role in acquiring ideas and values by which to live. In a dialogue, individuals became thinking participants in a quest for knowledge. Through relentless cross-examination, Socrates induced his partner in discourse to explain and justify his opinions rationally, for only thus did knowledge become a part of one's being.

Dialogue implied that reason was meant to be used in relations between human beings and that they could learn from each other, help each other, teach each other, and improve each other. It implied further that the human mind could and should make rational choices. To deal rationally with oneself and with others is the distinctive mark of being human. Through the dialectical method, people could make ethical choices, impose rules on themselves, and give form to their existence.

For Socrates, the highest form of excellence was taking control of one's life and shaping it according to ethical values reached through reflection. The good life, the moral life, is attained by the exercise of reason and by the development of intelligence—this precept is the essence of Socratic teaching. Socrates made the individual the center of the universe, reason central to the individual, and moral worth the central aim of human life. In Socrates, Greek humanism found its highest expression.

Condemned to Death.   Socrates devoted much of his life to what he believed was his mission: pricking the conscience of complacent Athenians and persuading them to think critically about how they lived their lives. "No greater good can happen to a man than to discuss human excellence every day,"[5] he said. Always self-controlled and never raising his voice in anger, Socrates engaged any willing Athenian in conversation about his values. Unlike the Sophists, who were paid

THE PARTHENON, ATHENS, 447–432 B.C. A masterpiece of the Doric style, the great temple dedicated to Athena Parthenos (the Maiden), the patron goddess of the city, was constructed through the efforts of Pericles. Its cult statue and the sculptural reliefs under its roofline were designed by the outstanding sculptor of the age, Phidias. In post-Hellenistic times, it served as a Christian church and then as a mosque, until it was destroyed in 1687. Between 1801 and 1812, the marble reliefs were removed by the Englishman Lord Elgin and now reside in the British Museum, in London. (Hirmer Verlag Fotoarchiv, München.)

professional teachers, Socrates never accepted a fee for his instruction. Through probing questions, he tried to stir people out of their complacency and make them realize how directionless and purposeless their lives were.

For many years, Socrates challenged Athenians without suffering harm, for Athens was generally distinguished by its freedom of speech and thought. In the uncertain times during and immediately after the Peloponnesian War, however,

not believing in the city's gods but in other, new divinities. Underlying these accusations was the fear that Socrates was a troublemaker, a subversive, a Sophist who threatened the state by subjecting its ancient and sacred values to the critique of thought.

Socrates denied the charges and conducted himself with great dignity at his trial, refusing to grovel and beg forgiveness. Instead, he defined his creed:

> *If you think that a man of any worth at all ought to . . . think of anything but whether he is acting justly or unjustly, and as a good or a bad man would act, you are mistaken. . . . If you were therefore to say to me, "Socrates, . . . we will let you go, but on the condition that you give up this investigation of yours, and philosophy. If you are found following these pursuits again you shall die." I say, if you offered to let me go on these terms, I should reply: . . . As long as I have breath and strength I will not give up philosophy and exhorting you and declaring the truth to every one of you whom I meet, saying, as I am accustomed, "My good friend, you are a citizen of Athens. . . . Are you not ashamed of caring so much for making of money and for fame and prestige, when you neither think nor care about wisdom and truth and the improvement of your soul?"*[6]

Convicted by an Athenian court, Socrates was ordered to drink poison. Had he attempted to appease the jurors, he probably would have been given a light punishment, but he would not disobey the commands of his conscience and alter his principles even under threat of death. Socrates' friends wanted to arrange his escape from prison, but he refused, for this would mean violating the city's laws—an act he considered unconscionable.

Socrates did not write down his philosophy and beliefs. We are able to construct a coherent account of his life and ideals largely through the works of his most important disciple, Plato.

Plato: The Rational Society

Plato (c. 429–347 B.C.) used his master's teachings to create a comprehensive system of philosophy, which embraced both the world of nature and

PHILOSOPHER (STATUETTE), C. 280 B.C. Greek artists were the first to excel in realistic portraiture. The philosopher is neither a divinely inspired seer nor a divine king, but a person in quest of knowledge.

(Image copyright © The Metropolitan Museum of Art/Art Resource, N.Y.)

Socrates made enemies. Several of the young men close to him were antidemocrats still mistrusted by some as a threat to the recently restored democracy. When Socrates was seventy, he was accused of corrupting the youth of the city and of

the social world. But Plato had a more ambitious goal than Socrates' moral reformation of the individual. He tried to arrange political life according to rational rules and held that Socrates' quest for personal morality could not succeed unless the community was also transformed on the basis of reason. In effect, Plato wanted to establish standards of thought and behavior for a city torn by moral and intellectual uncertainty. Many of the problems discussed by Western philosophers for the past two millennia were first raised by Plato. We focus on two of his principal concerns, the theory of Ideas and the theory of the just state.

Theory of Ideas.   Socrates had taught that universal standards of right and justice exist and are arrived at through thought. Building on the insights of his teacher Socrates and of Parmenides, who said that reality is known only through the mind, Plato postulated the existence of a higher world of reality, independent of the world of things that we experience every day. This higher reality, he said, is the realm of Ideas, or Forms—unchanging, eternal, absolute, and universal standards of beauty, goodness, justice, and truth. To live in accordance with these standards constitutes the good life; to know these Forms is to grasp ultimate truth.

Truth resides in this world of Forms and not in the world made known through the senses. For example, a person can never draw a perfect square, but the properties of a perfect square exist in the world of Forms. Also, a sculptor observes many bodies, and they all possess some flaw; in his mind's eye, he tries to penetrate the world of Ideas and to reproduce with art a perfect body. Again, the ordinary person only forms an opinion of what beauty is from observing beautiful things; the philosopher, aspiring to true knowledge, goes beyond what he sees and tries to grasp with his mind the Idea of beauty. Similarly, the ordinary individual has only a superficial understanding of justice or goodness; a true conception of justice or goodness is available only to the philosopher, whose mind can leap from worldly particulars to an ideal world beyond space and time.

Plato saw the world of phenomena as unstable, transitory, and imperfect, whereas his transcendent realm of Ideas was eternal and universally valid. For him, true wisdom was to be obtained

through knowledge of the Ideas, not the imperfect reflections of the Ideas perceived with the senses.

A champion of reason, Plato aspired to study human life and arrange it according to universally valid standards. In contrast to Sophist relativism, he maintained that objective and eternal standards do exist. Although Plato advocated the life of reason and wanted to organize society according to rational rules, his writing also reveals a religious-mystical side. At times, Plato seems like a mystic seeking to escape from this world into a higher reality, a realm that is without earth's evil and injustice.

Because Platonism is a two-world philosophy, which believes in a higher world as the source of values and in the soul's immortality, it has had an important effect on religious thought. Christian (as well as Jewish and Muslim) thinkers could harmonize Plato's stress on a higher nonmaterial reality and an immortal soul with their faith. In subsequent chapters, we examine the influence of Platonic otherworldliness on later philosopher-mystics and Christian thinkers.

The Just State.   In adapting the rational legacy of Greek philosophy to politics, Plato constructed a comprehensive political theory. What the Greeks had achieved in practice—the movement away from mythic and theocratic politics—Plato accomplished on the level of thought: the fashioning of a rational model of the state.

Like Socrates, Plato attempted to resolve the problem caused by the radical Sophists: the undermining of traditional values. Socrates tried to dispel this spiritual crisis through a moral transformation of the individual, whereas Plato wanted the entire community to conform to rational principles. Plato said that if human beings are to live an ethical life, they must do so as citizens of a just and rational state. In an unjust state, people cannot achieve Socratic wisdom, for their souls will mirror the state's wickedness.

Plato had experienced the ruinous Peloponnesian War and the accompanying political turmoil. He saw Athens undergo one political crisis after another; most shocking of all, he had witnessed Socrates' trial and execution. Disillusioned by the corruption of Athenian morality and politics, Plato refused to participate in political life. He came to believe that under the Athenian constitution neither the morality of the individual Athenian nor the good of the state could be enhanced and that Athens required moral and political reform founded on Socrates' philosophy. Like Socrates, and in contrast to the Sophists' relativism, Plato sought permanent truth and moral certainty.

In his great dialogue, *The Republic*, Plato devised an ideal state based on standards that would rescue his native Athens from the evils that had befallen it. *The Republic* attempted to analyze society rationally and to reshape the state so that individuals could fulfill the best within themselves and attain the Socratic goal of moral excellence. For Plato, the just state could not be founded on tradition (because inherited attitudes did not derive from rational standards) or on the doctrine of might being right (a principle taught by radical Sophists and practiced by Athenian statesmen). A just state, for Plato, conformed to universally valid principles and aimed at the moral improvement of its citizens, not at increasing its power and material possessions. Such a state required leaders distinguished by their wisdom and virtue, rather than by sophistic cleverness and eloquence.

Fundamental to Plato's political theory as formulated in *The Republic* was his criticism of Athenian democracy. An aristocrat by birth and temperament, Plato believed that it was foolish to expect the common man to think intelligently about foreign policy, economics, or other vital matters of state. Yet the common man was permitted to speak in the Assembly, to vote, and to be selected, by lot, for executive office. A second weakness of democracy was that leaders were chosen and followed for nonessential reasons, such as persuasive speech, good looks, wealth, and family background.

A third danger of democracy was that it could degenerate into anarchy, said Plato. Intoxicated by liberty, the citizens of a democracy could lose all sense of balance, self-discipline, and respect for law.

The citizens become so sensitive that they resent the slightest application of control as intolerable tyranny, and in their resolve to have no master they end up by disregarding even the law, written or unwritten.[7]

As liberty leads to license, Plato continued, the democratic society will deteriorate morally.

The parent falls into the habit of behaving like the child, and the child like the parent: the father is afraid of his sons, and they show no fear or respect for their parents, in order to assert their freedom. . . . To descend to smaller matters, the schoolmaster timidly flatters his pupils, and the pupils make light of their masters. . . . Generally speaking, the young . . . argue with . . . [their elders] and will not do as they are told; while the old, anxious not to be thought disagreeable tyrants, imitate the young and condescend to enter into their jokes and amusements.[8]

As the democratic city falls into disorder, a fourth weakness of democracy will become evident. A demagogue—often a wealthy, handsome war hero of noble birth with an ability to stir the multitude with words—will be able to gain power by promising to plunder the rich to benefit the poor. Increasingly, the tyrant throws off all constraints and uses his authority to satisfy his desire for power and possessions. To retain his hold over the state, the tyrant

begins by stirring up one war after another, in order that the people may feel their need of a leader, and also be so impoverished by taxation that they will be forced to think of nothing but winning their daily bread, instead of plotting against him.[9]

Because of these inherent weaknesses of democracy, Plato insisted that Athens could not be saved by more doses of liberty. He believed that Athens would be governed properly only when the wisest people, the philosophers, attained power.

Unless either philosophers become kings in their countries or those who are now called kings and rulers come to be sufficiently inspired with a genuine desire for wisdom; unless, that is to say, political power and philosophy meet together . . . there can be no rest from troubles . . . for states, nor yet, as I believe, for all mankind.[10]

Plato rejected the fundamental principle of Athenian democracy: that the average person is capable of participating sensibly in public affairs. People would not entrust the care of a sick person to just anyone, said Plato, nor would they allow a novice to guide a ship during a storm. Yet in a democracy, amateurs were permitted to run the government and to supervise the education of the young. No wonder Athenian society was disintegrating. Plato felt that these duties should be performed only by the best people in the city, philosophers, who would approach human problems with reason and wisdom derived from knowledge of the world of unchanging and perfect Ideas. Only these possessors of truth would be competent to rule, said Plato. Whereas Socrates believed that all people could base their actions on reason and acquire virtue, Plato maintained that only a few were capable of philosophical wisdom and that these few were the state's natural rulers.

The organization of the state, as formulated in *The Republic*, corresponded to Plato's conception of the individual soul, of human nature. Plato held that the soul had three major capacities: reason (the pursuit of knowledge), spiritedness (self-assertion, courage, ambition), and desire (the "savage many-headed monster" that relishes food, sex, and possessions). In the well-governed soul, spiritedness and desire are guided by reason and knowledge—standards derived from the world of Ideas.

Plato divided people into three groups: those who demonstrated philosophical ability should be rulers; those whose natural bent revealed exceptional courage should be soldiers; and those driven by desire, the great masses, should be producers (tradespeople, artisans, or farmers). In what was a radical departure from the general attitudes of the times, Plato held that men and women should receive the same education and have equal access to all occupations and public positions, including philosopher-ruler.

Plato felt that the entire community must recognize the primacy of the intellect and sought to create a harmonious state in which each individual performed what he or she was best qualified to do and preferred to do. This would be a just state, said Plato, for it would recognize human inequalities and diversities and make the best possible use of them for the entire community. Clearly,

this conception of justice was Plato's response to the radical Sophists, who taught that justice consisted of the right of the strong to rule in their own interest or that justice was doing whatever one desired.

In *The Republic*, philosophers were selected by a rigorous system of education open to all children. Those not demonstrating sufficient intelligence or strength of character were to be weeded out to become workers or warriors, depending on their natural aptitudes. After many years of education and practical military and administrative experience, the philosophers were to be entrusted with political power. If they had been properly educated, the philosopher-rulers would not seek personal wealth or personal power; their only concerns would be pursuing justice and serving the community. To prevent the philosopher-rulers from pursuing their own interests rather than the good of the community, they would not be permitted to own property or to have families. Since the children they sired would come from a community of wives, no one would know which child was his.

The philosophers were to be absolute rulers. Although the people would lose their right to participate in political decisions, they would gain a well-governed state, whose leaders, distinguished by their wisdom, integrity, and sense of responsibility, would seek only the common good. Only thus could the individual and the community achieve well-being.

Plato repudiated the fundamental principles of a free community: the right to participate in government, equality before the law, and checks on leaders' power. Even freedom of thought was denied the great mass of people in Plato's state. Philosopher-rulers would search for truth, but the people were to be told clever stories—"noble lies," Plato called them—to keep them obedient. However, the philosopher-rulers, said Plato, would not be seekers of power or wealth. It would not be in their character as wise and virtuous people, the best products of polis education, to behave like ruthless tyrants.

The purpose of *The Republic* was to warn Athenians that without respect for law, wise leadership, and proper education for the young, their city would continue to degenerate. Plato wanted to rescue the city-state from disintegration by re-creating the community spirit that had vitalized the polis—and he wanted to re-create it not on the basis of mere tradition but on a higher level, with philosophical knowledge. The social and political institutions of Athens, Plato thought, must be reshaped according to permanent and unalterable ideals of truth and justice, and this could be done only when power and wisdom were joined. He aimed to fashion a just individual and a just state by creating conditions that permitted reason to prevail over the appetites, self-interest, and class and party loyalties.

Aristotle: A Synthesis of Greek Thought

Aristotle (384–322 B.C.) stands at the apex of Greek thought because he achieved a creative synthesis of the knowledge and theories of earlier thinkers. Aristotle studied at Plato's Academy for twenty years. Later, he became tutor to young Alexander the Great, the son of Philip of Macedon. Returning to Athens after Alexander had inherited his father's throne, Aristotle founded a school, the Lyceum.

The range of Aristotle's interests and intellect is extraordinary. He was the leading expert of his time in every field of knowledge, with the possible exception of mathematics. Even a partial listing of his works shows the universal character of his mind and his all-consuming passion to understand the worlds of nature and of humankind: *Logic, Physics, On the Heavens, On the Soul, On the Parts of Animals, Metaphysics, Nicomachean Ethics, Politics, Rhetoric,* and *Poetics.*

Aristotle undertook the monumental task of organizing and systematizing the thought of the Pre-Socratics, Socrates, and Plato. He shared with the natural philosophers a desire to understand the physical universe; he shared with Socrates and Plato the conviction that reason was a person's highest faculty and that the polis was the primary formative institution of Greek life. Out of the myriad of Aristotle's achievements, we discuss only three: his critique of Plato's theory of Ideas, his ethical thought, and his political thought.

Critique of Plato's Theory of Ideas. Like
Democritus before him, Aristotle renewed confidence in **sense perception,** for which Plato had little respect; he wanted to swing the pendulum back from Plato's higher world to the material world. Possessing a scientist's curiosity to understand the facts of nature, Aristotle appreciated the world of phenomena, of concrete things. He respected knowledge obtained through the senses, as the following selection from his observations of a hen's embryo shows:

> *With the common hen after three days and three nights there is the first indication of the embryo. . . . Meanwhile the yolk comes into being . . . and, the heart appears, like a speck of blood, in the white of the egg. This point beats and moves as though endowed with life.*[11]

Aristotle retained Plato's stress on universal principles, but he wanted these principles to derive from human experience with the material world. To the practical and empirically minded Aristotle, the Platonic notion of an independent and separate world of Forms beyond space and time seemed contrary to common sense. To comprehend reality, said Aristotle, one should not escape into another world. For him, Plato's two-world philosophy suffered from too much mystery, mysticism, and poetic fancy; moreover, Plato undervalued the world of facts and objects revealed through sight, hearing, and touch, a world that was important to Aristotle. Like Plato, Aristotle desired to comprehend the essence of things and held that understanding universal principles is the ultimate aim of knowledge. But unlike Plato, he did not turn away from the world of things to obtain such knowledge.

For Aristotle, the Forms were not located in a higher world outside and beyond phenomena but existed in things themselves. He said that through human experience with such things as men, horses, and white objects, the essence of man, horse, and whiteness can be discovered through reason; the Form of Man, the Form of Horse, and the Form of Whiteness can be determined. These universals, which apply to all men, all horses, and all white things, were for both Aristotle and Plato the true objects of knowledge. For Plato, these Forms existed independently of particular objects; the Forms for men or horses or whiteness or triangles or temples existed, whether or not representations of these Ideas in the form of material objects were made known to the senses. For Aristotle, however, universal Ideas could not be determined without examination of particular things. Whereas Plato's use of reason tended to stress otherworldliness, Aristotle tried to bring philosophy back to earth.

By holding that certainty in knowledge comes from reason alone and not from the senses, Plato was predisposed toward mathematics and metaphysics—pure thought, which transcends the world of change and material objects. By stressing the importance of knowledge acquired through the rational examination of sense experience, Aristotle favored the development of empirical sciences—physics, biology, zoology, botany, and other disciplines based on the observation and investigation of nature and the recording of data. Aristotle maintained that theory must not conflict with facts and must make them more intelligible and that it was the task of science to arrange facts into a system of knowledge.

Ethical Thought. Like Socrates and Plato, Aristotle believed that a knowledge of **ethics** was possible and that it must be based on reason, for this is what distinguishes human beings from other forms of life. For him, ethical thought derived from a realistic appraisal of human nature and a commonsense attitude toward life. In *Nicomachean Ethics*, he offered this appraisal, as well as a practical guide to proper conduct. The good life, for Aristotle, was the examined life; it meant making intelligent decisions when confronted with specific problems. Individuals could achieve happiness when they exercised the distinctively human trait of reasoning, when they applied their knowledge relevantly to life, and when their behavior was governed by intelligence and not by whim, tradition, or authority.

Aristotle recognized that people are not entirely rational, that the human personality reveals a passionate element, which can never be eradicated or ignored. Aristotle held that surrendering completely to desire meant descending to the level of beasts, but that denying the passions and living as an ascetic was a foolish and unreasonable rejection of human nature. He maintained that by proper training people could learn to regulate their desires. They could achieve moral well-being, or virtue, when they avoided extremes of behavior and rationally chose the way of moderation, which

he defined as the mean between two extremes. For example, in one extreme, some people "become angry at the wrong things, more than is right, and longer, and cannot be appeased until they inflict vengeance or punishment." In the other extreme, foolish and slavish people endure every insult without defending themselves. Between these extremes is "the man who is angry at the right thing and with the right people, and, further as he ought, when he ought, and as long as he ought. . . . The good-tempered man tends to be unperturbed and not to be led by passion."[12] "Nothing in excess" is the key to Aristotle's ethics.

Aristotle believed that the contemplative life of the philosopher would yield perfect happiness. The pursuit of philosophical wisdom and beauty, he stated, offered "pleasures marvelous for their purity and their enduringness."[13] But Aristotle did not demand more from an individual than human nature would allow. He did not set impossible standards for behavior, recognizing that all persons cannot pursue the life of contemplation, for some lack sufficient leisure or intelligence. However, by applying reason to human affairs, all individuals could experience a good life.

Political Thought. Aristotle's *Politics* complements his *Ethics*. To live the good life, he said, a person must do so as a member of a political community. Only the polis would provide people with an opportunity to lead a rational and moral existence, that is, to fulfill their human potential. With this assertion, Aristotle demonstrated a typically Greek attitude. At the very moment when his pupil Alexander the Great was constructing a world-state that unified Greece and Persia, Aristotle defended the traditional system of independent city-states. Indeed, his *Politics* summed up the polis-centered orientation of Hellenic civilization.

Also in typically Greek fashion, Aristotle did not want women to participate in the political life of the city. Unlike Plato, who, in *The Republic*, gave women an equal opportunity with men to become philosopher-rulers, Aristotle, in his *Politics*, put women in an inferior category and maintained that the free male should rule over women. Though Aristotle taught that all human beings share in a rational soul, he felt that women, along with children and slaves, shared in it to a lesser degree.

Although the parts of the soul are present in all of them, they are present in different degrees. For the slave has no deliberative faculty at all; the woman has, but it is without authority, and the child has, but it is immature. . . . Clearly, then, moral virtue belongs to all of them; but the temperance of a man and of a woman, or the courage and justice of a man and of a woman, are not, as Socrates maintained, the same; the courage of a man is shown in commanding, of a woman in obeying. . . . All classes must be deemed to have their special attributes, as the poet says of women, "Silence is a woman's glory," but this is not equally the glory of man.[14]

Like Plato, Aristotle presumed that political life could be rationally understood and intelligently directed. In *Politics,* as in *Ethics,* he adopted a commonsense, practical attitude. He did not aim at utopia but wanted to find the most effective form of government for most men in normal circumstances. Exemplifying the polis outlook, Aristotle held that enhancing the good of the community is nobler and more virtuous than doing good for oneself, however worthy the act.

Aristotle emphasized the importance of the rule of law. He placed his trust in law rather than in individuals, for they are subject to unruly passions. Aristotle recognized that at times laws should be altered, but he recommended great caution; otherwise, people would lose respect for law and legal procedure.

For the law has no power to command obedience except that of habit, which can only be given by time, so that a readiness to change from old to new laws enfeebles the power of the law.[15]

Tyranny and revolution, Aristotle said, can threaten the rule of law and the well-being of the citizen. To prevent revolution, the state must maintain

the spirit of obedience to law, more especially in small matters; for transgression creeps in unperceived and at last ruins the state. [This cannot be done] unless the young are trained by habit and education in the spirit of the

constitution. [To live as one pleases] is contradictory to the true interests of the state. . . . Men should not think it slavery to live according to the rule of the constitution, for it is their salvation.[16]

Aristotle held "that the best political community is formed by citizens of the middle class [those with a moderate amount of property], and that those states are likely to be well-administered in which the middle class is large and stronger if possible than the other classes [the wealthy and the poor]." Both the rich, who excel in "beauty, strength, birth, [and] wealth," and the poor, who are "very weak or very much disgraced, [find it] difficult to follow rational principles. Of these two the one sort grow into violence and great criminals, the other into rogues and petty rascals." The rich are unwilling "to submit to authority . . . for when they are boys, by reason of the luxury in which they are brought up, they never learn even at school, the habit of obedience." Consequently, the wealthy "can only rule despotically." On the other hand, the poor "are too degraded to command and must be ruled like slaves."[17] Middle-class citizens are less afflicted by envy than the poor and are more likely than the rich to view their fellow citizens as equals.

ART

The classical age of Greek art spans the years from the end of the Persian Wars (479 B.C.) to the death of Alexander the Great (323 B.C.). During this period, standards were established that would dominate Western art until the emergence of modern art in the late nineteenth century.

Greek art coincided with Greek achievement in all other areas. Like Greek philosophy and politics, it too applied reason to human experience and made the transition from a mythopoeic-religious worldview to a world perceived as orderly and rational. It gradually transformed the supernatural religious themes with which it was at first preoccupied into secular human themes. Classical art was representational—that is, it strove to imitate reality, to represent the objective world realistically, as it appeared to the human eye.

Artists carefully observed nature and human beings and sought to achieve an exact knowledge of human anatomy; they tried to portray accurately the body at rest and in motion. They knew when muscles should be taut or relaxed, one hip lower than the other, the torso and neck slightly twisted—in other words, they succeeded in transforming marble or bronze into a human likeness that seemed alive. In addition to being realistic and naturalistic, Greek art was also idealistic, aspiring to a finer, more perfect representation of what was seen, depicting the essence and form of a thing more truly than it actually appeared. Thus, a Greek statue resembled no specific individual but revealed a flawless human form, without wrinkles, warts, scars, or other imperfections.

In achieving an accurate representation of objects and in holding that there were rules of beauty that the mind could discover, the Greek artist employed an approach consistent with the new scientific outlook. The Greek temple, for example, is an organized unity obeying nature's laws of equilibrium and harmony; classical sculpture captures the basic laws that govern life in motion. Such art, based on reason, which draws the mind's attention to the clear outlines of the outer world, also draws attention to the mind itself, making human beings the center of an intelligible world and the masters of their own persons.

Greek artists, just like Greek philosophers, proclaimed the importance and creative capacity of the individual. They exemplified the humanist spirit that characterized all aspects of Greek culture. Classical art placed people in their natural environment, made the human form the focal point of attention, and exalted the nobility, dignity, self-assurance, and beauty of the human being.

POETRY AND DRAMA

Through their awareness of human personality, poets and dramatists, like philosophers and artists, gave expression to the rise of the individual. One of the earliest and best of the Greek poets was Sappho, a woman who lived around 600 B.C. on the island of Lesbos. Sappho established a school to teach music and singing to well-to-do girls and to prepare them for marriage. With great tenderness, Sappho wrote poems of friendship and love: "Some say the fairest thing on earth is a troop of horsemen, others a band of foot-soldiers, others a squadron of ships. But I say the fairest thing is the beloved."[18] And of her daughter Cleïs, she wrote:

> I have a child; so fair
> As golden flowers is she,
> My Cleïs, all my care.
> I'd not give her away
> For Lydia's* wide sway
> Nor lands men long to see.[19]

Sappho's love poetry, addressed also to women, indicates that she was bisexual. This form of sexual behavior was tolerated in ancient Greece, says classicist Lyn Hatherly Wilson, "because it was not procreative, because it did not alter a woman's virginal status, or affect her entry into marriage and male/female relations, except in ways that were considered positive."[20] Sappho was the most prominent female poet in the ancient world. She was depicted on coins and in art, and Plato praised the beauty of her lyric poetry. Sometimes, however, she was treated in an uncomplimentary way by comic playwrights who thought it inappropriate for a woman to write poetry. Her influence endured for centuries: the Roman poets Catullus, Horace, and Ovid alluded to her.

Pindar (c. 518–438 B.C.) was another Greek lyric poet. In his poem of praise for a victorious athlete, Pindar expressed the aristocratic view of excellence. Although life is essentially tragic—triumphs are short-lived, misfortunes are many, and ultimately death overtakes all—man must still demonstrate his worth by striving for excellence.

> He who wins of a sudden, some noble prize
> In the rich years of youth
> Is raised high with hope; his manhood takes
>   wings;

*Ancient country in Asia Minor.

He has in his heart what is better than wealth
But brief is the season of man's delight.
Soon it falls to the ground;
Some dire decision uproots it.
—Thing of a day! such is man: a shadow in
  a dream.
Yet when god-given splendour visits him
A bright radiance plays over him, and how
  sweet is life![21]

The high point of Greek poetry is drama, an art form that originated in Greece. The Greek dramatist portrayed the sufferings, weaknesses, and triumphs of individuals. Just as a Greek sculptor shaped a clear visual image of the human form, so also a Greek dramatist brought the inner life of human beings, their fears and hopes, into sharp focus and tried to find the deeper meaning of human experience. Thus, both art and drama evidenced the growing self-awareness of the individual.

Drama originated in the religious festivals honoring Dionysus, the god of wine and agricultural fertility. A profound innovation in these sacred performances, which included choral songs and dances, occurred in the last part of the sixth century B.C. when Thespis, the first actor known to history, stepped out of the chorus and engaged it in dialogue. By separating himself from the choral group, Thespis demonstrated a new awareness of the individual.

With only one actor and a chorus, however, the possibilities for dramatic action and human conflicts were limited. Then Aeschylus introduced a second actor in his dramas, and Sophocles a third. Dialogue between individuals thus became possible. The Greek actors wore masks, and by changing them, each actor could play several roles in the same performance. This flexibility allowed the dramatists to depict the clash and interplay of human wills and passions on a greater scale. By the middle of the fifth century B.C., tragedies were performed regularly as civic festivals. The audience sat on wooden bleachers in an open-air, hillside theater (*theatron*). The acoustics of these stone theaters were so superb that a clear voice projected from the front could be heard, without amplification, in the last row. In the staging of these tragedies, the all-male chorus generally danced and sang in a circular area called the

orchestra ("dancing place"), which encircled an altar. Their costumes consisted of goat skins (only later did the costumes become elaborate), larger-than-life masks, and elevated shoes.

Because of the grandeur of the dramatists' themes, the eminence of their heroes, and the loftiness of their language, Greek spectators felt intensely involved in the lives portrayed. What they were witnessing in a **tragedy** went beyond anything in their ordinary lives, and they experienced the full range of human emotions.

A development parallel to Socratic dialectics—dialogue between thinking individuals—occurred in Greek drama. Through the technique of dialogue, early dramatists first pitted human beings against the gods and destiny. Later, by placing characters in conflict with one another, dramatists arrived at the idea of individuals as active subjects responsible for their behavior and decisions, which were based on their own feelings and thoughts. Greek tragedy evolved as a continuous striving toward humanization and individualization.

Like the natural philosophers, Greek dramatists saw an inner logic in the universe and called it Fate or Destiny. When people were stubborn, narrow-minded, arrogant, and immoderate, when their "word and deed" showed no respect for justice, when they dishonored the gods, they were punished. The order in the universe required it, said Sophocles.[22]

In being free to make decisions, the dramatist says, individuals have the potential for greatness, but in choosing wrongly, unintelligently, they bring disaster on themselves and others. Also like philosophy, Greek tragedy entailed rational reflection. Tragic heroes were not passive victims of fate. They were thinking human beings who felt a need to comprehend their position, explain the reasons for their actions, and analyze their feelings. The audience was prodded to think, for a tragedy depicted a clash of viewpoints that, as in the Assembly, the audience had to analyze before choosing sides.

The essence of Greek tragedy lies in the tragic hero's struggle against cosmic forces and insurmountable obstacles, which eventually crush him. But what impressed the Greek spectators (and impresses today's readers and viewers of Greek drama) was not the vulnerability or weaknesses

Hesiod

The poet Hesiod (eighth century B.C.) lived on a farm in Boetia, in central Greece, and wrote two major poems. *Theogony* deals with the formation of the universe, and *Works and Days* depicts the life of peasants.

Theogony is replete with mythical imagery, but for several reasons scholars regard it as a precursor of Greek philosophy. First, in explaining the origins of the world through the genealogy of the gods, Hesiod produced an ordered and structured mythology that can be interpreted as nascent rational speculation. Second, the gift of law bestowed by Zeus on humanity can be viewed as an early expression of natural law—the recognition of both a physical and a moral order inherent in the universe. Crucial

for philosophical thought, the concept of natural law that Hesiod expressed in mythical-religious terms was explicitly formulated in the rational categories of philosophy by Greek thinkers after Hesiod.

Whereas Homer's epics concentrate on heroes striving to win honor as defined by a chivalric aristocratic ideal, Hesiod's later poem, *Works and Days*, describes the daily ordeal of common folk struggling to feed their families. A man of the soil, Hesiod maintains that honest labor promotes the good life.

Although he was generally pessimistic, Hesiod believed that human beings could improve their lot if they embraced justice, which "is proved the best thing they have." An awareness of justice is what distinguishes human beings from other creatures.

of human beings, but their courage and determination in the face of these forces.

Aeschylus

Aeschylus (525–456 B.C.), an Athenian nobleman, had fought in the battle of Marathon. He wrote more than eighty plays, of which only seven survive. They have common themes. As an Athenian patriot, Aeschylus urged adherence to traditional religious beliefs and moral values. Like Solon, the statesman, he believed that the world was governed by divine justice, which could not be violated with impunity; when individuals evinced hubris (overweening pride or arrogance), which led them to overstep the bounds of moderation and to set themselves above the gods, they must be punished. Another principal theme was that through suffering came knowledge: the terrible consequences of sins against the divine order should remind all to think and act with moderation and caution.

Aeschylus' play *The Persians* dealt with an actual event, the defeat of the Persian emperor Xerxes by the Greeks. Xerxes' intemperate

ambition to become master of Asia and Greece conflicted with the divine order of the universe. For this hubris, Xerxes and his fellow Persians must pay.

> *A single stroke has brought about the ruin of great*
> *Prosperity, the flower of Persia fallen and gone.*[23]

The suffering of Xerxes should make people aware of what they can and cannot do.

> *And heaps of corpses even in generations hence*
> *Will signify in silence to the eyes of men*
> *That mortal man should not think more than mortal thoughts.*
> *For hubris blossomed forth and grew a crop of ruin,*
> *And from it gathered in a harvest full of tears.*
> *In face of this, when Xerxes, who lacks good sense, returns*
> *Counsel him with reasoning and good advice,*
> *To cease from wounding God with overboastful rashness.*[24]

*You, Perses, should store away in your mind all
  that I tell you,
and listen to justice, and put away
  all notions of violence.
Here is the law, as Zeus established it
  for human beings;
as for fish, and wild animals, and the flying
  birds,
they feed on each other, since there is no idea of
  justice among them;
but to men he gave justice, and she in the end is
  proved the best thing
they have. If a man sees what is right and
  is willing to argue it,
Zeus of the wide brows grants him prosperity.**

Human beings are faced with the choice
between diké (straight judgment and justice),
which safeguards society, and hubris (excessive pride), which destroys it. Honoring justice is what distinguishes a civilized society from a state of savagery.

Throughout *Theogony* and *Works and Days*, Hesiod used the language and imagery of myth to express curiosity about the genesis of the universe, concern for justice, and awareness of a universal moral order. In succeeding centuries, Greek thinkers would discuss these issues using the language and categories of philosophy.

---

*Hesiod, *Works and Days*, in *Hesiod*, trans. Richard Lattimore (Ann Arbor: University of Michigan Press, 1973), 51.

Whereas Aeschylean drama dealt principally with the cosmic theme of the individual in conflict with the moral universe, later dramatists, while continuing to use patterns fashioned by Aeschylus, gave greater attention to the psychology of the individual.

Sophocles

Another outstanding Athenian dramatist was Sophocles (c. 496–406 B.C.). His greatness as a playwright lay in both the excellence of his dramatic technique and the skill with which he portrayed character. The people that he created possessed violent passions and tender emotions; they were noble in their nature, though their actions showed human frailty. Sophocles consciously formulated a standard of human excellence: individuals should shape their character in the way a sculptor shapes a form, according to laws of proportion. Sophocles felt that when these principles of harmony were violated by immoderate behavior, a person's character would be thrown off balance and misfortune would strike. The physical world and human activities obey laws, said Sophocles, and human beings cannot violate these laws with impunity.

Whereas Aeschylus concentrated on religious matters and Euripides (see the next section) dealt with social issues, Sophocles wrote about the perennial problem of well-intentioned human beings struggling valiantly, but unwisely and vainly, against the tide of fate. His characters, bent on some action fraught with danger, resist all appeals to caution and inescapably meet with disaster.

In *Oedipus Rex*, first performed about 429 B.C., Sophocles probes deeply into the human psyche. Oedipus is warned not to pursue the mystery of his birth but insists on searching for the truth about himself: "Nothing will move me. I will find the whole truth." (He had unsuspectingly killed his father and married his mother.*)

*Sigmund Freud's interpretation of the Oedipus story has had a profound impact on psychoanalytic theory: "[Oedipus'] destiny moves us only because it might have been ours. . . . It is the fate of all of us, perhaps, to direct our first sexual impulse towards our mother and our first hatred and . . . murderous wish against our father. Our dreams convince us that this is so" (*The Interpretation of Dreams*).

SOPHOCLES. The great Athenian dramatist wrote 123 tragedies, only seven of which have survived.

For this determination, born more of innocence than arrogance, he will suffer. Events do not turn out, as Oedipus discovers, the way a person thinks and desires that they should; the individual is impotent before a relentless fate, which governs human existence. It seems beyond imagining that Oedipus, whom all envied for his intelligence, courage, and good works, would suffer such dreadful misfortune.

But tragedy also gives Oedipus the strength to assert his moral independence. Although struck down by fate, Oedipus remains an impressive figure. The tragedy's catharsis (the purging of the audience's emotions through a work of art) comes from Oedipus' choice of his own punishment, self-inflicted blindness. Oedipus demonstrates that he still possesses the distinctly human qualities of choosing and acting, that he still remains a free man responsible for his actions. Despite his misery, Oedipus is able to confront a brutal fate with courage and to demonstrate nobility of character.

Euripides

The rational spirit of Greek philosophy permeated the tragedies of Euripides (c. 485–406 B.C.). Like the Sophists, Euripides subjected the problems of human life to critical analysis and challenged human conventions. It was this critical spirit that prompted the traditionalist Aristophanes (see the next section) to attack Euripides for introducing the art of reasoning into tragedy. The role of the gods, women's conflicts, the horrors of war, the power of passion, and the prevalence of human suffering and weakness were carefully scrutinized in Euripides' plays. Euripides blends a poet's insight with a psychologist's probing to reveal the tangled world of human passions and souls in torment. Thus, in *Medea,* he presents the deepest feelings of a Greek woman (see Primary Source box).

Euripides recognized the power of irrational, demonic forces that seethe within people—what he called "the bloody Fury raised by fiends of Hell."[25] A scorned Medea, seeking revenge against her husband by murdering their children, says:

> *I know indeed what evil I intend to do,*
> *But stronger than all my afterthoughts is my*
>   *fury,*
> *Fury that brings upon mortals the greatest*
>   *evils.*[26]

In his plays, Euripides showed that the great tragedy of human existence is that reason can offer only feeble resistance against these compelling, relentless, and consuming passions. The forces that destroy erupt from the volcanic nature of human beings.

A second distinctive feature of Euripidean tragedy is its humanitarianism. No other Greek thinker expressed such concern for a fellow human being, such compassion for human suffering. In *The Trojan Women,* Euripides depicted war as agony and not glory, and the warrior as brutish and not noble. He described the torments of women, for whom war meant the loss of homes, husbands, children, and freedom. In 416 B.C., Athens massacred the men of the small island of Melos, sold its women and children into slavery, and sacked the city, actions that

Euripides, *Medea*

The Greek dramatist Euripides applied a keen critical spirit to the great question of individual life versus the demands of society. His play Medea *focuses on a strong-willed woman whose despair at being cast off by her husband leads her to exact a terrible revenge. But in the following passage,* Medea *might speak for the deepest feelings of any Greek woman.*

It was everything to me to think well of one
    man,
And he, my own husband, has turned out
    wholly vile.
Of all things which are living and can form a
    judgement
We women are the most unfortunate creatures.
Firstly, with an excess of wealth it is required
For us to buy a husband and take for our bodies
A master; for not to take one is even worse.
And now the question is serious whether we
    take
A good or bad one; for there is no easy escape
For a woman, nor can she say no to her
    marriage.
She arrives among new modes of behaviour
    and manners,
And needs prophetic power, unless she has
    learnt at home,

How best to manage him who shares the bed
    with her.
And if we work out all this well and carefully,
And the husband lives with us and lightly bears
    his yoke,
Then life is enviable. If not, I'd rather die.
A man, when he's tired of the company in his
    home,
Goes out of the house and puts an end to his
    boredom
And turns to a friend or companion of his own
    age.
But we are forced to keep our eyes on one
    alone.
What they say of us is that we have a peaceful
    time
Living at home, while they do the fighting in
    war.
How wrong they are! I would very much rather
    stand
Three times in the front of battle than bear one
    child.

Question for Analysis

1. According to this passage, what were the difficulties Greek women faced?

Euripedes, *Medea*, trans. Rex Warner (London: The Bodley Head, 1944), 18.

Euripides regarded as mindless savagery. *The Trojan Women*, performed a year later, warned Athenians:

> *How are ye blind,*
> *Ye treaders down of cities, ye that cast*
> *Temples to desolation, and lay waste*
> *Tombs, the untrodden sanctuaries where lie*
> *The ancient dead; yourselves so soon to die![27]*

By exposing war as barbaric, Euripides was expressing his hostility to the Athenian leaders who persisted in continuing the disastrous Peloponnesian War.

Aristophanes

Greek dramatists often served as political and social critics, none more so than Aristophanes (c. 448–c. 380 B.C.), the greatest of the Greek comic playwrights. He lampooned Athenian statesmen and intellectuals, censured government policies, and protested against the decay of traditional Athenian values. Behind Aristophanes' sharp wit lay a deadly seriousness, for there was much in Athens during the Peloponnesian War that angered him. As an aristocrat, he was repelled by Cleon, the common tanner who succeeded Pericles. As an admirer of the ancient values of honor, duty, and moderation, he was infuriated by corruption, which he attributed to the Sophists. As a man of common sense, he recognized that the Peloponnesian War must end. In the process of serving as a social critic, Aristophanes wrote some of the most hilarious lines in world literature.

In *Lysistrata,* an antiwar comedy, the women of Greece agree to abstain from having sexual relations with their husbands to compel the men to make peace. Lysistrata reveals the plan.

> *For if we women will but sit at home,*
> *Powdered and trimmed, clad in our daintiest*
>   *lawn,* *
> *Employing all our charms, and all our arts*
> *To win men's love, and when we've won it,*
>   *then*
> *Repel them firmly, till they end the war,*
> *We'll soon get Peace again, be sure of that.*[28]

After the plan has been implemented, many women, now sexually frustrated, seek to desert the temple where they have gathered. But the men also suffer.

> *Oh me! these pangs and paroxysms of love,*
> *Riving my heart, keen as a torturer's wheel!*[29]

Through these unorthodox methods, the women achieve their goal, peace. Performed during the darkest days of the war, this play reminded its audiences to concentrate their efforts in the real world on securing peace.

In *The Clouds,* Aristophanes ridiculed the Sophist method of education both for turning the youth away from their parents' values and for engaging the youth in useless, hair-splitting logic. To Aristophanes, the worst of the Sophists was Socrates, who is depicted in *The Clouds* as a fuzzy-minded thinker with both feet planted firmly in the clouds. Socrates is made to look

*Fine linen dress

ridiculous, a man who walks on air, contemplates the sun, and teaches such absurd things as "Heaven is one vast fire extinguisher" or "How many feet of its own a flea could jump." The Sophists in the play teach only how "to succeed just enough for my need and to slip through the clutches of the law." A student of these Sophists becomes "a concocter of lies . . . a supple, unprincipled, troublesome cheat."[30] To Aristophanes, Socrates was a subversive who caused Athenians to repudiate civil morality and to speculate about nonsense questions. Clearly, Aristophanes admired the Athens that had bested the Persians at the battle of Marathon and feared the rationalism that Euripides, the Sophists, and Socrates had injected into Athenian intellectual life.

HISTORY

The Mesopotamians and the Egyptians kept annals that purported to narrate the deeds of gods and their human agents, the priest-kings or god-kings. These chronicles, filled with religious sayings, royal records, and boastful accounts of military campaigns, are devoid of critical analysis and interpretation. The Hebrews valued history, but believing that God acted in human affairs, they did not remove historical events from the realm of religious-mythical thought. The Greeks initiated a different approach to the study of history. For the Greeks, history was not the record of God's wrath or benevolence—as it was for the Hebrews—but the actions solely of human beings. As the gods were eliminated from the natural philosophers' explanations for the origins of things in the natural world, mythical elements were also removed from the writing of history.

Greek historians asked themselves questions about the deeds of people, based their answers on available evidence, and wrote in prose, the language of rational thought. They not only narrated events but also examined them, says Italian historian Arnaldo Momigliano, with a "critical attitude . . . enabling [them] to distinguish between facts and fancies. To the best of my knowledge no historiography earlier than the Greek or independent of it developed these critical methods."[31]

In the same spirit, British philosopher and historian R. G. Collingwood states:

> *The Greeks quite clearly and consciously recognized both that history is, or can be, a science, and that it has to do with human actions. Greek history is not legend, it is research; it is an attempt to get answers to definite questions about matters of which one recognizes oneself as ignorant. It is not theocratic, it is humanistic; the matters inquired into are not of gods, they are of men. Moreover, it is not mythical. The events inquired into are not events in a dateless past, at the beginning of things; they are events in a dated past, a certain number of years ago. This is not to say that legend, either in the form of theocratic history or in the form of myth, was a thing foreign to the Greek mind. . . . But what is remarkable about the Greeks was not the fact that their historical thought contained a certain residue of elements which we should call non-historical, but the fact that side by side with these, it contained elements of what we call history.*[32]

In several respects, however, the Greeks were unhistorical. To them, history moved in cycles; events and periods repeated themselves. Unlike the Hebrews, they had little awareness of historical uniqueness and progression. Nor was history as vital to the Greeks as it was to the Hebrews. Greek philosophers preferred fixing their minds on eternal and changeless truths rather than on the vicissitudes of history. Aristotle said that poetry (which also included drama) is "more philosophic and of greater import than history, since its statements are of the nature of universals," whereas histories deal only with particular events.[33]

Herodotus

Often called "the father of history," Herodotus (c. 484–c. 424 B.C.) wrote a history of the Persian Wars. Herodotus valued the present and recognized that it is not timeless but has been shaped by earlier happenings. To understand the conflict between Persia and Greece, the most important event during his lifetime, he first inquired into the histories of these societies. Much of his information was derived from posing questions to natives of the lands he visited. Interested in everything, Herodotus frequently interlaced his historical narrative with a marvelous assortment of stories and anecdotes.

The central theme of Herodotus' *Histories* is the contrast between Near Eastern despotism and Greek freedom and the subsequent clash of these two worldviews in the Persian Wars. Certain of their superiority, the Greeks considered the non-Hellenic world to be steeped in ignorance and darkness. Herodotus, however, was generally free of this arrogance. A fair-minded, sympathetic, and tolerant observer, he took joy in examining the wide range of human character and experience.

Though Herodotus found much to praise in the Persian empire, he was struck by a lack of freedom and by what he considered barbarity. Herodotus emphasized that the mentality of the free citizen was foreign to the East, where men were trained to obey the ruler's commands absolutely. Not the rule of law but the whim of despots prevailed in the East. When a Persian official urged some Greeks to submit to Xerxes, Herodotus wrote that the Greeks said: "You understand well enough what slavery is, but freedom you have never experienced, so you do not know if it tastes sweet or bitter. If you ever did come to experience it, you would advise us to fight for it not with spears only, but with axes too."[34] Of all the Greek city-states, Herodotus admired Athens most. Freedom had enabled Athens to achieve greatness, said Herodotus, and it was this illustrious city that had rescued the Greek world from Persia.

Another theme evident in Herodotus' work was punishment for hubris. In seeking to become king of both Asia and Europe, Xerxes had acted arrogantly; although he behaved as if he were superhuman, "he too was human, and was sure to be disappointed of his great expectations."[35] Like the Greek tragedians, Herodotus drew universal moral principles from human behavior.

In several ways, Herodotus was a historian rather than a teller of tales. First, he recognized that there is value in studying and preserving the past. Second, he asked questions about the past, instead of merely repeating ancient legends; he tried to discover what had happened, analyzed the motivations behind actions, and searched for cause-and-effect connections. Third, he demonstrated at times a cautious and critical attitude toward his sources, refusing to rely on legends based on little or no objective evidence.

> *The course of my story now leads me to Cyrus: who was this man who destroyed the empire of Croesus, and how did the Persians win their predominant position in Asia? I could, if I wished, give three versions of Cyrus' history, all different from what follows; but I propose to base my account on those Persian authorities who seem to tell the simple truth about him without trying to exaggerate his exploits.*[36]

Fourth, rising above inherited prejudices and a narrow parochialism, he attempted to examine disinterestedly and critically the histories of both the Greeks and the Persians. Fifth, although the gods appeared in Herodotus' narrative, they played a far less important role than they did in Greek popular mythology. Still, by retaining a belief in the significance of dreams, omens, and oracles and by allowing divine intervention, Herodotus fell short of being a thoroughgoing rationalist. Herodotus' writings contain the embryo of rational history; Thucydides brought it to maturity.

Thucydides

Thucydides (c. 460–c. 400 B.C.) also concentrated on a great political crisis confronting the Hellenic world: the Peloponnesian War. Living in Periclean Athens, whose lifeblood was politics, Thucydides regarded the motives of statesmen and the acts of government as the essence of history. He did not just catalogue facts but also sought those general concepts and principles that the facts illustrated. His history was the work of an intelligent mind trying to make sense of his times.

Thucydides applied to the sphere of political history a rationalist empiricism worthy of the Ionian natural philosophers. He strove for factual accuracy and drew conclusions based on a critical analysis of events and motives. He

searched for the truth underlying historical events and attempted to present it objectively. From the Sophists, Thucydides learned that the motives and reactions of human beings follow patterns. Therefore, a proper analysis of the events of the Peloponnesian War would reveal general principles that govern human behavior and relations between states. He intended his history to be a source of enlightenment for future ages, a possession for all time, because the kinds of behavior that caused the conflict between Sparta and Athens would recur regularly throughout history, for human nature is unchanging and predictable.

> *Of the events of the war I have not ventured to speak from any chance information, nor according to any notion of my own; I have described nothing but what I either saw myself, or learned from others of whom I made the most careful and particular inquiry. The task was a laborious one, because eyewitnesses of the same occurrences gave different accounts of them, as they remembered or were [partial to] one side or the other. And very likely the strictly historical character of my narrative may be disappointing to the ear. But if he who desires to have before his eyes a true picture of the events which have happened, and of the like events which may be expected to happen hereafter in the order of human things shall pronounce what I have written to be useful, then I shall be satisfied. My history is an everlasting possession, not a prize composition which is heard and forgotten.*[37]

In Thucydides' history, there was no place for myths, for legends, for the fabulous—all of which were hindrances to historical truth. He recognized that a work of history was a creation of the rational mind and not an expression of the poetic imagination. The historian seeks to learn and to enlighten, not to entertain.

Rejecting the notion that the gods interfere in history, Thucydides looked for the social forces and human decisions behind events. Undoubtedly, he was influenced by Hippocratic doctors, who frowned on divine explanations for disease and distinguished between the symptoms of a disease and its causes. Whereas Herodotus occasionally lapsed into supernatural explanations, Thucydides wrote history in which the gods were absent, and he denied their intervention in human affairs. For Thucydides, history was the work of human beings, and the driving force in history was men's will to power and domination.

In addition to being a historian, Thucydides was also an astute and innovative political thinker with a specific view of government, statesmen, and international relations. He warned against the dangers of extremism unleashed by the strains of war, and he believed that when reason was forsaken, the state's plight would worsen. He had contempt for statesmen who waged war lightly, acting from impulse, reckless daring, and an insatiable appetite for territory. Consequently, he regarded the decision to attack Syracuse in Sicily, which cost so many lives, as a gross political blunder. Although Thucydides admired Athens for its democratic institutions, rule of law, sense of civic duty, and cultural achievements, he recognized an inherent danger in democracy: the emergence of demagogues, who rise to power by stirring up the populace and abuse their power when in office. He extended to international relations the Sophists' insight that people tend to act out of self-interest; national interest, he maintained, was the motivating force in relations between states. Further, he explicitly formulated the principle of balance of power as a basic formula governing international relations. What caused the Peloponnesian War, he said, was the sudden and spectacular increase of Athenian power and the Spartans' fear that this would upset the balance. Finally, Thucydides left us with an enduring insight: war unleashes terrible passions among ordinary people that culminate in slaughter and misery.

Political scientists, historians, and statesmen still turn to Thucydides for insights into the realities of power politics, the dangers of political fanaticism, the nature of imperialism, the methods of demagogues, and the effects of war on democratic politics.

THE GREEK ACHIEVEMENT: REASON, FREEDOM, HUMANISM

Like other ancient peoples, the Greeks warred, massacred, and enslaved; they could be cruel, arrogant, contentious, and superstitious; and they often violated their ideals. But their achievement was unquestionably of profound historical significance. Western thought essentially begins with the Greeks, who first defined the individual by the capacity to reason. It was the great achievement of the Greek spirit to rise above magic, miracles, mystery, authority, and custom and to discover the procedures and terminology that permit a rational understanding of nature and society. Every aspect of Greek civilization—science, philosophy, art, literature, politics, historical writing—showed a growing reliance on human reason and a diminishing dependence on the gods.

In Mesopotamia and Egypt, people had no clear conception of their individual worth and no understanding of political liberty. They were not citizens but subjects who marched to the command of a ruler whose power originated with the gods. Such royal power was not imposed on an unwilling population but was religiously accepted and obeyed.

Unlike in the Near East, monarchs were incidental to Greek political history, a development that enabled the Greeks to create both civic politics and political freedom. They saw the state as a community of free and equal citizens who made laws that served the common good. Disputes between citizens were decided by a jury of one's peers, not by the whims of a ruler or his officials. The citizens had no other masters but themselves. Denouncing arbitrary rule, they argued that power should be regulated by law and justice. The Greeks held that men are capable of governing themselves, and they regarded active participation in public affairs as a duty. For the Greeks, the state was a civilizing agent that permitted people to live the good life. Greek political thinkers arrived at a conception of the rational or legal state, in which law was an expression of reason, not of whim or divine commands; of justice, not of might; of the general good of the community, not of the self-interest of a particular class or individuals. At the beginning of the fourth century B.C., an Athenian orator eloquently captured the meaning of his city's political achievement. The Athenians, he said, "deemed that it was the way of wild beasts to be held subject to one another by force, but the duty of men to delimit justice by law, to convince by reason, and to serve these two by submitting to the sovereignty of law and the instruction of reason."[38] The ideas and terminology of this statement were totally alien to the political experience of the ancient Near East and remain an integral component of the Western democratic tradition. An offshoot of the Greek democratic experience was the emergence of political thought. Greek thinkers' discussions of justice, power, freedom, and the strengths and weaknesses of democracy are the foundation of Western political theory.

The Greeks also gave to Western civilization a conception of inner, or ethical, freedom. People were free to choose between shame and honor, cowardice and duty, moderation and excess. The heroes of Greek tragedy suffered not because they were puppets manipulated by higher powers but because they possessed the freedom of decision. The idea of ethical freedom reached its highest point with Socrates, who shifted the focus of thought from cosmology to the moral life. To shape oneself according to ideals known to the mind, to develop into an autonomous and self-directed person, became for the Greeks the highest form of freedom.

Underlying everything accomplished by the Greeks was a humanist attitude toward life. The Greeks expressed a belief in the worth, significance, and dignity of the individual. They called for the maximum cultivation of human talent, the full development of human personality, and the deliberate pursuit of excellence. In valuing human personality, the Greek humanists did not approve of living without restraints; they aimed at creating a higher type of man. Such a man would mold himself according to worthy standards; he would make his life as harmonious and flawless as a work of art. This aspiration required effort, discipline, and intelligence. Fundamental to the Greek humanist outlook was the belief that human beings could master themselves. Although people could not alter the course of nature, for there was an order to the universe over which neither human beings nor gods had control, Greek humanists believed that people could control their own lives. Contemporary humanists continue to derive inspiration and guidelines from the literary, artistic, and philosophical creations of ancient Greece.

Despite their lauding of the human being's creative capacities, the Greeks were not naïve about human nature. Rather, intensely aware of the individual's inherent capacity for evil, Greek thinkers repeatedly warned that without the restraining forces of law, civic institutions, moral norms, and character training, society would be torn apart by the savage elements within human nature.

By discovering theoretical reason, defining political freedom, and affirming the worth and potential of human personality, the Greeks broke with the past and founded the rational and humanist tradition of the West. "Had Greek civilization never existed," wrote poet W. H. Auden, "we would never have become fully conscious, which is to say that we would never have become, for better or worse, fully human."[39]

❖   ❖   ❖

NOTES

1. John N. Theodorakopoulos, "The Origins of Science and Philosophy," in *History of the Hellenic World: The Archaic Period* (University Park: Pennsylvania State University Press, 1975), 438.

2. Quoted in George Sarton, *A History of Science* (Cambridge, Mass.: Harvard University Press, 1952), 1:355–356.

3. Euripides, *Iphigenia at Aulis,* in *Ten Plays by Euripides,* trans. Moses Hadas and John McClean (New York: Bantam Books, 1960), 348, lines 1400–1401.

4. Excerpted in Kathleen Freeman, *Ancilla to the Pre-Socratic Philosophers* (Cambridge, Mass.: Harvard University Press, 1957), 157–158.

5. Plato, *Apology,* trans. F. J. Church, rev. R. D. Cummings (Indianapolis: Bobbs-Merrill, 1956), sec. 28.

6. Ibid., secs. 16–17.

7. Plato, *The Republic,* trans. F. M. Cornford (New York: Oxford University Press, 1945), 289.

8. Ibid.

9. Ibid., 293.

10. Ibid., 178–179.

11. *Historia Animalium,* in *Works of Aristotle,* trans. D'Arcy Wentworth Thompson (New York: Oxford University Press, 1962), 4:561.

12. *Nicomachean Ethics,* in *Basic Works of Aristotle,* ed. Richard McKeon (New York: Random House, 1941), 996.

13. Ibid., 1104.

14. *Politics,* in *Basic Works of Aristotle,* ed. McKeon, 1144–45.

15. Ibid., 1164.

16. Ibid., 1246, 1251.

17. Ibid., 1220–21.

18. Cited in Werner Jaeger, *Paideia: The Ideals of Greek Culture,* trans. Gilbert Highet (New York: Oxford University Press, 1945), 1:135.

19. *The Oxford Book of Greek Verse in Translation,* ed. T.F. Higham and C.M. Bowra (1938), Sappho, "A Girl" (6 lines from p. 211). By Permission of Oxford University Press.

20. Lyn Hatherly Wilson, *Sappho's Sweet Bitter Songs* (London and New York: Routledge, 1966), 70.

21. Cited in H. D. F. Kitto, *The Greeks* (Baltimore: Penguin Books, 1957), 174–175.

22. See Sophocles, *Oedipus the King,* trans. Bernard M. W. Knox (New York: Washington Square Press, 1959), 61.

23. Aeschylus, *The Persians,* trans. Anthony J. Podlecki (Englewood Cliffs, N.J.: Prentice-Hall, 1970), 49, lines 250–251.

24. Ibid., 96–97, lines 818–822, 829–831.

25. *Medea,* trans. Rex Warner, in *Euripides,* vol. 3 of *The Complete Greek Tragedies,* ed. David Grene and Richard Lattimore (Chicago: University of Chicago Press, 1959–1960), 101, line 1260.

26. Ibid., 96, lines 1078–80.

27. Euripides, *The Trojan Women,* trans. Gilbert Murray (New York: Oxford University Press, 1915), 16, lines 95–97.

28. *Lysistrata,* in *Five Comedies of Aristophanes,* trans. Benjamin Bickley Rogers (Garden City, N.Y.: Doubleday Anchor Books, 1955), 292.

29. Ibid., 320.

30. *The Clouds,* in *Five Comedies of Aristophanes,* trans. Rogers, 156–157, 169–170.

31. Arnaldo Momigliano, *The Classical Foundations of Modern Historiography* (Berkeley: University of California Press, 1990), 30.

32. R. G. Collingwood, *The Idea of History* (New York: Oxford University Press, 1956), 17–18.

33. Poetics, in *Basic Works of Aristotle,* ed. McKeon, 1464.

34. Herodotus, *The Histories,* trans. Aubrey de Sélincourt (Baltimore: Penguin Books, 1954), 458.

35. Ibid., 485.

36. Ibid., 53.

37. Thucydides, *The Peloponnesian War,* trans. B. Jowett (Oxford: Clarendon Press, 1881), bk. 1, chap. 22.

38. Quoted in Jennifer Tolbert Roberts, *Athens on Trial: The Antidemocratic Tradition in Western Thought* (Princeton, N.J.: Princeton University Press, 1994), 46.

39. W. H. Auden, ed., *The Portable Greek Reader* (New York: Viking, 1952), 38.

SUGGESTED READING

Brickhouse, Thomas C. and Nicholas D. Smith, *Plato's Socrates* (1994). Informed discussions of Socrates' methodology, psychology, ethics, religion, and politics.

Brunschwig, Jacques, and Geoffrey E. R. Lloyd, eds., *Greek Thought* (2000). Essays dealing with many areas of Greek thought.

Gottlieb, Anthony, *The Dream of Reason* (2000). Superb chapters on Greek philosophy.

Guthrie, W. K. C., *The Greek Philosophers from Thales to Aristotle* (1960). A short, reliable survey of Greek philosophy.

Jaeger, Werner, *Paideia: The Ideals of Greek Culture* (1939–1944). A three-volume work on Greek culture by a distinguished classicist. The treatment of Homer, the early Greek philosophers, and the Sophists in volume 1 is masterful.

Jones, W. T., *A History of Western Philosophy*, vol. 1 (1962). Clearly written; contains useful passages from original sources.

Kitto, H. D. F., *Greek Tragedy* (1954). A valuable introduction to Greek drama.

Levi, Peter, *The Pelican History of Greek Literature* (1985). Sound insights into Greek writers.

Romm, James, *Herodotus* (1998). A study of Herodotus the historian and story teller.

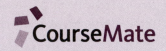

Chapter 5

The Hellenistic Age: Cultural Diffusion

Alexander the Great on Horseback. In conquering the lands from Greece to India, Alexander the Great displayed a military genius that would fascinate commanders from Caesar to Napoleon. (Alinari/Art Resource, N.Y.)

- **Alexander the Great**
- **Hellenistic Society**
- **Hellenistic Culture**
- **The Hellenistic Legacy**

Focus Questions

1. What are the basic differences between the Hellenic and the Hellenistic Ages?

2. How did Alexander the Great contribute to the shaping of the Hellenistic Age?

3. Why are the terms *individualism, universalism,* and *cosmopolitanism* used to characterize the Hellenistic Age?

4. What prescriptions did each of the Hellenistic philosophies offer for achieving happiness?

5. What is the enduring significance of Stoicism for the modern world?

Greek civilization, or Hellenism, passed through three distinct stages: the Hellenic Age, the Hellenistic Age, and the Greco-Roman Age. The **Hellenic Age** began about 800 B.C. with the early city-states, reached its height in the fifth century B.C., and endured until the death of Alexander the Great in 323 B.C. At that time, the ancient world entered the **Hellenistic Age**, which ended in 30 B.C., when Egypt, the last major Hellenistic state, fell to Rome. The **Greco-Roman Age** lasted five hundred years, encompassing the period of the Roman Empire up to the collapse of the Empire's western half in the last part of the fifth century A.D.

Although the Hellenistic Age absorbed the heritage of classical (Hellenic) Greece, its style of civilization changed. During the first phase of Hellenism, the polis was the center of political life. The polis gave Greeks an identity, and only within the polis could Greeks live a good and civilized life. With the coming of the Hellenistic Age, this situation changed. Kingdoms and empires eclipsed the city-state in power and importance. Cities retained a large measure of autonomy in domestic affairs but lost their freedom of action in foreign affairs. Dominated by monarchs, cities were no longer self-sufficient and independent communities as they had been in the Hellenic period. Monarchy—the essential form of government in the Hellenistic world—had not been admired by the Greeks of the Hellenic Age. They agreed with Aristotle that monarchy was suitable only for non-Greeks, who lacked the capacity to govern themselves.

As a result of Alexander the Great's conquests of the lands between Greece and India, tens of thousands of Greek soldiers, merchants, and administrators settled in eastern lands. Their encounters with the different peoples and cultures of the Near East widened the Greeks' horizon and weakened their ties to their native cities. Because of these changes, the individual had to define a relationship not to the narrow, parochial society of the polis, but to the larger world. The Greeks had to examine their place in a world more complex, foreign, and threatening than the polis. They had to fashion a conception of a community that would be more comprehensive than the city-state.

Hellenistic philosophers struggled with these problems of alienation and community. They

BATTLE OF ISSUS, ROMAN MOSAIC. The subject of the mosaic is believed to be Alexander's victory over the Persian king Darius III in 333 B.C. at the battle of Issus. On the right side of the mosaic, we see a realistic battle scene filled with both commotion and emotion. (Scala/Ministero per i Beni e le Attività culturali/Art Resource, N.Y.)

sought to give people the inner strength to endure in a world where the polis no longer provided security. In this new situation, philosophers no longer assumed that the good life was tied to the affairs of the city. Freedom from emotional stress—not active citizenship and social responsibility—was the avenue to the good life. This pronounced tendency of people to withdraw into themselves and seek emotional comfort helped shape a cultural environment that contributed to the spread and triumph of Christianity in the Greco-Roman Age.

In the Hellenic Age, Greek philosophers had a limited conception of humanity, dividing the world into Greeks and barbarians. In the Hellenistic Age, the intermingling of Greeks and peoples of the Near East—the fusion of different ethnic groups and cultures scattered over great distances—caused a shift in focus from the city to the **oikoumene** (the inhabited world); parochialism gave way to **cosmopolitanism** and **universalism** as people began to think of themselves as members of a world community. Philosophers came to regard the civilized world as one city, the city of humanity. This new concept was their response to the decline of the city-state and the quest for an alternative form of community.

By uniting the diverse nationalities of the Mediterranean world under one rule, Rome gave political expression to the Hellenistic philosophers' longing for a world community. But the vast and impersonal Roman Empire could not rekindle the sense of belonging, the certainty of identity, that came with being a citizen of a small polis. In time, a resurgence of the religious spirit, particularly in the form of Christianity, helped overcome the feeling of alienation by offering an image of community that stirred the heart.

ALEXANDER THE GREAT

After the assassination of Philip of Macedon in 336 B.C., his twenty-year-old son, Alexander, succeeded to the throne. Alexander inherited a proud and fiery temperament from his mother. From his tutor Aristotle, Alexander gained an appreciation for Greek culture, particularly the Homeric epics. Undoubtedly, the young Alexander was excited by these stories of legendary heroes, particularly of Achilles, and their striving for personal glory. Alexander acquired military skills and qualities of leadership from his father.

Alexander also inherited from Philip an overriding policy of state: the invasion of Persia. Such an exploit attracted the adventurous spirit of the young Alexander. A war of revenge against the Persians, who were masters of the Greek city-states of Asia Minor, also appealed to his Pan-Hellenic sentiments. Alexander was heir to the teachings of the fourth-century orator Isocrates, who urged a crusade against Persia to unite the Greeks in a common cause. Philip had intended to protect his hold on Greece by driving the Persians from Asia Minor. But Alexander, whose ambition knew no bounds, aspired to conquer the entire Persian Empire. Daring, brave, and intelligent, Alexander possessed the irrepressible energy of a romantic adventurer.

With an army of thirty-five thousand men, Alexander crossed into Asia Minor in 334 B.C. and eventually advanced all the way to India. In his military campaigns, which covered about ten thousand miles, Alexander proved himself to be a superb strategist and leader of men. Winning every battle, Alexander's army had carved an empire that stretched from Greece to India. Future conquerors, including Caesar and Napoleon, would read of Alexander's career with fascination and longing.

The world after Alexander differed sharply from that existing before he took up the sword. His conquests brought West and East closer together, marking a new epoch. Alexander himself helped implement this transformation, whether intentionally or unwittingly. He took a Persian bride, arranged for eighty of his officers and ten thousand of his soldiers to marry Asian women, and planned to incorporate thirty thousand Persian youths into his army. Alexander founded Greek-style cities in Asia, where Greek settlers mixed with the native population.

As Greeks acquired greater knowledge of the Near East, the parochialism of the polis gave way to a world outlook. As trade and travel between West and East expanded, as Greek merchants and soldiers settled in Asiatic lands, and as Greek culture spread to non-Greeks, the distinctions between barbarian and Greek lessened. Although Alexander never united all the peoples in a world-state, his career pushed the world in a new direction, toward a fusion of disparate peoples and the intermingling of cultural traditions.

HELLENISTIC SOCIETY

Competing Dynasties

In 323 B.C., Alexander, not yet thirty-three years old, died after a sickness that followed a drinking party. He had built an empire that stretched from Greece to the Punjab of India, but he was denied the time needed to organize effective institutions to govern these vast territories. After Alexander's premature death, his generals engaged in a long and bitter struggle to see who would succeed the conqueror. Since none of the generals or their heirs had enough power to hold together Alexander's vast empire, the wars of succession ended in a stalemate. By 275 B.C., the empire was fractured into three dynasties: the Ptolemies in Egypt, the Seleucids in western Asia, and the Antigonids in Macedonia. Macedonia—Alexander's native country—continued to dominate the Greek cities, which periodically tried to break its hold. Later, the kingdom of Pergamum, in western Asia Minor, emerged as the fourth Hellenistic monarchy. These Hellenistic kings were not native rulers enjoying local support (except in Macedonia) but were foreign conquerors. Consequently, they had to depend on mercenary armies and loyal administrators.

In the third century B.C., Ptolemaic Egypt was the foremost power in the Hellenistic world. The Seleucid Empire, which stretched from the Mediterranean to the frontiers of India and encompassed many different peoples, attempted to extend its power in the west but was resisted by the Ptolemies. Finally, the Seleucid ruler Antiochus III

(223–187 B.C.) defeated the Ptolemaic forces and established Seleucid control over Phoenicia and Palestine. Taking advantage of Egypt's defeat, Macedonia seized several of Egypt's territories.

Rome, a new power, became increasingly drawn into the affairs of the quarrelsome Hellenistic kingdoms. By the middle of the second century B.C., it had imposed its will on them. From that time on, the political fortunes of the western and eastern Mediterranean were inextricably linked.

Hellenistic society was characterized by a growing cosmopolitanism—a mingling of peoples, an interchange of cultures, and a broad outlook. Greek traditions spread to the Near East, while Mesopotamian, Egyptian, Hebrew, and Persian traditions—particularly religious beliefs—moved westward. A growing cosmopolitanism replaced the parochialism of the city-state. Although the rulers of the Hellenistic kingdoms were Macedonians and their high officials and generals were Greeks, the style of government was modeled after that of the ancient Middle Eastern kingdoms. In the Hellenic Age, the law had expressed the will of the community, but in this new age of monarchy, the kings laid down the law. To promote loyalty, the Macedonian rulers encouraged the Near Eastern cultic practice of worshiping the king as a god or as a representative of the gods. In Egypt, for example, the priests conferred on the Macedonian king the same divine powers and titles traditionally held by Egyptian pharaohs. In accordance with ancient tradition, statues of the divine king were installed in Egyptian temples, suffusing political power with supernatural authority, in marked contrast to the democratic spirit of the Greek Assembly.

Following Alexander's lead, the Seleucids founded cities in the east patterned after the city-states of Greece. The cities, which were often founded to protect trade routes and as fortresses against hostile tribes, adopted the political institutions of Hellenic Greece, including a popular assembly and a council. Hellenistic kings generally did not intervene in the cities' local affairs. Thousands of Greeks settled in these cities, which were Greek in architecture and contained Greek schools, temples, theaters where performances of classical plays were staged, and gymnasia. Gymnasia were essentially places to exercise, train in sports, and converse, but some had libraries and halls where public lectures and competitions of orators and poets were held. Hellenistic kings brought books, paintings, and statues from Greece to their cities. Hellenistic cities, inhabited by tens of thousands of people from many lands and dominated by a Hellenized upper class, served as centers and agents of Hellenism, which non-Greeks adopted. The ruling class in each Hellenistic city was united by a common Hellenism, which overcame national, linguistic, and racial distinctions. *Koine* (or shared language), a form of spoken Greek spread by soldiers, administrators, merchants, teachers, and others, became a common tongue throughout much of the Mediterranean world. Greek was the language both of government and culture.

Hellenistic cities engaged in economic activity on a much greater scale than the classical Greek city-states. Increased trade integrated the Near East and Greece into a market economy, and business methods became more developed and refined. The middle and upper classes enjoyed homes, furniture, and jewelry more elegant than those of Periclean Athenians, and some people amassed great fortunes. In contrast to the ideal of citizenship, which distinguished the fifth-century polis, many Greeks who settled in Egypt, Syria, and other eastern lands ran roughshod over civil law and moral values and engaged in competitive struggles for wealth and power.

The greatest city of the time and the one most representative of the Hellenistic Age was Alexandria, in Egypt, founded by Alexander. Strategically located at one of the mouths of the Nile, it became a hub of commerce and culture. The most populous city of the Mediterranean world, Alexandria had about 300,000 inhabitants fifty years after its founding. At the beginning of the Christian era, it contained perhaps a million people: Macedonians, Greeks, Romans, Jews, Syrians, Ethiopians, and Arabs.

Alexandria was an unrivaled commercial center; goods from the Mediterranean world, eastern Africa, Arabia, and India circulated in its marketplaces. Two handsome boulevards, squares, fountains, and great temples added to the city's beauty. Its library, created by the first two Ptolemies, had about half a million books. The library was part of a larger complex, the museum, which contained an astronomical observatory

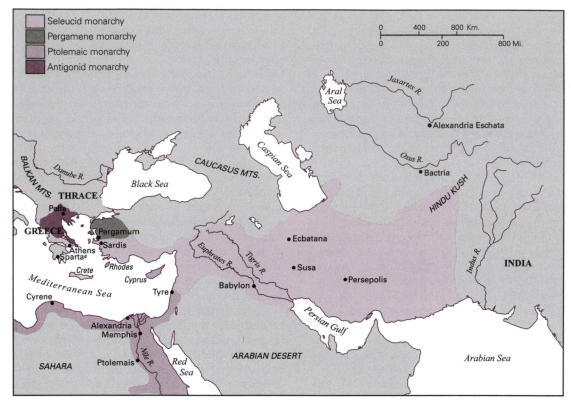

Map 5.1 **THE DIVISION OF ALEXANDER'S EMPIRE AND THE SPREAD OF HELLENISM** None of Alexander's generals could hold together the vast empire, which fractured into competing dynasties. (Copyright © 2013 Cengage Learning.)

and botanical and zoological gardens. Some of the greatest poets, philosophers, physicians, and scientists of the Mediterranean world utilized these facilities. Athens and other classical Greek cities seemed like provincial towns compared to Alexandria.

Aside from the proliferation of Greek urban institutions and ideas, Hellenistic cosmopolitanism expressed itself in an increased movement of peoples, the adoption of common currency standards, and an expansion of trade. International trade was made easier by improvements in navigation techniques, better port facilities, the extension of the monetary economy at the expense of barter, and the rapid development of banking. The makeup of Hellenistic armies also reflected the cosmopolitanism of the age. Serving the Hellenistic kings were men from lands stretching from India to the little-known areas north of the

Danube. In Egyptian and Syrian cities, a native elite emerged who spoke Greek, wore Greek-style clothes, and adopted Greek customs.

Cultural exchange permeated all phases of cultural life. Sculpture showed the influence of many lands. Historians wrote world histories, not just local ones. Greek astronomers worked with data collected over the centuries by the Babylonians. Like other Near Eastern people, the Jews—both those in Judea and the **Diaspora** (Jews who lived outside Palestine)—came under the influence of Hellenism. Some Jewish scholars, admiring Greek learning, expressed Jewish religious ideas in philosophical terms; God was identified with reason, and Moses' Law with the rational order of the universe. They wanted to show that Mosaic Law, revealed by God, was compatible with the truth discovered by natural reason. The Hebrew Scriptures were translated

NIKE, THE GODDESS OF VICTORY, ON A GOLD EARRING, HELLENISTIC PERIOD. The calm, timeless, idealized forms of classical period sculpture gave way to a new style—the Hellenistic, marked by more dynamic, emotion-laden realism. This new aesthetic form reflected the cosmopolitan character of the Greek culture that emerged from Alexander's conquests. (Museum of Fine Arts, Boston/Henry Lillie Pierce Fund, 98.788.)

into Greek—the *Septuagint*—for use by Greek-speaking Jews living in Alexandria and other areas outside of Judea. Greek words entered the Hebrew language, and newly constructed synagogues employed Hellenistic architectural styles.

Greeks increasingly demonstrated a fascination with Near Eastern religious cults. Philosophers helped break down the barriers between peoples by asserting that all inhabit a single fatherland. As the philosopher Crates said, "My fatherland has no single tower, no single roof. The whole earth is my citadel, a home ready for us all to live in."[1]

The spread of Greek civilization from the Aegean to the Indus River gave the Hellenistic world a cultural common denominator, but **Hellenization** did not transform the East and make it one with the West. Hellenization was limited almost entirely to the cities, and in many urban centers it was often only a thin veneer. Many non-Greeks learned Greek and received a Greek education, which was a necessity for advancement in the state bureaucracy, and some assumed Greek names. But for most, Hellenization did not go much deeper. The countryside lacked even the veneer of Greek culture. Retaining traditional attitudes, the countryside in the East resisted Greek ways. In the villages, local and traditional law, local languages, and family customs remained unchanged; religion, the most important ingredient of the civilizations of the Near East, also kept its traditional character, even if ancestral gods were given Greek names.

To be sure, Hellenistic society was male dominated, but the status of women did show some improvement over the classical period. Some royal mothers and daughters exercised political power, even if behind the scenes, and royal women had access to great wealth as indicated by their cash contributions to cities. Some non-royal ladies held important priestly offices, and far more than in the classical era, women contributed to high culture as poets, harpists, artists, and architects. Two of the new schools of philosophy, Epicureanism and Cynicism, welcomed female participation.

HELLENISTIC CULTURE

Literature, History, and Art

The Hellenistic Age saw a great outpouring of literary works. Callimachus (c. 305–240 B.C.), an Alexandrian scholar-poet, felt that no one could duplicate the great epics of Homer or the plays of the fifth-century B.C. dramatists. He urged poets to write short, finely crafted poems instead of composing on a grand scale. A student of his, Apollonius of Rhodes, took issue with him and wrote the *Argonautica*. This Homeric-style epic tells the story of Jason's search for the Golden Fleece.

The poet Theocritus (c. 315–250 B.C.), who lived on the island of Sicily, wrote pastorals that showed great sensitivity to natural beauty. He responded with uncommon feeling to the sky and wind, to the hills, trees, and flowers, and to the wildlife of the countryside.

DRUNKEN OLD WOMAN. Hellenistic genre sculpture depicted people in everyday situations as individuals, rather than as types. This sculpture of a drunken old woman is a marble copy of a third- or second-century B.C. Hellenistic work. (© imagebroker.net/SuperStock.)

The Athenian playwright Menander (c. 342–291 B.C.) depicted Athenian life at the end of the fourth century. Menander's plays, unlike Aristophanes' lampoons of inept politicians, dealt little with politics. Apparently, Menander reflected the attitude of his fellow Athenians, who, bored with public affairs, had accepted their loss of freedom to Macedonia and were preoccupied with their private lives. Menander dealt sympathetically with human weakness and wrote about stock characters: the clever slave, the young playboy, bragging soldiers, compassionate prostitutes, the elderly seducer, the heroine in trouble. Menander also expressed a warm concern for people, urging them to recognize the humanity of their fellows—whether Greeks, barbarians, or slaves—and to treat one another with kindness and respect.

The leading historian of the Hellenistic Age was Polybius (c. 200–118 B.C.), a Greek, whose history of the rise of Rome is one of the great works of historical literature (see Primary Source box). Reflecting the universal tendencies of the Hellenistic Age, Polybius endeavored to explain how Rome had progressed from a city-state to a world conqueror.

Hellenistic art, like Hellenistic philosophy, expressed a heightened awareness of the individual. Whereas Hellenic sculpture aimed to depict ideal beauty—the perfect body and face—Hellenistic sculpture, moving from idealism to realism, captured individual character and expression, often of ordinary people—an old fisherman, a crippled man, a drunken lady, a dwarf. Scenes of daily life were realistically portrayed. Wealthy merchants commissioned artists to embellish their private homes. Monarchs, eager to glorify their reigns, sought the services of eminent artists to produce royal portraits, victory monuments, paintings of great battles, temples, and tombs. Continuing a practice initiated during the Hellenic Age, Hellenistic cities commissioned artists. What was new, however, was the proliferation of portrait statues honoring prominent civic leaders, orators, poets, philosophers, and playwrights.

Science

During the Hellenistic Age, Greek scientific achievement reached its height. When Alexander invaded Asia Minor, the former student of Aristotle brought along surveyors, engineers, scientists, and historians, who continued with him into Asia. The vast amount of data in botany, zoology, geography, and astronomy collected by Alexander's staff stimulated an outburst of activity. To integrate so much information, scientists had to specialize in the various disciplines. Hellenistic scientists preserved and expanded the tradition of science developed in the Hellenic Age. They attempted a rational analysis of nature; they engaged in research, organized knowledge in logical fashion, devised procedures for mathematical proof, separated medicine from magic, grasped the theory of experiment, and applied scientific principles to mechanical devices. Hellenistic science, says historian Benjamin Farrington, stood "on the threshold of the modern world. When modern science began in the sixteenth century, it took up where the Greeks left off."[2]

Although Alexandria was the principal center of scientific research, Athens still retained some of its former luster in this area. After Aristotle died in 322 B.C., he was succeeded as head of the Lyceum by Theophrastus and then by Strato. Both wrote treatises on many subjects—logic, ethics, politics, physics, and botany. Theophrastus systematized knowledge of botany in a manner similar to Aristotle's treatment of animals. Strato is most famous for his study of physics. It is likely that Strato, in his investigation of physical problems, did not rely on logic alone but performed a series of experiments to test his investigations.

Because of its library, the finest in the ancient world, and its state-supported museum, Alexandria attracted leading scholars and superseded Athens in scientific investigation. The museum was really a research institute—the first institution in history specifically established for the purpose of scientific research—in which some of the best minds of the day studied and worked.

Alexandrian doctors advanced medical skills. They improved surgical instruments and techniques and, by dissecting bodies, added to anatomical knowledge. Through their research, they discovered organs of the body not known until then, made the distinction between arteries and veins, divided nerves into those comprising the motor and the sensory system, and identified the brain as the source of intelligence. Their investigations advanced knowledge of anatomy and physiology to a level that was not significantly improved until the sixteenth century A.D.

Knowledge in the fields of astronomy and mathematics also increased. Eighteen centuries before Copernicus, Alexandrian astronomer Aristarchus (310–230 B.C.) said that the sun was the center of the universe, that the planets revolved around it, and that the stars were situated at great distances from the earth. But these revolutionary ideas were not accepted, and the belief in an earth-centered universe persisted. In geometry, Euclid, an Alexandrian mathematician who lived around 300 B.C., creatively synthesized earlier developments. Euclid's hundreds of geometric proofs, derived from reasoning alone—his conclu-

sions flowed logically and flawlessly from given assumptions—are a profound witness to the power of the rational mind.

Alexander's expeditions had opened the eyes of Mediterranean peoples to the breadth of the earth and had stimulated explorations and geographic research. Eratosthenes (c. 275–194 B.C.), an Alexandrian geographer, sought a scientific understanding of this enlarged world. He divided the planet into climatic zones, declared that the oceans are joined, and with extraordinary ingenuity and accuracy measured the earth's circumference.

Archimedes of Syracuse (c. 287–212 B.C.), who studied at Alexandria, was a mathematician, a physicist, and an ingenious inventor. His mechanical inventions, including war engines, dazzled his contemporaries. However, Archimedes dismissed his practical inventions, preferring to be remembered as a theoretician. In one treatise, he established the general principles of hydrostatics, a branch of physics that deals with the pressure and equilibrium of liquids at rest.

Philosophy

Hellenistic thinkers preserved the rational tradition of Greek philosophy. Like their Hellenic predecessors, they regarded the cosmos as governed by universal principles intelligible to the rational mind. For the philosophers of both ages, a crucial problem was the achievement of the good life. Also, both Hellenic and Hellenistic thinkers sought rules for human conduct that accorded with rational standards; both believed that individuals attain happiness through their own efforts, unaided by the gods. In the tradition of Socrates, Hellenistic thinkers taught a morality of self-mastery. But although they retained the inheritance of the classical age, they also transformed it, for they had to adapt thought to the requirements of a cosmopolitan society.

In the Hellenic Age, the starting point of philosophy was the citizen's relationship to the city; in the Hellenistic Age, the point of departure was the solitary individual's relationship to humanity and the individual's personal destiny in a larger and more complex world. Philosophy tried to deal with the feeling of alienation—of not

Profile

Polybius

Rome's expansion from a city-state to a world empire that embraced many different nationalities and the extension of citizenship to non-Romans exemplified the universalism and cosmopolitanism of the Hellenistic Age. So too did Polybius' *Histories,* which sought to account for Rome's unprecedented accomplishment.

In 168 B.C. at the battle of Pynda, the Romans defeated Macedonia, which ruled Greece, ending its independence. After the battle, Polybius, along with a thousand other Greeks who had shown sympathy for Macedonia, was deported to Rome to be questioned. Protected by an influential Roman family, no harm came to him.

In the tradition of Thucydides, Polybius believed that a historian had a duty to teach moral lessons and to enlighten by pointing to general principles governing the course of historical events. Like Thucydides, he believed that there are lessons to be learned from a study of history and that his work would instruct current and future officials regarding the proper course of action under given circumstances. But whereas Thucydides wrote about the Peloponnesian War, which involved the Greek city-states, Polybius, reflecting the spirit of the Hellenistic Age, took the entire Mediterranean world as his subject. His aim was to recount how "the Romans succeeded in less than fifty-three years in bringing under their rule the whole inhabited world, an achievement which is without parallel in human history."* No question was of greater importance, he said, than to understand how Rome acquired this supremacy. Polybius stated explicitly that, unlike his predecessors who wrote specialized narrow studies dealing with aspects of Greek or Persian history, he was attempting a unique project—a systematic world history that "examine[s] the general and comprehensive

belonging—resulting from the weakening of the individual's attachment to the polis and to arrive at a conception of community that corresponded to the social realities of a world grown larger. Unlike Plato and Aristotle, Hellenistic philosophers were moralists, not great speculators and theorists. The Hellenistic schools of philosophy, in contrast to their predecessors, were far less concerned with the scientific understanding of nature. Also in contrast to earlier Greek thinkers, they were less concerned with political organization. Philosophy was now chiefly preoccupied with providing the individual with practical guidelines for living; it tried to alleviate spiritual uneasiness and loss of security. It aspired to make people ethically independent so that they could achieve happiness in a hostile and competitive world. As the philosopher Epicurus said: "Empty are the words of that philosopher who offers no therapy for human suffering. For just as there is no use in medical expertise if it does not give therapy for bodily disease, so too there is no use in philosophy if it does not expel the suffering of the soul."[3] To "expel the suffering of the soul"—to conquer fear and anxiety and to achieve happiness—said Hellenistic philosophers, people must not allow themselves to be troubled by cares and concerns that are ultimately trivial.

In striving for tranquility of mind and relief from conflict, Hellenistic thinkers reflected the general anxiety that pervaded their society. They retained respect for reason and aspired to the rational life, but by stressing peace of mind and the effort to overcome anxiety, they were performing a quasi-religious function. Philosophy was trying to provide comfort for the individual suffering from feelings of loneliness and insignificance. This attempt indicated that Greek civilization was undergoing a spiritual transformation. (We examine the full meaning of this transformation in Chapters 7 and 8.) The gravitation toward religion in an effort to relieve despair gathered momentum in the centuries that followed. Thus, Hellenistic philosophies helped prepare people to accept Christianity, which promised personal salvation. Ultimately, the Christian answer to the problems of alienation and the need for community would

110

scheme of events."[†] Such a study, he held, was an avenue to a wisdom closed to historians who write monographs on parochial, insignificant, and obscure topics.

Among the reasons Polybius gave for Rome's success was its political system, which balanced aristocratic and democratic elements: the Senate, representing the aristocracy, wielded great power, but the Assembly, representing the commoners, also played an important role in political life. Polybius held that such a political balance promoted loyalty and effective government. Polybius was greatly impressed with the Roman army. The discipline and dedication of citizen soldiers, he said, help explain Rome's success in creating a world empire.

---

*Polybius, *The Rise of the Roman Empire,* trans. Ian Scott-Kilvert (New York: Penguin Classics, 1979), 41.

[†]Ibid., 44.

---

predominate over the Greco-Roman attempt at resolution.

The Hellenistic world gave rise to four principal schools of philosophy: Epicureanism, Stoicism, Skepticism, and Cynicism.

Epicureanism. In the tradition of Plato and Aristotle, Epicurus (342–270 B.C.) founded a school in Athens at the end of the fourth century B.C. He broke with the attitude of the Hellenic Age in significant ways. Unlike classical Greek philosophers, Epicurus, reflecting the Greeks' changing relationship to the city, taught the value of passivity and withdrawal from civic life. To him, citizenship was not a prerequisite for individual happiness. Wise persons, said Epicurus, would refrain from engaging in public affairs, for politics is marred by clashing factions and treachery that deprive individuals of their self-sufficiency, their freedom to choose and to act. Nor would wise individuals pursue wealth, power, or fame, as the pursuit would only provoke anxiety. For the same reason, wise persons would not surrender to hate or love, desires that distress the soul. A wise person would also try to live justly, for one who behaves unjustly is burdened with troubles. Nor could there be happiness when one worried about dying or pleasing the gods.

To Epicurus, dread that the gods punished people in this life and could inflict suffering after death was the principal cause of anxiety. To remove this source of human anguish, he favored a theory of nature that had no place for supernatural intervention in nature or in people's lives. Therefore, he adopted the physics of Democritus, which taught that all things consist of atoms in motion. In a universe of colliding atoms, there could be no higher intelligence ordering things; there was no room for divine activity. Epicurus taught that the gods probably did exist but that they could not influence human affairs; hence, it was pointless to worry about them. Individuals should order their lives without considering the gods. Epicurus embraced atomism, not as a disinterested scientist aspiring to truth, but as a moral philosopher seeking to liberate emotional life from fear of the gods.

People could achieve happiness, said Epicurus, when their bodies were "free from pain" and their minds "released from worry and fear." Although Epicurus wanted to increase pleasure for the individual, he rejected unbridled hedonism. Because he believed that happiness must be pursued rationally, he thought that the merely sensuous pleasures with unpleasant aftereffects (such as overeating and excessive drinking) should be avoided. In general, Epicurus espoused the traditional Greek view of moderation and prudence. Most important for achieving the good life, said Epicurus, was the company of friends.

By opening his philosophy to men and women, slave and free, Greek and barbarian, and by separating ethics from politics, Epicurus fashioned a philosophy adapted to the post-Alexandrian world of kingdoms and universal culture.

Stoicism. Around the time of the founding of Epicurus' school, Zeno (335–263 B.C.) also opened a school in Athens. Zeno's teachings, called Stoicism, became the most important philosophy in the Hellenistic world. Epicurus backed away from civic participation and political life as snares that deprived the individual of self-sufficiency. Stoics, however, developed a new formula for the individual's membership in a political community. By teaching that the world constituted a single

Epicureanism: Living Well

Epicureanism was named for its founder, Epicurus, who established a school at Athens in 307 or 306 B.C. To achieve peace of mind, taught Epicurus, one should refrain from worrying about death or pleasing the gods, avoid intense involvements in public affairs, cultivate friendships, and pursue pleasure prudently. The following excerpts from Epicurus' works reveal his prescription for living well in a world grown more complex.

. . . We must grasp this point, that the principal disturbance in the minds of men arises because they think that these celestial bodies are blessed and immortal, and yet we have wills and actions and motives inconsistent with these attributes; and because they are always expecting or imagining some everlasting misery (inflicted on them by the gods), such as is depicted in legends, or even fear the loss of feeling in death . . . and, again, because they are brought to this pass not by reasoned opinion, but rather by some irrational presentiment . . . and, by learning the true causes of celestial phenomena and all other occurrences that come to pass from time to time, we shall free ourselves from all which produces the utmost fear in other men.

It is vain to ask of the gods what a man is capable of supplying for himself.

But the many at one moment shun death as the greatest of evils, at another yearn for it as a respite from the evils of life. But the wise man neither seeks to escape life nor fears the cessation of life, for neither does life offend him nor does the absence of life seem to be any evil.

A man cannot dispel his fear about the most important matters if he does not know what is the nature of the universe but suspects the truth of some mythical story. So that without natural science it is not possible to attain our pleasures unalloyed.

When, therefore, we maintain that pleasure is the end, we do not mean the pleasures-of-profligates and those that consist in sensuality, as is supposed by some who are either ignorant or disagree with us or do not understand, but freedom from pain in the body and from trouble in the mind.

Of all the things which wisdom acquires to produce the blessedness of the complete life, far the greatest is the possession of friendship.

We must release ourselves from the prison of affairs and politics.

A free life cannot acquire many possessions, because this is not easy to do without servility to mobs or monarchs. . . .

The noble soul occupies itself with wisdom and friendship. . . .

Questions for Analysis

1. What did Epicurus believe were the chief causes of emotional distress among human beings?
2. What advice did he offer for achieving inner peace and happiness?

Epicurus: The Extant Remains translated by Cyril Bailey (1926), 440 words from pp. 53, 85, 89, 101, 115, 117, 119. By permission of Oxford University Press.

society, Stoicism gave theoretical expression to the world-mindedness of the age. By arriving at the concept of a world-state, the city of humanity, Stoicism offered an answer to the problem of community and alienation posed by the decline of the city-state. By stressing gaining control over one's inner life in dealing with life's misfortunes, Stoicism offered an avenue to individual happiness in a world fraught with uncertainty.

At the core of Stoicism was the belief that the universe contained a principle of order, variously called Divine Reason (*Logos*), the Divine Fire, or God—more the fundamental force of the universe than a living being. This ruling principle underlay reality and permeated all things; it ordered the cosmos according to law. The Stoics reasoned that, being part of the universe, people too shared in the **Logos** that operated throughout

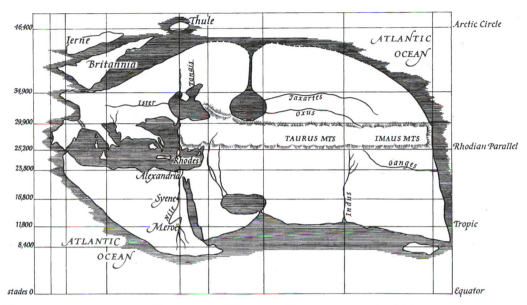

RECONSTRUCTION OF THE MAP OF THE WORLD BY ERATOSTHENES (C. 275–194 B.C.). Geographical knowledge expanded enormously among the Hellenistic Greeks. The first systematic scientific books on geography were credited to Eratosthenes, head of the Alexandrian library, the greatest scientific and humanistic research center in the Hellenistic world. Eratosthenes estimated the circumference of the earth with remarkable accuracy for his time. His map illustrates the limits of the world known to the Greeks. (From John Onians, *Art and Thought in the Hellenistic Age* [Thames and Hudson, 1979]. Reprinted by permission of Thames and Hudson Ltd.)

the cosmos. Inherent in every human soul and discovered through reason, the Logos enabled people to act virtuously and intelligently and to comprehend the principles of order that governed nature. This **natural law** provides human beings with an awareness of what is and is not correct behavior, especially when dealing with other human beings. Living in accordance with natural law is the avenue to both virtue and happiness. Natural law alone commands our ultimate obedience.

Since reason was common to all, human beings were essentially brothers and fundamentally equal. Reason gave individuals dignity and enabled them to recognize and respect the dignity of others. To the Stoics, all people, Greek and barbarian, free and slave, rich and poor, were fellow human beings, and one law, the law of nature, applied to all of them. What people had in common as fellow human beings far outweighed differences based on culture. All rational human beings were fellow citizens of a cosmopolis, a world community. Thus, the Stoics, like the Hebrews, arrived at the idea of a common humanity subject to the same moral obligations.

Pericles had spoken of the Athenians' obligation to abide by the laws and traditions of their city; Stoics, viewing people as citizens of the world, emphasized the individual's duty to understand and obey the natural law that governed the cosmos and applied to all. Socrates had taught a morality of self-mastery—reason exercising control over feelings; the Stoics spread Socrates' philosophy beyond Athens, beyond Greece, and enlarged it, offering it as a way of life for all. Like Socrates, the Stoics believed that a person's distinctive quality was the ability to reason and that happiness came from the disciplining of emotions by the rational part of the soul. Also like Socrates, the Stoics maintained that individuals should progress morally, thus perfecting their character.

MARBLE PORTRAIT OF EPICURUS. The direct gaze and inner calm of the philosopher suggest the essence of his teachings. Epicurus believed that happiness came from a rationally ordered life. He urged his followers to disengage from the uncertainties and stress of politics, business, family, and religion. (The Metropolitan Museum of Art/Art Resource, N.Y.)

In the Stoic view, wise persons ordered their lives according to the natural law—the Logos, or law of reason—that underlay the cosmos. To live in agreement with nature—that is, to follow the dictates of reason—was the aim of moral activity. This harmony with the Logos would give these individuals the inner strength to resist the torments inflicted by others, by fate, and by their own passionate natures. Self-mastery and inner peace, or happiness, would follow. Such individuals would remain undisturbed by life's misfortunes, for their souls would be their own. Even slaves were not denied this inner freedom; although their bodies were subjected to the power of their masters, their minds still remained independent and free.

Stoicism had an enduring influence on the Western mind. To some Roman political and legal thinkers, the Empire fulfilled the Stoic ideal of a world community, in which people of different nationalities held citizenship and were governed by a worldwide law that accorded with the law of reason, or natural law—a moral order operating throughout the universe. Stoic beliefs—that by nature we are all members of one family, that each person is significant, that distinctions of rank and race are of no account, and that human law should not conflict with natural law—were incorporated into Roman jurisprudence, Christian thought, and modern liberalism. There is continuity between the Stoic idea of natural law and the principle of inalienable rights, rights to which all are entitled by nature, stated in the American Declaration of Independence. In the modern age, the principle of natural law provided theoretical justification for human rights that are the birthright of each individual.

Skepticism. The Epicureans tried to withdraw from the evils of this world and to attain personal happiness by reducing physical pain and mental anguish. The Stoics sought happiness by actively entering into harmony with universal reason, that is, with nature. Both philosophies sought peace of mind, but the Stoics did not disengage themselves from political life and often exerted influence over Hellenistic rulers. Skepticism, another school of philosophy, attacked the Epicurean and Stoic belief that there is a definite avenue to happiness. Skeptics held that one could achieve spiritual comfort by recognizing that none of the beliefs by which people lived were true or could bring happiness. For the Skeptic, nothing can be known with certainty. Therefore, suspending judgment—that is, recognizing the existence of alternative viewpoints and disdaining a commitment to dogmatic beliefs—calms the mind and brings contentment.

Some Skeptics taught indifference to all theory and urged conformity to accepted views whether or not they were true. This attitude would avoid arguments and explanations. Gods might not exist, said the Skeptics, but to refuse to worship them or to deny their existence would only cause trouble; therefore, individuals should follow the crowd. The life of the mind—metaphysical speculation inquiring into the origin of things, and clever reasoning—did not bring truth or happiness, so why should one bother with it? Suspending judgment, recognizing the inability to understand, not committing oneself to a system of belief—by these means one could achieve peace of mind. Instead of embracing doctrines, said the Greek writer Lucian, individuals should go their way "with ever a smile and never a passion."[4] This was the position of those Skeptics who were suspicious of ideas, particularly all encompassing rational systems, and hostile to intellectuals.

The more sophisticated Skeptics did not run away from ideas but pointed out their limitations; they did not avoid theories but refuted them. In doing so, they did not reject reason. Rather, they focused on a problem of reason: whether indeed it could arrive at truth. Thus, Carneades of Cyrene (213–129 B.C.) insisted that all ideas, even mathematical principles, must be regarded as hypotheses and assumptions, not as absolutes. Just because the universe showed signs of order, Carneades argued, one could not assume that it had been created by God. Since there was never any certainty, only probability, morality should derive from practical experience rather than from dogma.

Cynicism. The Cynics were not theoretical philosophers but supreme individualists who rebelled against established values and conventions—against every barrier of society that restrained individuals from following their own natures. Cynics regarded laws and public opinion, private property and employment, and wives and children as hindrances to the free life. Extreme individualists, the Cynics had no loyalty to family, city, or kingdom and ridiculed religion, philosophy, and literature. They renounced possessions and showed no respect for authority. When Diogenes, a fourth-century B.C. Cynic, met Alexander the Great, he is supposed to have asked only that the great conqueror get out of his light.

Cynics put their philosophy into practice. They cultivated indifference and apathy and scorned wealth, fame, and noble birth. To harden themselves against life's misfortunes, they engaged in strenuous exercise, endured cold and hunger, and lived ascetically. Not tied down by property or employment,

Cynics wandered shoeless from place to place, wearing dirty and ragged clothes and carrying staffs. To show their disdain for society's customs, Cynics grew long scraggly beards, used foul language, and cultivated bad manners. Diogenes supposedly said: "Look at me, . . . I am without a home, without a city, without property, without a slave; I sleep on the ground; I have neither wife nor children, no miserable governor's mansion, but only earth, and sky, and one rough cloak. Yet what do I lack? Am I not free from pain and fear, am I not free?"[5]

In their attack on inherited conventions, Cynics strove for self-sufficiency and spiritual security. Theirs was the most radical philosophical quest for meaning and peace of soul during the Hellenistic Age.

THE HELLENISTIC LEGACY

The Hellenistic Age encompassed the period from the death of Alexander to the formation of the Roman Empire. During these three centuries, Greek civilization spread eastward as far as India and westward to Rome. As Greeks settled in the Near East and intermingled with Egyptians, Syrians, Persians, and others, the parochialism of the Greek polis gave way to a new cosmopolitanism, an interest in the culture of other ethnic groups, and to universalism, an awareness that people were members of a world community that transcended citizenship in one's native city. Both philosophy and the arts reflected these new concerns.

Rome, conqueror of the Mediterranean world and transmitter of Hellenism, inherited the universalist tendencies of the Hellenistic Age and embodied them in its law, institutions, and art. So too did Christianity, which welcomed converts from every ethnic background and held that God loved all people and that Christ died for all humanity. The Stoic idea of natural law that applies to all human beings and its corollary that human beings are fundamentally equal were crucial to the formulation of the modern idea that the individual is endowed with **natural rights** that no government can violate. A parallel can be drawn between the Hellenistic Age, in which Greek civilization spread to the Near East, and our own age, in which the ideas, institutions, and technology of Western civilization have been exported throughout the globe.

NOTES

1. Quoted in John Ferguson, *The Heritage of Hellenism* (New York: Science History Publications, 1973), 30.

2. Benjamin Farrington, *Greek Science* (Baltimore: Penguin Books, 1961), 301.

3. Quoted in Anthony Gottlieb, *The Dream of Reason* (New York: W. W. Norton, 2000), 283–284.

4. Quoted in J. H. Randall Jr., *Hellenistic Ways of Deliverance and the Making of the Christian Synthesis* (New York: Columbia University Press, 1970), 74.

5. Epictetus, *The Discourses as Reported by Arrian, the Manual and Fragments,* trans. W. A. Oldfather (Cambridge, Mass.: Harvard University Press, 1966), 2:147.

SUGGESTED READING

Bonnard, André, *Greek Civilization,* vol. 3 (1961). Self-contained chapters on various phases of late classical and Hellenistic periods.

Cartledge, Paul, *Alexander the Great* (2004). A recent biography.

Chamoux, François, *Hellenistic Civilization* (2003). Strong on the ways Greek ideas and cultural forms were received in different lands.

Ferguson, John, *The Heritage of Hellenism* (1973). A good introduction to Hellenistic culture.

Gergel, Tania, ed., Alexander *the Great: The Brief Life and Towering Exploits of History's Greatest Conqueror As Told by His Original Biographers* (2004). A convenient anthology of original sources.

Grant, Michael, *From Alexander to Cleopatra* (1982). A fine survey of all phases of Hellenistic society and culture.

Koester, Helmut, *Introduction to the New Testament,* vol. 1, *History, Culture, and Religion of the Hellenistic Age* (1982). An intelligent guide.

Tripolitis, Antonia, *Religions of the Hellenistic Age* (2002). An excellent survey.

Wallbank, F. W., *The Hellenistic World* (1982). A survey of the Hellenistic world that makes judicious use of quotations from original sources.

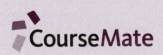

Chapter 6

The Roman Republic: City-State to World Empire

A Roman Warship with Legionnaires on a Relief from the Temple of Fortuna Primigenia, First Century B.C. Roman soldiers fought on sea as well as on land, conquering nations throughout the Mediterranean area during the eras of the Republic and the Empire. (Scala/Art Resource, N.Y.)

- **Evolution of the Roman Constitution**
- **Roman Expansion to 146 B.C.**
- **Culture in the Republic**
- **Collapse of the Republic**

Focus Questions

1. What was the significance of the conflict between plebeians and patricians?
2. What factors enabled the city-state of Rome to conquer Italy and the Mediterranean world?
3. What was the significance of Roman expansion?
4. What were the reasons for the collapse of the Roman Republic?

Rome's great achievement was to transcend the narrow political orientation of the city-state and to create a world-state that unified the different nations of the Mediterranean world. Regarding the polis as the only means to the good life, the Greeks had not desired a larger political unit and had almost totally excluded foreigners from citizenship. Although Hellenistic philosophers had conceived the possibility of a world community, Hellenistic politics could not shape one. Rome overcame the limitations of the city-state mentality and developed an empire-wide system of law and citizenship. The Hebrews were distinguished by their prophets and the Greeks by their philosophers. The Romans produced no Amos or Isaiah, and no Plato or Aristotle; their genius found expression in law and government and in the transmission of the Greek cultural achievement.

Historians divide Roman history into two broad periods: the period of the **Republic** began in 509 B.C. with the overthrow of the Etruscan monarchy; the period of the **Empire** began in 27 B.C., when Octavian (Augustus) became in effect the first Roman emperor, ending almost five hundred years of republican self-government. By conquering the Mediterranean world and extending Roman law and, in some instances, citizenship to different nationalities, the Roman Republic transcended the parochialism typical of the city-state. The Republic initiated the trend toward political and legal universalism, which reached fruition in the second period of Roman history, the Empire.

EVOLUTION OF THE ROMAN CONSTITUTION

By the eighth century B.C., peasant communities existed on some of Rome's seven hills near the Tiber River in central Italy. To the north stood Etruscan cities and to the south Greek cities. The more advanced civilizations of both Etruscans and Greeks were gradually absorbed by the Romans.

The origin of the Etruscans remains a mystery, although some scholars believe that they came from Asia Minor and settled in north-central Italy. From them, Romans acquired architectural styles and skills in road construction, sanitation,

Chronology 6.1 ✦ The Roman Republic

509 B.C.	Expulsion of the Etruscan monarch
450	Law of Twelve Tables
287	End of the Struggle of the Orders
264–241	First Punic War: Rome acquires provinces
218–201	Second Punic War: Hannibal is defeated
149–146	Third Punic War: destruction of Carthage
133–122	Land reforms by the Gracchi brothers; they are murdered by the Senate
88–83	Conflict between Sulla and the forces of Marius; Sulla emerges as dictator
79	After restoring rule by Senate, Sulla retires
73–71	Slave revolt is led by Spartacus
58–51	Caesar campaigns in Gaul
49–44	Caesar is dictator of Rome
31 B.C.	Antony and Cleopatra are defeated at Actium by Octavian

hydraulic engineering (including underground conduits), metallurgy, ceramics, and portrait sculpture. Symbols of authority and rule—purple robes, ivory-veneer chariots, thrones for state officials, and a bundle of rods and an ax held by attendants—were also borrowed from the Etruscans. Etruscan words and names entered into the Latin language, and Roman religion absorbed Etruscan gods.

The Etruscans had expanded their territory in Italy during the seventh and sixth centuries B.C., and they controlled the monarchy in Rome. However, defeated by Celts, Greeks, and finally Romans, the Etruscans had ceased to exercise any political power in Italy by the third century B.C.

Rome became a republic at the end of the sixth century B.C.—the traditional date is 509 B.C.—when the landowning aristocrats, or **patricians**, overthrew the Etruscan king. In the opening phase of republican history, religion governed the people, dictated the law, and legitimized the rule of the patricians—aristocrats by birth who regarded themselves as the preservers of sacred traditions. Gradually, the Romans loosened the ties between religion and politics and hammered out a constitutional system that paralleled the Greek achievement of rationalizing and secularizing politics and law. In time, the Romans, like the Greeks, came to view law as an expression of the public will and not as the creation of god-kings, priest-kings, or a priestly caste.

The impetus for the growth of the Roman constitution came from a conflict—known as the Struggle of the Orders—between the patricians and the commoners, or **plebeians.** At the beginning of the fifth century B.C., the patrician-dominated government consisted of two annually elected executives called consuls, the Centuriate Assembly, and the Senate. Patricians owned most of the land and controlled the army. The two consuls, who came from the nobility, commanded the army, served as judges, and initiated legislation. To prevent either consul from becoming an autocrat, decisions had to be approved by both of them. In times of crisis, the consuls were authorized by the Senate to nominate a dictator; he would possess absolute powers during the emergency, but these powers would expire after six months. The consuls were aided by other annually elected magistrates and administrators. The Centuriate Assembly was a popular assembly but, because of voting procedures, was controlled by the nobility. The Assembly elected consuls and other magistrates and made the laws, which also needed Senate approval. The Senate advised the Assembly but did not itself enact laws; it controlled public finances and foreign policy. Senators either were appointed for life terms by the consuls or were former magistrates. The Senate was the principal organ of patrician power.

The tension between patricians and commoners stemmed from plebeian grievances, which included enslavement for debt, discrimination in the courts, prevention of intermarriage with patricians, lack of political representation, and the absence of a written code of laws. Resenting their inferior status and eager for economic relief, the plebeians organized and waged a struggle for political, legal, and social equality. They had one decisive weapon: their threat to secede from Rome, that is, not to pay taxes, work, or serve in the army. Realizing that Rome, which was constantly involved in warfare on the Italian peninsula, could not endure without plebeian help, the pragmatic patricians begrudgingly made concessions. Thus, the plebeians slowly gained legal equality.

Early in the fifth century, the plebeians won the right to form their own assembly (the Plebeian Assembly, which was later enlarged and called the Tribal Assembly). This Assembly could elect tribunes, officials who were empowered to protect plebeian rights. As a result of plebeian pressure, in about 450 B.C., the first Roman code of laws was written. Called the Twelve Tables, the code gave plebeians some degree of protection against unfair and oppressive patrician officials, who could interpret customary law in an arbitrary way. Other concessions gained later by the plebeians included the right to intermarry with patricians; access to the highest political, judicial, and religious offices in the state; and the elimination of slavery as payment for debt. In 287 B.C., a date generally recognized as the termination of the plebeian-patrician struggle, laws passed by the Tribal Assembly no longer required Senate approval. Now the plebeians had full civil equality and legal protection, and their assembly had full power to enact legislation.

Despite these reforms, Rome was still ruled by an upper class. The oligarchy that now held power consisted of patricians and influential plebeians who had joined forces with the old nobility. Marriages between patricians and politically powerful plebeians strengthened this alliance. Generally only wealthy plebeians became tribunes, and they tended to side with the old nobility rather than

defend the interests of poor plebeians. By using bribes, the ruling oligarchy of patricians and wealthy plebeians maintained control over the Assembly, and the Senate remained a bastion of aristocratic power.

A patron–client relationship extending back to the days of the monarchy reinforced upper-class rule. In early Rome, a plebeian seeking protection for himself and his family in the courts looked to a patrician for assistance. In return, the plebeian gave his patrician patron both military and political support. Enduring over the centuries, the patron–client relationship assured powerful nobles of their commoner clients' support in the Assembly, and it provided clients with food, money, and protection.

Thus, from beginning to end, an upper class—sometimes expanded to allow entry of new talent and wealth—governed the Roman Republic. This aristocracy's view of liberty always remained elitist: freedom for Rome's best men to achieve virtue (*virtus*), dignity (*dignitas*), and fame (*fama*) by competing with one another for political power and privilege. Cicero (see below), himself a member of the ruling elite, aptly summed up its outlook: "the safety of the State depends upon the wisdom of its best men, especially since Nature has provided not only that those men who are superior in virtue and in spirit should rule the weaker, but also that the weaker should be willing to obey the stronger."[1] Like others of the upper class, Cicero held that "the perversity and rashness of popular assemblies" precluded them from governing effectively.[2] In the Greek cities, tyrants had succeeded in breaking aristocratic dominance, thereby clearing a pathway for democratic government. But in the Roman Republic, the nobility maintained its tight grip on the reins of power until the civil wars of the first century B.C.

Deeming themselves Rome's finest citizens, the ruling oligarchy led Rome during its period of expansion and demonstrated a sense of responsibility and a talent for statesmanship. In noble families, parents and elders prepared the young for public service. They recounted the glorious deeds of ancestors who had served Rome, and they reminded youngsters of their responsibility to bring additional honors to the family by winning distinction as a commander, orator, or jurist.

STATUE PORTRAIT, FIRST CENTURY A.D. The Romans valued family, city, and tradition. Here a noble proudly exhibits the busts of his ancestors. (Scala/Art Resource, N.Y.)

In this way, a son would prove his worth as a man and as a Roman.

During their two-hundred-year class struggle, the Romans forged a constitutional system based on civic needs rather than on religious mystery. The essential duty of government ceased to be the regular performance of religious rituals and became the maintenance of order at home and the preservation of Roman might and dignity in international relations. Although the Romans retained the ceremonies and practices of their ancestral religion—correct observance was a way of showing respect for tradition—public interest, not religious tradition, determined the content of law and was the standard by which all the important acts of the city were judged. When Romans chose a course of action in public life, they rarely took into consideration the fear of displeasing the gods. By the late Republic, Romans did not seem concerned about divine intervention in their daily lives; the prospect of divine punishment seemed quite remote. In the opening stage of republican history, law was priestly and sacred, spoken only by priests and known only to men of religious families. Gradually, as law was written, debated, and altered, it became disentangled from religion. Another step in this process of secularization and rationalization occurred when the study and interpretation of law passed from the hands of priests to a class of professional jurists, who analyzed, classified, systematized, and sought commonsense solutions to legal problems.

The Roman constitution was not a product of abstract thought, nor was it the gift of a great lawmaker such as the Athenian Solon. Rather, like the unwritten British constitution, the Roman constitution evolved gradually and empirically in response to specific needs. The Romans, unlike the Greeks, were distinguished by practicality and common sense, not by a love of abstract thought. In their pragmatic and empirical fashion, they gradually developed the procedures of public politics and the legal state.

Undoubtedly, the commoners' struggle for rights and power did arouse hatred on both sides. But in contrast to the domestic strife in Greek cities, Rome's class conflict did not end in civil war. This peaceful solution testifies to the political good sense of the Romans. Fear of foreign powers and the tradition of civic patriotism prevented the patrician–plebeian conflict from turning into a fight to the death. At the time of the class struggle, Rome was also engaged in the extension of its power over the Italian peninsula. Without civic harmony and stability, Rome could not have achieved expansion.

ROMAN EXPANSION TO 146 B.C.

By 146 B.C., Rome was the dominant state in the Mediterranean world. Roman expansion occurred in three main stages: the uniting of the Italian peninsula, which gave Rome the forces that transformed it from a city-state into a great power; the collision with Carthage, from which Rome emerged as ruler of the western Mediterranean; and the subjugation of the Hellenistic states, which brought Romans in close contact with Greek civilization. As Rome expanded territorially, its leaders enlarged their vision. Instead of restricting citizenship to people having ethnic kinship, Rome assimilated other peoples into its political community. Just as Roman law had grown to cope with the earlier grievances of the plebeians, so too it adjusted to the new situations resulting from the creation of a multinational empire. The city of Rome was evolving into the city of humanity—the cosmopolis envisioned by the Stoics.

The Uniting of Italy

During the first stage of expansion, Rome extended its hegemony over Italy, subduing in the process neighboring Latin kinsmen, semicivilized Italian tribes, the once-dominant Etruscans, and Greek city-states in southern Italy. At the beginning, Roman warfare was principally motivated by the hunger for more farmland. As Rome expanded and its territory and responsibilities increased, it was often drawn into conflict to protect its widened boundaries and its allies. Also fueling Roman expansion was an aristocratic ethos, which placed the highest value on glory and reputation. Demonstrating prowess in war, aristocrats believed, was the finest way to win the esteem of fellow Romans, bring honor to their families, and enhance their own political careers.

Rome's conquest of Italy stemmed in part from superior military organization, grueling training, and iron discipline. From the Greeks they acquired the most advanced methods of siegecraft. Also copying the Greeks, the Romans organized their soldiers into battle formations; in contrast, their opponents often fought as disorganized hordes, which were prone to panic and flight. Fighting as part of a unit strengthened the courage and confidence of the Roman soldier, for he knew that his comrades would stand with him. Roman soldiers who deserted their posts or fled from battle were punished and disgraced, an ordeal more terrible than facing up to the enemy. The promise of glory and rewards also impelled the Roman soldier to distinguish himself in battle.

Ultimately, Rome's success was due to the character of its people and the quality of its statesmanship. The Roman farmer-soldier was dedicated, rugged, persevering, and self-reliant. He could march thirty miles a day laden with arms, armor, and equipment weighing sixty pounds. In the face of danger, he remained resolute and tenacious, obedient to the poet Virgil's maxim: "Yield you not to ill fortune, but go against it with more daring." Romans willingly made sacrifices so that Rome might endure. In conquering Italy, they were united by a moral and religious devotion to their city strong enough to overcome social conflict, factional disputes, and personal ambition.

Despite its army's might, Rome could not have mastered Italy without the cooperation of other Italian peoples. Like other ancient peoples, Rome plundered, enslaved, and brutalized, at times with great ferocity. But it also endeavored, through generous treatment, to gain the loyalty of those it had conquered. Some defeated Italian communities retained a measure of self-government but turned the conduct of foreign affairs over to Rome and contributed contingents to the army when Rome went to war. Other conquered people received partial or full citizenship. In extending its dominion over Italy, Rome displayed a remarkable talent for converting former enemies into allies and eventually into Roman citizens. No Greek city had ever envisaged integrating nonnatives into its political community.

Polybius: The Roman Army

The discipline and dedication of the citizen soldiers help explain Rome's success in conquering a world empire. In the following account, Polybius (see Profile in Chapter 5) tells how the commanders enforced obedience and fostered heroism.

A court-martial composed of the tribunes immediately sits to try him [a soldier], and if he is found guilty, he is punished by beating (*fustuarium*). This is carried out as follows. The tribune takes a cudgel and lightly touches the condemned man with it, whereupon all the soldiers fall upon him with clubs and stones, and usually kill him in the camp itself. But even those who contrive to escape are no better off. How indeed could they be? They are not allowed to return to their homes, and none of their family would dare to receive such a man into the house. Those who have once fallen into this misfortune are completely and finally ruined. The *optio* [lieutenant] and the *decurio* [sergeant] of the squadron are liable to the same punishment if they fail to pass on the proper orders at the proper moment to the patrols and the *decurio* of the next squadron. The consequence of the extreme severity of this penalty and of the absolute impossibility of avoiding it is that the night watches of the Roman army are faultlessly kept. . . .

The Romans also have an excellent method of encouraging young soldiers to face danger. Whenever any have especially distinguished themselves in a battle, the general assembles the troops and calls forward those he considers to have shown exceptional courage. He praises them first for their gallantry in action and for anything in their previous conduct which is particularly worthy of mention, and then he distributes gifts such as the following: to a man who has wounded one of the enemy, a spear; to one who has killed and stripped an enemy, a cup if he is in the infantry, or horse-trappings if in the cavalry—originally the gift was simply a lance. These presentations are not made to men who have wounded or stripped an enemy in the course of a pitched battle, or at the storming of a city, but to those who during a skirmish or some similar situation in which there is no necessity to engage in single combat, have voluntarily and deliberately exposed themselves to danger.

At the storming of a city the first man to scale the wall is awarded a crown of gold. In the same way those who have shielded and saved one of their fellow-citizens or of the allies are honoured with gifts. . . . The men who receive these trophies not only enjoy great prestige in the army and soon afterwards in their homes, but they are also singled out for precedence in religious processions when they return. On these occasions nobody is allowed to wear decorations save those who have been honoured for their bravery by the consuls, and it is the custom to hang up the trophies they have won in the most conspicuous places in their houses, and to regard them as proofs and visible symbols of their valour. So when we consider this people's almost obsessive concern with military rewards and punishments, and the immense importance which they attach to both, it is not surprising that they emerge with brilliant success from every war in which they engage.

Question for Analysis

1. How did the Romans ensure good discipline and promote bravery among their soldiers?

Polybius, *The Rise of the Roman Empire*, trans. Ian Scott-Kilvert (New York: Penguin Books, 1984), 332–334.

The Italian Confederation formed by Rome was a unique and creative organization that conferred on Italians a measure of security and order previously unknown. Rome prevented internecine wars within the peninsula, suppressed internal revolutions within city-states, and protected the Italians from barbarians (Gallic invaders from the north). In the wars of conquest outside Italy, a share of the glory and plunder fell to all Italians, another benefit of the confederation.

By 264 B.C., Rome had achieved two striking successes. First, it had secured social cohesion by redressing the grievances of the plebeians. Second, it had increased its military might by conquering Italy, thus obtaining the human resources with which it would conquer the Mediterranean world.

Conquest of the Mediterranean World

When Rome finished unifying Italy, there were five great powers in the Mediterranean area: the Seleucid monarchy in the Near East, the Ptolemaic monarchy in Egypt, the kingdom of Macedonia, Carthage in the western Mediterranean, and the Roman-dominated Italian Confederation. One hundred twenty years later, by 146 B.C., Rome had subjected the other states to its dominion—"an event for which the past affords no precedent," said the contemporary Greek historian Polybius.

Roman expansion beyond Italy did not proceed according to predetermined design. Indeed, some Roman leaders considered involvement in foreign adventures a threat to both Rome's security and its traditional way of life. But it is difficult for a great power not to get drawn into conflicts as its interests grow, and, without planning it, Rome acquired an overseas empire.

Shortly after asserting supremacy in Italy, Rome engaged Carthage, the other great power in the western Mediterranean, in a prolonged conflict. Founded about 800 B.C. by Phoenicians, the North African city of Carthage had become a prosperous commercial center. Its wealth was derived from a virtual monopoly of trade in the western Mediterranean and along the western coasts of Africa and Europe. The Carthaginians (*Poeni* in Latin) had acquired an empire comprising North Africa and coastal regions of southern Spain, Sardinia, Corsica, and western Sicily.

War between the two great powers began because Rome feared Carthage's designs on the northern Sicilian city of Messana. Rome was apprehensive about the southern Italian city-states that were its allies, fearing that Carthage would use Messana either to attack them or to interfere with their trade. Rome decided that the security of its allies required intervention in Sicily.

The two powers had stumbled into a collision, the First Punic War (264–241 B.C.), that neither had deliberately sought. Although Rome suffered severe losses—including the annihilation of an army that had invaded North Africa and the destruction of hundreds of ships in battle and storms—the Romans never considered anything but a victor's peace. Drawing manpower from loyal allies throughout Italy, Rome finally prevailed over Carthage, which had to surrender Sicily to Rome. Three years later, Rome seized the islands of Corsica and Sardinia from a weakened Carthage. With the acquisition of these territories beyond Italy, which were made into provinces, Rome had the beginnings of an empire.

Carthaginian expansion in Spain in order to recoup wealth—Spain was rich in metals—and to obtain manpower for the depleted Carthaginian forces precipitated the Second Punic War (218–201 B.C.). Coming from Spain, the Carthaginian army was commanded by Hannibal (247–183 B.C.), whose military genius astounded the ancients. Hannibal led a seasoned army, complete with war elephants for charging enemy lines, through passes in the Alps so steep and icy that men and animals sometimes lost their footing and fell to their deaths. Some twenty-six thousand men survived the crossing into Italy; fifteen thousand more were recruited from Gallic tribesmen of the Po valley. At the battle of Cannae (216 B.C.), 50,000 Carthaginian mercenaries, principally Libyans, Numidians, Gauls, and Spaniards, faced some 60,000 Roman citizen-soldiers. In a brilliant encircling maneuver, the Carthaginian forces completely destroyed the largest army Rome had ever put into the field. The butchering by hand of the trapped Roman soldiers lasted for hours.

Romans were in a state of shock. Mixed with grief for the dead was the fear that Hannibal would crown his victory with an attack on Rome itself. To prevent panic, the Senate ordered women and children indoors, limited mourning to thirty days, and prepared to raise a new army. Adding to Rome's distress was the defection of many southern Italian allies to Hannibal.

These were the Republic's worst days. Nevertheless, says the Roman historian Livy, the Romans did not breathe a word of peace. Hannibal could not follow up his victory at Cannae with a finishing blow, for Rome wisely would

CAST MADE FROM TRAJAN'S COLUMN. Emperor Trajan (A.D. 98–117) constructed a column to commemorate his campaigns. One of the reliefs depicts a Roman fleet landing at the port of Acona. During the First Punic War, Rome had become a naval power able to counter Carthage's fleet. (© DeA Picture Library/Art Resource, N.Y.)

not allow its army to be lured into another major engagement. Nor did Hannibal possess the manpower to capture the city itself, with its formidable fortifications. In addition, most of Rome's Italian allies remained loyal, although many south Italian cities went over to Hannibal. Rome quickly raised and equipped new legions, even enlisting seventeen-year olds and promising freedom to slaves and amnesty to criminals who volunteered to serve. To finance the army, taxes were doubled and women surrendered their jewelry to the state. Most important, the Roman fleet prevented supplies from reaching the Carthaginians.

When Rome invaded North Africa, threatening Carthage, Hannibal was forced to withdraw his troops from Italy in order to defend his homeland. Hannibal, who had won every battle in Italy, was defeated by Scipio Africanus at the battle of Zama in North Africa in 202 B.C., ending the Second Punic War. Carthage was compelled to surrender Spain and to give up its elephants and its navy. Sheer determination, its vast reserves of manpower, and the state's willingness to garner its wealth to strengthen its legions explain Rome's victory.

The Second Punic War left Rome as the sole great power in the western Mediterranean; it also hastened Rome's entry into the politics of the Hellenistic world. In the year after Cannae, during Rome's darkest ordeal, Philip V of Macedonia formed an alliance with Hannibal. Fearing that the Macedonian ruler might have intentions of invading Italy, Rome initiated the First Macedonian War and won it in 205 B.C. To end Macedonian influence in Greece, which Rome increasingly viewed as a Roman protectorate, the Romans fought two other wars with Macedonia. Finally, in 148 B.C., Rome created the province of Macedonia.

Intervention in Greece led to Roman involvement in the Hellenistic kingdoms of the Near East and Asia Minor—Seleucia, Egypt, and Pergamum. The Hellenistic states became client kingdoms of Rome and consequently lost their freedom of action in foreign affairs.

Roman imperialism is a classic example of a great power being snared into overseas adventures. To achieve security, Rome protected its allies, prevented endemic warfare, and thwarted any would-be conquerors of Italy. In the course of these actions came considerable spoils of war, but Rome's principal motives for expansion were strategic and political, not economic.

In 146 B.C., the same year that Rome's hegemony over the Hellenistic world was assured, Rome concluded an unnecessary Third Punic War with Carthage. Although Carthage was by then a second-rate power and no longer a threat to Rome's security, Rome had launched this war of annihilation against Carthage in 149 B.C. The Romans were driven by old hatreds and the traumatic memory of Hannibal's near conquest. Rome sold Carthaginian survivors into slavery, obliterated the city, and turned the territory into the Roman province of Africa. Rome's savage and irrational behavior toward a helpless Carthage was an early sign of the deterioration of senatorial leadership; there would be others.

Rome had not yet reached the limits of its expansion, but there was no doubt that by 146 B.C. the Mediterranean world had been subjected to its will. No power could stand up to Rome.

Consequences of Expansion

As a result of Rome's eastern conquests, thousands of Greeks came to Rome; many were educated persons who had been enslaved because of the conquests. This influx accelerated the process of Hellenization—the adoption of Greek culture—which had begun earlier with Rome's contact with the Greek cities of southern Italy.

A crucial consequence of expansion was Roman contact with the legal experience of other peoples, including the Greeks. Roman jurists, demonstrating the Roman virtues of pragmatism and common sense, selectively incorporated into Roman law elements of the legal codes and traditions of these nations. Thus, Roman jurists empirically fashioned the *jus gentium*, the law of nations, or peoples, which gradually was applied throughout the Empire (see "Law," in Chapter 7).

Rome's conquests also contributed to the rise of a business class, whose wealth was derived from trade, army supply contracts, construction, and tax collecting in the provinces. Rome had no professional civil service, and the collection of public revenues was open to bidding—the highest bidder receiving a contract to collect customs duties, rents on public lands, and tribute in the provinces. The collector's profit came from milking as much tax money as he could from the provincials. These financiers belonged to a group called the Equites, which also included prosperous landowners. Generally, the interests of the Equites paralleled those of the ruling oligarchy. At times, however, they did support generals—notably Julius Caesar—who challenged senatorial rule.

The immense wealth brought to Rome from ransacked eastern cities and overworked Spanish silver mines gave the upper classes a taste for luxury. The rich built elaborate homes, which they decorated with fine furniture and works of art and staffed with servants, cooks, and tutors. They delighted in sumptuous banquets, which contained all types of delicacies. Wealthy matrons wore fancy gowns and elaborate hairstyles. These excesses prompted Roman moralists to castigate the people for violating traditional values. Moralists lamented that the new prosperity produced a deterioration in the Roman character.

Roman conquerors had transported to Italy hundreds of thousands of war captives, including Greeks, from all over the Empire. The enslavement and deportations would continue in the first century B.C. (Julius Caesar, for example, enslaved some one million Gauls.) It is estimated that between 80 and 8 B.C. more than two million enslaved aliens were transported to Italy. By the middle of that century, slaves constituted about one-third of Italy's population, compared with about 10 percent before the Second Punic War. The wars of conquest (and piracy) had made the slave trade a vast and lucrative commercial venture. Like the Greeks, Romans considered slavery indispensable for the preservation of civilized life. Roman jurists and intellectuals regarded the division of humanity into masters and slaves as a rule of nature and viewed the slave as an animate tool, an object that produced and served; like other forms of property, slaves could be sold or rented out by their masters. The more fortunate or more capable slaves worked as domestic servants, artisans, bookkeepers, scribes, and administrators; the luckless and more numerous, branded and chained, toiled from dawn to dusk on the growing number of plantations or died early laboring in mines under inhuman conditions. So brutal was their existence that they begged for death, reported a Roman observer. Except for the very poor, every free Roman owned at least one slave. Roman masters often treated their slaves brutally: torture was common, and masters sexually exploited both male and female slaves for their own pleasure or compelled them to work as prostitutes. But strong personal bonds between master and slave also existed—for example, there are accounts of slaves enduring torture and death to protect their masters from enemies.

Although slave uprisings were not common, their ferocity terrified the Romans. In 135 B.C., slaves in Sicily revolted and captured some key towns, defeating Roman forces before being subdued. In 73 B.C., gladiators led by Spartacus broke out of their barracks and were joined by tens of thousands of runaways. Spartacus aimed to escape from Italy to Gaul and Thrace, the homelands of many slaves. The slave army, which grew to some 150,000, defeated Roman armies and devastated southern Italy before the superior might of Rome prevailed. Some 6,000 of the defeated slaves were tortured and crucified on the road from Capua to Rome.

Republican Rome treated the people in overseas lands differently from its Italian allies. Italians were drafted into the Roman army, but provincials as a rule served only in emergencies, for Rome was not certain of their loyalty or of their readiness to meet Roman standards of discipline. Whereas Rome had been somewhat generous in extending citizenship to Italians, provincials were granted citizenship only in exceptional cases. All but some favored communities were required to pay taxes to Rome. Roman governors, lesser officials, and businessmen found the provinces a source of quick wealth; they were generally unrestrained by the Senate, which was responsible for administering the overseas territories. Exploitation, corruption, looting, and extortion soon ran rampant. "No administration in history has ever devoted itself so whole-heartedly to fleecing its subjects for the private benefit of its ruling class as Rome of the last age of the Republic," concludes E. Badian.[3] The Roman nobility proved unfit to manage a world empire.

Despite numerous examples of misrule in the provinces, Roman administration had many positive features. Rome generally allowed its subjects a large measure of self-government and did not interfere with religion and local customs. Usually, the Roman taxes worked out to be no higher, and in some instances lower, than those under previous regimes. Most important, Rome reduced the endemic warfare that had plagued these regions.

Essentially, Rome used its power for constructive ends: to establish order; to build roads, aqueducts, and public buildings; and to promote Hellenism. When Rome destroyed, it rebuilt creatively; when it conquered, it spread civilization and maintained peace. But no doubt its hundreds of thousands of prisoners of war, uprooted, enslaved, and degraded, did not view Roman conquest as beneficial; nor did the butchered Spanish tribesmen or the massacred Carthaginians.

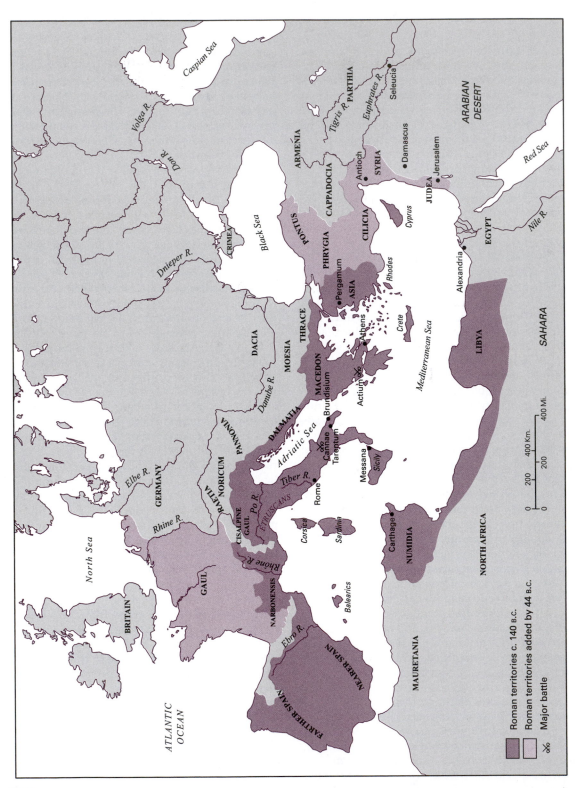

	Caspian Sea

ARABIAN DESERT

Volga R.

Don R.

PARTHIA

Tigris R.

Euphrates R.

• Seleucia

ARMENIA

CAPPADOCIA

• Damascus

SYRIA

Antioch

Red Sea

CRIMEA

Black Sea

PONTUS

CILICIA

JUDEA

• Jerusalem

Nile R.

Dnieper R.

PHRYGIA

Cyprus

EGYPT

Rhodes

Alexandria

DACIA

ASIA

• Pergamum

SAHARA

Danube R.

MOESIA

THRACE

Athens

Crete

LIBYA

Mediterranean Sea

Elbe R.

DALMATIA

MACEDON

Actium

Brundisium

GERMANY

VINONON

PANN

Adriatic Sea

Tarentum

Cannae

Messana

Sicily

RAETIA

NORICUM

Po R.

CISALPINE GAUL

ETRUSCANS

Tiber R.

Rome

North Sea

Rhine R.

Corsica

Sardinia

Carthage

NUMIDIA

NORTH AFRICA

Rhône R.

GAUL

NARBONENSIS

Balearics

BRITAIN

ATLANTIC OCEAN

Ebro R.

NEARER SPAIN

FARTHER SPAIN

MAURETANIA

400 Mi.

400 Km.

200

200

0

0

Roman territories c. 140 B.C.

Roman territories added by 44 B.C.

Major battle

RUINS IN SPAIN. This Roman aqueduct in Spain stands as an impressive reminder of the ancient Romans' engineering skills. (© Alan Copson/JAI/Corbis.)

To these hapless victims, Rome appeared as an evil oppressor, not as the creator of a cosmopolis that brought order and security.

CULTURE IN THE REPUBLIC

One of the chief consequences of expansion was increased contact with Greek culture. During the third century B.C., Greek civilization started to exercise an increasing and fruitful influence on the Roman mind. Greek teachers, both slave and free, came to Rome and introduced Romans to Hellenic cultural achievements. As they conquered the eastern Mediterranean, Roman generals began to ship libraries and works of art from Greek cities to Rome. Roman sculpture and painting imitated Greek prototypes. In time, Romans acquired from Greece knowledge of scientific thought, philosophy, medicine, and geography. Roman writers and orators used Greek history, poetry, drama, and oratory as models. The Elder Pliny (A.D. 23–79), who wrote on many topics but is most famous for *Natural History*, refers to Homer's poetry as "the most valuable work of the human mind."[4] Cicero, Rome's greatest orator, tells us that ambitious young men eager to learn the art of oratory but unaware of the existence of any "course of training or any rules of art . . . attain[ed] what skill they could by means of their natural ability. . . . But later, having heard the Greek orators, gained acquaintance with their literature and called in

◄ *Map 6.1* **ROMAN CONQUESTS DURING THE REPUBLIC** The conquest of Italy gave Rome the manpower to expand throughout the Mediterranean world. In the Second Punic War, Rome defeated its greatest rival, Carthage. (Copyright © 2013 Cengage Learning.)

Greek teachers, our people were fired with a really incredible enthusiasm for eloquence."[5]

Adopting the humanist outlook of the Greeks, the Romans came to value human intelligence and eloquent and graceful prose and poetry. Wealthy Romans retained Greek tutors, poets, and philosophers in their households and sent their sons to Athens to study. By the late Republic, educated Romans could speak and read Greek. Thus, Rome creatively assimilated the Greek achievement and transmitted it to others, thereby extending the orbit of Hellenism. To be sure, some conservative Romans were hostile to the Greek influence, which they felt threatened traditional Roman values that had accounted for Roman greatness. Cato the Elder (234–149 B.C.) and other Roman moralists denounced Socrates for undermining respect for Athenian law and warned that Greek philosophy might lure Roman youth into similar subversive behavior. Moreover, said these moralists, Greek philosophy, with its endless discussions of abstract themes, contrasted with the virtue most cherished by Romans—*gravitas*, or seriousness, which enabled Romans to conduct public affairs effectively. Philosophy seemed designed for a life of leisure and inaction, whereas a virtuous Roman was actively involved in practical civic matters. But the tide of Hellenism could not be stemmed.

Plautus (c. 254–184 B.C.), Rome's greatest playwright, adopted features of fourth- and third-century Greek comedy. His plays had Greek characters and took place in Greek settings; the actors wore the Greek style of dress. His characters resembled those found in Menander's comedies: a cunning slave, a lovesick youth, a foolish old man, a braggart soldier. The plots often consisted of a struggle between two antagonists over a woman or money, or both. The plays usually had the ending desired by the audience: the "good guy" won, and the "bad guy" received a fitting punishment. The pains of love were a common theme.

> *Not the throes of all mankind*
> *Equal my distracted mind.*
> *I strain and I toss*
> *On a passionate cross;*
> *Love's goad makes me reel,*
> *I whirl on Love's wheel,*
> *In a swoon of despair*

> *Hurried here, hurried there—*
> *Torn asunder, I am blind*
> *With a cloud upon my mind.*[6]

Terence (c. 185–159 B.C.), another playwright, was originally from North Africa and was brought to Rome as a slave. His owner, a Roman senator, provided the talented youth with an education and freed him. Terence demonstrated humaneness, a quality that can be seen in his attitude toward child rearing.

> *I give—I overlook; I do not judge it necessary*
> *to exert my authority in everything. . . . I think*
> *it better to restrain children through a sense*
> *of shame and liberal treatment than through*
> *fear. . . . This is the duty of a parent to ac-*
> *custom a son to do what is right rather of his*
> *own choice, than through fear of another.*[7]

Catullus (c. 84–c. 54 B.C.) is generally regarded as one of the greatest lyric poets in world literature. He was a native of northern Italy whose father had provided him with a gentleman's education. In his early twenties, Catullus came to Rome and fell in love with Clodia; she was the wife of the governor of Cisalpine Gaul, who was away at the time. For the older Clodia, Catullus was a refreshing diversion from her many other lovers. Tormented by Clodia's numerous affairs, Catullus struggled to break away from passion's grip.

> *I look no more for her to be my lover*
> *As I love her. That thing could never be.*
> *Nor pray I for her purity—that's over.*
> *Only this much I pray, that I be free.*
> *Free from insane desire myself, and guarded*
> *In peace at last. O heaven, grant that yet*
> *The faith by which I've lived may be*
> *   rewarded.*
> *Let me forget.*[8]

Lucretius (c. 96–c. 55 B.C.), the leading Roman Epicurean philosopher, was influenced by the civil war fostered by two generals, Marius and Sulla, which is discussed later in this chapter. Distraught by the seemingly endless strife, Lucretius yearned for philosophical tranquility. Like Epicurus, he believed that religion prompted people to perform evil deeds and caused them to experience terrible anxiety about death and eternal punishment. In his work *On the Nature of Things*, Lucretius expressed his appreciation of Epicurus. Like his mentor, Lucretius denounced superstition and religion for fostering psychological distress and advanced a materialistic conception of nature, one that left no room for the activity of gods—mechanical laws, not the gods, governed all physical happenings. To dispel the fear of punishment after death, Lucretius marshaled arguments to prove that the soul perishes with the body. He proposed that the simple life, devoid of political involvement and excessive passion, was the highest good and the path that would lead from emotional turmoil to peace of mind. Epicurus' hostility to traditional religion, disparagement of politics and public service, and rejection of the goals of power and glory ran counter to the accepted Roman ideal of virtue. On the other hand, his glorification of the quiet life amid a community of friends and his advice on how to deal with life's misfortunes with serenity had great appeal to first-century Romans like Lucretius, who were disgusted with civil strife.

Rome's finest orator, as well as a leading statesman, Cicero (106–43 B.C.) was an unsurpassed Latin stylist and a student of Greek philosophy. His letters, more than eight hundred of which have survived, provide modern historians with valuable insights into the politics of the late Republic. His Senate speeches have been models of refined rhetoric for all students of the Latin language. Cicero's discussion of such topics as republicanism, citizenship, friendship, virtue, duty, and justice had an enduring influence on Western moral and political thought. Dedicated to republicanism and public-spiritedness, Cicero sought to prevent one-man rule and in his writings exhorted fellow Romans to serve their city.

Cicero was drawn to Stoicism, the most influential philosophy in Rome. Stoicism's stress on virtuous conduct and performance of duty coincided with Roman ideals, and its doctrine of a natural law that applies to all nations, regardless of ethnicity or culture, harmonized with the requirements of a world empire. Cicero admired the Stoic goal of the self-sufficient sage who sought to accord his life with standards of virtue inherent in nature. Natural law commands people to do what is right and deters them from doing what is

wrong, and our gift of reason enables us to abide by its commands. Thus, knowledge and virtue are closely linked. Cicero adopted the Stoic belief that the law of the state should conform with the rational and moral norms embodied in natural law, for adherence to such rationally formulated law creates a moral bond among citizens.

He also shared the Stoic view that because natural law applies to all, we are all citizens of a single commonwealth and belong to a society of humanity. As he expressed it,

> *there is no difference in kind between man and man; for Reason, which alone raises us above the level of the beasts and enables us to draw inferences, to prove and disprove, to discuss and solve problems, and to come to conclusions, is certainly common to us all, and though varying in what it learns, at least in the capacity to learn it is invariable. . . . In fact, there is no human being of any race who, if he finds a guide, cannot attain virtue.*[9]

In the eighteenth century, the Founding Fathers of the United States praised Cicero's natural law philosophy, which coincided with their belief in inalienable rights; his condemnation of tyranny; and his advocacy of liberty, republicanism, and constitutional government.

COLLAPSE OF THE REPUBLIC

In 146 B.C., Roman might spanned the Mediterranean world. After that year, the principal concerns of the Republic were no longer foreign invasions but adjusting city-state institutions to the demands of empire and overcoming critical social and political problems at home. The Republic was unequal to either challenge. Instead of developing a professional civil service to administer the conquered lands, Roman leaders attempted to govern an empire with city-state institutions that had evolved for a different purpose. The established Roman administration proved unable to govern the Mediterranean world. In addition, Rome's ruling elites showed little concern for the welfare of their subjects, and provincial rule worsened as governors, tax collectors, and soldiers shamelessly exploited the provincials.

FORUM IN ROME. The forum, a large rectangular space that served as a marketplace, was the center of a Roman city. In Rome itself, the forum evolved into a political center surrounded by large public buildings. (Hiroshi Higuchi/Getty Images.)

During Rome's march to empire, all its classes had demonstrated a magnificent civic spirit in fighting foreign wars. With Carthage and Macedonia no longer threatening Rome, this cooperation deteriorated, as Cato the Elder had forewarned: "What was to become of Rome, when she should no longer have any state to fear?"[10] Internal dissension tore Rome apart as the drive for domination formerly directed against foreign enemies turned inward against fellow Romans. Civil war replaced foreign war.

The Romans had prevailed over their opponents partly because of their traditional virtues: resoluteness, simplicity of manners, and willingness to sacrifice personal interests for the good of Rome. But the riches flowing into Rome from the plundered provinces caused these virtues to decay, and rivalry for status and a frenzied pursuit of wealth overrode civic patriotism. This "perverted greed" and "lack of principle," said the poet Horace (65–8 B.C.), had caused "impious slaughter, . . . intestine [domestic] fury, . . . and lawless licence."[11] And the masses, landless and afflicted with poverty and idleness, withdrew their allegiance from the state.

In this time of agony, both great and self-seeking individuals emerged. Some struggled to restore the social harmony and political unity that had prevailed in the period of expansion. Others, political adventurers, attacked the authority of the Senate to gain personal power. The Senate, which had previously exercised leadership creatively and responsibly, degenerated into a self-serving oligarchy that resisted reform and fought to preserve its power and privilege.

Neither the Senate nor its opponents could rejuvenate the Republic. Eventually it collapsed, a victim of class tensions, poor leadership, power-hungry demagogues, and civil war. Underlying all these conditions were the breakdown of social harmony and the deterioration of civic patriotism. The Republic had conquered an empire only to see the character of its citizens decay. In a high moral tone, the historian Sallust (c. 86–34 B.C.) condemned the breakdown of republican values.

> *Growing love of money, and the lust for power which followed it, engendered every kind of evil. Avarice destroyed honor, integrity, and every other virtue, and instead taught men to be proud and cruel, to neglect religion, and to hold nothing too sacred to sell. Ambition tempted many to be false. . . . At first these vices grew slowly and some times met with punishments; later on, when the disease had spread like a plague, Rome changed: her government, once so just and admirable, became harsh and unendurable.[12]*

Crisis in Agriculture

The downhill slide of the Republic began with an agricultural crisis. During the long war with Hannibal in Italy, each side had tried to deprive the other of food supplies; in the process, they ruined farm land, destroyed farmhouses and farm equipment, and slaughtered animals. With many Roman soldier-farmers serving in the army for long stretches of time, fields lay neglected. Returning veterans with small holdings lacked the wealth to restore their land. They were forced to sell their farms to wealthy landowners at low prices.

Another factor that helped to squeeze out the owners of small farms was the importation of hundreds of thousands of slaves to work on large plantations called **latifundia**. This massive use

of slaves was unprecedented in Roman history. Farmers who had formerly increased their meager incomes by working for wages on neighboring large estates were no longer needed. Sinking ever deeper into poverty and debt, farmers gave up their lands and went to Rome, seeking work. The dispossessed peasantry found little to do in Rome, where there was not enough industry to provide them with employment and where much of the work was done by slaves. Congregated in rundown, crime-ridden slums and chronically unemployed, the urban poor faced a daily struggle for survival. The once sturdy and independent Roman farmer, who had done all that his country had asked of him, was becoming part of a vast urban underclass—destitute, embittered, and alienated. The uprooting of a formerly self-reliant peasantry was Hannibal's posthumous revenge on Rome; severing the civic bond, it would prove even more deadly than Cannae.

The Gracchan Revolution

In 133 B.C., Tiberius Gracchus (163–133 B.C.), who came from one of Rome's most honored families, was elected tribune. Distressed by the injustice done to the peasantry and recognizing that the Roman army depended on the loyalty of small landowners, Tiberius made himself the spokesman for land reform. He proposed a simple and moderate solution for the problem of the landless peasants: implementing an old law barring any Roman from using more than 312 acres of the state-owned land obtained in the process of uniting Italy. For many years, the upper class had ignored this law, occupying vast tracts of public land. By reenacting the law, Tiberius hoped to free land for distribution to landless citizens.

Rome's leading families viewed Tiberius as a revolutionary threatening their property and political authority. They thought him a dangerous democrat who would undermine the Senate, the seat of aristocratic power, in favor of the Assembly, which represented the commoners. When Tiberius sought reelection as a tribune, a violation of constitutional tradition, the senators were convinced that he was a rabble-rouser who aimed to destroy the republican constitution and become a one-man ruler. To preserve the status quo, with

Cleopatra

Cleopatra (69–30 B.C.), the Greek queen of Egypt, belonged to the Ptolemaic family, the Macedonian Greeks who ruled Egypt during the Hellenistic Age. Cleopatra spoke Greek, received a Greek education, and viewed herself as Greek, but in contrast to her Ptolemaic predecessors, she also learned to speak the Egyptian tongue. Aspiring to revive Ptolemaic power, which had once extended into Palestine and Lebanon, she had the political good sense to realize that this could not be accomplished by antagonizing Rome, which dominated the Mediterranean world.

Cleopatra became Julius Caesar's mistress when the Roman leader stopped at Alexandria. In 47 B.C., she bore a son, declaring that Caesar was the father, and in the next year she followed Caesar to Rome. Three years after Caesar's assassination, she became Mark Antony's lover and bore him twins. She worked closely with Antony, who competed with Octavian for control of the Roman world. At the naval battle of Actium in 31 B.C., Antony and Cleopatra escaped to Egypt, where Octavian pursued them. When Antony's forces either surrendered to Octavian without a fight or fled, Cleopatra barricaded herself inside her mausoleum. Thinking that she had killed herself, Antony plunged a sword into his body. A messenger told the dying Antony that Cleopatra was still alive and wished to see him. Slaves carried him to her. Because the mausoleum's doors were sealed, he had to be hoisted with great difficulty to an opening in the wall by Cleopatra and her female servants.

wealth and power concentrated in the hands of a few hundred families, senatorial extremists killed Tiberius and some three hundred of his followers, dumping their bodies into the Tiber.

The cause of land reform was next taken up by Gaius Gracchus (153–121 B.C.), a younger brother of Tiberius. An emotional and gifted speaker, Gaius won the support of the city poor and was elected tribune in 123 B.C. A more astute politician than his brother, Gaius increased his following by favoring the Equites, the new class of plebeian businessmen, and by promising full citizenship to all Italians. He aided the poor by reintroducing his brother's plan for land distribution and by enabling them to buy grain from the state at less than half the market price. But like his brother, Gaius aroused the anger of the senatorial class, which ordered his murder. After his death, three thousand of his followers were executed without trial.

By killing the Gracchi, the Senate had substituted violence for reason and made murder a means of coping with troublesome opposition. Soon the club and the dagger became common weapons in Roman politics, hurling Rome into an era of political violence that ended with the destruction of the Republic. Though the Senate considered itself the guardian of republican liberty, in reality it was expressing the determination of a few hundred families to retain their control over the state. This is a classic example of a once-creative minority clinging tenaciously to power long after it has ceased to govern effectively or to inspire allegiance. The Senate, which had led Rome to world dominance, became a self-seeking, unimaginative, entrenched oligarchy that was dragging the Republic and the Mediterranean world into disaster.

Rome in the first century B.C. was very different from the Rome that had defeated Hannibal. Entranced by luxuries flowing into Rome from its eastern conquests and determined to retain oligarchic rule, the senatorial families neglected their responsibility to the state. Many upper-class Romans, burning to achieve the dignity and glory that would mark them as great men, tried to climb onto the crowded stage of Roman politics, but the best roles were already reserved for members of the senatorial families. With so few opportunities, aspirants to political power stopped at nothing.

Roman politics in the century after the Gracchi was bedeviled by intrigues, rivalries, personal

Plutarch, the ancient biographer, described the scene:

Those that were present say that nothing was ever more sad than this spectacle, to see Antony, covered all over with blood and just expiring, thus drawn up, still holding up his hands to her, and lifting up his body with the little force he had left. . . . When she had got him up, she laid him on the bed, tearing all her clothes, which she spread upon him; and beating her breast with her hands, lacerating herself, and disfiguring her own face with the blood from his wounds, she called him her lord, her husband, her emperor.*

Antony died shortly afterward. Captured by the Romans, Cleopatra feared that Octavian would parade her in a victory celebration at Rome. To avoid such a humiliation, the proud Cleopatra poisoned herself, ending the Ptolemaic dynasty in Egypt. In a last letter, she requested to be buried beside Antony.

Cleopatra's life and death have intrigued historians; writers, including Shakespeare; and Hollywood producers. Her true character remains elusive. She had sufficient allure to attract both Caesar and Antony and sufficient ruthlessness to murder her younger brother, and co-ruler, in order to make her son co-ruler. No doubt her determination and ambition made her an equal partner with Antony in their political quest.

*Plutarch, *The Lives of Noble Grecians and Romans*, trans. John Dryden, rev. A. H. Clough (New York: The Modern Library, n.d.), 1148.

ambition, and violence. Political adventurers exploited the issue of cheap grain and free land in order to benefit their careers. Whereas the Gracchi were sincere reformers, these later champions of social reform were unscrupulous demagogues who cleverly charmed and manipulated the city poor with bread and circuses: low-cost food and free admission to games. These demagogues aspired to the tribunate of the plebes, an office possessing powers formidable enough to challenge the Senate and not too difficult to obtain since ten tribunes were elected each year. By riding a wave of popular enthusiasm, these political adventurers hoped to sweep aside the Senate and concentrate power in their own hands. The poor, denied land and employment, demoralized, alienated, and lulled into political ignorance by decades of idleness, food handouts, and free entertainment, were ready to back whoever made the most glittering promises. The Senate behaved like a decadent oligarchy, and the Tribal Assembly, which had become the voice of the urban mob, demonstrated a weakness for demagogues, an openness to bribery, and an abundance of deceit and incompetence. The Roman Republic had passed the peak of its greatness.

Rival Generals

Marius (157–86 B.C.), who became consul in 107 B.C., adopted a military policy that eventually contributed to the wrecking of the Republic. Until about 100 B.C., soldiers served essentially at their own expense, paying for their arms, armor, and food. This meant that only men of some substance could serve. Short of troops for a campaign in Numidia in North Africa, Marius disposed of the traditional property requirement for entrance into the army and filled his legions with volunteers from the urban poor, a dangerous precedent. These new soldiers, disillusioned with Rome, served only because Marius held out the promise of pay, loot, and land grants after discharge. In effect, they were Marius's clients. Their loyalty was not to Rome but to Marius, and they remained loyal to their commander only as long as he fulfilled his promises.

Marius set an example that other ambitious commanders followed. They saw that a general could use his army to advance his political career, that by retaining the confidence of his soldiers he could cow the Senate and dictate Roman policy. The army, no longer an instrument of government, became a private possession of generals. Seeing its authority undermined by generals appointed by the Assembly, the Senate was forced to seek army commanders who would champion the cause of senatorial rule. In time, Rome would be engulfed in civil wars as rival generals used their troops to strengthen their political affiliations and to further their own ambitions.

Meanwhile, the Senate continued to deal ineffectively with Rome's problems. When Rome's Italian allies—who had provided the manpower needed to conquer the Empire—pressed for citizenship, the Senate refused to make concessions. The Senate's shortsightedness plunged Italy into a savage war known as the Social War. As it ravaged the peninsula, the Romans reversed their policy and conferred citizenship on the Italians. The unnecessary and ruinous rebellion petered out.

While Rome was fighting its Italian allies, Mithridates, king of Pontus in northern Asia Minor, invaded the wealthy Roman province of Asia. In 88 B.C., he incited the local population to massacre eighty thousand Italian residents of the province, a devastating blow to Rome's economy and prestige. Mithridates and his forces crossed into Greece and occupied Athens and other cities. Faced with this crisis, the Senate entrusted command to Sulla (138–78 B.C.), who had distinguished himself in the Social War. But supporters of Marius, through intrigue and violence, had the order rescinded and the command given to Marius.

Sulla refused to accept his loss of command, which deprived him of honor and opportunity for riches; with his loyal troops, he proceeded to the capital. This was a fateful moment in Roman history: the first march on Rome by a Roman legion, the first prolonged civil war, and the first time a commander and his troops defied the government. The competition for honor, the overriding concern of Roman aristocrats, had taken Rome down a perilous path. Sulla won the first round. But when Sulla left Rome to fight Mithridates in Greece, Marius and his troops retook the city and, in a frenzy, lashed out at Sulla's supporters. The killing lasted for five days and nights.

Marius died shortly afterward. Sulla, on his return, quickly subdued Marius's supporters and became dictator of Rome. He instituted a terror that far surpassed Marius's violence. Without legal sanction and with cold-blooded cruelty, Sulla marked his opponents for death; the state seized their property and declared their children and grandchildren ineligible for public office.

Sulla resolved to use his absolute power to revive the Senate's rule and make it permanent. He believed that only rule by an aristocratic oligarchy could protect Rome from future military adventurers and assure domestic peace. Therefore, he restored the Senate's right to veto acts of the Assembly, limited the power of the tribunes and the Assembly, and, to prevent any march on Rome, reduced the military authority of provincial governors. To make the Senate less oligarchic, he increased its membership to six hundred. Having put through these reforms, Sulla retired.

Julius Caesar

The Senate failed to wield its restored authority effectively. The Republic was still menaced by military commanders who used their troops for their own political advantage, and underlying problems remained unsolved. In 60 B.C., a triumvirate, a ruling group of three—consisting of Julius Caesar (c. 100–44 B.C.), a politician; Pompey, a general; and Crassus, a wealthy banker—conspired to take over Rome. The ablest of the three was Caesar. Descended from an ancient noble family, Caesar had first gained public recognition for his demonstration of conspicuous bravery in Rome's assault on the rebellious Greek city of Mytilene. Upon returning to Rome, he distinguished himself as an orator—his star was rising.

Recognizing the importance of a military command as a prerequisite for political prominence, Caesar gained command of the legions in Gaul in 59 B.C. The following year he began the conquest of the part of Gaul not under Roman control, bringing the future France into the orbit of Greco-Roman civilization. The campaign was brilliantly described in his *Commentaries*, although, to be sure, the work was a deliberate attempt to apprise the Roman public of his military prowess. The successful Gallic campaigns and the invasion of Britain revealed Caesar's exceptional talent for generalship: he acted decisively, moved troops rapidly, and had excellent rapport with his men. By plundering Gaul, he also acquired a fortune

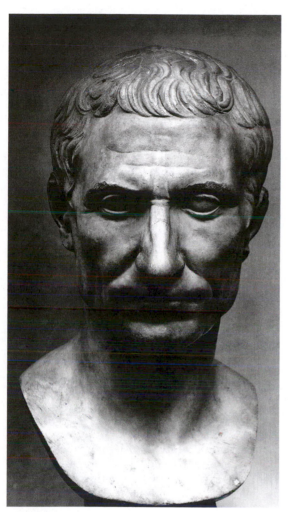

BUST OF CAESAR. Julius Caesar tried to rescue a dying Roman world by imposing strong rule. He paved the way for the transition from republican to imperial rule. (Scala/Art Resource, N.Y.)

marriage to Caesar's daughter Julia. After her death in 54 B.C., Pompey and Caesar grew apart. Pompey, who was jealous of Caesar's success and eager to expand his own power, drew closer to the Senate. Supported by Pompey, the Senate ordered Caesar to relinquish his command. Caesar realized that without his troops he would be defenseless; he decided instead to march on Rome. After Caesar crossed the Rubicon River into Italy in 49 B.C., civil war again ravaged the Republic. Pompey proved no match for so talented a general; the Senate acknowledged Caesar's victory and appointed him to be dictator, a legal office, for ten years.

Caesar realized that republican institutions no longer operated effectively and that only strong and enlightened leadership could permanently end the civil warfare destroying Rome. His reforms were designed to create order out of chaos. Caesar responded to the grievances of the provincial subjects by lowering taxes, making the governors responsible to him, restraining Roman businessmen from ruthlessly draining the provinces' wealth, and generously extending citizenship. To gain greater support for Rome, he also granted citizenship to more Italians. To aid the poor in Rome, he began a public works program, which provided employment and beautified the city. He also relocated more than a hundred thousand veterans and members of Rome's lower class to the provinces, where he gave them land. To improve administration, he reorganized town governments in Italy, reformed the courts, and planned to codify the law. He attempted to conciliate the senatorial class by treating former enemies with moderation and generosity.

In February 44 B.C., Rome's ruling class—jealous of Caesar's success and power and afraid of his ambition—became thoroughly alarmed when his temporary dictatorship was converted into a lifelong office. The aristocracy saw this event as the end of senatorial government and their rule, which they equated with liberty, and as the beginning of a Hellenistic type of monarchy. On March 15 of that year, a group of aristocrats, regarding themselves as defenders of centuries-old republican traditions and institutions, assassinated Caesar. The group included the general and orator Marcus Junius Brutus. Cicero expressed the feeling that motivated the conspirators.

that could be used to further his political career. Indeed, Caesar's victories alarmed the Senate, which feared that the popular general would use his devoted troops and soaring reputation to seize control of the state.

Meanwhile, the triumvirate had fallen apart. In 53 B.C., Crassus had perished with his army in a disastrous campaign against the Parthians in the East. The bonds between Pompey and Caesar were weak, consisting essentially of Pompey's

Our tyrant deserves his death, [for his] was the blackest crime of all. [Caesar was] a man who was ambitious to be king of the Roman people and master of the whole world. . . . The man who maintains that such an ambition is morally right is a madman, for he justifies the destruction of law and liberty.[13]

The Republic's Last Years

The assassination of Julius Caesar did not restore republican liberty but plunged Rome into renewed civil war. Thousands more died in battle or were killed in the proscriptions—lists of Roman citizens declared by their political enemies to be outlaws. Those proscribed had their property confiscated and could be executed. Two of Caesar's trusted lieutenants, Mark Antony and Lepidus, joined with Octavian, Caesar's adopted son, and defeated the armies of Brutus and Cassius, two conspirators in the plot against Caesar. After Lepidus was forced into political obscurity, Antony and Octavian fought each other, with control of Rome as the prize. In 31 B.C., at the naval battle of Actium in western Greece, Octavian crushed the forces of Antony and his wife, Egypt's Queen Cleopatra (who had earlier borne Julius Caesar's son). Octavian emerged as master of Rome and four years later became, in effect, the first Roman emperor. The Roman Republic, whose death throes had lasted for decades and kept the Mediterranean world in turmoil, had finally perished.

The Roman Republic, which had amassed power to a degree hitherto unknown in the ancient world, was wrecked not by foreign invasion but by internal weaknesses: the personal ambitions of power seekers; the degeneration of senatorial leadership and the transformation of political rivalry into violence and terror, in which opponents were condemned to death and their property confiscated; the formation of private armies, in which soldiers gave their loyalty to their commander rather than to Rome; the transformation of a self-reliant peasantry into an impoverished and demoralized city rabble; and the deterioration of the ancient virtues that had been the source of the state's vitality. Before 146 B.C., the threat posed by foreign enemies, particularly Carthage, had forced Romans to work together for the benefit of the state, and the equilibrium achieved during the patrician-plebeian struggle was maintained. This social cohesion broke down when foreign danger diminished. In the ensuing century of turmoil, the apparatus of city-state government failed to function effectively.

Thus, the high point of Roman rule was not achieved under the Republic. The city-state constitution of the Republic was too limited to govern an immense empire. Rome first had to surpass the narrow framework of city-state government before it could unite the Mediterranean world in peace and law. The genius of Augustus (Octavian), the first emperor, made this development possible.

❖ ❖ ❖

Notes

1. Cicero, *De Republica*, trans. Clinton Walker Keyes (Cambridge, Mass.: Harvard University Press, Loeb Classical Library, 1994), 79.

2. Ibid., 81.

3. E. Badian, *Roman Imperialism in the Late Republic* (Ithaca, N.Y.: Cornell University Press, 1971), 87.

4. Quoted in Alan Wardman, *Rome's Debt to Greece* (New York: St. Martin's Press, 1976), 62.

5. Cicero, *De Oratore,* trans. E. W. Sutton (Cambridge, Mass.: Harvard University Press, Loeb Classical Library, 1967), 14.

6. Quoted in J. Wright Duff, *A Literary History of Rome* (New York: Barnes and Noble, 1960), 136–137.

7. Terence, *The Brothers,* trans. H. T. Riley (London: Henry G. Bohn, 1853), 202–203.

8. Catullus, quoted in E. A. Havelock, *The Lyric Genius of Catullus* (New York: Russell and Russell, 1929), 63.

9. Cicero, *De Legibus,* trans. C. W. Keyes (Cambridge, Mass.: Harvard University Press, Loeb Classical Library, 1928), 329–330.

10. Quoted in Eli Sagan, *The Honey and the Hemlock* (New York: Basic Books, 1991), 25.

11. Horace, *The Odes and Epodes,* trans. C. E. Bennett (Cambridge, Mass.: Harvard University Press, 1988), ode 24, pp. 255–256.

12. Sallust, *The Conspiracy of Catiline,* trans. S. A. Handford (Baltimore: Penguin Books, 1963), 181–182.

13. Cicero, *De Officiis,* trans. Walter Miller (Cambridge, Mass.: Harvard University Press, Loeb Classical Library, 1913), 357.

SUGGESTED READING

Boren, H. C., *Roman Society* (1977). A social, economic, and cultural history of the Republic and the Empire, written with the student in mind.

Christ, Karl, *The Romans* (1984). A good survey.

Crawford, M., *The Roman Republic* (1982). A reliable survey, with many quotations from original sources.

Dupont, Florence, *Daily Life in Ancient Rome* (1989). Everyday private and public lives of Roman citizens.

Errington, R. M., *The Dawn of Empire: Rome's Rise to World Power* (1972). A study of Rome, the reluctant imperialist.

Grant, Michael, *History of Rome* (1978). A synthesis of Roman history by a leading classical scholar; valuable in regard to both the Republic and the Empire.

Holland, Tom, *Rubicon: The Last Years of the Roman Republic* (2003). Well-written and intelligent.

McGeouch, Kevin M., *The Romans* (2004). A comprehensive analysis of Roman society and culture in the Republic and the Empire.

Ogilvie, R. M., *Roman Literature and Society* (1980). An introductory survey of Latin literature.

Wood, Neal, *Cicero's Social and Political Thought* (1988). An important work for understanding ancient thought and Cicero's impact on later Western political philosophy.

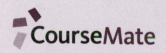

Go to the CourseMate website at **www.cengagebrain.com** for additional study tools and review materials—including audio and video clips—for this chapter.

Chapter 7

The Roman Empire: A World-State

Marcus Aurelius, Roman Emperor (161–180) In this relief, Marcus rides through the Roman Forum in ceremonial triumph after defending the Empire against barbarian incursions.

(Alfredo Dagli Orti/© The Art Archive/Corbis.)

Rome's republican institutions, designed for a city-state, proved incapable of coping with the problems created by the conquest of a world empire. Invincible against foreign enemies, the Republic collapsed from within. But after Octavian's brilliant statesmanship brought order out of chaos, Rome entered its golden age under the rule of emperors. For more than two hundred years, from 27 B.C. to A.D. 180, the Mediterranean world enjoyed unparalleled peace and stability. The Roman world-state, erected on a Hellenic cultural foundation and cemented with empirewide civil service, laws, and citizenship, gave practical expression to Stoic cosmopolitanism and universalism. Yet even this impressive monument had structural defects, and in the third century A.D. the Empire was wracked by crises from which it never fully recovered. In the fifth century, Germanic tribesmen overran the western half of the Empire, which had by then become a shadow of its former self.

During its time of trouble, Rome also experienced an intellectual crisis. Forsaking the rational and secular values of classical humanism, many Romans sought spiritual comfort in Near Eastern religions. One of these religions, Christianity, won out over its competitors and was made the official religion of the Empire. With the triumph of Christianity in the Late Roman Empire, Western civilization took a new direction. Christianity would become the principal shaper of the European civilization that emerged from the ruins of Rome.

AUGUSTUS AND THE FOUNDATIONS OF THE ROMAN EMPIRE

After Octavian's forces defeated those of Antony and Cleopatra at the battle of Actium in 31 B.C., no opponents could stand up to him. The century of civil war, political murder, corruption, and mismanagement had exhausted the Mediterranean world, which longed for order. Like Caesar before him, Octavian recognized that only a strong monarchy could rescue Rome from civil war and anarchy. But learning from Caesar's assassination, he also knew that republican ideals were far from dead. To exercise autocratic power openly, like a Hellenistic monarch, would have aroused the hostility of the

Chronology 7.1 ❖ The Roman Empire

27 B.C.	Senate grants Octavian the title Augustus, and he becomes, in effect, the first Roman emperor; start of the principate and the Pax Romana
A.D. 14	Death of Augustus; Tiberius gains the throne
66–70	Jewish revolt: Romans capture Jerusalem and destroy the second temple
79	Eruption of Mount Vesuvius and destruction of Pompeii and Herculaneum
132–135	Hadrian crushes another Hebrew revolt
180	Marcus Aurelius dies: end of the Pax Romana
212	Roman citizenship is granted to virtually all free inhabitants of Roman provinces
235–285	Military anarchy; Germanic incursions
285–305	Diocletian tries to deal with the crisis by creating a regimented state
378	Battle of Adrianople: Visigoths defeat the Roman legions
406	Imperial borders collapse, and Germanic tribes move into the Empire
410	Rome is plundered by Visigoths
455	Rome is sacked by Vandals
476	End of the Roman Empire in the West

Roman ruling class, whose assistance and goodwill Octavian desired.

Octavian demonstrated his political genius by reconciling his military monarchy with republican institutions: he held absolute power without abruptly breaking with a republican past. Magistrates were still elected, and assemblies still met; the Senate administered certain provinces, retained its treasury, and was invited to advise Octavian. With some truth, Octavian could claim that he ruled in partnership with the Senate. By maintaining the facade of the Republic, Octavian camouflaged his absolute power and contained senatorial opposition, which already had been weakened by the deaths of leading nobles in battle or in the purges that Octavian had instituted against his enemies. Moreover, Octavian's control over the armed forces made resistance futile, and the terrible violence that followed Caesar's assassination made senators amenable to change.

In 27 B.C., Octavian shrewdly offered to surrender his power, knowing that the Senate, purged of opposition, would demand that he continue to lead the state. By this act, Octavian could claim to be a legitimate constitutional ruler leading a government of law, not one of lawless despotism so hateful to the Roman mentality. In keeping with his policy of maintaining the appearance of traditional republican government, Octavian refused to be called king or even, like Caesar, dictator; instead, he cleverly disguised his autocratic rule by taking the inoffensive title *princeps* (first citizen). The Senate also honored Octavian by conferring on him the semireligious and revered name of *Augustus*. (The rule of Augustus and his successors is referred to as the *principate*.)

The reign of Augustus signified the end of the Roman Republic and the beginning of the Roman Empire—the termination of senatorial rule and aristocratic politics and the emergence of one-man rule. The old Roman aristocracy, decimated by war and the proscriptions employed by Antony, Lepidus, and Octavian, had to adjust to a political situation in which they no longer predominated. As the historian Tacitus recognized, Augustus accomplished a profound revolution in Roman political life: "The country had been transformed, and there was nothing left of the fine old Roman character. Political equality was a thing of the past; all eyes watched for imperial commands."[1] Under Augustus, who ruled

THE PANTHEON, C. A.D. 125. The Pantheon, the most complete surviving building of Roman antiquity, was built by Emperor Hadrian in the second century A.D. In the temple, Greek forms of ornamentation are combined with Roman building techniques. The vast hemispherical dome was constructed by pouring concrete into great wooden forms; then the interior was faced with marble. In contrast to a Greek temple, where the exterior is paramount, the Roman temple emphasizes interior space. (Alinari/Art Resource, N.Y.)

from 27 B.C. to A.D. 14, the power of the ruler was disguised; in ensuing generations, however, emperors would wield absolute power openly. As Rome became more autocratic and centralized, it took on the appearance of an oriental monarchy.

Augustus introduced the practice of emperor worship. In the eastern provinces, where Middle Eastern and Hellenistic monarchs had been traditionally regarded as divine, the person of Augustus was worshiped as a god. In Italy, where the deification of leaders was alien to the republican spirit, divine honors were granted to Augustus's genius, or spirit of leadership; once deceased, Augustus and his successors were deified. The imperial cult, with its ceremonies, processions, temples, and statues, strengthened the bonds of loyalty that

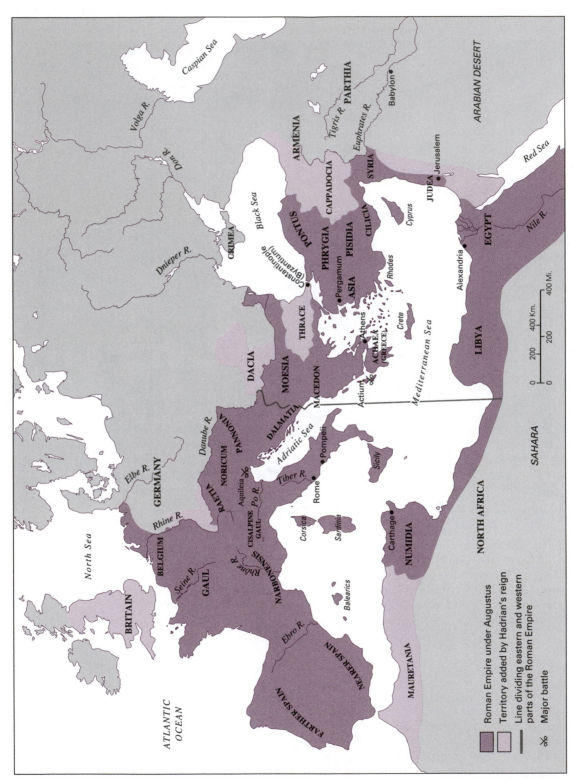

Caspian Sea

Volga R.

Don R.

ARMENIA

PARTHIA

Tigris R.

Euphrates R.

Babylon

Red Sea

Nile R.

ARABIAN DESERT

CAPPADOCIA

SYRIA

Jerusalem

JUDEA

PONTUS

PHRYGIA

PISIDIA

CILICIA

Cyprus

EGYPT

Dnieper R.

Black Sea

CRIMEA

Constantinople
(Byzantium)

Pergamum

ASIA

Rhodes

Alexandria

LIBYA

Rhine R.

THRACE

Athens

ACHAEA
(GREECE)

Crete

Mediterranean Sea

400 Mi.

DACIA

MOESIA

MACEDON

Actium

400 Km.

200

200

0

0

Danube R.

DALMATIA

Adriatic Sea

Pompeii

Sicily

SAHARA

GERMANY

PANNONIA

NORICUM

RAETIA

Aquileia

Po R.

Tiber R.

Rome

CISALPINE
GAUL

Corsica

Sardinia

NORTH AFRICA

Elbe R.

Rhine R.

BELGIUM

Seine R.

Rhône R.

NARBONENSIS

GAUL

Balearics

Carthage

NUMIDIA

North Sea

BRITAIN

Ebro R.

MAURETANIA

FARTHER SPAIN

NEARER SPAIN

ATLANTIC
OCEAN

Roman Empire under Augustus

Territory added by Hadrian's reign

Line dividing eastern and western
parts of the Roman Empire

Major battle

tied subjects to the emperor. By the third century, Italians and other peoples in the western territories generally viewed the living emperor as a god-king.

Despite his introduction of autocratic rule, Augustus was by no means a self-seeking tyrant, but a creative statesman. Heir to the Roman tradition of civic duty, he regarded his power as a public trust delegated to him by the Roman people. He was faithful to the classical ideal, which required that the state should promote the good life by protecting civilization from barbarism and ignorance; he sought to rescue a dying Roman world by restoring political order and reviving the moral values and civic spirit that had contributed to Rome's greatness.

To prevent a renewal of civil war and to safeguard the borders of the Empire, Augustus reformed the army. As commander in chief, he could guard against the reemergence of ambitious generals like those whose rivalries and private armies had wrecked the Republic. Augustus maintained the loyalty of his soldiers by ensuring that veterans, on discharge, would receive substantial bonuses and land in Italy or in the provinces. By organizing a professional standing army made up mostly of volunteers who generally served for twenty-five years, Augustus was assured a well-trained and loyal force capable of maintaining internal order, extending Roman territory, and securing the frontier.

For the city of Rome, Augustus had aqueducts and water mains built, which brought water to most Roman homes, and he beautified the city by restoring ancient monuments and temples and building new ones. He created a fire brigade, which reduced the danger of great conflagrations in crowded tenement districts, and he organized a police force to contain violence. He improved the distribution of free grain to the impoverished urban masses and financed the popular gladiatorial combats out of his own funds.

◀ *Map 7.1* THE ROMAN EMPIRE UNDER AUGUSTUS AND HADRIAN During the Pax Romana, the Roman Empire expanded beyond the Rhine and Danube Rivers, the imperial boundary during the reign of Augustus. (Copyright © 2013 Cengage Learning.)

In Italy, Augustus had roads repaired, and he fostered public works. He arranged for Italians to play a more important role in the administration of the Empire. For the Italians' security, his army suppressed brigandage, which had proliferated in the countryside during the preceding century of agony, and he guarded the northern borders from barbarian incursions.

By ending the civil wars and their accompanying devastation and by ruling out forced requisition of supplies and extortion of money, Augustus earned the gratitude of the provincials. Also contributing to his empirewide popularity were his efforts to correct tax abuse and to end corruption through improving the quality of governors and enabling aggrieved provincials to bring charges against Roman officials. An imperial bureaucracy, which enabled talented and dedicated men to serve the state, gradually evolved. In addition, Augustus continued the sensible practice of not interfering with the traditional customs and religions of the provinces. During his forty-year reign—the longevity itself was a stabilizing factor—Rome overcame the chaos of the years of revolution. The praise bestowed on him by grateful provincials was not undeserved. One decree from the province of Asia called Augustus

> *the savior of all mankind in common whose provident care has not only fulfilled but even surpassed the hopes of all: for both land and sea are at peace, the cities are teeming with the blessings of concord, plenty, and respect for law, and the culmination and harvest of all good things bring fair hopes for the future and contentment with the present.*[2]

THE PAX ROMANA

The brilliant statesmanship of Augustus inaugurated Rome's greatest age. For the next two hundred years, the Mediterranean world enjoyed the blessings of the **Pax Romana**, the Roman peace. The ancient world had never experienced such a long period of peace, order, efficient administration, and prosperity. Although both proficient and inept rulers succeeded Augustus, the essential features of the Pax Romana persisted.

Profile

Epictetus

Born a slave, Epictetus (c. A.D. 55–135) belonged to an official (himself a former slave) who served the emperors Nero and Domitian. Even before he was given his freedom, Epictetus received a good education from his master. In A.D. 89, Domitian, fearful that philosophers would cast doubt on the emperor's divinity, banished all philosophers from Rome and Italy. Epictetus moved to Epirus in Greece, where he attracted students. One student recorded and organized Epictetus's thoughts into eight books, four of which were lost. Epictetus presented his views in the form of maxims: admonitions from a teacher to his students to pursue the moral life. His ideas greatly influenced Marcus Aurelius, the Roman emperor and Stoic philosopher.

Like other Stoic philosophers, Epictetus was concerned with attaining peace of mind—an inner contentment that produces happiness. For Epictetus, happiness did not depend on material possessions, status, reputation, or the affection others have for us. By pursuing these externals, he said, we become subject to the people who are needed to procure them for us: "If you are absorbed in externals, you must necessarily be tossed up and down, according to the inclination of your master. Who is your master? Whosoever controls those things which you seek."*

Epictetus maintained that to achieve happiness we must reduce desires, shun things that are beyond our power to control, and deliberately strive for inner dignity and moral integrity. Human beings, said Epictetus, can shield themselves from life's uncertainties and misfortunes, even slavery, by taking control of the part of themselves that belongs to no one else: their minds. Epictetus defined man as a rational

The Successors of Augustus

The first four emperors who succeeded Augustus were related either to him or to his third wife, Livia. They constituted the Julio-Claudian dynasty, which ruled from A.D. 14 to 68. Although their reigns were marked by conspiracies, summary executions, and assassinations, the great achievements of Augustus were preserved and strengthened. The Senate did not seek to restore republicanism and continued to assist the princeps; the imperial bureaucracy grew larger and more professional; the army, with some exceptions, remained a loyal and disciplined force.

The Julio-Claudian dynasty came to an end in A.D. 68, when the emperor Nero committed suicide. Nero had grown increasingly tyrannical and had lost the confidence of the people, the senatorial class, and the generals, who rose in revolt. In the year following his death, anarchy reigned as military leaders competed for the throne. After a bloody civil war, the execution of two emperors, and the suicide of another, Vespasian gained the principate. Vespasian's reign (A.D. 69–79) marked the beginning of the Flavian dynasty. By rotating commanding officers and stationing native troops far from their homelands, Vespasian improved discipline and discouraged mutiny. By having the great Colosseum of Rome constructed for gladiatorial contests, he earned the gratitude of the city's inhabitants. Vespasian also had nationalist uprisings put down in Gaul and Judea.

In Judea, Roman rule clashed with Jewish religious-national sentiments. Recognizing the tenaciousness with which Jews clung to their faith, the Roman leaders deliberately refrained from interfering with Hebraic religious beliefs and practices. Numerous privileges, such as exemption from emperor worship because it conflicted with the requirements of strict monotheism, were extended to Jews not only in Judea but throughout the Empire. Sometimes, however, the Romans engaged in activities that outraged the Jews. For example, Pontius Pilate, the Roman procurator in

being. It is reason that distinguishes man from wild beasts and cattle. He wrote:

Take care, then to do nothing like a wild beast; otherwise you have destroyed the man; you have not fulfilled what your nature promises. Take care too, to do nothing like cattle; for thus likewise the man is destroyed. In what do we act like cattle? When we act gluttonously, lewdly, rashly, sordidly, inconsiderately, into what are we sunk? Into cattle. What have we destroyed? The rational being. When we behave contentiously, injuriously, passionately, and violently, into what we have sunk? Into wild beasts. . . . By all these means the nature of man is destroyed.[†]

---

*Epictetus, *Discourses*, based on translation of Thomas Wentworth Higginson (Roslyn, N.Y.: Walter J. Black, Classics Club, 1944), bk. 2, chap. 2, p. 92.

[†]Ibid., bk. 2, chap. 9, pp. 106–107.

Judea from A.D. 26 to 36, at one point ordered a Roman army unit into Jerusalem with banners bearing the image of the emperor. The entire Jewish nation was aroused. To the Jews, this display of a pagan idol in their holy city was an abomination. Realizing that the Jews would die rather than permit this act of sacrilege, Pilate ordered the banners removed. Another explosive situation emerged when the emperor Caligula (A.D. 37–41) ordered that a golden statue of himself be placed in Jerusalem's temple. Again, the order was rescinded when the Jews demonstrated their readiness to resist.

Relations between the Jews of Judea and the Roman authorities deteriorated progressively in succeeding decades. Militant Jews, who rejected Roman rule as a threat to the purity of Jewish life, urged their people to take up arms. Feeling a religious obligation to reestablish an independent kingdom in their ancient homeland and unable to reconcile themselves to Roman rule, the Jews launched a full-scale war of liberation in A.D. 66. In A.D. 70, after a five-month siege had inflicted terrible punishment on the Jews, Roman armies captured Jerusalem and destroyed the temple, the central site and focus of Jewish religious life. After the conquest of Jerusalem, some fortresses, including Masada on the western side of the Dead Sea, continued to resist. The defenders of Masada withstood a Roman siege until A.D. 73; refusing to become Roman captives, they took their own lives.

Vespasian was succeeded by his sons Titus (A.D. 79–81) and Domitian (A.D. 81–96). The reign of Titus was made memorable by the eruption of Mount Vesuvius, which devastated the towns of Pompeii and Herculaneum. After Titus's brief time as emperor, his younger brother Domitian became ruler. Upon crushing a revolt led by the Roman commander in Upper Germany, a frightened Domitian executed many leading Romans. These actions led to his assassination in A.D. 96, ending the Flavian dynasty. The Flavians, however, succeeded in consolidating and extending the borders of the Empire.

The Senate selected one of its own, Nerva, to succeed the murdered Domitian. Nerva's reign (A.D. 96–98) was brief and uneventful. But he introduced a wise practice that would endure until A.D. 180: he adopted as his son and designated as his heir a man with proven ability, Trajan, the governor of Upper Germany. This adoptive system assured a succession of competent rulers.

During his rule (A.D. 98–117), Trajan eased the burden of taxation in the provinces, provided for the needs of poor children, and had public works built. With his enlarged army, he conquered Dacia (parts of Romania and Hungary), where he seized vast quantities of gold and silver. He made the territory into a Roman province, adding to the large frontier Rome had to protect. The settlement of the region by many of Trajan's veterans led to its Romanization.

Trajan's successor, Hadrian (A.D. 117–138), abandoned what remained of Trajan's eastern conquests. He strengthened border defenses in Britain and fought the second Hebrew revolt in Judea (A.D. 132–135). After initial successes, including the capture of Jerusalem, the Jews were again defeated by superior Roman might. The majority of Palestinian Jews were killed, sold as slaves, or forced to seek refuge in other lands. The Romans renamed the province Syria Palestina; they forbade Jews to enter Jerusalem, except once a year, and encouraged non-Jews to settle the land. Although the Jews continued to maintain a presence in Palestine, they had become a dispossessed and dispersed people.

After Hadrian came another ruler who had a long reign, Antoninus Pius (A.D. 138–161). He introduced humane and just reforms. He set limits on the right of masters to torture their slaves to obtain evidence, and he established the principle that an accused person be considered innocent until proven guilty. During the reign of Antoninus, the Empire remained peaceful and prosperous.

Marcus Aurelius (A.D. 161–180), the next emperor, was also a philosopher whose *Meditations* eloquently expressed Stoic thought. Frequent strife marked his reign. Roman forces had to fight the eastern kingdom of Parthia. The Roman legions were victorious in this campaign but brought back from the East an epidemic that decimated the population of the Empire. Marcus Aurelius also had to deal with Germanic incursions into Italy and the Balkan Peninsula—incursions far more serious than any faced by previous emperors.

From the accession of Nerva in A.D. 96 to the death of Marcus Aurelius in A.D. 180, the Roman Empire was ruled by "the Five Good Emperors." During this period, the Empire was at the height of its power and prosperity, and nearly all its peoples benefited. The four emperors preceding Marcus Aurelius had no living sons, so they had resorted to the adoptive system in selecting successors, which served Rome effectively. But Marcus Aurelius chose his own son, Commodus, to succeed him. With the accession of Commodus—a misfit and a megalomaniac—in A.D. 180, the Pax Romana came to an end.

"The Time of Happiness"

The Romans called the Pax Romana "the Time of Happiness." They saw it as the fulfillment of Rome's mission: the creation of a world-state that provided peace, security, ordered civilization, and the rule of law. Roman legions defended the Rhine–Danube river frontiers from incursions by Germanic tribesmen, held the Parthians at bay in

the east, and subdued the few uprisings that occurred. Nerva's adoptive system of selecting emperors provided Rome with internal stability and a succession of emperors with exceptional ability. These Roman emperors did not use military force needlessly but fought for sensible political goals; generals did not wage war recklessly but tried to limit casualties, avoid risks, and deter conflicts by a show of force.

Constructive Rule. Roman rule was constructive. The Romans built roads—some fifty-three thousand miles of roads, from Scotland to the Euphrates—improved harbors, cleared forests, drained swamps, irrigated deserts, and cultivated undeveloped lands. The aqueducts they constructed brought fresh water for drinking and bathing to large numbers of people, and the effective sewage systems enhanced the quality of life. Goods were transported over roads made safe by Roman soldiers and across a Mediterranean Sea swept clear of pirates. A wide variety of goods circulated throughout the Empire. A stable currency, generally not subject to depreciation, contributed to the economic well-being of the Mediterranean world.

Scores of new cities sprang up, and old ones grew larger and wealthier. Although these municipalities had lost their power to wage war and had to bow to the will of the emperors, they retained considerable freedom of action in local matters. Imperial troops guarded against civil wars within the cities and prevented warfare between cities—two traditional weaknesses of city life in the ancient world. Some two thousand municipalities served as centers of Greco-Roman civilization, which spread to the farthest reaches of the Mediterranean, continuing a process initiated during the Hellenistic Age. Regions of North Africa, Gaul, Britain, and South Germany, hitherto untouched by Hellenism, were brought into the orbit of Greco-Roman civilization. Barriers between Italians and provincials broke down as Spaniards, Gauls, Africans, and other provincials rose to high positions in the army and in the imperial administration and even became emperors. Citizenship, generously granted, was finally extended to virtually all free people by an edict of A.D. 212.

ARCH OF TITUS, C. A.D. 81, CONCRETE FACED WITH MARBLE, ROME. The arch stands at the crest of the Sacred Way to commemorate Titus' successful capture of Jerusalem in A.D. 70. It was dedicated in A.D. 81 by his brother, the Emperor Domitian.
(Scala/Art Resource, N.Y.)

BASALT BUST OF LIVIA. Octavian's third wife, Livia (58 B.C.–A.D. 29), was admired for her wisdom and dignity, and the emperor valued her counsel.
(Alinari/Art Resource, N.Y.)

Improved Conditions for Both Slaves and Women.
Conditions improved for those at the bottom of society, the slaves. At the time of Augustus, slaves may have accounted for a quarter of the population of Italy. But their numbers declined as Rome engaged in fewer wars of conquest. The freeing of slaves also became more common during the Empire. Urban slaves, who were often skilled artisans, could be induced to work more effectively if there was the hope of **manumission**. Often, nobles liberated and set up in business skilled and enterprising slaves in return for a share of the profits. Freed slaves became citizens, with most of the rights and privileges of other citizens; their children suffered no legal disabilities. (The poet Terence, the Stoic philosopher Epictetus, and the father of the poet Horace were all freed slaves.)

During the Republic, slaves had been terribly abused; they were often mutilated, thrown to wild beasts, crucified, or burned alive. Several emperors issued decrees protecting slaves from cruel masters. Claudius forbade masters to kill sick slaves; Vespasian forbade masters to sell slaves into prostitution. Domitian prohibited the castration of slaves, and Hadrian barred the execution of slaves without a judicial sentence.

The status of women had been gradually improving during the Republic. In the early days of the Republic, a woman lived under the absolute authority first of her father and then of her husband. By the time of the Empire, a woman could own property and, if divorced, keep her dowry. A father could no longer force his daughter to marry against her will, although upper-class marriages were usually based on political and social considerations. Women could make business arrangements and draw up wills without the consent of their husbands. Roman women, unlike their Greek counterparts, were not secluded in their homes but could come and go as they pleased. Upper-class women of Rome had far greater opportunities for education than did those of Greece, and some formed groups that read and discussed poetry.

Supervising the household remained the principal responsibility of Roman women. The Romans regarded marriage as a sacred civic duty. Seeking to restore traditional values, Augustus issued decrees encouraging Romans to marry. Romans greatly admired the woman who loved only one man and had only one husband, but in reality promiscuity, adultery, divorce, and remarriage were quite common. A wife could obtain a divorce just as easily as her husband, but as a rule children remained with their father. Despite the frequency of divorce, there is evidence that husbands and wives held genuine affection for each other.

The history of the Empire, indeed Roman history in general, was filled with talented and influential women. Cornelia, the mother of Tiberius and Gaius Gracchus, influenced Roman politics through her sons. The historian Sallust said that Sempronia, the wife of a consul and the mother of Brutus, one of the assassins of Julius Caesar, was "well-educated in Greek and Latin literature. . . . She could write poetry, crack a joke, and converse at will. . . . She was in fact a woman of ready wit and considerable charm."[3] Livia, the dynamic wife of Augustus, was often consulted on important government matters, and during the third century there were times when women controlled the throne.

An Orderly World Community. From Britain to the Arabian Desert, from the Danube River to the sands of the Sahara, some fifty to seventy million people with differing native languages, customs, and histories were united by Roman rule into a world community. Unlike officials of the Republic, when corruption and exploitation in the provinces were notorious, officials of the Empire felt a strong sense of responsibility to preserve the Roman peace, institute Roman justice, and spread Roman civilization.

In creating a stable and orderly political community with an expansive conception of citizenship, Rome resolved the problems posed by the limitations of the Greek city-state: civil war, intercity warfare, and a parochial attitude that divided people into Greek and non-Greek. Rome also brought to fruition an ideal of the Greek city-state—the protection and promotion of civilized life. By constructing a world community that broke down barriers between nations, by preserving and spreading Greco-Roman civilization, and by developing a rational system of law that applied to all humanity, Rome completed the trend toward universalism and cosmopolitanism that had emerged in the Hellenistic Age. The Roman world-state was the classical mind's response to the problem of community posed by the decline of the city-state in the era of Alexander the Great. Aelius Aristides, a second-century rhetorician, although Greek, proudly considered himself a Roman and glowingly extolled the Roman achievement.

> *Neither sea nor any intervening distance on land excludes one from citizenship. No distinction is made between Asia and Europe in this respect. Everything lies open to everybody; and no one fit for office or a position of trust is an alien. . . . You have made the word "Roman" apply not to a city but to a universal people. . . . You no longer classify peoples as Greek or barbarian. . . . You have redivided mankind into Romans and non-Romans. . . . Under this classification there are many in each city who are no less fellow citizens of yours than those of their own stock, though some of them have never seen this city.*[4]

medicine, and geography. Roman writers used Greek models; sharing in the humanist outlook of the Greeks, they valued human achievement and expressed themselves in a graceful and eloquent style. The diffusion of Hellenism throughout the Mediterranean world produced a cultural unity among elites that underlay the Pax Romana. Roman cultural life reached its high point during the reign of Augustus, when Rome experienced the golden age of Latin literature.

Literature and History. At the request of Augustus, who wanted a literary **epic** to glorify the Empire and his role in founding it, Virgil (70–19 B.C.) wrote the *Aeneid*, a masterpiece in world literature. The *Aeneid* is a long poem that recounts the tale of Aeneas and the founding of Rome. The first six books, which describe the wanderings of Aeneas, a survivor of Troy, show the influence of Homer's *Odyssey*; the last six, dealing with the wars in Italy, show the *Iliad*'s imprint. Whereas Homer's epics focused on the deeds and misdeeds of heroic warriors, the *Aeneid* is a literary epic of national glory. The most profound ideas and feelings expressed in the *Aeneid* are Roman virtues—patriotism, devotion to the family, duty to the state, and a strong sense of religion. Intensely patriotic, Virgil ascribed to Rome a divine mission to bring peace and civilized life to the world, and he praised Augustus as a divinely appointed ruler who had fulfilled Rome's mission. The Greeks might be better sculptors, orators, and thinkers, said Virgil, but only the Romans knew how to govern an empire.

BAS-RELIEF FROM CONSTANTINE'S ARCH. Emperor Marcus Aurelius dispenses aid to needy citizens. (Alinari/Art Resource, N.Y.)

Roman Culture and Law During the Pax Romana

During the late Roman Republic, Rome had creatively assimilated the Greek achievement (see Chapter 6) and transmitted it to others who had little or no contact with Hellenism. Rome had acquired Greek scientific thought, philosophy,

For other peoples will, I do not doubt,
still cast their bronze to breathe with softer
features,
or draw out of the marble living lines, plead
causes better,
trace the ways of heaven with wands and tell
the rising
constellations; but yours will be the rulership
of nations,
remember, Roman, these will be your arts:
to teach the ways of peace to those you
conquer, to spare
defeated peoples, to tame the proud.[5]

Aelius Aristides: The Blessings of the Pax Romana

In the following reading, Aelius Aristides (A.D. 117–187), a Greek intellectual, glowingly praises the Pax Romana in an oration that was probably delivered in Rome. In the tradition of Roman orators, Aristides used hyperbole and exaggeration. Nevertheless, the oration does capture the universalism and cosmopolitanism that characterized the Roman Empire.

"But the most marvelous and admirable achievement of all, and the one deserving our fullest gratitude, is this. . . . You alone of the imperial powers of history rule over men who are free. You have not assigned this or that region to [unscrupulous governors]. . . . Just as citizens in an individual city might designate magistrates, so you, whose city is the whole world, appoint governors to protect and provide for the governed, as if they were elective, not to lord it over their charges. As a result, so far from disputing the office as if it were their own, governors make way for their successors readily when their term is up, and may not even await their coming. Appeals to a higher jurisdiction are as easy as appeals from parish to county. . . .

"But the most notable and praiseworthy feature of all, a thing unparalleled, is your magnanimous conception of citizenship. All of your subjects (and this implies the whole world) you have divided into two parts: the better endowed and more virile, wherever they may be, you have granted citizenship and even kinship; the rest you govern as obedient subjects. Neither the seas nor expanse of land bars citizenship; Asia and Europe are not differentiated. Careers are open to talent. . . . Rich and poor find contentment and profit in your system; there is no other way of life. Your polity is a single and all-embracing harmony. . . .

. . . "[You] established cities in diverse parts. The cities you filled with colonists; you introduced arts and crafts and established an orderly culture. . . . Your military organization makes all others childish. Your soldiers and officers you train to prevail not only over the enemy but over themselves. The soldier lives under discipline daily, and none ever deserts the post assigned him.

"You alone are, so to speak, natural rulers. Your predecessors were masters and slaves in turn; as rulers they were counterfeits, and reversed their positions like players in a ball game. . . . You have measured out the world, bridged rivers, cut roads through mountains, filled the wastes with posting stations, introduced orderly and refined modes of life. . . .

"Be all gods and their offspring invoked to grant that this empire and this city flourish forever and never cease until stones float upon the sea and trees forbear to sprout in the springtide. May the great Ruler and his sons be preserved to administer all things well."

Question for Analysis

1. What did Aristides find so admirable in Rome's imperial system?

Moses Hadas, ed., *A History of Rome: From Its Origins to 529 A.D. as Told by the Roman Historians* (Garden City, N.Y.: Doubleday Anchor Books, 1956), 143–145.

In his *History of Rome,* the historian Livy (59 B.C.–A.D. 17) also glorified Roman virtues, customs, and deeds. He praised Augustus for attempting to revive traditional Roman morality, to which Livy felt a strong attachment. Modern historians criticize Livy for failing to utilize important sources of information in this work, for relying on biased authorities, and for allowing fierce patriotism to warp his judgment. Although Livy was a lesser historian than Thucydides or Polybius, his work was still a major achievement, particularly in its depiction of the Roman character, which helped make Rome great.

An outstanding poet, Horace (65–8 B.C.) was the son of a freed slave. He broadened his education by studying literature and philosophy in Athens, and Greek ideals are reflected in his writings. Horace enjoyed the luxury of country estates, banquets, fine clothes, and courtesans, along with the simple pleasures of mountain streams and clear skies. His poetry touched on many themes—the joy of good wine, the value of moderation, and the beauty of friendship. Desiring to blend reason and emotion, Horace urged men to seek pleasurable experiences but to avoid extremes and to keep desire under rational control. He also reminded Romans of the terrible civil wars that had ruined the Republic.

> *What plain is not enriched with Latin blood, to bear witness with its graves to our unholy strife. . . . What pool or stream has failed to taste the dismal war! What sea has Italian slaughter not discolored! What coast knows not our blood!*[6]

Unlike Virgil, Livy, or Horace, Ovid (43 B.C.–A.D. 17) did not experience the civil wars during his adult years. Consequently, he was less inclined to praise the Augustan peace. His poetry showed a preference for romance and humor, and he is best remembered for his advice to lovers contained in his most famous work, *The Art of Love.* Written when Ovid was fifty years old, the work deals with the art of seduction. Book I tells how to attract a woman who is the object of a man's desire; Book II explains how a man can keep a woman's love; Book III advises women about men. To the man who wants to win a woman, Ovid gave this counsel:

> *First of all, be quite sure that there isn't a woman who cannot be won, and make up your mind that you will win her. Only you must prepare the ground.*
>
> *You must play the lover for all you're worth. Tell her how you are pining for her.*
>
> *Never cease to sing the praises of her face, her hair, her taper fingers, and her dainty foot.*
>
> *Tears too are a mighty useful resource in the matter of love. They would melt a diamond. Make a point, therefore, of letting your mistress see your face all wet with tears.*
>
> *Women are things of many moods. You must adapt your treatment to the special case.*[7]

The writers who lived after the Augustan age were of a lesser quality than their predecessors, although the historian Tacitus (A.D. 55–c. 118) was an exception. Sympathetic to republican institutions, Tacitus denounced Roman emperors and the imperial system in his *Histories* and *Annals.* In *Germania,* he turned his sights on the habits of the Germanic peoples. He described the Germans as undisciplined but heroic, with a strong love of freedom.

The satirist Juvenal (A.D. c. 55–138) attacked the evils of Roman society, such as the misconduct of emperors, the haughtiness of the wealthy, the barbaric tastes of commoners, and the failures of parents. He also described the noise, congestion, and poverty of the capital, as well as its criminal element.

> *But these aren't your only terrors. For you can never restrain*
> *The criminal element. Lock up your house, put bolt and chain*
> *On your shop, but when all's quiet, someone will rob you or he'll*
> *Be a cutthroat perhaps and do you in quickly with cold steel.*[8]

In addition, Juvenal expressed venomous views toward women. He describes the humiliations husbands must face—infidelity, poisonings, public harlotry, and being ignored, intimidated, and dominated. All of this, says Juvenal, is a consequence of a wife's failure to live up to the obligations of the married state—being silent, loyal, obedient, respectful of her husband, and caring for the children.

Philosophy. Stoicism was the principal philosophy of the Pax Romana, and its leading exponents were Seneca, Epictetus (A.D. c. 60–c. 117), and the emperor Marcus Aurelius. Perpetuating the rational tradition of Greek philosophy, Roman Stoics saw the universe as governed by reason, and they esteemed the human intellect. Like Socrates, they sought the highest good in this world, not in an afterlife, and envisioned no power above human reason. Moral values were obtained from reason alone. The individual was self-sufficient and depended entirely on rational faculties for knowing and doing good. Stoics valued self-sufficient persons who attained virtue and wisdom by exercising rational control over their lives. Roman thinkers also embraced the Stoic doctrine that all people, because of their capacity to reason, belong to a common humanity.

Lucius Annaeus Seneca (4 B.C.–A.D. 65), a student of rhetoric and philosophy, served the emperor Nero. After Nero accused him of participating in a conspiracy against the throne, Seneca was forced to commit suicide. Seneca's Stoic humanitarianism was expressed in his denunciation of the gladiatorial combats and in his concern for slaves. He urged Romans "to consider, that he whom you call your slave, is sprung from the same origin, enjoys the same climate, breathes the same air, and is subject to the same condition of life and death as yourself."[9]

The emperor Marcus Aurelius, the last of the great Stoics, also had to deal with serious problems confronting the Empire. While commanding troops engaged in fighting plundering tribesmen in the Balkans, he wrote in Greek the *Meditations*, a classic work of Stoic thought. In Stoicism, he sought the strength to overcome the burdens of ruling an empire, the fear of death, and the injustices and misdeeds committed by his fellows.

> *Hour by hour resolve firmly, like a Roman and a man, to do what comes to hand with correct and natural dignity, and with humanity, independence, and justice. Allow your mind freedom from all other considerations. This you can do, if you will approach each action as though it were your last, dismissing the wayward thought, the emotional recoil from the commands of reason, the desire to create an impression, the admiration of self, the discontent with your lot. See how little a man needs to master, for his days to flow on in quietness and piety: he has but to observe these few counsels, and the gods will ask nothing more.*[10]

Science. The two most prominent scientists during the Greco-Roman age were Ptolemy, the mathematician, geographer, and astronomer, who worked at Alexandria in the second century A.D., and Galen (A.D. c. 130–c. 201), who investigated medicine and anatomy. Ptolemy's thirteen-volume work, *Mathematical Composition*—more commonly known as the *Almagest*, a Greek-Arabic term meaning "the greatest"—summed up antiquity's knowledge of astronomy and became the authoritative text during the Middle Ages. In the Ptolemaic system, a motionless, round earth stood in the center of the universe, and the moon, sun, and planets moved about the earth in circles, or in combinations of circles. The Ptolemaic system was built on a faulty premise, as modern astronomy eventually showed. However, it did work—that is, it did provide a model of the universe that adequately accounted for most observed phenomena. The Ptolemaic system would not be challenged until the middle of the sixteenth century.

As Ptolemy's system dominated astronomy, so the theories of Galen dominated medicine down to modern times. By dissecting both dead and living animals, Galen attempted a rational investigation of the body's working parts. Although his work contains many errors, he made essential contributions to the knowledge of anatomy. Thanks to Arab physicians who preserved his writings during the Middle Ages, Galen's influence continued in the West into early modern times.

Art, Architecture, and Engineering. Romans borrowed art forms from other peoples, particularly the Greeks, but they borrowed creatively, transforming and enhancing their inheritance. Roman portraiture continued trends initiated during the Hellenistic Age. Imitating Hellenistic models, Roman sculptors realistically carved every detail of a subject's face: unruly hair, prominent nose, lines and wrinkles, a jaw that showed weakness or strength. Sculpture also gave expression to the imperial ideal. Statues of emperors conveyed nobility and authority; reliefs commemorating victories glorified Roman might and grandeur.

The Romans most creatively transformed the Greek inheritance in architecture. The Greek temple was intended to be viewed from the outside; the focus was exclusively on the superbly balanced exterior. By using arches, vaults, and domes, the Romans built structures with large, magnificent interiors. The vast interior, massive walls, and overarching dome of the famous Pantheon, a temple built in the early second century, during the reign of Hadrian, symbolizes the power and majesty of the Roman world-state.

The Romans excelled at engineering. They built amphitheaters, public baths, and aqueducts that carried water to Roman cities—some still survive. Roman engineers with an eye for natural barriers and drainage problems carefully selected routes and designed great embanked roads, the finest in the ancient world.

Law. Expressing the Roman yearning for order and justice, law was Rome's great legacy to Western civilization. Roman law passed through two essential stages: the formation of civil law (*jus civile*) and the formation of the law of nations (*jus gentium*). The basic features of the civil law evolved during the two-hundred-year Struggle of the Orders, at the same time that Rome was extending its dominion over Italy. The Twelve Tables, drawn up in the early days of the patrician–plebeian struggle (described at the beginning of Chapter 6), established for the Roman state written rules of criminal and civil law that applied to all citizens. Over the centuries, the civil law was expanded by statutes enacted by the assemblies, by the legal decisions of jurisdictional magistrates, by the rulings of emperors, and by the commentaries of professional jurists, who, aided by familiarity with Greek logic, engaged in systematic legal analysis.

During the period of the Republic's expansion outside Italy, contact with the Greeks and other peoples led to the development of the second branch of Roman law, jus gentium, which combined Roman civil law with principles selectively drawn from the legal tradition of Greeks and other peoples. Roman jurists identified the jus gentium with the natural law (*jus naturale*) of the Stoics. The jurists said that a law should accord with rational principles inherent in nature: uniform and universally valid standards that can be discerned by rational people. Serving to bind different peoples together, the law of nations harmonized with the requirements of a world empire and with Stoic ideals, as Cicero pointed out.

> *True law is right reason in agreement with nature; it is of universal application, unchanging and ever lasting. . . . And there will not be different laws at Rome and at Athens or different laws now and in the future, but one eternal and unchangeable law will be valid for all nations and all times.*[11]

The law of nations came to be applied throughout the Empire, although it never entirely supplanted local law. In the eyes of the law, a citizen was not a Syrian or a Briton or a Spaniard but a Roman. In effect, through jus gentium, an international law, Rome transformed what was a theoretical principle for the Stoics into a political reality.

After the fall of the western Roman Empire, Roman law fell into disuse in Europe. Gradually reintroduced in the twelfth century, it came to

THE COLOSSEUM, ROME, A.D. 70–80. The joint work of the emperor Vespasian and his sons Titus and Domitian, this huge amphitheater was the largest in the ancient world. It was the site of innumerable spectacles, sham sea battles, gladiatorial games, wild beast hunts, and the deaths of Christian martyrs.
(Scala/Art Resource, N.Y.)

form the basis of the common law in all Western European lands except Britain and its dependencies. Some provisions of Roman law are readily recognizable in modern legal systems, as the following excerpts illustrate:

Justice is a constant, unfailing disposition to give everyone his legal due.
No one suffers a penalty for what he thinks.
In the case of major offenses it makes a difference whether something is committed purposefully or accidentally.

The guilt or punishment of a father can impose no stigma upon the son, for every individual is subjected to treatment in accordance with his own action, and no one is made the inheritor of the guilt of another.
In inflicting penalties, the age . . . of the guilty party must be taken into account.[12]

Entertainment. Despite its many achievements, Roman civilization presents a paradox. On the one hand, Roman culture and law evidence high standards of civilization. On the other hand, the Romans institutionalized barbaric practices: battles to the death between armed gladiators and the tormenting and slaughtering of wild beasts.

The major forms of entertainment in both the Republic and the Empire were chariot races, wild animal shows, and gladiatorial combat. Chariot races were gala events in which the most skillful riders and the finest and best-trained stallions raced in an atmosphere of extreme excitement. The charioteers, many of them slaves hoping that victory would bring them freedom, became popular heroes. The rich staked fortunes on the races, and the poor bet their last coins.

The Romans craved brutal spectacles. One form of entertainment pitted wild beasts against each other or against men armed with spears. Another consisted of battles, sometimes to the death, between highly trained gladiators. The gladiators, mainly prisoners of war and condemned criminals, learned their craft at schools run by professional trainers. Some gladiators entered the arena armed with a sword, others with a trident and a net. The spectators were transformed into a frenzied mob that lusted for blood. If they were displeased with a losing gladiator's performance, they would call for his immediate execution.

Over the centuries, these spectacles grew more bizarre and brutal. Hundreds of tigers were set against elephants and bulls; wild bulls tore apart men dressed in animal skins; women battled in the arena; dwarfs fought each other. One day in the Colosseum, which could seat fifty thousand people, three thousand men fought one another; on the day the Colosseum opened in A.D. 80, nine thousand beasts were slaughtered. In fact, much of the African trade was devoted to supplying animals for the contests.

Few Romans questioned these barbarities, which became a routine part of daily life. Occasionally, however, thoughtful Romans had strong doubts. After watching a public spectacle, the Stoic philosopher Seneca wrote in disgust: "There is nothing more harmful to one's character than attendance at some spectacle, because vices more easily creep into your soul while you are being entertained. When I return from some spectacle,

I am greedier, more aggressive and . . . more cruel and inhuman."[13]

SIGNS OF TROUBLE

The Pax Romana was one of the finest periods in ancient history. But even during the Time of Happiness, signs of trouble appeared that would grow to crisis proportions in the third century.

Internal Unrest

The Empire's internal stability was always subject to question. Were the economic foundations of the Empire strong and elastic enough to endure hard blows? Could the Roman Empire retain the loyalty of so many diverse nationalities, each with its own religious and cultural traditions? Were the mass of people committed to the values of Greco-Roman civilization, or would they withdraw their allegiance and revert to their native traditions if imperial authority weakened?

Most people in the Mediterranean world welcomed Roman rule and could not conceive of a world without the Empire that brought them peace and security. Nevertheless, during the Pax Romana, dissident elements did surface, particularly in Gaul, Egypt, and Judea. Separatist movements in Gaul were crushed by Roman forces. To provide free bread for Rome's poor, Roman emperors exploited the Egyptian peasantry. Weighed down by forced labor, heavy taxes, requisitions, and confiscations, Egyptian peasants frequently sought to escape from farm work. And the Romans suppressed two uprisings by the Jews of Judea.

The unrest in Egypt, Gaul, and Judea demonstrated that not all people at all times welcomed the grand majesty of the Roman peace and that localist and separatist tendencies persisted in a universal empire. In the centuries that followed, as Rome staggered under the weight of economic, political, and military difficulties, these native loyalties reasserted themselves. Increasingly, the masses, and even the Romanized elite of the cities, withdrew their support from the Roman world-state.

Social and Economic Weaknesses

A healthy world-state required empirewide trade to serve as an economic base for political unity, expanding agricultural production to feed the cities, and growing internal mass markets to stimulate industrial production. But the economy of the Empire during the Pax Romana had serious defects. The means of communication and transportation were slow, which hindered long-distance commerce. Roman roads, built for military rather than commercial purposes, were often too narrow for large carts and in places were too steep for any vehicles. Consequently, transporting goods by land, even short distances, necessitated huge price increases that hampered trade. Many nobles, considering it unworthy for a gentleman to engage in business, chose to squander their wealth rather than invest it in commercial or industrial enterprises. Lacking the stimulus of capital investment, the economy could not expand.

Limited employment opportunities resulted from the Greco-Roman civilization's failure to improve its technology substantially and from reliance on slave labor. Also, because manual labor was considered degrading, fit only for a slave, there was little incentive for innovation that might have triggered economic growth and expanded employment opportunities. Because of these factors, millions of people simply did not engage in productive labor. Moreover, scarce employment left the masses with little purchasing power; this too adversely affected business and industry. Many unemployed inhabitants of Italian towns lived on free or cheap grain provided by the state. To feed this unemployed underclass, the government kept the price of grain artificially low. This practice discouraged farmers from planting more crops and expanding grain production and forced many of them to seek other livelihoods. As more farmers left the countryside, the towns became increasingly swollen with an impoverished proletariat. Rural areas eventually faced a serious shortage of laborers due to this population migration.

Ultimately, only a small portion of the urban population—landlords whose estates were outside the city, merchants, and administrators—reaped the benefits of the Roman peace. They basked in luxury, leisure, and culture. The urban poor, on the other hand, derived few of the economic gains and shared little in the political and cultural life of the city. The privileged classes bought off the urban poor with bread and circuses, but occasionally mass discontent expressed itself in mob violence. Outside the cities, the peasantry—still the great bulk of the population—was exploited to provide cheap food for the city dwellers.

Such a parasitical, exploitative, and elitist social system might function in periods of peace and tranquility, but could it survive crises? Would the impoverished people of town and country—the overwhelming majority of the population—remain loyal to a state whose benefits barely extended to them and whose sophisticated culture, which they hardly comprehended, virtually excluded them?

Cultural Stagnation and Transformation

Perhaps the most dangerous sign for the future was the spiritual paralysis that crept over the ordered world of the Pax Romana. A weary and sterile Hellenism underlay the Roman peace. The ancient world was undergoing a transformation of values that foreshadowed the end of Greco-Roman civilization.

During the second century A.D., Greco-Roman civilization lost its creative energies, and the values of classical humanism were challenged by mythic-religious movements. No longer regarding reason as a satisfying guide to life, the educated elite subordinated the intellect to feelings and an unregulated imagination. No longer finding the affairs of this world to have purpose, people placed their hope in life after death. The Roman world was undergoing a religious revolution and seeking a new vision of the divine.

The application of reason to nature and society, as we have seen, was the great achievement of the Greek mind. Yet despite its many triumphs, Greek rationalism never entirely subdued the mythic-religious mentality, which draws its strength from human emotion. The masses of peasants and slaves remained attracted to religious forms. **Ritual,** mystery, magic, and ecstasy never lost their hold on the ancient world—nor, indeed, have they on our own scientific and technological society. During the Hellenistic Age, the tide of rationalism gradually receded, and the nonrational, an ever-present undercurrent, showed renewed vigor. This resurgence of the mythical mentality could be seen in the popularity of the occult, magic, alchemy, and astrology. Feeling themselves controlled by heavenly powers, burdened by danger and emotional stress, and fearing fate as fixed in the stars, people turned for deliverance to magicians, astrologers, and exorcists.

They also became devotees of the many Near Eastern religious cults that promised personal salvation. More and more people felt that the good life could not be achieved by individuals through their own efforts; they needed outside help. Philosophers eventually sought escape from this world through union with a divine presence greater than human power. Increasingly, the masses, and then even the educated elite, came to believe that the good life could be found not on earth but only in a world beyond the grave. Seeing themselves as isolated souls wandering aimlessly in a social desert, people sought refuge in religion. Reason had been found wanting; the time for faith and salvation was at hand.

The Roman Empire had imposed peace and stability, but it could not alleviate the feelings of loneliness, anxiety, impotence, alienation, and boredom that had been gaining ground in the Mediterranean world since the fourth century B.C. A spiritual malaise descended on the Greco-Roman world. Among the upper classes, the philosophical and scientific spirit withered; rational and secular values were in retreat. Deprived of the excitement of politics and bored by idleness and pleasure, the best minds, says historian Michael Rostovtzeff,

lost faith in the power of reason. . . . Creative genius dwindled; science repeated its previous results. The textbook took the place of research; no new artistic discoveries were made, but echoes of the past were heard. . . . [Writers] amuse[d] the mind but [were] incapable of elevating and inspiring it.[14]

The Spread of Mystery Religions

The proliferation of Eastern mystery religions was a clear expression of this transformation of classical values. During the Hellenistic era, slaves, merchants, and soldiers brought many religious cults westward from Persia, Babylon, Syria, Egypt, and Asia Minor. The various mystery cults possessed many common features. Converts underwent initiation rites and were bound by oath to secrecy. The initiates, in a state of rapture, attempted to unite with the deity after first purifying themselves through baptism (sometimes with the blood of a bull), fasting, having their heads shaved, or drinking from a sacred vessel. Communion was achieved by donning the god's robe, eating a sacred meal, or visiting the god's sanctuary. This sacramental drama propelled initiates through an intense mystical experience of exaltation and rebirth. Cultists were certain that their particular savior-god would protect them from misfortune and ensure their soul's immortality.

Of special significance was the cult of Mithras, which had certain parallels with early Christianity and was its principal competitor. Originating in Persia, Mithraism spread westward into the Roman Empire. Because it stressed respect for the masculine virtues of bravery and camaraderie, it became particularly popular with the army. The god Mithras, whose birth date was celebrated on December 25, had as his mission the rescuing of humanity from evil. He was said to demand high standards of morality, to judge souls after death, and to grant eternal life to his faithful followers.

The popularity of magic and mystery demonstrates that many people in Roman society either did not comprehend or had lost faith in the rational and secular values of classical humanism. Religion proved more comforting to the spirit. People felt that the gods could provide what reason, natural law, and civic affairs could not: a sure way of overcoming life's misfortunes and discouragements, a guarantee of immortality, a sense of belonging to a community of brethren who cared, an exciting outlet for bottled-up emotions, and a sedative for anxiety at a time when dissatisfaction with the human condition showed itself in all phases of society and life.

The Spiritualization of Philosophy

The religious orientation also found expression in philosophy, which demonstrated attitudes markedly at odds with classical humanism. These attitudes, commonly associated with religion, included indifference to the world, withdrawal, and pessimism

HADRIAN'S WALL. Between A.D. 122 and 127, the Romans constructed an elaborate defensive system in Britain consisting of a wall of solid masonry and a series of forts. Built on high ground, Hadrian's Wall extended from the estuary of the Solway to that of the Tyne, a distance of seventy-three miles. (© Patrick Ward/Corbis.)

about the earthly state. From trying to understand nature and individuals' relationships to one another, the philosophers more and more aspired to a communion with a higher reality. Like the mystery religions, philosophy reached for something beyond this world in order to comfort the individual. In Neo-Platonism, which replaced Stoicism as the dominant school of philosophy in the late Roman Empire, religious yearnings were transformed into a religious system that transcended reason.

Plotinus (A.D. c. 205–c. 270), the most influential spokesman of Neo-Platonism, went far beyond Marcus Aurelius's natural religion; in aspiring to the ecstatic union of the soul with God, he subordinated philosophy to mysticism and the occult. Plato's philosophy, we have seen, contained both

a major and a minor key. The major key stressed a rational interpretation of the human community and called for reforming the polis on the basis of knowledge, whereas the minor key urged the soul to rise to a higher world of reality. Plotinus was intrigued by Plato's otherworldliness.

What Plotinus desired was union with the One, or the Good, sometimes called God—the source of all existence. Plotinus felt that the intellect could neither describe nor understand the One, which transcended all knowing, and that joining with the One required a mystical leap, a purification of the soul that dispensed with logic, evidence, and proof. This vision, which induced the soul to return to its true home, was for Plotinus something greater and more compelling than reason.

For Plotinus, philosophy became a religious experience, a contemplation of the eternal. His successors held that through acts of magic the soul can unite with the One. Compared with this union with the divine One, of what value was knowledge of the sensible world or a concern for human affairs? For Plotinus, the principal goal of life was not comprehension of the natural world or fulfillment of human potential or betterment of the human community but attaining spiritual truth—knowledge of the One—through a transrational experience. Neo-Platonism, concludes historian of philosophy W. T. Stace, "is founded upon . . . the despair of reason." It seeks to reach the Absolute not through reason but through "spiritual intoxication." This marks a radical transformation of philosophical thinking.

> *For philosophy is founded upon reason. It is the effort to comprehend, to understand, to grasp the reality of things intellectually. Therefore it cannot admit anything higher than reason. To exalt intuition, ecstasy, or rapture, above thought—this is the death of philosophy. . . . In Neo-Platonism, therefore, ancient philosophy commits suicide. This is the end. The place of philosophy is taken henceforth by religion.*[15]

By the time of the late Roman Empire, mystery religions intoxicated the masses, and mystical philosophy beguiled the educated elite. Classical civilization was being transformed. Philosophy had become subordinate to religious belief; secular values seemed inferior to religious experience. The earthly city had raised its eyes toward heaven. The culture of the Roman world was moving in a direction in which the quest for the divine was to predominate over all human enterprises.

THE DECLINE OF ROME

Third-Century Crisis

At the death of Marcus Aurelius in A.D. 180, the Empire was politically stable, economically prosperous, and militarily secure. In the third century, the ordered civilization of the Pax Romana ended. Several elements caused this disruption. The Roman Empire was plunged into military anarchy, raided by Germanic tribes, and burdened by economic dislocations. During these critical times, effective leadership was lacking, for the adoptive system abandoned by Marcus Aurelius was not restored.

The degeneration of the army was a prime reason for the third-century crisis. During the great peace, the army had remained an excellent fighting force, renowned for its discipline, organization, and loyalty. In the third century A.D., however, there was a marked deterioration in the quality of Roman soldiers. Lacking loyalty to Rome and greedy for spoils, soldiers used their weapons to prey on civilians and to make and unmake emperors. Fearful of being killed by their unruly troops who wanted spoils or of being murdered by a suspicious emperor, generals were driven to seize the throne. Once in power, they had to buy the loyalty of their soldiers and guard against assassination by other generals. From A.D. 235 to 285, military mutiny and civil war raged as legion fought legion. During this period, there were twenty-six soldier-emperors, twenty-five of whom died violently. The once stalwart army neglected its duty of defending the borders against barbarian incursions and disrupted the internal life of the Empire.

Perhaps the degeneration of the army can be explained by the liberal granting of citizenship. In A.D. 212, citizenship was extended to virtually all freeborn inhabitants of the Empire. Previously, many army recruits had been drawn from among provincials, who were attracted by the promise of citizenship and its advantages. These recruits generally were men of a high caliber who were interested in bettering themselves and their families' lot. With citizenship no longer an inducement for enlistment, says Edward T. Salmon,

> *recruits were now only too likely to be drawn from the lowest and most primitive elements . . . men of the rough and reckless type, who were joining the army chiefly in order to get weapons in their hands with which they would be able to extort for themselves an even greater share of the Empire's collective wealth . . . men who knew little and cared less about Rome's mission and who, when not preying upon the civilians, had not the slightest compunction about preying upon one another.*[16]

During the third century, Rome also had to deal with a revived Persian Empire that forced the Romans to shift large contingents of legions eastward. Taking advantage of the weakened borders and military anarchy, Germanic tribesmen crossed the Rhine–Danube frontier to loot and destroy. The Goths raided coastal cities of Asia Minor and Greece and even burned much of Athens. In the Western Empire, other Germanic tribes penetrated Gaul, Spain, and Italy and engaged the Romans in a full-scale battle near Milan. At the same time that the European defense lines were being breached, a reborn Persian Empire, led by the Sassanid dynasty, attacked and for a while conquered Roman lands in the east. Some sections of the Empire, notably in Gaul, attempted to break away; these moves reflected an assertion of local patriotism over Roman universalism. The "city of mankind" was crumbling.

These eruptions had severe economic repercussions. Cities were pillaged and destroyed, farmland ruined, and trade disrupted. To obtain funds and supplies for the military, emperors confiscated goods, exacted forced labor, and devalued the currency by reducing the gold and silver content of coins and adding base metals: zinc, tin, and lead. Cheap money caused a ruinous inflation, leading many people to turn to barter as a medium of exchange. These measures led many citizens to withdraw their loyalty from Rome.

Repeated invasions, civil war, pillage by Germanic tribes and by Roman soldiers, soaring prices, a debased coinage, declining agricultural production, disrupted transportation, and the excessive demands of the state caused economic havoc and famine in the cities. Compounding the problem was a great plague that spread across North Africa and the Balkans in midcentury. Driven to desperation by famine and plague, by invading barbarians and plundering Roman soldiers, and by the extortions and requisitions of government officials, many people fled the cities. The urban centers of the ancient world, creators and disseminators of high civilization, were caught in a rhythm of breakdown. As cities decayed, the center of life gravitated back to the countryside. Large, fortified estates, or villas, owned by the emperor or wealthy aristocrats, provided refuge for the uprooted and destitute of town and country. In the countryside, people had no deep

commitment to classical civilization, which had made little headway against native languages, religions, and manners.

During the third century A.D., the spiritual crisis intensified as the rational foundations of Greco-Roman civilization eroded further. People turned increasingly to the mystery cults, which offered relief from earthly misery, a sense of belonging, and a promise of immortality. In philosophy, creative energies were directed not toward a greater understanding of nature or society but toward a knowledge of the divine, which, taught the philosophers, was the path to happiness. Hellenism was breaking down.

Diocletian and Constantine: The Regimented State

The emperors Diocletian (A.D. 285–305) and Constantine (A.D. 306–337) tried to contain the awesome forces of disintegration. At a time when agricultural production was steadily declining, they had to feed the city poor and an expanded army of more than 500,000, strung out over the Empire. They also had to prevent renewed outbreaks of military anarchy, drive the Germans back across the Danube frontier, and secure the eastern region against renewed aggression from Persia. Their solution was to weaken municipal institutions, tighten the reins of central government, and extort more taxes and requisitions from the citizens. In the process, they transformed Rome into a bureaucratic, regimented, and militarized state, which some historians refer to as "a vast prison."

Ruling like a Near Eastern despot, Diocletian completed a trend that had been developing for generations. He imitated the pomp of the East, wore magnificent robes and jewels, and demanded that subjects prostrate themselves in his presence. Cities lost their traditional right of local self-government—a loss that also culminated an earlier trend. To increase the size of the army, Diocletian drafted prisoners of war and hired German mercenaries. He also established, on vacant or deserted Roman lands, colonies of Germans from which soldiers could be recruited. To ensure continuous production of food and goods, as well as the collection of taxes, the state forced unskilled workers and artisans to hold their jobs for life and to pass them on to their children. For the same reasons, peasants were turned into virtual serfs, bound to the land that they cultivated. An army of government agents was formed to hunt down peasants who fled the land to escape crushing taxes and poverty.

Also frozen into their positions were city officials, or *curiales*. They often found it necessary to furnish from their own pockets the difference between the state's tax demands and the amount that they could collect from an already over-taxed population. This system of a hereditary class of tax collectors and of crippling taxes to pay for a vastly expanded bureaucracy and military establishment enfeebled urban trade and industry. Such conditions killed the civic spirit of townspeople, who desperately sought escape. By overburdening urban dwellers with taxes and regulations, Diocletian and Constantine helped shatter the vitality of city life, on which Roman prosperity and civilization depended. During the Pax Romana, municipal authorities had enjoyed considerable autonomy; now the state bureaucracy extended its often onerous and rapacious power everywhere.

Rome was governed by a despotism characteristic of the Near East—a highly centralized monarchy regimenting the lives of its subjects. Whereas Augustus had upheld the classical ideal that the commonwealth was a means of fostering the good life for the individual, Diocletian adopted the Eastern attitude that the individual lives for the state. The absolutism inherent in the concept of the principate had eclipsed the republican elements that had endured in the Augustan political settlement.

To guard against military insurrection, Diocletian appointed a loyal general as emperor to govern the western provinces of the Empire while he ruled the eastern regions; although both emperors bore the title Augustus, Diocletian remained superior. (Each emperor then chose an heir-designate, who received his own territory to govern. For a time, the Empire was a tetrarchy—a government by four.) By building an imperial capital, Constantinople, at the Bosporus, a strait where Asia meets Europe, Constantine furthered this trend of dividing the Empire into eastern and western halves.

Tribal Migrations and Invasions

Nearly two centuries after Diocletian's reign, the Roman historian Zosimus described the emperor's accomplishment.

> *By the foresight of Diocletian the frontiers were everywhere studded with cities and forts and towers, and the whole army stationed along them. It was thus impossible for the barbarians to break through, since at every point they encountered an opposing force strong enough to repel them.*[17]

By imposing some order on what had been approaching chaos, Diocletian and Constantine prevented the Empire from collapsing. Rome was given a reprieve. A long period of peace might have brought economic recovery, but misfortune continued to burden Rome, and the process of breakdown and disintegration resumed.

In the last part of the fourth century, the problem of guarding the frontier grew more acute. The Huns, a nomadic people from central Asia, swept across the plains of Russia. With their formidible cavalry—the Huns were expert riders and archers—they subdued the Ostrogoths, a Germanic tribe that had established itself in Ukraine, and forced the Germanic Visigoths, who had migrated along the Danube in what is now Romania, to seek refuge within the eastern Roman Empire. Enraged by their mistreatment at the hands of Roman officials, the Visigoths took up arms. In 378, Goths and Romans fought each other in a historic battle at Adrianople. The Visigoths' cavalry cut to pieces the Roman forces, largely tribal mercenaries, and killed and captured perhaps as many as two-thirds of the Roman army. Emperor Valens perished in what was Rome's worst defeat since Cannae in the war with Hannibal. The Visigoths were on Roman territory to stay. The battle of Adrianople signified that Rome could no longer defend its borders. Since it was the Visigoth cavalry that prevailed over a Roman army composed mainly of foot soldiers, the battle also signified that cavalry had begun to supersede infantry as a principal instrument of warfare.

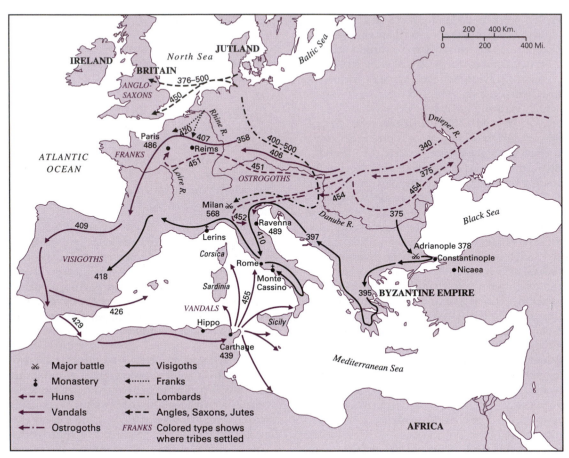

Map 7.2 INCURSIONS AND MIGRATIONS, C. A.D. 300–500 In the fifth century, Germanic tribes, seeking land and desperate to escape the Huns, overran the weakened Roman borders. (Copyright © 2013 Cengage Learning.)

Other Germanic tribes increased their pressure on the Empire's borders. Attracted by the warmer climate, riches, and advanced civilization of the Roman Empire, they were also looking for new lands to farm and were frightened by the advent of the Huns. The borders finally collapsed at the very end of 406 as Vandals, Alans, Suebi, and other tribes joined the Goths in devastating and overrunning the Empire's western provinces. In 408–409, the Visigoths, led by Alaric, besieged Rome itself, extorting huge sums in return for permitting food to enter the city. Then, in 410, they rampaged through the city, which for eight hundred years had remained free of foreign attack,

slaughtering, destroying, and plundering. Saint Jerome lamented: "Who could believe that Rome, built upon the conquest of the whole world, would fall to the ground? that the mother herself would become the tomb of her peoples?"[18]

Economic conditions continued to deteriorate. Cities in Britain, Gaul, Germany, and Spain lay abandoned. Other metropolises saw their populations dwindle and production stagnate. The great network of Roman roads was not maintained, and trade in the West almost disappeared or passed into the hands of Greeks, Syrians, and Jews from the East. Everywhere famine, the extortion of taxes by government officials, the proliferation of marauding outlaws (many of them driven from their homes by the excessive financial demands of the state bureaucracy), and murderous warfare added to the misery of the Roman populace and the decomposition and fragmentation of the Empire.

In 451, Attila (c. 406–453), who had united Mongol tribes, led his Huns into Gaul, where he suffered his only defeat at the hands of a coalition of Germans and the remnants of the Roman army. He died two years later, having come within a hairsbreadth of turning Europe into a province of a Mongolian empire. But Rome's misfortunes persisted. In 455, Rome was again pillaged, this time by the Vandals. Additional regions fell under the control of Germanic chieftains. Germanic soldiers in the pay of Rome gained control of the government and dictated the choice of emperor. In 476, Germanic officers overthrew the Roman emperor Romulus and placed a fellow German, Odoacer, on the throne. This act is traditionally regarded as the end of the Roman Empire in the West. By the end of the fifth century, the western empire had fragmented into separate Germanic kingdoms.

Reasons for Rome's Decline

What were the underlying causes of the decline and fall of the Roman Empire in the West? Surely, no other question has intrigued the historical imagination more than this one. Implicit in the answers suggested by historians and philosophers is a concern for their own civilization. Will it suffer the same fate as Rome?

To analyze so monumental a development as the fall of Rome, some preliminary observations are necessary. First, the fall of Rome was a process lasting hundreds of years; it was not a single event that occurred in A.D. 476. Second, only the western half of the Empire fell. The eastern half—wealthier, more populous, less afflicted with civil wars, and less exposed to barbarian invasions—survived as the Byzantine Empire until the middle of the fifteenth century. Third, no single explanation suffices to account for Rome's decline; multiple forces—internal problems and external threats—operated concurrently to bring about the fall.

The Role of the Germanic Tribes. Was Rome's fall suicide or murder? Did the Germans walk over a corpse, or did they contribute substantially to Rome's decline and fall? Undoubtedly, an empire enfeebled by internal rot succumbed to the Germanic migrations. Perhaps a stronger Rome might have secured its borders, as it had done during the Pax Romana. But the Germanic attacks occurred mainly in the west, and the western Empire, poorer and less populated than the eastern portion, reeled under these increasingly numerous and more severe barbarian onslaughts. The pressures exerted by the Germans along an immense frontier also aggravated Rome's internal problems. The barbarian attacks left border regions depopulated and impoverished, as expenditures for the military drained the western Empire's resources. The Empire imposed high taxes and labor services on its citizens in order to strengthen the armed forces, causing the overburdened middle and lower classes to hate the imperial government that took so much from them.

Moreover, as more and more territory fell to the barbarian invaders, the Roman state was deprived of badly needed tax revenues. Containing the threat from a revived Persian Empire made it more difficult for Rome to deal with the Germanic invaders: it necessitated stationing a large force on the eastern frontier that could have been deployed in the west, and it imposed a heavy financial burden on the Empire, preventing it from funding larger armies against the barbarians.

Spiritual Considerations. The classical mentality, once brimming with confidence about the potentialities of the individual and the power of the intellect, suffered a failure of nerve. The urban upper class, on whom the responsibility for preserving cosmopolitan Greco-Roman culture traditionally rested, became dissolute and apathetic and no longer took an interest in public life. The aristocrats secluded themselves behind the walls of their fortified country estates; many did not lift a finger to help the Empire. The townspeople demonstrated their disenchantment by avoiding public service and by rarely organizing resistance forces against the barbarian invaders. Hounded by the state and persecuted by the army, many farmers viewed the Germans as liberators. The great bulk of the Roman citizenry, disillusioned and indifferent, simply gave up, despite the fact that they overwhelmingly outnumbered the Germanic invaders.

Political and Military Considerations. The Roman government itself contributed to this spiritual malaise through its increasingly autocratic tendencies, which culminated in the regimented rule of Diocletian and Constantine. The insatiable demands and regulations of the state in the late Roman Empire sapped the initiative and civic spirit of its citizens. The ruined middle and lower classes withdrew their loyalty. For many, the state had become the enemy, and its administration was hated and feared more than the barbarians. Salvianus of Marseilles (c. A.D. 400–470), a monk from Gaul, described the disaffection toward Rome that led many to welcome the barbarians as liberators.

> *Meanwhile the poor are being robbed, widows groan, orphans are trodden down, so that many, even persons of good birth, who have enjoyed a liberal education, seek refuge with the enemy to escape death under the trials of general persecution. They seek among the barbarians the Roman mercy, since they cannot endure the barbarous mercilessness they find among the Romans. . . . So you find men passing over everywhere, now to the Goths . . . , or whatever other barbarians have established their power anywhere. . . . Hence the name of Roman citizen, once . . . much valued . . . , is now voluntarily repudiated and shunned, and is thought not merely valueless, but even almost abhorrent.*[19]

Related to the political decline was the government's inability to retain the allegiance of its armies and to control ambitious military commanders, who used their troops to seize the throne and its immense power. The internal security and stability of the Empire was thus constantly imperiled by army leaders more concerned with grandiose personal dreams than with defending the Empire's borders. These civil wars imposed terrible financial burdens on the Empire and gravely weakened the frontier defenses—compounding the problem of forces spread thinly over thousands of miles and presenting an invitation to the Germans to increase their pressure.

During the Pax Romana, superior training and organization, rigorous discipline, a professional system of command, and a network of walls and forts enabled the Roman legions to protect the frontiers against incursions. The Roman soldier, for whom discipline was a deeply ingrained tradition, knew that his comrades would not desert the field, no matter how hard the fighting—an attitude that usually meant certain victory against untrained barbarian hordes. However, in the Late Roman Empire, the quality of Roman soldiers deteriorated, and the legions failed to defend the borders, even though the Germanic invaders were fewer numerically. During the third century, the army consisted predominantly of the provincial peasantry. These nonurban, non-Italian, semicivilized soldiers, often the dregs of society, were not committed to Greco-Roman civilization. They had little comprehension of Rome's mission and at times used their power to attack the cities and towns and to prey on hapless citizens. The emperors also recruited large numbers of Germans into the army—barbarians had been used as auxiliary troops since Julius Caesar—to fill depleted ranks. Ultimately, the army consisted predominantly of barbarians, as both legionnaires and officers. Although these Germans made brave soldiers, they too had little loyalty to Greco-Roman civilization and to the Roman state. This deterioration of the Roman army occurred in part because many young citizens evaded conscription. No longer imbued with patriotism, they considered military service a servitude to be shunned.

The deterioration of the Roman army is seen also on the level of tactics. Roman soldiers continued to fight in organized units, but the training and discipline required for fighting in close-order formations had lapsed. Barbarian units serving with the Roman army under their own commanders did not easily submit to traditional discipline. Thus, Rome lost the tactical superiority that it had once enjoyed over the barbarians.

Economic Considerations. Contributing to the decline of the Roman Empire in the west were population decline, the lack of technological advance, the heavy burden of taxation, and economic decentralization, which abetted political decentralization.

During the late Roman Empire, the population shrank. The epidemic during the reign of Marcus Aurelius, which might have been the bubonic plague, lasted fifteen years. A second plague struck the Empire during the reign of Commodus, Marcus Aurelius's son. Other plagues in the middle of the third century and constant warfare further reduced the population. The birth rate did not rise to compensate for these losses. Worsening economic conditions and lack of hope in the future apparently discouraged people from increasing the size of their families.

The decline in population adversely affected the Empire in at least three important ways. First, at the same time that the population was declining, the costs of running the Empire were spiraling, a situation that created a terrible burden for taxpayers. Second, fewer workers were available for agriculture, the most important economic activity of the Empire. Third, population decline reduced the manpower available for the army, forcing emperors to permit the establishment of Germanic colonies within the Empire's borders to serve as feeders for the army. This situation led to the barbarization of the army.

The Roman peace brought stability, but it failed to discover new and better ways of producing goods and agricultural products. To be sure, some advances in technology did take place during the Hellenistic Age and the Pax Romana: rotary mills for grain, screw presses, and improvements in glass-blowing and field-drainage methods. But the high intellectual culture of Greece and Rome rested on a meager economic and technological foundation. The widespread use of slave labor probably precluded a breakthrough in technology, for slaves had little incentive to invent more efficient ways of producing. The upper classes, identifying manual labor with slavery, would not condescend to engage in the mechanical arts. This failure to improve the level of technology limited employment opportunities for the masses. Because the masses could not increase their purchasing power, business and industry were without a mass internal market that might have acted as a continual stimulus for the accumulation of capital and for economic expansion.

Instead of expanding industry and trade, towns maintained their wealth by exploiting the countryside. The Roman cities, centers of civilized life and opulence, lacked industries. They spent but did not produce. Provided with food and entertainment—"bread and circuses"—the unproductive city dwellers, driven out of the labor force by slavery and economic stagnation, were a heavy burden for the state. The towns were dominated by landlords whose estates lay beyond the city and whose income derived from grain, oil, and wine. Manufacturing was rudimentary, confined essentially to textiles, pottery, furniture, and glassware. The methods of production rarely improved; the market was limited; the cost of transportation, particularly by land, was high; and agricultural productivity was low—the labor of perhaps nineteen peasants was required to support one townsman. Such a fundamentally unhealthy economy could not weather the dislocations caused by uninterrupted warfare and the demands of the military and a mushrooming bureaucracy.

With the barbarians pressing on the borders, the increased military expenditures overstrained the Empire's resources. To pay for the food, uniforms, arms, and armor of the soldiers, taxes were raised, growing too heavy for peasants and townspeople, particularly since the large landowners did not pay their fair share. The state also requisitioned wood and grain and demanded that citizens maintain roads and bridges. The government often resorted to force to collect taxes and exact services. Crushed by these demands, many peasants simply abandoned their farms and sought the protection of large landowners or turned to banditry.

Making the situation worse was the administrative separation of the Empire into eastern and western parts, undertaken by Diocletian and Constantine. As a result, western emperors could no longer rely on financial aid from the wealthier east to pay for the defense of the borders. Slow communications and costly transport continued to hamper the empirewide trade, which was required to sustain political unity. Meanwhile, industries gravitated outward, to search for new markets in the frontier army camps and for new sources of slaves in border regions. This dispersion further weakened the bonds of economic unity. Gradually, trade became less international and more local, and provincial regions grew more self-sufficient. The strife of the third century intensified the drift toward economic self-sufficiency in the provinces, a condition that promoted localism and separatism.

Contributing to the economic decentralization was the growth of industries on latifundia, the large, fortified estates owned by wealthy aristocrats. Producing exclusively for the local market, these estates contributed to the impoverishment of urban centers by reducing the number of customers available to buy goods made in the cities. As life grew more desperate, urban craftsmen and small farmers, made destitute by the state, sought the protection of these large landlords, whose estates grew in size and importance. The growth of latifundia was accompanied by the decline of cities and the transformation of independent peasants into virtual serfs.

These great estates were also new centers of political power, which the imperial government could not curb. A new society was taking shape in the late Roman Empire. The center of gravity shifted from the city to the landed estate, from the imperial bureaucrat to the local aristocrat. These developments epitomized the decay of ancient civilization and presaged a new era, the Middle Ages.

THE ROMAN LEGACY

Rome left the West a rich heritage, which endured for centuries. The idea of a world empire united by a common law and effective government never died. In the centuries following the collapse of Rome, people continued to be attracted to the idea of a unified and peaceful world-state. By preserving and adding to the philosophy, literature, science, and arts of ancient Greece, Rome strengthened the basic foundations of the Western cultural tradition. Latin, the language of Rome, lived on long after Rome perished. The Western church fathers wrote in Latin, and during the Middle Ages, Latin was the language of learning, literature, and law. From Latin came Italian, French, Spanish, Portuguese, and Romanian. Roman law, the quintessential expression of Roman genius, influenced church law and formed the basis of the legal codes of most European states. Finally, Christianity, the core religion of the West, was born within the Roman Empire and was greatly influenced by Roman law (the church's **canon law** owed much to Roman jurisprudence) and organization (the pope, head of the church and ruling from Rome, was the counterpart of the Roman emperor, and bishoprics were established in regions that coincided with the Empire's administrative structure). The ideal of a single Christian society embracing many different nationalities, so dear to medieval thinkers, was superimposed on the model of the Roman Empire.

❖   ❖   ❖

NOTES

1. Tacitus, *The Annals of Imperial Rome,* trans. Michael Grant (Baltimore: Penguin Books, 1959), 31.

2. Cited in David Magie, *Roman Rule in Asia Minor* (Princeton, N.J.: Princeton University Press, 1950), 490.

3. Sallust, *The Conspiracy of Cataline,* trans. S. A. Handford (Baltimore: Penguin Books, 1963), 193.

4. Excerpted in Naphtali Lewis and Meyer Reinhold, eds., *Roman Civilization, Sourcebook II: The Empire* (New York: Harper and Row, 1966), 136.

5. *From The Aeneid of Virgil,* trans. Allen Mandelbaum, copyright © 1971 by Allen Mandelbaum. Used by permission of Bantam Books, division of Random House, Inc.

6. *The Odes and Epodes of Horace,* trans. C. E. Bennett (Cambridge, Mass.: Harvard University Press, Loeb Classical Library, 1914), 109.

7. *The Art of Love and Other Love Books of Ovid* (New York: Grosset and Dunlap, The Universal Library, 1959), 117–118, 130–132, 135.

8. *The Satires of Juvenal,* trans. Hubert Creekmore (New York: Mentor Books, 1963), 58–61.

9. Adapted from Seneca, *The Epistles,* trans. Thomas Morell (London: W. Woodfall, 1786), vol. 1, epistle 47.

10. Marcus Aurelius, *Meditations,* trans. Maxwell Staniforth (Baltimore: Penguin Classics, 1964), bk. 2.

11. Cicero, *De Republica,* trans. Clinton Walker Keyes (Cambridge, Mass.: Harvard University Press, Loeb Classical Library, 1994), 211.

12. Excerpted in Lewis and Reinhold, eds., *Roman Civilization, Sourcebook II: The Empire,* 535, 539, 540, 547, 548.

13. Seneca, *The Epistles,* vol. 1, epistle 7.

14. Michael Rostovtzeff, *Rome* (New York: Oxford University Press, 1960), 322.

15. W. T. Stace, *A Critical History of Greek Philosophy* (London: Macmillan, 1924), 377.

16. Excerpted in Mortimer Chambers, ed., *The Fall of Rome* (New York: Holt, Rinehart and Winston, 1963), 45–46.

17. Quoted in Stephen Williams, *Diocletian and the Roman Recovery* (New York: Methuen, 1985), 101.

18. Excerpted in James Harvey Robinson, ed., *Readings in European History* (Boston: Ginn, 1904), 45.

19. Salvian, *On the Government of God,* trans. Eva M. Sanford (New York: Octagon, 1966), 141–142.

SUGGESTED READING

Boardman, John, et al., eds., *The Oxford History of the Classical World* (1986). Essays on all facets of Roman culture.

Christ, Karl, *The Romans* (1984). Good chapters on social and cultural life in the Empire.

Clarke, M. L., *The Roman Mind* (1968). Studies in the history of thought from Cicero to Marcus Aurelius.

Ferrill, Arther, *The Fall of the Roman Empire: The Military Explanation* (1986). Examines the deterioraton of the Roman Army.

Galinsky, Karl, *Augustan Culture* (1996). Weaves together the history and culture of the period.

Goldsworthy, Adrian, *How Rome Fell* (2009). An important recent study of Rome's decline, paying special attention to Rome's frequent internal wars starting in the third century.

Grant, Michael, *The Fall of the Roman Empire* (1990). A clearly written synthesis.

Heather, Peter, *The Fall of the Roman Empire: A New History of Rome and the Barbarians* (2006). A readable, thoughtful analysis.

Jenkyns, Richard, ed., *The Legacy of Rome: A New Appraisal* (1992). Essays on Rome's influence upon later centuries.

Southern, Pat, *Augustus* (1998). A helpful biography.

White, Lynn, ed., *The Transformation of the Roman World* (1973). A useful collection of essays on the transformation of the ancient world and the emergence of the Middle Ages.

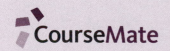

Chapter 8

Early Christianity: A World Religion

Christ Gives the Law to Saints Peter and Paul, fifth century, Santa Costanza, Rome. This mosaic portrays a haloed, beardless Christ bestowing the law in the manner of an emperor delivering an edict. (Vanni/Art Resource, N.Y.)

Focus Questions

1. How did Saint Paul transform a Jewish sect into a world religion?
2. What factors contributed to the triumph of Christianity in the Roman Empire?
3. How was early Christianity influenced by Judaism, Greek philosophy, and Hellenistic mystery religions?
4. What factors contributed to Christian anti-Judaism? What is the historical significance of the negative image of Jews and Judaism taught by early Christians?
5. What are the core features of Saint Augustine's theology?
6. What do the worldviews of Christianity and Greco-Roman humanism have in common? Why are they essentially different?

As confidence in human reason and hope for happiness in this world waned in the last centuries of the Roman Empire, a new outlook began to take hold. Evident in philosophy and in the popularity of Eastern religions, this viewpoint stressed escape from an oppressive world and communion with a higher reality. Christianity evolved and expanded within this setting of declining classicism and heightening otherworldliness. As one response to a declining Hellenism, Christianity offered a spiritually disillusioned Greco-Roman world a reason for living: the hope of personal immortality. The triumph of Christianity marked a break with classical antiquity and a new stage in the evolution of the West, for there was a fundamental difference between the classical and the Christian concepts of God, the individual, and the purpose of life.

THE ORIGINS OF CHRISTIANITY

A Palestinian Jew named Jesus was executed by the Roman authorities during the reign of Tiberius (A.D. 14–37), who succeeded Augustus. At the time, few people paid much attention to what proved to be one of the most pivotal events in world history. In the quest for the historical Jesus, scholars have stressed the importance of both his Jewishness and the religious ferment that prevailed in Palestine in the first century B.C. Jesus' ethical teachings are rooted in the moral outlook of the Old Testament prophets. Jesus, who prayed as a Jew, taught as a Jew to fellow Jews, and valued Jewish law and prophetic teachings, could only conceive of himself as a Jew. Hans Küng, the prominent Swiss student of religion, elaborates on this point.

> *Jesus was a Jew, a member of a small, poor, politically powerless nation living at the periphery of the Roman Empire. He was active among Jews and for Jews. His mother Mary, his father Joseph, his family, his followers were Jews. His name was Jewish (Hebrew Yeshu'a). . . . His Bible, his worship, his prayers were Jewish. In the situation at that time he could not have thought of any proclamation among the gentiles. His message was for the Jewish people, but for this people*

171

Chronology 8.1 ❖ Early Christianity

c. A.D. 29	Crucifixion of Jesus
c. 34–64	Missionary activity of Saint Paul
c. 66–70	The Gospel According to Mark is written
250–260	A decade of brutal persecution of Christians by the Romans
313	Constantine grants toleration of Christianity
c. 320	First convent is founded
325	Council of Nicaea rules that God and Christ are of the same substance, coequal and coeternal
391–392	Theodosius I prohibits public acts of pagan worship and the public profession of pagan religion; during his reign, Christianity becomes the state religion
430	Death of Saint Augustine
451	Council of Chalcedon rules that Christ is truly God and truly man
529	Saint Benedict founds monastery at Monte Cassino

in its entirety without any exception. From this basic fact it follows irrevocably that without Judaism there would be no Christianity. The Bible of the early Christians was the "Old Testament." The New Testament Scriptures became part of the Bible only by being appended to the Old. The gospel of Jesus Christ everywhere quite consciously presupposes the Torah and the Prophets.[1]

Judaism in the First Century B.C.

In the first century B.C., four principal social-religious parties, or sects, existed among the Palestinian Jews: Sadducees, Pharisees, Essenes, and Zealots. Composed of the upper stratum of Jewish society—influential landed gentry and hereditary priests, who controlled the temple in Jerusalem—the religiously conservative Sadducees insisted on a strict interpretation of **Mosaic Law** (Torah) and the perpetuation of temple ceremonies. Claiming to be the descendants of Sadok, the high priest of Solomon, Sadducees believed that they were maintaining the ancient Hebrew teachings concerning the Torah, which they interpreted literally. Rejecting the concepts of the resurrection of the dead and of an afterlife,

they held that God meted out rewards and punishments on earth. Challenging the aristocratic Sadducees, the Pharisees adopted a more liberal attitude toward Mosaic Law. They allowed discussion on varying interpretations of the Law and granted authority to oral tradition—an "oral Torah," which was communicated from one generation to another—as well as to written Scripture. Unlike the Sadducees, the Pharisees believed in life after death. The concept of personal immortality is barely mentioned in the Hebrew Scriptures. A later addition to Hebrew religious thought, probably acquired from Persia, the idea had gained wide acceptance by the first century A.D. The Pharisees had the support of most of the Jewish people. All later forms of Judaism developed from the Pharisees.

Besides the afterlife, another widely recognized idea in the first century B.C. was the belief in a **Messiah**, a redeemer chosen by God to liberate Israel from foreign rule. In the days of the Messiah, it was predicted, Israel would be free, the exiles would return, and the Jews would be blessed with peace, unity, and prosperity. The Messiah, in contrast to wicked Roman rulers, would govern justly and righteously.

The third religious party, the Essenes, established a semimonastic community near the Dead

Sarcophagus of Baebia Hertofila, Late Third Century, Museo Delle Terme, Rome. Symbolizing the Christian Eucharist, Jesus distributes the bread and the wine of the Last Supper to his disciples. (Scala/Art Resource N.Y.)

Sea. Like the Sadducees, they considered themselves to be the true descendants of Sadok, but they rejected the temple priests as corrupt. Only those priests affiliated with their sect were deemed pure. In 1947, leather scrolls in hermetically sealed cylinders were found near the Essene community of Qumran, about fourteen miles from Jerusalem, close to the Dead Sea. Dated from between c. 200 B.C. and A.D. 66–70, the *Wady Qumran Manuscripts*, commonly called the Dead Sea Scrolls, contain the oldest extant Hebrew manuscripts and also documents that are unique to the sect of the Essenes, founded by a man they refer to as "the Teacher of Righteousness." The Essenes believed in the physical resurrection of the body, like the Pharisees, but gave this doctrine a more compelling meaning by tying it to the immediate coming of God's kingdom. Certain that the Messiah was about to come, the Essenes saw themselves as the first generation of God's people.

By adding to our knowledge of Palestinian Judaism in the first century, the scrolls shed light on the period in which Christianity arose and the New Testament was written. Because of the similarity between many of the teachings of Jesus, particularly in the Sermon on the Mount, and the teachings of the Essenes' Teacher of Righteousness, some modern scholars have suggested that Jesus may have been a member of the Essene community. These scholars argue that the teachings of Jesus concerning the imminent coming of the kingdom of God parallel the messianic expectations of the Essenes.

The fourth sect, the Zealots, demanded that the Jews neither pay taxes to Rome nor acknowledge the authority of the Roman emperor. Devoted patriots, the Zealots engaged in acts of resistance to Rome, which culminated in the great revolt of A.D. 66–70, discussed in Chapter 7.

Jesus (c. 4 B.C.–c. A.D. 29) practiced his ministry within this context of Jewish religious-national expectations and longings. The hopes of Jesus' early followers encompassed a lower-class dissatisfaction with the aristocratic Sadducees; a Pharisee emphasis on prophetic ideals and the afterlife; an Essene preoccupation with the end-of-days, the nearness of God, and the need for repentance; and a conquered people's yearning for a Messiah who would liberate their land from Roman rule and establish God's reign.

Jesus: The Inner Person

Historians are able to speak with greater certainty about social-religious developments in Judea at the time of Jesus than they can about Jesus himself. In reconstructing what Jesus did and believed, the historian labors under a handicap, for the sources are few. Jesus himself wrote nothing, and nothing was written about him during his lifetime. In the generations following his death, both Roman and Jewish historians paid him scant attention. Consequently, virtually everything known about Jesus derives from the Bible's New Testament, which was written decades after Jesus' death by devotees seeking to convey a religious truth and to propagate a faith.

Modern historians in quest of the historical Jesus have rigorously and critically analyzed the New Testament; their analyses have provided some insights into Jesus and his beliefs. Nevertheless, much about Jesus remains obscure. Very little is known about his childhood. Like other Jewish youths, he was taught Hebrew religious-ethical thought and the many rules that governed daily life. At about the age of thirty, no doubt influenced by John the Baptist, who likely was once part of the Essene community, Jesus began to preach the coming of the reign of God and the need for people to repent—undergo moral transformation—so that they could enter God's kingdom. "Now after John was arrested, Jesus came into Galilee, preaching the gospel of God, and saying, 'The time is fulfilled, and the kingdom of God is at hand; repent, and believe in the gospel [good news]'" (Mark 1:14–15).[2]* This apocalyptic vision that the existing world was coming to an end and would be replaced by God's perfect kingdom had been preached by John the Baptist and other religious thinkers before him.

For Jesus, the coming of the kingdom was imminent; the process leading to the establishment of God's kingdom on earth had already begun. A new order would soon be established in which God would govern his people righteously and mercifully. Hence, the present moment became critical for him—a time for spiritual preparedness and repentance—because an individual's thoughts, goals, and actions would determine whether he or she

would gain entrance into the kingdom. People had to radically change their lives. They had to eliminate base, lustful, hostile, and selfish feelings; stop pursuing wealth and power; purify their hearts; and show their love for God and their fellow human beings.

Most likely Jesus' early followers perceived him as a prophet. Like the Hebrew prophets, Jesus saw ethics as the core of Mosaic Law: "So whatever you wish that men would do to you, do so to them; for this is the law and the prophets" (Matthew 7:12). Like the prophets, he denounced injustice and oppression, urged mercy and compassion, and expressed a special concern for the poor and downtrodden.

Jesus did not intend to lead his fellow Jews, who called him rabbi, away from their ancestral religion: "'Think not that I have come to abolish the law and the prophets; I have come not to abolish them but to fulfil them'" (Matthew 5:17). Although Jesus did not negate the Law, some of his interpretations offended Jewish leaders.

While not seeking to break with his past or to reject Jewish law, Jesus was distressed by the Judaism of his day. Following the prophets, the rabbis taught the Golden Rule, as well as God's love and mercy for his children, but it seemed to Jesus that these ethical considerations were being undermined by an exaggerated rabbinical concern with ritual, restrictions, and the fine points of the Law. Jesus believed that the center of Judaism had shifted from prophetic values to obedience to rules and prohibitions regulating the smallest details of daily life. (To Jewish leaders, of course, these detailed regulations governing eating, washing, Sabbath observance, family relations, and so forth were God's commands intended to sanctify all human activities.) To Jesus, such a rigid view of the Law distorted the meaning of prophetic teachings. Rules dealt only with an individual's visible behavior; they did not engage the person's inner being and lead to a moral transformation based on love, compassion, and selflessness. Observing the Lord's command to rest on the Sabbath—for example, by not eating an egg laid on Saturday or by not lifting a chair on that day—did not purify a person's heart.

For Jesus, the best way to realize the true meaning of Jewish law was through moral purity, which finds expression in a love for one's fellows. The inner person concerned Jesus, and it was an inner change that he sought: "For

*The biblical quotations in this chapter are taken from the Revised Standard Version of the Holy Bible.

from within, out of the heart of man, come evil thoughts, fornication, theft, murder, adultery, coveting, wickedness, deceit, licentiousness, envy, slander, pride, foolishness. All these evil things come from within, and they defile a man" (Mark 7:21–23). To Jesus, the spirit of Mosaic Law was more important than the letter of the Law; for him, right living and a pure loving heart were Judaism's true essence. With the fervor of a prophet, he urged a moral transformation of human character through a direct encounter between the individual and God. By preaching active love for others and genuine compassion for sufferers and by stressing a personal and intimate connection between the individual and God, Jesus associated himself more with the Hebrew prophetic tradition than with the Hebrew rituals, rules, and prohibitions that served to perpetuate a national and cultural tradition of a distinct people.

It was inevitable that Jewish scribes and priests, guardians of the faith, would regard Jesus, who had become a popular preacher, as a threat to ancient traditions. To Jewish leaders, he was a troublemaker and a subversive. They accused him of associating with social outcasts, sinners, and imperial tax collectors; undermining respect for the Sabbath by violating God's strict command prohibiting any form of labor on this holy day; proclaiming spiritual truth in his own name and on his own authority; and claiming that he, above all other men, had a special and intimate relationship with God and that by associating with him a sinner would be forgiven. Stated succinctly, Jewish leaders believed that Jesus was setting the authority of his person over Mosaic Law—an unpardonable blasphemy in their eyes. They saw Jesus as a false prophet who was leading the people astray.

The Romans, who ruled Palestine, had little interest in Jewish intrareligious disputes. They feared Jesus as a political agitator, as a charismatic leader who could ignite Jewish messianic expectations into a revolt against Rome. After Jewish leaders turned Jesus over to the Roman authorities, the Roman procurator, Pontius Pilate, sentenced him to death by crucifixion, a customary punishment for someone guilty of high treason. Jesus' execution was consistent with Roman policy in Judea, for the Romans routinely arrested and executed Jews suspected of inciting unrest against Roman rule. Inscribed on the cross on which he was crucified were the words "King of the Jews," a seemingly clear indication of why Pilate ordered his death. Although it is questionable if Jesus ever intended to challenge Roman authority, Pilate was taking no chances. He wanted to eliminate this popular leader before he might ignite a popular uprising.

Some Jews, believing that Jesus was an inspired prophet or even the long-awaited Messiah, had become his followers; the chief of these were the Twelve Disciples. At the time of Jesus' death, Christianity was not a separate religion but a small Hebrew sect with dim prospects for survival. What established the Christian movement and gave it strength was the belief of Jesus' followers that he was raised from the dead on the third day after he was buried. The doctrine of the resurrection enabled people to regard Jesus as more than a superb ethical soul, more than a righteous rabbi, more than a prophet, more than the Messiah; it made possible belief in Jesus as a divine **savior-god** who had come to earth to show people the way to heaven. For early Christians, Jesus' death and belief in his resurrection took on greater importance than his life. For these believers, Jesus the savior-god became the center of their emerging church.

There is no evidence that Jesus, who never preached to Gentiles, intended to establish a new church; this was accomplished by his followers. In the years immediately following the crucifixion, the religion of Jesus was confined almost exclusively to Jews, who could more appropriately be called Jewish-Christians. The word *Christian* came from a name given Jesus: *Christ* (the Lord's Anointed, the Messiah). Missionaries of this dissenting Christian movement within Judaism were called Apostles—those sent out to preach the gospel about Christ. They addressed themselves to Jews and to converts to Judaism who, because they did not adhere fully to Mosaic Law, were not wholly accepted by the Jewish community.

Before this new Jewish messianic movement could realize the universal implications of Jesus' teachings and become a world religion, as distinct from a reformist Jewish sect, it had to separate itself both ideologically and socially from the corporate body of Judaism. Instrumental in this

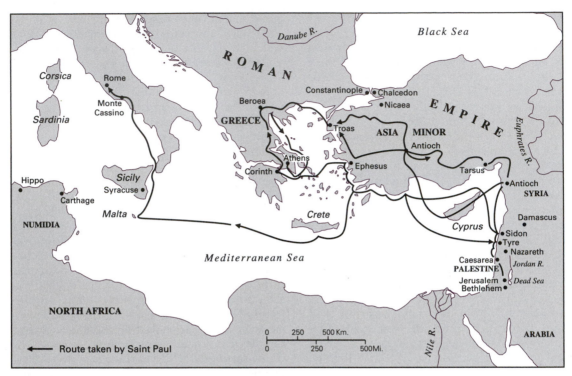

Map 8.1 **THE JOURNEYS OF SAINT PAUL** Paul, a Greek-speaking citizen of Rome and thus free to travel throughout the Empire, won converts to the new religion. (Copyright © 2013 Cengage Learning.)

development was the work of a Hellenized Jew named Saul, known to the world as Saint Paul.

Saint Paul: From a Jewish Sect to a World Religion

Saint Paul (A.D. c. 5–c. 67) came from the Greek city of Tarsus in southeastern Asia Minor. Originally called Saul, he belonged to the Diaspora, or the "Dispersion"—the millions of Jews living outside Palestine. Though the Jews of the Diaspora retained their ancient faith, they were also influenced by Greek culture. An example is the Alexandrian Jew Philo (c. 20 B.C.–c. A.D. 50), who tried to demonstrate that Hebrew Scriptures could be explained and justified in terms of Greek philosophy.

Non-Jews, or *Gentiles* (from Latin *gens,* or "nation"), who came into contact with Jews of

the Diaspora were often favorably impressed by Hebrew monotheism, ethics, and family life. Some Gentiles embraced Hebrew monotheism but refused to adhere to provisions of the Law requiring circumcision and dietary regulations. Among these Gentiles and non-Palestinian Jews who were greatly influenced by the Greco-Roman milieu, Jesus' Apostles would find receptive listeners.

Reared in Tarsus, a stronghold of Greek culture, Saul knew Greek well, but it is unlikely, despite a respectable writing style, that he had great knowledge of Greek literature, philosophy, and science. Trained in the outlook of the Pharisees, the young Saul went to Jerusalem to study with Rabban Gamaliel, an outstanding Pharisee teacher. In Jerusalem, Saul persecuted Jesus' followers in the time after his crucifixion, but then Saul underwent a spiritual transformation and became a follower of Jesus. Serving as a zealous missionary of Jewish

Saint Paul Mosaic from the Baptistry of the Arians, Ravenna, Italy. Inspired by Jesus' life and death, Paul taught that Jesus was a resurrected redeemer who held the promise of salvation for both Jews and Gentiles. (Scala/Art Resource N.Y.)

Christianity in the Diaspora, Saul, now called by his Roman name, Paul, preached to his fellow Jews in synagogues throughout the Roman Empire and wrote letters of advice back to the congregations he had started. Not having much success with his fellow Jews and recognizing that the Christian message applied to non-Jews as well, Paul urged spreading it to the Gentiles. His knowledge of Greek was of inestimable value in his missionary work with both Diaspora Jews and Gentiles.

Although he was neither the first nor the only missionary to the Gentiles, Paul was without doubt the most important. In the process of his missionary activity—and he traveled extensively throughout the Roman Empire—he formulated doctrines that represented a fundamental break with Judaism and became the heart of this new religion. Paul taught that all people, both Jews and Gentiles, were sinners as a consequence of Adam's original defiance of God; that Jesus had come to earth to save all people from sin and death; that by suffering and dying on the cross he had atoned for the sins of all and made it possible for people to have eternal life in heaven; and that by believing in Jesus people could gain this salvation. Alone, one was helpless, possessed by sin, unable to overcome one's wicked nature. Jesus was the only hope, said Paul. "Wretched man that I am! Who will deliver me from this body of death? Thanks be to God through Jesus Christ our Lord!" (Romans 7:24–25).

Christ: A Savior-God. To the first members of the Christian movement, Jesus was both a prophet who proclaimed the power and purpose of God and the Messiah whose coming heralded a new age. To Paul, Jesus was a resurrected redeemer who offered salvation to all peoples. Paul taught that the crucified Messiah had suffered and died for the sins of human beings; that through Jesus God had shown his love of humanity and revealed himself to all people, both Jews and Gentiles; and that this revelation supplanted the earlier one to the Jewish people.

Increasingly Jesus' followers came to view the sacrificed Messiah as a savior-god, indeed, as God incarnate. The idea of a slain savior-god was well known in the mystery religions of the eastern Mediterranean. Like these religions, Christianity initiated converts into the mysteries of the faith, featured a sacramental meal, and in time developed a priesthood. But the similarities between

Christianity and the mystery cults should not be overstressed since the differences are more profound.

Unlike the cultic gods, Jesus had actually lived in history. Hence, people could identify with him, which enormously increased the appeal of this new religion. Moreover, the deities of the mystery religions were killed against their will by evil powers. In Jesus, it was said, God had become a man and suffered pain and death out of compassion for human beings, to show a floundering humanity the way that would lead from sin to eternal life. This suffering Savior evoked from distressed human beings deep feelings of love and loyalty. Adherents of the mystery cults were not required to undergo a profound moral transformation. Christian converts, however, felt a compelling obligation to make their behavior, in the words of Paul, "worthy of the God who calls you" (Thessalonians 2:12) and to obey Jesus' command: "Be perfect as your heavenly Father is perfect" (Matthew 5:48). Finally, Christians, with their Jewish heritage, would tolerate no other divinity but God. Pagans, on the other hand, often belonged to more than one cult, or at least recognized the divinity of gods in other cults.

The Break with Judaism. In attempting to reach the Gentiles, Paul had to disentangle Christianity from a Jewish sociocultural context. Thus, he held that neither Gentile nor Jewish followers of Jesus were bound by the hundreds of rituals and rules that constitute Mosaic Law.* Paul saw no distinctive difference between Jew and Gentile; in his view, the ministry of Jesus was intended for all. As a consequence of Jesus' coming, Paul maintained, Mosaic regulations hindered missionary activity among the Gentiles. For Paul, not the Law of Moses but love of and faith in Christ was

the new avenue to God and salvation. The followers of Jesus fulfilled Hebrew history; they were the new Israel.

To Paul, the new Christian community was the true fulfillment of Judaism: it was the means to moral transformation and eternal life. The Jews regarded their faith as a national religion, bound inseparably with the history of their people. Paul saw the new Christian community not as a nation but as an oikoumene, a world community. Jesus fulfilled not only the messianic aspirations of the Jews but also the spiritual needs and expectations of all peoples. To this extent, Christianity shared in the universalism of the Hellenistic Age.

In preaching the doctrine of a risen Savior and insisting that Mosaic Law had been superseded, Paul (whatever his intentions) was breaking with his Jewish roots and transforming a Jewish sect into a new religion. Separating Christianity from Judaism enormously increased its appeal for non-Jews, who were attracted to Hebrew ethical monotheism but repelled by practices such as circumcision, dietary regulations, and other strict requirements of Mosaic Law. Paul built on Jesus' appeal for individual spiritual renewal and his empathy for all humanity (both also concerns of the ancient Hebrew prophets) to create a religion intended not for a people with its own particular history, culture, and land, but for all humankind.

THE SPREAD AND TRIUMPH OF CHRISTIANITY

By establishing Christianity's independence from Judaism and its practices, Paul made the new religion attractive to the Greco-Roman world. Originating in the first century, Christianity took firm root in the second, grew extensively in the third, and became the official religion of the Roman Empire at the end of the fourth century.

The Appeal of Christianity

The triumph of Christianity was related to a corresponding decline in the vitality of Hellenism and a shift in cultural emphasis—a movement from reason to emotion and revelation. Offering

*Paul's understanding of Mosaic Law is a matter of controversy. Some scholars argue that he regarded the Law as obsolete and broke with his ancestral faith. Other scholars, arguing that Paul did not forsake the Law, point to a famous passage: "Do we then nullify the law by this faith? Not at all! Rather we uphold the law" (Romans 3:31). Paul, who continually described himself as a Pharisee, lived an observant life and celebrated Jewish festivals. For these scholars, Paul never stopped revering the Torah but taught that Jesus, the Messiah, fulfilled the Torah's higher purpose—the biblical prophecy of the Messiah's coming.

comforting solutions to the existential problems of life and death, religion demonstrated a greater capacity than reason to stir human hearts. Hellenism had invented the tools of rational thought, but the power of mythical thought was never entirely subdued. By the Late Roman Empire, science and philosophy were unable to compete with mysticism, myth, and the divine.

This deterioration of the classical outlook was demonstrated by the growing popularity of Eastern religions and the spiritualization of philosophy. Mystery cults, which promised personal salvation, were spreading and gaining followers. Astrology and magic, which offered supernatural explanations for the operations of nature, were also popular. Stoicism and Epicureanism were performing a religious function by trying to help individuals overcome emotional stress, while Neo-Platonists yearned for a mystical union with the One. This recoil from rational and worldly values helped prepare the way for Christianity. In a culturally stagnating and spiritually troubled Greco-Roman world, Christianity gave new meaning to life and offered new hope to disillusioned men and women.

During the Hellenistic Age, the individual had struggled with the problems of alienation and lack of community. With the decline of the independent city-state, the individual searched for a new frame of reference, a new form of attachment. The Roman Empire represented one possible allegiance. But for many people, it was not a satisfying relationship; the individual found it difficult to be devoted to a political organization so vast, remote, and impersonal. The Christian message of a divine Savior and a concerned Father, as well as of brotherly love, inspired men and women who were dissatisfied with the world of the here and now—who felt no attachment to city or empire, derived no inspiration from philosophy, and suffered from a profound sense of loneliness. Christianity offered the individual what the city and the Roman world-state could not: an intensely personal relationship with God, an intimate connection with a higher world, and membership in a community of the faithful who cared for one another.

Stressing the intellect and self-reliance, Greco-Roman thought did not provide for the emotional needs of many people. Christianity addressed itself to this deficiency in the Greco-Roman outlook. Particularly those who were poor, oppressed, or enslaved were attracted to the personality, life, death, and resurrection of Jesus, his love for all, and his concern for suffering humanity. They found spiritual sustenance in a religion that offered a hand in love and taught that a person need not be well-born, rich, educated, or talented to be worthy, that God draws no distinction between the lowly poor and enslaved and the mightiest aristocrats. To people burdened with misfortune and terrified by death, Christianity held the promise of eternal life, a kingdom of heaven where they would be comforted by God the Father. Thus, Christianity gave to the common person what the aristocratic values of Greco-Roman civilization generally did not: hope, a sense of dignity, and inner strength. By and large, classical philosophy offered little compassion for the sufferer, but the cardinal principle of Christianity was that Jesus had endured earthly torments because of his love for all human beings and that even the lowliest could be redeemed.

Christianity succeeded not only through the appeal of its message but also through the power of its organization. To retain the devotion of the faithful, win new converts, protect itself from opponents, and administer its services, Christianity developed an organized body of followers. This body became the Christian church, which grew into a strong organization uniting the faithful. To city dwellers—lonely, alienated, disillusioned with public affairs; stranded mortals groping for a sense of community—the church that called its members "brother" and "sister" filled an elemental need of human beings to belong. Another attraction for Christian converts was the absence of painful or expensive initiation rites, such as those required for entrance into Mithraism, a leading rival (see "The Spread of Mystery Religions" in Chapter 7). Unlike Mithraism, the church also welcomed women converts, who were often the first to join and who brought their menfolk after them. Among the reasons that the church drew women was its command to husbands to treat their wives kindly, remain faithful, and provide for the children. Moreover, in the eyes of God, women were spiritually equal with men. The church also won new converts and retained the loyalty of its members by furnishing social services for the poor and infirm; welcoming slaves, criminals, sinners, and other outcasts; and offering community and comfort during difficult times.

Blandina

During the reign of the emperor Marcus Aurelius, a number of Christians in Lyons, Gaul, including Blandina, a frail young slave, were imprisoned and accused of engaging in cannibalism and incest. The Roman authorities tortured Blandina, hoping that she would implicate the Christian community in these abhorrent crimes. Despite the torments inflicted on her, Blandina would not speak falsely against her fellow Christians. The historian Eusebius described her terrible ordeal:

> Blandina was filled with such power that those who took it in turns to subject her to every kind of torture from morning to night were exhausted by their efforts and confessed themselves beaten—they could think of nothing else to do to her. They were amazed that she was still breathing, for her whole body was mangled and her wounds gaped; they declared that torment of any one kind was enough to part soul and body, let alone a succession of torments of such extreme severity. But the blessed woman, wrestling magnificently, grew in strength as she proclaimed her faith, and found refreshment, rest, and insensibility to her sufferings in uttering the words: "I am a Christian: we do nothing to be ashamed of."

For several days Blandina had to watch other Christians being whipped, roasted, and set upon by wild beasts in the amphitheater. Finally, after surviving

---

The ability of an evolving Christianity to assimilate elements from Greek philosophy and even from the mystery religions also contributed in no small measure to its growth. By becoming infused with Greek philosophy, Christianity could present itself in terms intelligible to those versed in Greek learning and thus attract educated people. Philosophers who converted to Christianity proved to be able defenders of their newly adopted faith. Because some Christian doctrines (the risen savior-god, the virgin and her child, life after death, communion with the divine), practices (purification through baptism), and holy days (December 25 was the birth date of the god Mithras) either paralleled or were adopted from the mystery religions, it became relatively easy to win converts from these rivals.

Christianity and Rome

At first, the Roman government, which was generally tolerant of religions, did not interfere much with the Christian movement. In fact, Christianity benefited in many ways from its association with the Roman Empire. Christian missionaries, among them some of the Twelve Disciples, who were the original followers of Christ, traveled throughout the Empire over roads and across seas made safe by Roman arms. The common Greek dialect, Koine, spoken in most parts of the Empire, facilitated the missionaries' task. Had the Mediterranean world been fractured into separate and competing states, the spread of Christianity might well have faced an insurmountable obstacle. The universalism of the Roman Empire, which made citizenship available to peoples of many nationalities, prepared the way for the universalism of Christianity, which welcomed membership from all nations. Early Christians grafted onto Rome's imperial mission a spiritual, evangelical cause: "Go ye therefore and teach all nations" (Matthew 28:19).

As the number of Christians increased, Roman officials began to fear the Christians as subversives, preaching allegiance to God and not to Rome, and as a self-absorbed sect that did not want to fit into the Empire. To many Romans, Christians were disloyal citizens, strange people who would not accept the state gods, would not engage in sacrifices to Roman divinities, scorned gladiatorial contests, stayed away from public baths, glorified nonviolence, refused to honor deceased emperors as gods, and worshiped a crucified criminal as Lord. Romans

similar torments, she was "dropped into a basket and thrown to a bull. Time after time the animal tossed her, but she was indifferent now to all that happened to her, because of her hope and sure hold on all that her faith meant, and of her communing with Christ. Then she, too, was sacrificed, while the heathen themselves admitted that never yet had they known a woman suffer so much or so long."*

**Eusebius, *The History of the Church from Christ to Constantine,* trans. G. A. Williamson (New York: New York University Press, 1966), 196, 202.*

ultimately found in Christians a scapegoat for the ills burdening the Empire, such as famines, plagues, and military reverses. Were not these afflictions divine punishment for Christians' refusal to honor ancestral gods and traditions? In an effort to stamp out Christianity, emperors occasionally resorted to persecution. Christians were imprisoned, beaten, starved, beheaded, burned alive, torn apart by wild beasts in the arena for the amusement of the Romans, and crucified. The authorities freed accused Christians who agreed to renounce their faith. But many Christians embraced the opportunity for martyrdom; they believed they were reenacting the passion of Jesus, who had sacrificed himself for humanity.

However, the early persecutions, beginning with those incited under Emperor Nero in A.D. 64, were local, did not cause much loss of life, and were too sporadic to impede the growth of Christianity. The persecutions in the mid-third century and during Diocletian's rule caused the brutal deaths of many Christians but did not last long enough to seriously threaten the new religion. Actually, they strengthened the determination of most of the faithful and won new converts, who were awed by the extraordinary courage of the martyrs willingly dying for their faith.

Unable to crush Christianity by persecution, Roman emperors decided to gain the support of the growing number of Christians within the Empire. In A.D. 313, Constantine, probably genuinely attracted to Christianity, issued the Edict of Milan, granting toleration to Christians. By allowing the free flow of Christian teachings and instituting legislation favorable to the church, Constantine and his successors accelerated the growth of Christianity and the Christianization of the Empire. By A.D. 392, Theodosius I had made Christianity the state religion of the Empire and declared the worship of pagan gods illegal. With Christianity in power, persecution did not end, but its target shifted to pagans, Jews, and Christians with unorthodox views. The polytheistic religions of the Roman world did not claim to possess an exhaustive truth—they did not assert that a particular god or a particular form of worship should prevail over all others and that wrongful religious expressions should be rooted out. People were relatively free to select their own credo and engage in their own acts of worship. Christianity, in contrast, possessing an exclusive attitude toward truth, felt compelled to cleanse society of false gods and beliefs. Such an outlook often led Christians to view nonbelievers as enemies of God deserving of punishment. Thus, mobs, often driven by fanatic clergy, hurled non-Christian writings into bonfires, destroyed pagan altars and sacred images, and squelched pagan rites and festivals. Emperors, often pushed by the clergy, passed decrees calling for fining, imprisoning, torturing, and executing adherents of pagan cults.

Christianity and Greek Philosophy

Christianity synthesized both the Hebrew and the Greco-Roman traditions. Having emerged from Judaism, Christianity assimilated Hebrew monotheism and prophetic morality and retained the Old Testament as the Word of God. Without this Hebraic foundation, Christianity cannot be understood. As the new religion evolved, it also assimilated elements of Greek philosophy. The ability to combine a historic Judaic monotheism, which had many admirers in the Gentile world, with Greek rational philosophy was a crucial reason for Christianity's triumph in the Roman Empire. But there was a struggle between conservatives, who wanted no dealings with pagan philosophy, and those

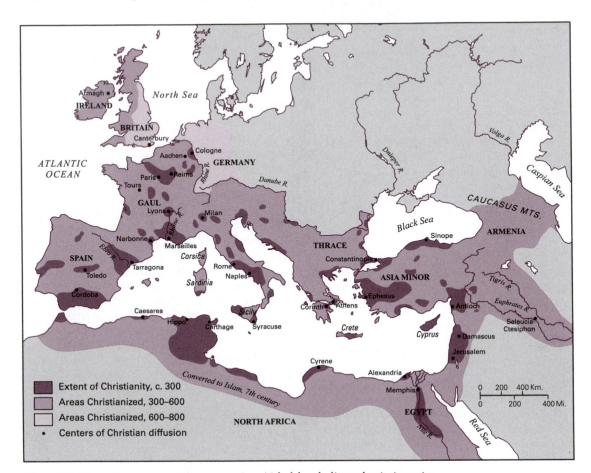

Map 8.2 THE SPREAD OF CHRISTIANITY Aided by dedicated missionaries, Christianity expanded throughout the Mediterranean world and later into Germanic lands. (Copyright © 2013 Cengage Learning.)

believers who recognized the value of Greek thought to Christianity.

To conservative church fathers—early Christian writers whose works are accepted as authoritative by the church—classical philosophy erred completely because it did not derive from divine revelation. As the final statement of God's truth, Christianity superseded both pagan philosophy and pagan religions. According to the church fathers, the simple peasant who accepted Christ possessed more knowledge than the most learned philosopher who did not. These conservatives feared that studying classical authors would contaminate Christian morality (did not Plato propose a community of wives, and did not the dramatists treat violent passions?) and promote heresy (was not classical literature replete with references to pagan gods?). For these church fathers, there could be no compromise between Greek philosophy and Christian revelation. For them, faith was more reliable than all the demonstrations of human reason. "What indeed has Athens to do with Jerusalem?" asked Tertullian (A.D. 150–225). "With our faith, we desire no further belief. For this is our faith that there is nothing which we ought to believe besides."[3]

Some church fathers, including several who had a Greek education, resisted this anti-intellectualism. Defending the value of studying classical literature, they maintained that such literature, if properly taught, could aid in the moral development of children because it presented many examples of virtuous deeds. Some church fathers claimed that Greek philosophy contained a dim glimmer of God's truth, a pre-Christian insight into divine wisdom. Christ had corrected and fulfilled an insight reached by the philosophical mind. Knowledge of Greek philosophy, they also contended, helped Christians explain their beliefs logically and argue intelligently with pagan critics of Christian teachings. Thus, Clement of Alexandria (c. A.D. 150–220) brought reason to the support of faith in his attempt to make Christianity more intellectually respectable in his world.

> *Rather, philosophy is a clear image of truth, a divine gift to the Greeks. Before the advent of the Lord, philosophy helped the Greeks to attain righteousness, and is now conducive to piety, it supplies a preparatory teaching for those who will later embrace the faith. God is the cause of all good things: some given primarily in the form of the Old and the New Testament; others are the consequence of philosophy. Perchance too philosophy was given to the Greeks primarily till the Lord should call the Greeks to serve him. Thus philosophy acted as a schoolmaster to the Greeks, preparing them for Christ, as the laws of the Jews prepared them for Christ.*[4]

Utilizing the language and categories of Greek philosophy, Christian intellectuals transformed Christianity from a simple ethical creed into a theoretical system, a theology. Greek philosophy enabled Christians to explain rationally God's existence and revelation in order to show that Christian teachings did not violate the laws of logic. Christ was depicted as the divine or incarnate Logos (reason) in human form. Educated believers could argue that the fundamental principles that Greek philosophers maintained operated in the universe were established by God the Father. The Stoic teaching that all people are fundamentally equal because they share in universal reason could be formulated in Christian terms: all are united in Christ. Christians could interpret the church to be the true fulfillment of the Stoic idea of a polity embracing the entire world. Stoic ethics, which stressed moderation, self-control, and brotherhood,

could be assimilated by Christian revelation. Particularly in Platonism, which drew a distinction between a world perceived by the senses and a higher order—a transcendent world that should be the central concern of human existence—Christian thinkers found a congenial vehicle for expressing Christian beliefs. The perfect and universal Forms, or Ideas, which Plato maintained were the true goal of knowledge and the source of ethical standards, were held by Christians to exist in God's mind.

That Greek philosophy had a strong hold on church doctrine was immensely important, for it meant that rational thought, the priceless achievement of the Greek mind, was not lost. But Greek philosophy had to sacrifice its ability to think freely to the needs of Christian revelation: reason had to serve faith. And in any conflict between reason and faith, faith would prevail. Although Christianity made use of Greek philosophy, Christian truth ultimately rested on faith, not reason. As Tertullian stated, it is precisely because faith in a crucified Lord contradicted all human logic that he would believe: "And the Son of God died; it is by all means to be believed, because it is absurd. And He was buried, and rose again; the fact is certain because it is impossible."[5]

THE GROWTH OF CHRISTIAN ORGANIZATION, DOCTRINE, AND ATTITUDES

Early in its history, the church gradually developed along hierarchical lines. Those members of the Christian community who had the authority to preside over the celebration of the Mass—breaking bread and offering wine as Christ had done in the Last Supper—were called either priests or bishops. Gradually, the designation *bishop* was reserved for the one clergyman in the community with the authority to resolve disputes over doctrines and practices. Regarded as the successors to Jesus' Twelve Disciples, bishops supervised religious activities within their regions. The most influential bishops ministered to the leading cities of the Empire: Rome, Alexandria, Antioch, and Milan. In creating a diocese that was supervised by a bishop and had its center in a leading city, the church adapted Roman administrative techniques.

The Primacy of the Bishop of Rome

The bishop of Rome, later called the *pope* ("father"), claimed primacy over the other bishops, maintaining that the Apostle Peter founded the Roman see (official seat of authority) and that both Peter and Paul were martyred in Rome. Moreover, as the traditional capital of the Empire, Rome seemed the logical choice to serve as the center of the church.

In developing the case for their supremacy over the church organization, bishops of Rome increasingly referred to the famous New Testament passage in which Jesus says to his disciple Simon (also called Peter): "'And I tell you, you are Peter, and on this rock I will build my church'" (Matthew 16:18). Because *Peter* in Greek means "rock" (*petra*), it was argued that Christ had chosen Peter to succeed him as ruler of the universal church. It was commonly accepted that Saint Peter had established a church in Rome and was martyred there, so it was argued further that the Roman bishop inherited the power that Christ had passed on to Peter. Thus, the argument continued, the bishop of Rome held a unique office: of all the bishops, only he had inherited the powers originally granted by Christ to Peter. Because the Apostles had been subordinate to Peter, so too must the bishops defer to Peter's successor.

The Rise of Monasticism

Some devout Christians committed to living a perfect Christian life were distressed by the wickedness of the world about them, including the moral laxity of those clergy who chased after wealth and pomp. Seeking to escape from the agonies and corruptions of this world, some ardent Christians withdrew to deserts and mountains in search of solitude and spiritual renewal. In their zeal to emulate Jesus' self-denial, they sometimes practiced extreme forms of asceticism: self-flogging, wearing spiked corsets, eating only herbs, or living for years atop a column high above the ground.

Gradually, colonies of these hermits sprang up, particularly in Egypt and Syria; in time, the leaders of these monastic communities drew up written rules for prayer and work. Saint Basil (c. 329–c. 379), a Greek who was bishop of Caesarea in Cappadocia (eastern Asia Minor), established the rules that became the standard for monasteries in the East. Basil required monks to refrain from bodily abuses and to engage in manual labor. Through farming, weaving, and construction, monks could make a monastery self-supporting and have the means to assist the needy. Aware of the lure of materialism and selfishness, Basil forbade his monks to own personal property other than clothing and insisted that they spend much of their time in silence.

The monastic ideal spread from east to west. The principal figure in the shaping of **monasticism** in the West was Saint Benedict (c. 480–c. 543), who founded a monastery at Monte Cassino, Italy, in 529. The Rule of Saint Benedict (see Primary Source box) required the monks to live in poverty and to study, labor, and obey the abbot, the head of the monastery. They had to pray often, work hard, talk little, and surrender private property. In imposing discipline and regulations, Benedict eliminated the excessive and eccentric individualism of the early monks. Benedict demonstrated the same genius for administration that the Romans had shown in organizing and governing their empire. Benedict's rule became the standard for monasteries throughout Western Europe.

Scriptural Tradition and Doctrinal Disputes

The earliest surviving Christian writings are Paul's Epistles, written some twenty-five to thirty years after the death of Jesus. Jesus' sayings were preserved by word of mouth. Sometime around A.D. 66–70, about forty years after the crucifixion, Saint Mark formulated the Christian message from this oral tradition and perhaps from some material that had been put in writing earlier. Later, Saint Matthew and Saint Luke, relying heavily on Mark's account, wrote somewhat longer Gospels. The Gospels of Mark, Matthew, and Luke are called *synoptic* because their approach to Jesus is very similar. The remaining Gospel, written by Saint John around A.D. 110, varies significantly from the synoptic Gospels. The Gospel of John uses the Stoic concept of Logos to present Jesus as the divine being. John identifies Jesus with the eternal word, or Logos, which became the incarnate Son of God: "In the beginning was the Word and the Word was with God, and the Word was God. . . . And the Word became Flesh and dwelt among us"

(John 1:1, 14). The synoptic Gospels; the Gospel According to Saint John; Acts of the Apostles; the twenty-one Epistles, including those written by Saint Paul; and Revelation constitute the twenty-seven books of the Christian New Testament. Christians also accepted the Old Testament of the Hebrews as God's Word. The New Testament was written not by historians with the critical spirit of a Thucydides or a Polybius but by men moved by the fervor of faith. Under these circumstances, it is understandable that it contains discrepancies, some nonhistorical legends, and polemics.

The early Christians had a Bible and a clergy to teach it. But the Holy Writ could be interpreted differently by equally sincere believers, and controversies over doctrine threatened the loose unity of the early church. The most important controversy concerned how people viewed the relationship between God and Christ. Arius (250–336), a Greek priest in Alexandria, led one faction; he denied the complete divinity of Christ, one of the basic tenets of the church. To Arius, Christ was more than man but less than God; the Father and the Son did not possess the same nature, or essence. Arius said that there was no permanent union between God and Christ; the Father alone is eternal and truly God.

The Council of Nicaea (325), the first assembly, or ecumenical council, of bishops from all parts of the Roman world, was called to settle the controversy. The council condemned Arius and ruled that God and Christ were of the same substance, coequal and coeternal. The position adopted at Nicaea became the basis of the Nicene Creed, which remains the official doctrine of the church. Although Arianism, the name given the heresy of Arius, won converts for a time, it eventually died out, helped along by persecution. This meant that the Catholic church alone would shape the distinctive character of the new civilization that emerged in the Middle Ages.

Christianity and Society

Although salvation was their ultimate aim, Christians still had to dwell within the world and deal with its imperfections. In the process, Christian thinkers challenged some of the mores of Greco-Roman society and formulated attitudes that would endure for centuries.

Influenced by passages in the New Testament that condemned acts of revenge and the shedding of blood, and concerned only with the heavenly kingdom, some early Christians refused military service. Others, however, held that in a sinful world, defense of the state was necessary, and without concealment or apology they served in the army. With the barbarians menacing the borders, Christian officials could not advocate nonviolence. Christian theorists began to argue that under certain circumstances—to punish injustice or to restore peace—war was just. But even such wars must not entail unnecessary violence.

Christians denounced the gladiatorial combats and contests between men and beasts as bloodlust and murder, and regarded attendance at these spectacles as tantamount to participating in murder. Nevertheless, these spectacles persisted even after the majority of the population had converted to Christianity. When the games finally ended, it was probably due more to the growing poverty of the western Empire than to the Christian conscience.

Numerous women joined the Christian movement and a number suffered martyrdom, but positions of authority were reserved for men, including ordination as priests. The early Christian view of women was rooted in the patriarchal tradition of Jewish society. Paul subjected the wife to her husband's authority. "Wives, be subject to your husbands, as to the Lord. For the husband is the head of the wife as Christ is the head of the church" (Ephesians 5:22–23). Paul wanted women to remain quiet at church meetings. "If there is anything they desire to know, let them ask their husbands at home. For it is shameful for a woman to speak in church" (1 Corinthians 14:35). But Paul also held that all are baptized in Christ: "There is neither Jew nor Greek, there is neither slave nor free, there is neither male nor female; for you are all one in Christ Jesus" (Galatians 3:28). Consequently, both sexes were subject to divine law, and both possessed moral autonomy. The early church held to strict standards on sexual matters. It condemned adultery and esteemed virginity pledged for spiritual reasons.

Christians waged no war against slavery, which was widely practiced and universally accepted in the ancient world. Paul commanded slaves to obey their masters, and many Christians, including leaders of local churches, were slave owners. Although

Saint Benedict of Nursia: The Christian Way of Life

In the following selection from his monastic book of rules, Saint Benedict of Nursia advises his monks on the attitudes and conduct necessary to live a virtuous Christian life.

What Are the Instruments of Good Works?

In the first place, to love the Lord God with the whole heart, whole soul, whole strength, then his neighbor as himself.

Then not to kill, not to commit adultery, not to steal, not to covet, not to bear false witness, to honor all men, and what anyone would not have done to him, let him not do to another. To deny himself, that he may follow Christ, to chasten the body, to renounce luxuries, to love fasting. To relieve the poor, to clothe the naked, to visit the sick, to bury the dead, to help in tribulation, to console the afflicted.

To make himself a stranger to the affairs of the world, to prefer nothing before the love of Christ, not to give way to anger, not to bear any grudge, not to harbour deceit in the heart, not to forsake charity. Not to swear, lest haply he perjure himself, to utter truth from his heart and his mouth. Not to return evil for evil, not to do injuries, but rather to bear them patiently, to love his enemies, not to curse against those that curse him, but rather to bless them, to endure persecution for righteousness' sake. Not to be proud, not given to wine, not gluttonous, not addicted to sleep, not slothful, not given to murmur, not a slanderer. To commit his hope to God; when he sees anything good in himself to attribute it to God, and not to himself, but let him always know that which is evil is his own doing; and impute it to himself. To fear the day of judgment, to dread hell, to desire eternal life with all spiritual longing, to have the expectation of death every day before his eyes. To watch over his actions at all times, to know certainly that in all places the eye of God is upon him; those evil thoughts which come into his heart to dash to pieces on Christ, and to make them known to his spiritual senior. To keep his lips from evil and wicked discourse, not to be fond of much talking, not to speak vain words or such as provoke laughter, not to love much or violent laughter. To give willing attention to the sacred readings, to pray frequently every day, to confess his past sins to God, in prayer, with tears and groanings; from thence forward to reform as to those sins.

Not to fulfill the desires of the flesh, to hate his own will, in all things to obey the commands of the abbot, even though he himself (which God forbid) should do otherwise, remembering our Lord's commands: "What they say, do; but what they do, do ye not." Not to desire to be called a saint before he is one, but first to be one that he may be truly called one; every day to fulfill the commands of God in his deeds, to love chastity, to hate no one, not to have jealousy or envy, not to love contention, to avoid self-conceit; to reverence seniors, to love juniors, to pray for enemies in the love of Christ, to be reconciled with his adversary, before the going down of the sun, and never to despair of the mercy of God. . . .

Question for Analysis

1. According to Saint Benedict, how should a Christian lead a virtuous life?

Oliver J. Thatcher, ed., *Library of Original Sources* (Milwaukee: University Research Extension, 1907), 4:133–134.

Christians did not try to alter the legal status of slaves, they did teach that slaves, too, were children of God; they sought their conversion; they urged owners not to treat slaves harshly; and they considered it a virtue for owners to free slaves. In the modern world, the Christian teaching that all persons are spiritually equal before God would arouse some Christians to fight for the abolition of slavery.

Christian theorists condemned sex outside of marriage, adultery, prostitution, homosexuality, and abortion, and insisted that the sex drive should be confined to reproduction, as Clement of Alexandria wrote: "Yet marriage in itself merits esteem and the highest approval, for the Lord wished men to 'be fruitful and multiply.' He did not tell them, however, to act like libertines, nor did He intend them to surrender themselves to pleasure as though born only to indulge in sexual relations. . . . To indulge in intercourse without intending children is to outrage nature."[6]

Christianity and the Jews

Increasingly, Christians identified opponents—Jews, pagans, and heretics—with Satan, the fallen angel, and viewed conflicts in a moral context: a struggle between God's faithful and Satan's servants. Over the centuries, the view that they were participants in a cosmic struggle between good and evil led Christians to demonize adversaries, a practice that exacerbated hatred and justified mistreatment and even massacre. Christian attitudes and behavior toward Jews poignantly illustrate this point.

Numerous links connect early Christianity and Judaism. Jesus himself and his earliest followers, including the Twelve Disciples, were Jews who were faithful to Jewish law. Jesus attended synagogue and frequently quoted the Hebrew Scriptures, which to him and his disciples was the authoritative word of God, to support a particular viewpoint. Jesus' message was first spread in synagogues throughout the Roman Empire. Early Christianity's affirmation of the preciousness of the human being, created in God's image; its belief that God rules history; its awareness of human sinfulness; its call for repentance; and its appeal to God for forgiveness are rooted in Judaism. The Christian reference to God as a "merciful Father" derives from Jewish prayer. Also rooted in Judaism are the moral norms

proclaimed by Jesus in the Sermon on the Mount and on other occasions. For example, "Thou shalt love thy neighbor as thyself" was the motto of the Jewish sage Hillel, a contemporary of Jesus, who founded a school. The great value that the Torah gives to charity was inherited by Christianity. Jesus' use of parables to convey his teachings, the concept of the Messiah, respect for the Sabbath, and congregational worship also stem from Judaism. Moreover, Christians viewed the Hebrew Scriptures as God's Word. In addition, a deep understanding of the New Testament requires knowledge of the Old Testament, for its thought and language permeate the Christian Gospels.

However, over the years, particularly after more and more non-Jews became followers of Christ, Christians forgot or devalued the Jewish roots of their faith, and some thinkers began to show hostility toward Judaism and Jews that had tragic consequences in later centuries. Several factors fueled this anti-Judaism: resentment against Jews for their refusal to embrace Jesus; the polemics of the Jewish establishment against followers of Jesus; the role in Jesus' death ascribed to Jews by the New Testament; resentment against those Christians who Judaized, that is, continued to observe Jewish festivals and the Jewish Sabbath, regard the synagogue as holy, and practice circumcision; and anger that Judaism remained a vital religion, for this undermined the conviction that Christianity was the fulfillment of Judaism and the one true faith.

What made Christian anti-Judaism particularly ominous was the effort of some theologians to demonize the Jewish people. The myth emerged that the Jews, murderers of the incarnate God who embodied all that was good, were a cursed people, children of the Devil, whose suffering was intended by God. Thus, Origen (c. 185–c. 251) maintained that "the blood of Jesus [falls] not only upon those who lived then but also upon all generations of the Jewish people following afterwards until the end of the world."[7] In the late fourth century, John Chrysostom described Jews as "inveterate murderers, destroyers, men possessed by the Devil. . . . [T]hey murder their offspring and immolate them to the devil." The synagogue, he said, was "the domicile of the devil as is also the soul of the Jews." Their rites are "criminal and impure," and their religion is "a disease." For the "odious assassination of Christ," there is "no expiation possible, . . . no pardon." Jews will live "under the yoke of servitude without end."[8] Since the Devil was very real to early and medieval Christians, the Jew became identified with evil. Christians developed a mindset, concludes the Reverend Robert A. Everett, that was "unable to see anything positive in Judaism. . . . Judaism and the Jewish people came to have no real value for Christians except as a negative contrast to Christianity."[9] Because of this "teaching of contempt" and the "diabolization of the Jew," the Christian ethic of love did not extend to Jews.

> *Once it is established that God has cursed the Jews, how can one argue that Christians should love them? If Jews have been fated by God to have . . . a long history of suffering, who are Christians to alter their history by doing anything to relieve Jewish suffering? The theology of victimization thus precludes Christian love as a basis of relating to Jews.*[10]

The diabolization of the Jew, which bore no relationship to the actual behavior of Jews or to their highly ethical religion, and the "theology of victimization," which held that the Jews were collectively and eternally cursed for denying Christ, became powerful myths, which, over the centuries, poisoned Christians' hearts and minds against Jews, spurring innumerable humiliations, persecutions, and massacres by Christians who believed that their actions were pleasing to God. Alongside this hatred of Jews and antipathy to their suffering, there also evolved the belief that the Jews, faithless and perfidious though they were, should be permitted to survive, for their dispersal among the nations was evidence of divine punishment and the truth of Christianity. Moreover, one day the Jews would see the light and convert to the true faith.

SAINT AUGUSTINE: THE CHRISTIAN WORLDVIEW

During the early history of Christianity, learned fathers of the church explained and defended church teachings. Most of the leading early fathers wrote in Greek, but in the middle of the fourth century, three great Latin writers—Saint Jerome, Saint Ambrose, and Saint Augustine—profoundly influenced the course of Christianity in the West.

As a youth, Saint Jerome (c. 340–420) studied Latin literature in Rome. Throughout his life, he remained an admirer of Cicero, Virgil, Lucretius, and other great Latin writers, and he defended the study of classical literature by Christians. Criticized for attacking the luxurious living and laxness of the clergy, he left Rome and established a monastery near Bethlehem, where he devoted himself to prayer and study. His greatest achievement was the translation of the Old and New Testaments from Hebrew and Greek into Latin. Jerome's text, the common, or Vulgate, version of the Bible, became the official edition of the Bible for the Western church.

Saint Ambrose (340–397), bishop of Milan, Italy, urged clerics not to pursue wealth but to practice humility and avoid favoring the rich over the poor. Ambrose sought to defend the autonomy of the church against the power of the state. Emperors are not the judges of bishops, he wrote. His dictum that "the Emperor is within the church, not above it" became a cardinal principle of the medieval church.

The most important Christian theoretician in the Late Roman Empire was Saint Augustine (354–430), bishop of Hippo, in North Africa. Born in the North African province of Numidia, Augustine attended school at Carthage, where he studied the Latin classics. Struggling to find meaning in a world that abounded with evil, Augustine turned to Manichaeism, an Eastern religious philosophy whose central doctrine was the struggle of the universal forces of light and good against those of darkness and evil. But Augustine still felt spiritually restless. In Milan, inspired by the sermons of Ambrose, he abandoned Manichaeism and devoted his life to following Christ's teachings. After serving as a priest, he was appointed bishop of Hippo in 395. At the turn of the fifth century, when the Greco-Roman worldview was disintegrating and the Roman world-state was collapsing, Augustine wrote his greatest and most influential work, *The City of God*. He became the chief architect of the Christian outlook that succeeded a dying classicism.

In 410, when Augustine was in his fifties, Visigoths sacked Rome—a disaster for which the classical consciousness was unprepared. Throughout the Empire, people panicked. Non-Christians blamed the tragedy on Christianity, saying that the

CHRIST ENTHRONED. This detail from the funerary sarcophagus of Junius Bassus, dating from A.D. 359, shows Christ sitting on a throne. (Hirmer Verlag Fotoarchiv, München.)

Christians had predicted the end of the world and by refusing to offer sacrifices to ancient gods had turned those deities against Rome. Even Christians expressed anxiety. Why were the righteous also suffering? Where was the kingdom of God on earth that had been prophesied in the Scriptures?

Augustine's *City of God* was a response to the crisis of the Roman Empire, just as Plato's *Republic* had been a reaction to the crisis of the Athenian polis. Whereas Plato expressed hope that a state founded on rational principles could remedy the abuses of Athenian society, Augustine maintained that the worldly city could never be the central concern of a Christian. The ideal state, he wrote, could not be realized on earth; it existed only in heaven. The misfortunes of Rome, therefore, should not distress a Christian unduly, for

Christianity belonged to the realm of the spirit and could not be identified with any state. The collapse of Rome did not diminish the greatness of Christianity because the true Christian was a citizen of a heavenly city that could not be pillaged by ungodly barbarians but would endure forever. Compared with God's heavenly city, Rome and its decline were unimportant. What really mattered in history, Augustine said, was not the coming to be or the passing away of cities and empires, but the individual's spiritual destiny, his or her entrance into heaven or hell.

Yet Augustine remained a man of this world. Although the earthly city was the very opposite of the heavenly city, he insisted that people must still deal with this earthly abode. Christians could not reject their city entirely but must bend it to fit a Christian pattern. The city that someday would rise from the ruins of Rome must be based on Christian principles. Warfare, economic activity, education, and the rearing of children should all be conducted in a Christian spirit. The church could not neglect the state but must guide it to protect human beings from their own sinful natures. The state must employ repression and punishment to restrain people, who were inherently sinful, from destroying one another. But the earthly city would never know tranquility, said Augustine, for it would always be inhabited predominantly by wretched sinners. People should be under no illusion that it could be transformed into the City of God. Because human beings are infected with sin, everywhere in human society we see

> love for all those things that prove so vain and . . . breed so many heartaches, troubles, griefs, and fears; such insane joys in discord, strife, and war; such wrath and plots of enemies . . . such fraud and theft and robbery; such perfidy . . . homicide and murder, cruelty and savagery, lawlessness and lust; all the shameless passions of the impure—fornication and adultery . . . and countless other uncleannesses too nasty to be mentioned; the sins against religion—sacrilege and heresy . . . the iniquities against our neighbors—calumnies and cheating, lies and false witness, violence to persons and property . . . and the innumerable other miseries and maladies that fill the world, yet escape attention.[11]

Augustine did not hold that Christ, by his sacrificial death, had opened the door to heaven for all. Most of humanity remained condemned to eternal punishment; only a handful were blessed with the gift of faith and the promise of heaven. Whereas the vast majority of people, said Augustine, were citizens of a doomed earthly city, the small number endowed with God's grace constituted the City of God. These people lived on earth as visitors only, for they awaited deliverance to the Kingdom of Christ, where together with the good angels and God they would know perfect happiness. But the permanent inhabitants of the earthly city were destined for eternal punishment in hell. A perpetual conflict existed between the two cities and between their inhabitants; one city

stood for sin and corruption, the other for God's truth and perfection. For Augustine, the highest good was not of this world but consisted of eternal life with God.

Augustine's distinction between this higher world of perfection and a lower world of corruption remained influential throughout the Middle Ages. But the church, rejecting Augustine's doctrine that only a limited number of people are predestined for heaven, emphasized that Christ had made possible the salvation of all who would embrace the precepts and injunctions of the church. Leading Protestant reformers of the sixteenth century, however, accepted Augustine's position.

Augustine repudiated the distinguishing feature of classical humanism: the autonomy of reason. For him, ultimate wisdom could not be achieved through rational thought alone. Reason had to be guided by faith. Without faith, there could be no true knowledge, no understanding. Philosophy had no validity if it did not first accept as absolutely true the existence of God and the authority of his revelation. Valid ethical standards could not be formulated by reason alone but were revealed to people by the living God. Christian truth did not rest on theoretical excellence or logical consistency; it was true because its source was God.

Augustine's belief contrasts with that of Socrates, who insisted that through rational reflection each individual could arrive at standards of good and evil. For the humanist Socrates, ultimate values were something that the individual could grasp through thought alone and could defend rationally. For Augustine, reason alone could not serve as a proper guide to life. He maintained that individuals, without divine guidance, lacked the capacity to comprehend ultimate truth or to regenerate themselves morally. Without God, they could not attain wisdom or liberate themselves from a wicked and sinful human nature: "the happiness of man can come not from himself but only from God, and . . . to live according to oneself is sin."[12]

Thus, in contrast to the classical view that asserted the primacy of reason, Augustine argued for the primacy of faith. He denied the classical view that reason *alone* could attain wisdom or could instruct people how to live. The wisdom that Augustine sought was Christian wisdom, God's revelation to humanity. The starting point for this wisdom, he said, was belief in God and

THE LADDER OF DIVINE ASCENT, TWELFTH-CENTURY ICON, ST. CATHERINE'S MONASTERY, MOUNT SINAI. Monks climbing a ladder to heaven, while demons are trying to prevent them from leaving earth. (Erich Lessing/Art Resource, N.Y.)

the Scriptures. For Augustine, secular knowledge for its own sake had little value; the true significance of knowledge lay in its role as a tool for comprehending God's will. Let us utilize truths useful to the faith that pagan philosophers might have chanced upon, he said. Augustine adapted the classical intellectual tradition to the requirements of Christian revelation.

With Augustine, the human-centered outlook of classical humanism, which for centuries had been undergoing transformation, gave way to a God-centered worldview. The fulfillment of God's will, not the full development of human talent, became the chief concern of life. The *City of God* encompassed several themes that would concern Christian thinkers for centuries: the meaning of history and the place of the individual, the state, and the church in God's plan.

Augustinian Christianity is a living philosophy because it still has something vital to say about the human condition. To those who believe that people have the intelligence and goodwill to transform their earthly city into a rational and just community that promotes human betterment, Augustine offers a reminder of human sinfulness, weakness, and failure. Nor will new and ingenious political and social arrangements alter a defective human nature. He cautions the optimist that progress is not certain; that people, weak and ever prone to wickedness, are their own worst enemies; that success is illusory; and that misery is the essential human reality.

CHRISTIANITY AND CLASSICAL HUMANISM: ALTERNATIVE WORLDVIEWS

Christianity and classical humanism are the two principal components of the Western tradition. The value that modern Western civilization places on the individual derives ultimately from classical humanism and the Judeo-Christian tradition. Classical humanists believed that human worth came from the capacity of individuals to reason and to shape their character and life according to rational standards. Christianity also places great stress on the individual. In the Christian view, God cares for each person; he wants people to behave righteously and to enter heaven; Christ died for all because he loves humanity. Christianity espouses active love and genuine concern for fellow human beings. Without God, people are as Augustine described them: "foul, crooked, sordid, . . . vicious." With God, the human personality can undergo a moral transformation and become loving, good, and free. The idea of a Christian conscience, prompted by God and transcending all other loyalties, reinforces respect for all human beings regardless of cultural and national differences. Also promoting respect for each person is the presupposition of natural equality stemming from the Christian belief that each individual, regardless of birth, wealth, or talent, is precious to God.

There are striking parallels between Christian and Stoic ethics. Both Christians and Stoics believed that there is an essential "brotherhood of man," that all human beings are related and possess a fundamental dignity. Both urged suppressing wild passions, expressing concern for others, living simply, and heeding the inner voice of conscience that commands human beings to do what is right.

But Christianity and classical humanism also represent two essentially different worldviews. The triumph of the Christian outlook signified a break with the essential meaning of classical humanism; it pointed to the end of the world of antiquity and the beginning of an age of faith, the Middle Ages. With the victory of Christianity, the ultimate goal of life shifted. Life's purpose was no longer to achieve excellence in this world through the full and creative development of human capacities, but to attain salvation in a heavenly city. A person's worldly accomplishments amounted to very little if he or she did not accept God and his revelation. The Christian ideal of the isolated and contemplative monk, who rejected the world in order to serve God, was alien to the spirit of classical humanism, which valued active citizenship and active participation in worldly activities. Equally foreign to the Greco-Roman mind was another idea introduced by Christianity: the need to escape from a sinful human nature, a consequence of Adam and Eve's defiance of God. This view of a corrupt human nature and an unclean human body, particularly in Augustine's formulation, became deeply embedded in the European mind during the Christian centuries—the Middle Ages.

In the classical view, history had no ultimate end, no ultimate meaning; periods of happiness and misery repeated themselves endlessly. In the Christian view, history is filled with spiritual meaning. It is the profound drama of individuals struggling to overcome their original sin in order to gain eternal happiness in heaven. History began with Adam and Eve's fall and would end when Christ returns to earth, evil is eradicated, and God's will prevails. For the Christian, Christ on the cross was both the central event and a turning point in world history.

Classicism held that there was no authority higher than reason, that individuals had within themselves, through unaided reason, the ability to understand the world and life. Christianity teaches that, without God as the starting point, knowledge is formless, purposeless, and prone to error. Classicism, unlike Judaism or Christianity, possessed no truths or moral precepts revealed by a divine power. Rather, classicism held that ethical standards were expressions of universal reason, laws of nature, which the human mind could discover. Through reason, individuals could discern the norms by which they should regulate their lives. Reason would enable them to govern desires and will; it would show where their behavior was wrong and teach them how to correct it. Because individuals sought what was best for themselves, they would obey the voice of reason. Christianity, on the other hand, maintains that ethical standards emanate from the personal will of God. Without submission to God's commands, people remain wicked forever; the human will, essentially sinful, cannot be transformed by the promptings of reason. Only when individuals turn to God for forgiveness and guidance can they find the inner strength to overcome their sinful nature. People cannot perfect themselves through scientific knowledge; it is spiritual insight and belief in God that they require and that must serve as the first principle of their lives. For classicism, the ultimate good was sought through independent thought and action; for Christianity, the ultimate good comes through knowing, obeying, and loving God.

Although some Christian thinkers dismissed Greek philosophy as erroneous and useless, others respected the Greek intellectual tradition and rejected attempts to eradicate it. Rather, they sought to fit it into a Christian framework—that is, rational inquiry must be guided by and never conflict with Christian teachings. By holding that the mind is limited in its capacity to think for itself and must be guided by faith and clerical authority, Christianity contributed to the waning of the classical tradition in the Late Roman Empire. For centuries, articles of faith would predominate over empirical observation and logic. Nevertheless, by preserving the Greek philosophical tradition— even if it remained subordinate to the Christian outlook—Christian thinkers performed a task of immense historical significance.

Christianity inherited the Hebrew view of the overriding importance of God for humanity: God, who is both lawgiver and judge, makes life intelligible and purposeful. For the Christian, God is a

PORTRAIT OF CHRIST. Painted on a ceiling in the Catacomb of Domitilla around the second century A.D., this is among the oldest surviving portraits of Jesus. (Scala/Art Resource, N.Y.)

living being, loving and compassionate, in whose company one seeks to spend eternity; one knows God essentially through faith and feeling. Although the Greek philosophers had a conception of God, it was not comparable to the God of the Hebrews and Christians. For the Greeks, God was a logical abstraction, a principle of order, the prime mover, the first cause, the mind of the universe, pure thought, the supreme good, the highest truth; God was a concept, impersonal, unfeeling, and uninvolved with human concerns. The Greeks approached God through the intellect, not the heart; they neither loved nor worshiped God. In addition, because religion was at the periphery, not the center, of classical humanism, the idea of God did not carry the same significance as it did for Christianity.

Christianity maintained that there was a prescribed way to worship the one true God, that belief in other gods was an abomination, and that nonbelievers (or infidels) and heretics were wicked sinners hated by God. Over the centuries, this outlook sanctioned fanaticism, persecution, and holy war, with accompanying massacres—a terrible legacy that constitutes the dark side of monotheism. Unlike the monotheistic faiths—Judaism, Christianity, and Islam—Greek and Roman polytheism had no concepts of **martyrdom** for the true faith and holy war against the infidel and consistently tolerated many different religious beliefs and practices as long as they did not threaten the state.

In the classical world, the political community was the avenue to justice, happiness, and self-realization. In Christianity, the good life was identified not with worldly achievement but with life eternal, and the ideal commonwealth could only be one that was founded and ruled by Christ. It was entrance into God's kingdom that each person must make the central aim of life. Christian thinkers viewed the state as an inferior community to their own—the church of Christ, which had ties to the spiritual realm, the highest good. Therefore, they held that secular power should submit to ecclesiastical authority. For the next thousand years, this distinction between heaven and earth, this otherworldly, theocentric outlook, would define the Western mentality.

In the Late Roman Empire, when classical values were in decay, Christianity was a dynamic and creative movement. Possessing both institutional and spiritual strength, Christianity survived the fall of Rome. Because it retained elements of Greco-Roman civilization and taught a high morality, Christianity served as a civilizing agent in the centuries that followed Rome's collapse. Indeed, Christianity was the essential shaper of the European civilization that emerged in the Middle Ages.

NOTES

1. Hans Küng, "Christianity and Judaism," in *Jesus' Jewishness,* ed. James H. Charlesworth (New York: Crossroad, 1991), 259.

2. The biblical quotations, used with permission, are from the Holy Bible, Revised Standard Version (New York: Thomas Nelson & Sons, 1952). The Revised Standard Version is the text used for biblical quotations throughout, except where noted otherwise.

3. Tertullian, "On Prescription Against Heretics," chap. 7, in *The Ante-Nicene Fathers,* ed. Alexander Roberts and James Donaldson (New York: Charles Scribner's Sons, 1918), 3:246.

4. Clement of Alexandria, *Stromata (Miscellanies),* trans. William Wilson, in *Ante-Nicene Christian Library,* vol. 4, *The Writings of Clement of Alexandria,* ed. Alexander Roberts and James Donaldson (Edinburgh: T & T Clark, 1867–1872), 303–304.

5. Tertullian, "On the Flesh of Christ," in *The Ante-Nicene Fathers,* ed. Roberts and Donaldson, 525.

6. From Clement of Alexandria, *Christ the Educator,* trans. Simon P. Woo, C. P. (New York: Fathers of the Church, 1954), 175.

7. *Origenis, Commentariorum in Evangelium Secundum Matthaeum, in Patrologiae Cursus Completus,* Series Graeca Prior, ed. J. P. Migne (Paris: Parisiorum, 1862), vol. 13 (trans. J. Castora), cols. 1494–1495, pars. 775–776.

8. Quoted in Edward H. Flannery, *The Anguish of the Jews* (London: Macmillan, 1965), 48.

9. Randolph Braham, ed., *The Origins of the Holocaust: Christian Anti-Semitism* (Boulder, Colo: Social Science Monographs and Institute for Holocaust Studies of the City University of New York, 1986), 36.

10. Ibid., 37.

11. Saint Augustine, *The City of God,* trans. Gerald G. Walsh et al., abridged (Garden City, N.Y.: Doubleday Image Books, 1958), 519.

12. Ibid., 300.

SUGGESTED READING

Armstrong, Karen, *A History of God* (1994). Good material on early Christianity.

Benko, Stephen, *Pagan Rome and the Early Christians* (1984). How Romans and Greeks viewed early Christianity.

Bettenson, Henry, and Chris Maunder, eds., *Documents of the Christian Church* (1999). A new edition of this invaluable reference work.

Chadwick, Henry, *The Early Church* (1967). A survey of early Christianity in its social and ideological context.

Charlesworth, James, ed., *Jesus' Jewishness* (1991). Essays by prominent scholars exploring the Jewish context of early Christianity.

Ferguson, Everett, ed., *Encyclopedia of Early Christianity* (1990). Entries on all aspects of early Christianity.

———, *Backgrounds of Early Christianity* (1993). A clear and thorough examination of the milieu in which Christianity was born.

Le Beau, Bryan F., Leonard Greenspoon, and Dennis Hamm, S. J., eds., *The Historical Jesus Through Catholic and Jewish Eyes* (2000). A collection of perceptive essays on Jesus' Jewish background.

Perkins, Pheme, *Reading the New Testament* (1978). Introduces the beginning student to the New Testament.

Perry, Marvin, and Frederick M. Schweitzer, eds., *Jewish-Christian Encounters Over the Centuries* (1994). Useful essays on Jesus, Paul, the Dead Sea Scrolls, and early Christian anti-Judaism.

Walsh, Michael, *The Triumph of the Meek: Why Early Christianity Succeeded* (1986). An informed and clearly written account of a major scholarly concern.

Wills, Garry, *What Jesus Meant* (2006). A fresh and intriguing reading of the gospels by an eminent Catholic intellectual.

———, *What Paul Meant* (2006). An interpretation of Paul's writings that sheds light on Jesus and his followers.

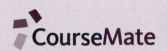

Go to the CourseMate website at **www.cengagebrain.com** for additional study tools and review materials—including audio and video clips—for this chapter.

Part Two

The Middle Ages: The Christian Centuries,

500 to 1400

500

600

700

800

900

1000

1100

1200

1300

Politics and Society

Germanic kingdoms established on former Roman lands (5th and 6th centuries)
Saint Benedict founds monastery at Monte Cassino (529)
Pope Gregory I sends missionaries to convert Anglo-Saxons (596)

Spread of Islam (622–732)

Charles Martel defeats Muslims at Tours (732)

Charlemagne crowned emperor of Romans
Alfred the Great, ruler of Saxon kingdom of Wessex (871–899)
Muslim, Magyar, and Viking invasions of Latin Christendom (9th and early 10th centuries)
Growth of feudalism (800–1100)

German king Otto I becomes first Holy Roman Emperor (962)

Split between the Byzantine and Roman churches (1054)
Norman conquest of England (1066)
Start of First Crusade (1096)

Philip Augustus expands central authority in France (1180–1223)
Development of common law and jury system in England (1100s)
Pontificate of Innocent III: height of papal power (1198–1216)

Magna Carta (1215)
Destruction of Baghdad by Mongols (1258)

Hundred Years' War (1337–1453)
Black Death (1347–1351)
Great Schism of papacy (1378–1417)

Thought and Culture

Boethius, *Consolation of Philosophy* (523)
Law code of Justinian (529)
Byzantine church Hagia Sophia (532–537)
Cassiodorus establishes a monastic library at Vivarium (540)

The Koran

Bede, *Ecclesiastical History of the English People* (c. 700)
Muslim Golden Age (700s and 800s)

Carolingian Renaissance (768–814)
Alfred the Great promotes learning in England (871–899)

Romanesque style in architecture (1000s and 1100s)

Flowering of medieval culture (12th and 13th centuries): universities, Gothic architecture, scholastic philosophy, revival of Roman law

Aquinas, *Summa Theologica* (1267–1273)

Dante, *Divine Comedy* (c. 1307–1321)
Chaucer, *Canterbury Tales* (c. 1388–1400)

Chapter 9

The Heirs of Rome: Byzantium, Islam, and Latin Christendom

Coronation of Charlemagne. (Scala/Art Resource, N.Y.)

- **Byzantine Civilization: The Medieval Christian East**
- **Islamic Civilization: Its Development and Dissemination**
- **Latin Christendom: The Rise of Europe**
- **The Church: Shaper of Medieval Civilization**
- **The Kingdom of the Franks**
- **Medieval Society**

Focus Questions

1. How did Latin Christendom blend Christian, Greco-Roman, and Germanic traditions?

2. In what ways were Greco-Roman ideas and institutions alien to Germanic traditions?

3. What was Byzantium's long-term influence on world history?

4. What does Islam have in common with Christianity? How do they differ?

5. What was the significance of medieval Muslim intellectual life?

6. What conditions led to the rise of feudalism and manorialism?

The triumph of Christianity, the decay of the Roman Empire, and the establishment of Germanic kingdoms on once-Roman lands constituted a new phase in Western history: the end of the ancient world and the beginning of the Middle Ages, a period that spanned a thousand years. In the ancient world, the locus of Greco-Roman civilization had been the Mediterranean Sea; the heartland of Western medieval civilization gradually shifted to the north, to regions of Europe that Greco-Roman civilization had barely penetrated. **Latin Christendom** (Western and Central Europe) was only one of three new civilizations based on religion that emerged after the decline of the Roman Empire; Byzantium and Islam were the other two. Both of these Eastern civilizations influenced the emerging Europe in important ways.

BYZANTINE CIVILIZATION: THE MEDIEVAL CHRISTIAN EAST

Although the Roman Empire in the West fell to the Germanic tribes, the eastern provinces of the Empire survived. They did so because they were richer, more urbanized, and more populous and because the main thrust of the Germanic and Hunnish invaders had been directed at the western regions. In the eastern parts, Byzantine civilization took shape. Its religion was Christian, its culture Greek, and its machinery of administration Roman. The capital, Constantinople, was built on the site of the ancient Greek city of Byzantium, on a peninsula in the Straits of Bosporus—the dividing line between Asia and Europe. Constantinople was a fortress city perfectly situated to resist attacks from land and sea.

During the Early Middle Ages (500–1050), Byzantine civilization was economically and culturally far more advanced than the Latin West. At a time when few westerners (Latin Christians) could read or write, Byzantine scholars studied the literature, philosophy, science, and law of ancient Greece and Rome. Whereas trade and urban life had greatly declined in the West, Constantinople was a magnificent Byzantine city of schools, libraries, open squares, and bustling markets.

Chronology 9.1 ❖ The Rise of Europe

496	Clovis adopts Roman Christianity
523	Boethius writes *Consolation of Philosophy*
540	Cassiodorus establishes a monastic library at Vivarium
596	Pope Gregory I sends missionaries to convert the Anglo-Saxons
717	Charles Martel becomes mayor of the palace under a weak Merovingian king
732	Charles Martel defeats the Muslims at Tours
751	Pepin the Short, with papal support, deposes the Merovingian ruler and becomes king of the Franks
755	Pepin donates to the papacy lands taken from the Lombards
768	Charlemagne becomes king of the Franks
774	Charlemagne defeats the Lombards
782	Alcuin of York heads Charlemagne's palace school
c. 799	Charlemagne subdues the Saxons
800	Charlemagne is crowned emperor of the Romans by Pope Leo III
814	Charlemagne dies and is succeeded by his son, Louis the Pious
840	Death of Louis the Pious: the empire is divided among his sons
c. 840s	Height of Viking attacks
c. 890	Magyars invade central Europe

Over the centuries, many differences developed between the Eastern church and the Roman church. The pope in Rome resisted domination by the Byzantine emperor, and the Byzantines denied the pope's claim to authority over all Christians. The two churches quarreled over ceremonies, holy days, and the display of holy images or icons. Fearing that some of his subjects were actually worshipping these images, in 726, Emperor Leo III ordered the destruction of all images of Christ, the Virgin, and the saints and persecuted monks who continued to venerate them. This decree greatly angered many Christians and the pope, who excommunicated Leo III. After a storm of protest convulsed the empire, the Empress Irene in 787 and the Empress Theodora in 843 restored the images. The iconoclastic struggle contributed to the rift between Byzantium and the papacy. The final break came in 1054 when the Christian church split into the Roman Catholic church in the West and the Eastern (Greek) Orthodox church in the East.

Political and cultural differences widened the rift between Latin Christendom and Byzantium. Latin Christians refused to recognize that the Byzantine emperors were, as they claimed, successors to the Roman emperors. In the Byzantine Empire, Greek was the language of religion and intellectual life; in the West, it was Latin.

Imperial Growth and Decline

Byzantine emperors were absolute rulers who held that God had chosen them to rule and to institute divine will on earth. As successors to the Roman emperors, they claimed to rule all the lands once part of the Roman Empire. The first great Byzantine ruler was Justinian, who reigned nearly forty years, from 527 to 565. Justinian often relied on the advice of his wife, Theodora. Theodora's background was unusual for an empress; she was not from the nobility but was the daughter of a bear trainer in the circus and had been an actress,

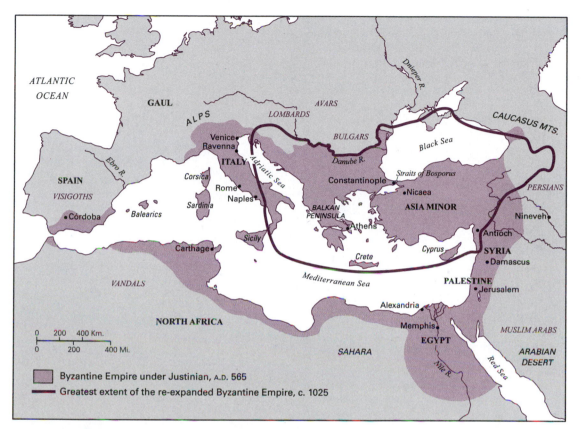

Map 9.1 **THE BYZANTINE EMPIRE** In the centuries after Justinian regained lands in the western Mediterranean that had been lost to Germanic invaders, the Byzantines faced attacks from Avars, Bulgars, Lombards, Persians, Arabs, Latin Christians, Seljuk Turks, and the Ottoman Turks, who captured Constantinople in 1453. (Copyright © 2013 Cengage Learning.)

a profession most people considered degrading. In a number of crises, the strong-willed and astute Theodora gave Justinian the courage to act decisively.

Justinian's most lasting achievement was the appointment of a commission of scholars to collect and codify Rome's ancient laws and the commentaries of learned jurists. The result was the *Corpus Juris Civilis,* which became the official body of law of the Byzantine Empire. In the twelfth century, it was gradually reintroduced into Western Europe, where it became the basis of civil law in many European lands.

Justinian sought to regain the lands in the western Mediterranean that had been conquered by Germanic invaders. During his reign, Byzantine forces retook North Africa from the Vandals, part of southern Spain from the Visigoths, and Italy from the Ostrogoths, establishing a western capital at Ravenna.

Besides draining the treasury, the long and costly wars led to the neglect of defenses in the Balkan Peninsula and the Near East. The Balkans were invaded by Slavic tribes from the Black Sea region and by Avars and Bulgars, originally from Central Asia; Syria was ravaged by the Persians.

RAVENNA MOSAICS. Theodora, Emperor Justinian's wife, was a strong-willed woman who exercised considerable authority and often advised her husband on matters of state. (North Wind Picture Archives/AP Images.)

Nor were the conquered territories in the west secure. The Germanic Lombards, who had moved into northern Italy in the late sixth century, conquered much Byzantine territory that had been recently recovered from the Ostrogoths. By 629, the Visigoths had driven the Byzantines from Spain.

In the early seventh century, the Byzantines faced a renewed threat from the Persians, who seized the Byzantine provinces of Syria, Palestine, and Egypt. In an all-out effort, however, Emperor Heraclius (610–641) regained the provinces and in 627 crushed the Persians near the ruins of the ancient city of Nineveh. But the exhausted Byzantine Empire had become vulnerable to the Muslim Arabs, who had moved swiftly out of the Arabian

Desert seeking to propagate Islam, their new faith (discussed later in this chapter).

By 642, the Arabs had stripped the Byzantine Empire of Syria, Palestine, and Egypt, and by the beginning of the eighth century, they had taken North Africa. Near the end of the seventh century and again in 717, the Muslims besieged Constantinople. But the Byzantine fleet was armed with a new weapon, "Greek fire"—a fiery explosive liquid shot from tubes—which set enemy ships aflame and made blazing pools on the water's surface. Thus, the light Byzantine ships were able to repulse the better-built Arabian ships.

The Arabs' failure to take Constantinople was crucial not only for the Byzantine Empire but also for the history of Christianity. Had this Christian

CHURCH OF THE HOLY WISDOM (HAGIA SOPHIA), CONSTANTINOPLE, 532–537. The largest church ever built in the Byzantine world, Hagia Sophia was constructed by Emperor Justinian. The interior of its immense dome was decorated with golden mosaics simulating the light of heaven. After the Turkish conquest of Constantinople in 1453, the mosaics were painted white, the church was converted into a mosque, and minarets (towers from which the faithful were summoned for prayer five times a day) were constructed. (© Peter M. Wilson/Corbis.)

fortress fallen in the eighth century, the Arabs would have been able to overrun the Balkan Peninsula and sail up the Danube River into the European heartland. After this defeat, however, Islamic armies largely concentrated their conquests outside Europe.

But soon new enemies threatened. By 1071, the Normans from France had driven the Byzantines from Italy. In the same year, the Seljuk Turks, a people from Central Asia who had adopted Islam, defeated the Byzantines in Asia Minor and subjugated most of the peninsula, the heart of the Byzantine Empire. Internal dissension, however, led to the breakup of the Seljuk Empire.

Seeking to exploit Seljuk weakness and to regain lost territories, the Byzantines appealed to Latin Christians for help. Although European Christians had little love for the Byzantines, they did want to free Christian holy places from the Muslims. For this purpose, they undertook a series of Crusades, beginning in the late eleventh century (see Chapter 10). In 1204, during the Fourth Crusade, Latin Christian knights—greedy for riches—and Venetian merchants—eager to gain control of the rich Byzantine trade—decided to take Constantinople rather than fight the Muslims.

The Latin Christians looted the city, destroying sacred books, vandalizing churches, and carrying huge amounts of gold, jewels, Christian relics, and works of art back to Western Europe. They also set up kingdoms on Byzantine lands and tried to force Latin forms of Christianity on the Byzantine Greeks. Not until 1261 were the westerners driven from Constantinople. The Byzantine Empire regained its independence, but its power was disastrously weakened. Crushing taxes, decreasing agricultural production, declining trade, and civil war continued to sap the tottering empire.

The deathblow to the empire was dealt by another group of Turks from central Asia. The Ottoman Turks had accepted Islam and had begun to build an empire. They drove the Byzantines from Asia Minor and conquered much of the Balkans. By the beginning of the fifteenth century, the Byzantine Empire consisted of only two small territories in Greece and the city of Constantinople. In 1453, the Ottoman Turks broke through Constantinople's great walls and plundered the city. After more than ten centuries, the Byzantine Empire came to an end.

The Bequest of Byzantium

During its thousand years, Byzantium made a significant impact on world history. First, it prevented the Muslim Arabs from advancing into Eastern Europe. Had the Arabs broken through Byzantine defenses, much of Europe might have been converted to the new faith of Islam. A far-reaching accomplishment was the codification of the laws of ancient Rome under Justinian. This monumental achievement preserved Roman law's principles of reason and justice. Today's legal codes in much of Europe and Latin America trace their roots to the Roman law recorded by Justinian's lawyers. The Byzantines also preserved the philosophy, science, mathematics, and literature of ancient Greece.

Contacts with Byzantine civilization stimulated learning in both the Islamic world to the east and Latin Christendom to the west. Speros Vryonis, a student of Byzantine civilization, states: "The Byzantines carried the torch of civilization unextinguished at a time when the barbarous Germanic and Slav tribes had reduced much of Europe to near chaos: and they maintained this high degree of civilization until Western Europe gradually emerged and began to take form."[1] Byzantium exerted an important religious, cultural, and linguistic influence on Latin Romanians, eastern Slavs (Russians and Ukrainians), and southern Slavs (Serbs and Bulgars). From Byzantium, the Slavs acquired legal principles, art forms, and an alphabet (the Cyrillic, based on the Greek) for writing their languages. (On the other hand, the western Slavs—Poles, Czechs, and Slovaks—came under the influence of Latin Christianity and Latin culture.)

ISLAMIC CIVILIZATION: ITS DEVELOPMENT AND DISSEMINATION

The Prophet: The Founding of a New Religion

The second Eastern civilization to arise after Rome's fall was based on the vital new religion of Islam, which emerged in the seventh century among the Arabs of Arabia. Its founder was Muhammad (c. 570–632), a prosperous merchant in Mecca, a trading city near the Red Sea. At times the introspective Muhammad withdrew from worldly affairs and devoted himself to meditation. He began to experience visions, which he interpreted as messages from God. When Muhammad was about forty, he believed that he was visited in his sleep by the angel Gabriel, who ordered him to "recite in the name of the Lord!" Transformed by this experience, Muhammad came to believe that he had been chosen as a prophet, the carrier of God's revelation.

Although most desert Arabs worshiped tribal gods, many Arabs, including Muhammad, in the towns and trading centers were familiar with Judaism and Christianity, and some had accepted the idea of one God. Rejecting the many deities of the tribal religions, Muhammad offered the Arabs a new monotheistic faith, Islam, which means "surrender to Allah (God)."

Islamic standards of morality and rules governing daily life are set by the Koran, the holy book that Muslims believe contains the words of

Allah as revealed to Muhammad. For Muslims, the Koran is both God's final word and infallible. Muslims see their religion as the completion and perfection of Judaism and Christianity; they believe both of those monotheistic predecessors were superseded by Allah's revelation to Muhammad. Muslims regard the ancient Hebrew prophets as sent from God and value their messages about compassion and the oneness of humanity. They also regard Jesus as a great prophet but do not consider him divine and view the Trinity as a form of polytheism. They see Muhammad as the last and greatest of the prophets and believe that he was entirely human, not divine. Muslims worship only Allah, the creator and ruler of heaven and earth, a single, all-powerful God who is merciful, compassionate, and just. According to the Koran, on the Day of Judgment, unbelievers and the wicked "shall dwell amidst scorching winds and seething water: in the shade of pitch-black smoke . . . sinners that deny the truth . . . shall eat . . . [bitter] fruit . . . [and] drink boiling water."[2] Faithful Muslims who have lived virtuously are promised paradise, which they believe to be a garden where they will experience bodily pleasures and spiritual delights.

An essential feature of Islam is the obligation of the faithful to obey the Five Pillars of the faith: (1) A Muslim must accept and repeat the statement of faith: "There is no God but Allah, and Muhammad is his Prophet." (2) At least five times a day, a believer must face the holy city of Mecca and pray. (3) Muslims have a religious duty to be generous to the poor. (4) During the holy month of Ramadan, believers should not eat or drink between sunrise and sunset. (5) Muslims are expected to make at least one pilgrimage to the holy city of Mecca.

Muhammad's religion began to win followers, but the ruling elite of Mecca would not accept this new faith. To escape persecution, Muhammad and his small band of followers left Mecca in 622 for Medina, a town about two hundred miles away. Their flight, known as the *Hegira,* or "emigration," is one of the most important events in Muslim history and is commemorated by yearly pilgrimages. The date of the Hegira became year one of the Muslim calendar.

In Medina, Muhammad gained converts and won respect as a judge, rendering decisions on

MOSQUE OF CÓRDOBA. The richness of Islamic culture and architecture is evident in Spain, where Muslim rule lingered until the conquest of Granada in 1492. The arch of alternating stone would find its way into Christian churches, most memorably at Vezelay in southern France. (Roger Viollet/Getty Images.)

such matters as family relations, property inheritance, and criminal behavior. Preaching a holy war against unbelievers, Muhammad urged followers to raid the trading caravans from Mecca and to subdue unfriendly Bedouin tribes. He tried to convert the Jews of Medina, but they would not accept him as a prophet and mocked his unfamiliarity with the Hebrew Scriptures and the learned writings of the rabbis. To a large extent, political considerations determined Muhammad's attitude toward Jews, who sided with his Meccan enemies. He expelled several thousand Jews from Medina, seized Jewish property, beheaded some six hundred Jewish men, and enslaved women and children. Later, he permitted the Arabian Jews the free exercise of their religion and guaranteed the security of their property. In 630, Mecca surrendered to a Muslim army virtually without a fight. Muhammad demonstrated leniency and forgiveness toward his former enemies and persecutors, a wise decision that helped gain him the support of the Meccans. Soon Bedouin tribes all over Arabia embraced Islam and recognized the authority of the Prophet Muhammad.

In a little more than two decades, Muhammad united the often feuding Arabian tribes into a powerful force dedicated to Allah and the spreading of the Islamic faith. After Muhammad's death in 632, his friend and father-in-law, Abu Bakr, became his successor, or caliph. Regarded as the defender of the faith, whose power derived from Allah, the caliph governed in accordance with Muslim law as defined in the Koran. Islam gave the many Arab tribes the unity, discipline, and organization to succeed in their wars of conquest. Under the first four caliphs, who ruled from 632 to 661, the Arabs, with breathtaking speed, overran Persia's empire, seized large parts of the Byzantine Empire, and invaded Europe.

Muhammad had conveyed to his followers their religious obligation to perform jihad, literally striving in the path of God. *Jihad* is a complex term whose two essential meanings are an internal striving by the individual for moral self-improvement and a collective military struggle to defend Islam against its enemies and to extend Muslim power over other lands so that all people will be subject to God's laws as revealed to Muhammad. Historically the doctrine of jihad held that the Islamic community (*umma*), the recipient of Allah's revelation was commanded to make Allah's directives supreme over the whole world. Either by conversion or conquest, infidels were destined to submit to Islamic jurisdiction.

Muslim warriors believed that they were engaged in a holy war to spread Islam to nonbelievers and that those who died in the jihad were assured a place in paradise. A desire to escape from the barren Arabian Desert and to exploit the rich Byzantine and Persian lands was another compelling reason for expansion. In the east, Islam's territory eventually extended into India and to the borders of China; in the west, it encompassed North Africa and most of Spain. The Muslims' northward push lost momentum and was halted in 717 by the Byzantines at Constantinople and in 732 by the Franks at the battle of Tours, in central France.

The Muslim State and Society

After the death of Muhammad, Muslims sought authoritative guidance on religious, social, and moral questions that the Koran did not specifically address. The most important source for such guidance was the *Hadith*—a collection of sayings, stories, and actions of the Prophet on a wide range of topics. The Koran coupled with the Hadith provided directions for a complete way of life for Muslims.

The Islamic state was a theocracy: government and religion were inseparable; there could be no distinction between secular and spiritual authority. Muslims viewed God as the source of all law and political authority and the caliph as his earthly deputy. Divine law regulated all aspects of human relations. The ruler who did not enforce Koranic law failed in his duties. Thus, Islam was more than a religion; it was also a system of government, society, law, and thought that bound its adherents into an all-encompassing community. Muslim jurists called for the creation of a single society governed by Islamic law. And this world-state had a religious obligation to subdue the non-Muslim world. This goal, to be achieved by jihad, endured in the Muslim mind over the centuries and is a principal aim of Muslim extremists today. The separation of church and state, which became firmly rooted in the West in modern times, still remains an alien concept in much of the Muslim world.

Over the centuries, many Christians and Jews living in Muslim lands, for a variety of reasons, some of them economic and social, converted to the new faith. Those who retained their ancestral faith had to accept a subordinate status—they could not bear arms, were assessed a special tax, at times were barred from testifying in court against a Muslim, and were required to wear a distinguishing mark on their clothing, a sign of their humiliation. Nevertheless, as "people of the book," Jews and Christians were protected communities, and despite instances of loss of property and life, including massacres, the two groups generally went about their business and practiced their religions relatively free of persecution. Generally Jews were physically safer in Muslim than in Christian lands.

Muslims perceived themselves as members of a single community of the faithful, but the emergence of sects ruptured the unity of Islam. The principal division—one that still incites bitter animosity—was between the Sunnis and the Shiites. The Sunnis, who were in the majority, followed traditional teachings and established practices as defined by the consensus of the Muslim community. The Shiites (*Shia* means "Party") maintained that not the existing caliphs but the descendants of Muhammad, starting with Ali, cousin and son-in-law of Muhammad and the fourth caliph, were the rightful rulers of the Islamic community.

Ali had been murdered in 661; his older son, in 669. The massacre in 680 of Ali's younger son, Husayn, and some of Husayn's followers and relatives gave rise to passionate devotion to the house of Ali, which is still expressed in processions, poetry, and self-mortification. To Shiites, the anniversary of Husayn's death remains the most important religious holiday in the Muslim calendar. Suffering and martyrdom are central to Shia.

Shiites viewed Ali and his descendants as *imams,* holy men, innocent of all sin, the most excellent of beings, selected by God to inherit Muhammad's spiritual and political powers. The imams linked the new generation with Muhammad's original inspiration. Shiites believed that without the imams' guidance, the true meaning of Islam could not be grasped.

The Muslim Golden Age

The Arabs who first burst into the Byzantine and Persian empires had no tradition of science or philosophy. But they were quick to absorb the learning of Byzantines and Persians who had preserved and studied ancient Greek works. In the eighth and ninth centuries, under the Abbasid caliphs based in Baghdad, Muslim civilization entered its golden age. Islamic civilization creatively integrated Arabic, Byzantine, Persian, and Indian cultural traditions. During the Early Middle Ages, when learning was at a low point in Western Europe, the Muslims forged a high civilization.

Muslim science, philosophy, and mathematics, based largely on the achievements of the ancient Greeks, made brilliant contributions to the sum of knowledge at a time when Latin Christendom had lost much of Greco-Roman thought and culture. The Muslims had acquired Greek learning from the older Persian and Byzantine civilizations, which had kept alive the Greek inheritance. By translating Greek works into Arabic and commenting on them, Muslim scholars performed the great historical task of preserving the philosophical and scientific heritage of ancient Greece. Muslim scholars, often affiliated with impressive universities, also creatively interpreted these Greek works and in some areas, particularly mathematics, pushed the frontiers of knowledge beyond what the Greeks had achieved. This intellectual heritage was passed on to Christian Europe, a transmission of immense historical significance, as the historian W. Montgomery Watt explains:

> When one becomes aware of the full extent of Arab experimenting, Arab thinking and Arab writing, one sees that without the Arabs European science and philosophy would not have developed when they did. The Arabs were no mere transmitters of Greek thought, but genuine bearers, who both kept alive the disciplines they had been taught and extended their range. When about 1100, Europeans became seriously interested in . . . science and philosophy . . . [they] had to learn all they could from the Arabs before they themselves could make further advances.[3]

There are numerous examples of Muslim brilliance in mathematics, medicine, science, and philosophy. From India, the Muslims acquired the concept of zero and "Arabic" numerals, passing these ideas on to the West. Euclid's *Elements,* the creative synthesis of Greek geometry, was translated into Arabic and studied by Muslim scholars who produced numerous commentaries on the work. Muslim mathematicians also did original work in algebra and trigonometry. Also translated into Arabic was another important Greek writing, Ptolemy's *Almagest,* which synthesized astronomical knowledge. Muslim astronomers corrected some of Ptolemy's calculations, pointed out theoretical inconsistencies, and explored problems he had not considered. In physics, the Muslim Arabs' most significant contribution was in the field of optics. Rejecting Euclid's and Ptolemy's explanation that the eye emits visual rays, they recognized that vision is a consequence of rays of light. Building on the medical knowledge of the Greeks, Muslim physicians became the best-trained and most skillful doctors of the time. Surgeons performed amputations, removed cancerous tissue, devised new medicines, and used anesthetics when performing operations. The best Muslim hospitals had separate wards for fevers, surgical cases, eye diseases, and dysentery. Well ahead of their time were those Muslim doctors who recommended humane treatment for the mentally ill. The Persian al-Razi, or Rhazes, who headed the hospital in Baghdad in the ninth century, wrote a medical encyclopedia in which he discussed measles, kidney stones, poisons, skin diseases, and ways of maintaining one's health. The works of Rhazes, translated into Latin, were widely consulted in Latin Christendom.

Muslim thinkers employed the categories of Greek philosophy to explain Islamic doctrine. Al-Farabi (c. 870–950), who wrote commentaries on Aristotle, offered proofs for God's existence based on Aristotelian logic that were later studied by medieval Christian philosophers. The most eminent Muslim thinker, Ibn-Sina, known to the West as Avicenna (980–1037), was a poet, doctor, scientist, and philosopher who wrote on every field of knowledge. His philosophical works, which relied heavily on Aristotle, had an important influence on medieval Christian thinkers. Another giant of Muslim learning was Ibn-Rushd, whom Westerners call Averroës (1126–1198). Averroës insisted that the Koran did not oppose the study of philosophy and held that the ancient Greeks—even though they were not Muslims—had discovered truth. His commentaries on Aristotle were studied in Western universities, where they sparked an important controversy (see page 265).

Mongol Invasions and Ottoman Dominance

The Arab empire, stretching from Spain to India, was unified by a common language (Arabic), a common faith, and a common culture. By the eleventh century, however, the Arabs began losing their dominance in the Islamic world. The Seljuk Turks, who had taken Asia Minor from the Byzantines, also conquered the Arabic lands of Syria, Palestine, and much of Persia. Although the Abbasid caliphs remained the religious and cultural leaders of Islam, political power was exercised by Seljuk sultans. In the eleventh and twelfth centuries, the Muslims lost Sicily and most of Spain to Christian knights, and European Crusaders carved out kingdoms in the Near East.

In the thirteenth century came a new wave of invaders, the Mongols from central Asia. Led by Genghis Khan, Mongolian archers, mounted on fast-moving ponies, poured across Asia into Muslim lands. By 1227, when Genghis Khan died, the eastern part of the Muslim world had fallen to the Mongols. After the death of Genghis Khan, some Mongol forces swept across Russia and threatened Central Europe; others continued to advance on Muslim lands in the Near East. Storming Baghdad in 1258, the Mongols burned, plundered, and killed with savage fury; among the fifty thousand people slaughtered was the last Abbasid caliph. The Mongols devastated the palaces, libraries, and schools that had made Baghdad the cultural capital of the Islamic world. A year later, they marched into Syria, again killing and looting. Their brutal advance westward was finally stopped in 1260 in Palestine by Egyptian forces.

By the beginning of the fourteenth century, the Mongols, who had by this time converted to Islam, remained in Persia and were unable to advance westward. In the late fourteenth century, however, the Mongols, under Tamerlane, again menaced the Near East. Another bloody conqueror, Tamerlane cowed opposition with huge pyramids built from the skulls of thousands of slaughtered victims. After Tamerlane's death in 1404, his empire disintegrated, and its collapse left the way open for the Ottoman Turks.

The Ottoman Empire reached its height in the sixteenth century with the conquest of Egypt, North Africa, Syria, and the Arabian coast. The

The Art of the Ancient World and the Middle Ages

1. Praxiteles. *Hermes with Young Dionysus*, c. 350 B.C. (Archaeological Museum, Olympia, Archaia, Greece/The Bridgeman Art Library.)

The art of the classical period (c. fifth century B.C.) was important not only to the ancient Greeks but also to the Romans and to later generations, from the Renaissance to the postmodern period of the late twentieth century. Through the ages, classical art has been kept alive—adopted, adapted, altered, and appreciated—by artists and craftspeople. Why has the classical style remained at the forefront of artistic endeavor?

The classical period has given us the first works of the Western world to represent the human form with accuracy. The body itself was the sculptors' subject. Their aim was to shape their marble so as to make a general and schematic figure lifelike. Classical sculpture has been a powerful learning device for aspiring artisans from Michelangelo to nineteenth-century artists such as Auguste Rodin. Ancient sculptures—and plaster casts made from them—have been used as teaching tools by educators since the Renaissance. Learning to draw from casts of ancient works was the traditional first step in an artist's education; even many abstract artists of the twentieth century had a solid grounding in works of the classical period.

2. Venus de Milo. Greek statue from the first century B.C., probably an imitation of a fourth-century work. (Vanni/Art Resource, N.Y.)

3. Lysippos. Roman copy of *Apoxyomenos (Scrapers)*, original c. 325–300 B.C. (Apoxyomenos (marble), Roman, (1st century AD)/Vatican Museums and Galleries, Vatican City, Italy/Bildarchiv Steffens Ralph Rainer Steffens/The Bridgeman Art Library International.)

The balanced, rhythmical composition of classical sculpture and architecture is another element that has influenced later artists. Earlier works—from the Greek Archaic period (sixth century B.C.) as well as from ancient Egypt and Mesopotamia—are solid, blocklike, and devoid of any sense of movement. Classical sculptors, by contrast, were able to bring the stone alive with innovative poses, luxuriant drapery, and a careful balancing between relaxation and tension.

The works of Praxiteles embody the ideal of classical sculpture and offer visual proof that the Greeks' search for beauty and truth extended beyond their literature and philosophy.

Praxiteles (fl. 375–330 B.C.) is renowned for the quality of his marble sculpture, such as *Hermes with Young Dionysus* (Figure 1),

considered one of his finest works. Little is known of Praxiteles himself, but much has been written about his art.

The Hermes statue has many of the attributes that distinguish the best classical sculpture. The stance is relaxed: an S-curve takes the weight off one leg and shifts it to the opposite hip. This *contrapposto,* or counterbalanced, pose draws attention to every part of the god's body. The turned and slightly tilted head is a departure from the fully frontal works of earlier periods. The drapery is a careful, three-dimensional rendering of drapery in vase painting from the same period. It is realistic and so fluid that viewers might forget they are looking at marble.

A roughly contemporary work, the *Venus de Milo* (Figure 2) by an unidentified artist, embodies many of the same principles as the Hermes figure. Venus puts her weight on one leg, tensing some muscles and relaxing others. Drapery loosely covers her waist and has the look of soft cotton.

A contemporary of Praxiteles, Lysippos (fl. fourth century B.C.), is credited with changing the "canon of proportions" established by his predecessor Polyclitus. The canon of proportions rules that earlier sculptors followed in carving their masterpieces, assured a certain uniformity in the rendering of the human form. Heads were always a certain proportion of the whole, eyes were placed at a certain level within the face, and so on. But the work of Lysippos is notably different.

One of Lysippos' best-known works, the *Apoxyomenos (Scraper)* (Figure 3), shows a youthful athlete cleaning himself with a *strigyl* (scraper) after exercising. What distinguishes this work from the works of other artists are the proportions. Lysippos' youth has a smaller head and a more slender body. Although he stands with his weight on one foot, his hips are not as sharply angled as the hips of other classical figures, in which the S-curve is more clearly pronounced. Even the face of the athlete foretells a new era in art. Unlike the serene, perfect faces of other classical figures, the Apoxyomenos' expression seems thoughtful and dreamy, not remote and dispassionate.

Distinguished by its portrayal of emotion and drama, *The Laocoön Group* (Figure 4) is one of the most famous works of Western art. Dated to the second century B.C., the work depicts the death of Laocoön, a priest of the god Apollo, and his twin sons, killed by sea serpents because they tried to prevent the entry into Troy of the huge wooden horse in which Greek warriors were concealed. The sculptors, Agesander, Atheodorou, and Polydoros of Rhodes, convey the violence and intensity of events through the exaggeration of facial features, musculature, and pose.

This work from the Hellenistic period differs from its classical predecessors in its emotionality and exaggeration of the human form. Laocoön's face shows anguish over the loss of his sons, and his muscles bulge as he strains to

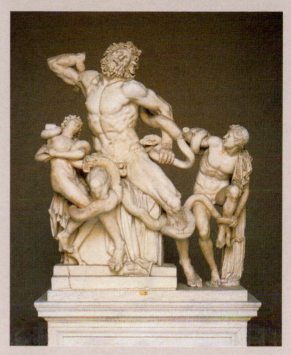

4. Hellenistic Sculpture. *The Laocoön Group*, second century B.C. (Scala/Art Resource, N.Y.)

wrest himself from the serpent's grasp. Laocoön's children are depicted as smaller than their father yet as fully mature men.

Many historians have described the art of Rome as unoriginal and deriving from classical Greek works. The Romans did make multiple copies of many Greek prototypes, but they also excelled in areas of the decorative arts in which we have no evidence of Greek virtuosity. The Romans developed distinctive styles in wall painting (fresco), mosaic, and minor metal arts; their contributions to architecture are also noteworthy.

Frescoes are made by painting directly on wet or damp plaster. Some fresco painters limit their work to small scenes; others cover entire walls with landscapes, people, and architectural elements. Roman fresco painters were adept at reproducing the look of marble and other materials. The *trompe l'oeil* (literally "fool the eye") style of Roman fresco painters demonstrates their skill at reproducing the world around them.

5. Detail of a Pompeian Wall Fresco, Lady Playing the Cithera, first century B.C. (© The Art Gallery Collection/Alamy.)

As can be seen in Figure 5, Roman painters were able to convincingly present three-dimensional objects on a two-dimensional surface. This first-century B.C. fresco, *Lady Playing the Cithera* (a harplike musical instrument), from a villa at Boscoreale, near Pompeii, is an excellent example of the fresco painter's art. Though painted on a flat surface, the chair is set at an angle and projects outward toward the viewer. The chair's three-dimensionality is further emphasized by the placement of the young attendant, who stands behind it, holding on to its back.

Roman sculptors tended to follow closely the classical Greek and Hellenistic traditions. Some art historians assert that originality in Roman sculpture is evident only in lifelike portrait busts of the emperors, often planted firmly on the necks of copies of Greek or Hellenistic gods and heroes. To an extent, this is the case with the life-size *Augustus of the Prima Porta* (Figure 6), a work probably completed during the reign of Augustus (27 B.C.–A.D. 14) or shortly after his death and deification. Many elements of this work are direct borrowings from classical and Hellenistic prototypes. It is

the head, however, that sets this work apart from its forebears. The face of Augustus is a lifelike representation of the emperor, if we assume that the great number of coins bearing Augustus's image offer an accurate likeness. Unlike Greek sculpture, which idealized the human form, this Roman work presents an image that would be recognized by all who viewed it.

Roman works such as the Augustus statue also served as illustrations of contemporary events. Carvings on the breastplate in *Augustus of the Prima Porta* portray the Romans' victory over the Parthians. Pictorial narratives of other Roman achievements were sculpted on freestanding columns and triumphal arches, as well as on the walls of buildings. In this way, Roman rulers were able to transmit news and information throughout their vast empire to people who could not read or who did not speak Latin.

The art and architecture of the Byzantine era and the Middle Ages show a transformation in subject matter. Christianity, with its theme of resurrection and salvation, dominated the period. Both Latin and Greek churches used art to spread Christian teachings and to buttress their authority. Because few people could read or write, both churches relied on sculpture, painting, and drawing to convey the essence of Christianity.

Figure 7, the mosaic *The Court of Justinian*, from the Church of San Vitale in the Italian city of Ravenna, shows the emperor Justinian and his attendants and dates to c. A.D. 547. The emperor stands in the center of the scene and is flanked by officials and local clergy. The contrast between this work and the Boscoreale fresco (Figure 5) is noteworthy. Here, the emphasis is on two-dimensionality and the vertical. All of the figures face front; there is little attempt to show depth or three-dimensionality, except for the somewhat unsuccessful overlapping of figures. These Byzantine figures, with small heads, tiny feet, and disproportionate arms, are elongated and slender, unlike the figures of the Roman painting or the Greek sculptures shown earlier.

As political and spiritual ruler of the Byzantine Empire, Justinian is flanked by twelve companions, drawing a parallel between him and Jesus Christ. His golden halo brings to mind the one usually shown around Christ's head; the attributes of Christianity, including a cross, a censer (incense burner), and a shield bearing a symbolic version of Jesus' name, remind viewers of Justinian's dual roles.

Easily recognized symbols and images such as the halo became part of a common language for transmitting the message of Christ and the church. This is exemplified by the *Enthroned Madonna and Child*, from the Byzantine school (Figure 8) in the thirteenth century, in which the Madonna is shown in what now seems to be a conventional pose—seated on an elaborate chair or throne, facing front, holding the child on her left knee, and supporting him with her left hand. The Madonna is heavily robed, but the artist was able to depict the clothes with the fluidity of the painter responsible for the Boscoreale fresco (Figure 5).

The *Enthroned Madonna and Child*'s origins are Eastern—the Byzantine school having developed in Byzantium, the capital of the eastern Roman Empire. Byzantium (renamed Constantinople in A.D. 330) had a certain sphere of influence in the West, attested to by the Ravenna mosaic (Figure 7), and, as a result, a fusion of Eastern and Western styles is evident in works such as the *Enthroned Madonna*. What is typically Byzantine about this work is the richness of color and the use of gold—in the background and in the Madonna's robes. The faces of the figures owe more to Western art, however. Soft modeling and careful shading make them look almost as if they were superimposed by another artist at another time.

The Last Supper of the thirteenth-century Magdalen Master (Figure 9) preserves the austere and otherworldly emphasis of the Eastern style exhibited by such works as the Ravenna Mosaic. It captures a pivotal moment, when Christ announces to his disciples that he will be betrayed by one of them, and instructs them to commemorate him by consuming bread and wine as his body and blood. (Compare with da Vinci's *Last Supper*, Figure 5 in the art essay "The Renaissance.") This event becomes

6. *Augustus of the Prima Porta.* (Scala/Art Resource, N.Y.)

the basis for the Christian sacrament of the Eucharist.

The painting is two-dimensional. There is no depth, no background, and no foreground. The table does not recede into the picture. The objects on its surface seem stacked vertically one on top of another. The tablecloth lacks texture. The figures seated at the table are immobile, rigid, lifeless, expressionless, severe, and monotonously spaced. There is a prevailing impersonality in the composition.

The painting perfectly exemplifies the characteristic style of Eastern and medieval art, which

7. Mosaic. *The Court of Justinian, c.* A.D. 547. (Scala/Art Resource, N.Y.)

is nonperspectival, usually two-dimensional, and profoundly impersonal.

At this point, Western art begins to undergo another transformation. Styles and subject matter change, paralleling developments in politics and society. Artists working at the end of the Middle Ages and on the verge of the Renaissance include the brothers Jan and Hubert van Eyck. Figure 10 shows *The Last Judgement* (c. 1420–1425), one panel of a diptych (a two-paneled work) painted by one or both of them (the other panel portrays the Crucifixion). *The Last Judgement* illustrates some of the stylistic elements that distinguish these artists. The image is divided in two horizontally. In the upper half, which represents heaven, the mood is one of calm and

order; below, on earth and in hell, pandemonium reigns. This suggestion of the promise of heaven and the threat of hell was intended to motivate people to heed Christian teachings and clerical authority.

The van Eycks portrayed this idea with a clarity and realistic feeling unseen in other works. Their virtuosity is paralleled by the work of a slightly earlier Italian artist, Giotto di Bondone (1267–1337), whose style also marked a definite break with his peers, and whose work stands on the cusp between the Renaissance and what preceded it.

Giotto's *Kiss of Judas*, in the Scrovengi Chapel in Padua, dates from 1305 (Figure 11). A work of the Late Middle Ages, or Gothic period, it represents a major shift in artistic

direction; its lifelike depiction of the human figures seen in the foreground anticipates later perspectival painting. To understand this change in representational art in the fourteenth century, it is necessary to remember what was happening in Italy at the time. Although the art was meant to reflect the kingdom of heaven, actual events in the kingdom on earth played a great role.

As noted earlier, Byzantium and Byzantine art influenced Italian art and society in the medieval period. Images, symbols, and techniques that flourished in Eastern workshops took root in Italy, culminating in what art historians call a neo-Byzantine style in the early thirteenth century, soon after the Crusaders conquered Constantinople in 1204. Italian artists adopted the Byzantine style, which had its roots in classical Greek prototypes. The combination of Byzantine, Greek, and native Italian styles produced the new way of seeing epitomized by Giotto.

8. Byzantine School. *Enthroned Madonna and Child*, thirteenth century. (Virgin and Child (tempera on panel), Byzantine, (14th century)/Church of Sveti Kliment, Ohrid, Macedonia/Giraudon/The Bridgeman Art Library International.)

9. Studio of Magdalen Master. *The Last Supper*, late thirteenth century. (Reunion des Musées Nationaux, Art Resource, N.Y.)

10. Hubert or Jan van Eyck. *The Last Judgement*, c. 1420–1425. (© The Metropolitan Museum of Art/Art Resource, N.Y.)

11. Giotto di Bondone. *Kiss of Judas*, c. 1305, Scrovengi Chapel, Padua, Italy. (Alinari/Art Resource, N.Y.)

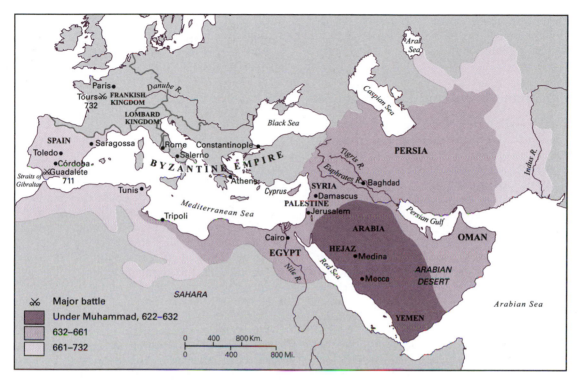

Map 9.2 THE EXPANSION OF ISLAM, 622–732 From 632 to 661, the Arabs, with breathtaking speed, overran the Persian Empire, seized some of Byzantium's provinces, and invaded southern Europe. Their northward momentum was halted in 717 by the Byzantines at Constantinople and in 732 by the Franks at the battle of Tours in central France. (Copyright © 2013 Cengage Learning.)

Turkish conquest of much of Hungary in the 1520s and the siege of Vienna (1529) spread panic in Europe. The Ottomans developed an effective system of administration but could not restore the cultural brilliance, the thriving trade, or the prosperity that the Muslim world had known under the Abbasid caliphs of Baghdad. The vitality that had kept the Muslim world more advanced than Western Europe for most of the Middle Ages dissipated.

LATIN CHRISTENDOM: THE RISE OF EUROPE

The centuries of cultural greatness of the Islamic and the Byzantine civilizations enriched the Western world. They did not, however, produce the major breakthroughs in science, technology, philosophy, economics, and political thought that gave rise to the modern world. That process was the singular achievement of Europe. During the Middle Ages, a common European civilization—Latin Christendom—evolved. It integrated Christian, Greco-Roman, and Germanic elements. Christianity was at the center of medieval civilization, Rome was the spiritual capital and Latin the language of intellectual life, and Germanic customs pervaded social and legal relationships.

During the Early Middle Ages (500–1050), Latin Christendom was culturally far behind the two Eastern civilizations and did not catch up until the twelfth century. In succeeding centuries, however, it produced the movements that ushered in the modern age: the Renaissance, the

Reformation, the Scientific Revolution, the Age of Enlightenment, the French Revolution, and the Industrial Revolution.

Political and Economic Transformation

From the sixth to the eighth century, Europeans struggled to overcome the disorder created by the breakup of the Roman Empire and the deterioration of Greco-Roman civilization. In the process, a new civilization, with its own distinctive style, took root. It grew out of the intermingling of Greco-Roman civilization, the Christian outlook, and Germanic traditions, although centuries would pass before it would come to fruition.

In the fifth century and after, Germanic invaders founded kingdoms in North Africa, Italy, Spain, Gaul, and Britain—lands formerly belonging to the Roman Empire. Even before the invasions, these Germanic tribes had acquired some knowledge of Roman culture and were attracted to it. Therefore, the new rulers sought not to destroy Roman civilization but to share in its advantages. For example, Theodoric the Great (474–526), the Ostrogoth ruler of Italy, retained the Roman Senate, civil service, and schools; and rich aristocratic Roman families continued to hold high government offices. The Burgundians in Gaul and the Visigoths in Spain maintained Roman law for their conquered subjects; and the Frankish ruler Clovis (c. 466–511) wore Roman imperial colors and took Roman titles. All the Germanic kingdoms tried to maintain Roman systems of taxation; furthermore, Latin remained the official language of administration.

However, torn by warfare, internal rebellion, and assassination, the Germanic kingdoms provided a poor political base on which to revive a decadent and dying classical civilization. Most of the kingdoms survived for only a short time and had no enduring impact. An exception to this trend occurred in Gaul and south-central Germany, where the most successful of the Germanic kingdoms was established by the Franks—the founders of the new Europe.

The Roman world was probably too far gone to be rescued, but even if it had not been, the Germans were culturally unprepared to play the role of restorer. By the end of the seventh century, the old Roman lands in Western Europe showed a marked decline in central government, town life, commerce, and learning. Though vigorous and brave, the Germanic invaders were essentially a rural and warrior people, tribal in organization and outlook. Their native culture, without cities or written literature, was primitive compared with the literary, philosophical, scientific, and artistic achievements of the Greco-Roman world. The Germans were not equipped to reform the decaying Roman system of administration and taxation or to cope with the economic problems that had burdened the Empire. Nor could they maintain roads and irrigation systems, preserve skills in the arts of stoneworking and glassmaking, or breathe new life into the dying humanist culture.

Roman ideas of citizenship and the legal state were totally alien to Germanic tradition. The Germans gave loyalty to their kin and to a tribal chief, not to an impersonal state that governed citizens of many nationalities. The king viewed the land he controlled as a private possession that could be divided among his sons after his death—a custom that produced numerous and devastating civil wars and partitions. Unlike the Romans, the Germanic invaders had no trained civil servants to administer the state and no organized system of taxation to provide a secure financial base for government.

The Germans also found Roman law strange, although the Germanic kingdoms did make attempts to retain Roman law codes. Roman law incorporated elements of Greek philosophy and was written, whereas Germanic law at the time of the invasions consisted of unwritten tribal customs. Roman law applied to all people throughout the Empire, regardless of nationality; a German could be judged only by the law of his own tribe. Roman judges investigated evidence and demanded proof; Germanic courts, in the absence of clear evidence, relied on trial by ordeal. In a typical ordeal, a bound defendant was thrown into a river. Sinking meant innocence; floating was interpreted as divine proof of guilt, because the pure water had "rejected" the evildoer. Although primitive by Roman standards, Germanic law did help lessen blood feuds between families. Before long, the Germanic kingdoms began to put customary tribal law, which had absorbed and continued to absorb elements from Roman law, into writing. Replacing Roman law and spreading throughout

Europe, Germanic law became an essential element of medieval society.

The distinguishing feature of classical civilization, its vital urban institutions, had deteriorated in the Late Roman Empire. The shift from an urban to a rural economy accelerated under the kingdoms created by Germanic chieftains. Although the Germanic kings retained Roman cities as capitals, they did not halt the process of decay that had overtaken urban centers. These rulers settled their people in the countryside, not in towns; they did not significantly utilize cities as instruments of local government; and they failed to maintain Roman roads. Although towns did not vanish altogether, they continued to lose control over the surrounding countryside and to decline in wealth and importance. They were the episcopal seats (sees) of bishops, rather than centers of commerce and intellectual life. Italy remained an exception to this general trend. There, Roman urban institutions persisted, even during the crudest period of the Early Middle Ages. Italian cities kept some metal currency in circulation and traded with one another and with Byzantium.

Shrinking commerce during the Early Middle Ages was part of the process of decline begun in the Late Roman Empire. Although commerce never wholly disappeared, it was predominantly localized. Furthermore, it was controlled by colonies of Jews, Syrians, and Greeks—a sign of the economic inertia of Latin Christians. From the last decade of the fifth century to the middle of the seventh century, Byzantine merchants established themselves in the western lands and exchanged papyrus, spices, and textiles for European slaves. Then, in the second half of the seventh century, this trade dropped off greatly; as Muslim power expanded to control the Mediterranean, Byzantine merchants had to turn eastward for markets. Thus, the bonds between East and West weakened, and Europe shifted its axis northward, away from the Mediterranean. Few goods exchanged hands, and few coins circulated; people produced for themselves what they needed.

The Waning of Classical Culture

Greco-Roman humanism, in retreat since the Late Roman Empire, continued its decline in the centuries immediately following Rome's demise. The old Roman upper classes abandoned their heritage and absorbed the ways of their Germanic conquerors, the Roman schools closed, and Roman law faded into disuse. Aside from clerics, few people could read and write Latin, and even learned clerics were rare. Europeans' knowledge of the Greek language was almost totally lost, and the Latin rhetorical style deteriorated. Many literary works of classical antiquity were either lost or unread. Raids by Germanic tribes and later by Muslims, Magyars, and Vikings (see below) devastated libraries. Many works by great authors were lost forever. For example, only seven of the one hundred dramas written by Sophocles have survived. Gone were attempts to understand the natural world through reason; magic and the occult prevailed among both pagans and Christians. The literature of the seventh century, concerned principally with the lives of saints, was devoid of the humanist themes that had motivated Greek and Roman poets and dramatists. European culture was much poorer than the high civilizations of Byzantium, Islam, and ancient Rome.

During this period of cultural poverty, the few persons who were learned generally did not engage in original thought but salvaged and transmitted remnants of classical civilization. Given the context of the times, this was a considerable achievement. These individuals retained respect for the inheritance of Greece and Rome while remaining devoted to Christianity. In a rudimentary way, they were struggling to create a Christian culture that combined the intellectual tradition of Greece and Rome with the religious teachings of the Christian church.

An important figure in the intellectual life of this transitional period was Boethius (480–c. 525), a descendant of a noble family. Boethius had received a classical education at the Platonic Academy at Athens before Emperor Justinian closed it in 529. He was the last Latin-speaking scholar of the Roman world to have mastered the Greek language and to have intimate knowledge of Greek philosophy. Later, Boethius served the Ostrogoth Theodoric I, who ruled Italy. Recognizing that Greco-Roman civilization was dying, Boethius tried to rescue the intellectual heritage of antiquity. He translated into Latin some of Aristotle's treatises on logic and wrote commentaries on

Aristotle, Cicero, and Porphyry (a Neo-Platonist philosopher). He also wrote treatises on theology and textbooks on arithmetic, astronomy, and music. A sudden turn of fortune deprived him of power, prestige, and possessions and confronted him with imminent death when Theodoric ordered him executed in 524 or 525 for allegedly participating in a plot against the throne.

While in prison awaiting execution, Boethius wrote *The Consolation of Philosophy,* which is regarded as one of the masterpieces of world literature. In it, Boethius pondered life's meaning: "Think you that there is any certainty in the affairs of mankind when you know that often one swift hour can utterly destroy a man?"[4] Alone in his dungeon, he turned for guidance and consolation to the philosophical training of his youth. He derived comfort from Lady Philosophy, who reassured him, in the tradition of Socrates and the Stoics, that "if then you are master of yourself, you will be in possession of that which you will never wish to lose, and which Fortune will never be able to take from you."[5] No tyrant can "ever disturb the peculiar restfulness which is the property of a mind that hangs together upon the firm basis of its reason."[6] In the life and thought of Boethius, the classical tradition lived on. He was a bridge between a classical civilization too weakened to be revived and a Christian civilization still in its embryonic stage.

Until the twelfth century, virtually all that Latin Christendom knew of Aristotle came from Boethius's translations and commentaries. Similarly, his work in mathematics, which contains fragments from Euclid, was the principal source for the study of that discipline in the Early Middle Ages. In his theological writings, he strove to demonstrate that reason did not conflict with orthodoxy—an early attempt to attain a rational comprehension of belief, or, as he expressed it, to join faith to reason. Boethius's effort to examine Christian doctrines rationally, a principal feature of medieval philosophy, would grow to maturity in the twelfth and thirteenth centuries. Writing in the sixth century, Boethius was a forerunner of this movement.

Cassiodorus (c. 490–575), a contemporary of Boethius, was born in southern Italy of a good family; he served three Ostrogoth kings. Although Cassiodorus wrote the twelve-volume *History of the Goths* and some theological treatises, his prime legacies were the establishment

of a monastic library containing Greek and Latin manuscripts and his advocacy of higher education to improve the quality of the clergy. In his educational writings, he justified the importance of studying secular literature as an aid to understanding sacred writings. Even though his works were not original, they did rescue some ideas of the ancients from oblivion; these ideas would bear fruit again in later centuries. Cassiodorus's plans for founding a university in Rome modeled after the one in Alexandria did not materialize; in fact, six hundred years would elapse before universities would arise in Latin Christendom. Leaving political office, Cassiodorus retired to a monastery, where he helped initiate the monastic practice of copying ancient texts. Without this tradition, many key Christian and Greco-Roman works would undoubtedly have perished.

In Spain, Isidore of Seville (c. 576–636) compiled an encyclopedia, *Etymologiae,* covering a diversity of topics, from arithmetic and God to furniture. Isidore derived his information from many secular and religious sources. Quite understandably, his work contained many errors, particularly in its references to nature. For centuries, though, the *Etymologiae* served as a standard reference work and was found in every monastic library of note.

The translations and compilations made by Boethius, Cassiodorus, and Isidore, the books collected and copied by monks and nuns, and the schools established in monasteries (particularly those in Ireland, England, and Italy) kept intellectual life from dying out completely in the Early Middle Ages. Amid the deterioration of political authority, the stagnation of economic life, and the decline in learning, a new civilization was emerging. Germanic and Roman peoples intermarried, and Roman, Germanic, and Christian traditions intermingled. But it was the church more than anything else that gave form and direction to the emerging civilization.

THE CHURCH: SHAPER OF MEDIEVAL CIVILIZATION

The Church as Unifier

Christianity was the integrating principle and the church was the dominant institution of the Middle Ages. During the Late Roman Empire, as the Roman state and its institutions decayed, the church gained power and importance; its organization grew stronger, and its membership increased. Unlike the Roman state, the church was a healthy and vital institution. The elite of the Roman Empire had severed their commitment to the values of classical civilization, whereas church leaders were intensely devoted to their faith.

During the invasions of the fifth and sixth centuries, the church, retaining an effective administrative system, assumed many political functions formerly performed by the Roman state and continued to convert the Germanic tribes. By teaching a higher morality, the church tamed the warrior habits of the Germanic peoples. By preserving some of the high culture of Greece and Rome, it opened Germans' minds to new ideas. A unifying and civilizing agent, the church provided people with an intelligible and purposeful conception of life and death. In a dying world, the church was the only institution capable of reconstructing civilized life.

Thus, the Christian outlook, rather than the traditions of the Germanic tribes, was the foundation of medieval civilization. During the course of the Middle Ages, people came to see themselves as participants in a great drama of salvation. There was only one truth: God's revelation to humanity. There was only one avenue to heaven, and it passed through the church. God had established the church to administer the rites through which his love was bestowed on people. The church had the awesome responsibility of caring for human souls. Without the church, it was believed, people would remain doomed sinners. To the medieval mind, society without the church was inconceivable. Membership in a universal church replaced citizenship in a universal empire. Across Europe, from Italy to Ireland, a new society centered on Christianity was forming.

Monks and the Papacy

Monks helped construct the foundations of medieval civilization. During the seventh century, intellectual life on the European continent continued its steady decline. In the monasteries of Ireland and England, however, a tradition of learning persisted. Early in the fifth century, Saint Patrick began the conversion of the Irish to Christianity. In Ireland, Latin became firmly entrenched as the language of both the church and scholars at a time when it was in danger of disappearing in many parts of Europe. Irish monks preserved and cultivated Latin and even kept some knowledge of Greek alive. Irish scholars engaged in biblical analysis, and, besides copying manuscripts, they decorated them, with an exquisite eye for detail. In England, the Anglo-Saxons, both women and men, who converted to Christianity mainly in the seventh century, also established monasteries that kept learning alive. Double monasteries existed, in which monks and nuns obeyed a common rule and one superior, sometimes an abbess. The Venerable Bede (673–735) wrote commentaries on Scripture and translated the fourth Gospel (Saint John's) into Anglo-Saxon. Bede is best known for his *Ecclesiastical History of the English People,* one of the finest medieval historical works.

In the sixth and seventh centuries, Irish and Anglo-Saxon monks and nuns built monasteries in continental Europe and converted people in the surrounding areas. They became the chief agents in Christianizing people in northern Europe. Thus, monks and nuns made possible a unitary European civilization based on a Christian foundation. By copying and preserving ancient texts, they also kept alive elements of ancient civilization.

During the Early Middle Ages, when cities were in decay, monasteries, whose libraries contained theological works and ancient Latin classics, were the main cultural centers; they would remain so until the rebirth of towns in the High Middle Ages. Monks instructed peasants in superior methods of farming and were partly responsible for the reclamation of lands that had been neglected or devastated during the great invasions and for the clearing of new lands. Monasteries also offered succor to the sick and the destitute and served as places of refuge for travelers. To the medieval mind, the monks' and nuns' selfless devotion to God, adoption of apostolic poverty, and dedication to prayer and contemplation represented the highest expression of the Christian way of life; it was the finest and most certain path to salvation. It was not uncommon for both men and women, with old age or even death approaching, to take the vows so that they might die as monks or nuns. Regarding the monks as soldiers in the

MONASTERY OF MONT ST. MICHEL. The monastic institutions throughout Western Europe stood firm amid the intellectual and cultural confusion of the Early Middle Ages. By copying ancient manuscripts and studying Latin, monks preserved elements of classical civilizations. (© Paul Almasy/Corbis.)

war against paganism, unorthodoxy, and heresy, the popes protected monasteries and encouraged their spread.

The Early Middle Ages was a formative period for the **papacy,** as well as for society in general. The status of the papacy was closely tied to events in Italy. In the late sixth century, the papacy was compelled to protect Rome and the surrounding territory from the Lombards, the last Germanic people to settle in once-Roman lands. At this critical stage, Gregory I, the Great (590–604), became pope. A descendant of a prominent Roman family and a monk, Gregory turned out to be one of the ablest medieval popes. He used Roman methods of administration effectively to organize and administer papal property in Italy, Sicily, Sardinia, Gaul, and other regions. The papacy owned huge estates worked by serfs. It also owned timberlands and mines, which provided the income for maintaining the clergy, churches, monasteries, hospitals, and orphanages in Rome and other places. Because of Gregory's efforts, the papacy became the leading financial institution of the day.

Gregory tried to strengthen the pope's authority within the church, insisting that all bishops and the Byzantine church in Constantinople were subject to papal authority. Establishing monasteries, he tightened the bonds between the monks and the papacy, and it was he who

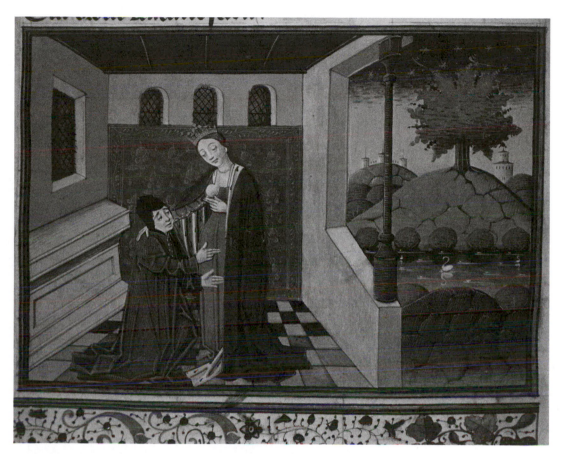

THE CONSOLATION OF PHILOSOPHY. Fortune turns her wheel as Philosophy consoles the imprisoned Boethius, who faces death. (Bridgeman-Giraudon/Art Resource, N.Y.)

dispatched Benedictine monks to England to win over the Anglo-Saxons. The newly established Anglo-Saxon church looked to Rome for leadership. Gregory realized that to lead Christendom effectively the papacy must exercise authority over churches outside Italy—a policy adopted by popes who succeeded him.

He was also an intellectual who wrote commentaries on the books of the Bible and authored many works dealing with Christian themes: the duties of bishops, the lives of saints and monks, miracles, and purgatory. Because of his many writings, Gregory is regarded as a father of the Latin church. An astute diplomat, he knew that

the papacy required the political and military support of a powerful kingdom to protect it from its enemies, especially the Lombards. Accordingly, he set his sights on an alliance with the Franks. Finally materializing 150 years later, this alliance between the papacy and Frankish kings helped shape medieval history.

THE KINGDOM OF THE FRANKS

From their homeland in the Rhine River valley, the Frankish tribes had expanded into Roman territory during the fourth and fifth centuries.

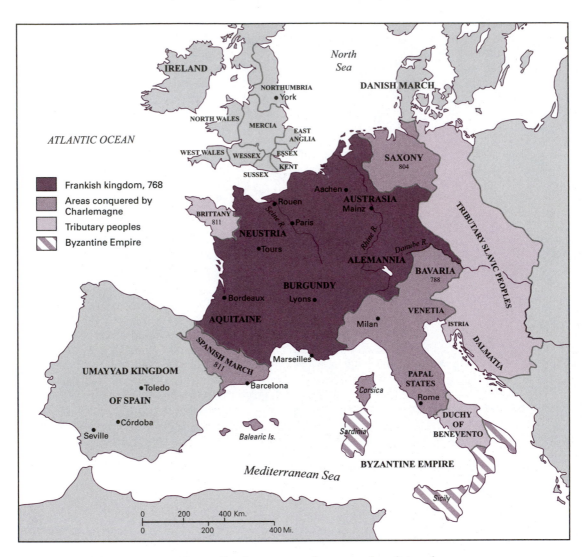

Map 9.3 **The Carolingian World** Resting more on the personal qualities of Charlemagne than on any firm economic or political foundation, the Carolingian empire did not survive the emperor's death in 814. (Copyright © 2013 Cengage Learning.)

The ruler Clovis united the various Frankish tribes and conquered most of Gaul. In 496, he converted to Roman Christianity. Clovis's conversion to Catholicism was an event of great significance. A number of other Germanic kings had adopted the Arian form of Christianity, which the church had declared heretical. By embracing Roman Christianity, the Franks became a potential ally of the papacy.

Clovis's successors could not maintain control over their lands, and power passed to the mayor of the palace, the king's chief officer. Serving as mayor of the palace from 717 to 741, Charles Martel subjected all Frankish lands to his rule. In addition, at the battle of Tours in 732, he defeated the Muslims. Although the Muslims continued to occupy the Iberian Peninsula, they would advance no farther north into Europe.

Charles Martel was succeeded by his son, Pepin the Short, who in 751 deposed the king. With the approval of the papacy and his nobles, Pepin was crowned king by Boniface, a prominent bishop. Two years later, Pope Stephen II anointed Pepin again as king of the Franks and appealed to him to protect the papacy from the Lombards. Pepin crossed into Italy, defeated the Lombards, and turned over captured lands to the papacy. This famous Donation of Pepin made the pope ruler of the territory between Rome and Ravenna, which became known as the Papal States.

The Era of Charlemagne

The alliance between the Franks and the papacy was continued by Pepin's successor, Charlemagne (Charles the Great), who ruled from 768 to 814. Charlemagne continued the Carolingian policy of expanding the Frankish kingdom. He destroyed the Lombard kingdom, added Bavaria to his kingdom, and, after long, terrible wars, compelled the Saxons to submit to his rule and convert to Christianity—thousands were beheaded when they were slow to choose between baptism or execution. He also conquered a region in northern Spain, the Spanish March, which served as a buffer between the Christian Franks and the Muslims in Spain.

Immense difficulties arose in governing the expanded territories. Size seemed an insuperable obstacle to effective government, particularly since Charlemagne's administrative structure, lacking trained personnel, was primitive by Islamic, Byzantine, or Roman standards. The empire was divided into about 250 counties administered by counts—nobles personally loyal to the ruler. Men from powerful families, the counts served as generals, judges, and administrators, implementing the king's decisions. To supervise the counts, Charlemagne created *missi dominici* (royal messengers)—generally two laymen and a bishop or abbot—who made annual journeys to the different counties. The purpose of the missi dominici was to prevent counts and their subordinates from abusing their power and undermining Charlemagne's authority.

On Christmas Day in Rome in the year 800, Pope Leo III crowned Charlemagne emperor of the Romans. The initiative for the coronation probably came from the papacy, not from Charlemagne. The meaning of this event has aroused conflicting opinions among historians, but certain conclusions seem justified. The title signified that the tradition of a world empire still survived despite the demise of the western Roman Empire three hundred years earlier. But because it was the pope who crowned Charlemagne, this meant that the emperor had a spiritual responsibility to spread and defend the faith. Thus, Roman universalism was fused with Christian universalism.

The Frankish Empire, of course, was only a dim shadow of the Roman Empire. The Franks had no Roman law or Roman legions; there were no cities that were centers of economic and cultural activity; and officials were not trained civil servants with a world outlook, but uneducated war chieftains with a tribal viewpoint. Yet Charlemagne's empire did embody the concept of a universal Christian empire, an ideal that would endure throughout the Middle Ages.

The crowning of a Germanic ruler as emperor of the Romans by the head of the church represented the merging of Germanic, Roman, and Christian traditions, which is the essential characteristic of medieval civilization. This blending of traditions was also evident on a cultural plane, for Charlemagne, a Germanic warrior-king, showed respect for classical learning and Christianity, both non-Germanic traditions.

Carolingian Renaissance

Charlemagne felt that it was his religious duty to raise the educational level of the clergy so that they understood and could properly teach the faith. To do so required overcoming the illiteracy or semiliteracy of clergymen and preparing sacred Scriptures that were uniform, complete, and free of errors. Charlemagne also fostered education to train administrators who would be capable of overseeing his empire and the royal estates; such men had to be literate. He himself learned Latin and spoke it fluently.

To achieve his purpose, Charlemagne gathered some of the finest scholars in Europe. Alcuin of York, England (735–804), was given charge of the palace school attended by Charlemagne and

Saint Boniface

Of the many English monks and nuns who converted inhabitants of the Netherlands and Germany, none was more important than Saint Boniface (c. 680–754). In 716, Boniface, then a monk called Wynfrid who had earned a reputation as a Latin scholar, left England for Frisia in order to restore the churches that had been destroyed when the Frisians revolted against Frankish rule and Christian proselytizing. Consecrated bishop in 722, he extended his missionary activity into Bavaria and Thuringia. Working closely with the papacy, he founded monasteries, including the famous Abbey of Fulda; converted pagans; and imposed Christian standards of behavior on both clergy and laypeople. For example, he prohibited idol worship and the selling of slaves to heathens for sacrifices. In a letter to Pope Zacharias, he expressed his displeasure with deacons who "have four or five concubines in their beds, still read the Gospel and are not ashamed or afraid to call themselves deacons—nay rather, entering upon the priesthood, they continue in the same vices, add sin to sin, declare that they also have a right . . . to celebrate mass."* He also denounced "any layman, be he emperor, king, official, or count [who] may capture a monastery from the power of a bishop, an abbot, or an abbess and begin to hold property bought by the blood of Christ—the ancient fathers called such a man a robber, sacrilegious, a murderer of the poor, a devil's wolf entering the sheepfold of Christ, to be condemned with the ultimate anathema before the judgment of Christ."†

Boniface maintained a correspondence with his cousin Lioba, an English-born nun, who became abbess of the convent Boniface founded at Tauberbischofsheim, near the Main River. Shortly before his death, Boniface visited with Lioba at her convent. He urged her not to "forsake the land of your pilgrimage. . . . Hold

his sons and daughters, high lords, and youths training to serve the emperor. Throughout France, Alcuin expanded schools and libraries, promoted the copying of ancient manuscripts, and imposed basic literary standards on the clergy.

The focus of the Carolingian Renaissance was predominantly Christian: an effort to train clergymen and improve their understanding of the Bible and the writings of the church fathers. This process raised the level of literacy and improved the Latin style. Most important, monastic copyists continued to preserve ancient texts, which otherwise might never have survived; the oldest surviving manuscripts of many ancient Greek and Roman works are Carolingian copies.

Compared with the Greco-Roman past, with the cultural explosion of the twelfth and thirteenth centuries, or with the great Italian Renaissance of the fifteenth century, the Carolingian Renaissance seems slight indeed. Although it did rediscover and revive ancient Roman works and adopt Roman architecture and artistic forms, it did not recapture the worldly spirit of Greece and Rome. Carolingian scholars did not engage in independent philosophical speculation or search for new knowledge, nor did they achieve that synthesis of faith and reason that would be constructed by the great theologians of the twelfth and thirteenth centuries. The Carolingian Renaissance did, however, reverse the process of cultural decay, which had characterized much of the Early Middle Ages. Learning would never again fall to the low level it had reached during the centuries following the decline of Rome.

During the era of Charlemagne, a distinct European civilization took root. It blended the Roman heritage of a world empire, the intellectual achievement of the Greco-Roman mind, Christian otherworldliness, and the customs of the Germanic peoples. This nascent civilization of Latin Christendom differed from Byzantine and Islamic civilizations, and Latin Christians were growing conscious of the difference. But the new medieval civilization was still centuries away from its high point, which would be reached in the twelfth and thirteenth centuries.

Charlemagne's empire also engendered the ideal of a unified Latin Christendom: a single

bravely to your course, carry on the good work day by day, and heed not the body's weakness. Time is not long, suffering is not hard, if your eyes are set upon eternity."[‡]

When Boniface died, Archbishop Cuthbert of Canterbury praised him for bringing "savage peoples from their long and devious wanderings in the wide abyss of eternal perdition into the glorious pathways of the heavenly fatherland by the inspiration of his holy words and by the example of his pious and gentle life."[§] When Lioba died in 780, she was buried at Fulda to be joined with Boniface.

The Letters of Saint Boniface, trans. Ephraim Emerton (New York: Columbia University Press, 1940), 80.

[†]Ibid., 140.

[‡]Quoted in Eleanor Duckett, *The Wandering Saints of the Early Middle Ages* (New York: Norton, 1959), 227.

[§]*The Letters of Saint Boniface,* 184.

Christian community under one government. This new collectivity would supersede the separate Germanic tribal units. Over the centuries, the pursuit of this ideal of a Christian world-state, Christendom, would inspire many people, both clergy and laity.

The Breakup of Charlemagne's Empire

After Charlemagne's death in 814, his son, Louis the Pious, inherited the throne. Louis aimed to preserve the empire, but the task was virtually impossible. The empire's strength rested more on the personal qualities of Charlemagne than on any firm economic or political foundation. In particular, it never developed an empirewide system of taxation, such as the one that had supported the Roman Empire for centuries. Moreover, the empire was simply too large and consisted of too many diverse peoples to be governed effectively. Besides Frankish nobles, who sought to increase their own power at the emperor's expense, Louis had to deal with his own rebellious sons. After

Louis died in 840, the empire was divided among the three surviving sons.

The Treaty of Verdun in 843 gave Louis the German the eastern part of the empire, which marked the beginning of Germany; to Charles the Bald went the western part, which was the start of France; and Lothair received the Middle Kingdom, which extended from Rome to the North Sea. The Middle Kingdom would become a source of conflict between France and Germany into the twentieth century. As central authority waned, large landowners increasingly exercised authority in their own regions. Simultaneous invasions from all directions furthered this movement toward localism and decentralization.

In the ninth and tenth centuries, Latin Christendom was attacked on all sides. From bases in North Africa, Spain, and Sicily, Muslims ravaged regions of southern Europe, even as far as the suburbs of Rome. They deported shiploads of Christians to North Africa to be sold in slave markets. The Magyars, originally from western Asia and linguistically related to Finns and Turks, crossed the Carpathian Mountains in the ninth century and established themselves on the plains of the Danube; their horsemen launched lightning raids into northern Italy, western Germany, and parts of France. Defeated in Germany in 933 and again in 955, the Magyars withdrew to what is now Hungary; they ceased their raids and adopted Christianity.

Still another group of invaders, the Northmen, or Vikings, sailed from Scandinavia in their long, open, wooden ships to raid the coasts and river valleys of Western Europe. Superb seamen, the Vikings crossed the North Atlantic and settled in Iceland and Greenland; from there, they almost certainly traveled to and landed on the coast of North America. In addition to their conquests and explorations, the Vikings also produced rich poetry, excelled at crafts, and contributed greatly to the revival of trade in the High Middle Ages.

In pursuit of slaves, jewels, and precious metals hoarded in monasteries, the Viking invaders plundered, destroyed, raped, and murdered. Villages were devastated, monasteries were looted and their libraries set ablaze, ports were ruined, and the population was decimated. Trade was at a standstill, coins no longer circulated, and farms were turned into wastelands. The European economy, already gravely weak, collapsed; the political authority of kings disappeared; and cultural life and learning withered.

These terrible attacks heightened political insecurity and accelerated anew the process of decentralization that had begun with the decline of Rome. During these chaotic times, counts came to regard as their own the land that they administered and defended for their king. At a time when monarchs could no longer guarantee the safety of their subjects, the inhabitants of a district looked on the count or local lord, frequently a former Carolingian official, as their ruler, for his men and fortresses protected them. In their regions, nobles exercised public power formerly held by kings, an arrangement later designated as *feudalism.*

Wherever great lords failed to protect their territories from neighboring counts or from invaders, political power was further fragmented. In other areas, local nobles chipped away at a count's authority in his county. In his region, the local lord, aided by warrior-knights, exercised virtually supreme authority; people turned to him for protection and for the administration of justice. Europe had entered an age of feudalism, in which the essential unit of government was not a kingdom but a local region, and political power lay in the hands of local lords.

MEDIEVAL SOCIETY

Arising during a period of collapsing central authority, invasion, scanty public revenues, and declining commerce and town life, feudalism attempted to provide some order and security. Feudalism was not a planned system devised logically from general principles but rather an improvised response to the challenge posed by ineffectual central authority. Feudal practices differed from locality to locality and in some regions barely took root. Although it was only a stopgap means of government, feudalism did bring some order, justice, and law during an era of breakdown, localism, and transition. It would remain the predominant political arrangement until kings reasserted their authority in the High and Late Middle Ages.

Feudalism made an enduring impact on Western civilization. It contributed to Western notions about honor, the deportment of gentlemen, and romantic love (see Chapter 11). Most important, feudal traditions laid the groundwork for the principle of limiting a king's power and for the practice of parliamentary government (see Chapters 10 and 12).

Feudalism was built on an economic foundation known as *manorialism.* Although pockets of free peasantry remained, a village community, or manor, consisting of serfs bound to the land became the essential agricultural arrangement for much of the Middle Ages. The manorial village was the means of organizing an agricultural society with limited markets and money. Neither lords nor priests performed economically productive work. Their ways of life were made possible by the toil of serfs.

Manorialism and feudalism presupposed a stable social order: clergy who prayed, lords who warred, and serfs who toiled. People believed that society functioned smoothly when individuals accepted their status and performed their proper role. In the words of an eleventh-century cleric,

> *Mankind, since the beginning of time has been divided in three, those who pray, those who cultivate, those who fight, and each of the three is comforted on either side by the two others. He who, forsaking the world, gives himself to a life of prayer owes it to the warriors that he is able to carry out his holy task in safety, while he owes his bodily nourishment to the farmers. Similarly, the farmers ascend to God through the prayers of the ecclesiastics and are defended by the weapons of the warriors. So also, the warriors are fed by the produce of the fields and benefit from the income therefrom, while the holy prayers of the pious whom they protect will expiate the crimes which they commit in battle.*[7]

A person's rights, duties, and relationship to law depended on his or her ranking in the social order. To change position was to upset the organic unity of society. And no one, serfs included, should be deprived of the traditional rights associated with his or her rank. This arrangement was justified by the clergy.

> *God himself has willed that among men, some must be lords and some serfs, in such a fashion that the lords venerate and love God, and that the serfs love and venerate their lord following the word of the Apostle; serfs obey your temporal lords with fear and trembling; lords treat your serfs according to justice and equity.*[8]

Bishop Adalbero of Laon: *The Tripartite Society*

Medieval thinkers came to see their society divided into three different but complementary groups: clergy, lords, and serfs. Each group had its own responsibilities—priests guided the souls of the faithful; lords protected society from its enemies; and the serfs' toil provided sustenance for everyone. Written in about 1020, the following statement by Bishop Adalbero of Laon, France, illustrates the tripartite nature of medieval society.

The community of the faithful is a single body, but the condition of society is threefold in order. For human law distinguishes two classes. Nobles and serfs, indeed, are not governed by the same ordinance. . . . The former are the warriors and the protectors of the churches. They are the defenders of the people, of both great and small, in short, of everyone, and at the same time they ensure their own safety. The other class is that of the serfs. This luckless breed possesses nothing except at the cost of its own labour. Who could, reckoning with an abacus, add up the sum of the cares with which the peasants are occupied, of their journeys on foot, of their hard labours? The serfs provide money, clothes, and food, for the rest; no free man could exist without serfs. Is there a task to be done? Does anyone want to put himself out? We see kings and prelates make themselves the serfs of their serfs; [but in truth] the master, who claims to feed his serf, is fed by him. And the serf never sees an end to his tears and his sighs. God's house, which we think of as one, is thus divided into three; some pray, others fight, and yet others work. The three groups, which coexist, cannot bear to be separated; the services rendered by one are a precondition for the labours of the two others; each in his turn takes it upon himself to relieve the whole. Thus the threefold assembly is none the less united, and it is thus that law has been able to triumph, and that the world has been able to enjoy peace.

Question for Analysis

1. According to Bishop Adalbero, what was the virtue of the triparite society?

Jacques Le Goff, *Medieval Civilization*, trans. Julia Barrow (Oxford: Blackwell, 1990), 255.

Vassalage

Feudal relationships enabled lords to increase their military strength. The need for military support was the principal reason for the condition of vassalage. A vassal was a knight who in a solemn ceremony pledged loyalty to a lord. This feature of feudalism derived from an ancient Germanic ceremony during which warriors swore personal allegiance to the head of the war-band. Among other things, the vassal gave military service to his lord and received in return a *fief*, which was usually land sufficient to support his needs. This fief was inhabited by peasants, and the crops that they raised provided the vassal with his means of support.

Besides rendering military assistance and supplying knights, the vassal owed several other obligations to his lord in return for the fief and the lord's protection. These duties included sitting in the lord's court and judging cases, such as the breach of feudal agreements between the lord and his other vassals; providing lodgings when the lord traveled through the vassal's territory; offering a gift when the lord's son was knighted or when his eldest daughter married; and raising a ransom should the lord be captured by an enemy.

Both lord and vassal felt honor-bound to abide by the oath of loyalty. It became an accepted custom for a vassal to renounce his loyalty to his lord if the latter failed to protect him from enemies, mistreated him, or increased the vassal's obligations as fixed by the feudal contract. Similarly, if a vassal did not live up to his obligations, the lord would summon him to his court, where the vassal would be tried

CHESS PIECES. These grim and foreboding chessmen depict the medieval nobility's concern with combat. (© The Trustees of the British Museum/Art Resource, N.Y.)

for treachery. If found guilty, he could lose his fief and perhaps his life. Sometimes disputes between vassals and lords erupted into warfare. Because a vassal often held land from more than one lord and sometimes was himself a lord to vassals, situations frequently became awkward, complex, and confusing. On occasion, a vassal had to decide to which lord he owed *liege homage* (prime loyalty).

As feudalism evolved, the king came to be regarded as the chief lord, who had granted fiefs to the great lords, who in turn had divided them into smaller units and regranted them to vassals. Thus, all members of the ruling class, from the lowliest knights to the king, occupied a place in the feudal hierarchy. In theory, the king was the highest political authority and the source of land tenure, but in actual fact he was often less powerful than other nobles of the realm.

Feudalism would decline when kings converted their theoretical powers into actual powers. The decline of feudalism was a gradual process; conflict between the crown and the aristocracy would persist, with varying degrees of intensity, for several centuries, but the future belonged to the centralized state being shaped by kings, not to feudal fragmentation.

Feudal Law

Feudal law, which incorporated many features of traditional Germanic law, differed markedly from Roman law. Roman law was universal, having been enacted by a central government for a world empire. It was also rational, for it sought to be in accord with natural law that applied to all; and it was systematic, for it offered a framework of standards that applied to individual cases. Feudal law, in contrast, was local, covering only a small region. Moreover, it was personal. In the Roman view, the individual as a citizen owed obligations to the state, whereas under feudalism, a vassal owed loyalty and service to a lord according to the terms of a personal agreement made between them.

In the feudal view, lords and kings did not make law; rather, they were guided by tradition and precedent. They discovered and confirmed law by examining ancient customs. Therefore, feudal patterns of landownership, military service, and wardship came to be regarded as an expression of ancient, unchanging, and inviolable custom. Consequently, if the vassal believed that his lord had violated the feudal agreement, that is, had broken faith with him and had transgressed tradition, the vassal would demand restoration of customary rights before an audience of his fellow vassals. Often lords battled one another, believing that they were defending their rights. Similarly, lords claimed the right to resist kings who did not honor their feudal agreements.

Feudal Warriors

Feudal lords viewed manual labor and commerce as degrading for men of their rank. They considered only one vocation worthy: that of warrior. Through combat, the lord demonstrated his valor, earned his reputation, measured his individual worth, derived excitement, added to his wealth, and defended his rights. Warfare was his whole purpose in life. During the twelfth century, to relieve the boredom of peacetime, nobles staged gala tournaments in which knights, fighting singly or in teams, engaged each other in battle to prove their skill and courage. The victors in these pageants gained prestige in the eyes of fellow nobles and admiring ladies and received prizes—falcons, crowns, and substantial amounts of money. The feudal glorification of combat became deeply ingrained in Western society and endured into the twentieth century. Over the centuries, a code of behavior, called *chivalry*, evolved for the feudal nobility. A true knight was expected to fight bravely, demonstrate loyalty to his lord, and treat other knights with respect and courtesy.

In time, the church interjected a religious element into the warrior culture of the feudal knight. It sought to use the fighting spirit of the feudal class for Christian ends: knights could assist the clergy in enforcing God's will. Thus, to the Germanic tradition of loyalty and courage was added a Christian component. As a Christian gentleman, a knight was expected to honor the laws of the church and to wield his sword in the service of God. He was supposed to protect women, children, and the weak and to defend the church against heretics and infidels. The very ceremony of knighthood was placed within a Christian framework. A priest blessed the future knight's arms and prayed that the knight would always "defend the Just and Right."

Regarding the private warfare of lords as lawless violence that menaced social life, the church, in the eleventh century, imposed strictures called the Peace of God and the Truce of God. These restrictions limited feudal warfare to certain days of the week and certain times of the year. Thus, the church tried to regulate warfare according to moral principles. Although only partially effective, these religious restraints did offer Christian society some respite from plundering and incessant warfare.

Noblewomen

Feudal society was very much a man's world. In theory, women were deemed to be physically, morally, and intellectually inferior to men; in practice, they were subjected to male authority. Fathers arranged the marriages of their daughters. Girls from aristocratic families were generally married at age sixteen or younger to a man often twice as old. The wife of a lord was at the mercy of her husband; if she angered him, she might expect a beating. A French law code of the thirteenth century stated: "In a number of cases men may be excused for the injuries they inflict on their wives, nor should the law intervene. Provided he neither kills nor maims her, it is legal for a man to beat his wife when she wrongs him."[9] Although the church taught that both men and women were precious to God and spiritual equals, church tradition also regarded women as agents of the Devil—evil temptresses who, like the biblical Eve, used their

NOBLEWOMEN. **At times, medieval ladies joined their husband's hunting party.** (akg-images)

sexuality to lure men into sin—and church law also permitted wife beating.

In Mary, the mother of Jesus, however, Christians had an alternative image of women to the image suggested by Eve, one that placed women in a position of honor. Devotion to the Virgin Mary reached its high point in the twelfth and thirteenth centuries with the growing belief in the Immaculate Conception (the idea, which later became a doctrine, that Mary was conceived free of original sin and remained free of sin throughout her life).* Moreover, medieval Christians believed that Mary, by dedicating her entire life to Jesus in his work of redemption, cooperated with him

in his ministry and could intercede with him in behalf of individual Christians. The numerous artistic depictions of Mary as the Mother of God and the Queen of Heaven, as well as the multitude of churches named after the Virgin, are evidence of the popular piety that the cult of Mary generated throughout the Middle Ages.

Aristocratic girls who did not marry often entered a convent. (Peasant daughters, because they were needed on the farm—they probably worked as hard and as well as men—rarely became nuns. Moreover, their parents could not afford the dowry, payable in land, cash, or goods, required by the convent for admission.) The nunneries provided an outlet for the talents of unmarried noblewomen. Abbesses demonstrated organizational skills in supervising the convent's affairs. Some nuns acquired an education and, like their male counterparts, copied manuscripts and thus preserved knowledge and ideas of the past. The nun Hroswitha (c. 935–c. 1001) of Gandersheim, in Saxony, Germany, produced poetry, history, and plays. Inspired by the Roman poet Terence, she wrote six dramas—the first since Roman times—along with a history of Germanic rulers and one of her own convent.

As the lady of the castle, the lord's wife performed important duties. She assigned tasks to the servants; made medicines; preserved food; taught young girls how to sew, spin, and weave (she was responsible for providing the lord and his companions with most of the clothes they required); and, despite her subordinate position, took charge of the castle when her husband was away. If the lord was taken prisoner in war, she raised the ransom to pay for his release. Sometimes she put on armor and went to war. For amusement, noblewomen enjoyed chess and other board games, played musical instruments, or embroidered tapestries to cover castle walls. A lady might also join her husband on the hunt, a favorite recreation of the medieval nobility.

Agrarian Life

The origins of manorialism can be traced in part to the Late Roman Empire, when peasants depended on the owners of large estates for protection and security. This dependence increased during the

*The Immaculate Conception did not become Roman Catholic dogma until 1854, when Pope Pius IX promulgated the bull *Ineffabilis Deus*.

Early Middle Ages, especially during the invasions of Northmen, Magyars, and Muslims in the ninth and tenth centuries. Peasants continued to sacrifice their freedom in exchange for protection, or, in some cases, they were too weak to resist the encroachments of local magnates. Like feudalism, manorialism was not an orderly system but consisted of improvised relationships and practices that varied from region to region.

A lord controlled at least one manorial village; great lords might control hundreds. A small manor included a dozen families; a large one, as many as fifty or sixty. The manorial village was never completely self-sufficient because salt, millstones, and metalware were generally obtained from outside sources; it did, however, constitute a balanced economic setting. Peasants grew grain and raised cattle, sheep, goats, and hogs; blacksmiths, carpenters, and stonemasons built and repaired dwellings and implements; the village priest cared for the souls of the inhabitants; and the lord defended the manor and administered the customary law.

The serf and his family lived in a dismal, one-room cottage that they shared with chickens and pigs. In the center burned a small fire, the smoke escaping through a hole in the roof. In cold weather when the fire was strong, the room filled with smoke. When it rained, water came through the thatched roof and turned the earthen floor into mud. The odor from animal excrement was ever present.

Poor roads, few bridges, and dense forests made travel difficult; thieves and warring knights made it unsafe. Peasants generally lived, worked, and died on the lord's estate and were buried in the village churchyard. Few had any contact with the world beyond the village of their birth. When a manor was attacked by another lord, the peasants found protection inside the walls of their lord's house. In many places, by the twelfth century, this building had become a well-fortified stone castle.

In return for protection and the right to cultivate fields and to pass these holdings on to their children, serfs owed obligations to their lord, and their personal freedom was restricted in a variety of ways. Bound to the land, they could not leave the manor without the lord's consent. Before serfs could marry, they had to obtain the lord's permission and pay a fee. The lord could select a wife for his serf and force him to marry her. Sometimes a serf, objecting to the lord's choice, preferred to pay a fine: "Thomas of Oldbury came on summons and was commanded to take Agatha of Halesowen to wife; he said he would rather be fined."[10] These rules also applied to serfs' children, who inherited their parents' obligations. In addition to working their allotted land, the serfs had to tend the fields reserved for the lord. Other services exacted by the lord included digging ditches, gathering firewood, building fences, repairing roads and bridges, and sewing clothes. Probably somewhat more than half of a serf's workweek was devoted to these labor obligations. Serfs also paid a variety of dues to the lord, most notably for using the lord's mill, bake-oven, and winepress.

Serfs did derive some benefits from manorial relationships. They received protection from roving brigands and warring nobles, and they possessed customary rights, which the lord generally respected, to cottages and farmland. But in a world periodically threatened with famine and epidemics, serfs faced an unrelenting struggle to survive, a struggle made all the more difficult by the contempt lords had for them. Medieval literature often depicted peasants as repulsive creatures—ugly, dirty, cowardly, and uncouth.

If a lord demanded more services or dues than were customary, or if he interfered with their right to cottages or strips of farmland, the peasants might demonstrate their discontent by refusing to work for the lord. Up to the fourteenth century, however, open rebellion was rare because lords possessed considerable military and legal power. The manorial system promoted attitudes of dependency and servility among the serfs; their hopes for a better life were directed toward heaven.

Medieval agriculture suffered from several deficiencies. Among them was the short supply of fertilizer; farmers depended solely on animal manure. Inadequate wooden plows and primitive methods of harnessing draft animals resulted in low yields. Yet as the Middle Ages progressed, important improvements in agriculture (discussed in Chapter 10) took place and had wide ramifications for medieval economic and social life. In the High Middle Ages, the revival of an urban economy and the reemergence of central authority would undermine manorial (and feudal) relationships.

NOTES

1. Speros Vryonis Jr., *Byzantium and Europe* (New York: Harcourt, Brace and World, 1967), 193.
2. *The Koran,* trans. N. J. Dawood (Baltimore: Penguin Books, 1961), 108–109.
3. W. Montgomery Watt, *The Influence of Islam on Medieval Europe* (Edinburgh: Edinburgh University Press, 1972), 43.
4. Boethius, *The Consolation of Philosophy,* trans. W. V. Cooper (New York: Modern Library, 1943), 26.
5. Ibid., 29.
6. Ibid., 34.
7. Quoted in Jean-Pierre Poly and Eric Bournazel, *The Feudal Transformation 900–1200,* trans. Caroline Higgitt (New York: Holmes and Meier, 1991), 149.
8. Quoted in V. H. H. Green, *Medieval Civilization in Western Europe* (New York: St. Martin's Press, 1971), 35.
9. Cited in Frances Gies and Joseph Gies, *Women in the Middle Ages* (New York: Thomas Y. Crowell, 1978), 46.
10. Quoted in G. G. Coulton, *Medieval Village, Manor, and Monastery* (New York: Harper Torchbooks, 1960), 82.

SUGGESTED READING

Angold, Michael, *Byzantium: The Bridge from Antiquity to the Middle Ages* (2001). An excellent introduction.

Collins, Roger, *Early Medieval Europe 300–1000* (1999). A clearly and expertly written text.

Fossier, Robert, ed., The *Cambridge Illustrated History of The Middle Ages, Vol. 1, 350–950* (2000). Excellent essays on major themes.

Gies, Frances, and Joseph Gies, *Life in a Medieval Castle* (1974). The castle as the center of medieval life; passages from journals, songs, and account books.

Holmes, George, ed., *The Oxford History of Medieval Europe* (1988). Essays by several scholars; good opening essay on transformation of the Roman world.

Lewis, A. R., *Emerging Medieval Europe* (1967). Good discussions of both economic and social changes.

Lewis, Bernard, ed. and trans., *Islam from the Prophet Muhammad to the Capture of Constantinople,* 2 vols. (1979). A valuable collection of original sources.

Lucas, Angela M., *Women in the Middle Ages* (1983). Women and religion, marriage, and letters.

Rowling, Marjorie, *Life in Medieval Times* (1973). All phases of medieval daily life.

Tierney, Brian, *Western Europe in the Middle Ages* (1970). An outstanding text.

Zacour, Norman, *An Introduction to Medieval Institutions* (1969). Comprehensive essays on all phases of medieval society.

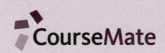

Chapter 10

The High Middle Ages: Vitality and Renewal

Miniature painting of Flemish citizens receiving a city charter, Chronique de Hainout, fifteenth century. (Bibliotheque Royal de Belgique.)

- **Economic Expansion**
- **The Rise of States**
- **The Growth of Papal Power**
- **Christians and Jews**

Focus Questions

1. What were the signs of vitality and recovery in European economic, political, and religious life during the High Middle Ages?

2. What factors contributed to the rise of towns? What was the significance of the medieval town?

3. Why was there a conflict between church and state during the Middle Ages?

4. What prompted lords and commoners to heed the papacy's call for a crusade?

5. What conditions led to the rise of states? What were the essential differences characterizing the development of medieval England, France, and Germany?

6. What factors led to the rise of anti-Semitism during the Middle Ages? How does anti-Semitism demonstrate the power of mythical thinking?

By the end of the eleventh century, Europe showed many signs of recovery and vitality. The invasions of Magyars and Vikings had ended, and powerful lords and kings imposed greater order on their territories. Improvements in technology and the clearing of new lands increased agricultural production. More food, the fortunate absence of plagues, and the limited nature of feudal warfare contributed to a population increase. The revival of long-distance trade and the emergence of towns were other visible signs of economic expansion. Offensives against the Muslims—in Spain, in Sicily, and (at the end of the century) in the Holy Land—demonstrated Europe's growing might and self-confidence. So too did the German conquest and colonization of lands on the northeastern frontier of Latin Christendom.

Reform movements strengthened the bonds between the church and the people and increased the power of the papacy. During the High Middle Ages (1050–1300), the pope, as Christ's deputy, sought to direct, if not rule, all Christendom. European economic and religious vitality was paralleled by a cultural flowering in philosophy, literature, and the visual arts. The civilization of Latin Christendom had entered its golden age.

ECONOMIC EXPANSION

A period of economic expansion, the High Middle Ages witnessed an agricultural revolution, a commercial revolution, the rebirth of towns, and the rise of an enterprising and dynamic middle class.

Agricultural Revolution

During the Middle Ages, important advances were made in agriculture. Many of these innovations occurred in the Early Middle Ages but were adopted only gradually and were not used everywhere. In time, however, they markedly increased production. By the end of the thirteenth century, medieval agriculture had reached a technical level far superior to that of the ancient world.

One innovation was a heavy plow that cut deeply into the soil. This new plow enabled farmers to work more quickly and effectively. As a

Chronology 10.1 ❖ The High Middle Ages

910	Founding of the Abbey of Cluny
962	Otto I crowned emperor of the Romans, beginning the Holy Roman Empire
987	Hugh Capet becomes king of France
1054	Split between the Byzantine and the Roman churches
1061–1091	Norman conquest of Sicily
1066	Norman conquest of England
1075	Start of the Investiture Controversy
1096	First Crusade begins
c. 1100	Revival of the study of Roman law at Bologna
1163	Start of the construction of the Cathedral of Notre Dame
1198–1216	Pontificate of Innocent III: height of the church's power
1267–1273	Saint Thomas Aquinas writes *Summa Theologica*
c. 1321	Dante completes *Divine Comedy*

result, they could cultivate more land, including the heavy, moist soils of northern Europe, which had offered too much resistance to the light plow. Another important advance in agricultural technology was the invention of the collar harness. The old yoke harness worked well with oxen but tended to choke horses, which, because they move faster and have greater stamina than oxen, are more valuable for agricultural work. The introduction of the horseshoe to protect the soft hooves of horses added to their ability to work on difficult terrain. The widening use of the water mill by the tenth century and the introduction of windmills in the twelfth century replaced ancient, less effective hand-worked mills for grinding grain.

The gradual emergence of the three-field system of managing agricultural land, particularly in northern Europe, increased production. In the old, widely used two-field system, half the land was planted in autumn with winter wheat, while the other half was left fallow to restore its fertility. In the new three-field system, one-third of the land was planted in autumn with winter wheat, a second third was planted the following spring with oats and vegetables, and the last third remained fallow. The advantages of the three-field system were that two-thirds of the land were farmed and only one-third was left unused and that the diversification of crops made more vegetable protein available.

Greater agricultural production reduced the number of deaths caused by starvation and dietary disease and thus contributed to a population increase. Grain surpluses also meant that draft animals and livestock could survive the winter. The growing numbers of animals provided a steady source of fresh meat and milk and increased the quantity of manure for fertilizer.

Soon the farmland of a manorial village could not support the growing village population. Consequently, peasants had to look beyond their immediate surroundings and colonize trackless wasteland. Lords vigorously promoted this conversion of uncultivated soil into agricultural land because it increased their incomes. Monastic communities also actively engaged in this enterprise. Almost everywhere peasants were draining swamps, clearing forests, and establishing new villages. Their endeavors during the eleventh and twelfth centuries

A Painting from an Anglo-Saxon Calendar, Eleventh Century. The heavy, iron-pointed, wheeled plough was of immense importance in extending farming to the heavier wet soils of northern Europe's lowlands. It made possible the growing agricultural exploitation of lands recovered from floodplains, forests, and marshes. (HIP/Art Resource, N.Y.)

brought vast areas of Europe under cultivation for the first time. New agricultural land was also acquired through expansion, the most notable example being the organized settlement of lands toward the east by German colonists.

The colonization and cultivation of virgin lands contributed to the decline of serfdom. Lords owned vast tracts of forests and swamps that would substantially increase their incomes if cleared, drained, and farmed. But serfs were often unwilling to move from their customary homes and fields to do the hard labor needed to cultivate these new lands. To lure serfs away from their villages, lords promised them freedom from most or all personal services. In many cases, the settlers fulfilled their obligations to the lord by paying rent rather than by performing services or providing foodstuffs, thus making the transition from serfs to freemen. In time, they came to regard the land as their own. As a result of these changing economic conditions, the percentage of French peasants who were serfs fell from 90 percent in 1050 to about 10 percent in 1350.

The improvement in agricultural technology and the colonization of new lands altered the conditions of life in Europe. Surplus food and the increase in population freed people to work at nonfarming occupations, making possible the expansion of trade and the revival of town life.

The Revival of Trade

Expanding agricultural production, the end of Viking attacks, greater political stability, the growth of a considerable money supply, and an increasing population produced a revival of commerce. During the Early Middle Ages, Italians and Jews kept alive a small amount of long-distance trade between Catholic Europe and the Byzantine and Islamic worlds. In the eleventh century, sea forces of Italian trading cities cleared the Mediterranean of Muslim fleets, which had blocked trade. As in Roman times, goods could circulate once again from one end of the sea to the other. The expanding population of northern Europe provided a market for Eastern silks, sugar, spices, and dyes, and Italian merchants were quick to exploit this demand.

By the start of the eleventh century, the European economy showed unmistakable signs of recovery from the disorders of the previous century. During the next two centuries, local, regional, and long-distance trade gained such momentum that some historians describe the period as a commercial revolution that surpassed the commercial activity of the Roman Empire during the Pax Romana. A class of traders emerged, many of them former serfs who had started trading by taking to the road as humble peddlers. Gradually they acquired business contacts in other lands, know-how, and ambition.

Crucial to the growth of trade were international fairs, where merchants and craftspeople set up stalls and booths to display their wares: swords, leather saddles, tools, rugs, shoes, silks, spices, furs, fine furniture, and other goods. Each fair lasted about three to six weeks; then the merchants would move on to another site. The Champagne region in northeastern France was the great center for fairs because the count of Champagne provided protection for merchants from thieves both en route to and at the fair, judges to guarantee the enforcement of contracts, and the necessary equipment, including covered stalls and accurate scales.

The principal arteries of trade flowed between the eastern Mediterranean and the Italian cities; between Scandinavia and the Atlantic coast; between northern France, Flanders, and England; and from the Baltic Sea in the north to the Black Sea and Constantinople via Russian rivers. The fine woolen cloth manufactured in Flanders provided the main stimulus for commerce along the Atlantic coast, and Flemish merchants prospered. In exchange for Flemish cloth, Scandinavians traded hunting hawks and fur; the English traded raw wools; and the Germans traded iron and timber. A wine trade also flourished between French vineyards and English wine merchants. Progress in navigation, including the use of the compass borrowed from the Arabs, and improvements in sails greatly aided long-distance commerce.

Because of their strategic position, Italian towns acted as intermediaries between the trade centers of the eastern Mediterranean and those of Latin Christendom. In Egyptian and North African ports, Italian merchants established enclaves where they set up permanent residence and conducted business. Luxury goods from as far away as India and China were transported to Italy by Italian ships and then taken overland to parts of Germany and France. In addition, the Italians extended their trade and increased their profits by sailing westward into the Atlantic Ocean and then north to the markets of Spain, the Netherlands, and England. On return voyages, they brought back wool and unfinished cloth, which in turn stimulated the Italian textile industry. Because individual merchants often lacked sufficient capital for these large-scale enterprises, groups of merchants formed partnerships. By enabling merchants to pool their capital, reduce their risks, and expand their knowledge of profit-making opportunities, these arrangements furthered commerce.

Increased economic activity led to other advances in business techniques. The development of banking and credit instruments made it unnecessary for merchants to carry large amounts of cash. The international fairs not only were centers of international trade but also served as capital markets for international credit transactions. The arrangements made by fair-going merchants to settle their debts were the origin of the bill of exchange, which allowed one currency to be converted into another. The invention of double-entry bookkeeping gave merchants an overview of their financial situation: the value of their goods and their ready cash. Without such knowledge, no large-scale commercial activity could be conducted on a continuous basis. Another improvement in business techniques was the formation of commercial law, which defined the rules of conduct for debts and contracts. Finally, a system of insurance emerged to provide protection for merchants whose goods were in transit. For a fee, a syndicate of brokers—the risk was too great for a single broker—would compensate the merchant whose cargo was lost at sea due to storms or piracy.

The Rebirth of Towns

In the eleventh century, towns emerged anew throughout Europe, and in the next century, they became active centers of commercial and intellectual life. Towns were a revolutionary force—socially, economically, and culturally. Because they provided new opportunities, other than food production, for commoners, towns contributed to the decline of manorialism. A new class of merchants and craftspeople came into being. This new class—the middle class—comprised those who, unlike the lords and serfs, were not affiliated with the land. The townsperson was a new type of person, with a value system different from that of the lord, the serf, or the cleric.

LOCAL MARKET IN FLORENCE. The birth of towns in the eleventh and twelfth centuries was a revolutionary development. Towns gave rise to a middle class that moved away from the outlook of traditional medieval society—clergy, lords, and peasants. This picture depicts the commercial vitality of a market in Florence. (Reunion des Musees Nationaux/Art Resource, N.Y.)

What spurred town growth was the increased food supply resulting from advances in agricultural technology. Surplus farm production meant that the countryside could support an urban population of artisans and professionals. Expanding trade also fostered urbanization. Towns emerged in places that were natural for trade: seacoasts, riverbanks, crossroads, and market sites. They also sprang up outside fortified castles and monasteries and on surviving Roman sites. The colonies of merchants who gathered at these locations were joined by peasants skilled in crafts or willing to work as laborers. From a medieval record comes this description of a town taking shape:

> After this castle was built, certain traders began to flock to the place in front of the gate to the bridge of the castle, that is merchants, tavernkeepers, then other outsiders drifted in for the sake of food and shelter of those who might have business transactions with the count, who often came there. Houses and inns were erected for their accommodation, since there was not room for them within the chateau. These habitations increased so rapidly that soon a large ville came into being.[1]

Medieval towns were protected from outside attack by thick, high walls, towers, and drawbridges. Most towns had a small population. The larger ones—Florence, Ghent, and Paris—had between fifty thousand and a hundred thousand inhabitants by the start of the fourteenth century; Venice and Milan had somewhat more than a hundred thousand. Covering only small areas, these walled towns were crowded with people. Booths and wares of merchants and artisans lined the narrow and crooked streets, which were strewn with refuse—animal blood and bones dumped by butchers, rotten fish discarded by fishmongers, and human waste thrown from windows. Such unsanitary conditions were a breeding ground for contagious disease.

During the day, the streets were jammed with merchants hawking their goods, women carrying baskets, men carting produce and merchandise, beggars pleading, children playing, and thieves lurking. A festive occasion, such as a procession honoring a patron saint, sometimes brought traffic to a standstill. A hanging—in Paris decomposing corpses on gallows were a permanent fixture—a beheading, or the burning of a heretic was looked upon as another festive occasion and always attracted a huge crowd. At night, the streets were deserted; few people ventured forth because the few elderly watchmen were no match for the numerous thieves. Even greater danger came from fires, which raged through overcrowded streets lined with wooden houses. Quarrels between individuals or groups were often settled violently.

Merchants and craftspeople organized guilds to protect themselves from outside competition. The merchant guild in a town prevented outsiders from doing much business. Craftsmen new to a town had to be admitted to the guild of their trade before opening a shop. Competition between members of the same guild was discouraged. To prevent any one member from making significantly more money than another, a guild required its members to work the same number of hours, pay employees the same wages, produce goods of equal quality, and charge customers a just price. These rules were strictly enforced. Guilds also performed social and religious functions. Guild members attended meetings in the guildhall, celebrated holidays together, and marched in processions. The guilds cared for members who were ill or needy and extended help to widows and children of deceased members.

Women took an active part in the economic life of towns, working with men, usually their husbands, in the various crafts—as cobblers, tailors, hatters, bakers, goldsmiths, and so forth. Women brewed beer; made and sold charcoal; sold vegetables, fish, and poultry; and ran inns. In many towns, the wives and widows of master craftsmen were admitted to guilds. These guildswomen had many of the privileges of a master, including the right to train apprentices.

Because many towns were situated on land belonging to lords or on the sites of old Roman towns ruled by bishops, these communities at first came under feudal authority. In some instances, lords encouraged the founding of towns, for urban industry and commerce brought wealth to the region. However, tensions soon developed between merchants, who sought freedom from feudal restrictions that interfered with their pursuit of financial gain, and lords and bishops, who wanted to preserve their authority over the towns. Townspeople, or burghers (a *burg* is a fortified town), refused to be treated as serfs bound to a lord and liable for personal services and customary dues. The burghers wanted to travel, trade, marry, and dispose of their property as they pleased; they wanted to make their own laws and levy their own taxes. Sometimes by fighting, but more often by payments of money, townspeople obtained charters from the lords giving them the right to set up their own councils. These assemblies passed laws, collected taxes, and formed courts, which enforced the laws. Towns became more or less self-governing municipalities, the first since Greco-Roman days.

The leading citizens of the towns, the patricians, were members of the merchant guilds who engaged in commerce, industry, and banking. Some patricians in the prosperous Italian towns enjoyed great wealth, owned considerable real estate, and conducted business transactions involving large sums. These people generally dominated town politics; often they obtained country estates and intermarried with the feudal aristocracy. Successful doctors and lawyers also belonged to the urban elite. Below them on the social scale were master craftsmen in the more lucrative crafts (goldsmiths, for example) and large retailers. Then came small retailers, masters in the less profitable crafts, and journeymen training to be masters. At the bottom were the laboring poor—the bulk of the population—who had no special skills and were subject to unemployment.

In virtually every medieval city, the church was the largest property owner. Because the church frowned on the pursuit of wealth, many businessmen had guilt pangs, particularly in old age, about the way they had earned their livelihood. Compounding their guilt and fear of hellfire was an awareness of having violated the church's strict prohibitions against practicing usury. To allay these concerns about the destiny of their souls, businesspeople often bequeathed money and property to the church. These bequests helped to finance hospitals and schools, which were the church's responsibility.

In a number of ways, towns loosened the hold of lords on serfs. "City air makes a man free," went a medieval proverb. Seeking freedom and fortune, serfs fled to the new towns, where, according to custom, lords could no longer reclaim them after a year and a day. Enterprising serfs earned money by selling food to townspeople. When the serfs acquired a sufficient sum of money, they bought their freedom from lords, who needed cash to pay for goods bought from merchants. Lords increasingly began to accept fixed cash payments from serfs in place of labor services or foodstuffs. As serfs met their obligations to lords with money, they gradually became rent-paying tenants and, in time, were no longer bound to the lord's land. The manorial system of personal relations and mutual obligations was disintegrating.

The activities of townspeople made them a new breed; they engaged in business and had money and freedom. Their world was the market rather than the church, the castle, or the manor. Townspeople were freeing themselves from the prejudices both of feudal aristocrats, who considered trade and manual work degrading, and of the clergy, who cursed the pursuit of riches as sordid and shameful and an obstacle to salvation. They revived the Greco-Roman ideal of active citizens devoted to their city. Processions, celebrations, and feasts commemorating holy days or memorable events in the town's history strengthened civic bonds. An emerging secular civic life, combined with the new value given to business and the need for some secular education in order to handle business transactions, produced a spiritual counterforce to Christian otherworldliness that would gain momentum in succeeding centuries. The townspeople were critical, dynamic, and progressive—a force for change.

THE RISE OF STATES

The revival of trade and the burgeoning of towns signaled a growing vitality in Latin Christendom. Another sign of strength was the greater order and security provided by the emergence of states.

While feudalism fostered a Europe that was split into many local regions, each ruled by a lord, the church envisioned a vast Christian commonwealth, **Respublica Christiana,** governed by an emperor who was guided by the pope. During the High Middle Ages, the ideal of a universal Christian community seemed close to fruition. Never again would Europe possess such spiritual unity.

But other forces were propelling Europe in a different direction. Aided by educated and trained officials who enforced royal law, tried people in royal courts, and collected royal taxes—all of which served to reduce the power of local lords—kings expanded their territory and slowly fashioned strong central governments. Gradually, subjects began to transfer their prime loyalty from the church and the lords to the person of the king. These developments laid the foundations of European states. Not all regions followed the same pattern. Whereas England and France achieved a large measure of unity during the Middle Ages, the areas that later became Germany and Italy remained divided, with numerous independent territories.

England

After the Roman legions abandoned England in the fifth century, the Germanic Angles and Saxons invaded the island and established several small kingdoms. In the ninth century, the Danes—one group of the Northmen who raided Western Europe—conquered most of Anglo-Saxon England. But the Saxon kingdom of Wessex, ruled by Alfred the Great (871–899), survived. To resist the Danes, Alfred strengthened his army and built a fleet. To stem the decline of learning that accompanied the Danish invasions, Alfred, like Charlemagne, founded a palace school, bringing to it scholars from other areas. Alfred himself studied Latin and translated a work of Pope Gregory I into Anglo-Saxon. He also had other works translated into Anglo-Saxon, including Boethius's *Consolation of Philosophy.* Alfred's descendants gradually regained land from the Danes and reestablished Anglo-Saxon control over the island.

In 1066, the Normans—those Northmen who had first raided and then settled in France—defeated the Anglo-Saxons in the battle of Hastings and became masters of England. Normans replaced the Anglo-Saxon aristocracy and ecclesiastical hierarchy. Determined to establish effective control over his new kingdom, William the Conqueror (1027–1087), duke of Normandy (in western France), kept one-sixth of conquered England for himself. In accordance with feudal practice, he distributed the rest among his Norman nobles, who swore an oath of loyalty to him and provided him with military assistance. But William made certain that no feudal baron had enough land or soldiers to threaten his power. The Norman conquest strengthened the king's position as never before.

To tighten royal control, William retained some Anglo-Saxon administrative practices. The land remained divided into *shires* (counties) administered by *sheriffs* (royal agents). This structure gave the king control over local government. To determine how much money he could demand, William ordered a vast census taken of people and property in every village. Census data, compiled in the *Domesday Book,* indicated the number of tenants, cattle, sheep, and pigs and the quantities of farm equipment throughout the realm. Thus, better than any other monarch of his day, William knew what the assets of his kingdom were. Because William conquered England in one stroke, his successors did not have to travel the long, painful road to national unity that French monarchs had to take.

Crucial to shaping national unity was the development of common law. When Henry I became king in 1100, England had conflicting baronial claims and legal traditions, which were a barrier to unity. These legal traditions included Anglo-Saxon law, feudal law introduced by the Normans from France, church law, and the commercial law emerging among the town businesspeople. During the reigns of Henry I (1100–1135) and Henry II (1154–1189), royal judges traveled to different parts of the kingdom. Throughout England, important cases began to be tried in the king's court rather than in local courts, thereby increasing royal power. The decisions of royal judges were recorded and used as guides for future cases. In this way, a law common to the whole land gradually came to prevail over the customary law of a specific locality. Because common law applied to all England, it served as a force for unity. It also provided a fairer system of justice. Common law remains the foundation of the English legal system

and the legal systems of lands settled by English people, including the United States.

Henry II made an early form of trial by jury a regular procedure for many cases heard in the king's court, laying the foundations of the modern judicial system. Twelve men familiar with the facts of the case appeared before the king's justices and were asked under oath if the plaintiff's statement was true. The justices based their decisions on the answers. Henry II also ordered representatives of a given locality to report under oath to visiting royal judges any local persons who were suspected of murder or robbery. This indictment jury was the ancestor of the modern grand jury.

The growth of an efficient financial administration paralleled the development of a strong judicial system. The Exchequer, the royal accounting office, was formed during the early years of Henry I's reign. Its officials saw to the collection of all revenues owed the king. Like the judges, these officials formed a class of professional administrators who were personally loyal to the king.

King John (1199–1216) inadvertently precipitated a situation that led to another step in the political development of England. Fighting a costly and losing war with the king of France, John had coerced his vassals into giving him more and more revenue; he had also punished some vassals without a proper trial. In 1215, the angry barons rebelled and compelled John to fix his seal to a document called Magna Carta, or Great Charter. Magna Carta is celebrated as the root of the uniquely English respect for basic rights and liberties. Although essentially a feudal document directed against a king who had violated feudal barons' rights, Magna Carta stated certain principles that eventually could be interpreted more widely.

Over the centuries, these principles were expanded to protect the liberties of the English against governmental oppression. Magna Carta stated that no unusual feudal dues "shall be imposed in our kingdom except by the common consent of our kingdom." In time, this right came to mean that the king could not levy taxes without the consent of Parliament, the governmental body that represents the English people. Magna Carta also provided that "no freeman shall be taken or imprisoned . . . save by the lawful judgment of his peers or by the law of the land." The barons who drew up the document had intended

WOMEN WORKERS. At times noble ladies fought side by side with men when their castle was attacked. Here women hurl rocks and shoot arrows at the attackers. (Bibliotheque Royale de Belgique.)

it to mean that they must be tried by fellow barons. As time passed, these words were regarded as a guarantee of trial by jury for all men, a prohibition against arbitrary arrest, and a command to dispense justice fully, freely, and equally. Implied in Magna Carta is the idea that the king cannot rule as he pleases but must govern according to the law: not even the king can violate the law of the nation. Centuries afterward, when the English sought to limit the king's power, they would interpret Magna Carta in this way.

Anglo-Saxon England retained the Germanic tradition that the king should consider the advice of the leading men in the land. William the Conqueror continued this practice by seeking the opinions of leading nobles and bishops. In the thirteenth century, it became accepted custom that the king should not decide major issues without consulting these advisers, who assembled together as the Great Council. Lesser nobility and townspeople also began to be summoned to meet with the king. These two groups were eventually called the House of Lords

(bishops and nobles) and the House of Commons (knights and burghers). Thus did the English Parliament evolve, and by the mid-fourteenth century, it was a permanent institution of government.

Frequently in need of money but unable to levy new taxes without the approval of Parliament, the king had to turn to that body for help. Parliament used this control over money matters to enhance its power. The tradition grew that the power to govern rested not with the king alone but with the king and Parliament together.

During the Middle Ages, England became a centralized and unified state. But the king did not have unlimited power; he was not above the law. The rights of the people were protected by certain principles implicit in the common law and Magna Carta and by the power of Parliament.

France

In the 150 years after Charlemagne's death, the western part of his empire, which was destined to become France, faced terrible ordeals. Charlemagne's heirs fought one another for the crown; the Vikings raided everywhere their ships would carry them; Muslims from Spain plundered the southern coast; and strong lords usurped power for themselves. With the Carolingian family unable to maintain the throne, the great lords bestowed the title of king on one of their own. In 987, they chose Hugh Capet (987–996), the count of Paris. Because many great lords held territories far larger than those of Hugh, the French king did not seem a threat to noble power. But Hugh strengthened the French monarchy by having the lords also elect his son as his co-ruler. This practice continued until it became understood that the crown would remain with the Capetian family.

With the accession of Louis VI (1108–1137), a two-hundred-year period of steadily increasing royal power began. Louis started this trend by successfully subduing the barons in his own duchy. A decisive figure in the expansion of French royal sway was Philip Augustus (1180–1223). Philip struck successfully at King John of England (of Magna Carta fame), who held more territory as feudal lord in France than Philip did. When William, duke of Normandy, conquered England in 1066, he became ruler of England and Normandy;

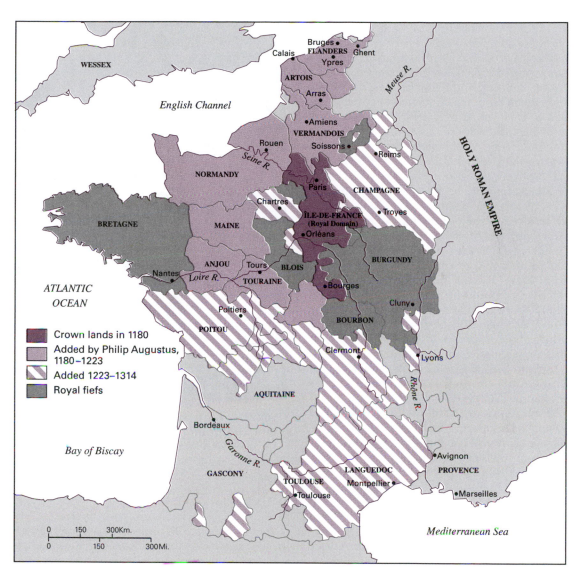

WESSEX

English Channel

Bruges •
Calais • **FLANDERS** • Ghent
Ypres •

Meuse R.

ARTOIS

Arras •

•Amiens
VERMANDOIS
Rouen • Soissons •
Seine R. • Reims

NORMANDY

Paris •
CHAMPAGNE
Chartres •
ÎLE-DE-FRANCE
(Royal Domain)
MAINE • Troyes

BRETAGNE

Orléans •

ANJOU Tours • **BLOIS** **BURGUNDY**
Nantes • *Loire R.*
TOURAINE
• Bourges
Cluny •

ATLANTIC
OCEAN

Poitiers •
BOURBON
POITOU

Clermont •
Lyons •

■ Crown lands in 1180
▨ Added by Philip Augustus, 1180–1223
▨ Added 1223–1314
■ Royal fiefs

AQUITAINE

Rhône R.

Bordeaux •

Avignon •

Bay of Biscay

Garonne R.

GASCONY
LANGUEDOC **PROVENCE**
TOULOUSE Montpellier •
• Toulouse • Marseilles

0   150   300Km.
0   150   300Mi.

Mediterranean Sea

HOLY ROMAN EMPIRE

Map 10.1 **THE KINGDOM OF FRANCE, 1180–1314** Through wars, alliances, and marriages, French kings expanded their territory. (Copyright © 2013 Cengage Learning.)

William's great-grandson Henry II acquired much of southern France through his marriage to Eleanor of Aquitaine (c. 1122–1204) in 1152. Thus, as a result of the Norman Conquest and intermarriage, the destinies of France and England were closely intertwined until the end of the Middle Ages. By stripping King John of most of his French territory (Normandy, Anjou, and much of Aquitaine),

Philip trebled the size of his kingdom and became stronger than any French lord.

Louis IX (1226–1270)—pious, compassionate, and conscientious and a genuine lover of peace—was perhaps the best-loved French monarch of the Middle Ages. Departing from feudal precedent, Louis issued ordinances for the entire realm without seeking the consent of his vassals.

One ordinance prohibited private warfare among the nobility. Another promoted the nationwide circulation of coins produced by royal mints. These ordinances furthered royal power and promoted order.

Under Louis IX and his successors, the power of the French monarch continued to grow. Kings added to their lands by warfare and marriage; they devised new ways of raising money, including taxing the clergy. A particularly effective way of increasing the monarch's power was by extending royal justice. In the thirteenth century, the king's court, the *parlement,* became the highest court in France. Quarrels between the king and his vassals were resolved in the parlement, and many cases previously tried in lords' courts were transferred to the king's court. Moreover, because the decision of feudal courts could be appealed to the parlement, lords no longer had the last say on legal questions.

At the beginning of the fourteenth century, Philip IV (the Fair) engaged in a struggle with the papacy (see page 279). Seeking to demonstrate that he had the support of his subjects, Philip summoned representatives of the church (First Estate), the nobility (Second Estate), and the townspeople (Third Estate) to meet in a national assembly known as the Estates General. This assembly would be called again to vote funds for the crown. Unlike the English Parliament, the Estates General never became an important body in French political life, and it never succeeded in controlling the monarch. Whereas the basis for limited monarchy had been established in England, no comparable checks on the king's power developed in France. By the end of the Middle Ages, French kings had succeeded in creating a unified state, but regional and local loyalties remained strong and persisted for centuries.

Germany

After the destruction of Charlemagne's empire, its German territories were broken into large duchies. Following traditional Germanic practice, the ruling dukes elected one of their own as king. The German king, however, had little authority outside his own duchy. Some German kings tried not to antagonize the dukes, but Otto the Great (936–973) was determined to control them. He entered into an alliance with German bishops and archbishops, who could provide him with fighting

THIRTEENTH-CENTURY POLITICS. The representative assembly, antecedent of the modern parliament, was an original achievement of the Middle Ages. Here the king of Aragon presides over the *cortes,* an assembly representing clergy, nobles, and townspeople. (MAS Barcelona/Institut Amattler d'Art Hispanic.)

men and trained administrators—a policy continued by his successors.

In 951, Otto marched into northern Italy in an attempt to assert his influence. Ten years later, he returned to protect the pope from his Italian enemies. In 962, emulating the coronation of Charlemagne, the pope crowned Otto "Emperor of the Romans" (later the title would be changed to "Holy Roman Emperor").

The revival of the empire meant that the history of medieval Germany was closely tied to that of Italy and the papacy. Otto and his successors wanted to dominate both Italy, which had been part of Charlemagne's empire, and the pope—an ambition that embroiled the Holy Roman Emperor in a life-and-death struggle with the papacy. The papacy allied itself with the German dukes and the Italian cities, enemies of the emperor. German intervention in papal politics and Italian lands was the principal reason that German territories did not achieve unity in the Middle Ages.

The Emergence of Representative Institutions

One great contribution of the Middle Ages to the modern world was the representative institution. Representative assemblies, or parliaments, had their beginnings at the end of the twelfth century in the Spanish kingdom of León. In the thirteenth century, they developed in other Spanish kingdoms—Castile, Aragon, Catalonia, and Valencia—as well as in Portugal, England, and the Holy Roman Empire. In the fourteenth century, parliaments formed in France and the Netherlands.

Kings generally came to accept the principles that parliamentary consent was required for levying taxes and that the king should consult parliament about important laws and obtain its approval. By and large, the parliaments had grown out of royal dependence on the nobility for military support. Because of this dependence, monarchs considered it wise to listen to the opinions of the lords. Consequently, it became customary for the king to summon councils to discuss matters of war and peace and other vital questions. Since the high clergy constituted an important group in the realm, they too were consulted. As towns gained in wealth and significance, townspeople were also asked to royal councils. Leading nobles came to represent the nobility as an order of society; members of the upper clergy—archbishops, bishops, and abbots—represented the entire clergy; and deputies from the towns represented the townspeople. An important tradition had been established: the duty of the monarch to seek advice and consent on issues of concern to his subjects. Perhaps the practice of representative government was influenced by those church lawyers who held that the pope should seek the guidance of the Christian community as expressed in church councils—meetings of representatives of the clergy.

To be sure, in succeeding centuries, parliaments would be either ignored or dominated by kings. Nevertheless, the principle of constitutional government—government by consent—was woven into the fabric of Western society. The representative parliament is unique to Western civilization; it has no parallel in the political systems of the non-European world. Originating in the Middle Ages, the representative assembly is a distinct achievement and contribution of Western civilization.

THE GROWTH OF PAPAL POWER

In the High Middle Ages, a growing spiritual vitality accompanied economic recovery and increasing political stability. It was marked by several developments. The common people were showing greater devotion to the church. Within the church, reform movements were attacking clerical abuses, and the papacy was becoming more powerful. A holy war against the Muslims was drawing the Christian community closer together. During this period, the church tried with great determination to make society follow divine standards: it tried to shape institutions and cultural expressions according to a comprehensive Christian outlook.

The Sacraments

As the sole interpreters of God's revelation and the sole ministers of his sacraments—sacred rites—the clergy imposed and supervised the moral outlook of Christendom. Divine grace was channeled through seven sacraments, which could be administered only by the clergy, the indispensable intermediary between individuals and God. On persons who resisted its authority, the church could impose the penalty of excommunication—expulsion from the church and denial of the sacraments, without which there could be no salvation.

The seven sacraments involved the church in the lives of individuals from birth to death. Baptism cleansed individuals—usually infants—of the stain of original sin. Confirmation granted additional **grace** to previously baptized young adults. Matrimony made marriage a holy union. Extreme unction, administered to the dying, was intended to remove the remains of sin. The sacrament of the Eucharist, derived from Gospel accounts of Christ's Last Supper, took place within a liturgical service, the Mass. In a solemn ceremony, bread and wine were miraculously transformed into the substance of the body and blood of Christ, which the priest administered, allowing believers to partake of Christ's saving grace. The sacrament of penance required sinners to show sorrow for their sins, to confess them to a priest, and to perform an act of contrition: prayer, fasting, almsgiving, or a pilgrimage to a holy shrine. Through the priest, the sinner could receive absolution and be rescued from spending eternity in hell. This sacrament enabled the church to enforce its moral standards throughout Latin Christendom. The final sacrament, ordination, consecrated men to serve as clergy.

Gregorian Reform

By the tenth century, the church was Western Europe's leading landowner, owning perhaps a third of the land in Italy and vast properties in other lands. However, the papacy was in no position to exercise commanding leadership over Latin Christendom. The office of pope had fallen under the domination of aristocratic families; they conspired and on occasion murdered in order to place one of their own on the wealthy and powerful throne of Saint Peter. As the papacy became a prize for Rome's leading families, it was not at all unusual for popes themselves to be involved in conspiracies and assassinations. Also weakening the authority of the papacy were local lords, who dominated churches and monasteries by appointing bishops and abbots and by collecting the income from church taxes. These bishops and abbots, appointed by lords for political reasons, lacked the spiritual devotion to maintain high standards of discipline among the priests and monks.

What raised the power of the papacy to unprecedented heights was the emergence of a reform movement, particularly in French and German monasteries. High-minded monks called for a reawakening of spiritual fervor and the elimination of moral laxity among the clergy. They particularly denounced the concern for worldly goods, the taking of mistresses, and the diminishing commitment to the Benedictine rule. Of the many monasteries that took part in this reform movement, the Benedictine monks of Cluny, in Burgundy, France, were the most influential.

In the middle of the eleventh century, popes came under the influence of the monastic reformers.

In 1059, a special synod, convened by the reform-minded Pope Nicholas II, moved to end the interference of Roman nobles and German Holy Roman Emperors in choosing the pope. Henceforth, a select group of clergymen in Rome, called *cardinals,* would be responsible for picking a new pontiff.

The reform movement found its most zealous exponent in the person of Hildebrand, who became Pope Gregory VII in 1073. Gregory insisted that human society was part of a divinely ordered universe, governed by God's universal law, and as the supreme spiritual leader of Christendom, the pope was charged with the mission of establishing a Christian society on earth. As successor to Saint Peter, the pope had the final word on matters of faith and doctrine. All bishops came under his authority; so too did kings, whose powers should be used for Christian ends. Disobeying the pope, God's viceroy on earth, constituted disobedience to God himself. The pope was responsible for instructing rulers in the proper use of their God-given powers, and kings had the solemn duty to obey these instructions. If the king failed in his Christian duty, the pope could deny him his right to rule. Responsible for implementing God's law, the pope could never take a subordinate position to kings.

Like no other pope before him, Gregory VII made a determined effort to assert the preeminence of the papacy over both the church hierarchy and secular rulers. This determination led to a bitter struggle between the papacy and the German monarch and future Holy Roman Emperor Henry IV. The dispute was a dramatic confrontation between two competing versions of the relationship between secular and spiritual authority.

Through his reforms, Gregory VII intended to improve the moral quality of the clergy and to liberate the church from all control by secular authorities. He forbade priests who had wives or concubines to celebrate Mass, deposed clergy who had bought their offices, excommunicated bishops and abbots who had received their estates from a lay lord, and expelled from the church lay lords who invested bishops with their office. The appointment of bishops, Pope Gregory insisted, should be controlled entirely by the church.

This last point touched off the conflict, called the Investiture Controversy, between King Henry and Pope Gregory. Bishops served a dual function. On the one hand, they belonged to the spiritual community of the church; on the other hand, as members of the nobility and holders of estates, they were also integrated into the feudal order. Traditionally, emperors had both granted bishops their feudal authority and invested them with their spiritual authority. In maintaining that no lay rulers could confer ecclesiastical offices on their appointees, Pope Gregory threatened Henry's authority.

In earlier times, seeking allies in the conflict with feudal nobility, German kings had made vassals of the upper clergy. In return for a fief, bishops had agreed to provide troops for a monarch in his struggle against the lords. But if kings had no control over the appointment of bishops—in accordance with Pope Gregory's view—they would lose the allegiance, military support, and financial assistance of their most important allies. To German monarchs, bishops were officers of the state who served the throne. Moreover, if they agreed to Gregory's demands, German kings would lose their freedom of action and be dominated by the Roman pontiff. Henry IV regarded Gregory VII as a fanatic who trampled on custom, meddled in German state affairs, and challenged legitimate rulers established by God, thereby threatening to subordinate kingship to the papacy.

With the approval of the German bishops, Henry called for Pope Gregory to descend from the throne of Saint Peter. Gregory in turn excommunicated Henry and deposed him as king. German lands were soon embroiled in a civil war as German lords used the quarrel to strike at Henry's power. Finally, Henry's troops crossed the Alps, successfully attacked Rome, and installed a new pope, who crowned Henry emperor of the Romans. Gregory died in exile in 1085.

In 1122, the papacy and Emperor Henry V reached a compromise. Bishops were to be elected exclusively by the church and invested with the staff and the ring—symbols of spiritual power—by the archbishop, not the king. This change signified that a bishop owed his role as spiritual leader to the church only. But the king would grant the bishop the scepter, to indicate that the bishop was also the recipient of a fief and the king's vassal, owing feudal obligations to the crown. This compromise, called the Concordat of Worms, recognized the dual function of the bishop as a spiritual leader in the church and a feudal landowner.

Similar settlements had been reached with the kings of France and England several years earlier.

The conflict between the papacy and the German rulers continued after the Concordat of Worms—a contest for supremacy between the heir of Saint Peter and the heir of Charlemagne. German monarchs wanted to control the papacy and the prosperous northern Italian cities. When Frederick I (1152–1190), known as Frederick Barbarossa (Red Beard), tried to assert authority over these cities, they resisted. In 1176, the armies of an alliance of Italian cities, supported by the pope, trounced Frederick's forces at the battle of Legnano. The Italian infantry showed that it could defeat knights on horseback, and Frederick was compelled to recognize the independence of the Italian cities. His numerous expeditions to Italy weakened his authority. German princes strengthened themselves at the expense of the monarchy, thereby continuing to preclude German unity.

The Crusades

Like the movement for spiritual renewal associated with the Cluniac reformers, the Crusades—wars to regain the Holy Land from the Muslims—were an outpouring of Christian zeal and an attempt by the papacy to assert its preeminence. Along with the renewal of commerce and the growth of towns, the Crusades were a sign of vitality and self-confidence in Western Europe. The victims of earlier Muslim attacks, Latin Christians now took the offensive. Furthermore, the Crusades were part of a general movement of European expansion during the High Middle Ages. Latin Christians were venturing forth as pioneers to open new lands to cultivation and as conquerors to expand the borders of Christendom.

By the middle of the eleventh century, forces from the cities of Genoa and Pisa had driven the Muslims from Sardinia. By 1091, Normans had taken Sicily from the Muslims and southern Italy from Byzantium. With the support of the papacy, Christian knights engaged in the long struggle to drive the Muslims from Spain; by 1248, after more than two centuries of conflict, only the small southern kingdom of Granada remained in Muslim hands. Germans conquered and colonized lands south of the Baltic coast inhabited by

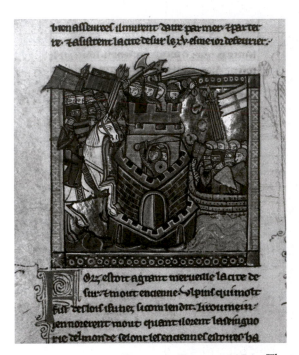

DEPICTION OF THE SIEGE OF TYRE IN 1124. The fall of the city gave Christians control of the Syrian coast. (Tyre being blockaded by the Venetian fleet and besieged by Crusader knighthood, from the Estoire d'Outremer (vellum and gold leaf), William of Tyre (c.1130–85)/Bibliotheque Nationale, Paris, France/The Bridgeman Art Library International.)

non-Christian Slavs, Balts, and Prussians. German settlers brought with them Christianity and German language and culture. They cleared vast tracts of virgin land for farming and established towns, bishoprics, and monasteries in a region where urban life had been virtually unknown.

In the eleventh century, the Seljuk Turks, who had earlier embraced Islam, conquered vast regions of the Near East, including Anatolia, a province of the Byzantine Empire. With the death of the Turkish sultan in 1092, the Seljuk Empire broke up, which reduced the pressure on Byzantium. Seeking to strengthen his army in preparation for the reconquest of Anatolia, Byzantine emperor Alexius appealed to Western rulers for mercenaries.

Pope Urban II, at the Council of Clermont (in France) in 1095, exaggerated the danger confronting Eastern Christianity. He called for a holy crusade against the heathen Turks, whom he accused of defiling and destroying Christian churches. Several months later, he expanded his objectives to include the conquest of Jerusalem. A Christian army, mobilized by the papacy to defend the faith and to regain the Holy Land from nonbelievers, accorded with the papal concept of a just war; it would channel the endemic violence of Europe's warrior class in a Christian direction. A crusade against the Muslims also held the promise of bringing the Eastern church, which had formally broken with Rome in 1054, under papal leadership. In organizing a crusade for Christian ends, Urban II, like Gregory VII in his struggle with Henry IV, sought to demonstrate the supremacy of the pope.

What motivated the knights and others who responded to Urban's appeal? To some younger sons with no hope of inheriting land at home, a crusade offered an opportunity to gain land by conquest. No doubt the Crusaders regarded themselves as armed pilgrims dedicated to rescuing holy places from the hated Muslims. Through the years, Christian pilgrims had made the journey to Jerusalem to do penance for crimes against the church and to demonstrate their piety. These pilgrims and other devout Christians found it deplorable that Christian holy places were controlled by heathen Muslims. Moreover, Urban declared that participation in a crusade was itself an act of penance, an acceptable way of demonstrating sorrow for sin. In their eagerness to recruit warriors, popular preachers went even further: they promised cancellation of penalties for sin. To a knight, a crusade was no doubt a great adventure that promised land, glory, and plunder, but it was also an opportunity to remit sins by engaging in a holy war. The enthusiasm with which knights became Christian warriors demonstrated the extent to which the warrior mentality of the nobles had become permeated by Christian principles.

Stirred by popular preachers, the common people also became gripped by the crusading spirit. The most remarkable of the evangelists was Peter the Hermit, who rode his donkey through the French countryside arousing the religious

Map 10.2 THE HOLY ROMAN EMPIRE, c. 1200 ▶
Unable to overcome the German princes, Holy Roman Emperors, unlike French and English rulers, could not build a unified state during the Middle Ages. Germany did not achieve unity until the late nineteenth century. (Copyright © 2013 Cengage Learning.)

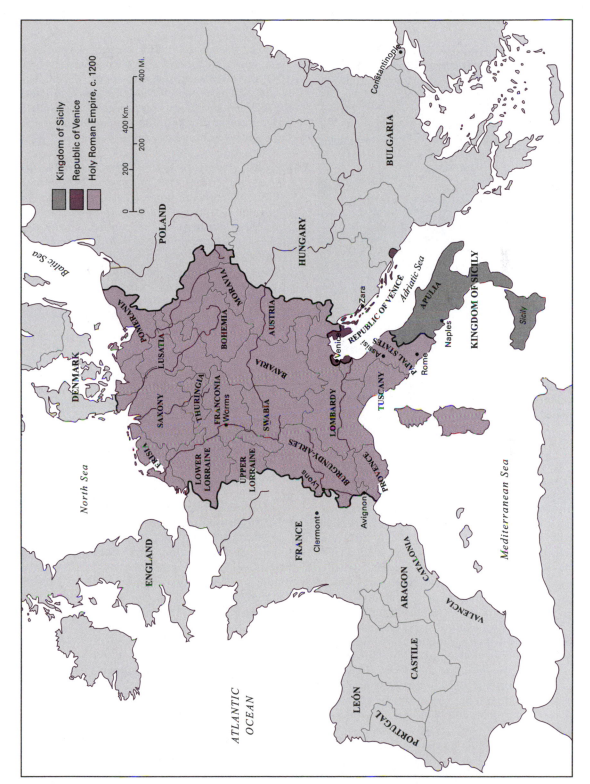

Kingdom of Sicily
Republic of Venice
Holy Roman Empire, c. 1200

400 Mi.
400 Km.
200
200
0
0

Baltic Sea

POLAND

Constantinople

BULGARIA

HUNGARY

POMERANIA

POLAND

MORAVIA

DENMARK

LUSATIA

BOHEMIA

AUSTRIA

Adriatic Sea

REPUBLIC OF VENICE

Zara

SAXONY

THURINGIA

FRANCONIA

Worms

BAVARIA

SWABIA

Venice

Assisi

PAPAL STATES

TUSCANY

LOMBARDY

APULIA

KINGDOM OF SICILY

Naples

Rome

North Sea

FRISIA

LOWER LORRAINE

UPPER LORRAINE

BURGUNDY-ARLES

PROVENCE

Lyons

FRANCE

Clermont

Avignon

Sicily

Mediterranean Sea

ENGLAND

CATALONIA

ARAGON

VALENCIA

CASTILE

LEÓN

PORTUGAL

*ATLANTIC
OCEAN*

243

CAPTURE OF JERUSALEM. Gripped by religious frenzy, the Crusaders, "dripping with blood," massacred the Muslim and Jewish inhabitants of Jerusalem. (Snark/Art Resource, N.Y.)

zeal of plain folk. Swayed by the old man's eloquence, thousands of poor people abandoned their villages and joined Peter's march to Jerusalem. As this army of the poor crossed Germany, the credulous peasants expected to find Jerusalem just beyond the horizon; some thought that Peter was leading them straight to heaven. While Peter's army made its way to Constantinople, another army of commoners recruited in Germany sought to do God's work by massacring the Jews of the Rhineland, despite the efforts of bishops to protect them. Unlike Peter's army, these commoners never reached Constantinople; after plundering Hungary, they were slaughtered by Hungarians (Magyars). Camped in the suburbs of Constantinople, Peter's restless recruits crossed from Byzantine-controlled land into Turkish territory, where they too were massacred. Faith alone could not win Jerusalem.

Departing later than the commoners, an army of knights assembled at Constantinople in the spring of 1097. After enduring the long march through

Anatolia, the Christian army arrived at Antioch in Syria, which it captured after a long siege. In June 1099, three years after Urban's appeal, the soldiers of the First Crusade (1096–1099) stood outside the walls of Jerusalem. Using siege weapons, they broke into the city and slaughtered Muslims and Jews. An eyewitness recorded the scene.

> *It was impossible to look upon the vast numbers of the slain without horror; everywhere lay fragments of human bodies, and the very ground was covered with the blood of the slain. It was not alone the spectacle of headless bodies and mutilated limbs strewn in all directions that roused horror in all who looked upon them. Still more dreadful was it to gaze upon the victors themselves, dripping with blood from head to foot, an ominous sight which brought terror to all who met them. . . .*
>
> *When at last the city had been set in order in this way, arms were laid aside. Then, clad in fresh garments, with clean hands and bare feet, in humility and contrition, [the victors] began to make the rounds of the venerable places which the Saviour had deigned to sanctify and make glorious with His bodily presence. With tearful sighs and heartfelt emotion they pressed kisses upon these revered spots.[2]*

Weakened by local rivalries and religious quarrels, the Muslim world failed to unite against the Christian invaders, who, besides capturing Jerusalem, carved out four small states in Syria and Palestine. How long could these Christian states, islands in a Muslim sea, endure against a Muslim counteroffensive?

Never resigned to the establishment of Christian states in their midst, Muslim leaders called for a jihad, or holy war. In 1144, one of the Crusader states, the County of Edessa, in Syria, fell to the resurgent forces of Islam. Alarmed by the loss of

***Map 10.3* THE ROUTES OF THE CRUSADES ▶**
In 1291, almost two hundred years after Pope Urban II's appeal for a crusade, the last Christian stronghold in the Near East had fallen.
(Copyright © 2013 Cengage Learning.)

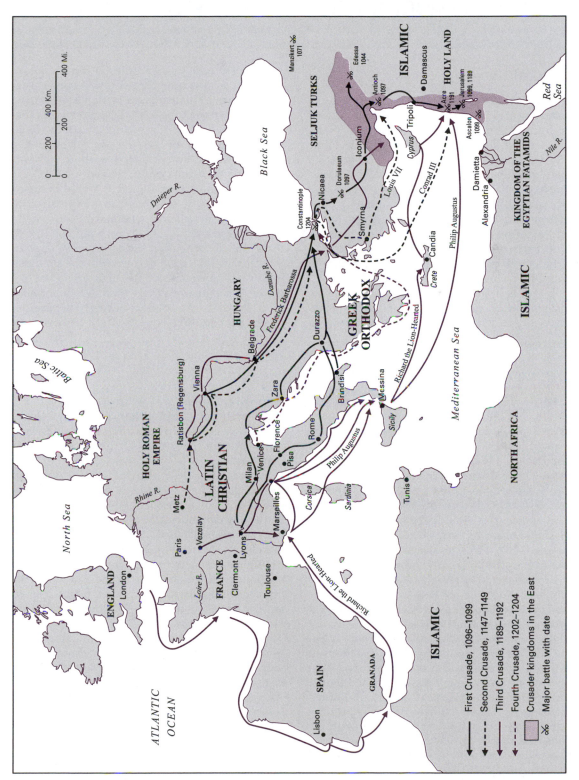

Black Sea

Baltic Sea

North Sea

ATLANTIC OCEAN

Dnieper R.

SELJUK TURKS

ISLAMIC

HOLY LAND

Red Sea

Manzikert 1071

Edessa 1044

Antioch 1097

Damascus

Jerusalem 1099, 1189

Acre 1191

Tripoli

Ascalon 1099

Cyprus

Nicaea

Dorulaeum 1097

Iconium

Smyrna

Constantinople 1204

GREEK ORTHODOX

Louis VII

Conrad III

Philip Augustus

Candia

Crete

KINGDOM OF THE EGYPTIAN FATIMIDS

Nile R.

Damietta

Alexandria

ISLAMIC

Richard the Lion-Hearted

Mediterranean Sea

HUNGARY

Frederick Barbarossa

Danube R.

Belgrade

Durazzo

Vienna

Ratisbon (Regensburg)

HOLY ROMAN EMPIRE

LATIN CHRISTIAN

Zara

Brundisi

Messina

Sicily

Metz

Rhine R.

Milan

Venice

Florence

Pisa

Rome

Corsica

Sardinia

Tunis

Philip Augustus

Marseilles

Paris

Vezelay

Lyons

Clermont

Toulouse

FRANCE

Loire R.

ENGLAND

London

NORTH AFRICA

ISLAMIC

Richard the Lion-Hearted

SPAIN

GRANADA

Lisbon

400 Mi.

400 Km.

200

200

0

0

First Crusade, 1096–1099

Second Crusade, 1147–1149

Third Crusade, 1189–1192

Fourth Crusade, 1202–1204

Crusader kingdoms in the East

Major battle with date

245

Saladin

Salah al-Din Yusuf (1137–1193), known to the Western world as Saladin, recaptured Jerusalem from the Franks in 1187. Born into a prominent Kurdish family, Saladin served the emir of Syria, whose troops invaded Egypt in 1167. Rising quickly, Saladin was appointed vizier of Egypt and then confirmed as sultan of Egypt and Syria. After extending his authority over Muslim-controlled territories of Egypt, Syria, and Palestine, Saladin, deeply committed to jihad, turned against the Franks. In particular, he vowed to liberate Islamic holy places in Jerusalem from Christian control.

In 1187, Saladin lured the Franks into an engagement at Hittin, near Tiberias, in northern Palestine. Marching all day, the exhausted and thirst-crazed Franks suffered terrible losses when, in desperation, they threw themselves at the prepared Muslim lines, which blocked the Franks from reaching Lake Tiberias and its life-giving water. After the victory at Hittin, Saladin's forces took several Christian strongholds, most of which surrendered without a fight. Then Saladin turned on Jerusalem.

Living up to his reputation as a man of honor and magnanimity, Saladin made the Christian inhabitants of Jerusalem a generous proposal. If the Franks surrendered, Christians would be free to leave the city with their property, and Christian pilgrims would not be harmed. But the Frankish lords would not surrender without a fight the city where Jesus had been crucified. On September 20, 1187, Saladin's soldiers besieged Jerusalem and began battering its walls. A Muslim historian

Edessa, Pope Eugenius II called for the Second Crusade (1147–1149), which was a complete failure.

After 1174, Saladin, a brilliant commander, became the most powerful leader in the Muslim Near East. In 1187, he invaded Palestine, annihilated a Christian army near Nazareth, and recaptured Jerusalem. In contrast to Christian knights of the First Crusade, who filled Jerusalem with blood and corpses, Saladin permitted no slaughter. The capture of Jerusalem led to the Third Crusade (1189–1192), in which some of Europe's most prominent rulers participated—Richard I, the Lion-Hearted, of England; Philip Augustus of France; and Frederick Barbarossa of Germany. The Crusaders captured Acre and Jaffa, but Jerusalem remained in Muslim hands.

Pope Innocent III, who called the Fourth Crusade (1202–1204), was enraged by the actions of the Crusaders. They had first attacked the Christian port of Zara, which was controlled by the king of Hungary, and then looted and defiled churches and massacred Byzantines in Constantinople. This shameful behavior, along with the belief that the papacy was exploiting the crusading ideal to extend its own power, weakened both the crusading zeal of Christendom and the moral authority of the papacy. It also left a legacy of bitterness and distrust that still taints relations between the Eastern Orthodoxy and other Christians.

Other Crusades followed, including even the Children's Crusade in 1212. Stirred by Stephen of Cloyes, a young shepherd boy who claimed that Christ had communicated with him, thousands of French peasant children, accompanied by priests, marched to Marseilles, where they expected the Mediterranean Sea to part, permitting them to continue their march to the Holy Land. When the miracle did not occur, the children boarded seven ships offered to them by William the Pig and Hugo the Iron, two seemingly pious townsmen. Two of the ships were lost in a terrible storm, and the other five were captured by Muslim pirates, with whom William and Hugo had worked out a deal. The children were sold into slavery in North Africa, and as far as is known, none ever returned (one priest eventually did).

Despite other crusades, the position of the Christian states in the Near East continued to deteriorate. In 1291, almost two centuries after Pope

noted: "Then began the fiercest struggle imaginable; each side looked on the fight as an absolute religious obligation. There was no need for a superior authority to drive them on."* On October 2, the Muslims rushed through the breached walls and captured the city. In stark contrast to the Christian conquest of Jerusalem in 1099, Saladin permitted no massacre and no plundering. The Franks could escape enslavement by paying a moderate ransom, and in an extraordinary display of tolerance, Saladin guarded Christian holy places from Muslims seeking revenge for earlier Frankish brutalities.

---

*Excerpted in Francesco Gabriel, ed., *Arab Historians of the Crusades* (Berkeley: University of California Press, 1969), 130.

Urban's appeal, the last Christian strongholds in the Near East fell.

The Crusades had some immediate effects on Latin Christendom. They may have contributed to the decline of feudalism and the strengthening of monarchy because many lords were killed in battle or squandered their wealth financing expeditions to the Holy Land. The Crusades did foster trade between Latin Christendom and the East, but the revival of trade had already begun and would have proceeded without the Crusades. The Crusades sparked an interest in geography and travel; introduced Westerners to new foods, clothing, and architecture; and became a theme in literature. Nevertheless, they did not significantly influence European intellectual progress. The Crusaders had no contact with Muslim centers of learning in the Near East; it was through Spain and Sicily that Muslim learning penetrated Latin Christendom and helped stimulate the cultural awakening of the twelfth and thirteenth centuries. Over the centuries, some have praised the Crusades for inspiring idealism and heroism. Others, however, have castigated the movement for corrupting the Christian spirit and unleashing religious intolerance and fanaticism—including the massacre of Jews in the Rhineland and of Muslims and Jews in Jerusalem—which would lead to strife in future centuries. The Crusades remain a crucial component of the ideology of contemporary Islamic extremists.

Dissenters and Reformers

Freedom of religion is a modern concept; it was totally alien to the medieval outlook. Regarding itself as the possessor and guardian of divine, and therefore ultimate, truth, the church felt a profound obligation to purge Christendom of **heresy**—beliefs that challenged Christian orthodoxy. To the church, heretics had committed treason against God and were carriers of a deadly infection. Heresy was the work of Satan; lured by false ideas, people might abandon the true faith and deny themselves salvation. The church could never create a Christian world community if heretics rebelled against clerical authority and created divisions among the faithful. In the eyes of the church, heretics not only obstructed individual salvation but also undermined the foundations of society. The church believed that it had a sacred duty to eradicate this moral defect.

To compel obedience, the church used its power of excommunication. An excommunicated person could not receive the sacraments or attend church services—fearful punishments in an age of faith. In dealing with a recalcitrant ruler, the church could declare an interdict on his territory, which in effect denied the ruler's subjects the sacraments (although exceptions could be made). The church hoped that the pressure exerted by an aroused populace would compel the offending ruler to mend his ways.

The church also conducted heresy trials. Before the thirteenth century, local bishops were responsible for locating heretics and putting them on trial. Gregory IX (1227–1241) started to use Franciscans and Dominicans (see page 249) as official investigators, in effect creating a permanent tribunal, the Inquisition, directly under the pope's authority. An inquisitor and his staff established themselves in a region suspected of heresy. After taking testimony, often in secret, the inquisitors summoned suspects to answer accusations made against them. The accused were not told the names of their accusers, nor could they have legal defense or examine evidence of witnesses. They were tortured (torture had been sanctioned by Roman law), and those who persisted in their beliefs might be turned over to the civil authorities to be burned at the stake.

Religious dissent in the Middle Ages was often reformist in character. Inspired by the Gospels, reformers criticized the church for its wealth and involvement in worldly affairs. They called for a return to the simpler, purer life of Jesus and the Apostles. Reform movements drew support from the new class of town dwellers; the church often rebuked the way of life in towns and only slowly adjusted to the townspeople's spiritual needs.

The Waldensians. In their zeal to emulate the moral purity and material poverty of the first followers of Jesus, reform-minded dissenters attacked ecclesiastical authority. The Waldensians, followers of Peter Waldo, a rich merchant of Lyons, were a case in point. Peter was greatly moved by a passage in Matthew: "If thou wilt be perfect go sell what thou hast and give to the poor and thou shalt have treasure in heaven" (19:22). In the 1170s, Peter distributed his property to the poor and attracted both male and female supporters. Like their leader, they committed themselves to poverty and to preaching the Gospel in the vernacular, or native tongue, rather than in the church's Latin, which many Christians did not understand. The Waldensians considered themselves true Christians, faithful to the spirit of the apostolic church. Repelled by Waldensian attacks against the immorality of the clergy and by the fact that these laypeople were preaching the Gospel without the permission of ecclesiastical authorities, the church condemned the movement as heretical. Despite persecution, however, the Waldensians continued to survive as a group in northern Italy.

The Cathari. Catharism was the most radical heresy to confront the medieval church. This belief represented a curious mixture of Gnosticism and Manichaeism—Eastern religious movements that had competed with Christianity in the days of the Roman Empire—and of doctrines condemned as heretical by the early church. Carried to Italy and southern France by Bulgarian missionaries, Catharism gained followers in regions where opposition to the worldliness and wealth of the clergy was already strong.

Cathari tenets differed considerably from those of the church. The Cathari believed in an eternal conflict between the forces of the god of good and those of the god of evil. Because the evil god, whom they identified with the God of the Old Testament, created the world, this earthly home was evil. The soul, spiritual in nature, was good but was trapped in wicked flesh. Because sexual activity was responsible for imprisoning the spirit in the flesh, the Cathari urged abstinence to avoid the birth of still another wicked human being. They also abstained from eggs, cheese, milk, and meat because these foods were the products of sexual activity. (This rigorous asceticism was demanded only of a select few, the *perfecti* [perfect ones]; simple believers could marry, and their diets were not restricted.) The Cathari taught that, since the flesh is evil, Christ would not have taken a human form; hence, he could not have suffered on the cross or have been resurrected. Nor could God have issued forth from the evil flesh of the Virgin. According to Catharism, Jesus was not God but an angel. In order to enslave people, the evil god created the church, which demonstrated its wickedness by pursuing power and wealth. They saw themselves as the true church, the successors of Jesus' apostles. Repudiating the existing church, the Cathari organized their own ecclesiastical hierarchy. People were impressed with the ascetic and moral lifestyle of the perfecti.

The center for the Catharist heresy was southern France, where a strong tradition of protest existed against the moral laxity and materialism of the clergy. When the Cathari did not submit to peaceful persuasion, Innocent III called on kings and lords to exterminate Catharism with the sword before the infection spread throughout Christendom. Lasting from 1208 to 1229, the war against the Cathari was marked by brutality and fanaticism. An army of crusading knights led by a papal legate assembled in northern France; it headed south, massacring heretics in the belief they were doing the work of God. Soon command of the crusading army passed to Simon de Montfort, a minor baron with great ambition. De Montfort slaughtered suspected heretics throughout the county of Toulouse, and for a short time he held the title of count of Toulouse. The crusading knights had effectively broken the power of the nobles who had protected the heretics. Innocent III sent legates to the region to arrest and try the Cathari. Under his successor, Dominican and Franciscan inquisitors completed the task of exterminating them virtually to the last person, a horrendous slaughter that some refer to as medieval genocide.

The Franciscans and the Dominicans. Driven by a zeal for reform, devout laypeople condemned the clergy for moral abuses. Sometimes their piety and resentment exploded into heresy; at other times, it was channeled into movements that served the church. Such was the case with the two great orders of friars, the Franciscans and the Dominicans.

Like Peter Waldo, Saint Francis of Assisi (c. 1181–1226) came from a wealthy merchant family. After undergoing an intense religious experience, Francis abandoned his possessions and devoted his life to imitating Christ. Dressed as a beggar, he wandered into villages and towns preaching, healing, and befriending. Unlike the monks who withdrew into walled fortresses, Francis proclaimed Christ's message to the poor of the towns. Like Peter Waldo, he preached a religion of personal feeling; like Jesus, he stretched out a hand of love to the poor, to the helpless, to the sick, and even to lepers, whom everyone feared to approach. The saintly Francis soon attracted disciples, called Little Brothers, who followed in the footsteps of their leader.

To suspicious churchmen, the Little Brothers seemed to be another heretical movement protesting against a wealthy and worldly church. However, Francis respected the authority of the priesthood and the validity of the sacraments. Recognizing that such a popular movement could be useful to the church, Innocent III allowed Francis to continue his mission. Innocent hoped that the Franciscans would help keep within the church those members of the laity who had deep religious feelings but were dissatisfied with the leadership of the traditional hierarchy.

As the Franciscans grew in popularity, the papacy exercised greater control over their activities; in time, the order was transformed from a spontaneous movement of inspired laymen into an organized agent of papal policy. The Franciscans served the church as teachers and missionaries in Eastern Europe, North Africa, the Near East, and China. The papacy set aside Francis's prohibition against the Brothers owning churches, houses, and lands corporately. His desire to keep the movement a lay order was abandoned when the papacy granted the Brothers the right to hear confession. Francis's opposition to formal learning as irrelevant to preaching Gospel love was rejected when the movement began to urge university education for its members. Those who protested against these changes as a repudiation of Francis's spirit were persecuted, and a few were even burned at the stake as heretics.

The Dominican order was founded by Saint Dominic (c. 1170–1221), a Spanish nobleman who had preached against the Cathari in southern France. Believing that those well versed in Christian teaching could best combat heresy, Dominic, unlike Francis, insisted that his followers engage in study. In time, the Dominicans became some of the leading theologians in the universities. Like the Franciscans, they went out into the world to preach the Gospel and to proselytize. Dominican friars became the chief operators of the Inquisition. For their zeal in fighting heresy, they were known as "hounds of the Lord."

Innocent III: The Apex of Papal Power

During the pontificate of Innocent III (1198–1216), papal theocracy reached its zenith. More than any earlier pope, Innocent made the papacy the center of European political life. In the tradition of Gregory VII, he forcefully asserted the theory of papal monarchy. As head of the church, Vicar of Christ, and successor of Saint Peter, Innocent claimed the authority to intervene in the internal affairs of secular rulers when they threatened the good order of Christendom. According to Innocent, the pope, "lower than God but higher than man . . . judges all and is judged by no one."[3]

Innocent applied these principles of papal supremacy in his dealings with the princes of Europe. When King Philip Augustus of France repudiated Ingeborg of Denmark the day after their wedding and later divorced her to marry someone else, Innocent placed an interdict on France to compel Philip to take Ingeborg back. For two decades, Innocent III championed Ingeborg's cause until she finally became the French queen. When King John of England rejected the papal candidate for

Pope Innocent III: "Royal Power Derives Its Dignity from the Pontifical Authority"

In the tradition of Gregory VII, Innocent III (1198–1216), the most powerful of medieval popes, asserted the claim for papal supremacy.

The Creator of the universe set up two great luminaries in the firmament of heaven; the greater light to rule the day, the lesser light to rule the night. In the same way for the firmament of the universal Church, which is spoken of as heaven, he appointed two great dignities; the greater to bear rule over souls (these being, as it were, days), the lesser to bear rule over bodies (those being, as it were, nights). These dignities are the pontifical authority and the royal power. Furthermore, the moon derives her light from the sun, and is in truth inferior to the sun in both size and quality, in position as well as effect. In the same way the royal power derives its dignity from the pontifical authority; and the more closely it cleaves to the sphere of that authority the less is the light with which it is adorned; the further it is removed, the more it increases in splendour.

Question for Analysis

1. Why were papal claims likely to stir a conflict with royal rulers?

Henry Bettenson and Chris Maunder, *Documents of the Christian Church* (New York: Oxford University Press, 1999), 123.

archbishop of Canterbury, Stephen Langton, Innocent first laid an interdict on the country. Then he excommunicated John, who expressed his defiance by confiscating church property and by forcing many bishops into exile. However, when Innocent urged Philip Augustus of France to invade England, John backed down. He accepted Innocent's nominee for archbishop, returned the property to the church, welcomed the exiles back, and, as a sign of complete capitulation, turned his kingdom over to Innocent to receive it back as a fief. Thus, as vassals of the papacy, John and his successors were obligated to do homage to the pope and to pay him a feudal tribute. Innocent also laid interdicts on the Spanish kingdoms of Castile and León and on Norway and strove to make the Holy Roman Emperor subservient to the papacy.

Innocent called the Fourth Crusade against the Muslims and a crusade against the heretical Cathari. The culminating expression of Innocent's supremacy was the Fourth Lateran Council, summoned in 1215. Comprising some twelve hundred clergy and representatives of secular rulers, the council issued several far-reaching decrees. It maintained that the Eastern Orthodox church was subordinate to the Roman Catholic church, prohibited the state from taxing the clergy, and declared laws detrimental to the church null and void. The council made bishops responsible for ferreting out heretics in their dioceses and ordered secular authorities to punish convicted heretics. Insisting on high standards of behavior for the clergy, it also required each Catholic to confess his or her sins to a priest at least once a year and to perform the prescribed penance. Through this directive, the church tightened its control over the conscience of Europe. The council also decreed that in the sacrament of the Eucharist the body and blood of Christ are actually present in the bread and wine used in the sacrament. This meant that the priest at the altar was God's agent in the performance of a wondrous miracle.

CHRISTIANS AND JEWS

In their relations with heretics, pagans, and Muslims, medieval Christians demonstrated a narrow and hostile attitude that ran counter to the Gospel message that all human beings were children of God and that Christ had suffered for all humanity.

Muslims were seen, in the words of Pope Urban II, as a "vile breed," "infidels," and "enemies of God." While the clergy denounced war among Christians, they considered it a duty to wage holy war against non-Christians. And knights regarded fighting the Muslims in Spain and the Holy Land as a heartfelt expression of their Christian ideals.

Medieval Christians also showed hatred for Jews—a visibly alien group in a society dominated by the Christian worldview. The First Crusade was a turning point for medieval Jews. Until then, there were few instances of organized violence against Jewish communities. If we are warring against God's enemies, reasoned zealous Crusaders, why not annihilate the Lord's enemies living in our midst? In 1096, bands of Crusaders, proclaiming that they were seeking vengeance against "Christ-killers," slaughtered Jews in French and German towns. The Crusaders were often aided by townspeople driven by hateful images of Jews and eager to seize Jewish property. The efforts of bishops to protect the Jews proved largely unsuccessful. In the German city of Mainz, more than a thousand Jews lost their lives. Some, in an act of martyrdom, chose to kill themselves and their children rather than submit to forced baptism or face a crueler death at the hands of the Crusaders. One contemporary wrote:

> I know not whether by a judgment of the Lord, or by some error of mind, they rose in a spirit of cruelty against the Jewish people scattered throughout these cities and slaughtered them without mercy, . . . asserting it to be their duty against the enemies of the Christian faith. . . . The Jews of [Mainz], knowing of the slaughter of their brethren, . . . fled in hope of safety to Bishop Rothard. . . . He placed the Jews in the very spacious hall of his own house, [but the Crusaders] attacked the Jews in the hall with arrows and lances. Breaking the bolts and doors, they killed the Jews, about seven hundred in number, who in vain resisted the force and attack of so many thousands. They killed the women, also, and with their swords pierced tender children of whatever age and sex.[4]

This venomous hatred of Jews unleashed by the First Crusade triggered numerous other massacres during the Middle Ages, at times fomented by clergy.

Viewing the Jews as possessions to be exploited, kings and lords taxed and fined them relentlessly and periodically expelled Jews from their territories in order to confiscate their property. In 1290, Jews were expelled from England, and in 1306, from France. Between 1290 and 1293, expulsions, massacres, and forced conversions led to the virtual disappearance of a centuries-old Jewish community life in southern Italy. In Germany, savage riots periodically led to the torture and murder of Jews. In 1348–1349, when the Black Death (see page 275) raged across Europe, Jews were accused of spreading the plague by poisoning well water; thousands of them were burned alive in Basel, Freiburg, Strasbourg, Mainz, and other towns.

Several factors contributed to anti-Jewish feelings during the Middle Ages. To medieval Christians, the Jews' refusal to embrace Christianity was an act of wickedness, particularly since the church taught that the coming of Christ had been prophesied by the Old Testament. Related to this prejudice was the portrayal of the crucifixion in the Gospels. In the minds of medieval Christians, the crime of deicide—the killing of God—eternally stained the Jews as a people; medieval Christians saw Jews as dangerous, criminal people rejected by God and deserving of ceaseless punishment. Christian theologians taught that they were to remain forever in subjection to Christians. It was just such a view that led town magistrates and princes periodically to confiscate Jewish property, at times after burning the helpless Jews alive in a public spectacle. The flames of hatred were fanned by the absurd allegation that Jews, made bloodthirsty by the spilling of Christ's blood, tortured and murdered Christians, particularly children, to obtain blood for ritual purposes. Although some popes condemned the charges as groundless, this blood libel was widely believed by the credulous masses and incited numerous riots, which led to the torture, burning alive, and expulsion of countless Jews and the pillaging of their property.

The role of Jews as moneylenders also provoked animosity toward them. Jews were increasingly excluded from international trade and most professions and were barred from the guilds and

ANTI-SEMITISM. Holding the Jews responsible for the Black Death, Christians committed mass murder. In Basel, several hundred Jews were herded into a wooden house and burned to death. Some six thousand Jews were burned alive in Mainz. Flames consumed another two thousand in a huge pyre outside Strasbourg, and their property was distributed to the local townspeople. In this picture depicting the slaughter of the Jews of Strasbourg, the townspeople evidently enjoy the spectacle. (Bibliothèque Royale de Belgique.)

in some areas from landholding as well. Hence, virtually the only means of livelihood open to them was moneylending—in reality an important activity in an expanding economy. This activity, which was in theory forbidden to Christians, aroused the hatred of the individual peasants, clergy, lords, and kings who did the borrowing.

The policy of the church toward the Jews was that they should not be harmed, and several medieval popes sought to protect Jewish life and property from wanton violence. But the church also wanted Jews to live in humiliation, a fitting punishment for their act of deicide and continued refusal to embrace Christianity. Thus, the Fourth Lateran Council barred Jews from public office, ordered them to remain off the streets during Christian festivals, and required them to wear a distinguishing badge on their clothing, a symbol of their

degradation. Christian art, literature, and religious instruction depicted the Jews in a derogatory manner, often identifying them with the Devil, who was very real and very terrifying to medieval Christians. Such people deserved no mercy, reasoned medieval Christians. Indeed, nothing was too bad for them. Because Jews were seen as evil allies of Satan engaged in a diabolical plot against God and Christendom, Jew-hatred was regarded as an expression of Christian virtue, a message routinely spread by preachers. Deeply etched into the minds and hearts of Christians, the distorted image of the Jew as a contemptible creature persisted in the European mentality into the twentieth century.

Despite their precarious position, medieval Jews maintained their faith, expanded their tradition of biblical and legal scholarship, and developed a flourishing Hebrew literature. The work of Jewish translators, doctors, and philosophers contributed substantially to the flowering of medieval culture in the High Middle Ages. The foremost Jewish scholar of the Middle Ages was Moses ben Maimon (1135–1204), also called by the Greek

name Maimonides (see profile in Chapter 11.) In both Muslim and Christian lands Maimonides achieved fame during his lifetime as a philosopher, theologian, mathematician, and physician.

NOTES

1. Quoted in J. W. Thompson, *Social and Economic History of the Middle Ages* (New York: Frederick Ungar, 1959), 2:772.
2. William of Tyre, *A History of Deeds Done Beyond the Sea,* trans. Emily Atwater Babcock and A. C. Krey (New York: Columbia University Press, 1943), 372, 373.
3. Excerpted in Brian Tierney, ed., *The Crisis of Church and State, 1050–1300* (Englewood Cliffs, N.J.: Prentice-Hall, 1964), 132.
4. Excerpted in A. C. Krey, ed., *The First Crusade: The Accounts of Eye-Witnesses and Participants* (Princeton, N.J.: Princeton University Press, 1921), 54–55.

SUGGESTED READING

Chazan, Robert, *Medieval Stereotypes and Modern Antisemitism* (1997). The deterioration of the image of the Jew in the High Middle Ages.

Duby, Georges, ed., *A History of Private Life*, vol. 2, *Revelations of the Medieval World* (1988). Among the topics discussed are sex, child-rearing, old age, and aristocratic households.

Fossier, Robert, ed., *The Cambridge Illustrated History of The Middle Ages*, vol. 2, *950–1250* (1997). Valuable essays.

Gimpel, Jean, *The Medieval Machine* (1977). Technological advances in the Middle Ages.

Lopez, R. S., *The Commercial Revolution of the Middle Ages, 950–1350* (1976). How an undeveloped society succeeded in developing itself.

Madden, Thomas E., ed., *Crusades* (2004). Essays by specialists on medieval crusading movements.

McCall, Andrew, *The Medieval Underworld* (2004). Accounts of witches, heretics, homosexuals, thieves and others considered on the margins of society.

Pernoud, Regine, ed., *The Crusades* (1964). A compilation of original sources.

Pounds, N. J. G., *An Economic History of Medieval Europe* (1974). A lucid survey.

Spufford, Peter, Power and Profit: *The Merchant in Medieval Europe* (2002). A detailed study replete with interesting accounts.

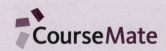

Chapter 11

The Flowering
of Medieval Culture:
The Christian Synthesis

School of Bologna manuscript illumination. (Bildarchiv Preussischer Kulturbesitz/Art Resource, N.Y.)

Focus Questions

1. What conditions contributed to the revival of learning during the High Middle Ages?
2. What were scholastic philosophers trying to accomplish?
3. How does the medieval view of the universe differ from the modern view?
4. How did religion pervade much of medieval philosophy, science, literature, art, and architecture?

Europe in the High Middle Ages showed considerable vitality. The population grew, long-distance trade revived, new towns emerged, states started to take shape, and papal power increased. The culminating expression of this recovery and resurgence was the cultural flowering in philosophy, the visual arts, and literature. Creative intellects achieved on a cultural level what the papacy accomplished on an institutional level: the integration of life around a Christian viewpoint. The High Middle Ages saw the restoration of some of the learning of the ancient world, the rise of universities, the emergence of an original form of architecture (the Gothic), and the erection of an imposing system of thought, called **scholasticism**. Medieval theologian-philosophers fashioned Christian teachings into an all-embracing philosophy, which represented the spiritual character of medieval civilization. They perfected what Christian thinkers in the Roman Empire had initiated and what the learned men of the Early Middle Ages were groping for: a synthesis of Greek philosophy and Christian **revelation**.

THE REVIVAL OF LEARNING

In the late eleventh century, Latin Christendom began to experience a cultural revival; all areas of life showed vitality and creativeness. In the twelfth and thirteenth centuries, a rich civilization with a distinctive style united the educated elite in the lands from England to Sicily. Gothic cathedrals, an enduring testament to the creativeness of the religious impulse, were erected throughout Europe. Universities sprang up in several cities. Roman authors were again read, and their style was imitated. The quality of written Latin—the language of the church, learning, and education—improved, and secular and religious poetry, both in Latin and in the vernacular, abounded. Roman law emerged anew in Italy, spread to northern Europe, and regained its importance (lost since Roman times) as worthy of study. Some key works of ancient Greece were translated into Latin and studied in universities. Employing the rational tradition of Greece, men of genius harmonized Christian doctrines and Greek philosophy. During this period, the status and influence of learned men grew considerably.

Map 11.1 MEDIEVAL CENTERS OF LEARNING Medieval universities established in the West a tradition of learning that has never died. There is direct continuity between the universities of our own day and the medieval centers of learning.

(Copyright © 2013 Cengage Learning.)

Several conditions contributed to this cultural explosion, known as the Twelfth-Century Awakening. As attacks of Vikings, Muslims, and Magyars ended and kings and great lords imposed more order and stability, people found greater opportunities for travel and communication. The revival of trade and the growth of towns created a need for literacy and provided the wealth required to support learning. Increasing contact with Islamic and Byzantine cultures in Spain and Sicily led to the translation into Latin of ancient Greek works preserved by these Eastern civilizations. By preserving Greek philosophy and science—and by commenting creatively on these classical works—Islamic civilization acted as a bridge between antiquity and the cultural revival of the High Middle Ages. The Twelfth-Century Awakening was also kindled by the legacy of the Carolingian Renaissance, whose cultural lights had dimmed but never wholly vanished in the period of disorder after the dissolution of Charlemagne's empire.

In the Early Middle Ages, the principal educational centers were the monastic schools. During the twelfth century, cathedral schools in towns gained importance. Paid a stipend by a local church, their teachers taught grammar, rhetoric, and logic. But the chief expression of expanding intellectual life was the university, a distinct creation of the Middle Ages.

The origins of the medieval university are obscure and varied. The first universities were not planned but grew spontaneously. They developed as students eager for knowledge and skills needed for high positions in government gathered around prominent teachers. The renewed importance of Roman law for business and politics, for example, drew students to Bologna to study with acknowledged masters.

The university was really a guild or corporation of masters or students who joined together to defend their interests against church or town authorities or the townspeople. A university might emerge when students united because of common needs, such as protection against townspeople who overcharged them for rooms and necessities. Organized into a body, students could also make demands on their instructors. At Bologna, professors faced fines for being absent or for giving lectures that drew fewer than five students; they were required to leave behind a deposit as security to ensure their return if they took a journey. A corporation of students formed the University at Bologna. The University of Paris, which evolved from the Cathedral School of Notre Dame, was the creation of a corporation of masters.

University students attended lectures, prepared for examinations, and earned degrees. They studied grammar, rhetoric, logic, arithmetic, geometry, astronomy, music, medicine, and, when ready, church law and theology, which was considered queen of the sciences. The curriculum relied heavily on Latin translations of ancient texts, chiefly the works of Aristotle. In mathematics and astronomy, students read Latin translations of Euclid and Ptolemy, while students of medicine studied the works of two great medical men of the ancient world, Hippocrates and Galen.

But sometimes students followed other pursuits. Instead of studying, they turned to drinking, gambling, and fighting. At Oxford University, it was reported that students "went through the streets with swords and bows and arrows and assaulted all who passed by."[1] Fathers complained that their sons preferred "play to work and strumming a guitar while the others are at their studies."[2] Students often faced financial problems, and they knew whom to ask for help: "Well-beloved father, to ease my debts . . . at the tavern, at the baker's, with the doctor . . . and to pay . . . the laundress and the barber, I send you word of greetings and of money."[3]

Universities performed a crucial function in the Middle Ages. Students learned the habit of reasoned argument. Universities trained professional secretaries and lawyers, who administered the affairs of church and state and of the growing cities; these institutions of learning also produced theologians and philosophers, who shaped the climate of public opinion. Since the curriculum and the texts studied were essentially the same in all lands, the learning disseminated by universities tightened the cultural bonds that united Christian Europe. Medieval universities established in the West a tradition of learning that has never died; there is direct continuity between the universities of our own day and the medieval ones.

THE MEDIEVAL WORLDVIEW

A distinctive worldview, based essentially on Christianity, evolved during the Middle Ages. This outlook differed from both the Greco-Roman and the modern scientific and secular views of the world. In the Christian view, not the individual but the Creator determined what constituted the good life. Thus, reason that was not illuminated by revelation was either wrong or inadequate, for God had revealed the proper rules for the regulation of individual and social life. Ultimately, the good life was not of this world but came from a union with God in a higher world. This Christian belief as formulated by the church made life and death purposeful and intelligible; it dominated the thought of the Middle Ages.

The Universe: Higher and Lower Worlds

Medieval thinkers sharply differentiated between spirit and matter, between a realm of grace and an earthly realm, between a higher world of perfection and a lower world of imperfection. Moral values derived from the higher world, which was also the final destination for the faithful. Two sets of laws operated in the medieval universe, one for the heavens and one for the earth. The cosmos was a giant ladder, with God at the summit; earth, composed of base matter, stood at the bottom, just above hell, where, farthest from God, dwelled Satan, his evil spirits, and the souls of the damned.

From Aristotle and Ptolemy, medieval thinkers inherited the theory of an earth-centered universe—the *geocentric theory*—which they imbued with Christian symbolism. The geocentric theory held that revolving around the motionless earth at uniform speeds were seven transparent spheres, in which were embedded each of the seven "planets"—the moon, Mercury, Venus, the sun, Mars, Jupiter, and Saturn. A sphere of fixed stars (that is, the stars, like chandeliers in a ceiling, stayed in a constant relationship to one another) enclosed this planetary system. Above the firmament of the stars were the three heavenly spheres. The outermost, the Empyrean Heaven, was the abode of God and the Elect. Through the sphere below—the Prime Mover—God transmitted motion to the planetary spheres. Underneath this was the lowermost sphere, the Crystalline Heaven, composed of a clear transparent substance.

An earth-centered universe accorded with the Christian idea that God created the universe for men and women and that salvation was the

GOD AS ARCHITECT OF THE UNIVERSE, FRENCH OLD TESTAMENT MINIATURE PAINTING, THIRTEENTH CENTURY. To the medieval Christian, God was the creator of the world. The universe had a known hierarchical order—a "great chain of being"—extending from God downward to the lowest form of being. (Osterreichische Nationalbibliothek, Vienna: Cod. 2554, fol. Iv.)

primary aim of life. Because God had created people in his image, they deserved this central position. Although they might be at the bottom of the cosmic ladder, only they, of all living things, had the capacity to ascend to heaven, the realm of perfection.

Also acceptable to the Christian mentality was the sharp distinction drawn by Aristotle between the world above the moon and the one below it. Aristotle held that terrestrial bodies were made of four elements: earth, water, air, fire. Celestial bodies, which occupied the region encompassing the moon and the area above, were composed of a fifth element, the ether—too clear, too pure, and too perfect to be found on earth. The planets and stars existed in a world apart; they were made of the divine ether and followed celestial laws, which did not apply to earthly objects. Whereas earthly bodies underwent change—ice converting to water, a burning log converting to ashes—heavenly objects were incorruptible, immune to all change. Unlike earthly objects, they were indestructible.

Heavenly bodies also followed different laws of motion than earthly objects. Aristotle said that it was natural for celestial bodies to move eternally in uniform circles, such motion being considered a sign of perfection. According to Aristotle, it was also natural for heavy bodies (stone) to fall downward and for light objects (fire, smoke) to move upward toward the celestial world; the falling stone and the rising smoke were finding their natural place in the universe. This view of the universe would be shattered by the Scientific Revolution of the sixteenth and seventeenth centuries.

The Individual: Sinful but Redeemable

At the center of medieval belief was the idea of a perfect God, who had conceived and created the universe, and wretched and sinful human beings. God had given Adam and Eve freedom to choose; rebellious and presumptuous, they had used their freedom to disobey God. In doing so, they made evil an intrinsic part of the human personality. But God, who had not stopped loving human beings, showed them the way out of sin. God became man and died so that human beings might be saved. Men and women were weak, egocentric, and sinful. With God's grace, they could overcome their sinful nature and gain salvation; without grace, they were utterly helpless.

The medieval individual's understanding of self stemmed from a comprehension of the universe as a **hierarchy** instituted by and culminating in God. On earth, the basest objects were lifeless stones devoid of souls; higher than stones were plants, endowed with a primitive type of soul, which allowed for reproduction and growth. Still higher were animals, which had the capacity for motion and sensation. The highest of the animals were human beings; unlike other animals, they could grasp some part of universal truth. Far superior to them were the angels, for they apprehended God's truth without difficulty. At the summit of this graduated universe was God, who was pure

Being, without limitation, and the source of all existence. God's revelation reached down to humanity through the hierarchical order. From God, revelation passed to the angels, who were also arranged hierarchically. From the angels, the truth reached men and women, grasped first by prophets and apostles and then by the multitudes. Thus, all things in the universe, from angels, men, and women to the lowest earthly objects, occupied a place peculiar to their nature and were linked by God in a great, unbroken chain.

Medieval individuals derived a sense of security from this hierarchical universe, in which the human position was clearly defined. Although they were sinners who dwelt on a corruptible earth, at the bottom of the cosmic hierarchy, they *could* ascend to the higher world of perfection above the moon. As children of God, they enjoyed the unique distinction that each human soul was precious; all Christians commanded respect, unless they were heretics. (A heretic forfeited dignity and could be justly executed.)

Medieval thinkers also arranged knowledge in a hierarchical order: knowledge of the spiritual surpassed all worldly knowledge, that is, all the sciences. Therefore, the true Christian understood that the pursuit of worldly knowledge could not proceed properly unless guided by divine revelation. To know what God wanted of the individual was the summit of self-knowledge and permitted entry into heaven. Thus, God was both the source and the end of knowledge. The human capacity to think and to act freely constituted the image of God within each individual; it ennobled man and woman and offered them the promise of associating with God in heaven.

True, human nobility derived from intelligence and free will. But if individuals disobeyed God, they brought misery on themselves. To challenge the divine will with human will constituted the sin of pride, contempt for God, and a violation of the divine order. Such sinful behavior invited self-destruction.

In the medieval view, neither nature nor the human being could be understood apart from God and his revelation. All reality emanated from God and was purposefully arranged in a spiritual hierarchy. Three great expressions of this view of life were scholastic philosophy, *The Divine Comedy* of Dante, and the Gothic cathedral.

PHILOSOPHY-THEOLOGY

Medieval philosophy, or scholasticism, applied reason to revelation. It explained and clarified Christian teachings by means of concepts and principles of logic derived from Greek philosophy. Scholastics tried to show that the teachings of faith, though not derived from reason, were not contrary to reason, that logic could confirm church dogma. They tried to prove through reason what they already held to be true through faith. For example, the existence of God and the immortality of the soul, which every Christian accepted as articles of faith, could also, they thought, be demonstrated by reason. In struggling to harmonize faith with reason, medieval thinkers constructed an extraordinary synthesis of Christian revelation and Greek thought.

The scholastic masters used reason not to challenge but to serve faith: to elucidate, clarify, and buttress it. They did not break with the central concern of Christianity, that of earning God's grace and achieving salvation. Although this goal could be realized solely through faith, scholastic thinkers insisted that a science of nature did not obstruct the pursuit of grace and that philosophy could assist the devout in the contemplation of God. They did not reject those Christian beliefs that were beyond the grasp of human reason and therefore could not be deduced by rational argument. Instead, they held that such truths rested entirely on revelation and were to be accepted on faith. To medieval thinkers, reason did not have an independent existence but ultimately had to acknowledge a suprarational, superhuman standard of truth; Greek philosophy had to be interpreted to accord with Christian revelation. They wanted rational thought to be directed by faith for Christian ends and guided by scriptural and ecclesiastical authority. Ultimately, faith had the final word.

Not all Christian thinkers welcomed the use of reason. Regarding Greek philosophy as an enemy of faith (would not reason lead people to question belief in miracles?), a fabricator of heresies (would not reason encourage disbelief in essential church teachings?), and an obstacle to achieving communion of the soul with God (would not a deviation from church teachings, under the influence of pagan philosophy, deprive people of salvation?), conservative theologians opposed the use

of reason to elucidate Christian revelation. For if reason could demonstrate the proof of Christian teachings, as its advocates insisted, it could also be used, warned conservatives, to challenge and reject those teachings. In a sense, the conservatives were right. By revitalizing Greek thought, medieval philosophy nurtured a powerful force that eventually would shatter the medieval concepts of nature and society and weaken Christianity. Modern Western thought was created by thinkers who refused to subordinate reason to religious authority. Reason proved to be a double-edged sword: it both ennobled and undermined the medieval worldview.

Saint Anselm and Abelard

An early scholastic, Saint Anselm (1033–1109) was abbot of the Benedictine monastery of Bec in Normandy. He used rational argument to serve the interests of faith. Like Augustine before him and other thinkers who followed him, Anselm said that faith was a precondition for understanding. Without belief, there could be no proper knowledge. He developed philosophical proof for the existence of God. Anselm argued as follows: We can conceive of no being greater than God. But if God were to exist only in thought and not in actuality, his greatness would be limited; he would be less than perfect. Hence, he exists. Anselm's motive and method reveal something about the essence of medieval philosophy. He does not begin as a modern might: "If it can be proven that God exists, I will adopt the creed of Christianity; if not, I will either deny God's existence (atheism) or reserve judgment (agnosticism)." Rather, Anselm accepts God's existence as an established fact because he believes what Holy Scripture says and what the church teaches. He then proceeds to employ logical argument to demonstrate that God can be known not only through faith but also through reason. He would never use reason to subvert what he knows to be true by faith. In general, this attitude would characterize later medieval thinkers, who also applied reason to faith.

As a young teacher of theology at the Cathedral School of Notre Dame, Peter Abelard (1079–1142) acquired a reputation for brilliance and combativeness. His tragic affair with Héloise, whom he tutored and seduced, has become one of the great

Peter Abelard: The Synthesis of Reason and Faith

Dialectics, a method of logical analysis, as applied to the Bible and the writings of early Christian thinkers, was brilliantly taught by Peter Abelard in the cathedral school at Paris. In his book Sic et Non *(Yes and No), Abelard listed some 150 questions on which the early church authorities had taken differing positions over the centuries. He suggested that these issues could be resolved by the careful application of the dialectical method to the language of the texts.*

Although he never intended to challenge the Christian faith, Abelard raised, with his critical scrutiny, fears that the dialectical approach would undermine faith and foster heresy, and he was forced to quit his teaching post. Nevertheless, the new scholastic rationalistic approach swept the schools of Europe. In the following reading, Abelard describes the critical use of rational methods in textual analysis.

We must be careful not to be led astray by attributing views to the [Church] Fathers which they did not hold. This may happen if a wrong author's name is given to a book or if a text is corrupt. For many works are falsely attributed to one of the Fathers to give them authority, and some passages, even in the Bible, are corrupt through the errors of copyists. . . . We must be equally careful to make sure that an opinion quoted from a Father was not withdrawn or corrected by him in the light of later and better knowledge. . . . Again the passage in question may not give the Father's own opinion, but that of some other writer whom he is quoting. . . .

We must also make a thorough inquiry when different decisions are given on the same matter under canon [church] law. We must discover the underlying purpose of the opinion, whether it is meant to grant an indulgence or exhort to some perfection. In this way we may clear up the apparent contradiction. . . . If the opinion is a definitive judgment, we must determine whether it is of general application or directed to a particular case. . . . The when and why of the order must also be considered because what is allowed at one time is often forbidden at another, and what is often laid down as the strict letter of the law may be sometimes moderated by a dispensation. . . .

Furthermore we customarily talk of things as they appear to our bodily senses and not as they are in actual fact. So judging by what we see we say it is a starry sky or it is not, and that the sun is hot or has no heat at all, when these things though variable in appearance are ever constant. Can we be surprised, then, that some matters have been stated by the Fathers as opinions rather than the truth? Then again many controversies would be quickly settled if we could be on our guard against a particular word used in different senses by different authors. . . .

A careful reader will employ all these ways of reconciling contradictions in the writings of the Fathers. But if the contradictions are so glaring that they cannot be reconciled, then the rival authorities must be compared and the view that has the heaviest backing be adopted. . . .

By collecting contrasting divergent opinions I hope to provoke young readers to push themselves to the limit in the search for truth, so that their wits may be sharpened by their investigation. It is by doubting that we come to investigate, and by investigating that we recognize the truth.

Questions for Analysis

1. Describe the methods of literary analysis promoted by Peter Abelard.
2. Why did Abelard's new method of textual analysis create so much controversy?

Excerpted in David Ayerst and A. S. S. Fisher, eds., *Records of Christianity*, vol. 2, *Christendom* (Oxford: Blackwell, 1977), 196–197.

Maimonides

Moses ben Maimon, also called by the Greek name Maimonides (1135–1204), was recognized as the foremost Jewish sage of his day. His works were also read and respected by Muslim and Christian thinkers, including Thomas Aquinas and Albert the Great. Born in Córdoba, Spain, then under Muslim rule, his family was forced to flee the country when the Almohads, a fanatical fundamentalist group from North Africa, conquered Córdoba and demanded that Jews and Christians convert or face death. Maimonides' family went into exile, moving about Spain and then emigrating to Morocco and later to a suburb of Cairo. When his brother David, a merchant, perished at sea with the family's fortune, Maimonides, who had read widely in Arabic translations of Greek and Muslim medical works, became a physician. Gaining a reputation, he served as court physician to Saladin and the Egyptian royal family.

During his lifetime, Maimonides achieved fame as a philosopher, theologian, mathematician, and physician. Maimonides was intimately familiar with the works of Arab philosophers and Arabic translations of ancient Greek philosophy, particularly Aristotle. Like Christian scholastics and Muslim philosophers, Maimonides tried to harmonize faith with reason, to reconcile the Hebrew Scriptures and the Talmud (Jewish biblical commentary) with the teachings of Aristotle.

romances in Western literature. Héloise had a child and entered a nunnery; Abelard was castrated on orders of Canon Fulbert, Héloise's guardian, and sought temporary refuge in a monastery. After resuming his career as a teacher in Paris, Abelard again had to seek refuge, this time for writing an essay on the **Trinity** that church officials found offensive. After further difficulties and flights, he again returned to Paris to teach dialectics. Not long afterward, his most determined opponent, Bernard of Clairvaux, accused Abelard of using the method of dialectical argument to attack faith. To Bernard, a monk and a **mystic**, subjecting revealed truth to critical analysis was fraught with danger.

> *The deepest matters become the subject of undignified wrangling. . . . Virtues and vices are discussed with no trace of moral feelings, the sacraments of the Church with no evidence of faith, the mystery of the Holy Trinity with no spirit of humility or sobriety: all is presented in a distorted form, introduced in a way different from the one we learned and are used to.*[4]

Hearkening to Bernard's powerful voice, the church condemned Abelard and confined him to a monastery for the rest of his days.

Abelard believed that it was important to apply reason to faith and that careful and constant questioning led to wisdom. Since all knowledge derives from God, said Abelard, it is good to pursue learning. In *Sic et Non* (Yes and No), he took 150 theological issues and, by presenting passages from the Bible and the church fathers, showed that there were conflicting opinions. He suggested that the divergent opinions of authorities could be reconciled through proper use of dialectics (see Primary Source box). But like Anselm before him, Abelard did not intend to refute traditional church doctrines. Reason would buttress, not weaken, the authority of faith. After his condemnation in 1141, Abelard wrote:

> *I will never be a philosopher, if this is to speak against St. Paul, I would not be an Aristotle if this were to separate me from Christ. . . . I have set my building on the cornerstone on which Christ has built his Church. . . . I rest upon the rock that cannot be moved.*[5]

The Recovery of Aristotle

During the Early Middle Ages, scholars in the Muslim world translated the works of Aristotle into Arabic and wrote commentaries on them.

Reflecting the value that Jews gave to education, Maimonides insisted that every Jewish man, whether he be rich or poor, old or young, healthy or unhealthy, and even if burdened with family responsibilities, was obliged to study daily the Hebrew Scriptures. Drawing on the deeply ingrained Jewish tradition calling for care for the poor, Maimonides listed eight degrees of almsgiving. The highest was to help a needy person become self-supporting. Just below was giving charity in such a way that both the donor and the recipient are unknown to each other.

In his numerous medical writings, Maimonides displayed a scientific bent in treating the sick, and to preserve health he urged drinking clean water, breathing fresh air, and eating healthy foods.

The preservation of ancient Greek thought was a major contribution of Islamic civilization. During the High Middle Ages, these works were translated into Latin by learned Europeans.

The introduction into Latin Christendom of the major works of Aristotle created a dilemma for religious authorities. Aristotle's comprehensive philosophy of nature and man, a product of human reason alone, conflicted in many instances with essential Christian doctrine. For Aristotle, God was an impersonal principle that accounted for order and motion in the universe, the unmoved mover. For Christianity, not only was God responsible for order in the physical universe, but he was also a personal being—a loving Father concerned about the deeds of his children. Whereas Christianity taught that God created the universe at a specific point in time, Aristotle held that the universe was eternal. Nor did Aristotle believe in the personal immortality of the soul, another cardinal principle of Christianity. For Aristotle, it was impossible for the soul to exist independently of the body.

Some church officials feared that the dissemination of Aristotle's natural philosophy would endanger faith. Would the teachings of Christ and the church fathers have to answer to pagan philosophy? Would Athens prevail over Jerusalem?

At various times in the first half of the thirteenth century, the teaching of Aristotle's scientific works was forbidden at the University of Paris. However, because the ban did not apply throughout Christendom and was not consistently enforced in Paris, Aristotle's philosophy continued to be studied.

Thomas Aquinas: The Synthesis of Faith and Reason

Rejecting the position of conservatives, who insisted that philosophy would contaminate faith, Saint Thomas Aquinas (c. 1225–1274) upheld the value of human reason and natural knowledge. He set about reconciling Aristotelianism with Christianity. Aquinas taught at Paris and at various institutions in Italy. His greatest work, *Summa Theologica*, is a systematic exposition of Christian thought and the crowning expression of the medieval attempt to integrate Aristotle with Christianity. As a devout Catholic and member of the Dominican order, he of course accepted the truth of revelation. He never used reason to undermine faith.

Aquinas divided revealed truth into two categories: beliefs whose truth can be demonstrated by reason and beliefs that reason cannot prove to be either true or false. For example, he believed that philosophical speculation could prove the existence of God and the immortality of the human soul but could not prove or disprove the doctrines of the Trinity, the **Incarnation,** and the **Redemption** because those articles of faith wholly surpassed the capacity of human reason. This fact, however, did not detract from their certainty. Doctrines of faith did not require rational proof to be valid. They were true because they originated with God, whose authority is unshakable.

Can the teachings of faith conflict with the evidence of reason? For Aquinas, the answer was emphatically no. He said that revelation could not be the enemy of reason because revelation did not contradict reason and reason did not corrupt the purity of faith. Revelation supplemented and perfected reason. If there appeared to be a conflict between philosophy and faith, it was certain that reason had erred somewhere, for the doctrines of faith were infallible. Since *both* faith and reason came from God, they were not in competition with each other but, properly understood, supported each other and formed an organic unity. Consequently, reason should not be feared, for it was another avenue to God. Because there was an inherent agreement between true faith and correct reason—they both ultimately stemmed from God—contradictions between the two were only a misleading appearance. Although philosophy had not yet been able to resolve the dilemma, for God no such contradictions existed. In heaven, human beings would attain complete knowledge, as well as complete happiness. While on earth, however, they must allow faith to guide reason; they must not permit reason to oppose or undermine faith.

Because reason was no enemy of faith, applying it to revelation need not be feared. As human reasoning became more proficient, said Aquinas, it also became more Christian, and apparent incompatibilities between faith and reason disappeared. Recognizing that both faith and reason point to the same truth, the wise person accepts the guidance of religion in all questions that relate directly to knowledge needed for salvation. There also existed a wide range of knowledge that God had not revealed and that was not required for salvation. Into this category fell much knowledge about the natural world of things and creatures, which human beings had perfect liberty to explore.

Thus, in exalting God, Aquinas also paid homage to human intelligence, proclaimed the value of rational activity, and asserted the importance of physical reality revealed through human senses. Consequently, he valued the natural philosophy of Aristotle. Correctly used, Aristotelian thought would assist faith. Aquinas's great effort was to synthesize Aristotelianism with the divine revelation of Christianity. That the two could be harmonized he had no doubt. He made use of Aristotelian categories in his five proofs of God's existence. In his first proof, for example, Aquinas argued that a thing cannot move itself. Whatever is moved must be moved by something else, and that by something else again. "Therefore, it is necessary to arrive at a first mover, moved by no other; and this everyone understands to be God."[6]

Aquinas upheld the value of reason. To love the intellect was to honor God and not to diminish the truth of faith. He had confidence in the power of the rational mind to comprehend most of the truths of revelation, and he insisted

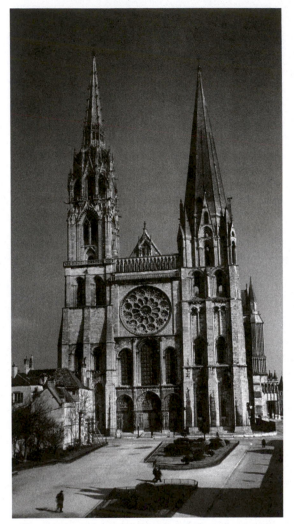

NOTRE-DAME DE CHARTRES, BEGUN C. 1194, CHARTRES, FRANCE. Because the two spires topping the west façade towers were constructed nearly four centuries apart, they provide an interesting contrast between early and late Gothic architecture. The simple north spire was built between 1160 and 1170; the south spire, constructed in the early sixteenth century, is a good example of the flamboyant Gothic style. (Nat Farbman/Time and Life Pictures/Getty Images.)

that in nontheological questions about specific things in nature—those questions not affecting salvation—people should trust only to reason and experience.

Aquinas gave new importance to the empirical world and to scientific speculation and human knowledge. The traditional medieval view, based largely on Saint Augustine, drew a sharp distinction between the higher world of grace and the lower world of nature, between the world of spirit and the world of sense experience. Knowledge derived from the natural world was often seen as an obstacle to true knowledge. Aquinas altered this tradition by affirming the importance of knowledge of the social order and the physical world. He gave human reason and worldly knowledge a new dignity. Thus, the City of Man was not merely a sinful place from which people tried to escape in order to enter God's city; it was worthy of investigation and understanding. But Aquinas remained a medieval thinker, for he always maintained that secular knowledge should be supervised and corrected by revealed truth, and he never questioned the truth of the medieval Christian view of the world and the individual. As historian Steven Ozment explains,

> *Aquinas brought reason and revelation together, but strictly as un-equals. . . . In this union, reason, philosophy, nature, secular man and the state ultimately had value only in subservience to the higher goals of revelation, theology, grace, religious man, and the church. . . . Thomist theology was the most sophisticated statement of the medieval belief in the secondary significance of the lay and secular world, a congenial ideology for a church besieged by independent and aggressive secular political powers.*[7]

Strict Aristotelianism: The Challenge to Orthodoxy

Some teachers in the Faculty of Arts at Paris, relying heavily on the commentaries of Averroës, the great Muslim thinker (see page 208), found Aquinas's approach of Christianizing or explaining away Aristotle unacceptable. Unlike Aquinas, they did not seek to reconcile Aristotle's philosophy with Christian dogma. They held that certain Aristotelian propositions contradicting faith were philosophically true, or at least could not be proven false. These teachers maintained that

it was impossible to refute these propositions by natural reason alone—that is, without recourse to faith. For example, by reason alone Aristotle had demonstrated that the world was eternal and that the processes of nature were unalterable. The first doctrine conflicted with the Christian belief that God created the universe at a point in time; the second conflicted with the belief that God could work miracles.

But these teachers did not take the next step and argue that Aristotle was correct and faith wrong. They maintained only that Aristotle's arguments could not be refuted by natural reason and that philosophers—as philosophers, not as Christians—should base their judgments on rational arguments only, not on miracles and revelation. These strict Aristotelians did not deny the truths of faith, but they did assert that natural reason could construct conclusive proofs for propositions that the church had explicitly stated to be false.

In 1277, the bishop of Paris condemned 219 propositions, many of them taught by these expositors of Aristotle at the University of Paris. Included in the condemnation were some propositions held by the great Aquinas. This move attempted to prevent Aristotle's philosophical naturalism from undermining Christian beliefs. Consequently, the condemnation was a triumph for conservative theologians, who had grown increasingly worried about the inroads made by Aristotelianism. To them, even the Christian Aristotelianism of Aquinas was suspect, for it could lead people astray, endangering their salvation.

Condemnations generally hinder the pursuit of knowledge, but, ironically, the condemnation of 1277 may have had the opposite effect. It led some thinkers to examine critically and reject elements of Aristotle's natural philosophy. This development may have served as a prelude to modern science, which, born in the sixteenth and seventeenth centuries, grew out of a rejection of Aristotelian physics.

SCIENCE

During the Early Middle Ages, few scientific works from the ancient world were available to Western Europeans. Scientific thought was at its lowest ebb since its origination more than a thousand years earlier in Greece. By contrast, both Islamic and Byzantine civilizations preserved and, in some instances, added to the legacy of Greek science. In the High Middle Ages, however, many ancient texts were translated from Greek and Arabic into Latin and entered Latin Christendom for the first time. The principal centers of translation were Spain, where Christian and Muslim civilizations intersected, and Sicily, which had been controlled by Byzantium up to the last part of the ninth century and then by Islam until Christian Normans completed the conquest of the island by 1091. Often learned Jews, who knew both Arabic and Latin, served as translators. These translations of ancient Greek scientific works and of Arabic commentaries stimulated interest in nature.

In the thirteenth and fourteenth centuries, a genuine scientific movement did occur. Impressed with the naturalistic and empirical approach of Aristotle, some medieval scholars spent time examining physical nature. Among them was the Dominican Albert the Great (Albertus Magnus). Born in Germany, Albert (c. 1206–1280) studied at Padua and taught at the University of Paris, where Thomas Aquinas was his student. To Albert, philosophy meant more than employing Greek reason to contemplate divine wisdom; it also meant making sense of nature. Albert devoted himself to mastering, editing, and commenting on the vast body of Aristotle's works.

While retaining the Christian stress on God, revelation, the supernatural, and the afterlife, Albert (unlike many earlier Christian thinkers) considered nature a valid field for investigation. In his writings on geology, chemistry, botany, and zoology, Albert, like Aristotle, displayed respect for the concrete details of nature, utilizing them as empirical evidence.

I have examined the anatomy of different species of bees. In the rear, i.e. behind the waist, I discovered a transparent, shining bladder. If you test this with your tongue, you find that it has a slight taste of honey. In the body there is only an insignificant spiral-shaped intestine and nerve fibers which are connected with the sting. All this is surrounded with a sticky fluid.[8]

Showing a modern-day approach, Albert approved of inquiry into the material world, stressed the value of knowledge derived from experience with nature, sought rational explanations for natural occurrences, and held that theological debates should not stop scientific investigations. He pointed to a new direction in medieval thought.

Robert Grosseteste (c. 1175–1253), chancellor of Oxford University, was also a scholar of the scientific movement. He declared that the roundness of the earth could be demonstrated by reason. In addition, he insisted that mathematics was necessary in order to understand the physical world, and he carried out experiments on the refraction of light.

Another Englishman, the monk and philosopher Roger Bacon (c. 1214–1294), foreshadowed the modern attitude of using science to gain mastery over nature. He recognized the practical advantages that might come and predicted these great changes.

Machines for navigation can be made without rowers so that the largest ships on rivers or seas will be moved by a single man in charge with greater velocity than if they were full of men. Also oars can be made so that without animals they will move with unbelievable rapidity. . . . Also flying machines can be constructed so that a man sits in the midst of the machine revolving some engine by which artificial wings are made to beat the air like a flying bird. Also a machine small in size can be made for walking in the sea and rivers, even to the bottom without danger.[9]

Bacon valued the study of mathematics and read Arabic works on the reflection and refraction of light. Among his achievements were experiments in optics and the observation that light travels much faster than sound. His description of the anatomy of the vertebrate eye and optic nerves was the finest of that era, and he recommended dissecting the eyes of pigs and cows to obtain greater knowledge of the subject.

The study of the ancient texts of Hippocrates and Galen and their Islamic commentators, particularly Avicenna's *Canon of Medicine*, which synthesized Greek and Arabic medicine, elevated medicine to a formal discipline. Although these texts contained numerous errors and contradictions, they had to be mastered, if only to be challenged, before modern medicine could emerge. In addition, medieval doctors dissected animals and, in the late fourteenth century, human bodies. From practical experience, medieval doctors, monks, and laypeople added to the list of plants and herbs that would ease pain and heal.

Medieval scholars did not make the breakthrough to modern science. They kept the belief that the earth was at the center of the universe and that different sets of laws operated on earth and in the heavens. Although some medieval thinkers explicitly urged seeking natural explanations to account for physical occurrences, medieval science was never wholly removed from a theological setting. Modern science self-consciously seeks the advancement of specifically scientific knowledge, but in the Middle Ages many questions involving nature were raised merely to clarify a religious problem.

Medieval scholars and philosophers, however, did advance knowledge about optics, the tides, and mechanics. They saw the importance of mathematics for interpreting nature, and they performed some experiments. By translating and commenting on ancient Greek and Arabic works, medieval scholars provided future ages with ideas to reflect on and to reject and surpass, a necessary precondition for the emergence of modern science.

Medieval thinkers also developed an anti-Aristotelian physics, which some historians of science believe influenced Galileo, the creator of modern mechanics, more than two centuries later. To explain why heavy objects do not always fall downward—why an arrow released by a bow moves in a straight line before it falls—Aristotle said that when the arrow leaves the bow, it separates the air, which then moves behind the arrow and pushes it along. Aristotle, of course, had no comprehension of the law of inertia, which, as formulated by Isaac Newton in the seventeenth century, states that a body in motion will continue in a straight line unless interfered with. Unable to imagine that being in motion is as natural a condition as being at rest, Aristotle concluded that an outside force must maintain continual contact with the moving object. Hence, the flying arrow requires the "air-engine" to keep it in motion.

In the fourteenth century, Jean Buridan, a professor at the University of Paris, rejected Aristotle's theory. Buridan argued that the bowstring transmits to the arrow a force called impetus, which keeps the arrow in motion. Whereas Aristotle attributed the arrow's motion to the air, which was external to the arrow, Buridan found the motive force to be an agent imparted to the arrow by the bowstring. Though still far from the modern theory of inertia, Buridan's impetus theory was an advance over Aristotle's air-engine. In the impetus theory, a moving body requires a cause to keep it in motion. In the theory of inertia, as noted above, once a body is in motion, no force is required to keep it moving in a straight line.

Late medieval physics went beyond Aristotle in other ways as well, particularly in the importance given to expressing motion mathematically. The extent to which late medieval thinkers influenced the thinkers of the Scientific Revolution is a matter of debate. Some historians view modern science as a child of the Middle Ages. Other historians believe that the achievements of medieval science were slim and that modern science owes very little to the Middle Ages.

THE RECOVERY OF ROMAN LAW

During the Early Middle Ages, Western European law essentially consisted of Germanic customs, some of which had been written down. Although some elements of Roman law endured as custom, the formal study of Roman law disappeared. The late eleventh and the twelfth centuries saw the revival of Roman law, particularly in Bologna, Italy. Irnerius lectured on the *Corpus Juris Civilis,* Roman laws and judicial commentaries codified by Byzantine jurists in the sixth century by order of the emperor Justinian. He made Bologna the leading center for the study of Roman law. Irnerius and his students applied to the study of law the methods of organization and logical analysis that scholastic theologians used in studying philosophical texts.

Unlike traditional Germanic law, which was essentially tribal law, Roman law assumed the existence of universal principles, which could be grasped by the human intellect and expressed in the law of the state. Roman jurists had systematically and rationally structured the legal experience of the Roman people. The example of Roman law stimulated medieval jurists to organize their own legal tradition. Intellectuals increasingly came to insist on both a rational analysis of evidence and judicial decisions based on rational procedures. Law codes compiled in parts of France and Germany and in the kingdom of Castile were influenced by the recovery of Roman law.

Roman law also influenced church law, which was derived from the Bible, the church fathers, church councils, and the decisions of popes. In the last part of the eleventh century, church scholars began to codify church (or canon) law and were helped by the Roman legal tradition.

LITERATURE

Medieval literature was written both in Latin and in the vernacular—the normal spoken language, as distinct from the language of learning. Much of medieval Latin literature consisted of religious hymns and dramas depicting the life of Christ and saints.

Medieval university students, like their modern counterparts, lampooned their elders and social conventions, engaged in drinking bouts, and rebelled against the rigors of study. They put their feelings into poetry written in Latin. For them, youth and study did not mix.

> Let's away with study,
>   Folly's sweet.
> Treasure all the pleasure of our youth:
>   Time enough for age
> To think of Truth.
> So short a day,
> And life so quickly hasting
> And is study wasting
>   Youth that would be gay![10]

And, of course, their thoughts turned to romance.

> All I care for is to play,
>   Gaze upon my treasure,
> Now and then to touch her hand,
>   Kiss in modest measure;
> But the fifth act of love's game,
>   Dream not of that pleasure![11]

Poor or errant students who had given up their studies roamed the roads as free spirits. These vagabonds sometimes composed poetry that ridiculed clerics and sang the praises of wine, gambling, and women.

> Down the highway-broad I walk,
> Like a youth in mind,
> Implicate myself in vice,
> Virtue stays behind,
> Avid for the world's delight
> More than for salvation,
> Dead in soul, I care but for
> Body's exultation.[12]

Vernacular literature emerged in the High Middle Ages. The French *chansons de geste*—epic poems of heroic deeds that had first been told orally—were written in the vernacular of northern France. The poems dealt with Charlemagne's battles against the Muslims, with rebellious nobles, and with feudal warfare. The finest of these epic poems, *The Song of Roland*, expressed the feudal ethic: loyalty to one's lord and devotion to Christianity were the highest virtues and treachery an unpardonable crime.

The *Nibelungenlied*, the best expression of the heroic epic in Germany, is often called "the *Iliad* of the Germans." Like its French counterpart, it dealt with heroic feats.

> In stories of our fathers, high marvels we are
>   told
> Of champions well-approved in perils
>   manifold.
> Of feasts and merry meetings, of weeping and
>   of wail,
> And deeds of gallant daring I'll tell you in my
>   tale.[13]

The *roman*—a blending of old legends, chivalric ideals, and Christian concepts—combined love with adventure, war, and the miraculous. Among the romans were the tales of King Arthur and his Round Table. Circulating by word of mouth for centuries, these tales spread from the British Isles to France and Germany.

Another form of medieval poetry, which flourished particularly in Provence, in southern France, dealt with the romantic glorification of women. Sung by troubadours, many of them nobles, the

MILLEFLEURS TAPESTRY: TWO MUSICIANS, SCHOOL OF THE LOIRE, FRANCE, C. 1500. The courtly love tradition, in which women were worshipped and untouchable, inspired poetry. Troubadours sang this poetry, which expressed a changing attitude toward women. By inviting poets to their courts and writing poetry themselves, noblewomen actively influenced the rituals and literature of courtly love. (© The Collection of the Frick Art and Historical Center, Pittsburgh, Pennsylvania.)

courtly love poetry expressed a changing attitude toward women. Although medieval men generally regarded women as inferior and subordinate, courtly love poetry ascribed to noble ladies superior qualities of virtue. To the nobleman, the lady became a goddess worthy of devotion, loyalty, and worship. He would honor her and serve her as he did his lord; for her love, he would undergo any sacrifice. Troubadours sang love songs that praised ladies for their beauty and charm and expressed both the joys and the pains of love.

> *I sing of her, yet her beauty*
> *is greater than I can tell,*
> *with her fresh color, lively eyes,*
> *and white skin, untanned*
> *and untainted by rouge.*

> *She is so pure and noble*
> *that no one can speak ill of her.*
> *But above all, one must praise,*
> *it seems to me, her truthfulness,*
> *her manners and her gracious speech*
> *for she never would betray a friend.*[14]

Noblewomen actively influenced the rituals and literature of courtly love. They often invited poets to their courts and wrote poetry themselves. Sometimes a lady troubadour expressed disdain for her husband and desire for the knight whom she truly loved.

> *I should like to hold my knight*
> *Naked in my arms at eve,*
> *That he might be in ecstasy*
> *As I cushioned his head against my breast,*
> *For I am happier far with him*
> *Than Floris with Blancheflor;*
> *I grant him my heart, my love,*
> *My mind, my eyes, my life.*

> *Fair friend, charming and good,*
> *When shall I hold you in my power?*
> *And lie beside you for an hour*
> *And amorous kisses give to you;*
> *Know that I would give almost anything*
> *To have you in my husband's place,*
> *But only if you swear*
> *To do everything I desire.*[15]

Ladies demanded that knights treat them with gentleness and consideration and that knights dress neatly, bathe often, play instruments, and compose (or at least recite) poetry. To prove worthy of his lady's love, a knight had to demonstrate patience, charm, bravery, and loyalty. It was believed that a knight would ennoble his character by devoting himself to a lady.

Courtly love involved not a husband–wife relationship but a noble's admiration and yearning for another woman of his class. Among nobles, marriages were arranged for political and economic reasons. The rituals of courtly love, it has been suggested, provided an outlet for erotic feelings condemned by the church. They also enhanced the skills and refined the tastes of the noble. The rough warrior acquired wit, manners, charm, and a facility with words. He was becoming a courtier and a gentleman.

THE VISITATION, WEST PORTAL, REIMS CATHEDRAL, C. 1225–1245. The reflection of Roman art exhibited by these statues of the expectant mothers (Mary and Elizabeth) of Jesus and John the Baptist suggests that the sculptor was well versed in the classical tradition. The carving of the draperies and the poses of the figures reveal classical traits, but instead of being idealizations, the figures display human warmth. (Scala/Art Resource/N.Y.)

The greatest literary figure of the Middle Ages was Dante Alighieri (1265–1321) of Florence. Dante appreciated the Roman classics and wrote not just in Latin, the traditional language of intellectual life, but also in Italian, his native tongue. In this respect, he anticipated the Renaissance. In the tradition of the troubadours, Dante wrote poems to his beloved Beatrice.

In *The Divine Comedy,* Dante synthesized the various elements of the medieval outlook and summed up, with immense feeling, the medieval understanding of the purpose of life. Written while Dante was in exile, *The Divine Comedy* describes the poet's journey through hell, purgatory, and paradise. Dante arranges hell into nine concentric circles; in each region, sinners are punished in proportion to their earthly sins. The poet experiences all of hell's torments—burning sand, violent storms, darkness, and fearful monsters that whip, claw, bite, and tear sinners apart. The ninth circle, the lowest, is reserved for Lucifer and traitors. Lucifer has three faces, each a different color, and two bat-like wings. In each mouth, he gnaws on the greatest traitors in history: Judas Iscariot, who betrayed Jesus, and Brutus and Cassius, who assassinated Caesar. Those condemned to hell are told: "All hope abandon, ye who enter in."

In purgatory, Dante meets sinners who, although they undergo punishment, will eventually enter paradise. He and Beatrice ascend to the highest heaven, a realm of light that radiates truth, goodness, and gentleness. In paradise, the poet meets the great saints and the Virgin Mary. He glimpses the Vision of God. In this mystical experience, the aim of life is realized.

ARCHITECTURE

Two styles of architecture evolved during the Middle Ages: Romanesque and Gothic. The **Romanesque** style dominated the eleventh century and the greater part of the twelfth. In imitation of ancient Roman structures, Romanesque buildings used massive walls to support stone barrel-and-groin vaults with rounded arches. Thick walls were needed to hold up the great weight of the roofs. Because the walls had few spaces for windows, little light entered the interior of Romanesque buildings.

The development of the pointed arch permitted supports that lessened the bearing pressure of the roof on the walls. This new style, called **Gothic,** allowed buildings to have lofty, vaulted ceilings and huge windows, which permitted sunlight to flood the interior. Whereas Romanesque buildings produced an impression of massive solidity, Gothic buildings created an illusion of lightness and upward motion. The Gothic cathedral gave visual expression to the medieval conception of a hierarchical universe. As the historian Joan Gadol puts it, "Inside and out, the Gothic cathedral is one great movement upward through a mounting series of grades, one ascent through horizontal levels marked by arches, galleries, niches, and towers. . . . [T]he material ascends to the spiritual, the natural is assumed into the supernatural—all in a graduated rise."[16] This illusion of upward reach to the heavens is created by the tall and narrow proportions of the interior spaces, the springing pointed arches, and the marching patterns of closely spaced columns and colonnettes.

The magnificently designed stained-glass windows and complex sculptural decoration of Gothic cathedrals depicted scenes from the Bible and the lives of saints, as well as scenes from daily life, for the worshipers, many of whom were illiterate. The reduction of wall space, which allowed these massive glass illustrations, was made possible by the flying buttresses on the buildings' exteriors. These great arcs of masonry carry the weight and thrust of the stone vaults out to the exterior walls. The light cage of buttresses surrounding the cathedral makes the exterior silhouette appear as airy and diffuse as the interior spaces. The architects and builders thought only of honoring God, not themselves; their identity remains a mystery.

Gothic cathedrals took many decades to complete and required donations from the devout.

Only in an age of intense religious faith could such energy have been spent to glorify God. These vast building projects, many of them in northern France, were made possible by economic prosperity. Funds were raised from a variety of sources. Cathedrals owned income-producing properties, such as farmland, mills, and forests, and received donations from pilgrims visiting the relics of famous saints. Clerics also collected tolls and taxes on goods shipped to fairs through their region.

The Gothic style was to remain vigorous until the fifteenth century, spreading from France to England, Germany, Spain, and beyond. Revived from time to time thereafter, it has proved to be one of the most enduring styles in Western art and architecture.

Not too long ago, some intellectuals viewed the Middle Ages as a period of ignorance and superstition, an era of cultural sterility that stood between the high civilizations of ancient Greece and Rome and the modern West. This view of the Middle Ages as a dark age has been abandoned, and quite properly so, for the High Middle Ages saw the crystallization of a rich and creative civilization. To be sure, its religious orientation sets it apart both from classical civilization and from our own modern secular and scientific civilization. But the *Summa Theologica* of Aquinas, *The Divine Comedy* of Dante, and the Gothic cathedral all attest to the creativeness and genius of the medieval religious spirit.

❖ ❖ ❖

NOTES

1. Quoted in G. G. Coulton, *Life in the Middle Ages* (New York: Macmillan, 1928), 1:74.

2. Quoted in Charles Homer Haskins, *The Rise of Universities* (Ithaca, N.Y.: Cornell University Press, 1957), 79.

3. Quoted in Coulton, *Life in the Middle Ages,* 3:113.

4. Quoted in Anders Piltz, *The World of Medieval Learning* (Oxford: Blackwell, 1981), 83.

5. Quoted in David Knowles, *The Evolution of Medieval Thought* (New York: Vintage Books, 1964), 123.

6. *Summa Theologica,* excerpted in *Introduction to Saint Thomas Aquinas,* ed. Anton C. Pegis (New York: Modern Library, 1948), 25.

7. Steven Ozment, *The Age of Reform* (New Haven, Conn.: Yale University Press, 1980), 20.

8. Quoted in Piltz, *The World of Medieval Learning,* 176.

9. Quoted in A. C. Crombie, *Medieval and Early Modern Science* (Garden City, N.Y.: Doubleday Anchor Books, 1959), 1:55–56.

10. Quoted in Marcia L. Colish, *Medieval Foundations of the Western Intellectual Tradition, 400–1400* (New Haven, Conn.: Yale University Press, 1997), 202.

11. Excerpted in David C. Riede and J. Wayne Baker, eds., *The Western Intellectual Tradition* (Dubuque, Ia.: Kendall/Hunt, 1980), 1:62.

12. Excerpted in E. H. Zeydel, ed., *Vagabond Verse: Secular Latin Poems in the Middle Ages* (Detroit: Wayne State University Press, 1966), 61.

13. *The Fall of the Nibelungers,* trans. William Nanson Lettsom (London: Williams and Norgate, 1890), 1.

14. Excerpted in Anthony Bonner, ed., *Songs of the Troubadours* (New York: Schocken Books, 1972), 42–43.

15. Quoted in Frances Gies and Joseph Gies, *Women in the Middle Ages* (New York: T. Y. Crowell, 1978), 45.

16. Joan Gadol, *Leon Battista Alberti, Universal Man of the Early Renaissance* (Chicago: University of Chicago Press, 1969), 149–150.

SUGGESTED READING

Bonner, Anthony, ed., *Songs of the Troubadours* (1972). Collection of troubadour poetry.

Colish, Marcia L., *Medieval Foundations of the Western Intellectual Tradition, 400–1400* (1997). A lucid account; highly recommended.

Cook, William R. and Ronald B. Herzman, *The Medieval World View: An Introduction* (1983). A lucid summary of the medieval outlook; excellent for students.

Copleston, F. C., *A History of Medieval Philosophy* (1974). A lucid, comprehensive survey of medieval philosophy.

Gilson, Etienne, *Reason and Revelation in the Middle Ages* (1966). A superb brief exposition of the medieval philosophical tradition.

Gimpel, Jean, *The Cathedral Builders* (1984). The financial, political, and spiritual forces behind the building of cathedrals.

Harren, Michael, *Medieval Thought: The Western Intellectual Tradition from Antiquity to the Thirteenth Century* (1992). An up-to-date introduction to the major themes of medieval thought.

Pieper, Josef, *Scholasticism* (1964). Written with intelligence and grace.

Piltz, Anders, *The World of Medieval Learning* (1981). A valuable survey of medieval learning intended for non-specialists.

Wieruszowski, Helene, *The Medieval University* (1966). A good survey, followed by documents.

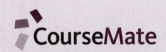

Chapter 12

The Late Middle Ages: Crisis and Dissolution

The Jacquerie Enraged French peasants attack the castle of a lord.

(© Mary Evans Picture Library/The Image Works.)

- **An Age of Adversity**
- **The Decline of the Papacy**
- **The Breakup of the Thomistic Synthesis**
- **The Middle Ages and the Modern World: Continuity and Discontinuity**

Focus Questions

1. Why is the fourteenth century described as an age of adversity?

2. What led to the decline of the medieval papacy? What is the historical significance of this development?

3. What is the significance of thinkers who challenged the Thomistic synthesis?

4. What is the legacy of the Middle Ages to the modern world?

5. How does the characteristic outlook of the Middle Ages differ from that of the modern age?

By the start of the fourteenth century, Latin Christendom had experienced more than 250 years of growth. On an economic level, agricultural production had expanded, commerce and town life had revived, and the population had increased. On a political level, kings had become more powerful, bringing greater order and security to large areas. On a religious level, the papacy had demonstrated its strength as the spiritual leader of Christendom, and the clergy had been reformed. On a cultural level, a unified worldview, blending faith and reason, had been forged.

During the Late Middle Ages, roughly the fourteenth and early fifteenth centuries, medieval civilization was in decline. The fourteenth century, an age of adversity, was marked by crop failures, famine, population decline, plagues, stagnating production, unemployment, inflation, devastating warfare, and abandoned villages. Violent rebellions by the poor of the towns and countryside were ruthlessly suppressed by the upper classes. The century witnessed flights into mysticism, outbreaks of mass hysteria, and massacres of Jews; it was an age of pessimism and general insecurity. The papacy declined in power, heresy proliferated, and the synthesis of faith and reason, erected by Christian thinkers during the High Middle Ages, began to disintegrate. These developments were signs that the stable and coherent civilization of the thirteenth century was drawing to a close.

But all was not decline and gloom. On the positive side, representative institutions developed, and thinkers showed a greater interest in the world of nature. And in Italy, the dynamic forces of urbanism and secularism were producing a period of cultural and humanistic flowering known as the Renaissance.

AN AGE OF ADVERSITY

Economic Problems, the Black Death, and Social Tension

In the Late Middle Ages, Latin Christendom was afflicted with severe economic problems. The earlier increases in agricultural production did not continue. Limited use of fertilizers and limited knowledge of conservation exhausted the topsoil.

Chronology 12.1 ❖ The Late Middle Ages

1303	The French attack papal summer palace at Anagni
1309–1377	Babylonian Captivity: the popes, all French, reside at Avignon and are influenced by the French monarchy
1323–1328	Peasants' Revolt in Flanders
1328	End of France's Capetian dynasty; Edward III of England tries to gain the French throne
1337–1453	Hundred Years' War between England and France
1346	Battle of Crécy: the English defeat the French
1347–1351	Black Death reaches Italian ports and ravages Europe
1356	Battle of Poitiers: the English defeat the French
1358	Jacquerie, the French peasants' revolt
1377	Pope Gregory XI returns papacy to Rome
1378	Florentine laborers revolt
1378–1417	Great Schism: Christendom has two and then three popes
1381	English peasants revolt
1382	Weavers revolt in Ghent
1415	Battle of Agincourt: Henry V of England defeats the French; Jan Hus, a Bohemian religious reformer, is burned at the stake
1429	Joan of Arc liberates Orléans
1431	Joan of Arc is condemned as a witch
1453	The English are driven from France, except Calais: end of the Hundred Years' War
1460	Pope Pius II condemns the Conciliar Movement as heretical

As more grazing land was converted to the cultivation of cereals, animal husbandry decreased, causing a serious shortage of manure needed for arable land. Intermittent bouts of prolonged heavy rains and frost also hampered agriculture. From 1301 to 1314, there was a general shortage of food, and from 1315 to 1317, famine struck Europe. People subsisted by scavenging. On roads and in villages, people died of starvation, and the dead remained unattended. Throughout the century, starvation and malnutrition were widespread. In Bruges, for example, two thousand of the town's thirty-five thousand inhabitants died of starvation.

Other economic problems abounded. A shortage of silver, caused by technical problems in sinking deeper shafts in mines, led to the debasement of coins and spiraling inflation, which hurt the feudal nobility in particular. Prices for manufactured luxury goods, which the nobility craved, rose rapidly. At the same time, the dues that the nobility collected from peasants diminished. To replace their revenues, lords and knights turned to plunder and warfare.

Compounding the economic crisis was the Black Death, or bubonic plague, a bacillus carried by fleas on black rats. The disease probably first struck Mongolia in 1331–1332, and from there it crossed into Russia. Carried back from Black Sea ports, the plague reached Sicily in 1347 and then spread swiftly throughout much of Europe

John Wycliff: Concerning the Pope's Power

John Wycliffe (c. 1320–1384), a respected English theologian challenged the church's core doctrine that salvation was attainable only by adhering to its sacraments as administered by the clergy. Anticipating the Protestant Reformation of the sixteenth century, Wycliffe maintained that inspiration from Scripture, not obedience to the church, was the path to salvation. He specifically rejected the church doctrine that the clergy were indispensable intermediaries between human beings and God. In calling for a return to the spiritual purity of the early Christians, he attacked the luxurious life style of bishops and the pope. The following text, originally written in Middle English, was rendered into Modern English by Alfred J. Andrea.

Christ was a very poor man from His birth to His death and forswore worldly riches and begging . . . but Antichrist, in contrast to this, from the time that he is made pope to the time of his death, covets worldly wealth and tries in many shrewd ways to gain riches. Christ was a most meek man and urged that we learn from Him, but people say that the pope is the proudest man on earth, and he makes lords kiss his feet, whereas Christ washed His apostles' feet. Christ was a most unpretentious man in life, deeds, and words. People say that this pope is not like Christ in this way, for whereas Christ went on foot to cities and little towns alike, they say this pope desires to live in a castle in a grand manner. Whereas Christ came to John the Baptist to be baptized by him, the pope summons people to come to him wherever he might be, yea, as though Christ Himself, and not the pope, had summoned them to Him. Christ embraced young and poor in token of his humility; people say that the pope desires to embrace worldly prestige and not good people for the sake of God, lest he dishonor himself. Christ was busy preaching the Gospel, and not for worldly prestige or for profit;

through human contact. Some historians contend that the Black Death may have consisted of two diseases, the bubonic plague and anthrax, which was transmitted by eating meat from diseased cattle. The first crisis lasted until 1351, and other serious outbreaks occurred in later decades. The crowded cities and towns, where sewage made rats more fecund, had the highest mortality rate—as much as sixty percent. Perhaps twenty million people—about one-quarter to one-third of the European population—perished in the worst disaster in recorded history caused by natural forces. Contemporaries viewed the disaster as divine punishment for humanity's sins.

Overwhelmed by terror, people abandoned their sick children, spouses, and parents. Panic-stricken people drifted into debauchery, lawlessness, and frenzied forms of religious life. Confidence in the church declined as many priests fled, depriving the sick of spiritual comfort and the dying of last rites. Organized bands of flagellants marched from region to region beating themselves and one another with sticks and whips in a desperate effort to appease God, who, they believed, had cursed them with the plague. Expressing the pervasive gloom and pessimism of these times, art concentrated on morbid scenes of decaying flesh, open graves laden with worm-eaten corpses—even the Madonna was represented as a corpse being eaten by snakes and frogs—dances of death, and the torments of hell. Sometimes this hysteria was directed against Jews, who were accused of causing the plague by poisoning wells. Terrible massacres of Jews, often by mass burnings, occurred despite the pleas of the

people say that the pope allows this, but he would gladly make laws to which he gives more prestige and sanction than Christ's law. Christ so loved His flock that He laid down his life for them and suffered sharp pain and death in order to bring them to bliss. People say that the pope so loves the prestige of this world that he grants people absolution that guarantees a straight path to Heaven so that they might perform acts that redound to his honor. And so this foolishness could be the cause of the death, in body and soul, of many thousands of people. And how does he follow Christ in this way? Christ was so patient and suffered wrongs so well that He prayed for His enemies and taught His apostles not to take vengeance. People say that the pope of Rome wishes to be avenged in every way, by killing and by damning and by other painful means that he devises. Christ taught people to live well by the example of His own life and by His words, for He did what He taught and taught in a manner that was consonant with His actions. People say that the pope

acts contrary to this. His life is not an example of how other people should live, for no one should live like him, inasmuch as he acts in a manner that accords to his high state. In every deed and word, Christ sought the glory of God and suffered many assaults on His manhood for this goal; people say that the pope, to the contrary, seeks his own glory in every way, yea, even if it means the loss of the worship of God. And so he manufactures many groundless gabblings.

If these and similar accusations are true of the pope of Rome, he is the very Antichrist and not Christ's vicar on earth.

Questions for Analysis

1. Why was John Wycliffe critical of the church?
2. Why did the church regard his teachings as a serious threat to its mission?

Source: From Alfred Andrea, *The Medieval Record*, 1E. © 1997 Wadsworth, a part of Cengage Learning, Inc. Reproduced by permission. www.cengage.com/permissions.

papacy. Whole Jewish communities in Germany and Switzerland were exterminated. Invited by Duke Casimir II, who hoped they would stimulate economic activity, many Jews fled to Poland.

The millions of deaths caused production of food and goods to plummet. However, depopulation was a boon for surviving artisans, who found opportunities and higher wages in depopulated towns desperate for skilled workers. A diminishing labor pool also benefited peasants, who were able to attain lighter burdens from strapped lords, and free peasants who toiled as laborers demanded higher wages. The combination of lower agricultural prices and increasing wages hurt aristocratic landowners. As their agricultural income lessened, nobles tried to make peasants bear the brunt of the crisis. A law decreed in England in

1349 required peasants to work for lords at fixed wages. Similar regulations of wages in German, Spanish, and Portuguese principalities aggravated tensions between peasants and nobles.

Economic and social tensions, some of them antedating the Black Death, escalated into rebellions. Each rebellion had its own specific causes, but a general pattern characterized the uprisings in the countryside. When kings and lords, breaking with customary social relationships, imposed new and onerous regulations, the peasants rose in defense of their traditional rights. No doubt their revolt was also fueled by an instinctive hatred for the haughty lords, who, for centuries, had treated peasants with contempt. In 1323, the lords' attempt to reimpose old manorial obligations infuriated the free peasants of Flanders,

THE GREAT PLAGUE. The Black Death, or bubonic plague, devastated Europe, carrying off entire villages. A new piety swept through European art in the plague's aftermath. The elegant French courtly love style was replaced by morbid scenes of decaying flesh and suffering saints. (Snark/Art Resource, N.Y.)

whose condition had improved in earlier decades. The Peasants' Revolt lasted five bloody years. In 1358, French peasants took up arms in protest against the plundering of the countryside by soldiers. Perhaps twenty thousand peasants died in the uprising known as the Jacquerie. In 1381, English peasants revolted, angered over legislation that tied them to the land and imposed new taxes. John Ball, who claimed to be a priest, expressed egalitarian sentiments.

> *My good friends, things cannot go on well in England, nor ever will until everything shall be in common; when there shall neither be vassal nor lord, and all distinctions leveled; when the lords shall be no more masters than ourselves. But ill have they used us! and for what reason do they thus hold us in bondage? Are we not all descended from the same parents, Adam and Eve? and what can they show, or what reasons give, why they should be more the masters than ourselves? except, perhaps, in making us labor and work, for*

> *them to spend. . . . They have handsome manors, when we must brave the wind and rain in our labors in the field; but it is from our labor they have wherewith to support their pomp.*[1]

Like the revolts in Flanders and France, the uprising in England failed. To the landed aristocracy, the peasants were sinners attacking a social system ordained by God. Possessing superior might, the nobility suppressed the peasants, sometimes with savage cruelty.

Social unrest afflicted the towns as well as the countryside. The wage earners of Florence (1378), the weavers of Ghent (1382), and the poor of Paris (1382) rose up against the ruling oligarchy. These revolts were generally initiated not by the poorest and most downtrodden but by those who had made some gains and were eager for more. The rebellions of the urban poor were crushed just like the peasant uprisings.

The Hundred Years' War

Compounding the adversity was the series of conflicts known as the Hundred Years' War (1337–1453). Because English kings ruled parts of France, conflicts between the two monarchies were common. In the opening phase of the war, the English inflicted terrible defeats on French knights at the battles of Crécy (1346) and Poitiers (1356). Using longbows, which allowed them to shoot arrows rapidly, English archers cut down wave after wave of charging French cavalry. The war continued on and off throughout the fourteenth century. During periods of truce, gangs of unemployed soldiers roamed the French countryside killing and stealing, actions that precipitated the Jacquerie.

After the battle of Agincourt (1415), won by the English under Henry V, the English controlled most of northern France. It appeared that England would shortly conquer France and join the two lands under one crown. At this crucial moment in French history, a young, illiterate peasant girl, Joan of Arc (1412–1431), helped rescue France. Believing that God commanded her to drive the English out of France, Joan rallied the demoralized French troops, leading them in battle. In 1429, she liberated the besieged city of Orléans. Later she was captured and imprisoned by the English, and in 1431 she was condemned as a heretic and a witch by a hand-picked church court and was burned at the stake. Inspired by Joan's death, the French drove the English from all French territory except the port of Calais.

During the Hundred Years' War, French kings introduced new taxes, which added substantially to their incomes. These monies furnished them with the means to organize a professional army of well-paid, loyal troops. By evoking a sense of pride and oneness in the French people, the war also contributed to a growing, but still incomplete, national unity. The English, too, emerged from the war with a greater sense of solidarity, and Parliament, because it had to finance the war, gained in stature. However, the war had horrendous consequences for the French peasants. Thousands of farmers were killed, and valuable farmland was destroyed by English armies and marauding bands of mercenaries. In a portentous development, the later stages of the Hundred Years' War saw the use of gunpowder and heavy artillery.

THE DECLINE OF THE PAPACY

The principal sign of breakdown in the Late Middle Ages was the waning authority and prestige of the papacy. In the High Middle Ages, the papacy had been the dominant institution in Christendom, but in the Late Middle Ages, its power disintegrated. The medieval ideal of a unified Christian commonwealth guided by the papacy was shattered. Papal authority declined in the face of the growing power of kings, who championed the parochial interests of states. The papacy's prestige and its capacity to lead diminished as it became more embroiled in European politics. Many pious Christians felt that the pope behaved more like a secular ruler than like an Apostle of Christ. Political theorists and church reformers further undermined papal authority.

Conflict with France

Pope Boniface VIII (1294–1303) vigorously upheld papal claims to supremacy over secular rulers. In the famous bull *Unam Sanctam* (1302), he declared:

> *If the earthly power errs, it shall be judged by the spiritual power . . . but [the pope] can be judged only by God not by man. . . . Whoever therefore resists this power so ordained by God resists the ordinance of God. . . . Therefore, we declare, state, define, and pronounce that it is altogether necessary to salvation for every human creature to be subject to the Roman Pontiff.*[2]

But in trying to enforce this idea of papal supremacy on proud and increasingly powerful kings, Boniface suffered defeat and humiliation.

Philip IV of France (1285–1314) taxed the church in his land to raise revenue for war. In doing so, he disregarded the church prohibition against the taxing of its property without papal permission. In 1296, in the bull *Clericis Laicos*, Pope Boniface VIII decreed that kings and lords who imposed taxes on the clergy and the clergy who paid them would be excommunicated. Far from bowing to the pope's threat, Philip acted forcefully to assert authority over the church in his kingdom. Boniface backed down from his position, declaring that the French king could tax the clergy in times of national emergency. Thus, the matter was resolved to the advantage of the state.

A second dispute had more disastrous consequences for Boniface. Philip tried and imprisoned a French bishop despite Boniface's warning that this was an illegal act and a violation of church law and tradition, which held that the church, not the state, must judge the clergy. Philip summoned the first meeting of the Estates General to gain the backing of the nation. Shortly afterward, Boniface threatened to excommunicate Philip. The outraged monarch raided the papal summer palace at Anagni in September 1303 and captured the pope. Although Boniface was released, this shocking event proved too much for him, and a month later he died.

Boniface's two successors, Benedict XI (1303–1304) and Clement V (1305–1314), tried to conciliate Philip. In particular, Clement decided to remain at Avignon, a town on the southeastern French frontier, where he had set up a temporary residence.

From 1309 to 1377, a period known as the Babylonian Captivity, the popes were all French and resided in Avignon, not Rome. During this time, the papacy, removed from Rome and

A DEAD MAN BEFORE HIS JUDGE: A MINIATURE PAINTING FROM THE ROMAN BOOK OF HOURS, FRANCE, C. 1420. God the Father, bearing the orb and sword of universal sovereignty, hears the final prayer of a dying man and sends an angel to liberate the man's soul from the clutches of a demon. A preoccupation with death and demons was characteristic of late medieval Christian art. (© Art Media/ HIP/The Image Works.)

deprived of revenues from the Papal States in Italy, was often forced to pursue policies favorable to France. The growing antipapalism among the laity further damaged the papal image. Laypeople were repelled by the luxurious style of living at Avignon and by the appointment of high churchmen to lands where they did not know the language and showed little concern for the local population. Criticism of the papacy increased.

The conflict between Boniface and Philip provoked a battle of words between proponents of papal supremacy and defenders of royal rights. The most important critique of clerical intrusion into worldly affairs was *The Defender of the Peace* (1324) by Marsiglio of Padua (c. 1290– c. 1343). Marsiglio held that the state ran according to principles that had nothing to do with religious commands originating in a higher realm. Religion dealt with a supernatural world and with principles of faith that could not be proved by reason, wrote Marsiglio. Politics, in contrast, dealt with a natural world and with the affairs of the human community. Political thinkers should not try to make the earthly realm conform to articles of faith. According to Marsiglio, the state was self-sufficient; it needed no instruction from a higher authority. Thus, Marsiglio denied the essential premises of medieval papal political theory: that kings received their power from God; that the pope, as God's vicar, was empowered to guide kings; that the state, as part of a divinely ordered world, must conform to and fulfill supranatural ends; and that the clergy were above the laws of the state. Marsiglio viewed the church as a spiritual institution with no temporal power. "Christ himself," said Marsiglio, "refuse[d] rulership in this world . . . and taught that all men, both priests and non-priests, should be subject . . . to the coercive judgment of the rulers of this world."[3] Marsiglio even went so far as to suggest that the church should be subordinate to the state; his concept of an autonomous state that did not answer to clerical authority anticipates modern political thought.

The Great Schism and the Conciliar Movement

The Avignon popes were often competent men who, despite the hard times that had overtaken the papacy, tried to bolster papal power. They tightened their hold over church administration by reserving for themselves certain appointments and collections of fees formerly handled by local bishops. Through a deliberate effort at financial centralization, including the imposition of new taxes and the more efficient collection of old ones, the Avignon popes substantially increased papal income.

Although Pope Gregory XI returned the papacy to Rome in 1377, the papacy was to suffer

Prominent churchmen urged the convening of a general council to end the disgraceful schism, which obstructed the papacy from performing its sacred duties. Held in 1409 and attended by hundreds of churchmen, the Council of Pisa deposed both Urban and Clement and elected a new pope. Since neither deposed pope recognized the council's decision, Christendom then had three popes. A new council was called at Constance in 1414. In the struggle that ensued, each of the three popes either abdicated or was deposed in favor of an appointment by the council. In 1417, the Great Schism ended.

During the first half of the fifteenth century, church councils met at Pisa (1409), Constance (1414–1418), and Basel (1431–1449) in order to end the schism, combat heresy, and reform the church. The Conciliar Movement attempted to transform the papal monarchy into a constitutional system in which the pope's power would be regulated by a general council. Supporters of the movement held that the papacy could not reform the church as effectively as a general council representing the clergy. But the Conciliar Movement ended in failure. As the Holy Roman Emperor and then the French monarch withdrew their support from the councils, the papacy regained its authority over the higher clergy. In 1460, Pope Pius II condemned the Conciliar Movement as heretical.

Deeply embroiled in European power politics and the worldly life of Renaissance Italy, the papacy often neglected its spiritual and moral responsibilities. Many devout Christians longed for religious renewal and a return to simple piety; the papacy did not hear this cry for reform. The papacy's failure to provide creative leadership for reform made possible the Protestant Reformation of the sixteenth century. By splitting Christendom into Catholic and Protestant, the Reformation destroyed forever the vision of a Christian world commonwealth guided by God's vicar, the pope.

Fourteenth-Century Heresies

Another threat to papal power and to the medieval ideal of a universal Christian community guided by the church came from radical

PORTRAIT OF JOAN OF ARC: WITCH OR SAINT? Claiming that heavenly voices had called upon her to lead the armies of France to victory over the English, a young peasant girl, Joan of Arc, persuaded the French crown prince to give her command of the army. Victorious in battle, she fulfilled all that was required of her, including the crowning of the new King at Rheims. Captured soon after, she was tried as a witch by an English-dominated court and executed in Rouen in 1431. She has been a heroine and inspiration to many modern artists, poets, and dramatists. (The Art Archive/Archives Nationales Paris/Marc Charmet.)

another humiliation: the Great Schism. Elected pope in 1378, Urban VI immediately displayed tactlessness, if not mental imbalance, by abusing and even imprisoning cardinals. Fleeing from Rome, the cardinals declared that the election of Urban had been invalid and elected Clement VII as the new pope. Refusing to step down, Urban excommunicated Clement, who responded in kind. To the utter confusion and anguish of Christians throughout Europe, there were now two popes: Urban ruling from Rome and Clement from Avignon.

reformers who questioned the function and authority of the entire church hierarchy. These heretics in the Late Middle Ages were forerunners of the Protestant Reformation. The two principal dissenters were the Englishman John Wycliffe (c. 1320–1384) and the Czech Jan Hus (c. 1369–1415).

By stressing a personal relationship between the individual and God and by claiming that the Bible itself, rather than church teachings, is the ultimate Christian authority, Wycliffe, a respected English theologian teaching at the University of Oxford, challenged the fundamental position of the medieval church: that the avenue to salvation passed through the church alone. He argued that Scripture, which was the final authority, needed no further development by church authorities and that the sacraments are not necessary for salvation. He denounced the wealth of the higher clergy and sought a return to the spiritual purity and material poverty of the early church. To Wycliffe, the wealthy, elaborately organized hierarchy of the church was unnecessary and wrong. The splendidly dressed and propertied bishops bore no resemblance to the simple people who first followed Christ. Indeed, these worldly bishops, headed by a princely and tyrannical pope, were really anti-Christians, the "fiends of Hell." Wycliffe wanted the state to confiscate church property and the clergy to embrace poverty. By denying that priests changed the bread and wine of Communion into the substance of the body and blood of Christ, Wycliffe rejected the special powers of the clergy.

In Bohemia, Wycliffe's ideas were enthusiastically received by Czech reformers led by Jan Hus. Like Wycliffe, Hus advocated vernacular translations of the Bible, which would be accessible to common people, and he upbraided the upper clergy for their luxury and immorality.

Both movements were declared heretical. The church deprived the Lollards—an order of poor priests that spread Wycliffe's teachings—of their priestly functions. In the early fifteenth century, some of Wycliffe's followers were burned at the stake, as was Jan Hus. Nevertheless, the church could not crush the dissenters' followers or eradicate their teachings. To some extent, the doctrines of the Reformation would parallel the teachings of Wycliffe.

THE BREAKUP OF THE THOMISTIC SYNTHESIS

In the Late Middle Ages, the papacy lost power as kings, political theorists, and religious dissenters challenged papal claims to supreme leadership. The great theological synthesis constructed by the scholastic theologians of the twelfth and thirteenth centuries was also breaking down. The process of fragmentation evident in the history of the church took place in philosophy as well.

Saint Thomas Aquinas's system culminated the scholastic attempt to show the basic agreement of philosophy and religion. In the fourteenth century, a number of thinkers cast doubt on the possibility of synthesizing Aristotelianism and Christianity, that is, reason and faith. Consequently, philosophy grew more analytical and critical. Denying that reason could demonstrate the truth of Christian doctrines with certainty, philosophers tried to separate reason from faith. Whereas Aquinas had said that reason proved or clarified much of revelation, fourteenth-century thinkers asserted that the basic propositions of Christianity were not open to rational proof. Whereas Aquinas had held that faith supplemented and perfected reason, some philosophers were now proclaiming that reason often contradicted faith.

Duns Scotus (1265–1308), a Scottish Franciscan, held that human reason cannot prove that God is omnipotent, that he forgives sins, that he rewards the righteous and punishes the wicked, or that the soul is immortal. These Christian doctrines, which scholastic philosophers believed could be proven by reason, were for Scotus the province of revelation and faith, not reason.

To be sure, this new outlook did not urge abandoning faith in favor of reason. Faith had to prevail in any conflict with reason because faith rested on God, the highest authority in the universe. But the relationship between reason and revelation was altered. Articles of faith, it was now held, had nothing to do with reason; they were to be believed, not proved. Reason was not an aid to theology but a separate sphere of activity. This new attitude snapped the link between reason and faith that Aquinas had so skillfully forged. The scholastic synthesis was disintegrating.

The chief proponent of the new outlook was William of Ockham (c. 1285–1349). In contrast to Aquinas, Ockham insisted that natural reason could not prove God's existence, the soul's immortality, or any other essential Christian doctrine. Reason could say only that God probably exists and that he probably endowed humankind with an immortal soul. But it could not prove these propositions with certainty. The tenets of faith were beyond the reach of reason, said Ockham; there was no rational foundation to Christianity. For Ockham, reason and faith did not necessarily complement each other as they did for Aquinas; it was neither possible nor helpful to join reason to faith. Ockham, however, sought not to undermine faith—only to disengage it from reason.

In the process of proclaiming the authority of theology, Ockham furthered the use of reason to comprehend nature. His approach, separating natural knowledge from religious dogma, made it easier to explore the natural world empirically without fitting it into a religious framework. Thus, Ockham is a forerunner of the modern mentality, which is characterized by a separation of reason from religion and an interest in the empirical investigation of nature.

THE MIDDLE AGES AND THE MODERN WORLD: CONTINUITY AND DISCONTINUITY

Medieval civilization began to decline in the fourteenth century, but no "dark age" comparable to the three centuries following Rome's fall descended on Europe; its economic and political institutions and technological skills had grown too strong. Instead, the waning of the Middle Ages opened up possibilities for another stage in Western civilization: the modern age.

The modern world is linked to the Middle Ages in innumerable ways. European cities, the middle class, the state system, English common law, universities—all had their origins in the Middle Ages. During medieval times, important advances were made in business practices, including partnerships, systematic bookkeeping, and the bill of exchange, which paved the way for modern banking. By translating and commenting on the writings of Greek and Arabic thinkers, medieval scholars preserved a priceless intellectual heritage without which the modern mind could never have evolved. In addition, numerous strands connect the thought of the scholastics and that of early modern philosophers.

Feudal traditions lasted long after the Middle Ages. Up to the French Revolution, for instance, French aristocrats enjoyed special privileges and exercised power over local government. In England, the aristocracy controlled local government until the Industrial Revolution transformed English society in the nineteenth century. Retaining the medieval ideal of the noble warrior, aristocrats continued to dominate the officer corps of European armies through the nineteenth century and even into the twentieth. Aristocratic notions of duty, honor, loyalty, and courtly love have endured into our own day.

During the Middle Ages, Europeans began to take the lead over the Muslims, the Byzantines, the Chinese, and all other peoples in the use of technology. Medieval technology and inventiveness stemmed in part from Christianity, which taught that God had created the world specifically for human beings to subdue and exploit. Consequently, medieval people tried to employ animal power and labor-saving machinery to relieve human drudgery. Moreover, Christianity taught that God was above nature, not within it, so the Christians faced no spiritual obstacle to exploiting nature—unlike, for instance, the Hindus. In contrast to classical humanism, the Christian outlook did not consider manual work degrading; even monks combined it with study.

The Christian stress on the sacred worth of the individual (each person had an immortal soul that was God's concern), on human equality (differences in rank and birth were of no account to God on **Judgment Day**), and on the higher law of God (divine precepts had a greater pull on conscience than did the state's laws) has never ceased to influence Western civilization. Even though in modern times the various Christian churches have not often taken the lead in political and social reform, the ideals identified with the Judeo-Christian tradition have become part of the Western heritage. As such, they have inspired social reformers who may no longer identify with their ancestral religion.

In structuring canon (church) law into a coherent and rational system, church jurists provided a model for legal systems in emerging European states. Moreover, specific elements of canon law have become an integral part of modern Western law. Medieval jurists, for example, argued for the replacement of trials by ordeals of fire or water, which were central to ancient Germanic folk law, with rational trial procedures and insisted that marriages based on fraud or duress could be invalidated.

Believing that God's law was superior to state or national decrees, medieval philosophers provided a theoretical basis for opposing tyrannical kings who violated Christian principles. The idea that both the ruler and the ruled are bound by a higher law would, in a secularized form, become a principal element of modern liberal thought.

Feudalism also contributed to the history of liberty. According to feudal custom, the king, as a member of the feudal community, was duty-bound to honor agreements made with his vassals. Lords possessed personal rights, which the king was obliged to respect. Resentful of a king who ran roughshod over customary feudal rights, lords also negotiated contracts with the crown, such as Magna Carta (1215), to define and guard their customary liberties. To protect themselves from the arbitrary behavior of a king, feudal lords initiated what came to be called *government by consent* and the *rule of law*.

During the Middle Ages, then, there gradually emerged the idea that law was not imposed on inferiors by an absolute monarch but required the collaboration of the king and his subjects; that the king, too, was bound by the law; and that lords had the right to resist a monarch who violated agreements. A related phenomenon was the rise of representative institutions, with which the king was expected to consult on the realm's affairs. The most notable of such institutions was the British Parliament; though subordinate to the king, it became a permanent part of the state. Later, in the seventeenth century, Parliament would successfully challenge royal authority. Thus, continuity exists between the feudal tradition of a king bound by law and the modern practice of limiting the authority of the head of state.

Although the elements of continuity are clear, the characteristic outlook of the Middle Ages is as different from that of the modern age as it was from the outlook of the Greco-Roman past. Religion—often expressing a disdain of earthly pursuits and a preoccupation with the world to come—was the integrating feature of the Middle Ages, whereas science and secularism—a preoccupation with worldly life—determine the modern outlook. The period from the Italian Renaissance of the fifteenth century through the eighteenth-century Age of Enlightenment saw a gradual breaking away from the medieval worldview—a rejection of the medieval conception of nature, the individual, and the purpose of life. The transition from medieval to modern was neither sudden nor complete, for there are no sharp demarcation lines separating historical periods. Although many distinctively medieval ways endured in the sixteenth, seventeenth, and even eighteenth centuries, these centuries saw as well the rise of new intellectual, political, and economic forms, which marked the emergence of **modernity**.

Medieval thought began with the existence of God and the truth of his revelation as interpreted by the church, which set the standards and defined the purposes for human endeavor. The medieval mind rejected the fundamental principle of Greek philosophy: the autonomy of reason. Without the guidance of revealed truth, reason was seen as feeble. Philosophical inquiry was permissible only if the mind arrived at clerically approved conclusions.

Scholastics engaged in genuine philosophical speculation and demonstrated impressive signs of logical thinking, but they did not allow philosophy to challenge the basic premises of their faith. For them, the dissemination of views that contradicted church doctrine had to be prohibited lest they corrupt the mind of the faithful. Unlike either ancient or modern thinkers, medieval scholars ultimately believed that reason alone could not provide a unified view of nature or society. A rational soul had to be guided by a divine light. For all medieval philosophers, the natural order depended on a supernatural order for its origin and purpose. To understand the natural world properly, it was necessary to know its relationship to the higher world. The discoveries of reason had to accord with Scripture as interpreted by the church. In medieval thought, says the historian-philosopher Ernst Cassirer,

WISDOM URGES MEDIEVAL SCHOLARS FORWARD. During the Middle Ages, Europeans made considerable advances in technology. The astrolabe, suadrant, sundials, and mechanical clocks shown here exemplify medieval technical skills. (Bibliothèque Royale de Belgique.)

> *neither science nor morality, neither law nor state, can be erected on its own foundations. Supernatural assistance is always needed to bring them to true perfection. . . . Reason is and remains the servant of revelation; within the sphere of natural intellectual and psychological forces, reason leads toward, and prepares the ground for, revelation.*[4]

In the modern view, both nature and the human intellect are self-sufficient. Nature is a mathematical system that operates without miracles or any other form of divine intervention. To comprehend nature and society, the mind needs no divine assistance; it accepts no authority above reason. The modern mentality finds it unacceptable to reject the conclusions of science on the basis of clerical authority and revelation or to ground politics, law, or economics on religious dogma. It refuses to settle public issues by appeals to religious belief, which is now seen as a strictly private concern.

The medieval philosopher understood both nature and society to be a hierarchical order. The heavens were qualitatively superior in purpose and substance to the earthly realm. God was the source of moral values, and the church was responsible for teaching and upholding these ethical norms. Kings acquired their right to rule from God. The entire social structure constituted a hierarchy: the clergy, the highest order, guided society according to Christian standards; lords defended Christian society from its enemies; and serfs, lowest in the social order, toiled for the good of all. In the hierarchy of knowledge, a lower form of knowledge derived from the senses, and the highest type of knowledge, theology, dealt with God's revelation. To the medieval mind, this hierarchical ordering of nature, society, and knowledge had a divine sanction.

Rejecting the medieval division of the universe into higher and lower realms and superior and inferior substances, the modern view postulated the uniformity of nature and of nature's

Joan of Arc

A crucial phase in the Hundred Years' War occurred in 1415 when England inflicted an overwhelming defeat on the French at Agincourt. The victorious English imposed on the French the Treaty of Troyes (1420). Its terms stipulated that the daughter of Charles VI, the French monarch, would marry the English ruler, Henry V, and that their future son would reign over the dual monarchy of England and France. This provision deprived Charles VI's only living son, the dauphin Charles, from succeeding to the throne. From Bourges in central France, the dauphin continued the struggle against the English invaders and their Burgundian allies. In 1428, the English besieged Orléans in preparation for an attack on Bourges. The dauphin's position seemed hopeless.

At this critical moment, Joan of Arc appeared on the scene. Born to a peasant family in northern France, Joan very early demonstrated extreme piety. At age thirteen, she experienced revelations—voices from angels and saints who guided her behavior. When she was about sixteen, her voices instructed her to raise the siege of Orléans and have Charles anointed king of France at Rheims. Joan the maid, as she was called, attracted followers who believed that Joan was sent by God to rescue Orléans from the English.

Demonstrating great resolve, Joan, dressed in men's clothing and accompanied by believers in her mission, made the arduous journey to the dauphin's castle. Charles reluctantly granted an audience to Joan, whom some of his counselors considered mad. After listening to Joan detail her divine mission, Charles had her examined by his clerks and sages, who reported that the uneducated, but devout, peasant girl was neither a heretic nor a sorceress. With the military position worsening, the desperate dauphin provided Joan with an army—perhaps this religiously inspired maid had indeed been sent by God. Wearing a full set of armor and wielding a lance, Joan demonstrated remarkable leadership and courage, which inspired her troops. She also showed a facility for military planning. To the inhabitants of Orléans, it seemed that God had provided them with a deliverer. When she entered the city, crowds pressed to touch her. Aided by the citizens of Orléans, Joan's army attacked the English fortifications. Hit by

laws: the cosmos knows no privilege of rank; heavenly bodies follow the same laws of nature as earthly objects. Space is geometric and homogeneous, not hierarchical, heterogeneous, and qualitative. The universe was no longer conceived as finite and closed but as infinite, and the operations of nature were explained mathematically. The modern thinker studies mathematical law and chemical composition, not grades of perfection. Spiritual meaning is not sought in an examination of the material world. Roger Bacon, for example, described seven coverings of the eye and then concluded that God had fashioned the eye in this manner in order to express the seven gifts of the Spirit. This way of thinking is alien to the modern outlook. So too is the medieval belief that natural disasters, such as plagues and famines, are God's punishments for people's sins.

The outlook of the modern West also broke with the rigid division of medieval society into three orders: clergy, nobles, and commoners. The intellectual justification for this arrangement, as expressed by the English prelate John of Salisbury (c. 1115–1180), has been rejected by modern westerners: "For inferiors owe it to their superiors to provide them with service, just as the superiors in their turn owe it to their inferiors to provide them with all things needful for their protection and succor."[5] To be sure, Christian theorists also maintained that as God's children, all human beings are in principle equal in God's eyes. Opposing the feudal principle that an individual's obligations and rights are a function of his or her rank in society, the modern view stressed equality of opportunity and equal treatment under the law. It rejected the idea that society should be guided

an arrow above the breast, Joan had the wound dressed and immediately returned to the fray. In a decisive encounter, the maid grabbed her standard from a squire and led a successful assault on an English fortress. Soon after, the English abandoned the siege: the maid's forces had liberated the city. Several months later, Joan achieved her greatest victory, an open-field battle at Patay, which caught the English by surprise. Following the battle, the dauphin was crowned Charles VII at Rheims.

Meanwhile, in the ongoing conflict with the English and Burgundians, Joan could not escape a Burgundian siege and was taken prisoner. Charles VII made no effort to ransom Joan; he simply abandoned her. Purchasing the now-famous prisoner from the Burgundians, the English organized a show trial in Rouen, conducted by learned but hostile French clerics, to prove that the despised Joan was a heretic and a witch. The proceedings took about five months. During that time, Joan wore leg irons; at night in her dungeon, her jailers chained the leg irons to the foot of the bed. During the interrogation, Joan displayed remarkable self-control, dignity, cleverness, and even eloquence and humor, which often exasperated the inquisitors. The inquisitors asked Joan if she would defer to the church when told that her voices were illusions; Joan replied that her voices had not commanded her to disregard the church but she served the Lord first, a rebellious act that amounted to heresy.

When the judges accused her of lying and threatened to inflict torture unless she altered her statements, Joan replied: "Truly, though you were to have my limbs torn off and send the soul out of my body, I should not say otherwise; and if I did tell you otherwise, I should always thereafter say that you had made me speak so by force."*

After the judges ruled that she had been doing the work of the Devil, Joan was declared a heretic and condemned to burn at the stake. The sentence was carried out on May 30, 1431, and her ashes were thrown into the Seine. In 1456, the church nullified the condemnation, and in 1920 Joan was declared a saint.

_____

*Quoted in Régine Pernoud, *Joan of Arc: By Herself and Her Witnesses*, trans. Edward Hyans (Lanham, Md.: Scarborough House, 1994), 206.

by clergy who were deemed to possess a special wisdom, by nobles who were entitled to special privileges, and by monarchs who were thought to receive their power from God.

The modern West also rejected the personal and customary character of feudal law. As the modern state developed, law assumed an impersonal and objective character. For example, if the lord demanded more than the customary forty days of military service, the vassal might refuse to comply because he would see the lord's request as an unpardonable violation of custom and agreement, as well as an infringement on his liberties. In the modern state, with a constitution and a representative assembly, if a new law increasing the length of military service is passed, it merely replaces the old law. People do not refuse to obey it because the government has broken faith or violated custom.

In the modern world, the individual's relationship to the universe has been radically transformed. Medieval people lived in a geocentric universe that was finite in space and time. The universe was small, enclosed by a sphere of stars, beyond which were the heavens. The universe, it was believed, was some four thousand years old, and, in the not-too-distant future, Christ would return and human history would end. People in the Middle Ages knew why they were on earth and what was expected of them; they never doubted that heaven would be their reward for living a Christian life. Preparation for heaven was the ultimate aim of life. J. H. Randall Jr., a historian of ideas, eloquently sums up the medieval view of a purposeful universe in which the human being's position was clearly defined.

The world was governed throughout by the omnipotent will and omniscient mind of God, whose sole interests were centered in man, his trial, his fall, his suffering and his glory. Worm of the dust as he was, man was yet the central object in the whole universe. . . . And when his destiny was completed, the heavens would be rolled up as a scroll and he would dwell with the Lord forever. Only those who rejected God's freely offered grace and with hardened hearts refused repentance would be cut off from this eternal life.[6]

This comforting medieval vision is alien to the modern outlook. Today, in a universe some thirteen to fourteen billion years old, in which the earth is a tiny speck floating in an endless cosmic ocean, where life evolved over tens of millions of years, many westerners no longer believe that human beings are special children of God; that heaven is their ultimate goal; that under their feet is hell, where grotesque demons torment sinners; or that God is an active agent in human history. To many intellectuals, the universe seems unresponsive to the religious supplications of people, and life's purpose is sought within the limits of earthly existence. Science and secularism have driven Christianity and faith from their central position to the periphery of human concerns.

In the nineteenth and twentieth centuries, Christian thinkers lamented the waning of faith. Distressed by all-consuming secularism, crude materialism, and vicious class and national antagonisms, these thinkers attributed the ills of the modern West to a diminishing commitment to Christianity and called for spiritual renewal. Some of them, looking back nostalgically to the Middle Ages, when life had an overriding religious purpose and few doubted the truth of Christian teachings, contended that the modern West would benefit from a reaffirmation of those Christian concerns and values that had energized medieval society.

The modern outlook developed gradually in the period from the Renaissance to the eighteenth-century Age of Enlightenment. Mathematics rendered the universe comprehensible. Economic and political thought broke free of the religious frame of reference. Science became the great hope of the future. The thinkers of the Enlightenment wanted to liberate humanity from superstition, ignorance, and traditions that could not pass the test of reason. They saw themselves as emancipating culture from theological dogma and clerical authority. Rejecting the Christian idea of a person's inherent sinfulness, they held that the individual was basically good and that evil resulted from faulty institutions, poor education, and bad leadership. Thus, the concept of a rational and free society in which individuals could realize their potential slowly emerged.

❖ ❖ ❖

NOTES

1. Jean Froissart, *Chronicles of England, France, Spain* (London: Henry G. Bohn, 1849), 653.

2. Excerpted in Brian Tierney, ed., *The Crisis of Church and State, 1050–1300* (Englewood Cliffs, N.J.: Prentice-Hall, 1964), 189.

3. Marsilius of Padua, *Marsilius of Padua: The Defender of the Peace,* trans. Alan Gewirth (New York: Columbia University Press, 1956), 2:119.

4. Ernst Cassirer, *The Philosophy of the Enlightenment* (Boston: Beacon Press, 1955), 40.

5. John of Salisbury, *Policraticus,* trans. John Dickinson (New York: Russell and Russell, 1963), 243–244.

6. J. H. Randall Jr., *The Making of the Modern Mind* (Boston: Houghton Mifflin, 1940), 34.

SUGGESTED READING

Bowsky, W. M., ed., *The Black Death* (1971). Readings on the impact of the plague.

Goodich, Michael, ed., *Other Middle Ages: Witnesses at the Margin of Medieval Society* (1998). Selections dealing with disenfranchised members of medieval society in the High and Late Middle Ages.

Cantor, Norma F., *In the Wake of the Plague: The Black Death and the World It Made* (2001). A readable and current synthesis of latest scholarship.

Holmes, George, *Europe: Hierarchy and Revolt, 1320–1450* (1975). A good survey of the period.

Lerner, Robert E., *The Age of Adversity* (1968). A short, readable survey of the fourteenth century.

Nirenberg, David, *Communities of Violence: Persecution of Minorities in the Middle Ages* (1996). Focuses on medieval beliefs that triggered violent attacks on minorities.

Ozment, Steven E., *The Age of Reform, 1250–1550* (1980). An intellectual and religious history of late medieval and Reformation Europe.

Pegg, Mark Gregory, *A Most Holy War: The Albigensian Crusade and the Battle for Christendom* (2008). A gripping narrative of medieval mass murder.

Russell, Burton Jeffrey, *Witchcraft in the Middle Ages* (1972). Describes the development of a phenomenon that is deeply rooted in the nonrational.

Spinka, M., *John Hus and the Czech Reform* (1941). A reliable work on Hus and the Hussite wars.

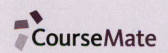

Part Three

Early Modern Europe: From Renaissance to Enlightenment

1350–1789

1300

1400

1500

1600

1700

Politics and Society

Hundred Years' War (1337–1453)

War of Roses in England (1455–1485)
Rule of Ferdinand and Isabella in Spain
  (1469–1516)
Charles VIII of France (1483–1498)
Henry VII; beginning of Tudor dynasty in
  England (1485–1509)
French invasion of Italy (1494)
Columbus reaches America (1492)

Henry VIII of England (1509–1547)
Francis I of France (1515–1547)
Charles V, Holy Roman emperor (1519–
  1556)
Henry VIII of England breaks with Rome
  (1529–1536)
Council of Trent (1545–1563)
Treaty of Augsburg in Germany (1555)
Philip II of Spain (1556–1598)
Elizabeth I of England (1558–1603)
Religious wars in France (1562–1598)
Revolt of the Netherlands from Spain
  (1566–1609)
Defeat of Spanish Armada (1588)

Thirty Years' War (1618–1648)
English revolutions (1640–1660, 1688–1689)
Louis XIV of France (1643–1715)
Peter the Great of Russia (1682–1725)

War of Spanish Succession (1702–1714)
War of Austrian Succession (1740–1748)
Frederick the Great of Prussia (1740–1786)
Maria Theresa of Austria (1740–1780)
Seven Years' War (1756–1763)
Catherine the Great of Russia (1762–1796)
American Declaration of Independence (1776)
American Revolution (1776–1783)
Beginning of French Revolution (1789)

Thought and Culture

Italian Renaissance begins (c. 1350)

Early Renaissance artists: Brunelleschi,
  Masaccio, van Eyck
Printing with movable type (c. 1445)
Humanists: Valla, Pico della Mirandola
Late Renaissance artists: Botticelli,
  Leonardo da Vinci, Michelangelo,
  Raphael, Bellini, Giorgione, Titian
Renaissance spreads to northern Europe
  (late 15th–early 16th centuries)

Humanists: Castiglione, Erasmus,
  Montaigne, Rabelais, More, Machiavelli,
  Cervantes, Shakespeare
Luther writes Ninety-Five Theses (1517)
Calvin, *The Institutes of the Christian Religion*
  (1536)
Copernicus, *On the Revolution of the
  Heavenly Spheres* (1543)

Scientists: Kepler, Galileo, Newton
Philosophers: Bacon, Descartes, Spinoza,
  Hobbes, Bayle, Locke

Enlightenment thinkers: Voltaire,
  Montesquieu, Rousseau, Diderot, Hume,
  Adam Smith, Thomas Jefferson, Kant

Chapter 13

The Renaissance: Transition to the Modern Age

The School of Athens, *by Raphael (1483–1520). The ancient Greek philosophers, with Plato and Aristotle at the center, are depicted here, assembled in classical grandeur. Painted to decorate the Vatican, the papal palace in Rome, the picture exudes the Renaissance reverence for classical antiquity and reflects the widely held view that ancient philosophy represented a foreshadowing of Christianity and was essentially in harmony with it.* (Alinari/Art Resource, N.Y.)

- **Italy: The Birthplace of the Renaissance**
- **The Renaissance Outlook: Humanism and Secular Politics**
- **The Spread of the Renaissance**
- **The Renaissance and the Modern Age**

Focus Questions

1. What conditions gave rise to the Italian Renaissance?
2. What is the historical significance of Renaissance humanism?
3. How did Machiavelli's political thought mark a break with the medieval outlook?
4. What were the effects of the printing press on European civilization?

From the Italian Renaissance of the fifteenth century through the Age of Enlightenment of the eighteenth century, the outlook and institutions of the Middle Ages disintegrated and distinctly modern forms emerged. The radical change in European civilization could be seen on every level of society. On the economic level, commerce and industry expanded greatly, and capitalism in some countries largely replaced medieval forms of economic organization. On the political level, central government grew stronger at the expense of feudalism. On the religious level, the rise of Protestantism fragmented the unity of Christendom. On the social level, middle-class townspeople, increasing in number and wealth, were playing a more important role in economic and cultural life. On the cultural level, the clergy lost its monopoly on learning, and the otherworldly orientation of the Middle Ages gave way to a secular outlook in literature and the arts. Theology, the queen of knowledge in the Middle Ages, surrendered her crown to science. Reason, which in the Middle Ages had been subordinate to revelation, asserted its independence.

Many of these tendencies manifested themselves dramatically during the Renaissance. The word *renaissance* means "rebirth," and it is used to refer to the attempt by artists and thinkers to recover and apply the ancient learning and standards of Greece and Rome. In historical terms, the Renaissance is both a cultural movement and a period. As a movement, it was born in the city-states of northern Italy and spread to the rest of Europe. As a period, it ran from 1350 to 1600. Until the late fifteenth century, the Renaissance was restricted to Italy. What happened there in the fourteenth and fifteenth centuries sharply contrasts with civilization in the rest of Europe, which, until the end of the fifteenth century, still belonged to the Late Middle Ages.

The nineteenth-century historian Jacob Burckhardt in his classic study *The Civilization of the Renaissance in Italy* (1860) held that the Renaissance was the point of departure for the modern world. During the Renaissance, said Burckhardt, individuals showed increasing concern with worldly life and self-consciously aspired to shape their destinies—attitudes that are the key to modernity.

Burckhardt's thesis has been challenged, particularly by medievalists, who view the Renaissance

Chronology 13.1 ❖ The Renaissance

1200–1300	Bologna, Padua, and Ravenna become centers of legal studies
1300–1450	Republicanism reigns in northern Italian city-states
1304–1374	Petrarch, "father of humanism"
1378	Ciompi revolt in Florence
c. 1407–1457	Lorenzo Valla, author of *Declamation Concerning the False Decretals of Constantine*
c. 1445	Johann Gutenberg invents movable metal type
1454	Peace of Lodi is signed
1494	Charles VIII of France invades northern Italy; Pope Julius II commissions frescoes by Michelangelo for the Vatican's Sistine Chapel
1513	Machiavelli writes *The Prince*
1528	*The Book of the Courtier*, by Baldesar Castiglione, is published
1535	Sir Thomas More, English humanist and author of *Utopia*, is executed for treason

as an extension of the Middle Ages, not as a sudden break with the past. These critics argue that Burckhardt neglected important links between medieval and Renaissance culture. One distinguishing feature of the Renaissance, the revival of classical learning, had already emerged in the High Middle Ages to such an extent that historians speak of "the renaissance of the twelfth century" and the "Twelfth-Century Awakening." The Renaissance owes much to the legal and scholastic studies that flourished in the Italian universities of Padua and Bologna before 1300. Town life and trade, hallmarks of Renaissance society, were also a heritage from the Middle Ages.

To be sure, the Renaissance was not a complete and sudden break with the Middle Ages. Many medieval ways and attitudes persisted. Nevertheless, Burckhardt's thesis that the Renaissance represents the birth of modernity has much to recommend it. Renaissance writers and artists themselves were aware of their age's novelty. They looked back on the medieval centuries as "the Dark Ages" that followed the grandeur of ancient Greece and Rome, and they believed that they were experiencing a rebirth of cultural greatness. Renaissance artists and writers were fascinated by the cultural forms of Greece and Rome; they sought to imitate **classical** style and to capture the secular spirit of antiquity. In the process, they broke with medieval artistic and literary forms. They valued the full development of human talent and expressed fresh excitement about the possibilities of life in this world. This outlook represented a new trend in European civilization.

The Renaissance, then, was an age of transition that saw the rejection of certain elements of the medieval outlook, the revival of classical cultural forms, and the emergence of distinctly **modern** attitudes. As mentioned earlier, this rebirth began in Italy during the fourteenth century. It gradually spread north and west to Germany, France, England, and Spain during the late fifteenth and sixteenth centuries.

ITALY: THE BIRTHPLACE OF THE RENAISSANCE

The city-states of northern Italy that spawned the Renaissance were developed urban centers where the elite had the wealth, freedom, and inclination to cultivate the arts and to enjoy the fruits of worldly life. In Italy, moreover, reminders of ancient Rome's grandeur were visible everywhere. Roman roads, monuments, and manuscripts intensified Italians' links to their Roman past.

The Political Evolution of the City-States

During the Middle Ages, the feudal states of northern Italy had been absorbed into the Holy Roman Empire. They continued to owe nominal allegiance to the German emperor during the early Renaissance. But protracted wars with the papacy had sapped the empire's vitality. Its consequent weakness allowed the states of northern Italy to develop as autonomous political entities. The weakening of the papacy in the fourteenth century also promoted this development.

In their size and their varied types of governments, the city-states in northern Italy resembled those of ancient Greece. Among the more important were Rome, Milan, Florence, Venice, Mantua, Ferrara, Padua, Bologna, and Genoa. They differed markedly from most of Europe in two fundamental respects.

First, by the late eleventh and twelfth centuries, these city-states were flourishing commercial and banking centers and monopolized trade in Mediterranean areas, including trade between the East and the West. Merchant fleets, especially those of Venice and Genoa, carried goods from ports in the eastern Mediterranean westward into the Atlantic and from there north to the Baltic Sea. In contrast to the rest of Europe, the wealth of these cities lay not in land but in commerce and industry. When popes, monarchs, and feudal magnates of Europe needed money, they borrowed it from Italian, especially Florentine, merchant-bankers.

Second, the predominance of business and commerce within these city-states meant that the feudal nobility, which held the land beyond the city walls, played a much lesser role in government than they did elsewhere in Europe. By the end of the twelfth century, the city-states no longer were dominated by the feudal nobility, or landed aristocracy. The aristocracy and the rich merchants had to share power, and when their alliances broke down, as they often did, the two groups struggled for power based on their opposing interests and outlooks. The interests of the smaller merchants and the artisans in the towns also had to be catered to. When they were not, those groups rioted and rebelled, as they did, for instance, in 1378, during the revolt of the *Ciompi* (wool-workers) in Florence.

Politically, the city-states in northern Italy were inherently unstable. The instability had two sources: internal conflicts between merchants and nobles and external rivalries among the city-states themselves. The city-states managed to keep both the papacy and the Holy Roman Empire at bay, sometimes by playing one giant against the other. But the price of this continued independence was that the city-states, without any externally imposed power structure, had to seek their own solutions to their instability. Out of this situation came experiments in the form and technique of government. The origins of modern political thought and practice can be discerned in this experimentation, which is an important link between the Renaissance and the modern age.

The political experimentation in the northern Italian city-states can usefully, if only roughly, be divided into two periods: the first (1300–1450) marked by the defense of **republicanism**; the second (1450–1550), by the triumph of **despotism**. By the end of the twelfth century, the city-states had adopted a fairly uniform pattern of republican self-government built around the office of a chief magistrate. Elected by the citizens on the basis of a broad franchise, the chief magistrate ruled with the advice of two councils—a large public one and a small secret one. His powers were tightly circumscribed by the **constitution**; with his term of office restricted ordinarily to six months, he could be removed from government or punished at the end of his tenure.

The city-states not only developed republican institutions but also devised important theories to defend and justify their liberty and self-government in the face of their external enemies, the papacy and the empire. With the emperor, they argued that their customary feudal subjection to imperial authority must be radically adjusted to fit the changed reality that they were in fact self-governing. With the papacy, they contended that Christ had denied all political jurisdiction to the clergy, including the pope, and that this fact undercut the papal claim to political control in Italy and elsewhere.

However, given the city-states' internal instability and rivalry, their republicanism proved precarious. During the fourteenth and early fifteenth centuries, the republican institutions in one city after another toppled in favor of despotic rule.

Three conditions were responsible for this development. First, class war between rich merchants and nobles caused one group or the other, or both, to seek a resolution of the crisis by turning to one-person rule. Second, the economic disasters, famine, and disease of the period from 1350 to 1450 encouraged the drift toward despotism. Northern Italy was particularly hard hit by the bubonic plague. The citizenry lost faith in the ability of short-term republican governments to cope with such emergencies and put its trust in long-term, one-man rule. Third, and perhaps most important, the city-states, in wars with their rivals, had come to rely on mercenary troops. The leaders of those troops, the notorious *condottieri*—unschooled in and owing no loyalty to the republican tradition—simply seized power during emergencies.

Some city-states held out for a long time against the trend toward despotism. Among those that did, Florence was by far the most successful. In the process, the Florentines developed new arguments and theories for the maintenance of republicanism and liberty (discussed later in this chapter). But by the middle of the fifteenth century, even Florentine republicanism was giving way before the intrigues of a rich banking family, the Medicis. They had installed themselves in power in the 1430s, with the return of Cosimo de' Medici from exile. Cosimo's grandson, Lorenzo the Magnificent, completed the destruction of the republican constitution in 1480, when he managed to set up a government staffed by his own supporters.

The one city-state where republicanism survived until the advent of Napoleon was Venice. Protected from the rest of Italy by lagoons, Venice during the Middle Ages controlled a far-flung and exceptionally lucrative seagoing trade and a maritime empire stretching along the Adriatic and the

PORTRAIT OF A MAN, CALLED *THE SOLDIER*, 1475, BY ANTONELLO DA MESSINA (D. 1479). This soldier could have been either a mercenary, hired to fight for pay, or a citizen-soldier who ideally would have fought not just for money but out of loyalty to his city-state, and who, as such, was thought to be the embodiment of civic virtue—honest, strong, and brave. (The Art Archive/Musee du Louvre, Paris/Alfredo Dagli Orti.)

eastern Mediterranean seas. Venetian maritime commercial successes were matched by political ones at home. For centuries, Venice managed to govern itself without a major upheaval; its republican constitution made this stability possible. Its chief executive offices, the Council of Ten, were elective, but after 1297 both these offices and the electorate were narrowly restricted by law to old patrician families. Venice was an aristocratic **republic**. The government proved remarkably effective because the ruling elite was able to instill in its young a sense of public duty that was passed on from one generation, and one century, to the next. Because Venetian government was at once stable and republican, it served as a model to republican theorists in seventeenth- and eighteenth-century Europe.

◀ *Map 13.1* ITALIAN CITY-STATES, C. 1494
During the Renaissance, Italy was divided between large kingdoms in the south, dominated by the Spanish monarchy, and smaller city-states in the north, each with its own government and army and often hostile to one another. The French king Charles VIII took advantage of these divisions by invading and occupying much of northern Italy beginning in 1494. (Copyright © 2013 Cengage Learning.)

Aside from Venice, the city-states in northern Italy were not only internally unstable but also constantly warring with one another. By the middle of the fifteenth century, however, five major powers had emerged from the fighting: the kingdom of Naples and Sicily in the south; the Papal States, a papacy-controlled territory running across the center of the Italian peninsula; and the city-states of Florence, Venice, and Milan in the north. In 1454, these five powers, largely through the efforts of Cosimo de' Medici, concluded the Peace of Lodi. For the next forty years, they were relatively peaceful, until the French king Charles VIII invaded northern Italy in 1494.

The Peace of Lodi endured so long thanks to diplomacy. The essential techniques of modern diplomacy were worked out and applied in the second half of the fifteenth century in Italy. The practices of establishing embassies with ambassadors, sending and analyzing intelligence reports, consulting and negotiating during emergencies, and forming alliances all developed during this period. Some historians also see this time in Italian history as the seedbed for the notion of balance of power, which eventually became fundamental to the diplomacy of all Europe. Later, in the early modern period, European governments formed alliances so that no single state or group of allied states could dominate the Continent. Some elements of this balance of power were anticipated in the struggles among the Italian city-states.

Renaissance Society

The new way of life in the city-states paralleled developments in relations among them. Prosperous merchants played a leading role in the political and cultural life of the city. With the growth of commerce and industry, the feudal values of birth, military prowess, and a fixed hierarchy of lords and vassals decayed in favor of ambition and individual achievement, whether at court, in the counting-house, or inside the artist's studio. The old feudal chivalric code was not destroyed but transformed to serve different purposes.

The new urban, commercial **oligarchies** could not justify their power in the old way, through heredity. Moreover, they had to function within the inherently unstable political climate of the city-states. Faced with this dual problem, the oligarchs fell back on the feudal idea of honor and developed elaborate codes. These codes differed in significant ways from their medieval antecedents. First came a depreciation (though never a complete elimination) of birth as a basis of merit and a corresponding emphasis on effort, talent, and (in the case of the artist) creative genius. Second, honor was no longer defined in narrow, largely military terms; it was expanded to include both the civic and courtly virtues of the worthy citizen and courtier and the artistic achievement of the painter, sculptor, architect, and poet.

The new code, however, did remain elitist and even aristocratic. Indeed, the new oligarchs of the Renaissance, because of their newness and insecurity, were all the more anxious to adopt the aristocratic outlook of the old nobility. The *nouveaux riches* (newly rich) aped the feudal aristocracy in dress and manners, even as they accommodated the code of knightly chivalry to the demands of a new urban and commercial culture. Renaissance society was a highly unstable compound of old and new.

Marriage and Family Life. City life profoundly altered family structures, marriage patterns, and relations between the sexes. Elsewhere in Europe, most people still lived on the land and tended to marry early in order to produce large families to work the fields. But in cities, early marriage could be a liability for a man who was attempting to make his fortune. The results were that older men married young brides and that wives usually outlived their husbands. Because a widow inherited her husband's property, she was not pressed to remarry and was likely to bring up her children in a single-parent household. According to the historian David Herlihy, the fact that so many women were responsible for nurturing their children may have encouraged the development of the Renaissance ideal of a gentleman, which emphasized civility, courtliness, and an appreciation of art, literature, and the feminine graces.

The large number of single, relatively prosperous, and leisured adults probably explains why Renaissance cities were reputed for sodomy, prostitution, and triangles involving an older husband, a young wife, and a young lover. Such sexual behavior was encouraged by the relative anonymity of the large cities and by the constant influx of young men of talent from the country districts.

Whatever the effect on their sons, upper-class women enjoyed greater freedom in greater numbers than they had since the fall of Rome. If they were married, they had the income to pursue pleasure in the form of clothes, conversation, and romance. If a well-to-do husband died while his wife was still young, she had no financial reasons to remarry and was free, to a degree previously unknown, to go her own way.

Patronage of the Arts.   Members of the urban upper class became patrons of the arts, providing funds to support promising artists and writers. Urban patricians, whose wealth was based on commerce and banking, not land, had become dominant in both republican Florence and despotic Milan. Unable to claim power by birth or to rely on traditional loyalties, they looked to culture to provide the trappings and justification of power.

For the newly rich, art could serve a political function. In its sheer magnificence, art could manifest power. Art, like literature, could also serve as a focus of civic pride and patriotism. Just as insecure rulers contended on the battlefield, they competed for art and artists to bolster their egos. Art became a desirable political investment, especially when, in the fifteenth century, economic investments were not offering as much return as they had a century or two before. The popes invested in art as well. Having lost the battle for temporal dominion in Europe, the papacy concentrated on increasing its direct dominion in Italy by consolidating and expanding the Papal States. As an adjunct to this policy, the popes heaped wealth on artists to enhance papal prestige. Indeed, the popes became the most lavish patrons of all, as the works of Michelangelo, Botticelli, and Raphael testify.

The result of this new patronage by popes and patricians was an explosion of creativity. The amount, and especially the nature, of this patronage also helped shape both art and the artist. For the first time since antiquity, portraiture became a separate genre and was developed much further than ever before. Patrician rivalry and insecurity of status, fed by the Renaissance ethic of achievement and reward, produced a scramble for honor and reputation. This fostered the desire to be memorialized in a painting, if not in a sculpture. A painter like Titian was in great demand.

Secularism.   Renaissance society was marked by a growing **secular** outlook. Intrigued by the active life of the city and eager to enjoy the worldly pleasures that their money could obtain, wealthy merchants and bankers moved away from the medieval preoccupation with salvation. Although they were neither nonbelievers nor atheists, for them religion increasingly had to compete with worldly concerns. Consequently, members of the urban upper class paid religion less heed or at least did not allow it to interfere with their quest for a full life. The challenge and pleasure of living well in this world seemed more exciting than the promise of heaven. This outlook found expression in Renaissance art and literature.

Individualism.   Individualism was another hallmark of Renaissance society. Urban life released people of wealth and talent from the old constraints of manor and church. The urban elite sought to assert their own personalities, discover and express their individual feelings, and demonstrate their unique talents. They strove to win fame and glory and to fulfill their ambitions. This Renaissance ideal was explicitly elitist. It applied only to the few, entirely disregarding the masses, and it valued what was distinctive and superior in an individual, not what was common to all. Concerned with the distinctions of the few, it did not consider the needs or rights of the many. Individualism became deeply embedded in the Western soul and was expressed by artists who sought to capture individual character, by explorers who ventured into uncharted seas, by conquerors who carved out empires in the New World, and by merchant-capitalists who amassed fortunes.

THE RENAISSANCE OUTLOOK: HUMANISM AND SECULAR POLITICS

Humanism

The most characteristic intellectual movement of the Renaissance was *humanism,* an educational and cultural program based on the study of ancient Greek and Roman literature. The humanist attitude toward antiquity differed from the attitude of medieval scholars, who had taken pains to

Leonardo Bruni: Study of Greek Literature and a Humanist Educational Program

Leonardo Bruni (1374–1444) was a Florentine humanist who extolled both intellectual study and active involvement in public affairs, an outlook called civic humanism. In this excerpt from his History of His Own Times in Italy, *Bruni expresses the humanist's love for ancient Greek literature and language.*

Love for Greek Literature

Then first came a knowledge of Greek, which had not been in use among us for seven hundred years. Chrysoloras the Byzantine,* a man of noble birth and well versed in Greek letters, brought Greek learning to us. When his country was invaded by the Turks, he came by sea, first to Venice. The report of him soon spread, and he was cordially invited and besought and promised a public stipend, to come to Florence and open his store of riches to the youth. I was then studying Civil Law,† but . . . I burned with love of academic studies, and had spent no little pains on dialectic and rhetoric. At the coming of Chrysoloras I was torn in mind, deeming it shameful to desert the law, and yet a crime to lose such a chance of studying Greek literature; and often with youthful impulse I would say to myself: "Thou, when it is permitted thee to gaze on Homer, Plato and Demosthenes,‡ and the other [Greek] poets, philosophers, orators, of whom such glorious things are spread abroad, and speak with them and be instructed in their admirable teaching, wilt thou desert and rob thyself? Wilt thou neglect this opportunity so divinely offered? For seven hundred years, no one in Italy has possessed Greek letters; and yet we confess that all knowledge is derived from them. How great advantage to your knowledge, enhancement of your fame, increase of your pleasure, will come from an understanding of this tongue? There are doctors of civil law everywhere; and the chance of learning will not fail thee. But if this one and only doctor of Greek letters disappears, no one can be found to teach thee." Overcome at length by these reasons, I gave myself to Chrysoloras, with such zeal to learn, that what through the wakeful day I gathered, I followed after in the night, even when asleep.

Questions for Analysis

1. Why was it so important to Leonardi Bruni to learn to read Greek?
2. Who are the ancient Greek thinkers whom Bruni singles out for special praise?

*Chrysoloras (c. 1355–1415), a Byzantine writer and teacher, introduced the study of Greek literature to the Italians, helping open a new age of Western humanistic learning.

†*Civil Law* refers to the Roman law as codified by Emperor Justinian in the early sixth century A.D. and studied in medieval law schools.

‡Demosthenes (384–322 B.C.) was an Athenian statesman and orator whose oratorical style was much admired by Renaissance humanists.

Henry Osborn Taylor, *Thought and Expression in the Sixteenth Century* (New York: Frederick Ungar, 1930), 1:36–37.

fit classical learning into a Christian worldview. Renaissance humanists did not subordinate the classics to the requirements of Christian doctrines; rather, they valued ancient literature for its own sake—for its clear and graceful style and its insights into human nature. From the ancient classics, humanists expected to learn much that could not be provided by medieval writing: for instance, how to live well in this world and how to perform one's civic duties. For the humanists, the classics were a guide to the good life, the active life. To achieve self-cultivation, to write well, to speak well, and to live well, it was necessary to know the classics. In contrast to scholastic philosophers, who used Greek philosophy to prove the truth of Christian doctrines, Italian humanists used classical learning to nourish their new interest in a worldly life.

Whereas medieval scholars were familiar with only some ancient Latin writers, Renaissance humanists restored to circulation every Roman work that could be found. Similarly, knowledge of Greek was very rare in Latin Christendom during the Middle Ages, but Renaissance humanists increasingly cultivated the study of Greek in order to read Homer, Demosthenes, Plato, and other ancients in the original.

Although predominantly a secular movement, Italian humanism was not un-Christian. True, humanists often treated moral problems in a purely secular manner. Yet in dealing with religious and theological questions, they did not challenge Christian belief or question the validity of the Bible. They did, however, attack scholasticism for its hair-splitting arguments and preoccupation with trivial questions. They stressed instead a purer form of Christianity, based on direct study of the Bible and writings by the church fathers.

The early humanists, sometimes called the fathers of humanism, were Petrarch (1304–1374) and Boccaccio (1313–1375). Petrarch, Boccaccio, and their followers carried the recovery of the classics further by making a systematic attempt to discover the classical roots of medieval Italian rhetoric. Petrarch's own efforts to learn Greek were largely unsuccessful, but by encouraging his students to master the ancient tongue, he advanced humanist learning. Petrarch was particularly drawn to Cicero, the ancient Roman orator. Following the example of Cicero, Petrarch insisted that education should consist not only of learning and knowing things but also of learning how to communicate one's knowledge and how to use it for the public good. Therefore, the emphasis in education should be on rhetoric and moral philosophy, wisdom combined with eloquence. As Bartolommeo della Fonte (1446–1513), professor of rhetoric at Florence, said, such a program of instruction would fit a man for effective rule: that is, "to punish the wicked, to care for the good, to embellish his native land and to benefit all mankind."[1] Thus, Petrarch helped make Ciceronian values dominant among the humanists. His

followers set up schools to inculcate the new Ciceronian educational ideal.

Implicit in the humanist educational ideal was a radical transformation of the medieval (Augustinian) view of humanity. According to this view, since human beings were completely subject to divine will, not only were they incapable of attaining excellence through their own efforts and talents, but it was also wrong and sinful for them even to try. In contrast, the humanists, recalling the classical Greek concept of arête, made the achievement of excellence through individual striving the end not only of education but also of life itself. Moreover, because individuals were capable of this goal, it was their duty to pursue it as the end of life, although the pursuit was not effortless and indeed demanded extraordinary energy and skill.

People were deemed capable of excellence in every sphere and duty-bound to make the effort. This emphasis on human creative powers was one of the most characteristic and influential doctrines of the Renaissance. A classic expression of it is found in the *Oration on the Dignity of Man* (1486) by Giovanni Pico della Mirandola (1463–1494). Man, said Pico, has the freedom to shape his own life. Pico has God say to man: "We have made you a creature" such that "you may, as the free and proud shaper of your own being, fashion yourself in the form you may prefer."[2]

Pico also spelled out another implication of man's duty to realize his potential: through his own exertions, man can come to understand and control nature. One of the new and powerful Renaissance images of man was as the *magus,* the magician. The vision of the mastery of nature would continue to inspire experimentalists, such as Francis Bacon, and natural philosophers, such as Robert Boyle and Isaac Newton, until at least the early eighteenth century. A major psychological driving force of the Scientific Revolution, this vision stemmed in large part from the philosophy of Italian humanists such as Pico.

The attack on the medieval scholastics was implicit in the humanist educational ideal. From the humanist perspective, scholasticism failed not only because its terms and Latin usage were barbarous but also because it did not provide useful knowledge. This humanist emphasis on the uses of knowledge offered an additional stimulus to science and art.

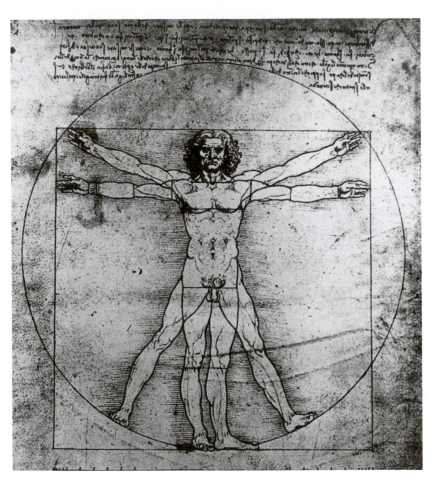

LEONARDO DA VINCI, *THE PROPORTIONS OF MAN*. Leonardo was fascinated by the human body. In his notebook, his written observations are accompanied by this marvelous drawing of the body, conceived and framed with realism and proportion. (Hulton Archive/Handout/Getty Images.)

But the new humanist and heroic image of human beings was deeply compromised and conflicted in one major area: the subject of women and gender relations. During the Renaissance, there were a few powerful female rulers, such as Elizabeth I, queen of England (1558–1603), and Catherine de' Medici, who became the regent (ruler) of France after her husband Henri II's untimely death in 1559. However, they were the exceptions. Politics and especially monarchical rule were always considered a male monopoly from which women should be excluded because they were inferior beings unsuited to holding such power.

Some aristocratic women patronized humanist scholars. Margaret Beaufort (1443–1509), mother of an English king, founded two colleges that fostered the new learning in England. Catherine of Aragon (1485–1536), the first wife of Henry VIII, king of England (1512–1547), surrounded herself with leading humanists, such as Desiderius Erasmus (1466–1536) and Juan Vives (1492–1540). The latter wrote for her a book entitled *The Instruction of a Christian Woman* (1523), which summarized humanist teaching on the subject. Vives insisted that women should be educated so that they could read serious books on religion and philosophy. But for him, like so many others, the goals of female education should be very limited. Men, he said, must be educated to act in the world and to govern. In contrast, women should be taught virtue—that is, devotion to home and family—and cheerful obedience to their husbands. In particular, women, according to Vives, should never be taught rhetoric, which was thought to be the key discipline in training men to become strong and effective leaders. Such rhetorical training would be wasted on women because their place was in the home and not in public life.

Such split thinking was repeated over and over again throughout the Renaissance. For example, Erasmus, the foremost European humanist, advocated female education, not so that educated women could act in the world but because reading was a way to banish idleness at home and was preferable to such tasks as knitting and sewing. Erasmus's friend Sir Thomas More (1478–1535) insisted on educating his daughters to a high level, not so that they could cut a figure on the public stage, but to make them better wives and daughters, that is, more virtuous and obedient. As female humanists in England and Italy, if not elsewhere, said at the time, men were jealous of educated women and afraid of losing control over them.

There were, however, a very few exceptions to this cramped and hostile view of female potential. The German physician Heinrich Cornelius Agrippa von Nettesheim (1486–1535), for instance, wrote *On the Nobility and Excellence of Women* in 1529. In this work, he held that although women are biologically different from men, they are not intellectually inferior to them. He went on to argue for the full equality of the sexes, a radical claim very far from mainstream, and even educated, opinion. Long before Agrippa, Christine de Pizan (1364–c. 1430), an extraordinary French female humanist, attacked the ancient prejudice that men are by nature not only stronger but also wiser than women. As she said in her great book, *The City of Ladies*, written in 1404, "[N]either the loftiness nor the lowliness of a person lies in the body according to sex, but in the perfection of conduct and virtues."[3] In other words, a person's worth is not about gender but about behavior. Despite this brilliant insight, which breaks through to an almost modern view of gender equality, even de Pizan could not hold

her ground but fell back on the deep-seated prejudices of her time. She said that men and women from time immemorial have played distinctly different roles in society, and so it should ever be: men are ordained to rule; women, to follow and obey. This is God's will. Thus, with the plausible exception of Agrippa, there were no modern feminists in the Renaissance, even at its most radical. The Renaissance humanists may have been overwhelmingly antifeminist, but they were also, at least in Florence and Venice, staunch republican political idealists.

In fourteenth- and fifteenth-century republican Florence, at least until the Medicis took control, Petrarchan humanism was not meant for a court elite. Humanism was a civic idea: to educate and inform citizens so that they could contribute to the common good to the greatest possible extent. In this sense, humanism was put in the service of republican values and the republican cause, and the mixture of the two is what has come to be called *civic humanism* by recent historians. This civic ideal developed furthest in the Florentine republic.

By the second half of the fifteenth century, as the Medicis gained increasing control, the civic ideal was being replaced by an ideal more fitting to the times, the ideal of princely rule. This ideal borrowed much from civic humanism, even though it was directed toward princes and courtiers and not toward citizens. The emphasis on the pursuit of virtue and honor continued. Like the ideal gentleman, the ideal prince would evolve through humanistic education, which would so prepare him for the struggle between virtue and fortune that virtue would prove victorious.

The similarities between the civic and princely ideals, however, were not as important as the differences. The aim of princely rule was not liberty but peace and security, and the best means to this end was not a republic but hereditary monarchy. This new princely ideal was reflected in a new spate of advice books, the most influential of which was *The Book of the Courtier*, written between 1513 and 1518 by Baldesar Castiglione (1478–1529). These books promoted the notion that the ideal ruler should be universally talented and skillful, equally commanding on the battlefield, at court, and in the state and virtuous throughout. These advice books, especially

Castiglione's, were to serve as indispensable handbooks for courtiers and would-be gentlemen in Renaissance Italy and throughout the rest of Europe for centuries.

A Revolution in Political Thought

One advice book transcended all the others: *The Prince,* written in 1513 by the Florentine Niccolò Machiavelli (1469–1527). It offered an indictment of the humanist ideal of princely rule and in so doing made some fundamental contributions to political theory. Indeed, Machiavelli may be called the first major modern political thinker. To Machiavelli, the humanist ideal was naïve in its insistence on the prince's virtues and eloquence to the exclusion of all other considerations. He attacked the medieval and humanist tradition of theoretical politics.

> *Since my intention is to say something that will prove of practical use to the inquirer, have thought it proper to represent things as they are in real truth, rather than as they are imagined. Many have dreamed up republics and principalities which have never in truth been known to exist; the gulf between how one should live and how one does live is so wide that a man who neglects what is actually done for what should be done learns the way to self-destruction.*[4]

NICCOLÒ MACHIAVELLI (1469–1527). Machiavelli looked back to the ancient Roman republic for his ideals and spent his life serving the city-state of Florence, but as the author of *The Prince*, his name became a byword for atheism and deceit. "Machiavellian" is still used to describe an unscrupulous politician. (Scala/Art Resource, N.Y.)

Politics, Machiavelli argued, requires the rational deployment of force, as well as, and even prior to, the exercise of virtue.

On this point, Machiavelli's advice is quite specific. He wrote *The Prince* in part as a plea. Since 1494, Italy had fallen prey to France and Spain. Their great royal armies overpowered the mercenary armies of the city-states and proceeded to lay waste to Italy in their struggle for domination of the peninsula. To prevent this, Machiavelli said, the Italians should unite behind a leader—the prince—whose first act would be to disband the mercenaries and forge a new citizen army worthy of the glorious Roman past and capable of repelling the "barbarian" invasion. "Mercenaries," Machiavelli claimed, "are useless and dangerous." They are useless because "there

is no . . . inducement to keep them on the field apart from the little they are paid, and this is not enough to make them want to die for you." And they are dangerous because their leaders, the infamous condottieri, "are anxious to advance their own greatness" at the expense of the city-state. Reliance on mercenaries was the sole cause of "the present ruin of Italy," and the cure lay in the creation of a national militia, led by a prince.[5]

This prince had to be both wily and virtuous, not just virtuous (as humanists had said): "The fact is that a man who wants to act virtuously in every way necessarily comes to grief among so many who are not virtuous." So Machiavelli scandalized Christian Europe by asserting that "if a prince wants to maintain his rule he must learn how not to be virtuous, and to make use of this or

The Renaissance

1. Filippo Brunelleschi, Church of San Lorenzo, interior, looking toward the apse, Florence, Italy.
(Erich Lessing/Art Resource, N.Y.)

The most vivid image of the Renaissance is conveyed through its architecture, sculpture, and painting. Renaissance examples of all three art forms display a style that stressed proportion, balance, and harmony. These artistic values were achieved through a new, revolutionary conceptualization of space and spatial relations. To a considerable extent, Renaissance art also reflects the values of Renaissance humanism in the use of classical models in architecture, in the rendering of the nude human figure, and in the heroic vision of human beings.

Medieval art sought to represent spiritual aspiration; the world was a veil merely hinting at the other, perfect, eternal world. Renaissance art expresses spiritual aspiration, but its setting and character differ altogether. This world is no longer a veil but the *place* where people live, act, and worship. The reference is less to the other world and more to this world, and people are treated as creatures who find their spiritual destiny as they fulfill their human one.

Renaissance artists produced revolutionary discoveries that served as the foundation of Western art up to the twentieth century. In art, as in philosophy, the Florentines played a leading role in this esthetic transformation. The first major contributor to Renaissance painting was the Florentine painter Giotto (c. 1276–1337). (See Figure 11 in the first art essay.) Giotto developed several

2. Donatello, *David*, c. 1425–1430. (Scala/Art Resource, N.Y.)

techniques of perspective, representing three-dimensional figures and objects on two-dimensional surfaces so that they appear to stand in space. Giotto's figures look remarkably alive. They are drawn and arranged in space to tell a story, and the expressions they wear and the illusion of movement they convey heighten the dramatic effect. The dramatic work of Giotto marked the end of the stiff, otherworldly style of the Middle Ages. The artists who followed Giotto diverged from his style and subject matter. Although Christianity was still an important theme, Renaissance artists also depicted subjects from Greek and Roman mythology as well as scenes from everyday life.

Painting, sculpture, architecture, and the minor arts evolved at a different pace throughout this period. It was not as if all artists declared themselves to be Renaissance figures simultaneously. Instead, styles changed with new artistic sensibilities, technological advances, and the requests of new patrons.

Rarely can one ascribe the development of an entire period of art to a single individual. Such is the case of Renaissance architecture, however. Filippo Brunelleschi (c. 1377–1446) began his career as a sculptor in Florence. He turned to architecture sometime after 1402 and traveled to Rome, where he studied the remains of imperial Roman buildings and monuments. Brunelleschi learned the theory of scientific perspective, perhaps while trying to draw on paper three-dimensional images of the monuments. He also developed a method of building double domes linked to reinforce each other. This lightened the weight of the dome, allowing the structure beneath to be built with fewer supporting elements.

One of the earliest expressions of his architectural skill can be seen in the Church of San Lorenzo in Florence (1421–1469) (Figure 1). Thanks to the benevolence of the Medici family, Brunelleschi was granted license to design an entire building himself. The Church of San Lorenzo was a new structure, not an adaptation of or an addition to an older, medieval building. Although some of its elements may have derived from earlier prototypes, the new building was distinct in its symmetry and regularity. Its floor plan shows a markedly regular repetition of equal-size squares to establish the nave, transept, and aisles. The centrally planned chapel, with its strict adherence

3. Masaccio, *The Holy Trinity*, 1425. (Scala/Art Resource, N.Y.)

to mathematical proportion, distinguishes the Church of San Lorenzo from the medieval Gothic cathedral. Brunelleschi's ability to grasp the concept of perspective in two dimensions is translated into three dimensions by the strong use of line and rhythmical arches that draw the eye to the altar.

Brunelleschi effected the same fusion of antique and Christian as his contemporaries did in other fields. Poets and writers experimented with classical and Christian styles; so too did Brunelleschi. Note, for example, the Corinthian capitals topping the San Lorenzo columns, whereas the floor plan is in the shape of a cross.

Architecture was not the only medium that combined experimentation and echoes of the past; sculpture did as well. Whereas Brunelleschi can be viewed as the father of Renaissance architecture, a host of sculptors advanced the Renaissance style in their medium. Prominent among them in the early Renaissance was Donatello (1386–1466), whose works distinguished him as a master even in his own time. The bronze *David* (c. 1425–1430) (Figure 2) is perhaps the most controversial of his best-known sculptures. The first life-size, freestanding nude sculpture since antiquity, this work is still something of an enigma.

Art historians assume that the statue was to have been exhibited outdoors, or at least in a central location, because it was meant to be viewed from all sides. The young David is wearing only a hat and high boots. Unlike the well-muscled athletes of the classical period, however, he is slender and slight, an adolescent instead of a developed adult. Donatello does pay homage to classical prototypes in the stance of his David— a *contrapposto,* or counterbalanced, pose, in which the weight on the legs is uneven (compare David's stance with Hermes' stance in Figure 1 of the first art essay).

Symbolic devices provide the key to the significance of the sculpture. David represents the city of Florence itself, and the helmet of Goliath under his feet represents the duchy of Milan, which at the time was at war with Florence. David's nudity may allude to the city's classical past, and the wreathed hat may suggest victory.

In painting, experiments in depth and linear perspective stand out as the major developments. Artists were seeking ways of making two-dimensional surfaces seem three-dimensional.

4. Pietro Perugino, *The Delivery of the Keys*, 1481. (Scala/Art Resource, N.Y.)

Brunelleschi was the first to develop a system in which all parallel lines of a scene converge in one central point on the horizon; other artists adopted his scheme and carried it further.

The Holy Trinity (Figure 3), a fresco by Masaccio (1401–1428), a brilliant young artist who died at the age of twenty-seven, advanced further Brunelleschi's experiments with linear perspective. Masaccio takes a central Christian spiritual idea, the Trinity—God the Father, the Son, and the Holy Spirit—and materializes and humanizes it.

He depicts a crucified Christ on the cross with God the Father standing behind him, and the Holy Spirit descending as a dove on Christ's head. The figures of Christ, the onlooking Madonna, St. John, even the figure of God the Father, standing behind Christ on an elevated platform, are human, material figures in a three-dimensional space.

The illusion of spatial depth is created by the architectural parameters of an overarching barrel-vaulted ceiling divided into squares diminishing in size.

Masaccio here provides a point of departure for subsequent art. Henceforth, artists will increasingly portray visual space within the three-dimensional perspectival format suggested by Masaccio, and human beings as real people, solid in form and realistic in anatomy, bones, muscles, and expressions.

Pietro Perugino's *The Delivery of the Keys* (1481) (Figure 4), a fresco from the Sistine Chapel in the Vatican, illustrates the enthusiasm with which other artists achieved perspective. Note that all the parallel lines in the foreground converge at the church in the center of the background. The viewer's eye is drawn into the

5. Leonardo da Vinci, *The Last Supper*, c. 1495–1498. (© The Gallery Collection/Corbis.)

painting, and figures seem real, not flat. Compare this portrayal with the flat and linear rendering of Justinian and his retinue in the mosaic from Ravenna. There, the effect is two-dimensional, and the viewer does not expect to see beyond the layer of figures. In the Perugino, by contrast, the figures are full and exist in a three- dimensional space.

The works of Leonardo da Vinci (1452–1519)—his drawings, paintings, sculpture, innumerable inventions, and copious writings—exemplify the Renaissance spirit. He expands the idea of three-dimensional, perspectival space to include the living form of things, their mathematical proportions. He announced a new way of looking at nature and the individual. For Leonardo, visual art offered a means of arriving at nature's truths. Truth was attained when the artist brought both human reason and creative capacity to bear on the direct experience of the senses. Leonardo examined objects in all their diversity and represented them realistically. He visually delineated the natural world with unprecedented scientific

precision, and he asserted his spiritual and intellectual freedom to do so. Through his art, Leonardo helped lay the foundations for modern science.

Leonardo's *The Last Supper* (Figure 5) affords a stark contrast to that of the Magdalen Master (compare with Figure 9 in the first art essay), providing a basis for gauging the distance traversed by Western art from the Middle Ages to modernity. Leonardo's version is explosive, and the scene is depicted vibrantly. The figures, in agitated motion, arranged in three-dimensional space, huddled into four groups, exhibit a wide range of postures, attitudes, and individual reactions to Christ's pronouncement that someone among them would betray him.

Leonardo has transformed medieval and Eastern two-dimensional space into the full-volumed three-dimensional space of the modern world and the lifeless, impersonal forms of medieval and Eastern art into unique individual personalities, their feelings captured at the very instant of their reaction to Christ's announcement.

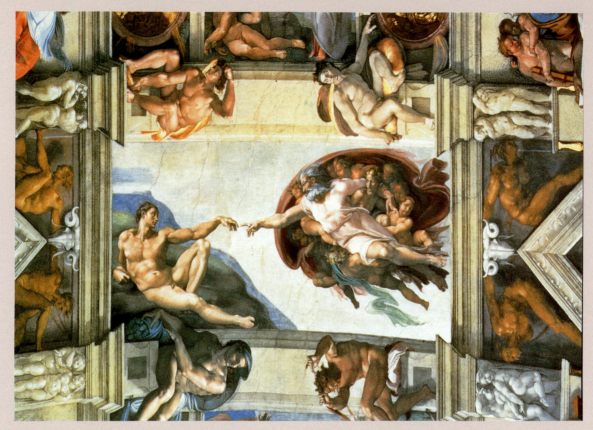

6. Michelangelo Buonarroti, *Creation of Adam*, 1510. (Sistine Chapel Ceiling: Creation of Adam, 1510 (fresco) (post restoration), Buonarroti, Michelangelo (1475–1564)/Vatican Museums and Galleries, Vatican City, Italy/The Bridgeman Art Library International.)

By the end of the fifteenth century, Renaissance art in Italy had reached its height. The High Renaissance flowered in the visual arts as well as in other areas of culture. Michelangelo, Titian, and Giorgione are among the best-known artists of this era.

The works of Michelangelo Buonarroti (1475–1564)—paintings, sculpture, literature, and architecture—epitomize the Renaissance. Looking at his paintings—for instance, *Creation of Adam* (1510) (Figure 6) on the ceiling of the Vatican's Sistine Chapel—a viewer is struck by the extent to which he learned from the art of the ancient world. Nevertheless, Michelangelo's reliance on the classical is subordinate to his Renaissance vantage point. Here, the figures float freely

through a celestial landscape and depict the biblical story of creation.

But the artists of the Renaissance looked to the classical past not only for technique; they also borrowed and adapted subject matter. Unlike the art of the Middle Ages, which concentrated on Christian themes, Renaissance paintings also illustrated the myths of ancient Greece and Rome.

The Venetian artist Titian (1488/90–1576) was well known for his use of both mythology and biblical themes. His *Bacchus and Ariadne* (1523) (Figure 7) illustrates his independence from the stylistic conventions of other High Renaissance schools. Titian offers a sensual rendering of the classical tale, in which the young Ariadne marries Bacchus (Dionysus), the god of wine, after being

7. Titian, *Bacchus and Ariadne*, 1523. (Erich Lessing/Art Resource, N.Y.)

abandoned by the Greek king Theseus. Titian's use of *chiaroscuro* (alternating areas of light and dark) is pronounced. The general feeling of the work is much looser and freer than the feelings of the carefully constructed canvases produced by his contemporaries. The painting also has a roughness, as though it were unfinished—a quality that marks a departure from the meticulously realistic works of other High Renaissance artists.

As the artistic styles of the Italian Renaissance spread northward, they were adapted and superimposed on a different set of political and religious circumstances, resulting in a fusion of Renaissance method and local themes. Pieter Brueghel the Elder's (1525/30–1569) *Hunters in the Snow* (1565) (Figure 8) exemplifies this trend. The artist

uses line and motion as Titian did. But the image he presents, although it contains many elements of the old style, looks ahead to the future.

Brueghel had spent almost two years studying in Italy, where he developed a technique for dealing with the problem of landscape. In his treatment of objects in three-dimensional space, he created a recessional movement that dominates the painting. The viewer's eye is drawn into the painting at an angle from the foreground to the background through myriad intermediate, diminishing shapes—dogs, human figures, trees, houses, a flying bird—all unified by one sweeping, sloping, downward motion. Brueghel thus achieves a perspectival depth that is entirely new, relying not on the correlation of stratified forms from left to

8. Pieter Brueghel the Elder, *Hunters in the Snow*, 1565. (Erich Lessing/Art Resource, N.Y.)

right, but on the recession of foreshortened forms. In this painting, the artist has surpassed the medieval representation of space in two dimensions and has produced a boundless three-dimensional space that belongs to the modern age.

By the late fifteenth and the sixteenth centuries, the styles of the Renaissance spread from Italy to the Low Countries (the Netherlands, Belgium, and Luxembourg), Germany, France, England, and Spain. These styles were not exported wholesale; rather, elements of the Renaissance fused with local traditions to produce new styles and variants of the Italian themes. What is consistent from one country to the next, however, is the extent to which Renaissance art really was a rebirth—a departure from the style of the medieval period.

not according to his need."[6] Even more shocking, the prince must know how to dissemble, that is, to make all his actions appear virtuous, whether they are so or not. In ironic parody of conventional advice-book wisdom, Machiavelli argued that a ruler must cultivate a *reputation* for virtue rather than virtue itself. In this connection, Machiavelli arrived at a fundamental political truth: politics (and especially the relationship between the ruler and the ruled) being what it is, the road to success for the prince lies in dissimulation (the art of appearance and cover-up). As he put it, "Everyone sees what you appear to be, few experience what you really are. And those few dare not [contradict] the many who are backed by the majesty of the state."[7] Here again the Renaissance arrived at modernity.

Machiavelli broke with both the medieval and the humanist traditions of political thought. He was a secularist who tried to understand and explain the state without recourse to Christian teachings. Influenced by classical thought, especially the works of Livy, he rejected the prevailing view that the state is God's creation and the ruler should base his policies on Christian moral principles. For Machiavelli, religion was not the foundation for politics but merely a useful tool in the prince's struggle for success. The prince might even dissemble, if he thought he had to, in matters of faith, by appearing pious, whether he was or not, and by playing on and exploiting the piety of his subjects.

THE SPREAD OF
THE RENAISSANCE

The Renaissance spread to Germany, France, England, and Spain in the late fifteenth and the sixteenth centuries. In its migration northward, Renaissance culture adapted itself to conditions unknown in Italy, such as the growth of the monarchical state and the strength of **lay piety**. In England, France, and Spain, Renaissance culture tended to be court centered and hence antirepublican, as it was, for instance, under Francis I in France and Elizabeth I in England. In Germany and the Rhineland, no monarchical state existed, but a vital tradition of lay piety was present in the

Low Countries. For example, the Brethren of the Common Life was a lay movement emphasizing education and practical piety. Intensely Christian and at the same time anticlerical, the people in such lay movements found in Renaissance culture tools for sharpening their wits against the clergy—not to undermine the faith but rather to restore it to its apostolic purity.

Thus, northern humanists were profoundly devoted to ancient learning, just as the humanists in Italy had been. But nothing in northern humanism compares to the paganizing trend associated with the Italian Renaissance. The northerners were chiefly interested in the problem of the ancient church and, in particular, the question of what constituted original Christianity. They sought a model in the light of which they might reform the corrupted church of their own time.

Everywhere, two factors operated to accelerate the spread of Renaissance culture after 1450: growing prosperity and the printing press. Prosperity, brought on by peace and the decline of famine and plague, led to the founding of schools and colleges. The sons (women were excluded) of gentlemen and merchants were sent to school to receive a humanistic education imported from Italy. The purpose of such education was to prepare men for a career in the church or the civil service of the expanding state and for acceptance into higher social spheres.

Printing with movable type, which was invented in the middle of the fifteenth century, quickened the spread of Renaissance ideas. Back in the Late Middle Ages, the West had learned, through the Muslims from the Chinese, of printing, paper, and ink. However, in this block printing process, a new block had to be carved from wood for each new impression, and the block was discarded as unusable as soon as a slightly different impression was needed. About 1445, Johann Gutenberg (c. 1398–1468) and other printers in Mainz in the Rhineland invented movable metal type to replace the cumbersome blocks. It was possible to use and reuse the separate pieces of type—as long as the metal in which they were cast did not wear down—simply by arranging them in the desired order.

With the advent of the printing press, the book-publishing industry began to develop. The first printed books were religious: Bibles,

Profile

A Renaissance Man

Leonardo da Vinci (1452–1519) is a supreme example of the so-called "universal man," someone wonderfully gifted who could excel in any number of fields. Because he was born illegitimate, he was disqualified from being trained in a learned profession such as law or medicine. But recognizing his immense talent, his father saw to it that he was apprenticed to Andrea del Verrocchio (1435–1488), the esteemed Florentine painter and sculptor, who carefully developed Leonardo's skills in the visual arts. Once Leonardo had been fully trained, it is said, Verrocchio was so struck by the beauty of his pupil's work that he decided never to paint again.

Given Leonardo's restless energy and insatiable curiosity, his genius could not be channeled in only one or a few directions. He quickly gained a reputation for tremendous skill in both science and art and was highly sought after. Florence was ruled by the Medicis, and Milan was ruled by the Sforzas. Leonardo worked for both, and briefly for the Medici pope Leo X (1513–1521) in Rome as well. He spent the last three years of his life in the pay of the French king Francis I (1515–1547), living in luxury at the French court and advising his patron on a variety of building projects.

Leonardo was a quick study and took advantage of opportunities for learning wherever he found them. At the Milanese court of the Sforzas, he met Luca Pacioli (1445–1517), the foremost Renaissance mathematician, who taught him geometry and the power of numbers to explain the world. Leonardo became committed to the view that mathematics provides the basis for true understanding in every field, not only in the physical and biological sciences but in painting and music as well. Leonardo had a large library and read widely, but he also believed that there was no substitute for studying nature firsthand and making experiments in order to obtain true and certain knowledge of things.

Leonardo was deeply interested in everything, and no subject was off limits. He studied human sexuality and, in his unpublished notebooks, made scientific drawings of a human fetus in the womb, male erections, and a couple having sex. One of his main fields of

sermons, and prayer books. But other kinds soon followed because there was a ready market for books on a great variety of secular subjects. The market was enormous and continued to expand during the sixteenth century. Printed books were much cheaper than the earlier hand-copied ones, and many more people could now afford to buy them. Publishers catered to every taste in reading—learned and popular, technical and imaginative, serious and light. Books became big business, driven by both consumer demand and the profit motive. Fifteen or twenty million books had already been published by 1500, and another 150 million more a century later.

Not only were books cheaper and more numerous, but printing also made it easier to learn to read. Literacy rates were still very low, especially among women and the poor, but the clerical and genteel monopoly on reading had been broken. More and more books were also published in the **vernacular** (rather than Latin), which helped standardize written language and stimulated the development of national literatures all across Europe. Printing, moreover, provided a surer basis for scholarship and prevented the further corruption of texts through hand copying. By giving all scholars the same text to work from, it made progress in critical scholarship and science faster and more reliable.

But in early modern Europe, printing was not an unmixed blessing. Elite opinion was often divided, or at least ambivalent, on the issue. Printing was an obvious boon; the authorities, however, saw the need for censorship, for imposing controls on what was published. Today, ours

investigation was human anatomy, both for how it could inform his painting and for what it could tell him about the aging process. Once he discovered a one-hundred-year-old man in a hospital in Florence and waited expectantly for his death so that he could examine his blood vessels. By comparing the corpses of the very young and the very old, he was the first to describe the disease known as arteriosclerosis, the hardening of the arteries. At this time, the church took a dim view of the carving up of human remains.

Much of Leonardo's effort was spent on practical design projects, large and small. In the prosperous and warring Italian city-states, there was always a need for industrial machinery, military fortifications, and weapons, and he received as many commissions for engineering work as he did for works of art. In 1502, he served as a military engineer to the commander of the papal army, the ruthless Cesare Borgia (d. 1507). The next year the Florentine government hired him to divert the course of the River Arno in order to cut off access to the sea by the city-state of Pisa, with which Florence was then at war. On this project, which was not successful, he collaborated with another famous Florentine, Machiavelli (see the section "A Revolution in Political Thought").

The list of Leonardo's ideas for new mechanical devices is staggering. He made some four hundred detailed drawings of machines. A short list of his proposals gives a hint of the range of his inventiveness. He came up with suggestions for a robot, a lifting fork, various cranes, machinery for making cloth, improvements on the printing press, a prototype of a car powered by springs and gears, a bicycle, and a flying machine. And then there were his ideas for weapons, including armored tanks, battering rams, scaling ladders, cannons, catapults, crossbows, and a submarine.

For all his inventive energy, Leonardo was notorious for procrastinating and sometimes never finishing his commissions for artworks and building projects, so the number of his surviving paintings is very small. This meager output has always been looked on as a great loss because his finished work sets such a high standard, including such incomparable paintings as *The Last Supper, Mona Lisa*, and *St. John the Baptist*.

is a **pluralistic** society that values new ideas and a variety of opinions, even differences of opinion, at least up to a point. Early modern Europeans were not so tolerant; in fact, they were suspicious of intellectual novelty and variety and sometimes downright hostile to **heterodox** thinking. For centuries, leaders in church and state had tried to build unity by enforcing Christian **orthodoxy** and punishing heresy. The motto of the French monarchy aptly sums up the point: "One king, one law, one faith." The Catholic church established an *Index of Prohibited Books* in the mid-sixteenth century, and books such as Machiavelli's *The Prince* were put on the list. Protestant authorities also set up machinery for regulating the book trade. Printers of "dangerous" books were punished, sometimes executed, and their book stocks confiscated. All intellectual life would be stifled by this atmosphere: the tension between the power of print and the desire to control opinion.

Erasmian Humanism

To Desiderius Erasmus (c. 1466–1536) belongs the credit for making Renaissance humanism an international movement. He was educated in the Netherlands by the Brethren of the Common Life, which was one of the most advanced religious movements of the age, combining mystical piety with rigorous humanist pedagogy. Erasmus traveled throughout Europe as a humanist educator and biblical scholar. Like other Christian humanists, he trusted the power of words and used his pen to attack scholastic theology and clerical abuses and to promote his philosophy of Christ.

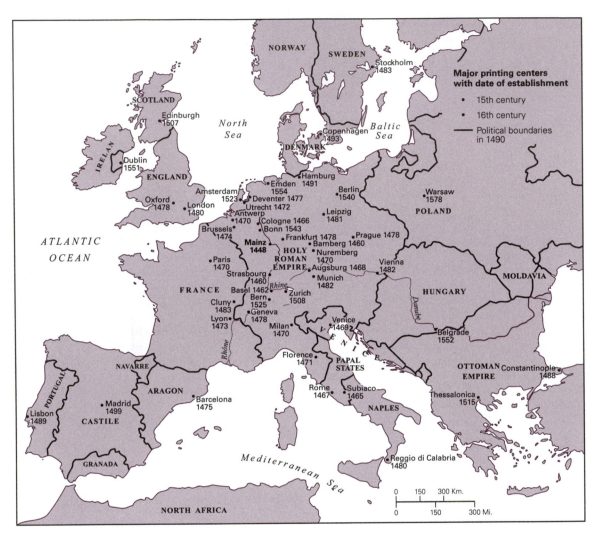

Map 13.2 **The Growth of Printing in Europe** The printing press was invented in the mid-fifteenth century, and its use had spread across Europe in less than a century. Even by 1500, some twenty million books had already been printed using the new technology. (Copyright © 2013 Cengage Learning.)

His weapon was satire, and his *Praise of Folly* and *Colloquies* won him a reputation for acid wit vented at the expense of conventional religion.

True religion, Erasmus argued, does not depend on dogma, ritual, or clerical power. Rather, it is revealed clearly and simply in the Bible and therefore is directly accessible to all people, from the wise and great to the poor and humble. Nor is true religion opposed to nature. Rather, people

are naturally capable of both apprehending what is good as set forth in the Scriptures and living in accordance with it. Perfect harmony between human nature and true religion allows humanity to attain, if not perfection, at least the next best thing, peace and happiness in this life.

This clear but quiet voice was drowned out by the storms of the Reformation (see Chapter 14), and the weight Erasmus gave to the individual's natural capacities could not hold its own before the renewed emphasis on human sinfulness and dogmatic theology. Erasmus was caught in the middle and condemned by both sides; for him, the Reformation was both a personal and a historical tragedy. He had worked for peace and unity and was treated to a spectacle of war and fragmentation. Erasmian humanism, however, survived these horrors as an ideal, and during the next two centuries, whenever thinkers sought toleration and rational religion (Rabelais and Montaigne, for instance), they looked back to Erasmus for inspiration.

French Humanism

German and French humanists pursued Christian humanist aims. They used humanist scholarship and language to satirize and vilify medieval scholastic Christianity and to build a purer, more scriptural Christianity. These northern humanists had great faith in the power of words. The discovery of accurate biblical texts, it was hoped, would lead to a great religious awakening. Protestant reformers, including Martin Luther, relied on humanist scholarship.

French thinkers of the next generation exploited and carried the humanist legacy in more radical directions. Among them, two were outstanding: Michel de Montaigne (1533–1592) and François Rabelais (c. 1494–1553). Both thought and wrote in reaction to the religious wars resulting from the Reformation. In the face of competing religious dogmatisms—Catholic, Protestant, and sectarian—Montaigne advanced a skepticism in which he maintained that one can know little or nothing with certainty. He therefore advocated political quietism and acceptance of Christianity on faith. This skepticism also entailed tolerance. An individual was not fully responsible for his or her beliefs, given that they were the product of frail reason and force of circumstance. Thus, Montaigne argued, people should not be punished for their beliefs, and the only ones who deserved to be severely dealt with were the dogmatists in religion. These people deserved to be punished because their certainty and self-righteousness flew in the face of a fundamental epistemological fact: that

PORTRAIT OF ERASMUS (1523) BY HANS HOLBEIN THE YOUNGER. Erasmus was the leading early sixteenth-century Christian humanist. He insisted that all Christians should strive to think rationally and to live peacefully with one another, despite their differences. (© INTERFOTO/Alamy.)

reason cannot be relied on, especially in matters of religion.

Montaigne was not a systematic philosopher but devoted himself to what he could learn by Socratic self-examination, the results of which he set down in his *Essays*. In their urbane and caustic wit and their intense self-absorption, the *Essays* betray a crucial shift in humanist thought, which became more pronounced in the next century. Gone is the optimism and emphasis on civic virtue of the High Renaissance. In their place come skepticism and introspection, the attempt to base morality on the self rather than on public values. As Montaigne says, "Let us learn to be no more avid of glory than we are capable of it."[8] This shift, produced by the increasing scale and violence of religious war, represented a retreat from the idealism of Renaissance humanism.

Rabelais took a different route from Montaigne's. In response to religious dogmatism, he asserted the essential goodness of the individual and the right to be free to enjoy the world rather than being bound down, as John Calvin later would have it, by fear of a vengeful God. Rabelais's folk-epic, *Gargantua and Pantagruel,* in which he celebrates earthly and earthy life, is the greatest French work of its kind and perhaps the greatest in any literature. Rabelais said that, once freed from dogmatic religion, people could, by virtue of their native goodness, build a paradise on earth and disregard the one dreamed up by theologians. In *Gargantua and Pantagruel,* he imagined a monastery where men and women spend their lives "not in laws, statutes, or rules, but according to their own free will and pleasure." They sleep and eat when they desire and learn to "read, write, sing, play upon several musical instruments, and speak five or six . . . languages and compose in them all very quaintly." They observe one rule: "do what thou wilt."[9]

Spanish Humanism

Spanish humanism represents a special case. The church hierarchy gained such a tight grip in Spain during the late fifteenth and early sixteenth centuries that it monopolized humanist learning and exploited it for its own repressive purposes. In contrast to Germany, France, and England, there was little or no room for a dissenting humanist voice. The mastermind behind this authoritarian Spanish humanism was Cardinal Francisco Jiménez de Cisneros (1436–1517). Jiménez founded the University of Alcalá, not far from Madrid, for the instruction of the clergy. He also sponsored and published the Complutensian Polyglot Bible, with Hebrew, Latin, and Greek texts in parallel columns. Jiménez, like Christian humanists elsewhere, sought to enlighten the clergy through a return to the pure sources of religion, and he saw his Polyglot Bible as one of the chief means of realizing that goal.

A century after Jiménez, Miguel de Cervantes Saavedra (1547–1616) produced his great novel, *Don Quixote,* in which he satirized the ideals of knighthood and chivalry. Don Quixote, the victim of his own illusions, roams the countryside looking for romance and an opportunity to prove his knightly worth. To Quixote's servant Sancho Panza,

PORTRAIT OF SIR THOMAS MORE **(1527) BY HANS HOLBEIN THE YOUNGER.** In England, More and Erasmus were close friends and colleagues, united in their devotion to humanistic scholarship and a Christian idealism that preached rational religion and life lived in service to the larger community.

(The Art Archive/Frick Collection, New York/Superstock)

Cervantes assigned the role of pointing up the inanity of his master's quest by always acting prudently and judging according to common sense. Despite his earthy realism, however, Panza must share his master's misfortunes—so much for realism in a world run by men full of illusions. Cervantes's satire is very gentle. That knightly valor was still a valid subject for satire indicates how wedded Spain was even in the early seventeenth century to the conservative values of its crusading past.

English Humanism

Christian humanism in England sharply contrasted with that in Spain. It was developed by secular men in government as much as by clerics, and its objectives were often opposed to authority and tradition. Various Italian humanists came to England during the fifteenth century as bishops, merchants, court physicians, or artists. Englishmen also studied in Italy, especially in Florence, and introduced the serious humanistic study of the classics at Oxford University toward the end of the century.

The most influential humanist of the early English Renaissance was Sir Thomas More (1478–1535), who studied at Oxford. His impact arose from both his writing and his career. Trained as a lawyer, he became a successful civil servant and member of Parliament. His most famous book is *Utopia,* the major utopian treatise to be written in the West since Plato's *Republic* and one of the most original works of the entire Renaissance.

Many humanists had attacked private wealth as the source of pride, greed, and human cruelty. But in *Utopia,* More went further. He argued that an acquisitive society is by nature both unjust and unprosperous. "For, when everyone is entitled to get as much for himself as he can, all available property . . . is bound to fall into the hands of a small minority, which means that everyone else is poor." The unscrupulous few win out over the many who remain honest and decent. For More, the conclusion was inescapable: "I am quite convinced that you will never get a fair distribution of goods . . . until you abolish private property altogether."[10] But to balance things out, he stated the economic case against communism as well. In the absence of a profit motive, "there would always tend to be shortages because nobody would work hard enough. . . . Then when things really got short, the . . . result would be a series of murders and riots."[11] But More accused those who took this view of lacking the imagination to conceive of a truly just society. In *Utopia,* he set out to make up for this deficiency by inventing an ideal society in which private ownership was abolished and poverty eliminated because everyone had to work in order to eat. Such a system even produced surpluses, which allowed people the leisure for instruction and recreation.

More succeeded Cardinal Wolsey as lord chancellor under Henry VIII. But when the king broke with the Roman Catholic church, More resigned, unable to reconcile his conscience with the king's rejection of papal supremacy. Three years later, in July 1535, More was executed for treason for refusing to swear an oath acknowledging the king's ecclesiastical supremacy.

William Shakespeare (1564–1616), widely considered the greatest playwright the world has ever produced, gave expression to conventional Renaissance values: honor, heroism, and the struggle against fate and fortune. But there is nothing conventional about Shakespeare's treatment of characters possessing these virtues. His greatest plays, the tragedies (*King Lear, Julius Caesar,* and others), explore a common theme: men, even heroic men, despite virtue, are able only with the greatest difficulty, if at all, to overcome their human weaknesses. What fascinated Shakespeare was the contradiction between the Renaissance image of nobility, which is often the self-image of Shakespeare's heroes, and man's capacity for evil and self-destruction. Thus, Ophelia says of Hamlet, her lover, in the play of the same name:

> O, what a noble mind is here o'erthrown!
> The courtier's, soldier's, scholar's, eye,
>   tongue, sword;
> The expectancy and rose of the fair state,
> The glass of fashion and the mould of form,
> The observ'd of all observers, quite, quite down!
> [And] I, of ladies most deject and wretched,
> That suck'd the honey of his music vows,
> Now see that noble and most sovereign
>   reason,
> Like sweet bells jangled, out of tune and harsh;
> That unmatch'd form and feature of blown
>   youth
> Blasted with ecstasy. O, woe is me,
> T' have seen what I have seen, see what I see![12]

The plays are intensely human—so much so that humanism fades into the background. Thus, art transcends doctrine to represent life itself.

THE RENAISSANCE AND THE MODERN AGE

The Renaissance, then, marks the birth of modernity—in art, in the idea of the individual's role in history and nature, and in society, politics, war, and diplomacy. Central to this birth is a bold new view of human nature: individuals in all endeavors are free of a given destiny imposed by God from the outside—free to make their own destiny, guided only by the example of the past, the force of present circumstances, and the drives of their own inner nature. Individuals, set free from theology, are seen to be the products, and in turn the shapers, of history. Their future is not wholly determined by Providence but is partly the work of their own free will.

Within the Italian city-states, where the Renaissance was born, rich merchants were at least as important as the church hierarchy and the old nobility. The city-states were almost completely independent because of the weakness of church and empire. So the northern Italians were left free to invent new forms of government, in which merchant-oligarchs, humanists, and condottieri played a more important part than priests and nobles, who dominated politics in the rest of Europe. Along with the inventiveness, however, this newness and lack of tradition produced disorder and violence. Condottieri grabbed power from hapless citizens, and republics gave way to despotism.

But the problems created by novelty and instability demanded solutions, and the wealth of the cities called forth the talent to find them. Commercial wealth and the new politics produced a new culture: Renaissance art and humanism. Talented individuals—scholars, poets, artists, and government officials—returned to classical antiquity, which in any case lay near at hand in Italy and Greece. Ancient models in art, architecture, literature, and philosophy provided answers to their questions. This return to antiquity also entailed a rejection of the Middle Ages as dark, barbarous, and rude. The humanists clearly preferred the secular learning of ancient Greece and Rome to the clerical learning of the more recent past. The reason for this was obvious: the ancients had the same worldly concerns as the humanists; the scholastics did not.

The revival of antiquity by the humanists did not mean, however, that they identified completely with it. The revival itself was done too self-consciously for that. In the very act of looking back, the humanists differentiated themselves from the past and recognized that they were different. They were in this sense the first modern historians because they could study and appreciate the past for its own sake and, to some degree, on its own terms.

A Word of Caution

We have emphasized in this chapter that the Renaissance, especially in Italy, represented a sharp and deliberate break with medieval tradition. Thinkers crawled out from under that tradition and adopted striking new views in many fields, as, for instance, in art and science, philosophy and religion, politics and education. The result was the beginnings of a new kind of high culture, less religious and more secular, with more emphasis on individualism, artistic creativity, and political realism. The starting point for this development was to a large degree a rediscovery of the classics, that is, the writings of ancient Greek and Roman thinkers. These works were taught and translated as never before since the fall of the Roman Empire and the onset of the so-called Dark Ages a thousand years before. In other words, educated Europeans laid the foundations for a new Renaissance culture by reviving a once-powerful, dead culture and being inspired and instructed by it. Renaissance men and women undertook this project and saw it through more or less on their own initiative and without help from the outside. The Renaissance, in this view, was largely a European affair and the achievement of the northern Italian city-states in the first instance.

There is much to be said for this picture, but it is not the last word on the subject because, as historians are becoming more and more aware, southern Europe, including Italy, France and Spain, in the centuries before the Renaissance, was engaged in large-scale trade with a non-European culture, namely, the Muslim civilization stretching across the Middle East and Mediterranean. Based on Islam, this was a great civilization that had developed from the seventh century and that never experienced the long decline that Christian Europe suffered in the early Middle Ages. Instead, the Muslims conquered the Middle East and North Africa and eventually Sicily and Spain. They built up great cities like Baghdad in the east, Cairo and Alexandria in Egypt, and Córdoba in southern Spain, all linked together by a flourishing trade throughout the Mediterranean. As prosperity increased in these cities, so did education, scholarship, and research. Schools and hospitals were founded for teaching and healing and large libraries created to facilitate study and learning. In the tenth century, the great library in Muslim Córdoba already had a collection of between 400,000 and 600,000 items, thus dwarfing the holdings of any library in Christian Europe at the time. As in Europe, much of this Muslim scholarship was based on ancient Greek and Latin manuscripts that were carefully preserved, translated into Arabic, and copied. But this educational tradition never died in Muslim lands as it had in Christian Europe. So when Europeans, led by the northern Italian city-states, rediscovered ancient literature and philosophy, they did not have to rely upon themselves alone but could also draw on Muslim sources for this ancient learning, where it was still being used and taught.

The Mediterranean was a "lake" in which goods like grain, oil, and wine were traded between Europeans in the north and Muslims in the south. Venice and Bologna in Italy established themselves as two of the principal hinges in this trade. Not only were goods and money exchanged, but also information, books, and knowledge. Much further west, scholars, Italian and otherwise, rushed to Spain, and especially to Córdoba, to use its great library and to get to know the works of antiquity, Aristotle especially (see pp. 85–87 and pp. 207–208).

During the Renaissance European scholars could draw upon texts, translations and scholarship made available to them over the centuries by contact between Europeans and Muslims, both through trade and by direct intellectual exchange. This is not to detract from the European Renaissance and its achievements, from which, after all, so much of the modern world emerged, including the very idea of modernity itself. This was in large part the invention of the northern Italian city-states, but it happened with considerable support from Muslim sources. To acknowledge this complicates matters somewhat and makes for a still unfinished, and less Eurocentric, story.

❖ ❖ ❖

Notes

1. Quoted in Quentin Skinner, *The Foundations of Modern Political Thought*, 2 vols. (Cambridge: Cambridge University Press, 1978), 1:89.

2. Giovanni Pico della Mirandola, *Oration on the Dignity of Man*, trans. A. Robert Caponigri (Chicago: Henry Regnery, 1956), 7.

3. Quoted in Margaret King, *Women of the Renaissance* (Chicago: University of Chicago Press, 1991), 221.

4. Niccolò Machiavelli, *The Prince,* trans. George Bull (Harmondsworth, England: Penguin Books, 1961), 90–91.

5. Ibid., 77–78.

6. Ibid., 91.

7. Ibid., 101.

8. Quoted in Eugen Weber, ed., *The Western Tradition,* 2 vols., 4th ed. (Lexington, Mass.: D. C. Heath, 1990), 1:395.

9. François Rabelais, *Gargantua and Pantagruel,* trans. Sir Thomas Urquhart (1883), bk. 1, chap. 57.

10. Thomas More, *Utopia,* trans. Paul Turner (Harmondsworth, England: Penguin Books, 1965), 66.

11. Ibid., 67.

12. From *Hamlet, Prince of Denmark,* in *The Complete Plays and Poems of William Shakespeare,* ed. William Allan Neilson and Charles Jarvis Hill (Boston: Houghton Mifflin, 1942), 1067.

Suggested Reading

Brucker, Gene A., *Renaissance Florence,* rev. ed. (1983). An excellent analysis of the city's economic and social structure, its political and religious life, and its cultural achievements.

Febvre, Lucien, and Henri-Jean Martin, *The Coming of the Book: The Impact of Printing, 1450–1800* (1997). Covers all aspects of "the print revolution."

Goody, Jack, *The Eurasian Miracle* (2010). Takes the long view and traces the origins of modernity back to the Bronze Age, offering food for thought.

Hale, John, *The Civilization of Europe in the Renaissance* (1995). An informed and entertaining survey, full of interesting illustrations.

King, Margaret L., *Women of the Renaissance* (1991). A useful survey of a burgeoning field of scholarship.

Schiffman, Zachary S., ed., *Humanism and the Renaissance* (2002). Excellent selection of brief historical interpretations of a big subject.

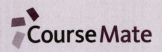

Go to the CourseMate website at www.cengagebrain.com for additional study tools and review materials—including audio and video clips—for this chapter.

Chapter 14

The Reformation: The Shattering of Christian Unity

St. Bartholomew's Day Massacre, *1572, by François Dubois (1529–1584).*

(St. Bartholomew's Day Massacre, 24th August 1572 (oil on panel), Dubois, Francois (1529–1584)/Musée d'
Archéologie et d'Histoire, Lausanne, Switzerland/Giraudon/The Bridgeman Art Library International.)

Focus Questions

1. What is a Protestant?
2. Why did the Protestant Reformation occur when it did?
3. What are the differences among a Lutheran, a Calvinist, and an Anglican?
4. What were the characteristics of the Radical Reformation?
5. Did Catholics and Protestants approach the modern world differently?

By the early sixteenth century, the only European institution that transcended geographic, ethnic, linguistic, and national boundaries was under severe attack from reformers. For centuries, the Catholic church, with its center in Rome, had extended its influence into every aspect of European society, culture, and politics. Reformers said that the church's desire to amass wealth and power appeared to outweigh its commitment to the search for holiness in this world and salvation in the next. Preoccupied by wealth, addicted to international power, and protective of their own interests, the clergy, from the pope down, took a battering from the church's critics. Humanists, made self-confident by the new learning and historical knowledge gathered during the Renaissance, called for reform and renewal, setting the stage for the Protestant Reformation. Eventually, though, the Reformation deviated significantly from what the Renaissance humanists had in mind. It brought into being a new form of Christianity, Protestantism, rather than reform of the Catholic church from within.

Schooled in new critical techniques, humanists used them to undermine the authenticity of documents that supposedly justified papal authority. Lorenzo Valla, for instance, disproved the validity of the Donation of Constantine (see "Humanism," in Chapter 13). But the fraud that especially vexed the humanists lay not on parchment but in the very practices by which the clergy governed the faithful.

The Protestant Reformation did not originate in elite circles of humanistic scholars. It began in German-speaking Europe with Martin Luther, an obscure monk and a brilliant theologian. Luther rejected the church's claim that it was the only vehicle for human salvation, and he defied the pope's right to silence, reprimand, and excommunicate any Christian who rejected papal authority or denied the truth of certain church teachings. After much soul-searching, in 1517 Luther proclaimed his *Ninety-Five Theses*. This set of short propositions started a public rebellion against the church's authority that in less than one decade shattered irrevocably the religious unity of Christendom. This rebellion also worked a quiet revolution in the lives of men and women. Marriage rather than celibacy for the clergy became an ideal, as did preaching, Bible-reading,

Chronology 14.1 ✦ The Reformation

1381	English peasants revolt and support John Wycliffe, an early reformer
1414–1418	Council of Constance
1415	Hus burned at the stake
1431–1449	Council of Basel
1517	Martin Luther writes the *Ninety-Five Theses*, and the Reformation begins; thousands of printed copies circulate
1520	Pope Leo X excommunicates Luther
1524–1526	German peasants revolt
1526	Hungary falls to the Ottoman Turks, and its Diet is dissolved; it is powerless to stop the spread of Lutheranism
1529	English Parliament accepts Henry VIII's Reformation
1534	Henry VIII is declared head of the Church of England; Francis I of France declares Protestants heretics; Ignatius Loyola founds the Society of Jesus; Anabaptists, radical reformers, capture Münster in Westphalia
1536	John Calvin publishes *Institutes of the Christian Religion*
1536–1564	Calvin leads the Reformation in Geneva with William Farel
1545–1563	Council of Trent
1553–1558	Mary, Catholic queen of England, persecutes Protestants; many flee to Geneva
1555	Peace of Augsburg
1561	Scotland turns Presbyterian under John Knox
1562–1598	French wars of religion between Catholics and Protestants are settled by the Edict of Nantes in 1598; in the same period the Dutch revolt against Spain
1640–1660	English Revolution; rise and defeat of the Puritans

and education. People felt less intimidated by clerical authority but may have privately questioned and chastised themselves. For help they turned to the Bible. Pitted against the church, the Reformation and then the Catholic response dominated European history throughout much of the sixteenth century.

THE MEDIEVAL CHURCH IN CRISIS

By the Late Middle Ages, the church had entered a time of crisis. Theologians and political theorists rejected the pope's claim to supremacy over kings and to spiritual sovereignty over all of Western Christendom. They argued that the church had become inefficient and corrupt, and they blamed the papacy in Rome. Some reformers sought to wrest power from the pope and give it to a general council of the church's hierarchy. Before 1480, this was one of the aims of the Conciliar Movement. However, the Councils of Constance and of Basel failed to leave a meaningful inheritance to the church, largely because the special interests of kings and the papacy undercut the councils' authority. By 1500, the failure of the Conciliar Movement meant that reforming the church from within would be very difficult. A broader reformation required defiant action and outreach to the faithful. The recent invention of printing gave literate people access to the writings of the reformers and their Catholic adversaries.

Wycliffe and Hus

Prior to Luther, the two most significant attempts to reform the church occurred first in the thirteenth century and then again in the late fourteenth century in England and Bohemia. In France, Waldo (d. 1218) led a band of reformers, the Waldensians, who wanted the Bible to be read in French and who laid emphasis on inner spirituality. As late as the 1680s, the French church, aided by the army, attempted to stamp out what it regarded as a form of Protestantism. In the fourteenth century, the leaders of two new movements, John Wycliffe in England and Jan Hus in Bohemia, were theologians who attacked vital church doctrines and practices. Wycliffe and Hus made heresy intellectually respectable. The influence of Wycliffe's and later Hus's movements also contributed to the long-term success of Protestantism in England and to its short-term success in portions of Eastern Europe. Hus laid the ground for the conversion of the Hungarian nobility. Even without access to printing, both Wycliffe and Hus appealed for mass support, prefiguring the populist quality of the Reformation.

John Wycliffe (c. 1320–1384), a master at Oxford University, attacked the church's authority by arguing simply that the worldly church did not control eternal destiny or the soul's access to grace. He said that salvation came only to those who possess faith, a gift freely given by God and not contingent on the church's rituals or sacraments. This position downgraded the clergy. Wycliffe attacked the church's wealth and argued that all true believers in Christ were equal and, in effect, Christ's priests. To make faith accessible to them, Wycliffe and his followers translated portions of the Bible into English. Wycliffe's preachings foreshadowed the teachings of Luther and the practices of the English Reformation.

Wycliffe received staunch support from some members of the English nobility. However, when his ideas were taken up by articulate peasants during an abortive peasants' revolt in 1381, Wycliffe lost many powerful backers. In the end, his attempt to reform the church by bringing it under secular control failed. Partly because he retained strong supporters and was more interested in scholarship than leadership, Wycliffe survived the failure of his movement and died a natural death. His ideas remained alive in popular religious beliefs, and his followers, called Lollards, have been credited with laying a foundation on which Protestant reformers of the sixteenth century could build.

A harsher fate awaited the Bohemian (Czech) reformer Jan Hus (c. 1369–1415): he was burned at the stake in 1415. Partly influenced by Wycliffe's writings, Hus, in his native Prague, attacked the sacramental system of the church, as well as its wealth and power. A popular preacher, he argued for Bohemian independence at a time when the Holy Roman Emperor sought to continue his control over that territory. After Hus's execution, his followers broke with the Roman Catholic church. The Bohemian church became independent from Rome, and the Hussites prepared the ground for the success of the Protestant Reformation. Until well into the seventeenth century, Bohemia remained a battleground of popular Protestantism against the official church.

Mysticism and Humanism

Wycliffe's and Hus's reform attempts coincided with a powerful new religiosity. Late medieval mystics sought to have immediate and personal communication with God and to renew the church's spirituality. Many late medieval mystics were women who, by virtue of their sex, were deprived of a clerical role in governing the church. First mysticism and then Protestantism offered women a way of expressing their independence in religious matters.

The church hierarchy had a deep distrust of mysticism. If people could experience God directly, they would have little need for the church and its rituals. In the fourteenth century, mystical movements seldom became heretical. But in the sixteenth and seventeenth centuries, radical reformers, some of them women preachers, often found in Christian mysticism a powerful alternative to the control and consolation offered by priests and the sacraments.

THE SACRED HEART OF JESUS, A HAND-COLORED WOODCUT SOLD AS AN INDULGENCE, NUREMBERG, 1480s. The sale of indulgences to erase purgatory time disgusted Martin Luther. He also condemned the veneration of relics—objects associated with the life of Christ or his saints, even bones and hair. Rival churches often claimed to have "the only authentic" head of a certain saint. (The Metropolitan Museum of Art, Bequest of James Clark McGuire, 1931. Photograph © The Metropolitan Museum of Art, New York/Art Resource, N.Y.)

In the Low Countries, the Brethren of the Common Life propounded a religious movement known as the *devotio moderna,* which was inspired by mysticism. A semimonastic order of laity and clergy, the Brethren embraced a practical piety, dedicating their lives to the service of the entire community. With their teaching, they trained a new generation of urban-based scholars and humanists, including Erasmus, who were severe critics of the church.

The humanist Erasmus of Rotterdam thought that critical words should be enough to show the clergy the folly of their ways, which he ridiculed in *The Praise of Folly* (1509). Yet neither mysticism, with its emphasis on inner spirituality, nor humanism, with its stress on classical learning, captured the attention of learned ordinary Europeans. A successful reform movement required leaders with a common touch and an aggressive temperament who could do battle with political realities and win lay support against the vast power of the church. Such leaders took solace in *millenarianism,* the belief that after the Last Judgment Christ would institute a thousand-year rule of saints on earth. Its believers found a radical and religious justification for attacking established institutions and institutional corruption. The end of the world would be ushered in by righteous reformers whose time had come.

The End of the World

In the movements inspired by Wycliffe and Hus, as well as in the peasant revolts often spurred by economic grievances, a sense of urgency became apparent. Millenarians, inspired by the biblical prophecies, looked forward to the moment of divine intervention when the world would be destroyed, sinfulness overwhelmed, and a paradise on earth created where God's chosen would rule. Millenarian reformists, some quite radical, took prophecies accepted but not promoted by the church and reinterpreted them to express their vision of a just society where religion aids the poor and oppressed. Protestant reformers reinterpreted Catholic millenarian doctrine. According to them, Christ would condemn the rich and propertied and establish a new society, not in heaven but on earth, which the poor would inherit, and for a thousand years—a millennium—the poor would rule in Christ's kingdom.

By 1500, the biblical concept of the Antichrist and the image of the whore of Babylon, both a part of **millenarian thinking,** became a shorthand for the corruption of the church. When Luther and other reformers in the early sixteenth century called the pope himself the Antichrist or the whore of Babylon, they drew upon the millenarian tradition of reform and protest that had existed in the West for centuries.

THE LUTHERAN REVOLT

Only an attack on papal and clerical authority could strike at the church's power. To succeed, the attack had to address the multitudes while appealing to princes. Heresy had to be made respectable and compelling. Such a feat required someone whose inner spiritual struggle highlighted the church's failure to care for souls, someone who could translate the agony of the search for salvation into language accessible to all Christians. Martin Luther (1483–1546) had experienced a personal crisis of faith, and he possessed the will, the talent, and the intellectual vigor to offer it as an example for other Christians. Luther wrote voluminously and talked freely to his friends and students. Using this mass of recorded material, historians have been able to reconstruct the life and personality of this Augustinian friar and theologian who began the Reformation (see Primary Source feature).

Luther: Humanist, Prophet, and Conservative

Martin Luther was born in eastern Germany to relatively uneducated parents of humble origins. His strict father, Hans Luther, was exceptionally ambitious. Born a peasant, he left the land and became a miner and finally a manager of several mines in the booming late-fifteenth-century German mine industry. Like many of the newly rich, Hans Luther had ambitious plans for his son; he wanted Martin to attain the status of an educated man and become a lawyer. Luther's mother was intensely pious, thus putting Luther in close touch with German popular religion.

At the university, Luther embarked on an ambitious intellectual career that was to make him one of the foremost theologians and biblical scholars of his day. At first, he studied law, and, of course, he read the humanists, including Erasmus.

But a rebellious streak surfaced. In 1504, at the age of twenty-one, Luther suddenly abandoned his legal studies to enter the Augustinian monastery at Erfurt. The actual decision was made swiftly. In later life, Luther recounted that the decision had been made in fear, as a vow to Saint Anne in the midst of a fierce lightning storm, by a young man convinced that his death at that moment would bring him eternal damnation. Why Luther thought he was damned is not known, but his guilt conspired with his vivid imagination to kindle what must have been a growing resentment against his father's domination. Challenging authority became a habit for Luther.

Luther was also a millenarian; he thought that he was living in the last days of the world. Eventually, as he became the leader of an international religious movement, Luther grew convinced that he was the long-foretold, divinely ordained prophet chosen to announce the coming Final Judgment. When he became the strong leader of the German Reformation, he also had to take political stands and pick his allegiances. Without hesitation and with deep conviction, Luther chose to preserve the social order, to support the power of princes and magistrates, and to maintain social hierarchy. Yet he took on papal authority and the power of the Holy Roman Emperor.

Luther's Break with Catholicism

As he prayed, Luther grew increasingly terrified by the possibility of his damnation. As a monk, he sought union with God, and he understood the church's teaching that salvation depended on faith, works (meaning acts of charity, prayer, fasting, and so on), and grace. He participated in the sacraments of the church, and through them sought God's grace. Indeed, after his ordination, Luther administered the sacraments. Yet he still felt the weight of his sins, and the church seemed unable to relieve that burden.

Even the mystery of the Mass and the conversion of bread and wine into the body and blood of Christ brought Luther little inner peace. Seeking solace and salvation, he increasingly turned to reading the Bible. Two passages spoke directly to him: "For therein is the righteousness of God revealed from faith to faith: as it is written, 'He who through faith is righteous shall live'" (Romans 1:17); and "They are justified by his grace as a gift, through the redemption which is in Christ Jesus" (Romans 3:24). In faith and grace, Luther found, for the first time in his adult life, some hope for his own salvation. These biblical passages said to him that faith, freely given only by God through Christ, gives salvation and that human beings, powerless because of their fallen and sinful nature, are rescued by divine mercy. Neither the pope nor the sacraments give what only God can provide—salvation.

The concept of salvation by faith alone satisfied Luther's spiritual quest. Practicing good works such as prayer, fasting, pilgrimages, and receiving the sacraments would not in themselves lead to grace. No amount of good works, however necessary for Christian unity, would bring salvation. Through reading the Bible and through faith alone, the Christian could find the purpose of earthly existence. For Luther, the true Christian was a courageous figure who faced the terrifying quest for salvation armed only with the hope that God had granted the gift of faith. The new Christian served others, not to bargain with good works for salvation, but solely to fulfill the demands of Christian love. Nuns left their convents and married in the belief that their faith and service to the community would save them. Priests also left the church to become, like Luther, leaders of their own churches. Luther's odyssey laid out a new Protestant piety that embraced activity in the world.

Pursuing his theological and biblical studies, Luther became a professor at the nearby university at Wittenberg, in Saxony, and a preacher in that city's church. He shared his personal struggle with his students and his congregations. At the University of Wittenberg and in the province of Saxony in general, Luther found an audience receptive to his views, and his popularity and reputation grew. Before 1517, he was considered a dynamic and controversial preacher, whose passionate interest lay in turning Christians away from their worldly pleasures and from reliance on good works while focusing their attention on Christ and the truth contained within Scripture. After 1517, Luther became internationally famous; eventually the church deemed him a heretic.

The Reformation began in 1517 with Luther's attack on the church's practice of selling indulgences. The church taught that some individuals go directly to heaven, some go directly to hell, and others go to heaven after spending time in purgatory. Punishment in purgatory is necessary for those who sinned excessively but had the good fortune to repent before death. Naturally, people worried about how long they might have to suffer in purgatory. Indulgences were intended to remit portions of that time and punishment and were granted by the church to those who prayed, attended Mass, and performed acts of charity—including making monetary offerings to the church itself. Could the church be selling and people buying admittance to heaven?

In the autumn of 1517, a friar named Tetzel was selling indulgences near Wittenberg. Some of the money went to rebuilding Saint Peter's Basilica in Rome, and the rest was for paying off debts incurred by a local archbishop when he purchased his office from the pope. Although Luther did not know about the purchase, he was incensed both by Tetzel's crude manner and by his flagrant exploitation of the people's ignorance and what Luther deemed his misuse of their money. Luther launched his attack on Tetzel and the selling of indulgences by tacking on the door of the Wittenberg castle church his *Ninety-Five Theses*.* He also sent a copy to the local archbishop. Luther's theses (propositions) challenged the entire notion of selling indulgences not only as a corrupt practice but also because it rested on a theologically unsound assumption—namely, that salvation could be bought and sold, that is, earned by the good work of supporting the church. Luther was blunt with the church's hierarchy and, in particular, with the papacy: he challenged its sole authority to save souls and to guard entrance into heaven. By his logic, indulgences were worthless.

Luther's argument in all his writings rested on the belief that Christian salvation through personal piety requires contrition for sins and trust in God's mercy and grace. He also believed that no good work earned salvation. The church, in contrast, held that *both* faith and good works were necessary for salvation. Luther further insisted that every individual could discover the meaning of the Bible unaided by the clergy. The church maintained that only the clergy could read

---

*Some scholars debate whether this public display ever occurred, but the document itself was soon printed and widely circulated.

Martin Luther: *Disputation of Doctor Martin Luther on the Power and Efficacy of Indulgences* (1517)

Out of love for the truth and the desire to bring it to light, the following propositions will be discussed at Wittenberg, under the presidency of the Reverend Father Martin Luther, Master of Arts and of Sacred Theology, and Lecturer in Ordinary on the same at that place. Wherefore he requests that those who are unable to be present and debate orally with us, may do so by letter.

In the Name our Lord Jesus Christ. Amen.

1. Our Lord and Master Jesus Christ . . . willed that the whole life of believers should be repentance.

2. This word cannot be understood to mean sacramental penance, i.e., confession and satisfaction, which is administered by the priests.

3. Yet it means not inward repentance only; nay, there is no inward repentance which does not outwardly work divers mortifications of the flesh.

4. The penalty [of sin], therefore, continues so long as hatred of self continues; for this is the true inward repentance, and continues until our entrance into the kingdom of heaven.

5. The pope does not intend to remit, and cannot remit any penalties other than those which he has imposed either by his own authority or by that of the Canons.

6. The pope cannot remit any guilt, except by declaring that it has been remitted by God and by assenting to God's remission; though, to be sure, he may grant remission in cases reserved to his judgment. If his right to grant remission in such cases were despised, the guilt would remain entirely unforgiven.

7. God remits guilt to no one whom He does not, at the same time, humble in all things and bring into subjection to His vicar, the priest.

8. The penitential canons are imposed only on the living, and, according to them, nothing should be imposed on the dying.

9. Therefore the Holy Spirit in the pope is kind to us, because in his decrees he always makes exception of the article of death and of necessity.

10. Ignorant and wicked are the doings of those priests who, in the case of the dying, reserve canonical penances for purgatory.

11. This changing of the canonical penalty to the penalty of purgatory is quite evidently one of the weeds that were sown while the bishops slept.

Questions for Analysis

1. What does it mean to say that the pope cannot remit our guilt? If not through the pope, then how will humans be forgiven?

2. What is Luther's view of the clergy?

Works of Martin Luther, trans. and ed. Adolph Spaeth, L. D. Reed, Henry Eyster Jacobs, et al. (Philadelphia: A. J. Holman, 1915), 1:29–38.

and interpret the Bible properly. Luther argued that in matters of faith there was no difference between the clergy and the laity; indeed, each person could receive faith directly and freely from God. The church held that the clergy and the sacraments were intermediaries between individuals and God: Christians reached eternal salvation through the church and its clergy. For Luther, no priest, no ceremony, no sacrament, and certainly no confinement in convents or monasteries could bridge the gulf between the Creator and his creatures, and the possibility of personal damnation

Tetzel Selling Letters of Indulgence. This engraving shows activities in the pope's audience-viewing room. Peasants and religious men are giving money to the church and receiving blessings after making their payments. (Kean Collection/Staff/ Getty Images.)

and penitent supplicant implied God's favor. In Luther's doctrine of faith, the notion of *predestination* is barely beneath the surface. Luther never chose to bring forth the implications of his doctrine. His contemporary, the great French theologian John Calvin, however, made predestination central to his version of reformed Christianity. This belief made salvation an intensely personal matter—some might say an intensely terrifying or liberating matter.

Predestination is such a difficult doctrine that discussion about it continues today. Predestination rests on the assumption that God is all-knowing, eternal, his will absolute: he gives faith to whomever he chooses and does so for his own inscrutable reasons. Because God's existence and will are timeless, God knows the fate of every person even as individuals are searching for salvation. Given God's foreknowledge, it may be said that every person is predestined for either heaven or hell. But for believers, the question remains: how can individuals know whether God has chosen them for salvation?

Luther said simply that men and women should hope and trust in salvation but certainty would be granted only after death. For subsequent reformers predestination made Protestant doctrine logical and created an identifying experience for all true Christians. Calvin and his followers, who by 1650 became numerically the largest group of European and American Protestants, believed firmly that some are chosen and others damned—but no one should presume one way or another.

The Creation and Spread of Lutheranism

In 1517, Luther could not foresee what he had started, that the Reformation was under way. Quickly translating his theses from Latin into German, his students printed and distributed them throughout Germany. Local church authorities recognized in Luther a serious threat and prepared to silence him. But Luther was tenacious; he began to write and preach his theology with increasing vigor. With the aid of the printing press, by 1525 there were probably three million Protestant pamphlets circulating in Germany. Students

remained a distinct reality. Hope lay only in a personal relationship between the individual and God, as expressed through faith in God's mercy and grace. In Luther's view, no church could mediate that faith for the individual, and to that extent Luther's theology destroyed the foundations of the church's spiritual power. By declaring that clergy and church rituals do not hold the key to salvation, Luther rejected the church's claim that it alone offered the way to eternal life.

But Who Is Saved?

If faith alone, freely given by God, brings salvation to the believer, how can a person know whether he or she has faith? Luther seemed content to assert that the search itself by a pious

and well-wishers from Eastern Europe as well as Germany flocked to Wittenberg.

At this point, politics intervened. Recognizing that his life might be in danger if he continued to preach without a protector, Luther appealed for support to Prince Frederick, the elector of Saxony. The elector was a powerful man in international politics—one of the seven lay and ecclesiastical princes who chose the Holy Roman Emperor. Frederick's support for his most famous university professor convinced church officials, including the pope, that this friar had to be handled cautiously.

The years 1518 and 1519 were momentous ones for the Holy Roman Empire. Before his death in 1519, the Holy Roman Emperor Maximilian I wanted to see his grandson Charles, king of Spain, elected to succeed him. The papacy at first opposed Charles's candidacy, even looking to Frederick of Saxony as a possible alternative. Frederick wisely declined. However, because he was one of the seven electors, the contenders—Charles, Francis I of France, and Henry VIII of England—counted on him for his vote. Charles bribed the electors and won the title. Therefore, during this crucial period and for years afterward, he had to proceed cautiously on issues that might offend powerful German princes.

These political considerations explain the delay in Luther's official condemnation and excommunication by the pope. When in late 1520 the pope finally acted, it was too late; Luther had been given the time needed to promote his views. He proclaimed that the pope was the Antichrist and that the church was the "most lawless den of robbers, the most shameless of all brothels, the very kingdom of sin, death and Hell."[1] When the papal bull excommunicating him was delivered, Luther burned it.

Luther and his followers established congregations for Christian worship throughout Germany. To find protectors, in 1520 Luther published the *Address to the Christian Nobility of the German Nation.* In it, he appealed to the German princes to cast off their allegiance to the pope, who, he argued, had used taxes and political power to exploit them for centuries. His appeal tapped into the resentment against foreign papal intervention that had long festered in Germany. Luther also wrote to the German people

about the meaning of his personal experience as a Christian. In *The Freedom of a Christian Man* (1520), he called on Germans to strive for true spiritual freedom through faith in Christ, to discipline themselves, to obey legitimate political authority, and to perform good works according to the dictates of Christian love. In these treatises, Luther made his political conservatism clear: he wanted to present no threat to legitimate authority, that is, to the power of German princes.

In 1521, Charles V, the Holy Roman Emperor and a devout Catholic, summoned Luther to Worms, giving him a pass of safe conduct. In that imperial city Luther faced the charge of heresy, both an ecclesiastical and a civil offense. As he traveled to Worms, crowds of well-wishers cheered his way. Then standing before the emperor and his court, Luther was supposed to recant. His careful and defiant reply became his most famous statement: "Unless I am convinced of error by the testimony of Scripture or by clear reason . . . I cannot and will not recant anything, for it is neither safe nor honest to act against one's conscience. God help me."

Shortly after this confrontation with the emperor, Luther went into hiding to escape arrest. In that one-year period, he translated the New Testament into German. With it, he offered literate Germans the opportunity to take the same arduous spiritual odyssey that he had undergone and to join him as a new type of Christian. These followers, or Lutherans, were eventually called *Protestants,* those who protested against the established church, and the term became generic for all supporters of the Reformation.

Religious Reform or Social Revolution?

Luther looked to every level of German society for support. In a country of many small towns with printing presses, the literate urban population responded dramatically to his call. Led by city fathers and preachers, individuals converted to the new Protestant churches or turned their own Catholic church into a Protestant one. The new faith made men and women bold. When a teenage boy married of his own will without consulting his family in Nuremberg, he defended his actions by saying that God "ordained that it happen this way by his divine will."[2] Priests were now expected to marry. Even though Protestants insisted that women marry and be silent and obedient, a Swiss Protestant woman who refused marriage justified her wanting to remain "masterless" by saying: "Those who have Christ for a master are not masterless."

Luther was a brilliant preacher, and clearly his message could inspire people to be defiant as well as devout. Protestantism came to be seen not only as a source of personal revitalization and salvation but also as a force that could renew society and government.

The same issues that moved Germans to leave the church appealed to people in towns and cities in Austria, Hungary, Poland, the Netherlands, and Switzerland. Even in Paris and London, as well as in northern Italy by the late 1520s, followers or readers of Luther could easily be found, and lives changed profoundly. Katharina von Bora, who married Martin Luther, was so devoted to the Lutheran cause that Luther called her his "Moses." There were thousands of devout and defiant Katharinas throughout Europe.

Despite repression by the Catholic church and the weight of habit and tradition, in 1550 Protestants were probably in the majority in some German towns, in much of Hungary and Bohemia, in Sweden, and in various Swiss cantons. In France, more than a million people converted to Calvin's version of Protestantism. Dutch city dwellers turned to it as well, much to the horror of their Spanish king. How could this have happened in one generation?

In the sixteenth century, any new religious or political movement needed the support of the nobility. Early on, Luther appealed to them, and they responded. Their motives ranged from piety to political ambition. The Reformation provided the nobility with the unprecedented opportunity to confiscate church lands, eliminate church taxes, and gain the support of their subjects by serving as leaders of a popular and dynamic religious movement. The Reformation also gave the nobles a way to resist the Catholic Holy Roman Emperor Charles V, who wanted to extend his authority over the German princes. Resenting Italian domination of the church, many other Germans who supported Martin Luther believed that they were freeing German Christians from foreign control. The same spirit motivated the nobility in France, the Low Countries, Poland, and Lithuania.

First and foremost, however, Lutheranism was a popular evangelical movement. Its battle cry became "The Word of God"; faith and the Bible were its hallmarks. Luther turned his wrath on the "detestable tyranny of the clergy over the laity; [the clergy] almost look upon them as dogs, unworthy to be numbered in the Church along with themselves. . . . They dare to command, exact, threaten, drive, and oppress, at their will."[3]

Those were fighting words—but uttered by a political conservative, who hesitated to challenge secular authority. To Luther, the good Christian must be an obedient citizen. The freedom of the Christian lay inward, a spiritual freedom. Yet Luther could not stop his ideas from spreading to the poor and the peasantry, often by word of mouth. The population of Germany was about 16 million, of which probably no more than 400,000 could read. For the illiterate and largely rural people, Lutheranism came to mean not only religious reform but also an evangelical social movement that would address their poverty. In addition, the peasants believed that the end of the world was near and that God would soon impose justice. Millenarianism and poverty inspired social revolution.

Although Luther had spoken forcefully about Christians' discontent with their church, he never understood that to the poor and socially oppressed, the church's abuses were visible signs of the poverty and exploitation they encountered in their daily lives. The wealthy feudal lords who dominated every aspect of their existence, as well as the prosperous townspeople who bought their labor for the lowest possible wages, seemed no different from the venal clergy; indeed, in some cases the lord was also a local bishop.

In the early sixteenth century, a rapid population explosion throughout Europe had produced severe inflation, high unemployment, and low wages. The poor got poorer. The peasantry in Germany was probably worse off than the peasantry in England and the Low Countries. In 1524, long-suffering peasants openly rebelled against

Katharina von Bora

Katharina von Bora (1499–1552) and Martin Luther had a marriage that, though imperfect, well represents the Protestant model. Although Katharina came from a noble background, her family was not well-off. After a few years of religious education, she entered a nunnery—a common choice for women without dowries for marriage. Katharina and other women in the convent soon became disillusioned with the cloistered life. Somehow, Martin Luther learned of their plight and decided to help. In April 1523, he aided eleven nuns—among them Katharina—in their escape from the cloister. Legend has it that they hid in empty smoked herring barrels.

Two years later, Katharina and Martin were married. Their marriage became a love match that lasted all of their lives. Katharina and Martin became role models for other Protestant clergy. Protestant doctrine taught women that marriage and child-rearing, combined with obedience to one's husband, led to holiness. Katie, as Martin called her, ran a household with more than forty rooms, in addition to buying and running a farm. She raised six children and was a devoted Protestant wife. Her last recorded words are "I will stick to Christ as a burr to a topcoat." Beginning with Katharina and Martin, Protestant ministers married, raised families, and served their congregations who supported them.

their lords. The peasants' revolt spread to more than one-third of Germany; some 300,000 people took up arms against their masters. They were inspired by Luther's successful confrontation with the church. Had he not chastised the nobles for failing to care for the poor as commanded in the Gospel?

Luther, however, had no intention of associating his movement with a peasant uprising and thereby alienating the nobility from the Reformation. Luther virulently attacked the rebellious peasants, urging the nobility to become "both judge and executioner" and to "knock down, strangle, and stab . . . and think nothing so venomous, pernicious, Satanic as an insurgent. . . . Such wonderful times are these that a prince can merit heaven better with bloodshed than another with prayer."[4] By 1525–1526, the peasants had been put down by the sword. Thousands died or were left homeless, and many were permanently alienated from Lutheranism. Because of the failure of the revolt, the German peasantry remained relatively backward and oppressed well into the nineteenth century. In Germany, the Reformation meant

religious reform, not social revolution or even social reform, and it became increasingly an urban phenomenon.

THE SPREAD OF
THE REFORMATION

Lutheranism spread in waves and in every direction out from Wittenberg, the training ground for Luther's clergy. In northern Europe, cut off from the south by the Alps and the Pyrenees, the Reformation spread rapidly. In southern Europe, where the church and the Inquisition were strongest, the Reformation made fewer inroads in Italy or Spain. Thus, the spread of Protestantism had a pattern. It grew strong in northern Germany, Scandinavia, the Netherlands, Scotland, and England but failed in Ireland and the Romance countries, though not without a struggle in France.

Protestantism also appeared simultaneously in different places—a sure indication of its popular roots. For example, in the Swiss city of Zurich, the priest and reformer Ulrich Zwingli (1484–1531)

ICONOCLAST FURY. In the sixteenth century, reformers tore out the statues and stained glass in Protestant churches, arguing that decoration distracts from the Bible and the Word of God. To this day, Protestant churches remain less decorated than Catholic ones. (The Granger Collection, New York.)

preached faith and not good works and saw the Bible as the key to divine will and law. Like Luther, he looked for an alternative to the doctrine of *transubstantiation*—the priest's transformation of Communion bread and wine into the substance of Christ's body and blood. It gave enormous power to the priesthood. But the two reformers differed bitterly over the form and meaning of the ceremony. Zwingli radically altered the Communion service, and it became solely a commemoration of the Last Supper. Their quarrel highlights that the reformers, as predicted by the Catholic church, could not agree on the meaning of the Bible or on the ritual expressions they would give their new versions of Christianity.

Zwingli died on the battlefield in a war to defend the Reformation. His teachings laid the foundation for a thorough reformation in Switzerland,

and the major reform movement of the next generation, Calvinism, benefited from Zwingli's reforms. Both forms of the Reformation spread into Eastern Europe.

In Germany, the strife created by the Reformation was settled, though not to everyone's satisfaction, by the Peace of Augsburg (1555). It decreed, by the famous dictum *cuius regio, eius religio* ("whoever rules, his religion"), that each territorial prince should determine the religion of his subjects. Broadly speaking, northern Germany became largely Protestant, and Bavaria and other southern territories remained in the Roman Catholic church. The victors were the local princes. Toward the end of his life, Charles V expressed bitter regret for not intervening more forcefully in those early years. The decentralization of the empire and its division into Catholic and Protestant areas blocked German unity until the last part of the nineteenth century. In Eastern Europe, both forms of Christianity showed hostility to Islam, and it was returned in kind.

Calvin and Calvinism

The success of the Reformation outside Germany and Scandinavia derived largely from the theological rigor of John Calvin (1509–1564), a French scholar and theologian. By the 1530s, Lutheran treatises circulated widely in Paris. Some university students, including the young John Calvin, seized upon Luther's ideas.

Calvin was born into a French family of bourgeois status; his father, somewhat like Luther's, was self-made and ambitious. A lawyer and administrator, the elder Calvin served ecclesiastical authorities until a dispute led to his excommunication. He desired prosperous careers for his sons. John first studied to be a priest and then, at his father's insistence, took up the study of law at the University of Orléans. Unlike the rebellious Luther, Calvin waited until his father's death to return to Paris and resume his theological studies. Even more so than Luther, Calvin was trained as a humanist. He knew the ancient languages, as well as philosophy and theology, and he knew the Bible. From all those sources, Calvin fashioned the most logically compelling version of Protestantism to come out of the Reformation.

Sometime in 1533 or 1534, Calvin met French followers of Luther and became convinced of the truth of the new theology. He took to the streets to spread his beliefs, and within a year he and his friends were in trouble with the authorities. Calvin was arrested but released because of insufficient evidence.

King Francis I, a bitter rival of the Holy Roman Emperor, could countenance Protestantism in Germany but would never permit disruptive religious divisions in France. Riots had already broken out in Paris between Catholics and supporters of the Reformation. In 1534, the French church, backed by a royal decree, declared the Protestants heretics and subjected them to arrest and execution.

Within a year, young Calvin abandoned his literary studies to become a preacher of the Reformation. Calvin explained his conversion as an act of God: "He subdued and reduced my heart to docility, which, for my age, was overmuch hardened in such matters."[5] Calvin emphasized the power of God over sinful and corrupt humanity; his God thundered and demanded obedience, and the terrible distance between God and the individual was mediated only by Christ.

In his search for spiritual order and salvation, Calvin spoke to his age. His anxiety was widely shared. He feared disorder and ignorance, sinfulness, and simply the unpredictable quality of human existence. The only solution to anxiety lay in unshakable faith in God, knowledge of his laws, and absolute adherence to righteous conduct. We must see God's order everywhere, especially in nature, in "the symmetry and regulation" of the universe.[6] Faith in God is so obviously our salvation that, according to Calvin, only the damned, the reprobate, would turn their back on him and live in disorder. Calvin assured his congregations that God "will give a good result to everything we do. . . . God will cause our enterprises to prosper when our purpose is right and we attempt nothing except what he wills."[7] With Calvin, the doctrine of predestination became the centerpiece of Protestant theology: some people are saved, others damned at birth; inward belief and outward righteousness and integrity may signal a person's fate, but God alone knows what the future holds.

The social and political implications of predestination were immediate: Calvinists became militant Protestants capable of ruling their towns or cities with the same iron will they used to control their unruly passions. Like Luther, Calvin always stressed that Christians should obey legitimate political authority. But Calvinists were individuals who assumed that unfailing dedication to God's law could signal salvation; their obedience to human laws would always be contingent on their inner sense of righteousness. Thus, Calvinism made for stern followers, active in their churches and willing to suppress vice in themselves and others. Calvinism also could produce revolutionaries willing to defy any temporal authorities seen to violate God's laws. Obedience to Christian law

THE NEW CHAPEL ON THE KALVERSTRAAT, DRAWN BY JAN GOEREE AND ENGRAVED BY BERNARD PICART. This Protestant chapel in Amsterdam, which was drawn in the early eighteenth century, tells us much about early Calvinism. It was austere, exacting, and ordered, and it emphasized the Word of God, not ceremonies. (Interior of the Church of St. Bavo in Haarlem, 1665 (oil on panel), Berckheyde, Job (1630–93)/© Gemaeldegerie Alte Meister, Dresden, Germany/© Staaliche Kunstsammlungen, Dresden/The Bridgeman Art Library International.)

became the dominating principle of Calvin's life. Rigorous enforcement of the law ensured obedience to God's law; the local Calvinist church became an alternative to the power of the Catholic church.

The political situation in France forced Calvin to leave. After his flight from Paris, he finally sought safety in Geneva, a small, prosperous Swiss city near the French border. It was a logical choice. Before Calvin's arrival, Geneva's citizens were in revolt against their Catholic bishops. The French-born reformer William Farel implored Calvin to stay to continue the work of the Reformation. Together, they became leaders of the Protestant movement in Geneva. After many setbacks, Calvin emerged as the most dynamic agent of reform in the city. Until his death in 1564, his beliefs and actions ruled Geneva's religious and social life.

Calvin established an unofficial Calvinist *theocracy*—a society in which Calvinist elders regulated citizens' personal and social lives and did so through church courts that were independent of state institutions. Older, pious, male members of the community governed the city.

These elders of the Calvinist church imposed strict discipline in dress, sexual mores, church attendance, and business affairs; they severely punished irreligious and sinful behavior. This rigid discipline contributed to Geneva's prosperity; indeed, Calvin instituted the kind of social discipline that some of the merchants had always wanted. Prosperous merchants, as well as small shopkeepers, saw in Calvinism a series of doctrines that justified the self-discipline they already exercised in their own lives and wished to impose on the unruly masses. They particularly approved of Calvin's economic views, for Calvin, unlike the Catholic church, saw nothing sinful in commercial activities and even gave his assent to the practice of charging interest.

Geneva became the center of international Protestantism. Calvin trained a new generation of Protestant reformers of many nationalities who carried his message back to their homelands. Calvin's *Institutes of the Christian Religion* (1536), in its many editions, became (after the Bible) the leading textbook of the new theology. In the second half of the sixteenth century, Calvin's theology of predestination spread into France, England, Scotland, the Netherlands, and parts of the Holy Roman Empire.

Calvin opposed violence against the legitimate authority of magistrates. Yet when monarchy became a persecutor, his followers felt compelled to respond. Calvinist theologians became the first political theoreticians of modern times to publish cogent arguments for opposition to monarchy and eventually for political revolution. In France and later in the Netherlands, Calvinism became a revolutionary ideology, complete with an underground organization of dedicated followers who challenged monarchical authority. (In the seventeenth century, the English version of Calvinism—Puritanism—performed the same function.) In certain circumstances, Calvinism supplied the moral force to support the individual against the claims of the monarchical state.

France

Although Protestantism was illegal in France after 1534, its persecution was halfhearted and never systematic. The Calvinist minority in France, the Huguenots, became a well-organized underground movement that attracted nobles, city dwellers, some peasants, and especially women. Huguenot churches, often under the protection of powerful nobles, assumed an increasingly political character in response to the monarchy-sponsored persecution. By 1559, French Protestants had organized and challenged their persecutors, King Henry II and the Guise—one of the foremost Catholic families in Europe, tied by marriage and conviction to the Spanish monarchy and its rigorous form of Catholicism. Guise power in the French court meant that all Protestant appeals for lenient treatment went unheeded, and in 1562 civil war erupted between Catholics and Protestants. What followed was one of the most brutal religious wars in the history of Europe. In 1572, an effort at conciliation through the marriage of a Protestant leader into the royal family failed when Catholics, urged on by the queen mother, Catherine de' Medici, murdered the assembled Protestant wedding guests. Over the next week, a popular uprising left thousands of Protestants dead; the streets, according to eyewitness accounts, were stained red with blood. These murders and the ensuing slaughter, known as the Saint Bartholomew's Day Massacre, inspired the pope to have a Mass said in thanksgiving for a Catholic "victory." Such was the extent of religious hatred in late-sixteenth-century Europe.

After nearly thirty years of brutal fighting throughout France, victory went to the Catholic side—but just barely. Henry of Navarre, the Protestant bridegroom who in 1572 had managed to escape the fate of his supporters, became King Henry IV, but only after reconverting to Catholicism. He established a tentative peace by granting Protestants limited toleration. In 1598, he issued the Edict of Nantes, the first document in any nation-state that attempted to institutionalize a degree of religious toleration. In the seventeenth century, the successors of Henry IV (he was assassinated by a priest in 1610) gradually weakened the edict and then in 1685 revoked it. The foundations of toleration, in theory and practice, remained tenuous in early modern France. Every French king of the seventeenth century tried to decrease the number of Protestants. In 1685, more than 150,000 fled to the Protestant areas of Europe or the American colonies.

England

The Reformation in England differed profoundly from the Continental Reformations. The king, Henry VIII (1509–1547), and not clergymen in revolt, made it happen. The pope refused to grant Henry an annulment of his marriage to his first wife, who had failed to produce a male heir. So this self-confident Renaissance king, bent on having a new wife and new sources of revenue, removed the English church from papal jurisdiction.

Unlike the French and Spanish kings, the English Tudors never frightened the papacy. Henry VII (1485–1509), the first Tudor monarch, and his son, Henry VIII, enjoyed a good measure of control over the English church but never played a major role in European and papal politics. When Henry VIII decided that he wanted a divorce (he called it an annulment) from the Spanish princess Catherine of Aragon in 1527–1528, the pope in effect ignored his request. Henry had neither power nor theology on his side. As the pope stalled, Henry grew more desperate; he needed a male heir and presumed that the failure to produce one lay with his wife. At the same time, he desired Anne Boleyn. But Spain's power over the papacy ensured that Henry's pleas for an annulment would go unheeded.

The English possessed a tradition of opposing the church that went back to Wycliffe in the fourteenth century. Aware of that long tradition, Henry VIII arranged to grant himself a divorce by severing England from the Roman Catholic church. To do so, he summoned Parliament, which in turn passed a series of statutes drawn up at his initiative and guided through Parliament by his political adviser, Thomas Cromwell. Beginning in 1529, Henry convinced Parliament to accept his Reformation, and so began an administrative and religious revolution. In 1534, Henry had himself declared supreme head of the Church of England (also known as the Anglican church). In 1536, he dissolved English monasteries and seized their property, which was distributed or sold to his loyal supporters. In most cases, it went to the lesser nobility and landed gentry. By involving Parliament and the gentry, Henry VIII turned the Reformation into a national movement.

In the eleven years after Henry's death in 1547, three more Tudor monarchs ascended the throne of England. Henry was succeeded by his sickly son, Edward VI, a Protestant, who reigned from 1547 to 1553. On his death, Edward was succeeded by his Catholic half sister, Mary (1553–1558), the daughter of Henry VIII and Catherine of Aragon, the divorced first wife, who had been sent into exile. Allied with the remaining Catholic minority in England, Mary persecuted Protestants severely. On her death, she was succeeded by her Protestant half sister, Elizabeth I (1558–1603), Henry's daughter by Anne Boleyn, and England became a Protestant country again.

The Church of England as it developed in the sixteenth century differed only to a limited degree in its customs and ceremonies from the Roman Catholicism that it replaced. Sections of the English population, including aristocratic families, remained Catholic and even used their homes as centers for Catholic rituals performed by clandestine priests. Thus, the exact nature of England's Protestantism became a subject of growing dispute. Was the Anglican church to be truly Protestant? Was its hierarchy to be responsive to, and possibly even appointed by, the laity? Were its services and churches to be simple, lacking in "popish" rites and rituals and centered only on Scripture and sermon? Was Anglicanism to conform to Protestantism as practiced in Switzerland, either in Calvinist Geneva or in Zwinglian Zurich? The clergy, especially the English bishops, would accept no form of Protestantism that might limit their ancient privileges, ceremonial functions, and power. Mary's persecutions, however, had forced leading English Protestants into exile in Geneva and into the arms of the Calvinist church.

Despite these religious issues, which were raised by the growing number of English Calvinists, or Puritans, as they were called, Elizabeth's reign was characterized by a heightened sense of national identity and by only the limited persecution of Catholics. At this same time, Calvinism flourished in Scotland. In Ireland, some elites and most peasants remained staunch Catholics.

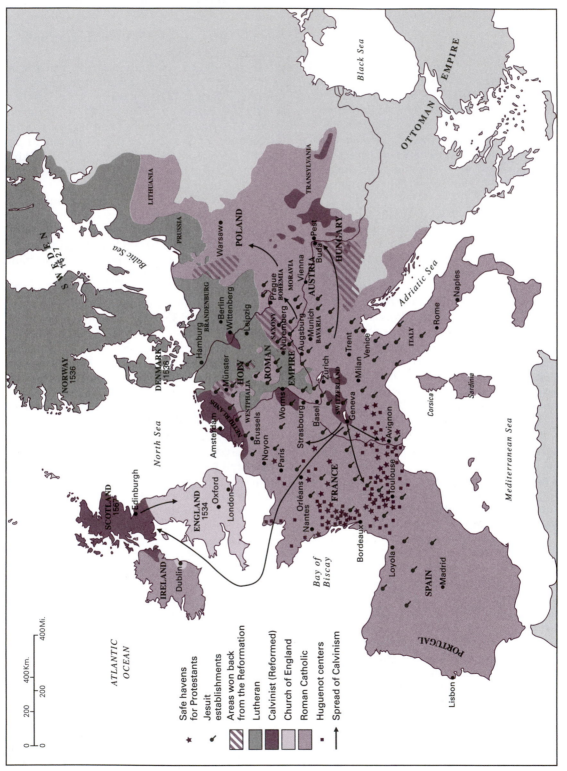

Black Sea

OTTOMAN EMPIRE

LITHUANIA

PRUSSIA

Warsaw

POLAND

TRANSYLVANIA

Pest

HUNGARY

Buda

AUSTRIA

Vienna

MORAVIA

BOHEMIA

Prague

Adriatic Sea

SWEDEN 1527

Baltic Sea

BRANDENBURG

Berlin

Wittenberg

Hamburg

Leipzig

SAXONY

Nuremberg

Augsburg

Munich

BAVARIA

Trent

Rome

ITALY

Naples

NORWAY 1536

DENMARK 1536

Münster

HOLY ROMAN EMPIRE

Worms

Zurich

SWITZERLAND

Milan

Venice

Corsica

Sardinia

WESTPHALIA

Strasbourg

Basel

Geneva

Avignon

Mediterranean Sea

North Sea

EAST FRIESLAND

Amsterdam

Brussels

Noyon

Paris

ENGLAND 1534

Oxford

London

Orléans

Nantes

FRANCE

Toulouse

SCOTLAND 1567

Edinburgh

IRELAND

Dublin

ATLANTIC OCEAN

Bay of Biscay

Bordeaux

Loyola

SPAIN

Madrid

PORTUGAL

Lisbon

400 Mi.

400 Km.

200

200

0

0

Safe havens for Protestants

Jesuit establishments

Areas won back from the Reformation

Lutheran

Calvinist (Reformed)

Church of England

Roman Catholic

Huguenot centers

Spread of Calvinism

Southern and Eastern Europe

In Spain and Italy, where the Inquisition was powerful, the Reformation struggled but failed to take hold. In Venice, as late as the 1560s, it was possible to find Protestants of all sorts—Lutherans, Calvinists, radical millenarians. We know about them from the interrogation reports filled out by their Catholic inquisitors. The Italian Inquisition had the backing of the papacy and the populace. Humanism, which might have given support to Protestantism, had never possessed a popular base in Italy, and the universities and printing presses, so vital to the Reformation north of the Alps, remained firmly under clerical control.

Luther's writings circulated in Spain for a time, but there, too, the authorities, both lay and clerical, quickly and thoroughly stamped out Protestantism. In the Middle Ages, the Spanish church and state had successfully joined in a religious and nationalist crusade to drive out the Muslims, and this effort forged strong links between the Spanish monarchy and the church. About a quarter of the Spanish population held a church office of one kind or another, and the church owned half of Spain's land. Allied with the state, the Inquisition enforced public and private morality. In southern Europe, the Reformation simply could not evade clerical authorities.

In Eastern Europe, the pattern was quite different and more complex than in Italy and Spain. In Hungary, warfare between Christians and Turks led to the collapse of the nobility, three-quarters of whom were killed in one battle in 1526. The weakness of Austrian Hapsburg authority in the country, coupled with the demise of the local elite, created a power vacuum into which the Reformation rushed.

Hungarian reformers such as Mathias Biró (1523–1545) and Stephen Kis (1505–1572) studied with Luther in Wittenberg and returned to Budapest to preach the Lutheran gospel. But as the number of their converts grew, Catholic and Turkish authorities became alarmed. They imprisoned

◀ *Map 14.1* **The Protestant and Catholic Reformations** Europe fractured into competing camps, and religious warfare became a way of life. (Copyright © 2013 Cengage Learning.)

Map 14.2 **Inner Austria and Adjacent Territories** The Protestant Reformation sought converts throughout Hapsburg Europe and also confronted Islam in the Ottoman Empire. In both places, the Reformation was only minimally successful—Hungary is a major exception—and by the end of the century the Hapsburgs acquired a large portion of that country. (Copyright © 2013 Cengage Learning.)

Kis and Biró, confiscated their libraries, and fought the Reformation at every turn. Yet the Protestants did make converts among the Hungarian nobility, as well as among the townspeople. Not until the seventeenth century and the Hapsburg-led Counter-Reformation did Hungary return to the church. Even in the eighteenth century, during the Enlightenment, Hungarian Protestants were influential in the intellectual life of the country.

The pattern of the Reformation in Eastern Europe followed that in the rest of the continent. It began in the cities, succeeded where it was supported by the nobility or where traditional authority was weak, and lasted when it took root among the general population. In Poland, that pattern occurred; in neighboring Lithuania, only the nobility, already immensely powerful, took up Protestantism. When the church, led by the Jesuits, fought back, it easily triumphed in those areas where the Reformation lacked popular support. Very slowly, Poland was brought back into the church; in Lithuania, by the late sixteenth century, Protestantism had all but disappeared. The Catholic version of reformation had demonstrated its considerable appeal.

The Radical Reformation

The mainstream of the Protestant Reformation can be described as *magisterial* because the leading reformers generally supported established political authorities, whether they were territorial princes or urban magistrates. For the reformers, human freedom was a spiritual, not a social, concept. Yet the Reformation did help trigger revolts among the artisan and peasant classes of Central and then Western Europe. Indications are that church doctrine had not made great inroads into the folk beliefs of large segments of the European masses. For example, some peasants held the very un-Christian beliefs that Nature was God or that witches had as much spiritual power as priests did. By the 1520s, several radical reformers arose, often from the lower classes of European society, and they channeled popular religion and folk beliefs into a new version of reformed Christianity that spoke directly to the temporal and spiritual needs of the oppressed.

Some beliefs constituted what may be called the *Radical Reformation*. Appealing to the poor and oppressed, the radicals argued that ordinary men and women, even if illiterate, have certain knowledge of their salvation through an *inner light,* a direct communication from God to his chosen "saints"—men and women predestined for salvation. That knowledge makes the saint free. For the radicals, spiritual freedom paralleled their demands for social and economic freedom and equality. Protestantism, radically interpreted, proclaimed the righteousness and the priesthood of all believers. It said that all people can have faith if God wills it and that God would not abandon the wretched and humble of the earth.

The radicals said, as did the Bible, that the poor shall inherit the earth, which is ruled at present by the Antichrist, and that the end of the world had been proclaimed by Scripture. The saint's task was to purge this earth of evil to make it ready for Christ's Second Coming. For the radicals, the faith-alone doctrine meant certain salvation for the poor and lowly, and the Scriptures became an inspiration for social revolution. The doctrine could also inspire quietism, retreat from this world in anticipation of a better world to come. Luther, Calvin, and the other reformers vigorously condemned the social doctrines preached by the radical reformers, whether activist or quietist.

The largest group in the Radical Reformation prior to 1550 has the general name of Anabaptists. On receiving the inner light—the message of salvation—the Anabaptist felt born anew and yearned to be rebaptized. This notion had a revolutionary implication: the first infant baptism—thought to ensure allegiance to an established church (Protestant or Catholic)—did not count. The Anabaptist was a new Christian led by the light of conscience to seek the reform and renewal of all institutions in preparation for the Second Coming of Christ. Millenarian doctrines about the end of the world provided a sense of time and urgency.

In 1534, Anabaptists captured the city of Münster in Westphalia, near the western border of Germany. They seized the property of nonbelievers, burned all books except the Bible, and in a mood of jubilation and sexual excess openly practiced a repressive (as far as women were concerned) polygamy. All the while, the Anabaptists proclaimed that the Day of Judgment was close at hand. The radical leaders at Münster were men totally unprepared for power. They were defeated by the army led by a Lutheran prince, Philip of Hesse, and the local Catholic bishops brutally suppressed them. In early modern Europe, *Münster* became a byword for dangerous revolution. In Münster today, the cages still hang from the church steeple where the Anabaptist leaders were tortured and left to die as a warning to all would-be imitators.

By the late sixteenth century, many radical movements had either gone underground or grown quiet. But a century later, during the

English Revolution of 1640 to 1660, the beliefs and political goals of the Radical Reformation resurfaced, threatening to push the political revolution in a direction that its gentry leaders desperately feared. Although the radicals failed in England, they left a tradition of democratic and antihierarchical thought. The radical assertion that saints, who have received the inner light, are the equal of anyone, regardless of social status, helped shape modern democratic thought.

THE CATHOLIC RESPONSE

As late as the 1530s, the Catholic church hesitated, uncertain that the Protestant Reformation would gain strength or attract so many powerful noble families. Initially, the energy for reform came from ordinary clergy, as well as from laypeople such as Ignatius Loyola (1491–1556), rather than from the hierarchy or the established religious orders. Clergy and especially the laity gave renewed energy to Catholicism. Trained as a soldier, the Spanish reformer Loyola created a new religious order. He fused the intellectual rigor of humanism with a reformed Catholicism, forming a renewed spirituality with wide appeal. Founded in 1534, the Society of Jesus, commonly known as the **Jesuits**, became the backbone of the Catholic Reformation (also called the *Counter-Reformation*) in southern and Western Europe.

The Jesuits strove to bypass local corruption and appealed to the papacy to lead a truly international movement to revive Christian universalism. The Jesuits saw most clearly the bitter fragmentation produced by the Reformation. Moreover, they perceived one of the central flaws in Protestant theology. Predestination offered salvation to the literate and prosperous laity and, at least in theory, to the poor as well. However, it also included the possibility of despair for the individual and a life tormented by the fear of inescapable damnation. In response, the Jesuits offered hope: a religious revival based on ceremony, tradition, and the priestly power to offer forgiveness.

Jesuits became confessors to princes and urged them to strengthen the church in their territories. They developed a pragmatic theology that permitted "small sins" in the service of an ultimately just cause. In this way, the Jesuits, by the seventeenth century, became the greatest teachers in Europe and also the most controversial religious group within the church. Were they the true voice of a reformed church, or did they have nefarious intentions, as their critics claimed? Did they seek political power of their own, making themselves the Machiavellian servants of princes? It was a controversy that continued well into the eighteenth century. Urged on by Catholic reformers, the church finally convened a council at Trent. It tackled corrupt practices and renewed Catholic spirituality throughout the West.

As a result of the Catholic revival, new schools and universities appeared, as did newly designed churches. The revival even fostered a distinct style of art and architecture: cherubic angels grace the ornate decor of Counter-Reformation churches; heaven-bound saints beckon the penitent. This baroque style, so lavish and emotive, sought to move the heart, just as Protestant preachers sought to move the intellect. The baroque constituted a powerful response to the Protestant message that religion is ultimately a private, psychological matter; instead, religion should move the emotions and inspire devotion to God and the church.

By the 1540s, the Counter-Reformation was well under way. The attempt to reform the church from within combined several elements—some benign, others bellicose. The leaders of this Catholic movement attacked many of the same abuses that Luther targeted, but they avoided a break with the doctrinal and spiritual authority of the pope and the clergy.

At the same time, the Counter-Reformation also turned aggressive and hostile toward Protestants. The church tried to counter the popular appeal of Protestantism by offering dramatic, emotional, and even sentimental piety to the faithful. For individuals who were unmoved by this appeal to sentiment or by the church's more traditional spirituality, and for those who allied themselves with Protestant heresy, the church resorted to sterner measures. The Inquisition expanded its activities, and wherever Catholic jurisdiction prevailed, unrepentant

THE INQUISITION. This image of the Inquisition came from a French Protestant engraver who had been forced to flee France because of his religion. Clearly he saw the practices of the Inquisition as part of a continuous pattern of religious persecution by authorities with far too much power. (© Bettmann/Corbis.)

heretics—Protestants, especially Jews, and even Muslims—were subject to death or imprisonment. Catholics did not hold a monopoly on persecution: wherever Protestantism obtained official status—in England, Scotland, Ireland, and Geneva, for instance—Catholics or religious radicals also faced persecution. Calvin, for example, approved the execution in 1563 of the naturalist and skeptic Michael Servetus, who opposed the doctrine of the Trinity. (In 1600, the Catholic church in Italy burned Giordano Bruno for similar reasons.)

Aside from torture and imprisonment, one of the Catholic church's main tools was censorship. By the 1520s, the impulse to censor and burn dangerous books intensified as the church tried to prevent the rapid spread of Protestant ideas. In the rush to eliminate heretical literature, the church condemned the works of reforming Cath-

olic humanists as well as those of Protestants. The *Index of Prohibited Books* became an institutional part of the church's life. Over the centuries, the works of many leading European thinkers were placed on the *Index,* which was abolished only in 1966.

The Counter-Reformation policies of education, vigorous preaching, church building, and self-reform but also torture, persecution, and censorship all succeeded in bringing thousands of people, Germans and Bohemians in particular, back into the church. Furthermore, the church implemented concrete changes in policy and doctrine. In 1545, the Council of Trent met to reform the church and strengthen it so as to better confront the Protestant challenge. Over the years, the council modified and unified church doctrine; abolished many corrupt practices, such as the selling of indulgences; and vested final authority in the papacy, thereby reasserting its power. The Council of Trent invigorated the church and gave it doctrinal clarity on such matters as the roles of faith and good works in attaining salvation. It made the church into the final arbiter of the Bible and demanded that texts be taken literally wherever possible. Galileo Galilei, the Italian physicist and astronomer, was to experience great difficulties in the next century because a literally read Bible implied that the motion of the earth contradicted Scripture.

After Trent the church sought to offer a clear voice amid the babble of Protestant tongues. All compromise with Protestantism was rejected (not that Protestants were anxious for it). The Reformation had split Western Christendom irrevocably.

THE REFORMATION AND THE MODERN AGE

At first glance, the Reformation would seem to have renewed the medieval stress on other-worldliness and reversed the direction toward a secularized humanism that the Renaissance had taken. Yet a careful analysis shows decisively modern elements in Reformation thought, as well as antiauthoritarian tendencies in its political history. The Reformation shattered the religious unity of Europe, the cornerstone of medieval culture, and further weakened the principal authority in medieval society, the church. The political power of the church waned considerably. To this day, Western Europe reveals both Catholic and Protestant traditions. Although doctrinal rigidity (and, in many places, church attendance) has largely disappeared, the split between the southern Catholic countries and the mostly Protestant north is still visible, if only in various customs and rituals. In Eastern European countries, where the churches, both Catholic and Protestant, emerged as powerful political forces, governments had to be cautious in dealing with them. During the 1980s, German Lutheran and Polish Catholic churches became focal points for anti-Soviet activities. Today, Northern Ireland stands as the sole reminder of the religious tensions that had once plagued the whole of Christian Europe. Even there, however, religious tensions appear to be waning. The challenge has now become to accept the Muslim minorities found in every European city, and to avoid a revival of anti-Semitism.

By strengthening the power of monarchs and magistrates at the expense of religious authority, the Reformation furthered the growth of the modern state. Protestant rulers completely repudiated the pope's claim to temporal power and extended their authority over Protestant churches in their lands. In predominantly Catholic lands, the church reacted to the onslaught of Protestantism by supporting the monarchies, but at the same time it preserved a significant degree of political independence. Protestantism did not create the modern secular state; it did, however, help free the state from subordination to religious authority. Such autonomy is an essential feature of modern and secular political life.

Indirectly, Protestantism contributed to the growth of political liberty: another ideal, though not always a reality, in the modern West. To be sure, neither Luther nor Calvin championed political freedom. Nevertheless, tendencies in the Reformation provided a basis for challenging monarchical authority. During the religious wars, both Protestant and Catholic theorists supported resistance to monarchs whose edicts, they believed, defied God's Law. Moreover, the Protestant view that all believers—laity, clergy, lords, and kings—were masters of their own spiritual destiny eroded hierarchical authority and became compatible with emerging constitutional government.

The Reformation also contributed to the creation of an individualistic ethic. Protestants sought an unmediated relationship with God and interpreted the Bible for themselves. Facing the prospect of salvation or damnation entirely on their own, without the church to provide sacramental aid, and believing that God had chosen them to be saved, Protestants developed inner confidence and assertiveness. This religious individualism was the counterpart of the intellectual individualism of the Renaissance humanists.

The Protestant ethic of the Reformation developed concurrently with a new economic system. Theorists have argued ever since about whether the new individualism of the Protestants brought on the growth of capitalism or whether the capitalistic values of the middle class gave rise to the Protestant ethic. In the middle of the nineteenth century, Karl Marx theorized that Protestantism gave expression to the new capitalistic values of the bourgeois: thrift, hard work, self-reliance, and rationality. Hence, Marx argued, the success of Protestantism can be explained by reference to the emergence of Western capitalism.

In 1904–1905, the German sociologist Max Weber argued that Marx had got it backward—that Protestantism enhanced the work ethic of capitalism, not vice versa.[8] Weber perceived in the Protestant ethic of the Reformation the spirit of a nascent capitalism. He saw the spirit of capitalism embodied in the entrepreneur, the parvenu, the self-made person. Such people strive for business success and bring to their enterprises self-discipline and self-restraint. They make profit not for pleasure but for the sake of more profit. They bring to their enterprises moral virtues of striving, frugality, and honesty. For Weber, Protestants made the best capitalists because predestination made them *worldly ascetics:* Christians forced to find salvation without assistance and through activity in this world. The reformers had condemned the monastery as an unnatural life; their concomitant emphasis on human sinfulness established a psychology of striving that could be channeled only into worldly activity. The characteristics of the modern world—individual expression, economic development, and scientific learning—were to become most visibly present in Western European Protestant cities, such as London, Amsterdam, and Geneva. By 1700, both the Protestant entrepreneur and the Protestant intellectual began to endorse religious toleration, freedom in trade as well as learning, and scientific investigation.

The tension between the Roman church and Protestantism set the former in the direction of opposing modernity. By 1800, the papacy in Rome—but by no means all Catholics—viewed change with deep suspicion and came to believe that churches, whether Protestant or Catholic, had a right to interfere in the political process in order to stem the tide toward irreligion.

❖   ❖   ❖

NOTES

1. *The Freedom of a Christian Man* (1520), in *Martin Luther: Selections from His Writings,* ed. John Dillenberger (New York: Doubleday, 1961), 46.

2. Steven Ozment, ed., *Three Behaim Boys: Growing Up in Early Modern Germany* (New Haven, Conn.: Yale University Press, 1990), 79.

3. Martin Luther, *On the Babylonish Captivity of the Church,* quoted in Eugen Weber, ed., *The Western Tradition,* 2 vols., 4th ed. (Lexington, Mass.: D. C. Heath, 1990), 1:338.

4. Martin Luther, *Luther's Works,* ed. Robert Schultz (Philadelphia: Fortress Press, 1967), 46:50–52.

5. François Wendel, *Calvin* (Paris: Presses Universitaires de France, 1950), 20.

6. Quoted in William J. Bouwsma, *John Calvin: A Sixteenth-Century Portrait* (New York: Oxford University Press, 1988), 104.

7. Ibid., 96.

8. See Max Weber, *Protestant Ethic and the Spirit of Capitalism,* trans. Talcott Parsons (New York: Charles Scribner's Sons, 1958).

SUGGESTED READING

Brown, Silvia, *Women, Gender, and Radical Religion in Early Modern Europe* (2007). A set of essays that show the possibilities opened to women who followed the Radical Reformation.

Cottret, Bernard, *Calvin: A Biography* (2000). A superb French historian shows Calvin as a remote, even shy man. The case of Servetus is well handled.

MacCulloch, D., *Reformation: Europe's House Divided* (2003). An excellent, detailed general survey.

Malcolmson, Christina, *Heart-Work: George Herbert and the Protestant Ethic* (1999). A story about the self-fashioning of a devout Protestant.

John D. Roth and James M. Stayer, eds. *A Companion to Anabaptism and Spiritualism, 1521–1700* (2007). Useful essays that give a closer look at the Anabaptists.

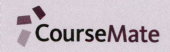

Chapter 15

European Expansion: Economic and Social Transformations

The Blacksmith's Shop, *attributed to Antoine Le Nain or Louis Le Nain (both d. 1648) This is a portrait of a blacksmith at work with his family in his shop and, as such, offers a rare pictorial glimpse into the lives and work of the skilled men and women who played an important role in the early modern European economic expansion, brought on by the increase in population and rising consumer demand for goods. The painter invests the human subjects of this group portrait with a quiet dignity that also effectively dignifies the blacksmith's skill and craft. Gravity and decorum have been achieved by framing the picture in a robustly neoclassical style that was usually reserved for depictions of the higher levels of society, namely the church and the aristocracy.* (Alfredo Dagli Orti/© The Art Archive/Corbis.)

- **European Expansion**
- **The Price Revolution**
- **The Expansion of Agriculture**
- **The Expansion of Trade and Industry**
- **The Growth of Capitalism**
- **The Elite and the People**
- **Economic and Social Transformations**

Focus Questions

1. What were the new forces for expansion operating in early modern Europe?

2. How did the Spanish and Portuguese overseas expansion compare in terms of the motives, the areas of expansion, and the character of the two empires?

3. How did slavery in the future United States compare with slavery in South America and the Caribbean?

4. What was the price revolution, what caused it, and what were its effects on agriculture, trade, and industry?

5. How and why did the traditional relationship between the people and their rulers begin to change in the sixteenth century, and with what result?

6. What accounts for the witch craze and its subsequent decline? Why were most of its victims women?

7. What were the long-term effects of European expansion during this period?

D uring the period from 1450 to 1750, Western Europe entered an era of overseas exploration and economic expansion that transformed society. By 1450, Europe had recovered from the severe contraction of the fourteenth century, produced by plague and marginal agriculture, and was resuming the economic growth that had been the pattern in the twelfth and early thirteenth centuries. This new period of growth, however, was no mere extension of the earlier one but a radical departure from medieval economic forms.

Overseas exploration changed the patterns of economic growth and society. European adventurers discovered a new way to reach the rich trading centers of India by sailing around Africa. They also conquered, colonized, and exploited a new world across the Atlantic. These discoveries and conquests brought about an extraordinary increase in business activity and the supply of money, which stimulated the growth of capitalism. People's values changed in ways that were alien and hostile to the medieval outlook. By 1750, the model Christian in northwestern Europe was no longer the selfless saint but the enterprising businessman. The era of secluded manors and walled towns was drawing to a close. A world economy was emerging in which European economic life depended on the market in Eastern spices, African slaves, and American silver. During this age of exploration and commercial expansion, Europe generated a peculiar dynamism unmatched by any other civilization. A process was initiated that, by 1900, would give Europe mastery over most of the globe and wide-ranging influence over other civilizations.

The economic expansion from 1450 to 1650 or 1700 did not, however, raise the living standards of the masses. The vast majority of the people, 80 to 90 percent, lived on the land, and their main business was the production of primary goods: food, especially **grain production**, and wool. For most of these people, life hovered around the **subsistence level**, sometimes falling below subsistence during times of famine and disease. Whenever the standard of living improved, any surplus resources were soon taken up by the survival of more children and hence more mouths to feed. The beneficiaries of the commercial expansion, those whose income rose, were the rich, especially the *nouveaux riches* (newly rich).

Chronology 15.1 ❖ The Commercial Revolution

1394–1460	Henry the Navigator, prince of Portugal, encourages expansion into Africa for gold and for his anti-Muslim crusade
1430	The Portuguese expand into the Canaries and the Azores
1488	Bartholomeu Dias reaches the tip of Africa
1492	Christopher Columbus reaches the Caribbean island of Hispaniola on his first voyage; the Jews are expelled from Spain; Granada, the last Muslim kingdom in Spain, is conquered, completing the Reconquest
1497	Vasco da Gama sails around the Cape of Good Hope (Africa) to India
1509	The Portuguese defeat the Muslim fleet at Diu in the Indian Ocean
1513	Balboa discovers the Pacific Ocean at the Isthmus of Panama
1519–1521	Hernando Cortés conquers the Aztecs in Mexico
1520–1521	Magellan's soldiers circumnavigate the globe
1531–1533	Francisco Pizarro conquers the Incas in Peru
1545	Silver is discovered by the Spaniards at Potosí, Peru
1552	Silver from the New World flows into Europe via Spain, contributing to a price revolution
1590s	The Dutch develop shipping carriers for grain
1602–1609	Dutch East India Company is founded; Bank of Amsterdam is founded, expanding credit
1651	Navigation Act is passed in England to accomplish the goals of mercantilism
1694	Bank of England is founded

In these respects, then, early modern Europe was comparable to an underdeveloped country today whose society consists of two main economic groups: a small, wealthy elite and a large and growing population that exists on the margin of subsistence and is racked by recurrent hunger and disease. Developments during overseas exploration and economic expansion should be viewed in the context of these social conditions.

EUROPEAN EXPANSION

During the Middle Ages, the frontiers of Europe had expanded, even if only temporarily in some instances. The Crusaders carved out feudal kingdoms in the Near East. Christian knights pushed back the Muslims on the Iberian Peninsula and drove them from Mediterranean islands. Germans expanded in the Baltic region at the expense of non-Christian Balts, Prussians, and Slavs. Genoa and Venice established commercial ports in the Adriatic Sea, the Black Sea, and the eastern Mediterranean. In the fifteenth and sixteenth centuries, Western Europeans embarked on a second and more lasting movement of expansion, which led them onto the uncharted waters of the Atlantic, Indian, and Pacific oceans. Combined forces propelled Europeans outward and enabled them to dominate Asians, Africans, and American Indians.

Forces Behind Expansion

The population of Western Europe increased rapidly between 1450 and 1600, at all levels of society. Among the gentry (hereditary landlords), population growth was translated into land hunger. As the numbers of those in the landed classes exceeded the supply of available land, the sons of the aristocracy looked beyond Europe for the lands and fortunes denied them at home. Nor was it unnatural for them to do so by plunder and conquest; their ancestors had done the same thing for centuries. Exploits undertaken and accomplished in the name of family, church, and king were deemed legitimate, perhaps the most legitimate, ways of earning merit and fame, as well as fortune. So the gentry provided the leadership—Hernando Cortés is an example—for the expeditions to the New World.

Merchants and shippers, as well as the sons of the aristocracy, had reason to look abroad. Trade between Europe, Africa, and the East had gone on for centuries, but always through intermediaries, who increased the costs and decreased the profits on the European end. Gold had been transported by Arab nomads across the Sahara from the riverbeds of West Africa. Spices had been shipped from India and the East Indies by way of Muslim and Venetian merchants. Western European merchants now sought to break those monopolies by going directly to the source: to West Africa for gold, slaves, and pepper, and to India for pepper, spices, and silks. Moreover, the incentive for such commercial enterprise grew because between 1450 and 1600 the wealth of prosperous Europeans increased dramatically. This wealth was translated into new purchasing power and the capacity to invest in foreign ventures that would meet the rising demand for luxury goods among the prosperous.

The centralizing monarchical state also played its part in expansion. Monarchs who, like Ferdinand and Isabella of Spain, had successfully established **royal hegemony** at home sought opportunities to extend their control overseas. The Spanish rulers looked over their shoulders at their neighbors, the Portuguese, and this competition spurred the efforts of both countries in their drive to the East. Later, the Dutch, the English, and the French engaged in a century-long rivalry. From overseas empires came gold, silver, and commerce that paid for ever more expensive royal government at home and for war against rival dynasties abroad.

Finally, religion helped the expansion. The crusading tradition was well established, especially on the Iberian Peninsula, where a five-hundred-year struggle known as the Reconquest had taken place to drive out the Muslims. Cortés, for example, saw himself as following in the footsteps of Paladin Roland, a medieval military hero who had fought to drive back Muslims and pagans. The Portuguese, too, were imbued with the crusading mission. Prince Henry the Navigator hoped that the Portuguese expansion into Africa would serve two purposes: the discovery of gold and the extension of Christianity at the expense of Islam. In this second aim, his imagination was fired by the legend of Prester John, which told of an ancient Christian kingdom of fabled wealth in the heart of Africa. If the Portuguese could reach that land, Prince Henry reckoned, the two kingdoms would join in a crusade against Islam.

Thus, expansion involved a mixture of economic, political, and religious forces and motives. The West had a crusading faith; divided into a handful of competing, warlike states, it expanded by virtue of forces built into its structure and culture. But besides the will to expand, the West also possessed the technology needed for successful expansion. This factor distinguished the West from China and the lands of Islam and helps explain why the West, rather than the Eastern civilizations, launched an age of conquest resulting in global mastery.

Not since the Early Middle Ages had there been such a rapid technological revolution as that which began in the fifteenth century. Europeans had already learned about gunpowder from the Chinese in the late thirteenth century, and by the fifteenth century, its military application had become widespread. The earliest guns were big cannons meant to knock holes in the walled defenses characteristic of the Middle Ages. In the sixteenth and seventeenth centuries, handheld firearms (particularly the musket) and smaller, more mobile field artillery were perfected. Dynastic and religious wars and overseas expansion kept demand for armaments high, and as a result, the armament industry was important to the growth of trade and manufacturing.

Another technological development during the period from 1400 to 1650 was the sailing ship. The vessels of the ancient world had been driven primarily by oars and human energy. Called galleys, they were suitable for the shorter distances, calmer waters, and less variable conditions of the Mediterranean and the Black and Red Seas—but not for the Atlantic and other great oceans, which Europeans began to ply in the early sixteenth century. Moreover, by the fifteenth century in Western Europe, labor was in short supply, making it difficult to recruit or condemn men to the galleys. For these reasons, the Portuguese, the Dutch, and the English abandoned the galley in favor of the sailing ship.

The sail and the gun were crucially important in allowing Europeans to overcome non-Europeans and penetrate and exploit their worlds. Western Europeans combined these devices in the form of the gunned ship. Not only was the sailing vessel more maneuverable and faster in the open seas than the galley, but the addition of guns gave it another tactical advantage over its rivals. The galleys of the Arabs in the Indian Ocean and the junks of the Chinese were not armed with guns below deck for firing at a distance to cripple or sink the enemy. In battle, they relied instead on the ancient tactic of coming up alongside the enemy vessel, shearing off its oars, and boarding to fight on deck.

The gunned ship gave the West naval superiority from the beginning. The Portuguese, for example, made short work of the Muslim fleet sent to drive them out of the Indian Ocean in 1509. That victory at Diu, off the western coast of India, indicated that the West not only had found an all-water route to the East but also was there to stay. Material and religious motives led Europeans to explore and conquer; superior technology ensured the success of their enterprises.

The Portuguese Empire

Several reasons account for Portugal's overseas success. Portugal's long Atlantic coastline ensured that its people would look to the sea—initially for fishing and trade and then for exploration. A sunny climate also spurred seafaring and commercial expansion. Portugal was northern Europe's closest supplier of subtropical products: olive oil, cork, wine, and fruit. The feudal nobility, typically antagonistic to trade and industry, was not as powerful in Portugal as elsewhere in Europe. Although feudal warriors had carved

Portugal out of Moorish Iberia in the twelfth century, their descendants were blocked from further interior expansion by the presence of the strong Christian kingdom of Castile in the east. The only other outlet for expansion was the sea.

Royal policy also favored expansion. The central government promoted trading interests, especially after 1385, when the merchants of Lisbon and the lesser ports helped establish a new dynasty in opposition to the feudal aristocracy. In the first half of the fifteenth century, a younger son of the king, named Prince Henry the Navigator (1394–1460) by English writers, sponsored voyages of exploration and the nautical studies needed to undertake them. In these endeavors, he spent his own fortune and the wealth of the church's crusading order that he headed. Prince Henry sought to revive the anti-Muslim crusade, to which Portugal owed its existence as a Christian state. This connection between the medieval Crusades and the early modern expansion of Europe ran through Portuguese and Spanish history.

As early as the fifteenth century, the Portuguese expanded into islands in the Atlantic Ocean. In 1420, they began to settle Madeira and raise food there, and in the 1430s they pushed into the Canaries and the Azores in search of new farmland and slaves for their colonies. In the middle decades of the century, they moved down the West African coast to the mouth of the Congo River and beyond, establishing trading posts as they went.

By the last quarter of the century, they had developed a viable imperial economy among the ports of West Africa, their Atlantic islands, and Western Europe—an economy based on sugar, black slaves, and gold. Africans panned the gold in the riverbeds of central and western Africa, and the Portuguese purchased it at its source. They paid in cloth and slaves at a profit of at least 500 percent. Then the Portuguese transported the gold to Europe, where they sold it for even more profit. Slaves figured not only in the purchase of gold but also in the production of sugar. On their Atlantic islands, the Portuguese grew sugar cane and little else by the end of the century, as a cash crop for European consumption, and slaves were imported from West Africa to do the work. There was also a lively trade in slaves to Portugal itself and elsewhere in southern Europe.

THE PORTUGUESE IN INDIA. A charming watercolor by a Portuguese traveler in India, this painting mixes what to Western eyes was strange and foreign with the more familiar. The elephant, the clothes, and the elaborate parasols held high by turbaned servants may have seemed exotic, but the hunt, the horse, and the hunting dogs had their counterparts in Western European landed society. (Biblioteca Casanatense, Rome/Photo: Humberto Nicoletti Serra.)

The Portuguese did not stop in western Africa. By 1488, Bartholomeu Dias had reached the southern tip of the African continent; a decade later, Vasco da Gama sailed around the Cape of Good Hope and across the Indian Ocean to India. By discovering an all-water route to the East, Portugal broke the **commercial monopoly** on Eastern goods that Genoa and Venice had enjoyed.

In search of spices, the Portuguese went directly to the source, to India and the East Indies. As they had done along the African coast, they established fortified trading posts—most notably at Goa, on the western coast of India (Malabar) and at Malacca (now Singapore), on the Malay Peninsula.

Demand for spices was insatiable. Pepper and other spices are relatively unimportant items in the modern diet, but in the era before refrigeration, fresh meat was available only at slaughtering time, customarily twice a year. The rest of the year the only meat available, for those who could afford it at all, was dried, stringy, and tough; spices made meat and other foods palatable.

The infusion of Italian, particularly Genoese, investment and talent contributed to Portuguese expansion. As Genoese trade with the Near East, especially the Black Sea, shrank due to the expansion of the Ottoman Empire, Genoese merchants shifted more and more of their capital and mercantile activities from the eastern to the western Mediterranean and the Atlantic—that is, to Spain and Portugal and their possessions overseas. This shift is evident in the life of Christopher Columbus

PORTRAIT OF A MAN, SAID TO BE CHRISTOPHER COLUMBUS (1519), BY SEBASTIANO DEL PIOMBO. Christopher Columbus was a Genoese navigator and explorer whose transatlantic voyages opened the way for European conquest and colonization of the Americas. (Christopher Columbus (oil on panel), Piombo, Sebastiano del (S. Luciani) (c.1485–1547)/Metropolitan Museum of Art, New York, USA/Peter Newark Pictures/The Bridgeman Art Library International.)

(1451–1506), a Genoese sailor, who worked in Portugal before finally winning acceptance at the court of Castile in Spain for his scheme to find a westward route to the spices of the East.

The Spanish Empire

Spain stumbled onto its overseas empire, which nonetheless proved to be the biggest and richest of any until the eighteenth century. Columbus won the support of Isabella, queen of Castile. But on his first voyage (1492), he landed on a large Caribbean island, which he named Española (Little Spain), or Hispaniola. To the end of his life, even after subsequent voyages, Columbus believed that the West Indies were part of the East. Two forthcoming events would reveal that Columbus

had discovered not a new route to the East but new continents: Vasco Nuñez de Balboa's discovery of the Pacific Ocean at the Isthmus of Panama in 1513 and Ferdinand Magellan's circumnavigation of the globe (1520–1521) through the strait at the tip of South America that now bears his name.

The Spanish and the Portuguese were not the first outsiders to explore and settle in the New World. Archaeological evidence indicates that there may have been several voyages undertaken from China, Ireland, Wales, and West Africa in the previous millennium. The Viking expeditions led by Leif Erikson and his brothers in the first decade of the eleventh century are well documented. The Vikings, originally from Scandinavia, sailed in small boats from Greenland and settled near the mouth of the St. Lawrence River in what is now southeastern Canada. But these earlier expeditions all ended in failure due to war with native Indians, hunger, and disease. The factors that gave the Spanish and the Portuguese permanent success in the New World stand out in sharp relief against these earlier failures—guns, sails, horses, crusading and missionary zeal, and royal power capable of mobilizing enough men and resources for the long haul.

The Spanish found no spices in the New World, but they were more than compensated by the abundant land and the large quantities of precious metals. Stories of the existence of larger quantities of gold and silver to the west lured the Spaniards from their initial settlements in the Caribbean to Mexico. In 1519, Hernando Cortés landed on the Mexican coast with a small army. During two years of campaigning, he managed to defeat the native rulers, the Aztecs, and to conquer Mexico for the Spanish crown. A decade later, Francisco Pizarro achieved a similar victory over the mountain empire of the Incas in Peru. Both Cortés and Pizarro exploited the

Map 15.1 **PORTUGUESE AND SPANISH EMPIRE ▶ BUILDING, 1415–1635** Not only did Spain and Portugal carve out empires in different parts of the world, but, as the map shows, they also built two different kinds of empires. Portugal established small colonies along the seacoast. Spain went in for conquering and governing large territories and large populations in the New World.

(Copyright © 2013 Cengage Learning.)

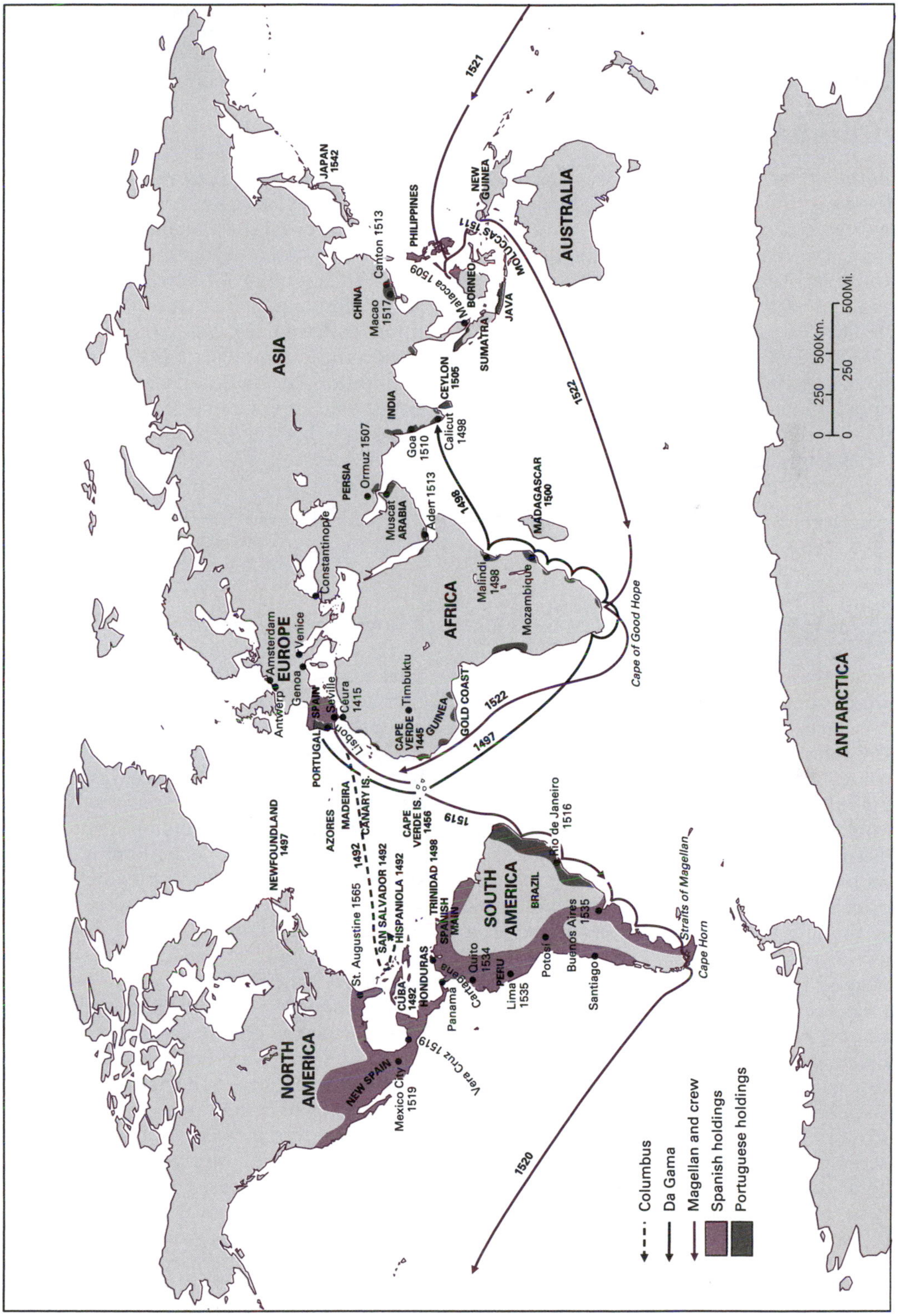

1521

JAPAN 1542

Canton 1513

CHINA

Macao 1517

PHILIPPINES

MOLUCCAS 1511

NEW GUINEA

AUSTRALIA

Borneo

Malacca 1509

JAVA

SUMATRA

CEYLON 1505

1522

INDIA

Ormuz 1507

Goa 1510

Calicut 1498

1498

PERSIA

Muscat

Aden 1513

ARABIA

Constantinople

ASIA

MADAGASCAR 1500

Malindi 1498

Mozambique

AFRICA

Cape of Good Hope

EUROPE

Amsterdam • Venice

Antwerp • Genoa

SPAIN

Seville

Ceuta 1415

Timbuktu

CAPE VERDE 1445

GUINEA

GOLD COAST

1522

PORTUGAL

Lisbon

1497

1519

AZORES

MADEIRA

CANARY IS.

CAPE VERDE IS. 1456

CAPE VERDE 1498

NEWFOUNDLAND 1497

St. Augustine 1565

SAN SALVADOR 1492

CUBA 1492

HISPANIOLA 1492

TRINIDAD 1498

SPANISH MAIN

HONDURAS

Cartagena

NORTH AMERICA

NEW SPAIN

Mexico City 1519

Vera Cruz 1519

Panama

Quito 1534

PERU

Lima 1535

Potosí

SOUTH AMERICA

BRAZIL

Rio de Janeiro 1516

Buenos Aires 1535

Santiago

Straits of Magellan

Cape Horn

1520

ANTARCTICA

500 Mi.

500 Km.

250

250

0

0

--- Columbus

→ Da Gama

→ Magellan and crew

Spanish holdings

Portuguese holdings

Bartolomé de las Casas

Bartolomé de las Casas (1474–1566), a Dominican friar excited in his youth by Columbus's discoveries, set out for the New World in 1502 and spent the rest of his life as a missionary to the American Indians. Not only did he preach to them and convert them to Christianity, but, appalled by the cruelty of the Spanish conquest, he also joined others in his order in defending the Indians against their oppressors.

Some argued that the brutal treatment of the Indians, the confiscation of their lands, and even their enslavement were justified because the Indians fit Aristotle's definition of "natural slaves":

people whose behavior and customs, such as human sacrifice, betrayed them as being less than rational and therefore subhuman. In book after book, de las Casas attacked such views. He pointed out that the Indians often lived up to a higher standard of civilized life than supposedly civilized European Christians—for example, in sexual conduct, choice of rulers, military discipline, child-rearing, and (something especially important to a monk) giving relief to the poor. In addition, de las Casas was impressed by the Incas' feats of engineering, especially the highways they had built through the Andes, which excelled anything he had seen that the Romans had done.

hostility that the subject tribes of Mexico and Peru felt toward their Aztec and Incan overlords, a strategy that accounts to some extent for the Spaniards' success. But the most important reason was probably the spread of infectious diseases among the native population, including the armies—diseases carried by the Europeans to which the Indians apparently had little or no resistance and that so weakened them that the Spanish forces could win despite being vastly outnumbered. This is one of the signal examples in world history where a nonhuman biological agency brought about a decisive turning point in the flow of events.

For good reasons, the Mexican and Peruvian conquests became the centers of the Spanish overseas empire. First, there were the gold hoards accumulated over the centuries by the rulers of these lands for religious and ceremonial purposes. Once these supplies were exhausted, the Spanish discovered silver at Potosí in Upper Peru in 1545 and at Zacatecas in Mexico a few years later. From the middle of the century, the annual treasure fleets sailing to Spain became the financial bedrock of Philip II's war against the Muslim Turks and the Protestant Dutch and English.

Not only gold and silver lured the Spanish to the New World. The crusading tradition also acted as a spur. Cortés, Pizarro, and many of their followers were *hidalgos*—lesser gentry whose status depended on the possession of landed estates and whose training and experience taught that holy war was a legitimate avenue to wealth and power. Their fathers had conquered Granada, the last Muslim kingdom in Spain, in 1492; they had expelled the Jews the same year and had carried the Christian crusade across to North Africa. The conquest and conversion of the peoples of the New World was an extension of the crusading spirit that marked the five previous centuries of Spanish history. The rewards were the propagation of the true faith, service to the crown, land grants, and control over the inhabitants, who would work the fields.

The conquerors initially obtained two kinds of grants from the crown: *encomiendas* and *estancias*. The latter were land grants, either of land formerly belonging to the native priestly and noble castes or of land in remoter and less fertile regions. Encomiendas were royal grants of authority over the natives. Those who received such authority, the *encomenderos*, promised to give protection and instruction in the Christian religion to their charges. In return, they gained the power to extract labor and tribute from the peasant masses, who were worked beyond their capacity.

The royal grants of encomiendas during the first generation of Spanish settlement were

This radical champion of Indian rights also dreamed of building a New Jerusalem in the New World. He called for the creation of a new kind of empire, in which Philip II would still be emperor but most of the Spanish colonists would be forced to leave. The missionaries would stay on, protected by a small Spanish army, to guide the Indians toward realizing this millennial vision. For his contemporaries, the most extreme aspect of the view de las Casas propounded was that the Indians should regain possession of all the land the Spanish had taken, including rights to all the gold and silver that lay beneath.

partially responsible for the decimation of the native peoples in the New World within a century of European occupation. Between 1500 and 1600, the number of natives shrank from about twenty million to perhaps no more than two million. The major cause of this catastrophe, however, was not forced labor but the diseases introduced from Europe—dysentery, malaria, hookworm, and smallpox—against which the natives had little or no natural resistance. But syphilis was probably transmitted the other way, that is, from the New World to the Old. Beginning in the 1540s, the position of the natives gradually improved as the crown withdrew grants that gave authority over the natives and took increasing responsibility for controlling the Indians.

Power and wealth became concentrated in fewer and fewer hands. As the Spanish landholders lost authority over the native population to royal officials and their associates, the latter gained substantially in power and privilege. As recurrent depressions ruined smaller landowners, they were forced to sell out to their bigger neighbors. On their conversion to Christianity, the Indians were persuaded to give more and more land to the church. Thus, Spanish America became permanently divided between the privileged elite and the impoverished masses.

Black Slavery and the Slave Trade

One group suffered even more than the Indians: the black slaves originally brought over from West Africa. During the long period of their dominance in North Africa and the Middle East (from the seventh to the nineteenth century), the Muslim states relied on slave labor and slave soldiers from black Africa south of the Sahara. Blacks were captured and transported across the Sahara to be sold in the slave markets of North Africa. It was common for such slaves, especially soldiers, to be eventually freed by their Muslim masters, a practice sanctioned by the Koran. Thus it was necessary to replenish the stock of slaves from south of the Sahara in every generation. At its height in the eighteenth century, this trans-Saharan trade may have risen to some ten thousand slaves a year.

But this annual traffic was eventually dwarfed by the slave trade between West Africa and the European colonies in the New World, which began in earnest in the early sixteenth century. The Portuguese dominated the Atlantic slave trade for a century and a half after 1450; during that time, it never rose beyond some five thousand black slaves a year. The Dutch edged out the Portuguese in the seventeenth century and competed with the French and the British for dominance. In the eighteenth century, the British gained control of at least 50 percent of the trade. As Roland Oliver notes in *The African Experience*, "By the end of the seventeenth century, stimulated by the growth of plantation agriculture in Brazil and the West Indies, Atlantic shipments had increased to about thirty thousand a year, and by the end of the eighteenth century they were nearly eighty thousand."[1]

Captured in raids by black African slavers, the victims were herded into specially built prisons on the West African coast. Those accepted for sale were "marked on the breast with a red-hot iron, imprinting the mark of the French, English or Dutch companies so that each nation may distinguish their own property."[2] Across the centuries, some 11 or 12 million blacks in all were exported to the New World. Of these, some 600,000 ended up in the thirteen colonies of British North America, forming the basis of the slave population of the new United States at the end of the American Revolution.

The conditions of the voyage from Africa, the so-called middle passage, were brutal. Crammed into the holds of ships, some 13 to 30 percent

Seventeenth-Century Slave Traders: Buying and Transporting Africans

Dealing in slaves was a profitable business that attracted numerous entrepreneurs. The following account was written by a slave trader in the seventeenth century.

As the slaves came down to Fida from the inland country, they are put into a booth, or prison, built for that purpose, near the beach, all of them together; and when the Europeans are to receive them, they are brought out into a large plain, where the surgeons examine every part of every one of them, to the smallest member, men and women being all stark naked. Such as are allowed good and sound, are set on the one side, and the others by themselves; which slaves so rejected are called Mackrons, being above thirty five years of age, or defective in their limbs, eyes or teeth; or grown grey, or that have venereal disease, or any other imperfection. These being so set aside, each of the others, which have passed as good, is marked on the breast, with a red-hot iron, imprinting the mark of the French, English, or Dutch companies, that so each nation may distinguish their own, and to prevent their being chang'd by the natives for worse, as they are apt enough to do. In this particular, care is taken that the women, as tenderest, be not burnt too hard.

The branded slaves, after this, are returned to their former booth, where the factor [agent] is to subsist them at his own charge, which amounts to about two-pence a day for each of them, with bread and water, which is all their allowance. There they continue sometimes ten or fifteen days, till the sea is still enough to send them aboard; . . . and when it is so, the slaves are carried off by parcels, in bar-canoes, and put aboard the ships in the road. Before they enter the canoes, or come out of the booth, their former Black masters strip them of every rag they have, without distinction of men or women. . . .

The Blacks of Fida are so expeditious at this trade of slaves that they can deliver a thousand every month. . . . If there happens to be no stock of slaves at Fida, the factor must trust the Blacks with his goods, to the value of a hundred and fifty, or two hundred slaves; which goods they carry up into the inland, to buy slaves, at all the markets, for above two hundred leagues up the country, where they are kept like cattle [are kept] in Europe; the slaves sold there being generally prisoners of war, taken from their enemies, like other booty, and perhaps some few sold by their own countrymen, in extreme want, or upon a famine; so also some as a punishment of heinous crimes: tho' many Europeans believe their parents sell their own children, men their wives and relations, which, if it ever happens, is so seldom, that it cannot justly be charged upon a whole nation, as a custom and common practice.

Questions for Analysis

1. How, why, and by whom are the slaves branded?
2. Who are those called "Black masters," and what role do they play in the slave trade?
3. Where do the slaves come from, and how do they initially come to be enslaved?

Elizabeth Donnan, ed., *Documents Illustrative of the Slave Trade* (Washington, D.C.: Carnegie Institution of Washington, 1935), 1:293–294.

of blacks died on board. On arrival in the New World, slaves were greased with palm oil to improve their appearance and paraded naked into the auction hall for the benefit of prospective buyers, who paid top prices for "the strongest, youthfullest, and most beautiful."[3] The standard workload for slaves everywhere was ten or eleven hours a day, six days a week. But some distinction must be made between slavery in the American South and elsewhere in the New World.

In Brazil and the West Indies, slaves were worked to exhaustion and death and then replaced. Slaves formed a large majority there and were concentrated on very large plantations. Revolts were frequent but were always crushed and savagely punished. In the American South, by contrast, slaves were a minority dispersed over relatively small holdings; large plantations were few. As a result, revolts and deadly epidemics were rare. After 1808, when the United States abolished the external slave trade, slaveholders could not ruthlessly exploit their slaves if they were to meet the growing need for workers caused by the increasing industrial demand for raw cotton. By 1830, the slave population of the southern states rose through natural increase to more than two million, which represented more than one-third of all slaves in the New World.

Why had the Atlantic slave trade grown to such a large volume by the eighteenth century? On the American side, economics provide the answer. In the New World, fields and mines had to be worked, but since the native population had been decimated, an enormous labor shortage existed. Black slaves were imported to satisfy the demand. Not only were they plentiful and cheap to maintain, but they were also skilled in farming and mining and could withstand tropical heat, insects, and disease, including the infections brought over from Europe to which the Indians had succumbed.

On the African side, how did suppliers continue to meet this large and growing New World demand? First, the demand was greater for males than for females, and males constituted two-thirds of those transported. Since all African peoples were polygynous (men might take more than one wife), the women and girls left behind in Africa continued to reproduce, so the population did not shrink, and there was always a supply of blacks to be captured and enslaved. Second, by 1700, a new factor was introduced, one that proved decisive: guns, imported from Europe, were now commonly traded for slaves. With the guns, the West African rulers built armies for capturing other peoples to sell to the Europeans, while protecting themselves from being enslaved by rival forces. The desire for profit led to the need for more captives to sell for still more firearms to take still more slaves. All the ingredients were now in place for a deadly arms race, and the result was "a spiral of mounting violence," which could not be broken.[4] But from the point of view of the Atlantic trade, this grisly scenario guaranteed a steady supply of human cargo to satisfy a steeply rising New World demand.

THE PRICE REVOLUTION

Linked to overseas expansion was another phenomenon: unprecedented inflation during the sixteenth century, known as the *price revolution*. Evidence is insufficient on the general rise in prices. Cereal prices, however, multiplied by eight times or more in certain regions during the sixteenth century and continued to rise, though more slowly, during the first half of the next century. After 1650, prices leveled off or fell in most places. This pattern continued throughout the eighteenth century in England and off and on in France up to the Revolution. Economic historians have generally assumed that the prices of goods other than cereals increased by half as much as grain prices. Because people at that time did not understand why prices rose so rapidly, inflation was not subject to control.

Like colonization, the price revolution played an enormous role in the commercial revolution and may have resulted partially from the silver mining conducted in New Spain. The main cause of the price revolution, however, was population growth during the late fifteenth and sixteenth centuries.

The population of Europe almost doubled between 1460 and 1620; then it leveled off and decreased in some places. The patterns of population growth and of cereal prices thus correspond in the sixteenth and seventeenth centuries. Before the middle of the seventeenth century, the number of mouths to feed outran the capacity of agriculture to supply basic foodstuffs, causing the vast majority of people to live close to subsistence. Until food production could catch up with the increasing population, prices, especially those of the staple food, bread, would continue to rise.

Why population grew so rapidly in the fifteenth and sixteenth centuries is not known, but we do know the reasons for the population decline in

A NEW WORLD SUGAR REFINERY, BRAZIL. Sugar was the main and most profitable crop of plantation agriculture until the late eighteenth century, when cotton took the lead, at least in some places. On the plantation, the cane was not only grown but also processed into a variety of products—sugar, molasses, and rum—that were exported to Europe to meet a rising demand. Black slaves did the work under efficient but brutal conditions and often at great profit to the plantation owners. (The Art Archive/Biblioteca Nacional Madrid/Gianni Dagli Orti.)

the seventeenth century. By then, the population had so outgrown the food supply that scarcity began to take its toll. Malnourishment, starvation, and disease pushed the death rate higher than the birth rate. With time, of course, prices decreased as population and hence demand declined in the 1600s.

The other principal cause of the price revolution was probably the flow of silver into Europe from the New World by way of Spain beginning in 1552. But as a cause, the influx of silver lies on shakier ground than the inflationary effects of an expanding population. Increases in production and consumption following the growth in population would, to some degree, have necessitated an increase in the money supply to accommodate the greater number of commercial transactions. At some point, it is assumed, the influx of silver exceeded the necessary expansion of the money supply and itself began contributing to the inflation. The most that can be said now is that the price revolution was caused by *too many people with too much money chasing too few goods*. The effects of the price revolution were momentous.

THE EXPANSION OF AGRICULTURE

The price revolution had its greatest effect on the land. Rising roughly twice as much as the prices of other goods, food prices spurred ambitious farmers to take advantage of the situation and produce for the expanding market. The opportunity for profit drove some farmers to work harder and manage their land better, and the impact of the price revolution came from that incentive. The most important changes occurred in England and the Netherlands.

The Old Pattern of Farming

All over Europe, landlords held their properties in the form of manors. A particular type of rural society and economy evolved on these manors in the Late Middle Ages. By the fifteenth century, much manor land was held by peasant-tenants according to the terms of a tenure known in England as *copyhold*. The tenants had certain hereditary rights to the land in return for the performance of certain services and the payment of certain fees to the landlord. Principal among these rights was the use of the commons—a tract of land consisting of pasture, woods, and a pond—by all tenants of a manor. For the copyholder, access to the commons often made the difference between subsistence and real want because the land tilled on the manor might not produce enough to feed a family.

Arable land was worked according to ancient custom. The land was divided into strips, and each peasant of the manor was assigned a certain number of strips. This whole pattern of peasant tillage and rights in the commons was known as the *open-field system*. After changing little for centuries, it was met head-on by incentives generated by the price revolution.

Enclosure

The open-field system, geared to providing subsistence for local villages, prevented large-scale farming for distant markets. The commons could not be diverted to the production of crops for sale, and the division of arable land into strips made it difficult to engage in profitable commercial agriculture. In the sixteenth century, English landlords aggressively pursued the possibilities for profit resulting from the inflation of farm prices and launched a two-pronged attack against the open-field system in an effort to transform their holdings into market-oriented, commercial ventures. First, they resorted to *enclosure*, fencing off the commons and thereby depriving their tenant peasantry of the use of the common land. Restriction of rights to the commons deprived tenants of critically needed produce. Then landlords changed the conditions of tenure from copyhold to leasehold. Copyhold was heritable and fixed; leasehold was not. When a lease came up for renewal, the landlord could raise the rent beyond the tenant's capacity to pay. Both acts of the landlord forced peasants off the manor or into the landlord's employ as farm laborers. Rural poverty and violence increased because of the mass evictions of tenant farmers.

With tenants gone, fields could be incorporated into larger, more productive units. Subsistence farming gave way to commercial agriculture: the growing of a surplus for the marketplace. Landlords would either hire laborers to work recently enclosed fields or rent these fields to prosperous farmers in the neighborhood. Either way, landlords stood to gain. They could hire labor at bargain prices because of the swelling population and the large supply of peasants forced off the land by enclosure. If landlords chose to rent out their fields, they also profited. Prosperous farmers, who themselves grew for the market, could afford to pay higher rents than the previous tenants, the subsistence farmers, and they were willing to pay more because farm prices tended to rise even faster than rents.

The existence of prosperous farmers, known collectively as the *yeomanry*, was crucial to the commercialization of farming in England. Yeomen were men who might not own much land but

THE HARVESTERS, 1565, BY PIETER BRUEGHEL THE ELDER (D. 1569). This painting shows crops being harvested by peasants in the Netherlands. Agriculture was the basis of all economic life in early modern Europe, and the Netherlands was one of the places where advanced farming techniques were applied to maximizing food production to feed a growing population. (Image copyright © The Metropolitan Museum of Art/Art Resource, N.Y.)

rented enough to produce a marketable surplus, sometimes a substantial one. They emerged as a discernible rural group in the High Middle Ages and were a product of the unique English inheritance custom of *primogeniture*, observed by peasantry and gentry alike.

Because of the rights of primogeniture, the eldest son inherited his parents' entire estate, and younger sons had to fend for themselves. Thus, land remained undivided, and heirs often had enough land to produce a surplus for sale. Many a gentleman landowner enclosed his fields, not to work them himself, but to rent them to neighboring yeomen at rates allowing him to keep abreast of spiraling prices. Yeomen were better suited to work the land than the landlord, depending on it as they did for their livelihood.

One other process growing out of the price revolution promoted enclosure and the commercialization of farming. Rising prices forced less businesslike landlords, who did not take advantage of the profits to be made from farming, to sell property in order to meet current expenses. The conditions of the price revolution thus tended to put an increasing amount of land into more productive hands.

Convertible Husbandry

In the Netherlands, the effect of the price revolution on agriculture was as dramatic and important as in England. By the seventeenth century, the Dutch population had soared, and the majority of people had moved to the cities. As a result, a situation affecting all Europe—the problem of land use—became vitally important, especially as there was so little land to start with. The Dutch continued their efforts to reclaim land from the sea, as they had begun to do in the Middle Ages. More significant, however, was their development, in the fifteenth and sixteenth centuries, of a new kind of farming known as *convertible husbandry*. This farming system employed a series of innovations that replaced the old three-field system of crop rotation, which had left one-third of the land unplanted at any given time. The new techniques allowed farmers to cultivate all their land every year and diversified agriculture.

Convertible husbandry alternated the planting of soil-depleting cereals with the planting of soil-restoring legumes and grazing. For a couple of years, a field would be planted in cereals; in the third year, peas or beans would be sown to return essential nitrogen to the soil; then for the next four or five years, the field would become pasture for grazing animals, whose manure would further restore the soil for replanting cereals and restarting the cycle. Land thus returned to grain produced much more than land used in the three-field system. This method of increasing **productivity**, when exported from the Netherlands and applied in England and France between 1650 and 1750, played an essential role in the complicated process by which these countries eventually became industrialized, for industrialization requires agriculture productive enough to feed large, non-farming urban populations.

THE EXPANSION OF TRADE AND INDUSTRY

The conditions of the price revolution also caused trade and industry to expand. Population growth, which exceeded the capacity of local food supplies, stimulated commerce in basic foodstuffs—for example, the Baltic trade with Western Europe. Equally important as a stimulus to trade and industry was the growing income of landlords, merchants, and, in some instances, peasants. This income created a rising demand for consumer goods, which helps explain several activities already mentioned. For example, the Portuguese spice trade with the East and the sugar industry in the Portuguese islands developed because prosperous people wanted such products. Higher income also created a demand for farm products other than cereals—meat, cheese, fruit, wine, and vegetables—and for fine cloth. The resulting land use reduced the area available for grain production and contributed to the rise in bread prices, which meant even larger profits.

Another factor propelling commercial and industrial expansion was the growth of the state. With increasing amounts of tax revenue to spend, the expanding monarchies of the sixteenth and seventeenth centuries bought more and more supplies—ships, weapons, uniforms, paper—and so spurred economic development.

The Domestic System

Along with commercial and industrial expansion came a change in the nature of the productive enterprise. Just as the price revolution produced, in the enclosure movement, a reorganization of agriculture and agrarian society, it similarly affected trade and manufacturing. The reorganization there took place especially in the faster-growing industries—woolen and linen textiles—where an increasingly large mass market outpaced supply and thus made prices rise. This basic condition of the price revolution operated, just as it did in food production, to produce expansion. In the textile industries, increasing demand promoted specialization. For example, eastern and southwestern England made woolens, and northwestern France and the Netherlands produced linen.

Markets tended to shift from local to regional or even to international, a condition that gave rise to the merchant-capitalist. Merchant-capitalists' operations, unlike those of local producers, extended across local and national boundaries. Such mobility allowed these capitalists to buy or produce goods where costs were lowest and to sell where prices and volume were highest. Because of the size and range of a business, an individual capitalist could control the traditional local producers, who increasingly depended on the capitalist for the widespread marketing of their expanded output.

This procedure, which was well developed by the seventeenth century, gave rise to what is known as the domestic system of cottage industry. The manufacture of woolen textiles is a good example of how the system worked. A merchant-capitalist would buy raw wool from English landlords, who had enclosed the common grazing land on their manors to take advantage of the rising price of wool. The merchant's agents collected the wool and took it (put it out) to nearby villages for spinning, dyeing, and weaving. The work was done in the cottages of peasants, many of whom had been evicted from the surrounding manors as a result of enclosure and therefore had to take whatever work they could get at whatever wages they were offered. When the wool was processed into cloth, it was picked up and shipped to market.

The domestic system represents an important step in the evolution of capitalism. It was not industrial capitalism, because there were no factories and the work was done by hand rather than by power machinery; nevertheless, the domestic system significantly broke with the medieval guild system. The new merchant-capitalists saw to it that the work was performed in the countryside, rather than in the cities and towns, to avoid guild restrictions on output, quality, pay, and working conditions. The medieval distinction between a master and an apprentice who would someday replace the master in the guild framework gave way to the distinction between the merchant-owner (the person who provided the capital) and the worker (the person who provided the labor in return for wages and would probably never be an owner).

Enclosure also served to capitalize industry. Mass evictions lowered the wages of cottage workers because labor was so plentiful. This condition provided an additional incentive for merchant-capitalists to invest in cottage industry. The changes in farming, however, were much more important to the economic development of Europe than the changes in industry because agriculture represented a much larger share of total wealth.

Innovations in Business

A cluster of other innovations in business life, some of them having roots in the Middle Ages, accompanied the emergence of the merchant-capitalist and the domestic system. Banking operations grew more sophisticated. It became possible for depositors to pay their debts by issuing written orders to their banks to make transfers to their creditors' accounts—the origins of the modern check. Accounting methods also improved. The widespread use of double-entry bookkeeping made errors immediately evident and gave a clear picture of the financial position of a commercial enterprise. Although known in the ancient world, double-entry bookkeeping was not widely practiced in the West until the fourteenth century. In this and other business practices, the lands of southern Europe, especially Italy, were the forerunners; their accounting techniques spread to the rest of Europe in the sixteenth century.

Business practices related to shipping also developed in the fourteenth century. A system of **maritime** insurance, without which investors would have been highly reluctant to risk their money on expensive vessels, evolved in Florence. By 1400, maritime insurance had become a regular item of the shipping business, and it was destined to play a major role in the opening of Atlantic trade. At least equally important to overseas expansion were business enterprises known as joint-stock companies, which allowed small investors to buy shares in a large venture. These companies made possible the accumulation of the huge amounts of capital needed for large-scale operations such as the building and deployment of merchant fleets—amounts quite beyond the resources of one person.

Patterns of Commercial Development

Responses to the price revolution in trade and industry hinged on social and political conditions and thus differed in various parts of Europe. In the United Provinces (the Netherlands) and England, there were far fewer strictures on trade and industry than in France and Spain, as will be explained later in this chapter. So in the sixteenth and seventeenth centuries, England and the United

Provinces were better placed than France and Spain to take advantage of conditions favorable for business expansion. In the United Provinces, favorable conditions resulted from the weakness of Dutch feudal culture and values in comparison with commercial ones, the small land area, and a far larger percentage of urban population than elsewhere in Western Europe.

England's advantage derived from another source: not the weakness of the landed gentry but its habits. Primogeniture operated among the owners of large estates just as it did among the yeomanry, with much the same effect. Younger sons were forced to make their fortunes elsewhere. Those who did so by going into business would often benefit from an infusion of venture capital that came from their elder brothers' landed estates. And, of course, capital was forthcoming from such quarters because of the profitable nature of English farming. In a reverse process, those who made fortunes in trade would typically invest money in land and rise gradually into landed society. The skills that had brought wealth in commerce would then be applied to new estates, usually with equal success.

England and the Netherlands. In both England and the United Provinces, the favorable conditions led to large-scale commercial expansion. In the 1590s, the Dutch devised a new ship, the *fluit*, or flyboat, to handle bulky grain shipments at the lowest possible cost. This innovation permitted them to capture the Baltic trade, which became the main source of their phenomenal commercial expansion between 1560 and 1660. Equally dramatic was their commercial penetration of the East. Profits from the European carrying trade built ships that allowed the Dutch first to challenge and then to displace the Portuguese in the spice trade with the East Indies during the early seventeenth century. The Dutch chartered the United East India Company in 1602 and established trading posts in the islands—the beginnings of the Dutch empire, which lasted until World War II.

The English traded throughout Europe in the sixteenth and seventeenth centuries, especially with Spain and the Netherlands. The staples of this trade were raw wool and woolens, but increasingly the trade included such items as ships and guns. The seventeenth century saw the foundation of a British colonial empire along the Atlantic seaboard in North America, from Maine to the Carolinas, and in the West Indies, where the English managed to dislodge the Spanish in some places.

In seventeenth-century England, the central government increasingly took the side of the capitalist producer. At the beginning of the century, the king had imposed feudal fees on landed property, acted against enclosures, and granted **monopolies** in trade and manufacture to court favorites, which restricted opportunities for investment. The king also spent revenues on maintaining an unproductive aristocracy. But by the end of the century, because of the revolutionary transfer of power from the king to Parliament, economic policy more closely reflected the interests of big business, whether agricultural or commercial. Landowners no longer paid feudal dues to the king. Enclosure went on unimpeded, and in fact was abetted, by parliamentary enactment.

The Navigation Act, first passed in 1651, allowed all English shippers to carry goods anywhere, replacing the old system that had restricted trade with certain areas to specific traders. The act also required that all goods be carried in English ships, enabling merchants, as Christopher Hill writes, "to buy English and colonial exports cheap and sell them dear abroad, to buy foreign goods cheap and sell them dear in England."[5] English shippers also gained the profits of the carrying trade, one factor leading to the displacement of the Dutch by the English as the leading power in international commerce after 1660.

France and Spain. France benefited from commercial and industrial expansion, but not to the same degree as England. The principal reason for the difference was the aristocratic structure of French society. Family ties and social intercourse between aristocracy and merchants, such as existed in England, were largely absent in France. Consequently, the French aristocracy remained contemptuous of commerce. Also inhibiting economic expansion were the guilds—remnants of the Middle Ages that restricted competition and production. In France, there was relatively less opportunity than in England for merchant-capitalists operating outside the guild structures.

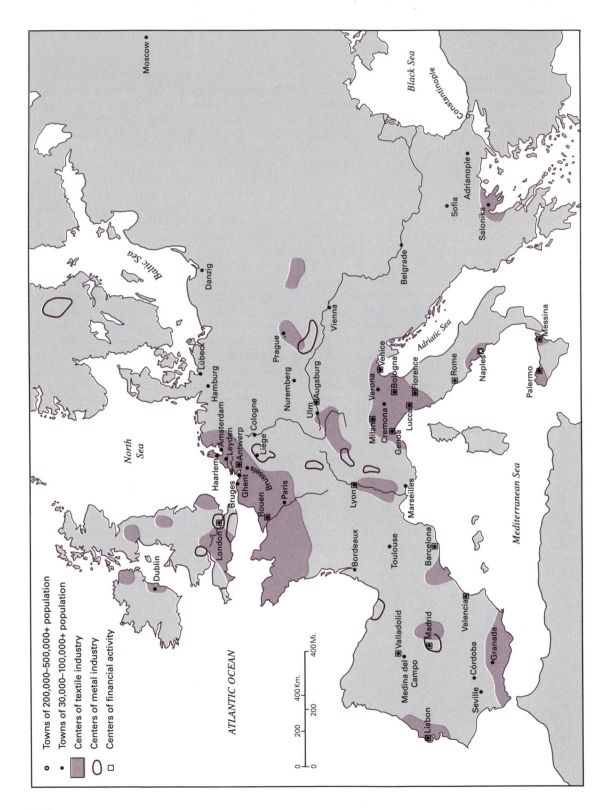

Black Sea

Constantinople

Moscow

Baltic Sea

Danzig

Lübeck

Hamburg

Sofia

Adrianople

Salonika

Belgrade

Vienna

Prague

Nuremberg

Ulm

Augsburg

Adriatic Sea

Verona

Venice

Bologna

Milan

Cremona

Lucca

Florence

Rome

Naples

Genoa

Messina

Palermo

Haarlem

Amsterdam

Leyden

Cologne

Antwerp

Liège

Ghent

Brussels

Bruges

Rouen

Paris

Lyon

Marseilles

London

North Sea

Dublin

Bordeaux

Toulouse

Barcelona

Valencia

Madrid

Valladolid

Medina del Campo

Granada

Córdoba

Seville

Lisbon

Mediterranean Sea

ATLANTIC OCEAN

Towns of 200,000–500,000+ population
Towns of 30,000–100,000+ population
Centers of textile industry
Centers of metal industry
Centers of financial activity

400 Mi.

400 Km.

200

200

Spain presents an even clearer example of the failure to grasp the opportunities afforded by the price revolution. By the third quarter of the sixteenth century, Spain possessed the makings of economic expansion: unrivaled amounts of capital in the form of silver, a large and growing population, rising consumer demand, and a vast overseas empire. These factors did not bear fruit because the Spanish value system regarded business as a form of social heresy. The Spanish held in high esteem gentlemen who possessed land gained through military service and crusading ardor, which enabled them to live on rents and privileges. Commerce and industry remained contemptible pursuits.

Numerous wars in the sixteenth century (with France, the Lutheran princes, the Ottoman Turks, the Dutch, and the English) increasingly strained the Spanish treasury, despite the annual shipments of silver from the New World. Spain spent its resources on maintaining and extending its imperial power and Catholicism rather than on investing in economic expansion. In the end, the wars cost even more than Spain could handle. The Dutch for a time, and the English and the French more permanently, displaced Spain as the great power. The English and the Dutch had taken advantage of the opportunities presented by the price revolution; the Spanish had not.

THE GROWTH OF CAPITALISM

What Is Capitalism?

The changes described—especially in England and the Netherlands—represent a crucial stage in the development of the modern economic system known as **capitalism**. This is a system of *private enterprise*: the main economic decisions (what, how much, where, and at what price to produce,

◀ *Map 15.2* INDUSTRIAL CENTERS IN THE SIXTEENTH CENTURY This map of Europe (c. 1500) indicates the population of the most important cities (Naples is the largest). It also shows the centers of three kinds of industry: textiles, metals, and finance. Cloth making (textile production) was the most important industry in Europe in the early modern period. (Copyright © 2013 Cengage Learning.)

buy, and sell) are made by private individuals in their capacity as owners, workers, or consumers. Capitalism is also said to be a system of *free enterprise*: the basic decisions are not left only to individuals; these decisions are also made in response to market forces. People are free, in other words, to obey the law of supply and demand. When goods and labor are scarce, prices and wages rise; when they are plentiful, prices and wages fall.

In the Middle Ages, capitalistic enterprise was not widespread because the market was severely restricted, and, consequently, so was the operation of market forces. The vast majority of people lived as self-sufficient subsistence farmers (peasants or serfs) on the land. There was some trade and a few small cities, especially in Italy, where capitalistic enterprise was conducted, but this commerce accounted for only a tiny fraction of total economic activity. Even in the cities, capitalistic forms of enterprise were hampered by guild restrictions, which set limits on production, wages, and prices without regard to market forces. In addition, the economic decay of the fourteenth and early fifteenth centuries did not predispose those who had surplus money to gamble on the future.

But conditions changed in certain quarters beginning in the fifteenth and sixteenth centuries, generating the incentive to invest—to take risks for future profit rather than to consume. This process was due, more than anything else, to the economic situation prevailing in Europe between 1450 and 1600.

The Fostering of Mercantile Capitalism

Several conditions sustained the incentive to invest and reinvest—a basic factor in the emergence of modern capitalism. One was the price revolution, stemming from a supply of basic commodities that could not keep pace with rising demand. Prices continued to climb, creating the most powerful incentive of all to invest rather than to consume. Why spend now, those with surplus wealth must have asked, when investment in commercial farming, mining, shipping, and publishing (to name a few important outlets) is almost certain to yield greater wealth in the future? The price revolution reduced the risk involved in investment, thus helping overcome the reluctance of the wealthy to engage in capitalistic enterprise.

Another condition that encouraged investment was the distribution of wealth in a way that promoted investment. Three distinct patterns of distribution worked to this effect. First, inflation widened the gap between the rich and the poor during the sixteenth century; the rich who chose to invest garnered increasing amounts of wealth, which probably added to their incentive to continue investing. Because of the growing population and the resulting shortage of jobs, employers could pay lower and lower wages; thus, again, their profits increased, encouraging reinvestment. Merchant-capitalists were an important group of investors who gained from these conditions. As they grew, they were able to exercise a controlling influence in the marketplace because they operated on a large scale, regionally to internationally; thus, they were able to dictate terms of production and employment, displacing the local guilds. This displacement was also favorable to investment and growth. Mercantile capitalism did not benefit everyone equally; in fact, it produced increasing inequities between rich and poor, owners and workers, and independent merchant-capitalists and members of local guilds.

The second pattern of wealth distribution that encouraged investment, especially in England, grew out of the practice of primogeniture. The concentration of inherited property in the hands of the eldest child (usually the oldest son) meant that he had sufficient wealth to be persuaded to invest at least part of it. Any younger sons were left to make their own way in the world and often turned their drive and ambition into profits.

Finally, a pattern of international distribution of wealth promoted investment in some lands. The classic example is that of Spain in relation, say, to England. Spain in the sixteenth century devoted its wealth and energies to religious war and empire and relied on producers elsewhere for many of its supplies. So Spanish treasure was exported to England to pay for imports, stimulating investment there rather than in Spain. Capitalism did not develop everywhere at the same pace, and as the Spanish case shows, the very conditions that discouraged it in one place encouraged it somewhere else.

Two additional stimuli for investment came from governments. First, governments acted as giant consumers, whose appetites throughout the early modern period were expanding. Merchants, who supplied governments with everything from guns to frescoes, not only prospered but reinvested as well because of the constancy and growth of government demand. Governments also sponsored new forms of investment, whether to satisfy the taste for new luxuries at the king's court or to meet the requirements of the military. Moreover, private investors reaped incalculable advantages from overseas empires. Colonies supplied cheap raw materials and cheap (slave) labor and served as markets for exports. They greatly stimulated the construction of ships and harbor facilities and the sale of insurance.

The second government stimulus comprised state policies meant to increase investment, which they no doubt sometimes did, though not always. Collectively, these policies constitute what is known as *mercantilism*: the conscious pursuit by governments of courses of action supposed to augment national wealth and power. One characteristic expression of mercantilism was the pursuit of a favorable balance of international payments. According to conventional wisdom, wealth from trade was measured in gold and silver, of which there was believed to be a more-or-less fixed quantity. The state's goal in international trade became to sell more abroad than it bought, that is, to establish a favorable balance of payments. When the amount received for sales abroad was greater than the amount spent for purchases, the difference would be an influx of precious metal into the state. By this logic, mercantilists were led to argue for the goal of national sufficiency: a country should try to supply most of its own needs to keep imports to a minimum. This argument, of course, ignored the fact that, in international trade, the more a country buys, the more it can sell because its purchases abroad create purchasing power for its goods overseas.

Mercantilism did have a positive side. Governments increased economic activity by employing the poor, subsidizing new industries, and chartering companies to engage in overseas trade. Particularly valuable were the steps taken by states to break down local trade barriers, such as guild regulations and internal tariffs, in an attempt to create national markets and internal economic unity.

The English, moreover, saw that mercantilistic calculations of national wealth should be made over the long run. For example, Thomas Mun (1571–1641) argued that a country might import more than it exported in the short run and still come out ahead in the end because raw materials that are imported and then reprocessed for export would eventually yield a handsome profit.

In addition, Mun was one of the first to discern the virtues of *consumerism,* a phenomenon that is still extremely important for achieving sustained economic growth. Speaking of foreign trade, he maintained that the more English merchants did to advertise English goods to potential customers, the greater the overseas market for those goods would be. In other words, demand can be *created.* Just as there is an urge to invest and make profits, so there is an appetite to consume and enjoy the products of industry, and both inclinations have played their part in the growth of capitalism. Nor was the message restricted to the foreign market. Between 1660 and 1750, England became the world's first consumer society: more and more people had more and more money to spend, and they acquired a taste for conspicuous consumption (which previously had always been confined to the aristocracy). Discretionary goods were available—lace, tobacco, housewares, flowers—and consumers wanted them. Concomitantly, just as today, the stronger the stimulus to buy, the harder the consumer worked, which induced further growth.

The price revolution, the concentration of wealth in private hands, and government activity combined to provide the foundation for sustained investment and for the emergence of mercantile capitalism. This new force in the world should not be confused with industrial capitalism. The latter evolved with the first Industrial Revolution in eighteenth-century England, but mercantile capitalism paved the way for it.

THE ELITE AND THE PEOPLE

Traditional Popular Culture

Europe's economic expansion was accompanied by equally important social and cultural changes in the relations between ordinary people and their rulers, whether kings, nobles, landlords, or clergy. Throughout the Middle Ages, there had always been two cultures: the elite culture of the royal court, the feudal lords, and the educated clergy, and the popular culture of largely illiterate peasants and artisans.

Over the centuries, the common people had evolved a distinctive culture, which their rulers patronized and, to some degree, participated in. This popular culture consisted of a mosaic of the customs of various groups of people—shepherds, peasants, cobblers, weavers, miners—each group with its own traditions. Even a youth culture of apprentices was to be found in the towns. Furthermore, besides the settled culture of the villages and towns, there was a vagabond culture of sailors, soldiers, beggars, thieves, and other "masterless men."[6]

The prosperous and the powerful called on the services of learned professionals—clergy, physicians, and lawyers. Ordinary people had their own humbler and cheaper equivalents—lay preachers, folk healers, and witches (that is, sorcerers and fortunetellers). The royal courts, manor houses, monasteries, and universities were centers of elite culture. Ordinary people worked, played, and worshiped in meaner settings: the village church, the tavern, the street, and especially the marketplace or village square. In the church and churchyard, they danced, feasted, and performed religious pageants; in the tavern and street, they gossiped, played games, watched puppet shows, staged cockfights, listened to folk preachers, and consulted healers, astrologers, and magicians.

Certain special occasions granted people the freedom to express themselves. Beginning in the thirteenth century, the most important of these occasions was the carnival, the three- to six-day festival preceding the onset of **Lent.** The carnival was a time of revelry and ritual processions through church and streets, excessive eating and drinking, and a sharp increase in sexual activity. It was also a time during which ordinary people, at least in their parades and public displays, engaged in what was called "turning the world upside down." So, for instance, in a procession a horse would be made to walk backward with its rider facing its tail. Popular illustrations of the era show a son beating his father, a pupil beating his teacher, servants giving orders to their masters, the laity preaching to the clergy, the husband minding the baby, and the wife smoking and holding a gun. What does all this mean? Was it a safety valve, allowing the people to blow off the steam generated by an otherwise oppressive and monotonous existence? Perhaps, but it sometimes led to real violence, and the elite, by the sixteenth century at any rate, looked on such behavior as subversive and fraught with danger. As a noble said on the occasion of the carnival at Palermo in 1648, "On the pretext of these assemblies of the people for these ridiculous spectacles, factious spirits would be able . . . to encourage some new riot."[7]

Nor was the carnival the only occasion for this ritual mockery of authority. The calendar year was punctuated by the observance of religious feast days on which similar behavior took place. So, for instance, in France, on the Feast of Fools (the Innocents) on December 28, an abbot or bishop of fools was elected, and a mock Mass took place in which the clergy dressed in women's clothes, played cards, ate sausages, sang ribald songs, and cursed their congregations instead of blessing them.

Among the most prevalent popular traditions was the ritual mockery of marriage known as the *charivari*. Only unconventional marriages qualified for such rude treatment at the hands of one's neighbors: an old man and a young wife, a second marriage, a husband beaten or cuckolded by his wife. The charivari consisted of a ritual procession in which the victim or his effigy would be mounted backward on an ass and drawn through the streets accompanied by "rough music" (the beating of pots and pans). Charivaris were sometimes conducted at the expense of tax collectors, preachers, and landlords. Here then was a kind of popular justice, another version of the world turned upside down.

The Reform of Popular Culture

Throughout the Middle Ages and until the early sixteenth century, elite culture and popular culture existed in more-or-less stable balance. Indeed, the two worlds, high and low, occupied considerable common ground. Landlords and clergy took part in village games and feasts and shared with their inferiors an outlook that stressed communal

values: pulling together in a subsistence world, making sure that everyone had enough for survival, and extending relief to those in need. The emphasis was on communalism, not individualism, especially in the countryside.

In the sixteenth century, however, a drastic change took place in the attitude of the elite toward ordinary people. No longer willing to patronize and foster popular culture, the elite became increasingly suspicious of and hostile to it. This shift occurred for two reasons. The first was the elite's fear of the growing numbers of the poor and fear of the growing numbers of people, some poor and some not, who, inspired by the new religious movements and the new printed literature, were beginning to question the old authorities and sometimes even joined in rebellion against them. Encouraged by the greater accessibility of printed books and by the Protestant emphasis on Bible reading, more and more people became literate, and a popular literature of religious instruction, astrological almanacs, and chivalric romances poured from the presses to meet the growing demand. On this score, too, the authorities had their misgivings; books of the right sort were acceptable, even useful, but a little learning was thought to be a dangerous thing.

The second reason for the shift in elite attitudes toward ordinary people was not fear but hope. Not only were the elite alarmed by the growing poverty and unrest among the people, but they also thought that they knew how to control the unrest and even perhaps in some measure overcome it. Just as religion inspired the people, so the Reformation, the Counter-Reformation, and the Christian humanism of the Renaissance inspired leaders to reform society and in particular to attack popular culture for being both too pagan and too disorderly. The customs of the people, it was thought, needed to be purified and made more decent and sober, and the people themselves needed to be disciplined so that they might become obedient subjects of king and church. Society came to be seen as divided between **the godly** (among whom the elite included themselves) and the ungodly multitude, who needed to be controlled and, if possible, educated for service in the Christian commonwealth.

What followed was a wide-ranging onslaught against all forms of traditional popular

PEASANT FESTIVAL, 1640, BY DAVID TENIERS THE YOUNGER (1610–1690).
This scene depicts peasant revelry, the rural village at play. The common folk
are eating, drinking, and dancing outside what looks like a country tavern.
Hardworking farmworkers no doubt deserved their day off. Notice in the lower
left of the picture a small group of gentry who owned the land on which the
peasants worked. Such landlords indulged the peasants in their merrymaking,
but warily and only up to a point because they feared the possibility of a riot and
popular rebellion. (akg-images/Joseph Martin.)

culture—what one historian has called "the triumph of Lent" over "the world of Carnival."[8] This
reform movement included attacks on popular festivals, **lay preaching,** and "the world turned up side
down." The Florentine ruler Girolamo Savonarola,
a few days before the carnival of 1496, preached
a sermon recommending that "boys should collect alms for the respectable poor, instead of mad

pranks, throwing stones and making floats."[9] A
century later, in England, Phillip Stubbe drew up
a comprehensive indictment of May games, Lords
of Misrule, Christmas feasting, church ales, wakes,
bearbaiting, cockfighting, and dancing. Popular religious dramas disappeared in northern Italy during the third quarter of the sixteenth century and
in England by the end of that century.

The new bureaucratic state joined the clergy in the reforming enterprise. In the sixteenth and seventeenth centuries, many forms of behavior that had been thought of as spiritual sins became secular crimes as well, subject to prosecution and punishment by the state. These newly criminalized activities included adultery, **blasphemy**, sodomy, infanticide, and witchcraft. In this period, too, public brothels, which had existed for centuries, were gradually shut down, a process beginning in Lutheran Germany between 1530 and 1560. The state enforced what the new moral puritanism decreed.

Witchcraft and the Witch Craze

The prosecution of witches constitutes a particularly important chapter in this attack on popular culture. Although it had always been suspect, witchcraft had been a part of traditional village culture for centuries. There were two kinds of witchcraft, known at the time as black and white. The white variety involved healing and fortune-telling. Black witchcraft conjured evil powers by a curse or by the manipulation of objects, such as the entrails of animals.

The medieval church developed a more theological and sinister interpretation of the phenomenon: that witches conspired with the Devil to work against God and human society, held secret meetings, and had carnal relations with the Devil. In the late twelfth century, Christian thinkers began to emphasize the idea of a Devil who roamed the world at the head of an army of demons, attempting to undermine the saving mission of Christ and tempting people to sin. Witches were regarded as those who had succumbed to temptation and entered into a pact to worship Satan in place of God. This worship was thought to take place at secret, nocturnal meetings (the legendary witches' Sabbats), during which witches and demons were supposed to engage in sexual orgies, sacrifice infants, and desecrate the Eucharist.

As early as the thirteenth century, bishops and popes prosecuted witches for heresy. Confessions were usually extracted by means of torture. Those found guilty were burned at the stake (on the Continent) or hanged (in England), and their property was confiscated by the authorities.

The church held that a witch's "only hope of salvation was to be arrested and to recant before her execution. By such reasoning the torment and killing of witches was for their own good as well as that of God and society."[10]

The growth of printed literature on the subject of witchcraft was especially influential in the spread of the church's view that witchcraft involved a diabolical plot. In 1486, there appeared a handbook called *Malleus Maleficarum* (*The Hammer of Witches*) by two German Dominicans who claimed to show what witches did at the Devil's behest. These Dominicans had tried almost fifty people for witchcraft, all but two of them women.

By the sixteenth century, the linkage of women to witchcraft had been firmly established. Men could also be accused of the crime, but almost everywhere that witches were tried in the sixteenth and seventeenth centuries, more than 75 percent were women, often elderly widows and spinsters. The so-called witch craze is a phenomenon of these two centuries, when perhaps as many as 110,000 people were prosecuted and 60,000 executed all over Europe.

Why were most of the accused women? No doubt this pattern reflected an ancient prejudice that women were less rational and more lustful than men and so more susceptible to the Devil's wiles. As the authors of *The Hammer of Witches* declared, "Witchcraft comes from carnal lust, which is in woman insatiable."[11]

One view of English witch-hunts during the period may help explain the predominance of women among the accused. In traditional society, widows and the elderly were objects of local charity. An old woman, so the theory goes, would beg for alms and be rebuffed by a more prosperous neighbor; later, some misfortune would befall the neighbor, and he would blame it on the old woman, accusing her of witchcraft as a way of assuaging his guilt for having refused her request for help. According to this interpretation, such behavior characterizes a period of rapid transition from communal subsistence to an ethic of economic individualism that demanded that each person look out for himself or herself. Just such a period in England coincided with the large number of witchcraft prosecutions brought against poor old women.

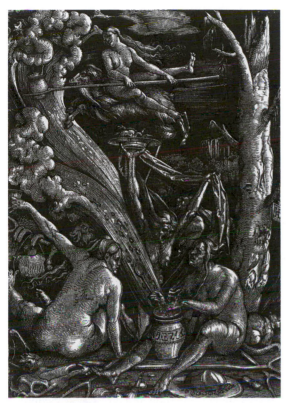

***Witches' Sabbat* (1510) by Hans Baldung Grien (1485–545).** This woodcut depicts both learned and popular beliefs concerning witches. For example, the night ride through the air, the naked feasting, and orgiastic concourse with the Devil all reflect the view that witchcraft was an extremely dangerous heresy that sought to overthrow Christianity and put Devil worship in its place. (Réunion des Musées Nationaux/Art Resource, N.Y.)

By 1700, the witch craze had ended in Western Europe—first in Holland, the most tolerant country, and in Spain, the most intolerant because the Spanish Inquisition provided another focus for persecutions. Two factors probably helped put an end to the witch-hunts.

First, the religious turmoil unleashed by the Reformation, on which the witch craze fed, also triggered an intellectual backlash that led some to wonder whether **fanaticism** had not gotten the better of reason and to call for a tempering of inflamed passions and the exercise of a greater degree of skepticism in matters of faith. "It is rating our conjectures too high to roast people alive for them," the skeptic Michel de Montaigne exclaimed.[12] Thus, judges in seventeenth-century France imposed stricter tests and demanded that more conclusive evidence be presented before convicting people tried for witchcraft. In 1682, Louis XIV himself declared the phenomenon to be a kind of fraud.

Second, during the last half of the seventeenth century, another shift was taking place in relations between the elite and the common people. The elite began to associate belief in astrology, magic, and witches with the people. Both cultures had once shared these beliefs, but now the elite spurned them as representing so many vulgar superstitions. This shift owed something to the growth of **skepticism** and the impact of science. It also indicated a hardening of the lines drawn between the two cultures and a greater willingness by the elite to accept, if not foster, the resulting divisions. By the early eighteenth century, although almost nobody would admit to having given up the belief in the existence of witches, serious discussion, let alone prosecution, of witchcraft cases had been read out of polite society. The reason was not that the belief had been proved wrong, but that to talk about it, except by way of ridicule, was deemed unseemly. The belief in witchcraft declined in part by being rendered taboo in the upper reaches of society. It lost its appeal as much through social **snobbery** as through science and skepticism.

ECONOMIC AND SOCIAL TRANSFORMATIONS

The transformations considered in this chapter were among the most momentous in the world's history. In an unprecedented development that may never be repeated, one small part of the world, Western Europe, became lord of the sea-lanes, master of many lands throughout the globe, and banker and profit-taker in an emerging world economy. Western Europe's global hegemony was to last well into the twentieth century. By conquering and settling new lands, Europeans exported Western culture around the globe, a process that accelerated in the twentieth century.

The overseas expansion had profound effects. The native populations of the New World were decimated. To ease the labor shortage, millions of blacks were imported from Africa to work as slaves on plantations and in mines. Black slavery would produce large-scale effects on culture, politics, and society, which have lasted to the present day.

The widespread circulation of plant and animal life also had great consequences. Horses and cattle were introduced into the New World. (The Aztecs were so amazed to see a man on horseback that they thought horse and rider were one demonic creature.) In return, the Old World sampled such novelties as corn, the tomato, and, most important, the potato, which was to become a staple of the northern European diet. Manioc, from which tapioca is made, was transplanted from the New World to Africa, where it helped sustain the population.

Western Europe was wrenched out of the subsistence economy of the Middle Ages and launched on a course of sustained economic growth. This transformation resulted from the grafting of traditional forms, such as primogeniture and holy war, onto new forces, such as global exploration, price revolution, and convertible husbandry. Out of this change emerged the beginnings of a new economic system, mercantile capitalism, which in large measure provided the economic thrust for European world predominance and paved the way for the Industrial Revolution of the eighteenth and nineteenth centuries.

Finally, these economic changes were accompanied by a major shift in relations between the rulers and the ruled. For centuries, the elite had tolerated and even patronized the culture of the common people. But under the impact of the commercial revolution and the Reformation, the authorities became increasingly suspicious of the people and undertook to purify and reform popular culture. The degree to which they succeeded remains an open question. But the gap between the elite and the people widened as the elite found less and less in popular culture to identify with and more and more to condemn or try to undo. The elite distanced themselves from ordinary people even as they attempted to impose their will. The result was the emergence of two separate cultures, divorced from and hostile to each other. Only in moments of mass hysteria, such as during the witch craze, could the people and their rulers join forces against a common and defenseless victim.

❖   ❖   ❖

NOTES

1. Roland Oliver, *The African Experience* (New York: HarperCollins, 1991), 123.

2. Quoted in Basil Davidson, *Africa in History* (New York: Collier Books, 1991), 215.

3. Quoted in Richard S. Dunn, *Sugar and Slaves* (Chapel Hill: University of North Carolina Press, 1972), 248.

4. Quoted in Davidson, *Africa in History,* 223.

5. Christopher Hill, *Reformation to Industrial Revolution* (Baltimore: Penguin Books, 1969), 159–160.

6. Christopher Hill, *The World Turned Upside Down* (New York: Viking, 1972), chap. 3.

7. Quoted in Peter Burke, *Popular Culture in Early Modern Europe* (New York: Harper and Row, 1978), 203.

8. Ibid., chaps. 7–8.

9. Ibid., p. 217.

10. Jeffrey B. Russell, *A History of Witchcraft* (London: Thames and Hudson, 1980), 78.

11. Quoted in Margaret L. King, *Women of the Renaissance* (Chicago: University of Chicago Press, 1993), 155.

12. Quoted in Russell, *A History of Witchcraft,* 73.

SUGGESTED READING

Bernard, Carmen, *The Incas: People of the Sun* (1994). Richly illustrated.

Burke, Peter, *Popular Culture in Early Modern Europe* (1994). A fascinating account of the social underside from the Renaissance to the French Revolution.

Cipolla, Carlo M., *Guns, Sails, and Empires* (1967). Establishes links between technological innovation and overseas expansion from 1400 to 1700.

Davis, Ralph, *The Rise of the Atlantic Economies* (1973). A reliable survey of early modern economic history.

Elliott, John H., *Empires of the Atlantic World: Britain and Spain in America 1492–1830* (2007). Wide-ranging and well informed.

Horton, James Oliver, and Lois E. Horton, *Slavery and the Making of America* (2004). A rich tapestry of incident and insight.

Wulffson, Don, *Before Columbus: Early Voyages to the Americas* (2008). An archaeological approach to overseas discovery and settlement which is very accessible to students.

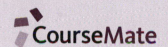

Chapter 16

The Rise of Sovereignty: Transition to the Modern State

Anton von Maron, Kaiser Joseph II (1741–1790). There is a standard pose intended to show the power of all absolute but reasonable monarchs. They live in elegant surroundings; they look earnest and strong. They use images to evoke their benevolence, hence the statue in back of Joseph II. (Imagno/Gerhard Trumler/Getty Images.)

Focus Questions

1. How did monarchs build strong states?

2. What enabled Spain to rise to greatness, and why was this greatness short-lived?

3. What were the achievements and failures of Louis XIV's reign?

4. What is the enduring historical significance of the English Revolution of the seventeenth century? How have historians quarreled about it?

5. What were the distinguishing features of Prussia and Russia by the early eighteenth century?

6. What was the role of the lesser nobility in the process of state formation?

From the thirteenth to the seventeenth century, a new and unique form of political organization emerged in the West: the **dynastic**, or national, **state**, which, through taxes and war, harnessed the power of its nobility and the material resources of its territory. The state was simply a large territory, generally with people speaking the same language who could very gradually imagine themselves as part of a community. Indeed, the European monarchs encouraged such thinking. Their right to rule had been established centuries earlier when a dynasty was founded, generally by the most militarily powerful nobleman. Under the laws and rights governing birth, the state became an entity inherited from generation to generation; thus, a dynasty was born. The power of the West to explore and dominate other lands and peoples would have been impossible without the backing provided by the European states. They directed the energies of merchants and landed elites into national service and international competition. A degree of domestic stability ensued, and the states encouraged commerce and industry, which could in turn be taxed. Although they nurtured the aristocracy, many states also required that both lord and peasant serve in national armies bent upon foreign conquest as well as defense. States need not have been dynastic; witness, for example, the emergence of the Dutch Republic, which was led by elite families. But by the late fifteenth century, most of the European states became the inheritance of dynastic kings.

Monarchs and their courts became centers of gravity in the process of state formation. The centralized governments that emerged generally embraced a system best described as **absolutism**. Under the impact of absolutism, kings seemed invincible. Out of their courts came the administration of justice, the power to collect taxes, foreign policy, laws governing the content of books and the press, and even laws regulating the forms of dress permitted to various classes and occupations. Despite the appeal of such kingly power, one other form of government emerged in early modern Europe: *republican,* or *constitutional,* states. By 1800, the future lay with this other, more participatory system. Republican government gave more power to landed or mercantile elites than to kings and their courts.

369

Chronology 16.1 ❖ The Rise of Monarchical Sovereignty

1469	Ferdinand and Isabella begin their rule of Castile and Aragon
1485	Henry VII begins the reign of the Tudor dynasty in England
1517	The Protestant Reformation starts in Germany
1519	Charles V of Spain becomes Hapsburg emperor of the Holy Roman Empire
1556–1598	Philip II of Spain persecutes Jews and Muslims
1559	Treaty of peace between France and Spain
1560–1609	The Netherlands revolts against Spanish rule
1562–1589	Religious wars in France
1572	Saint Bartholomew's Day Massacre: Queen Catherine of France thought to have ordered thousands of Protestants executed
1579	*Vindiciae contra Tyrannos*, published by Huguenots, justifies regicide; it will be translated and republished during the English Revolution
1588	English fleet defeats the Spanish Armada
1590s	A reaction in Russia against Ivan IV, the Terrible
1593	Henry IV of France renounces his Protestantism to restore peace in France
1598	French Protestants granted limited religious toleration by the Edict of Nantes
1630	King Charles I in England attempts to govern without Parliament
1640–1660	Revolution in England
1648	Treaty of Westphalia ends Thirty Years' War; guarantees the independence of the Dutch Republic
1649	Charles I, Stuart king of England, is executed by an act of Parliament
1649–1660	England is co-ruled by Parliament and the army under Oliver Cromwell
1660	Charles II returns from exile and becomes king of England
1683	Turks attack Vienna and are defeated
1685	Louis XIV of France revokes the Edict of Nantes
1688–1689	Revolution in England: end of absolutism; religious toleration for all Protestants
1699	Treaty of Karlowitz marks Austrians' victory over Turks and affirms Austria's right to rule Hungary, Transylvania, and parts of Croatia
1701	Louis XIV tries to bring Spain under French control
1702–1714	War of the Spanish Succession establishes a balance of power between England and France

Although kings in some medieval lands had begun to forge national states, medieval political forms differed considerably from the systems that developed in the early modern period. During the Middle Ages, feudal lords gave homage to their kings but ruled unencumbered over their local territories. Medieval representative assemblies, which met occasionally to give advice to kings, at times acted as a brake on the king's power. City-states enjoyed considerable autonomy. The clergy supported the monarch but governed in separate spiritual realms. The papacy challenged the authority of those monarchs who, it believed, did not fulfill their duty to rule in accordance with Christian teachings. In early modern times, powerful monarchs gradually subdued these competing systems of local authority and established strong central governments.

MONARCHS AND ELITES AS STATE BUILDERS

At first, kings drove the development of states. European elites, whether landed or urban, grudgingly gave allegiance to these ambitious, and at times ruthless, authority figures. In general, a single monarch seemed the only alternative to the even more brutal pattern of war and disorder so basic to the governing habits of the feudal aristocracy. But it was essential that the kings of Europe subordinate the aristocracy to their needs and interests and gain firm control over the Christian churches in their territories. Gradually, religious zeal was made compatible with, and largely supportive of, the state's goals rather than with papal dictates or even universal Christian aspirations. The demise of medieval representative assemblies—with the notable exception of the English Parliament and the Dutch Estates General—is a dramatic illustration of how monarchs subjected to their will all other political authorities, whether local, regional, or national. Parliaments gave one representative one vote, whereas Estates General voted by a collective process whereby one social estate or one province cast only one vote (polling its members to do so). The actual votes cast could be as few as three in the French case or seven for the number of Dutch provinces voting in The Hague. Few Estates General survived the seventeenth century. They were not in the monarch's interest.

Monarchs employed a variety of tools for extending their power. All encouraged the use of vernacular languages—English, French, or Spanish, for example—to foster a common identity, as well as to counteract the church's monopoly over the international language of the time, Latin. But more important than words were arms. The foundations of monarchical power lay in the standing army and the taxation that paid for the military. The goal of the monarch was to have independent wealth and power. In general, only war justified taxes. The rise and fall of the great European powers of the early modern period—first Spain and then the Dutch Republic, as well as France and England—can be traced directly in the fortunes of their armies on the battlefield and the fullness of the king's or state's treasury. Only the rise of the **Dutch Republic** broke with the pattern of king–army–taxes as the key to the creation of a centralized state. The Dutch case rested on local elites–army–taxes. The rich, urban, Protestant elite lent the state money at interest to wage a struggle for independence against Spain. In the process, the Dutch created the first system of national bonds and a citizen-financed national debt. A nation was created, but one without a king or a strong central government. Local elites held most of the power, just as they held the state bonds.

Where early modern monarchs succeeded in subduing, reconstituting, or destroying local aristocratic and ecclesiastical power systems, strong dynastic states emerged. Where the monarchs failed, as they did in the **Holy Roman Empire** and Italy, no viable states evolved until well into the nineteenth century. Those failures derived from the independent authority of local princes or city-states and, in the case of Italy, from the decentralizing influence of papal authority. In the Holy Roman Empire, feudal princes found allies in the newly formed Protestant communities, and in such a situation, religion worked as a decentralizing force. Once given the power to determine the local religion, many German princes also maintained their peasants as virtual serfs.

Early modern kings needed to gain control over religious authorities. They did not separate church and state (as was later done in the United States); rather they linked their subjects' religious identity with national identity. For example, in England, by the late seventeenth century, to be a true Protestant was to be a true English subject, while in Spain the same equation operated for the Catholic (as opposed to the Muslim or the Jew, who came to be regarded as non-Spanish). Even in the Dutch Republic, where a real, if limited, religious toleration prevailed, all the municipal, regional, and national offices were held by Protestants.

In the thirteenth century, most Europeans still identified themselves with their localities: their villages, manors, or towns. Their allegiance went to their local lord or bishop. They knew little, and probably cared less, about the activities of the king and his court, except when the monarch called on them for taxes or military service. By the late seventeenth century, in contrast, aristocrats in many European countries defined their political power in relation to king and court. By then, the lives of very ordinary people had been touched by national systems of tax collection, by the doctrines and practices of national churches, and by military conscription.

Increasingly, middle-class town dwellers, the **bourgeoisie**, also realized that their prosperity hinged, in part, on court-supported foreign and domestic policies. If the king assisted their commercial ventures, urban dwellers supported the growth of a strong central state. In only two states, England and the Dutch Republic, did landed and mercantile elites share in the process of governing by the late seventeenth century.

By that time commercial rivalry among states and colonial expansion were directly related to the ability of landed and commercial elites to protect their interests under the mantle of the state, and to the state's willingness to encourage world trade in order to enrich its own treasury. Monarchs and the states they helped create ushered in the modern world just as surely as did commercial expansion, capitalism, and science. They also enshrined political power as a masculine and familial preserve that could be inherited.

THE RISE AND FALL OF HAPSBURG SPAIN

The Spanish political experience of the sixteenth century exemplifies the interconnectedness of king, army, church, and taxation. It was also one of the most spectacular examples in history of the rise and equally dramatic fall of a great power. The Spanish kings turned a dynastic state into an empire. First Spain burst through its frontiers and encompassed Portugal, part of Italy, the Low Countries, and enormous areas of the New World. Spain became an intercontinental empire—the first in the West since Roman times. Until 1469, however, although Spanish was widely spoken on the Iberian Peninsula, Spain did not exist as a political entity. Then in that year, Ferdinand, heir to the throne of Aragon, married his more powerful and prosperous cousin, Isabella, heiress of Castile. Yet even after the unification of Castile and the crown of Aragon (encompassing Catalonia, Aragon, and Valencia), relations among the fiercely independent provinces of Spain were often tense. Only through dynastic marriage of their offspring to a German-speaking family of central Europe, the Hapsburgs, did the Spanish monarchs emerge on the international scene. Marriage and inheritance were key pieces in the puzzle of state development.

Ferdinand and Isabella: Unity and Purity of "Blood" and Religion

During their rule (1479–1516), Ferdinand and Isabella put in place a dynastic state and laid the foundation for the Spanish Empire and Spanish domination of European affairs throughout the sixteenth century. Together, they sought to build the army and consolidate the state by waging a campaign to reconquer Spanish territory still held by the Muslims. At the same time, they strove to bring the church into alliance with the state and forge a Spanish identity based on "blood" ancestry as well as religion. A person was considered Spanish only if no Jews or non-Spaniards could be found in the family lineage. The roots of racism lie deep in European religious and political history.

Spanish rulers also had to bring the church's interests in line with their own. Whereas other Europeans, partly under the impact of the Renaissance, questioned the church's leadership and attacked its corruption, the Catholic Kings (as Ferdinand and Isabella were called) reformed the church and made it their servant. The crusade

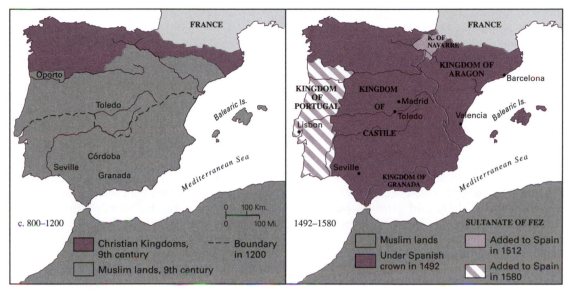

Map 16.1 SPAIN FROM THE NINTH TO THE SIXTEENTH CENTURY Spain became a nation gradually, and eventually Portugal split away to become a separate state.

against the Muslims pleased the militant Spanish church. Popular piety and royal policy led in 1492 to a victory over Granada, the last Muslim-ruled territory of Spain. In the same year, the Spanish state expelled the Jews from its territory.

The five-hundred-year struggle for Christian hegemony in the Iberian Peninsula left the Spanish fiercely religious and strongly suspicious of foreigners. Despite centuries of intermarriage with non-Christians, by the early sixteenth century, purity of blood and orthodoxy of faith became necessary for, and synonymous with, Spanish identity. The Spanish state and church actively engaged in persecuting Muslims and Jews, who for centuries had contributed substantially to Spanish cultural and economic life.

In 1492, the crown expelled some 150,000 Jews (some estimates are considerably higher). The thousands of Jews who underwent conversion were watched by a church tribunal, **the Inquisition**, for signs of backsliding. The clerical inquisitors employed brutal means of interrogation and torture, such as waterboarding, to ferret out newly converted Christians and their descendants who were suspected of secretly practicing Judaism. Death by fire, sometimes in elaborate

public ceremonies, was the ultimate penalty. Muslims also bore the pain of persecution: forced conversions, investigations, torture, and executions conducted by the Inquisition and, finally, mass expulsion in 1609 through 1614. The Inquisition represented the repressive side of the Spanish genius for conquest and administration, and its shadow stretched down through the centuries well into the twentieth, as witnessed by the support the Spanish clergy gave to the far-right regime of Francisco Franco (d. 1975). By contrast, today Spain is a flourishing democracy.

The wars against the Muslims rendered the Spanish army one of the finest in Europe. With a superior army, the great magnates pacified, and the church and the Inquisition under monarchical control, the Catholic Kings expanded their interests and embarked on an imperialist foreign policy in Europe and the New World. It had extraordinary consequences. Ultimately, Spain became dominant in the Americas. Intent on expanding their territory, Ferdinand and Isabella gambled on Columbus's voyage to what he and they thought was a new passage to India. The gamble paid off in the discovery of what eventually came to be known as North and South America. Beginning in 1519 in Mexico, the conquistador Hernando Cortés, using only six hundred foot soldiers and sixteen horses, defeated the Aztec nation. This feat was partly due to the superiority of Spanish technology, but also to the condition of the Aztec nation, which was struggling to maintain a hold over its own people and over scores of other Mexican tribes that it had, in some cases, brutally subdued. *Hidalgos,* members of the minor aristocracy, led the Spanish forces. As younger sons of impoverished aristocrats, war was their means to riches and land. Unlike the great and wealthy aristocrats, they would serve the crown at home and abroad as soldiers and often as bureaucrats. Their loyalty to the king was matched only by their fierce ambition. The Spanish hidalgos had their counterparts in France and elsewhere. The bureaucracy and army of the early modern states were very important avenues for lesser nobles to obtain and keep elite status.

The Reign of Charles V: Hapsburg, King of Spain, and Holy Roman Emperor

Through a series of shrewd marriage agreements for their children, Ferdinand and Isabella laid the foundation of their dynasty while at the same time strengthening their international alliances. As a result, their grandson, Charles, who ruled from 1516 to 1556, inherited Spain, the Netherlands, Austria, Sardinia, Sicily, the kingdom of Naples, and Franche-Comté. In 1519, the same year as the conquest of Mexico, he was also elected Holy Roman Emperor (partly through bribery). Thus, he became the most powerful monarch in Europe. But in the course of his reign, problems emerged that would eventually lead to Spain's decline and weaken the Hapsburg dynasty, to which he had been heir through marriage.

Charles's inheritance was simply too vast to be governed effectively. The Lutheran Reformation in Germany proved to be the first successful challenge to Hapsburg power. It opened the first phase in the religious and political struggle between Catholic Spain and Protestant Europe. That struggle, which dominated the last half of the sixteenth century, ultimately reduced Spanish

influence and led to the loss of the northern Low Countries and the further decentralization of the Holy Roman Empire.

The achievements of Charles V's reign rested on the army and bureaucracy. The Hapsburg Empire in the New World was vast and, on the whole, was effectively administered and policed, partly by the Catholic clergy. Out of a sprawling empire, with its exploited native populations, came the greatest flow of gold and silver the world had ever witnessed. Constant warfare in Europe, particularly in Italy and against the Turks in the Mediterranean, coupled with the immensity of the Spanish administrative network, required a steady intake of capital. But in the long run, this easy access to income was detrimental to the Spanish economy. There was no incentive for the development of domestic industry, entrepreneurship, or international commerce. Indeed, the influx of gold fostered an inflationary spiral. Constant war perpetuated a social order geared to the aggrandizement of a military class rather than to the development of a commercial class. Although war expanded Spain's power in the sixteenth century, it also sowed the seeds for the financial crises of the 1590s and beyond, and for the eventual decline of Spain as a world power.

Philip II

The reign of Philip II (1556–1598) was pivotal and exposed the strengths and weaknesses of the Spanish state. Philip II inherited the throne from his father, Charles V, who left his son with a large empire in both the Old World and the New. Philip II's zeal for Catholicism ruled his private conduct and infused his foreign policy. With the necessary revenue in hand, he launched an offensive against the Turks and international Protestantism.

To Philip II, being truly Spanish meant being Christian in faith and blood; the racist tendencies already evident in the later fifteenth century gained full expression during his reign. Increasingly, the country came to be ruled by an exclusive class of **Old Christians**, who claimed to be untainted because for centuries they had refused to marry Muslims or Jews, even if Jews were converts to Christianity—*New Christians*, as they were called. The Old Christians controlled the

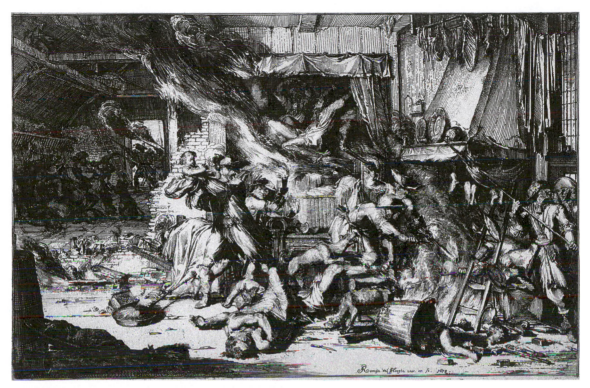

ROMEYN DE HOOGHE, *ATROCITIES OF WAR*, 1673. Nothing fueled Protestant zeal more than the history and images that depicted the Spanish assault on the Low Countries in the 1580s. Here, nearly one hundred years after the persecution of Dutch Protestants by the Spanish army, the most talented engraver of the late seventeenth century depicted the horrors inflicted on the Dutch during their revolt from Spain. (Fine Arts Museum of San Francisco, Achenbach Foundation for Graphic Arts, 1963.30.15279.)

church, religious orders, and the Inquisition. Tradition enabled them to preserve an imperial system urgently in need of reform.

Morose and withdrawn, Philip II worked incessantly without any obvious pleasures. He took a fine comb to his ministers' reports, yet despite all the editing, he was strangely indecisive. Some problems remained unsolved for years; frustrated advisers begged the king to take action.

In the 1560s, Philip sent the largest land army ever assembled in Europe into the Netherlands in order to crush Protestant-inspired opposition to Spanish authority. The ensuing revolt of the Netherlands lasted until 1609, and in losing the Netherlands, Spain lost its industrial heartland. In 1576 and again in 1585, the Spanish army, in a desperate attempt to defeat the rebels, sacked Antwerp, the leading commercial and banking city in northern Europe. Within ten years, Antwerp's trade and many of its educated and commercial elite went to Amsterdam, a Protestant stronghold. Amsterdam replaced Antwerp as an international capital and became the center of the new Dutch Republic. Its stock exchange dominated global commerce into the late eighteenth century, when it was replaced by London.

By the 1580s, Philip's foreign policy followed his religious zeal. He intervened in the French religious wars on the Catholic side, although his intervention gave little to Spain in the way of power or influence. Philip's religious fervor also led to the disastrous attempt in 1588 to invade England with an armada.

For Philip, an assault on Protestant England constituted a holy crusade against the "heretic and bastard" Queen Elizabeth; he particularly resented English assistance to Protestant rebels in the Dutch wars. Sailing from Lisbon in May, the Spanish Armada, twenty-two thousand men strong, met with humiliating defeat. Its large ships could not negotiate the treacherous English Channel, and the English ships easily outmaneuvered them, breaking their formation by crashing fire ships into them. Moreover, strong winds, typical for May, drove the Armada out of striking position.

The defeat had a psychological effect throughout Europe. The Spanish openly pondered what they had done to incur divine displeasure. Protestant Europe, however, hailed the victory as a sign of its election, and the "Protestant wind" stirred by divine intervention entered the mythology of English nationalism. In the rise and fall of nations, self-assurance has played a crucial, if inexplicable, role. The cultural renaissance associated with the England of Shakespeare owed its vigor and confidence in part to its pride at being Protestant and independent of Spanish influence.

The End of the Spanish Hapsburgs

After the defeat of the Armada, Spain gradually and reluctantly abandoned its imperial ambitions in northern Europe. By the first quarter of the seventeenth century, enormous weaknesses had surfaced in Spanish economic and social life. From the 1590s onward, bankruptcy reappeared while the agricultural economy, at the heart of any early modern nation, stagnated. At the height of its power, Spain had never devoted enough attention to increasing domestic production.

Despite these setbacks, Spain became an aggressor during the Thirty Years' War (1618–1648), at its heart a religious struggle for mastery over the Holy Roman Empire. The Austrian branch of the Catholic Hapsburg family joined forces with their Spanish cousins, and neither the Protestant

Swedes and Germans nor the Dutch could stop them. Only French participation in the Thirty Years' War on the Protestant side tipped the balance decisively against the Hapsburgs. In the course of the war, large portions of what is today Germany were destroyed, and its population fled or was killed. Spanish aggression brought no victories, and with the Peace of Westphalia (1648), Spain officially recognized the independence of the Netherlands and cut its ties with the Austrian branch of the family.

By 1660, the domination of Europe by the Spanish Hapsburgs had come to an end. The rule of the Protestant princes had been secured in the Holy Roman Empire; the largely Protestant Dutch Republic flourished; Portugal and its slave colony of Brazil were independent of Spain; and dominance over European affairs had passed to France. The quality of material life in Spain deteriorated rapidly, and the ever-present gap between the rich and the poor widened. The traditional aristocracy and the church retained their land and power but failed conspicuously to produce effective leadership. With decline came rigidity of institutions and values. Spain remained authoritarian far longer than other European countries. Democratic revolutions did not occur in a country dominated exclusively by the landed elite and the church. The commercial elite, which became increasingly important in England, the Netherlands, and France, failed to develop in monarchical and agricultural Spain.

The Spanish experience illustrates two aspects of the history of state formation. First, the state as empire can survive and prosper only if the domestic economic base continues to expand. Second, living off subjugated colonies ultimately means economic stagnation and can lead to technological backwardness at home.

In general, states with a vital and aggressive mercantile class generally prospered in the early modern period. In such states, the landed elite was joined by a commercial elite. The latter comprised those who invested, or even participated, in the market and manufacturing, whether at home or abroad. In Spain, however, the old aristocracy and the church continued to dominate and control society and its mores. They not only despised manual labor and profit-taking through trade but also showed little interest in science and technology.

THE GROWTH OF FRENCH POWER

Two states in the early modern period succeeded most effectively in consolidating the power of their central governments: France and England. Each became a model of a very different form of statehood. The English model evolved into a constitutional monarchy. Parliament limited the king's power, and the rights of the English people were protected by law and tradition. The French model emphasized at every turn the glory of the king and, by implication, the **sovereignty** of the dynastic state and its right to stand above the interests of its subjects. France's monarchy became absolute, although very gradually. Only by the 1660s did the court and king achieve political hegemony.

When Hugh Capet became king of France in 987, as an aristocrat he was merely first among equals. From this small power base, more symbolic than real, Hugh Capet's successors extended their territory and dominion at the expense of aristocratic power. To administer their territories, the Capetians established an efficient bureaucracy composed of townsmen and trustworthy lesser nobles who, unlike the great feudal lords, owed their wealth and status directly to the king. These royal officials, essential to monarchical power, collected the king's feudal dues and administered justice. At the same time, French kings emphasized that they had been selected by God to rule, a theory known as the *divine right of kings*. This theory conferred sanctity, and the French kings used it to enforce their commands over rebellious lords and to resist papal claims of dominance over the French church.

Yet medieval French kings never sought absolute power. Only during the reign of Louis XIV (d. 1715) did the power base of the French monarchy consolidate. The king and his court, as well as his representatives in the provinces, managed to rule without formal consultations with their subjects. In the Middle Ages, the French monarchs recognized the rights of, and consulted with, local representative assemblies, which represented the three estates, or orders, in society. These assemblies (whether regional or national) consisted of deputies drawn from the various elites: the clergy as the first estate, the nobility as the second estate, and the rest of the population as the third estate. The Estates met as circumstances—such as wars, taxes, or local disputes—warranted, and the Estates General was always summoned by the king. Medieval French kings consulted these assemblies mainly to give legitimacy to their demands and credibility to their administration. They also recognized that the courts—especially the highest court, the Parlement of Paris—had the right to administer the king's justice with a minimum of royal interference. Medieval kings were never the originators of law; they were its guarantors and administrators.

In France, war served the interests of a monarchy bent on consolidating its power and authority. As a result of the Hundred Years' War (1337–1453), the English were eventually driven from France, their claims to the French throne dashed. In the process of war, the French monarchy grew richer. War enabled the French kings to levy new taxes, often enacted without the consent of the Estates General, and to maintain a large standing army under royal command. The Hundred Years' War also inspired allegiance to the king as the visible symbol of France. The war heightened the French sense of national identity; the English were a common enemy, discernibly different in manners, language, dress, and appearance.

Religion and the French State

In every emergent state, tension existed between the monarch and the papacy. At issue was control over the church within that territory—over its personnel, its wealth, and, of course, its pulpits, from which an illiterate majority learned what their leaders wanted them to know, religious doctrines but also the role of obedience to civil authority. The monarch's power to make church appointments could ensure a complacent church, one that was willing to preach about the king's divine right to rule and that would offer no resistance to his authority. Centuries of tough bargaining with the papacy paid off when, in 1516, Francis I (1515–1547) concluded the Concordat of Bologna, by which Pope Leo X permitted the French king to nominate, and therefore effectively to appoint, his choice of bishops in the French church.

The Concordat of Bologna laid the foundation for the *Gallican church*—a term signifying the immense power and authority of the Catholic Church in France as sanctioned and overseen by the French kings. By the early sixteenth century, religious homogeneity had strengthened the central government at the expense of papal authority. This ecclesiastical and religious settlement lay at the heart of monarchical authority. Consequently, by the 1520s, the Protestant Reformation threatened the very survival of France as a unified state. Throughout the early modern period, French kings assumed that France must be governed by one king, one faith, and one set of laws. Any alternative to that unity offered the aristocracy or the clergy the opportunity to channel religious dissent into their service at the expense of royal authority. Once linked, religious and political opposition to any central government could be extremely dangerous.

During the decades that followed, partly through the efforts of the Huguenot (Protestant) underground and partly because the French king and his ministers vacillated in their attempts at persecution, the Protestant minority grew in strength and dedication. By challenging the authority of the Catholic Church, Protestants were also inadvertently challenging royal authority; the Gallican church and the French monarchy supported each other. Protestantism became the basis for a political movement of an increasingly revolutionary nature.

From 1562 to the final peace of 1598, France experienced waves of religious wars; the king lost control over vast areas of the kingdom. In 1579, extreme Huguenot theorists published the *Vindiciae contra Tyrannos*. This anonymous attack on the rights of kings, combined with a call to action, was the first of its kind in early modern times. It justified rebellion against, and even the execution of, an unjust king. European monarchs might claim power and divinely sanctioned authority, but by the late sixteenth century, their subjects had available the moral justification to oppose their monarch's will, by force if necessary. Significantly, this same treatise was translated into English in 1648, a year before Parliament publicly executed Charles I, king of England.

The French monarchy foundered in the face of a combined religious and political opposition. The era of royal supremacy ushered in by Francis I came to an abrupt end during the reign of his successor, Henry II (1547–1559). Wed to Catherine

de' Medici, a member of the powerful Italian banking family, Henry occupied himself not with the concerns of government but with the pleasures of the hunt. The sons who succeeded Henry—Francis II (1559–1560), Charles IX (1560–1574), and Henry III (1574–1589)—were uniformly weak. In this power vacuum, their mother, Catherine, emerged as virtual ruler—a queen despised as an Italian, a woman, and a backstairs intriguer. One of the most hated figures of her day, Catherine de' Medici defies dispassionate assessment. She or her son ordered the execution of Protestants by royal troops in Paris—the beginning of the infamous Saint Bartholomew's Day Massacre (1572). The massacre of more than five thousand Protestants became both a symbol and a legend in subsequent European history: a symbol of the excesses of religious zeal and a legend of Protestant martyrdom, which gave renewed energy to the cause of international Protestantism.

The civil wars begun in 1562 continued after the massacre. They dragged on until the death of the last Valois king in 1589. The Valois failure to produce a male heir to the throne placed Henry, duke of Bourbon and a Protestant, in line to succeed to the French throne. Realizing that the overwhelmingly Catholic population would not accept a Protestant king, Henry (apparently without much regret) renounced his adopted religion and embraced the church. His private religious beliefs may never be known, but outward conformity to the religion of the Catholic majority offered peace and the reestablishment of political stability. Under the reign of Henry IV (1589–1610), a form of religious toleration returned. Henry granted it to his Protestant subjects through the Edict of Nantes (1598), but they were never welcomed in significant numbers into the royal bureaucracy. Throughout the seventeenth century, every French king attempted to undermine the Protestants' regional power bases and ultimately to destroy their religious liberties.

Louis XIV: The Consolidation of French Monarchical Power

The defeat of Protestantism as a national force set the stage for the final consolidation of the French state under the great Bourbon kings,

THE HALL OF MIRRORS IN THE ROYAL PALACE AT VERSAILLES. Immense and grand, Versailles was the wonder of the age. Like the person of the king, it said to his subjects: I am grandeur incarnate. Even by today's standards, it was an impressive building, both inside and out. (© Massimo Listri/Corbis.)

Louis XIII and Louis XIV. Louis XIII (1610–1643) depended on an efficient and trustworthy bureaucracy, a renewable treasury, and constant vigilance against the localized claims to power by the great aristocracy and Protestant cities and towns. Cardinal Richelieu, who served as the young Louis XIII's chief minister from 1624 to 1642, became the great architect of French absolutism.

Richelieu's political morality rested on one principle, embodied in a phrase he invented: *raison d'état*, reason of state. Richelieu applied the principle as he brought under the king's control the disruptive and antimonarchical elements within French society. He increased the power of the central bureaucracy; attacked the power of independent, and often Protestant, towns and

cities; and harassed their Huguenot inhabitants. Above all, he humbled the great nobles by limiting their effectiveness as councilors to the king and prohibiting their traditional privileges, such as using a duel rather than court action to settle grievances. Reason of state also guided Richelieu's foreign policy. It required that France turn against Catholic Spain and join the Protestant, and hence anti-Spanish, side in the Thirty Years' War. This led to a decisive victory for French power on the Continent.

Richelieu died in 1642, and Louis XIII the following year. Mazarin, a cardinal who had never been ordained a priest and was an Italian by birth, took charge during the minority of Louis XIV (he was five years old when Louis XIII died) and continued Richelieu's policies. Mazarin's heavy-handed actions produced a rebellious reaction, the *Fronde*, a series of street riots that eventually cost the government control over Paris and lasted from 1648 to 1653. Centered in Paris and supported by the great aristocracy, the courts, and the city's poorer classes, the Fronde threatened to develop into a full-scale uprising. It might have done so but for one crucial factor: its leadership was divided. Court judges (lesser nobles who had often just risen from the ranks of the bourgeoisie) deeply distrusted the great aristocrats and refused in the end to make common cause with them, and both groups feared disorders among the urban masses. Early modern states faced deep trouble only when the elites united against them.

When Louis XIV finally came to the throne in 1661, he vowed that what he had witnessed in Paris, when the Fronde brought street rioters to the palace windows, would never be repeated. Aided by his minister of finance, Jean Baptiste Colbert, Louis XIV crafted the absolutist state. He became the source of all power. Local elites or officials were expected to look to the central government for everything, from taxes to noble titles and exclusive privileges for perfume manufacturing or coal extraction. Provincial bureaucrats reported to ministers based in Paris. Indeed, even road engineers were sent out from Paris. The army was made larger and more professional, gaining, in addition, an architecture and engineering corps. The state also established a military school and sponsored academies for science, literature, and language. Intellectuals received court patronage and pensions, but only if they said what the crown wanted to hear. Colbert turned intelligence gathering into an art.

Under Louis XIV, the state became the major player in everything, from dredging the rivers to awarding manufacturing monopolies. No absolute monarch in Western Europe had ever before held so much personal authority or commanded such a vast and effective military and administrative machine. Louis XIV's reign finished the process of increasing monarchical authority. Intelligent, cunning, and possessing a unique understanding of the requirements of his office, Louis XIV became the envy of his age.

Perhaps the most brilliant of Louis XIV's many policies was his treatment of members of the aristocracy. He simply dispensed with their services as influential advisers. He treated them to elaborate rituals, feasts, processions, displays, and banquets, but as they played, their power dwindled. The wiser aristocrats stayed home on their estates. For those who ventured to Versailles in search of power and glory, the possibility of financial ruin loomed. Few could keep up with the level of the king's spending.

Louis XIV's domestic policies, not surprisingly, centered on the incessant search for new revenues. Versailles and its banquets cost a fortune. So too did his wars, which Louis XIV waged to excess. He relied on the brilliant Colbert, who improved methods of tax collecting, promoted new industries, and encouraged international trade. Such ambitious national policies were possible because Louis XIV inherited the efficient system of administration that had been introduced by Richelieu. Instead of relying on the local aristocracy to collect royal taxes and to administer royal policies, Richelieu had appointed the king's own men as *intendants*—functionaries with wide powers who were dispatched into the provinces. At first, their mission had been temporary and their success minimal, but gradually, they became a permanent feature of royal administration. During the reign of Louis XIV, the country was divided into thirty-two districts, controlled by intendants. Operating with a total bureaucracy of about a thousand officials and no longer bothering even to consult the parlements (courts of law) or the Estates, Louis XIV ruled absolutely.

Why did such a system of absolute authority work? The peasants occasionally revolted, but why did the old aristocracy not rise in rebellion? For the aristocrats, the loss of political authority was not accompanied by a comparable loss in wealth and social position; indeed, quite the contrary was true. During the seventeenth century, the French nobility—2 percent of the population—controlled approximately 20 to 30 percent of the total national income. The church, too, fared well under Louis, receiving good tax arrangements, provided it preached about the king's divinely given rights. Although there were peasant upheavals throughout the century, the sheer size of the royal army and police—more than 300,000 by the end of Louis's reign—made successful revolt nearly impossible. When, in the early 1700s, a popular religious rebellion led by Protestant visionaries broke

Louis XIV, *Instructions for the Dauphin*

In the Instructions for the Dauphin *of 1665, Louis XIV boasted to his heir that he understood the key to successful kingship.*

[Successful kingship lies in being] informed of everything, listening to the lowliest of my subjects, always knowing the number and character of my troops and the condition of my strongholds, constantly issuing orders for all their needs, dealing directly with foreign envoys, receiving and reading dispatches, drafting some of the replies personally and giving the substance of the others to my secretaries, regulating the collections and the expenditures of my state, having those whom I place in important positions report directly to me, maintaining greater secrecy in my affairs than any of my predecessors, distributing graces as I choose, and keeping my servants, unless I am mistaken—although showered with graces for themselves and their families—in modesty far removed from the loftiness and from the power of prime ministers.

Questions for Analysis

1. Could any one human being do all that Louis XIV claimed he was doing?
2. Why is Louis XIV concerned to keep his servants away from his prime ministers?

Jacob Soll, *The Information Master: The Rise and Fall of Jean-Baptiste Colbert's Secret State Library* (Ann Arbor: University of Michigan Press, 2010).

out in the south, royal troops crushed it. Thus, absolutism rested on the complicity of the old aristocracy, the self-aggrandizement of government officials, the church's doctrines, the revenues squeezed out of the peasantry, and the power of a huge military machine.

Yet Louis XIV's system was fatally flawed. Without any effective check on his power and on his dreams of international conquest, no limit was imposed on the state's capacity to make war or spend money. By the 1680s, his domestic and foreign policies turned violently aggressive. In 1685, he revoked the Edict of Nantes, and thousands of French Protestants fled or were imprisoned. In 1689, he embarked on a military campaign to gain territory from the Holy Roman Empire. And in 1701, he tried to bring Spain under the control of the Bourbon dynasty. Louis XIV, however, underestimated the strength of his northern rivals, England and the Dutch Republic. Their combined power, in alliance with the Holy Roman Empire and the Austrians, defeated Louis XIV's ambitions and left his treasury empty. In the winter of 1709–1710, famine stalked the land.

The War of the Spanish Succession was fought on the battlefields of northern Europe. Out of it, the Austrians acquired the southern Netherlands (Belgium) and thus a buffer against the possibility of a French overrun of the Low Countries. Most dramatically, however, the war created a balance of power in Europe. Britain emerged as a major force in European affairs, the counterweight against the French colossus. Anglo-French rivalry dominated the international politics of the eighteenth century, creating a fragile balance of power in the Atlantic world.

Louis XIV's participation in these long wars emptied the royal treasury. By the late seventeenth century, taxes had risen intolerably and were levied mostly on those least able to pay: the peasants. In the early 1700s, the combination of taxes, bad harvests, and plague led to widespread poverty, misery, and starvation in large areas of France. Thus, for the great majority of French people, absolutism meant a decline in living standards and a significant increase in mortality rates. Absolutism also required surveillance of the population. Royal authorities censored books; spied on heretics, Protestants, and freethinkers; and even tortured and executed opponents of state policy.

By 1715, France was a tightly governed society whose treasury was bankrupt. Protestants had been driven into exile or forced to convert. Strict

LOUIS XIV. By every gesture and pose, Louis XIV sought to display grandeur and to embody monarchy. His dress and affect were meant to awe and intimidate. (Bridgeman-Giraudon/Art Resource, N.Y.)

censorship laws closely governed publishing, causing a brisk trade in clandestine books and manuscripts. Direct taxes burdened the poor and were legally evaded by the aristocracy. Critics of state policy within the church had been effectively marginalized. And over the long run, foreign wars had brought no significant gains.

In the France of Louis XIV, the dynastic and absolutist state reached maturity and began to display some of its classic characteristics: centralized bureaucracy; royal patronage to enforce allegiance; a system of taxation universally but inequitably applied; and suppression of political opposition, either through the use of patronage or, if necessary, through force. On a more positive note, the state cultivated the arts and sciences as a means of increasing national power and prestige. Together, these policies enabled France and its monarchs to achieve political stability, enforce a uniform system of law, and channel the country's

wealth and resources into the service of the state as a whole (see Primary Source box).

Nonetheless, at his death in 1715, Louis XIV left a bureaucracy and onerous taxation that were vastly in need of overhaul. But because this system favored the church and the nobility, reforming it was virtually impossible. The pattern of war, excessive taxation of the lower classes, and spending beyond revenues had damaged France's finances. Yet the bureaucracy of the absolutist state continued to grow and extend its influence into every area of trade. To this day, perfectly preserved pieces of silk and cotton cloth from every French province sit in the Parisian archives of the government. They had been sent there for inspection. Only when the king's ministers had approved the samples could the cloth from which they had been cut be sold in the open market, with the king's seal. By the 1780s, manufacturers clamored for freer markets; fewer, or at least faster, inspections; and more freedom to experiment. They smuggled and cheated the inspectors while looking across the Channel with envy at the power, wealth, and freedom of England's industry and its merchants. The discontent of French manufacturers contributed to the causes of the French Revolution of 1789.

THE GROWTH OF LIMITED MONARCHY AND CONSTITUTIONALISM IN ENGLAND

England achieved national unity earlier than any other major European state. Its island geography freed it from the border disputes that plagued emerging states in Continental Europe. By an accident of fate, its administrative structure also developed in such a way as to encourage centralization. In 1066, William, duke of Normandy and vassal to the French king, had invaded and conquered England, acquiring at a stroke the entire kingdom. In contrast, the French kings took centuries to make the territory of France their domain.

As conquerors, the Norman kings intermarried with their powerful subjects, such as earls and barons, and consulted with the church and the nobility. By the middle of the thirteenth century, these consultations, or *parlays,* came to be called *parliaments.* Increasingly, kings invited parliament's representatives from the counties—knights and

De France wreedheid tot Bodegrave en Swammerdam geschiedt in den Jaare 1672.

ENGRAVING OF THE FRENCH INVASION OF THE DUTCH REPUBLIC IN 1672, BY BERNARD PICART. France's bellicosity against its neighbors was graphically depicted in this engraving, which depicts a scene from the French invasion of the Dutch Republic in 1672. This image may have been propaganda, but it was effective in branding the French king, Louis XIV, as a tyrant. (Fine Arts Museum of San Francisco, Achenbach Foundation for Graphic Arts A059746.)

burgesses. Gradually, these lesser-than-noble but landed and prominent representatives came to regard Parliament as a means of redressing their grievances. In turn, the later medieval kings saw Parliament as a means of exercising control and raising taxes. By 1297, the Lords (the upper house) and the Commons (the lower house) had obtained the king's agreement that no direct taxes could be levied without their consent. By the fourteenth century, Parliament had become a permanent institution of government. Its power

was entirely subservient to the crown, but its right to question royal decisions had been established.

The English Parliament and Constitution

The medieval English Parliament possessed two characteristics that distinguished it from its many Continental counterparts, such as the various French Estates. The English Parliament was national, not

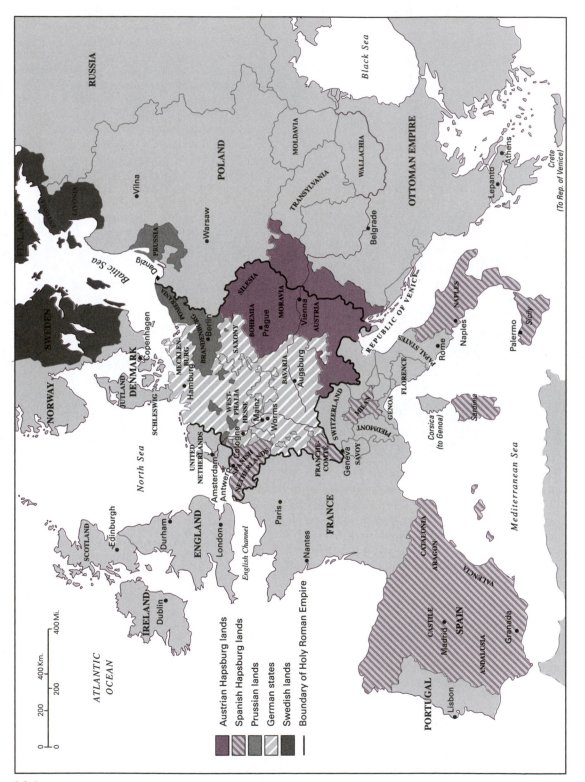

RUSSIA

Black Sea

FINLAND

Baltic Sea

SWEDEN

NORWAY

DENMARK

North Sea

SCOTLAND

Edinburgh•

IRELAND

Dublin •

ENGLAND

London •

Durham •

English Channel

POLAND

Vilna •

•Warsaw

LIVONIA

PRUSSIA

Danzig•

POMERANIA

BRANDENBURG

Berlin •

MECKLEN-
BURG

Copenhagen •

JUTLAND

SCHLESWIG

Hamburg •

WEST-
PHALIA

HESSE

Cologne •

Mainz •

Worms •

SAXONY

SILESIA

MORAVIA

BOHEMIA

Prague •

BAVARIA

Augsburg •

SWITZERLAND

Geneva •

Vienna •

AUSTRIA

MOLDAVIA

TRANSYLVANIA

WALLACHIA

Belgrade •

OTTOMAN EMPIRE

REPUBLIC OF VENICE

PAPAL STATES

Rome •

FLORENCE

GENOA

MILAN

PIEDMONT

SAVOY

FRANCHE-
COMTÉ

UNITED
NETHERLANDS

Amsterdam •

Antwerp •

SPANISH
NETHERLANDS

Paris •

Nantes •

FRANCE

*Corsica
(to Genoa)*

Sardinia

Naples •

NAPLES

Palermo •

Sicily

Lepanto •

Athens •

*Crete
(To Rep. of Venice)*

Mediterranean Sea

*ATLANTIC
OCEAN*

PORTUGAL

Lisbon •

SPAIN

Madrid •

CASTILE

ANDALUSIA

Granada •

VALENCIA

CATALONIA

ARAGON

400 Mi.

200

200

400 Km.

0

0

■ Austrian Hapsburg lands
▨ Spanish Hapsburg lands
▨ Prussian lands
▨ German states
▨ Swedish lands
— Boundary of Holy Roman Empire

provincial; more important, its representatives were elected across caste lines, with voting rights dependent on property, not on noble birth or status. These representatives voted as individuals rather than collectively as clergy, nobles, or commoners—that is, as Estates. In the Middle Ages, Parliament and the monarchy were interdependent; they were seen not as rivals but as complementary forms of centralized government. That very interdependence, however, would ultimately lead to conflict.

The constitution, too, emerged during the Middle Ages in England. It comprised unwritten and written precedents, laws, and royal acts that came to embody the basic principles of government. In contrast to the French model, England developed into a *constitutional* monarchy. The most famous document, Magna Carta (1215), guaranteed certain aristocratic privileges and was read at the opening meeting of almost every Parliament the king called. The theoretical foundation for the constitution—which was never a written document—grew out of legal practices and customs described under the generic term *common law*. Whereas feudal law applied only to a local region, common law extended throughout the realm and served as a unifying force.

The Tudor Achievement

Despite having a Parliament and constitution, England in the fifteenth century could be a lawless place where local noblemen made war on their neighbors largely unchecked by central government. One such war, the War of the Roses (1455–1485), pitted two noble families against each other in a struggle for domination. Out of it, the Tudors emerged triumphant, in the person of Henry VII (1485–1509), who spent much of his reign consolidating and extending his authority. He revitalized and remade the institutions of central government. Henry VII's goal was to check the unruly nobility. Toward this end, he brought commoners into the government. These commoners, unlike the great magnates, could be channeled into royal service because they craved what the king offered: financial

HENRY VIII. Although the ruler of a second-rate power, Henry VIII sought to impress upon his subjects that he was a new and powerful monarch. He sought to compete in style, if not in power, with the French and the Spanish kings. (Walker Art Gallery, National Museums Liverpool.)

rewards and elevated social status. Although they did not fully displace the aristocracy, commoners were brought into Henry VII's inner circle, into the Privy Council, into the courts, and eventually into all the highest offices of the government. The strength and efficiency of Tudor government were shown during the Reformation, when Henry VIII (1509–1547) made himself head of the English church. This giant step toward increasing royal power grew out of the restored order and stability imposed by his father.

◀ *Map 16.2* EUROPE, 1648 By 1648, Europe was exhausted by war. (Copyright © 2013 Cengage Learning.)

The Henrican and Protestant Reformation in England was a revolution in royal, as well as ecclesiastical, government. It defeated a main obstacle to monarchical authority: the power of the papacy. At the same time, the Reformation greatly enhanced the power of Parliament. Henry VIII used Parliament to make the Reformation because he knew that he needed the support of the lords, the country gentry, and the merchants. Parliament's participation in the Reformation gave it a greater role and sense of importance than it had ever possessed in the past. Nonetheless, the final outcome of this administrative revolution enhanced monarchical power. By the end of his reign, Henry VIII easily possessed as much power as his French rival, Francis I. Indeed, until the early seventeenth century, the history of monarchical power in England, with its absolutist tendencies, was remarkably similar to the Continental pattern. No one could imagine the instability that lay ahead.

At Henry's death, the Tudor bureaucracy and centralized government were strained to the utmost, yet they survived. The government weathered the reign of Henry's sickly son, Edward VI (1547–1553), and the extreme Protestantism of some of his advisers, and it survived the brief and deeply troubled reign of Henry's first daughter, Mary (1553–1558), who brutally tried to return England to Catholicism. At Mary's death, England stood dangerously close to the religious instability and sectarian tension that would undermine the French kings during the final decades of the sixteenth century.

Henry's second daughter, Elizabeth I (1558–1603), initiated a period of peace and religious stability. The Elizabethan period brought a heightened sense of national identity. The English Reformation enhanced that sense, as did the increasing fear of foreign invasion by Spain. The fear was real enough and lessened only with the defeat of the Spanish Armada in 1588. For the English, the victory seemed like that of David over Goliath, and its value was both symbolic and real. Just as the Spanish agonized about what they had done to offend God, the English smugly concluded that they had pleased him. In the seventeenth century, the English would look back on Elizabeth's reign as a golden age. It was the calm before the storm. In the seventeenth century, a prosperous commercial class emerged, and it would demand a greater say in government operations.

The social and economic changes of the Elizabethan age can be seen, in microcosm, by looking at the Durham region in northern England. From 1580 to 1640, a new coal-mining industry developed there through the efforts of entrepreneurs—gentlemen with minor lands who, with the aid of engineers, exploited their mineral resources. The wool trade also prospered in Durham. By 1600, social and political tensions had developed. The wool merchants and the entrepreneurial gentry were demanding a greater say in governing the region. They were opposed by the traditional leaders of Durham society: the bishops and the dozen or so aristocratic families with major landholdings and access to the court in London.

This split can be described as one between "court" and "country." In this context, *court* refers to the traditional aristocratic magnates, the church hierarchy, and royal officialdom, and *country* denotes a loose coalition of merchants and rising agricultural and industrial entrepreneurs from the prosperous gentry class, whose economic worth far exceeded their political power. The pattern found in Durham was repeated in other parts of England, generally where industry and commerce grew and prospered. The gentry gained social status and wealth. In the seventeenth century, these social and economic tensions between court and country would help foment revolution. Indeed, English historians have argued that one needs look no further than the new merchant class for the roots of the civil wars of the 1640s.

By the early seventeenth century in England, the descendants of the old feudal aristocracy differed markedly from their Continental counterparts. Isolation from the great wars of the Reformation had produced an aristocracy less militaristic and more ceremonial and commercial in orientation. Furthermore, the lesser ranks of the landowning aristocracy, gentlemen without titles (the gentry), had prospered significantly in Tudor times. In commercial matters, they were often no shrewder than the great landed magnates, but they had in Parliament, as well as in their counties, an effective and institutionalized means of expressing their political interests. The great nobles, in contrast, had largely abandoned the sword as the primary expression of their political authority without putting anything comparable in its place. Gradually, political initiative was slipping away from the great lords and into the hands of a gentry that was commercially and agriculturally innovative as well as fiercely protective of its local base of political power.

At Elizabeth's accession, male contemporaries worried in print whether she would be up to the task of ruling and urged her court and Privy Council to keep her in line. They were in for a shock as Elizabeth proved to be one of the most able monarchs; she did not hesitate to set policy as she saw fit, much to the annoyance of her advisers. Even the earl of Leicester, widely regarded as one of her suitors, said in 1578 that "our conference with her Majesty about affairs is both seldom and slender."

Elizabeth faced the possibility of rebellion led by her Catholic cousin, Mary Queen of Scots, and in the end, Elizabeth saw to her execution. Elizabeth's greatest test came in 1588 when the Spanish king, Philip II, sent his Armada to invade England for the purpose of restoring it to Catholicism. Consulting her astrologers but armed for battle, Elizabeth rallied the country, and the English fleet got very lucky. A gale-force wind blew the Spanish ships out of striking distance of the mouth of the Thames River, and the Armada was virtually destroyed. The wind that blew that day became known as "the Protestant wind," and Elizabeth went down in history as "good Queen Bess."

Even more so than her father, Elizabeth secured England, though not Ireland, for the Protestant cause. She also gave her name to the age, and Elizabethan England flourished culturally. During her reign, William Shakespeare wrote many of his greatest plays and the London theatre blossomed.

Religion played a vital role in this realignment of political interests and forces. Many of the old aristocracy clung to the Anglicanism of the Henrican Reformation, with bishops and liturgy intact, and some even clung to Catholicism. The newly risen members of the gentry found in the Protestant Reformation a form of religious worship more suited to their independent spirit. They felt that it was their right to appoint their own preachers and that the church should reflect local tastes and beliefs rather than doctrines and ceremonies inherited from a discredited Catholicism. In late Tudor times, gentry and merchant interests

fused with Puritanism—the English variety of Calvinism—to produce a political-religious vision with ominous potential. Some historians have argued that, not a new merchant class, but religious tensions account for the civil wars. They add to that argument the errors in judgment made by Charles I.

The English Revolutions, 1640–1660 and 1688–1689

The religious and political forces threatening the monarchy were dealt with ineffectively by the first two Stuart kings: James I (1603–1625) and Charles I (1625–1649). Like their Continental counterparts, both believed in royal absolutism. Essentially, these Stuart kings tried to do in England what Louis XIV later did in France: establish crown and court administrators as the sole governing bodies within the state. The Stuarts, however, lacked an adequate financial and institutional base for absolutism, not least of all a standing army. Nor did they possess the vast independent wealth of the French kings.

Through the established church, the Stuarts preached the doctrine of the divine right of kings. James I, an effective and shrewd administrator, conducted foreign policy without consulting Parliament. In a speech before Parliament, he stated that "it is sedition in subjects to dispute what a king may do in the height of his power. . . . I will not be content that my power be disputed upon."[1]

James I made the standard moves toward creating an absolute monarchy: he centralized and consolidated the power of the government and tried to win over the aristocracy by giving them new offices and titles. To merchants, he gave royal monopolies for everything from soap to coal. James I did not have a sufficient economic base to pay for his largesse. His son and successor, Charles I, had the same problem. But Charles suspended Parliament in 1629 and attempted to rule through his advisers. He had two major goals: to rid the nation of Puritans and to root out the "country" opposition. Charles also tried to collect taxes without Parliament's consent. These policies ended in disaster; by 1640, the Puritans and the gentry opposition had grown closer together.

Elizabeth I, Queen of England (1558–1603)

Born in 1533, Elizabeth, the daughter of Henry VIII and his second wife, Anne Boleyn, was raised as a Protestant by her father. Fidelity to the Anglican Church may have been basic to Henry's interests, but fidelity to his marriage vows was not. He put Anne Boleyn to death on charges of treason. His marriage to her had led to England's break with the Roman Catholic Church, which would not grant him a divorce from his first wife, Catherine of Aragon, with whom he had failed to produce a male heir. When Henry's second marriage also did not produce the male heir he so deeply desired, he tired of Elizabeth's mother. Hence her tragic end.

The church of Rome regarded Elizabeth as a bastard and never accepted Henry's self-decreed divorce from his first wife. Not surprisingly, in her youth, Elizabeth came to fear marriage and to regard her claim to the English throne as precarious. She became queen in 1558—after the deaths of her half sister, Mary, and half brother, Edward, each of whom had short, tumultuous reigns.

Elizabeth watched and waited, knowing that unless assassinated she would someday be queen. She saw that intervention into the private religious beliefs of her subjects would lead to turmoil and persecution. She vowed never to repeat the mistakes especially of her half-sister, Mary, who persecuted and executed Protestant leaders.

With Elizabeth's accession to the throne, England and Wales returned to the fold of the Henrican Reformation, repudiating the efforts of Queen Mary to force them to revert to Roman Catholicism. Because Mary executed Protestant leaders, she went down in history as "Bloody Mary." Elizabeth recognized that as a woman, she would have to make alliances and never allow herself to be perceived as weak. Yet the obvious form of alliance, that of marriage to a foreign prince, made her hesitate, probably out of fear that she too would somehow meet the sad fate of her mother. Her steady hand gave England an era of relative peace complete with a flourishing of the arts and letters. By the end of her reign, many courtiers were discontent, but not the mass of population who had come to revere her.

The first English Revolution began in 1640 because Charles I needed money to defend the realm against a recent Scottish invasion. Being staunch Calvinists, the Scots had rebelled against Charles's religious policies and thought that his Anglicanism was a barely concealed Catholicism. Moreover, their clan leaders saw rebellion as a way to get back at the Stuart kings, who long had been a thorn in their side, first when they ruled in Edinburgh and now from their base in London. Charles had no alternative but to call Parliament, and it could now dictate the terms: if Parliament received no concessions from Charles, then it would raise no money to fight the Scots, who were also demanding payment for every day they occupied the northern territory. Parliament countered the king's requests with demands for rights: consultations with Parliament in matters of taxation, trial by jury, habeas corpus, and a truly Protestant church responsive to the beliefs and interests of its laity. Charles refused these demands, viewing them as an assault on royal authority. He even tried to arrest the leaders of Parliament. In 1642, civil war began. Directed by Parliament and financed by taxes and the merchants, the war was fought by the New Model Army, led by Oliver Cromwell (1599–1658), a Puritan squire with a gift for military leadership.

The two English revolutions became part of a constitutional crisis that lasted two generations. The crisis began in 1640, degenerated into civil war in 1642, and culminated in regicide in 1649. After the restoration of monarchy in 1660, the crisis flared up again in 1679 through 1681 and was finally resolved by the revolution of 1688–1689—sometimes called the Glorious Revolution. The crisis affected England, Scotland, Ireland, and Wales differently, but in all cases, it led to the consolidation of English power over these territories. Perhaps the native Irish fared worst of all as Cromwell drove thousands to the barren western part of the island.

The civil wars of the 1640s generated a new type of military organization. The New Model Army was financed by Parliament's rich supporters and led by gentlemen farmers. Its ranks were filled by religious zealots, along with the usual cross section of poor artisans and day laborers. This citizen army defeated the king, his aristocratic followers, and the Anglican Church's hierarchy. After his defeat, Charles refused to compromise with his Parliamentary captors.

In January 1649, Charles I was publicly executed by order of Parliament. During the interregnum (time between kings) of the next eleven years, Parliament joined with the army to govern the country as a republic. As power was distributed between the army and Parliament, Cromwell proved to be the key player. He had the support of the army's officers and some of its rank and file, and he had been a member of Parliament for many years. However, he gained control over the army only after it was purged of radical groups. Some of these radicals, known as Levellers, wanted to level society, that is, to redistribute property by ending monopolies and to give the vote to all male citizens. In the context of the 1650s, Cromwell was a moderate republican who also believed in limited religious toleration for Protestants, yet history has painted him, somewhat unjustly, as a military dictator.

Both English revolutions were led by a loose coalition of urban merchants and landed gentry imbued with the strict Protestantism of the Continental Reformation. In the 1650s, their success was jeopardized by growing discontent from the poor, who made up the rank and file of the army and demanded that their grievances be rectified. The radicals of the first English Revolution—men such as Gerrard Winstanley, the first theoretician of social democracy in modern times, and John Lilburne, the Leveller—demanded redistribution of property, even communal property; voting rights for the majority of the male population; and abolition of religious and intellectual elites, whose power and ideology supported the interests of the ruling classes. The radicals rejected Anglicanism and moderate Puritanism; they opted instead for radical politics and free lifestyles. They spurned marriage, and the Quakers even allowed women to preach. They, in effect, created a revolution within the revolution. The radicals terrified devoted Puritans such as Cromwell. By 1660, two years after Cromwell's death, the country was adrift, without effective leadership.

Parliament, having secured the economic interests of its constituency (gentry, merchants, and some small landowners), chose to restore court and crown and invited the exiled son of the executed king to return to the kingship. Having learned the lesson his father had spurned, Charles II (1660–1685) never instituted royal absolutism, although he did try to minimize Parliament's role in the government. His court was a far more open institution than his father's had been, for Charles II feared a similar death.

Charles's brother James II (1685–1688), however, was a foolishly fearless Catholic and an admirer of French absolutism. Having gathered at his court a coterie of Catholic advisers (among them Jesuits) and supporters of royal prerogative, James attempted to bend Parliament and local government to the royal will. James's Catholicism, modeled on French Gallicanism, was the crucial element in his failure. The Anglican Church would not back him, and political forces similar to those that had gathered against his father, Charles I, in 1640 descended on him. But back in the 1650s, the ruling elites had learned their lesson: civil war would produce social discontent among the masses. The upper classes wanted to avoid open warfare and to preserve the monarchy as a constitutional authority but not as an absolute one. Puritanism, with its sectarian fervor and its dangerous association with republicanism, was allowed to play no part in the second English Revolution of 1688–1689.

In early 1688, Anglicans, some aristocrats, and opponents of royal prerogative (members of the Whig party, along with a few Tories) formed a conspiracy against James II. Their purpose

OLIVER CROMWELL. Cromwell wore the simple black of the Puritan gentry and sought to portray himself as a pious warrior. Yet in this portrait, he does have a somewhat regal bearing, and his task demanded that he act like a king without ever becoming one. (akg-images.)

was to invite his son-in-law, William of Orange, *stadholder* (head) of the Netherlands and husband of James's Protestant daughter Mary, to invade England and rescue its government from James's control. The final outcome of this invasion was determined by William and his conspirators, in conjunction with a freely elected Parliament. This dangerous plan succeeded for three main reasons: William and the Dutch desperately needed English support against the threat of a French invasion; James had lost the loyalty of key men in the army, powerful gentlemen in the counties, and the Anglican Church; and the political elite was committed and united in its intentions. William and Mary were declared king and queen by act of Parliament, and William defeated James II's army in Ireland. The

last revolution in English history defeated royal absolutism forever. Ironically, while political freedom increased in England, Scotland soon lost its parliament, and Catholics in Ireland were systematically repressed.

This bloodless revolution—the Glorious Revolution—created a new political and constitutional reality. Parliament gained the rights to assemble regularly and to vote on all matters of taxation; the rights of habeas corpus and trial by jury (for men of property and social status) were also secured. These rights were in turn legitimated in a constitutionally binding document, the Bill of Rights (1689). All Protestants, regardless of their sectarian bias, were granted toleration.

The Revolution Settlement of 1688–1689 resolved the profound constitutional and social tensions of the seventeenth century and laid the foundations of the English government that exists today. The year 1688 saw the creation of a new public and political order that would become the envy of enlightened reformers. The Glorious Revolution, says the historian Steve Pincus, succeeded when popular uprisings "that involved the spectrum of English society, from humble men and women who volunteered with their pitchforks . . . to wealthy businessmen and aristocratic landowners" drove out James II and his version of monarchical absolutism.[2] Throughout the eighteenth century, England was ruled by kings and Parliaments that represented the interests of the mercantile and the landed whose prosperity ensured social and political stability. While religion had been important, the English Revolution gave legitimacy to monied and landed interests.

In the end, the English revolutions established English parliamentary government and the rule of law; they also provided a degree of freedom for the propertied. In retrospect, we can see that absolutism according to the French model probably never had a chance in England. England had too many gentlemen who possessed enough land to be independent of the crown, yet not so much that they could control whole sections of the kingdom. In addition, monarchs had no effective standing army. But to contemporaries, the issues seemed different: English opponents of absolutism spoke of their rights as granted by their ancient constitution and feudal law, of the need to make the English church truly Protestant, and, among the radicals, of the right of lesser men to establish their property. These opponents possessed an institution—Parliament—through which they could express their grievances. Eventually, they also acquired an army, which waged war to protect property and commercial rights. In 1689, the propertied classes invented limited monarchy and a constitutional system based on laws made by Parliament and sanctioned by the king. Very gradually, the monarchical element in that system would yield to the power and authority of parliamentary ministers and state officials. 1688–1689 has been called the "bloodless revolution," but that vastly underestimates the level of violence that gripped the country.

In the nineteenth and twentieth centuries, parliamentary institutions would be gradually and peacefully reformed to express a more democratic social reality. The events of 1688 and 1689 have rightly been described as "the year one," for they fashioned a system of government that operated effectively in Britain and could also be adopted elsewhere with modification. The British system became a model for other forms of representative government that were adopted in France and in the former British colonies, beginning with the United States. It was the model that offered a viable alternative to absolutism.

THE NETHERLANDS: A BOURGEOIS REPUBLIC

One other area in Europe developed a system of representative government that also survived until late in the eighteenth century. The Netherlands (the Low Countries, that is, the seven Dutch provinces and Belgium) had been part of Hapsburg territory since the fifteenth century. When Charles V ascended the Spanish throne in 1516, the Netherlands emerged as the economic linchpin of the Spanish empire. Spain exported wool and bullion to the Low Countries in return for manufactured textiles, hardware, grain, ships,

and naval stores. Flanders, with Antwerp as its capital, was the manufacturing and banking center of the Spanish empire.

To the north, cities such as Rotterdam and Amsterdam built and outfitted the Spanish fleet. In The Hague, printers published the Bible in Spanish and in Dutch or Flemish (actually the same language). But in the north, too, Protestantism made significant inroads.

During the reign of Charles V's successor, Philip II, a tightly organized Calvinist minority, with its popular base in the cities and its military strategy founded on sea raids, at first harassed and then aggressively challenged Spanish power. In the 1560s, the Spanish responded by trying to export the Inquisition into the Netherlands and sending an enormous standing army there under the duke of Alva. It was a classic example of overkill; thousands of once-loyal Flemish and Dutch subjects turned against the Spanish crown. The people either converted secretly to Calvinism or aided the revolutionaries. Led by William the Silent (1533–1584), head of the Orange dynasty, the seven northern provinces (Holland, Zeeland, Utrecht, Gelderland, Overijssel, Friesland, and Groningen) joined in the Union of Utrecht (1579) to protect themselves against Spanish aggression. Their determined resistance, coupled with the serious economic weaknesses of the overextended Spanish empire, eventually produced unexpected success for the northern colonies. They also formed the first state to articulate the notion that the government should leave people to their religious preferences.

By 1609, the seven northern provinces were effectively free of Spanish control and loosely tied together under a republican form of government. Seventeenth-century Netherlands (that is, the Dutch Republic) became a prosperous bourgeois state. Rich from the fruits of manufacture and trade in everything from tulip bulbs to ships— and, not least, slaves—Dutch merchants ruled their cities and provinces with a fierce pride. By the early seventeenth century, this new, highly urbanized nation of only 1.2 million people was practicing the most innovative commercial and financial techniques in Europe.

In this fascinating instance, capitalism and Protestantism fused to do the work of princes;

the Dutch state emerged without absolute monarchy, and indeed in opposition to it. From that experience, the ruling Dutch oligarchy retained a deep distrust of hereditary monarchy and of central government. The exact position of the House of Orange remained a vexing constitutional question until well into the eighteenth century. The oligarchs and their party, the Patriots, favored a republic without a single head, ruled by them locally and in the Estates General. The Calvinist clergy, old aristocrats, and a vast section of the populace—all for very different reasons—wanted the head of the House of Orange to govern as stadholder of the provinces—in effect, as a limited monarch in a republican state. These unresolved political tensions between the center and the localities prevented the Netherlands from developing a form of republican government to rival the stability of the British system of limited monarchy. The Dutch achievement came in other areas, particularly in art and technological innovation.

Calvinism had provided the ideology of revolution and national identity. Capital, in turn, created a unique cultural milieu in the Dutch urban centers of Amsterdam, Rotterdam, Utrecht, and The Hague. Wide toleration without a centralized system of censorship made the Dutch book trade, which often disseminated works by refugees from the Spanish Inquisition and later by French Protestants, the most vital in Europe right up to the French Revolution. By 1700, half the books published in Europe were printed in the Dutch Republic. And the sights and sounds of a prosperous population, coupled with a politically engaged and rich bourgeoisie, fed the imagination, as well as the purses, of various artistic schools. Rembrandt van Rijn, Jan Steen, Frans Hals, Jan Vermeer, and Jan van de Velde are at the top of a long list of great Dutch artists—many of them also refugees. They left timeless images portraying the people of the only republican state to endure in the course of the seventeenth century. By 1650, the Dutch Republic had become the richest state in Europe, possibly in the world. Only after the invasion by the French revolutionaries in 1795 did the Dutch Republic confront the weaknesses of highly localized government and the absence of a constitution.

THE HOLY ROMAN EMPIRE: THE FAILURE TO UNIFY GERMANY

In contrast to the English, French, Spanish, and Dutch experiences in the early modern period, the Germans failed to achieve national unity. This failure to unify is tied to the history of the Holy Roman Empire. That union of various central European territories was created in the tenth century, when Otto I, in a deliberate attempt to revive Charlemagne's empire, was crowned "emperor of the Romans" by the pope. Later, the title was changed to "Holy Roman Emperor." The empire consisted of mostly German-speaking principalities.

Otto and his medieval successors busied themselves not with administering their territories but with attempting to gain control over the rich Italian peninsula and dealing with the challenges presented by powerful popes. Meanwhile, members of the German nobility extended and consolidated their rule over their peasants and over various towns and cities within the empire. Their aristocratic power remained a constant obstacle to German unity. Only by incorporating the nobility into the fabric of the state's power, court, and army and by sanctioning their oppressive control of the peasants would Holy Roman Emperors very gradually manage to create a unified German state.

In the medieval and early modern periods, the Holy Roman Emperors depended on powerful noble lords—including archbishops and bishops—for support because the office of emperor was elective, not hereditary. German noble princes—including the archbishops of Cologne and Mainz, the Hohenzollern ruler of Brandenburg, and the duke of Saxony, electors responsible for choosing the Holy Roman Emperor—were fiercely independent. All regarded themselves as autonomous powers. These decentralizing tendencies were highly developed by the thirteenth century, and the emperors gradually realized that they were losing control of the outer frontiers of the empire. The French had conducted a successful military incursion into northern Italy and on the western frontier of the empire. Hungary had fallen to the Turks, and the Swiss, given their terrain, were impossible to beat into submission. At the same time, the Hapsburgs maneuvered themselves into a position from which they could monopolize the imperial elections.

The Holy Roman Empire in the reigns of the Hapsburg emperors Maximilian I (1493–1519) and Charles V (1519–1556) might have achieved a degree of cohesion comparable with that in France and Spain. Certainly, the impetus of war—against France and against the Turks—required the creation of a large standing army and the taxation to maintain it. Both could have worked to the benefit of a centralized, imperial power. But the Protestant Reformation, which began in 1517, meshed with already well-developed tendencies toward local independence and destroyed the last hope of Hapsburg domination and German unity. Members of the German nobility used the Reformation as a vindication of their local power, and indeed, Martin Luther made just such an appeal to their interests.

At precisely the moment in the 1520s when Charles V had to act with great determination to stop the spread of Lutheranism, he was at war with France over its claims to Italian territory. Charles had no sooner won his Italian territories, in particular the rich city-state of Milan, than he had to make war against the Turks, who in 1529 besieged Vienna. Not until the 1540s was Charles V in a position to attack the Lutheran princes. By then, they had solidified their position and united for mutual protection.

War raged in Germany between the Protestant princes and the imperial army led by Charles V. In 1551, Catholic France entered the war on the Protestant side, and Charles had to flee for his life. Defeated, Charles later abdicated and retired to a Spanish monastery. The Treaty of Augsburg (1555) gave every German prince the right to determine the religion of his subjects. The princes had won their local territories, and a unified German state was never constructed by the Hapsburgs.

When Charles V abdicated in 1556, he divided his kingdom between his son Philip and his brother Ferdinand. Philip inherited Spain and its colonies, as well as the Netherlands. Ferdinand acquired the Austrian territories. The Spanish and Austrian branches of the Hapsburg family defined their interests in common and often waged war accordingly. The enormous international power of the Hapsburgs faltered only in the German states

within the Holy Roman Empire. Throughout the sixteenth century, the Austrian Hapsburgs barely managed to control these sprawling and deeply divided German territories. Protestantism, as protected by the Treaty of Augsburg, and the powerful German nobility continued to prevent the creation of a German state.

The Austrian Hapsburg emperors always sought to enhance the power of the Catholic Church and to court the favor of local interests opposed to the nobility. No Hapsburg was ever more fervid in that regard than the Jesuit-trained Archduke Ferdinand II, who ascended the throne of the Holy Roman Empire in Vienna in 1619. He immediately embarked on a policy of Catholic revival and used Spanish officials as his administrators. His policies provoked within the empire a thirty-year-long war that engulfed the whole of Europe.

The Thirty Years' War (1618–1648) began when the Bohemians attempted to put a Protestant king on their throne. The Austrian and Spanish Hapsburgs reacted by sending an army into Bohemia, and suddenly the whole empire was forced to take sides along religious lines. The Bohemian nobility, after centuries of enforcing serfdom, failed to rally the rural masses behind them, and victory went to the emperor. Bohemia and the German states suffered almost unimaginable devastation; ravaging Hapsburg armies sacked and burned three-fourths of each kingdom's towns and practically exterminated its aristocracy.

Until the 1630s, it looked as though the Hapsburgs would succeed in enhancing their power and promoting centralization. But the intervention of Lutheran Sweden, led by Gustavus Adolphus and encouraged by France, wrecked Hapsburg ambitions. The ensuing military conflict devastated vast areas of northern and central Europe. The civilian population suffered untold hardships: soldiers raped women and pillaged the land, and thousands of refugees fled. Partly because the French finally intervened directly, the Spanish Hapsburgs emerged from the Thirty Years' War with no benefits. At the Treaty of Westphalia (1648), their Austrian cousins reaffirmed their right to govern the eastern states of the kingdom, with Vienna as their capital. Austria took shape as a dynastic state, and the German territories in the empire remained fragmented by the independent interests of their largely recalcitrant feudal nobility. In consequence, the Thirty Years' War shaped the course of German history into the late nineteenth century.

THE EMERGENCE OF AUSTRIA AND PRUSSIA

Austria

As a result of the settlement at Westphalia, the Austrian Hapsburgs gained firm control over most of Hungary and Bohemia, where they installed a virtually new and foreign nobility. At the same time, they strengthened their grip on Vienna. In one of the few spectacular successes achieved by the Counter-Reformation, the ruling elites in all three territories were forcibly, or in many cases willingly, converted back to Catholicism. At long last, religious predominance could be used as a force—long delayed by the pull of the Protestant Reformation—for the creation of the Austrian dynastic state.

One severe obstacle remained: the military threat posed by the Turks, who sought to control much of Hungary. In 1683, the Turks again besieged Vienna, but a Catholic and unified Austrian army, composed of a variety of peoples and assisted by the Poles, managed to defeat the Turks and recapture the whole of Hungary and Transylvania and part of Croatia. Austria's right to govern these lands was firmly accepted by the Turks at the Treaty of Karlowitz (1699). Islam had been beaten back to the frontiers of Eastern Europe.

The Austrian Hapsburgs and their victorious army emerged into the larger arena of European power politics. In 1700, at the death of the last Spanish Hapsburg, Leopold I sought to place his second son, Archduke Charles, on the Spanish throne. But this attempt brought Leopold into a violent clash with Louis XIV. Once again, Bourbon and Hapsburg rivalry, a dominant theme in early modern history, provoked a major European war.

In the War of the Spanish Succession (1702–1714), the Austrians joined forces with the English and the Dutch against the French. The allies gained much: Austria acquired what is now Belgium as a colony and pieces of Italy, including Milan. The Austrians did not capture the Spanish

MARIA THERESA AND JOSEPH. By the middle of the eighteenth century, the nuclear family was being valorized even among the monarchs of Europe. Here Maria Theresa and Joseph pose with their family. (Reunion des Musees Nationaux/Art Resource, N.Y.)

throne, but they did become a major force in European power politics, later to be challenged by Prussia. The English and Dutch subdued French ambitions and formed an alliance that lasted for fifty years. In retrospect, we can see the war as the beginning of England's rise to the status of a world power; ironically, by the 1730s, the Dutch Republic had entered a period of economic decline.

Prussia

Prussia was a state within the Holy Roman Empire, and its territorial ambitions could be checked by the other princely states or the empire. Although Prussia developed an absolute monarchy like France's, its powerful aristocracy acquiesced to monarchical power only in exchange for guarantees of their feudal power over the peasantry. In 1653, the Prussian nobility granted the Hohenzollern ruler of Prussia power to collect taxes for the maintenance of a strong army, but only after he issued decrees rendering serfdom permanent.

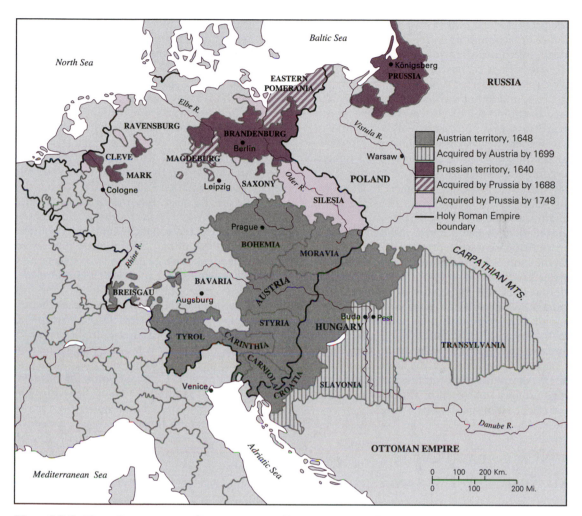

Map 16.3 THE GROWTH OF AUSTRIA AND BRANDENBURG-PRUSSIA, c. 1650–1750 This growth laid the foundation for modern Germany and also for tension between Christianity and Islam. (Copyright © 2013 Cengage Learning.)

The Hohenzollerns, the ruling dynasty of Prussia, had had a most inauspicious beginning in the later Middle Ages. These rulers were little more than dukes in the Holy Roman Empire until 1415, when Holy Roman Emperor Sigismund made one of them an imperial elector with the right to choose imperial successors. For centuries, the Hohenzollerns had made weak claims to territory in northern Germany. They finally achieved control over Prussia and certain other smaller principalities by claiming the inheritance of one wife (1608) and by single-minded, ruthless aggression.

The most aggressive of these Hohenzollerns was the elector Frederick William (1640–1688), who played a key role in forging the new Prussian state. Frederick William inherited the territories of the beleaguered Hohenzollern dynasty, whose main holding, Brandenburg in Prussia, was very poor in natural resources. Indeed, Prussia barely survived the devastation wreaked by the Thirty Years' War, especially the Swedish army's occupation of the electorate.

Distaste for foreign intervention in Prussia, and for the accompanying humiliation and excessive taxes, prompted the Junker class (the landed Prussian nobility) to support national unity and strong central government. However, they would brook no threat to their economic control of their lands and peasants. Frederick William's policy of foreign war, taxes, and military conscription led to an increase in the power of the central government. But in Prussia, in contrast to lands to the west, the bureaucracy was entirely military. No clerics or rich bourgeois shared power with the Junkers. The pattern initiated by the Great Elector (Frederick William) would be continued in the reigns of his successors: Frederick I (d. 1713), Frederick William I, and Frederick the Great.

In the older dynastic states, absolute monarchs tried to dispense with representative institutions once the monarchy had grown strong enough. So too did Frederick William (1713–1740) finally undercut the Prussian provincial assemblies, the *Landtage,* which still had some power over taxation and army recruitment. He was able to do so only by integrating the landowning Junker class into the government and the army by keeping the taxpaying peasants in the status of serfs. A military elite with little interest in reform and a landed nobility supported by the labor of its serfs lay at the heart of the Prussian state.

RUSSIA: GREAT NOBLES AND STARVING PEASANTS

Though remote from developments in Western Europe, Russia in the early modern period possessed characteristics remarkably similar to those of Western European states. It relied on absolute monarchy reinforced by a feudal aristocracy. As in Europe, the power of the aristocracy to wreak havoc had to be checked and its energies channeled into the state's service. But the Russian pattern of absolutism broke with the Western model and resembled that adopted in Prussia, where serfdom increased as the power of centralized monarchy grew. The monarchy secured aristocratic cooperation in the state's growth by enforcing serfdom.

Late in the sixteenth century, Ivan the Terrible (1547–1584) sought to impose a tsarist autocracy. He waged a futile war against Sweden and created an internal police force, which he entrusted with the administration of central Russia. His failure in war and an irrational policy of repression (fueled in part by his mental instability) doomed his attempt to impose absolutism. Much of Ivan's state building was undone with his death, which launched the Time of Troubles, a period of foreign invasion and civil warfare that endured for years.

Order was restored in 1613, when the Romanovs gained the support of the aristocracy. The accession of Michael Romanov as tsar marks the beginning of the Romanov dynasty and the emergence of a unified Russian state. Of that dynasty, by far the most important ruler was Peter the Great (1682–1725). He journeyed throughout Western Europe and sought to imitate its political and cultural institutions. He ruthlessly suppressed the independent aristocrats while inventing new titles and ranks for his supporters. He reformed the army in accordance with military standards in Western Europe and he made the peasants into the personal property of their lords. From 1700 to 1707, taxes on the peasants multiplied fivefold. Predictably, the money went toward the creation of a professional army along European lines and toward making war. The preparation led this time to victory over the Swedes. Finally, Peter brought the Russian Orthodox Church under the control of the state by establishing a new office, called the Holy Synod; its head was a government official. He built St. Petersburg in imitation of Western cities and endowed its cultural institutions.

Peter managed to wed the aristocracy to the absolutist state, and the union was so successful that strong Russian monarchs in the eighteenth century, such as Catherine the Great, could embrace enlightened reforms without jeopardizing the stability of their regimes. Once again, repression and violence in the form of taxation, serfdom, and war led to the creation of a dynastic state—one that proved least susceptible to reform and was eventually dismantled in 1917 by the Russian Revolution.

THE STATE AND MODERN POLITICAL DEVELOPMENT

By the early seventeenth century, Europeans had developed a sophisticated concept of the *state:* an active political entity to which its subjects owed duties and obligations. That concept became the foundation of the modern science of politics. The one essential ingredient of the Western concept of the state, as it emerged in the early modern period, was the notion of *sovereignty:* the state defined itself as supreme within its borders and over other institutions and organizations. By implication, even the church was allowed to exist only if it recognized the state's authority. The art of government thus entailed molding powerful elites into service to the state. The sovereign state, its power enhanced by war and taxation, became the basic unit of political authority in Europe and eventually the American republic.

Interestingly, the concept of human liberty, now so basic to global human rights, was not articulated first in the sovereign states of Europe. Rather, the idea was largely an Italian creation, discussed with great vehemence by Italian theorists of the later Middle Ages and the Renaissance. These humanists lived and wrote in the independent city-states, and they often aimed their treatises against the encroachments of the Holy Roman Emperor—in short, against princes and their search for absolute power. In the sixteenth and seventeenth centuries, the idea of liberty was rarely discussed and was generally found only in the writings of Dutch and French Calvinist opponents of absolutism. Not until the mid-seventeenth century in England did a body of political thought emerge that placed human liberty as a central political value within the state—a state governed by mere mortals and not by divinely sanctioned and absolute kings. In general, despite the English and Dutch developments, absolutism in its varied forms (Spanish, French, Prussian, Russian), often supported by national churches, dominated the political development of early modern Europe.

Although first articulated in the Italian republics and then enacted briefly in England and more durably in the Netherlands, the republican ideal did not gain acceptance as a viable alternative to absolutism until the European Enlightenment of the eighteenth century. In essence, the republican ideal placed the state in the service of those who support and create it. In the democratic and republican revolutions of the late eighteenth century, Western Europeans and Americans repudiated monarchical systems of government and opted for republics. By then, princes and military

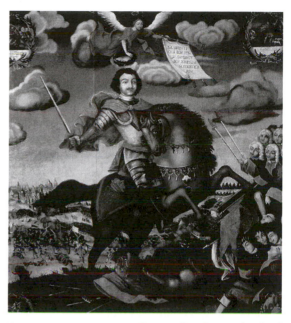

PETER THE GREAT. Peter the Great looked westward and outward and sought to modernize Russia. (The Art Archive/Russian Historical Museum Moscow/Alfredo Dagli Orti.)

elites had outlived their usefulness in many parts of Europe. The states they had created, mostly to further their own interests, had become larger than their creators. Eventually, the national states of Western Europe, as well as of the Americas, proved able to survive and prosper without kings or aristocrats, although they retained the administrative and military mechanisms so skillfully and relentlessly developed by early modern kings and their court officials.

By the eighteenth century, the state, not the locality, had become the focal point of Western political life. Peace in Europe and its colonies depended on the art of balancing the powers of the various states so that no single state could expect to win domination, or *hegemony,* over all the others. Whenever a European state believed that it could dominate in Europe or expand its colonies abroad, war resulted. In early modern times, first the Spanish under Charles V and Philip II and then the French under Louis XIV sought, and for a brief time achieved, hegemony over European politics. Ultimately, however, these great states with inadequate taxing powers faltered because of the internal financial pressures that warmaking created. Nonetheless, the belief persisted, until 1945, that one state could dominate Western affairs. In the twentieth century, that belief produced not simply war but world war. By then, the power of Western states and, among others, their Japanese imitators had overtaken vast areas of the world, and the ability to impose a balance of power became a matter of world survival. The militarism at the basis of globally ambitious state power led into the nuclear age.

NOTES

1. Quoted from *True Law of Free Monarchies,* excerpted in Marvin Perry et al., *Sources of the Western Tradition* (Boston: Houghton Mifflin, 1999), 358–359.
2. Steve Pincus, *1688. The First Modern Revolution* (New Haven, CT: Yale University Press, 2009), p. 483.

SUGGESTED READING

Adams, Julia, *The Familial State: Ruling Families and Merchant Capitalism in Early Modern Europe* (2005). The first account to show the role of gender and family loyalty in the formation of three states: France, England, and the Dutch Republic.

Bucholz, Robert, *Early Modern England, 1485–1714: A Narrative History* (2009).

Harkness, Deborah, *The Jewel House: Elizabethan London and the Scientific Revolution* (2007). A fascinating look at the intellectual and social dynamism of the period.

Koenigsberger, H. G., *Monarchies, States, Generals, and Parliaments* (2001). An excellent survey of the various forms of early modern government by a master historian.

Soll, Jacob, *The Information Master: The Rise and Fall of Jean-Baptiste Colbert's Secret State Library* (2010). A compelling account of spying, intrigue and sheer brilliance at administration.

http://www.history.ac.uk/projects/bbih. The best collection of books and articles on British and Irish history.

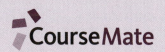

Go to the CourseMate website at **www.cengagebrain.com** for additional study tools and review materials—including audio and video clips—for this chapter.

Chapter 17

The Scientific Revolution: The Universe Seen as a Mechanism

The late 18th century poet and engraver, William Blake imaged Newton as the "first man" who followed the laws of geometry to fashion the world. Here Newton uses the simple compass of the mason to put his design onto the world. (Tate, London/Art Resource, N.Y.)

- **Medieval Cosmology**
- **A New View of Nature**
- **The Newtonian Synthesis: Experiment, Mathematics, and Theory**
- **Biology, Medicine, and Chemistry**
- **Bacon and Descartes: Prophets of the New Science**
- **The Social Implications of the Scientific Revolution**
- **The Meaning of the Scientific Revolution**

Focus Questions

1. What were the basic features of the medieval view of the universe?
2. Who were the leading figures of the Scientific Revolution, and what were their accomplishments?
3. What was the relationship between science and alchemy during this period?
4. Why was the Scientific Revolution a decisive force in the shaping of the modern approach to industry?

*I*n the fifteenth century, the medieval view of the world began to disintegrate. By the late seventeenth century, educated Europeans no longer believed in it. Thus, the collapse of medieval institutions such as feudalism and serfdom had an intellectual parallel. No set of ideas were as important in shaping the modern worldview as those associated with Scientific Revolution of the seventeenth century. They made physical nature a valid object for experimental and empirical inquiry and mathematical calculation. For the new science to arise, a philosophical break with the medieval conception of nature had to occur. The medieval approach to nature sought to explain nature's appearances. To the naked eye, the earth seems to be in the center of our universe. Medieval philosophy explained how and why the earth was in the center, and how and why heavy bodies fell toward it and light ones rose away from it. The philosophical revolution of the seventeenth century demolished such explanations. At the heart of the Scientific Revolution lay the assumption that appearances could lie, that truth depended upon seeing the universe as an abstract entity: as matter in motion, as geometrical shapes, and as weight and number. The universe became a mechanism.

The Scientific Revolution brought a new, **mechanical conception of nature** that enabled Westerners to discover and explain the laws of nature mathematically. Nature came to be composed solely of matter, whose motion, occurring in space and measurable by time, is governed by the push and pull of bodies and by laws of force. This philosophically elegant construction unified nature as composed of atoms, knowable and even possibly manageable. It led to the formulation of a unified science of mechanics that could be employed in an industrial setting.

The new science rested on a distinctive and replicable methodology. First, it was empirical, and gradually it became experimental. Because of successful observations and experiments performed by scientists and natural philosophers such as Galileo Galilei, William Harvey, Robert Boyle, and Isaac Newton, science acquired its still-characteristic methods of observation, experimentation, and replication. By the late seventeenth century, a serious interest in the physical order required actually doing—and recording—rigorous and systematic experiments or, at the least, observing the behavior of physical phenomena. Regularity and order appeared to be embedded in nature, measurable and quantifiable.

Mathematics increasingly became the language of the new science. For centuries, Europeans had used first geometry and then algebra to explain certain physical phenomena. With the Scientific Revolution came a new mathematics, the infinitesimal **calculus**. Even more important, philosophers became increasingly convinced that all nature—moving physical objects, as well as invisible forces—could be described mathematically. By the late seventeenth century, even geometry had become so complex that the gifted philosopher John Locke (1632–1704), a friend of Isaac Newton, could not understand the sophisticated mathematics used in the *Principia*. A new scientific culture had been born. During the eighteenth-century Enlightenment (Chapter 18), the model of nature offered by science implied progress. If physical nature could be known, why not human nature and human institutions?

MEDIEVAL COSMOLOGY

The unique character of the modern scientific outlook contrasts sharply with the medieval understanding of the natural world and its physical properties. It rested on Christian thought combined with theories derived from ancient Greek writers, such as Aristotle and Ptolemy.

Aristotle (384–322 B.C.) had argued that nature possessed inherent, purposeful tendencies. A stone falls because it is absolutely heavy; fire rises because it is absolutely light. Weight is an inherent property of a physical thing; therefore, motion results from the properties of bodies, and not from the forces that impinge on them. It follows (logically but incorrectly) that if the medium through which a body falls is taken as a constant, then the speed of its fall could be doubled if its weight were doubled. Only rigorous experimentation refuted this erroneous, but commonsensical, concept of motion.

Aristotle's physics complemented his *cosmology*, or world picture. The earth, being the heaviest object, lay stationary and suspended at the center of the universe. The sun, planets, and moon

revolved in circles around the earth. Aristotle presumed that because the planets were perfectly round, always in motion, and seemingly never altered, the most natural movement for them should be perfect, that is, circular.

Aristotle could put the earth at the center of the universe and make it stationary because he presumed its absolute heaviness; all other heavy bodies that he had observed fell toward it. Aristotle believed that everything in motion had been moved by another object that was itself in motion—a continuing chain of movers and moved. By inference, this belief led back to some object or being that began the motion. Christian philosophers of the Middle Ages argued that Aristotle's Unmoved Mover must be the God of Christianity. Aristotle, a pagan Greek, knew nothing of a personal God nor an afterlife of rewards or punishments. He believed that the universe was eternal rather than created at a specific point in time, and he would have found the Christian identification of God as the Mover meaningless.

Although Aristotle's cosmology never gained the status of orthodoxy among the ancient Greeks, by the second century A.D. in Alexandria, Greek astronomy became codified and then rigid. Ptolemy of Alexandria produced the *Almagest* (A.D. 150), a handbook of Greek astronomy based on the theories of Aristotle. The crucial assumption in the *Almagest* was that a motionless earth lay at the center of the universe and that the planets moved about it in a series of circular orbits, interrupted by smaller circular orbits, called epicycles. The epicycles explained why at certain times a planet was visibly closer to the earth. As Ptolemy put it, if the earth moved, "living things and individual heavy objects would be left behind . . . [and] the earth itself would very soon have fallen completely out of the heavens."[1] By the Late Middle Ages, Ptolemy's handbook contained standard astronomical wisdom. As late as the 1650s, more than a hundred years after the Polish astronomer Nicolaus Copernicus had argued mathematically that the sun was the center of the universe, educated Europeans in most universities still believed that the earth held the central position. By 1750, the earth-centered universe had fallen to the status of a superstition.

In the thirteenth century, mainly through the philosophical efforts of Thomas Aquinas

(1225–1274), Aristotle's thought was adapted to Christian beliefs, often in ingenious ways. Aquinas emphasized that order pervaded nature and that every physical effect had a physical cause. Aquinas and his followers, who were called **scholastics**, searched for causes—again, to ask *why* things move, rather than *how* they move. Aquinas insisted that nature proves God's existence; God is the First Cause of all physical phenomena. The world picture taught by the scholastics in their schools affirmed the earth and humankind as the center of the Christian drama of birth, death, and salvation.

Medieval thinkers integrated the cosmology of Aristotle and Ptolemy into a Christian framework that drew a sharp distinction between the world beyond the moon and the earthly realm. Celestial bodies were composed of the divine ether, a substance too pure and too spiritual to be found on earth; heavenly bodies, unlike earthly bodies, were immune to all change and obeyed different laws of motion. The universe was divided into a higher world of the heavens and a lower world of earth. Earth could not compare with the heavens in spiritual dignity, but God had nevertheless situated it in the center of the universe. Earth deserved this position of importance; only here did Christ live and die for humankind. This concept of the physical universe collapsed under the impact of the new science.

Also shattered by the new **natural philosophy** was the belief that all reality, natural as well as human, could be described as consisting of *matter* and *form*. Following Aristotle, the scholastics argued that matter was inchoate, lifeless, and indistinguishable. Only form gave it shape and identity. A table, for instance, possessed a recognizable shape and could be identified as a table because it possessed the form of tableness. A human being existed only because the matter of the body was given life by the soul, by its form. This doctrine was central to medieval philosophy and theology. Important beliefs were justified by it. For example, the church taught that the priest, when performing the sacrament of the **Eucharist**, had the power to transform bread and wine into the body and blood of Christ. This was possible because, theologians argued, the matter of the bread and wine looked the same, but its form was changed by the power of the priest. Consequently, the Mass could

be explained without recourse to blind faith, or worse, magic. Similarly, medieval people believed that the king's power resided within him; kingness was part of his essence. Likewise, nobility was a quality said to be inherent in the person of the nobleman or noblewoman. The mechanical philosophy of Galileo, Boyle, and Newton, which was central to the Scientific Revolution, denied the very existence of forms. Matter was simply composed of tiny **corpuscles**, or **atoms**, hard and impenetrable, governed by the laws of impact or force. Such a conception of nature threatened whole aspects of medieval and even Christian doctrine; ultimately, in social terms, the implications of the mechanical and atomic philosophy proved to be democratic.

A NEW VIEW OF NATURE

Renaissance Neo-Platonism

Italian Renaissance thinkers rediscovered the importance of the ancient Greek philosopher Plato (c. 429–347 B.C.). Plato taught that the philosopher must look beyond the appearances of things to an invisible reality, which is abstract, simple, rational, and best expressed mathematically. For Plato, the greatest achievements of the human mind were mathematics and music; both revealed the inherent harmony and order within nature.

Renaissance Platonists interpreted Plato from a Christian perspective, and they believed that the Platonic search for truth about nature, about God's work, was but another aspect of the search for knowledge about God. The Italian universities and academies became centers where the revival of Plato flourished among teachers and translators, who came to be known as **Neo-Platonists**. Central to their humanist curriculum was the study of philosophy, mathematics, music, Greek and Latin, and in some cases Arabic. Those languages made available the world of pagan, pre-Christian learning and its many different philosophies of nature. The leading thinkers of the Scientific Revolution were all influenced by Renaissance Neo-Platonism. They revered Plato's search for an abstract and mathematically elegant truth. They returned to the ancient thinkers for an alternative to Aristotle. Some of the ancients had been atomists; a few had even argued that the sun might be at the center of the universe. They had also invented geometry.

With the impulse to mathematize nature came the desire to measure and experience it. The rediscovery of nature found expression in the study of human anatomy, as well as in the study of objects in motion. Renaissance art shows the fruits of this inquiry, for artists tried to depict the human body as exactly as possible and yet to give it ideal form. The revival of artistic creativity associated with the Renaissance is linked to an interest in the natural world and to Neo-Platonism.

Magic, Alchemy, and the Search for Nature

One other body of thought and practice had been available in European civilization for centuries. Derived from Arabic sources, alchemy taught a basic pharmacology that depended upon the constant distillation of common substances to produce more pure and powerful remedies. Alchemists were needed in the study of minerals, in agriculture, and of course most importantly in medicine. Alchemy also had its critics, who were irritated by the claim made by some alchemists that it was possible to turn base metals into gold. Only the truly pious practitioner could unlock the mysteries of gold or find an elixir of life that would ensure longevity. But critics cast a cold eye on such claims.

Isaac Newton for much of his life saw no contradiction in searching for the mathematical laws of nature while practicing alchemy—the search for a way to transform ordinary metals into gold—which was also the origin of modern chemistry. Gradually, the emphasis on the search for gold fell by the wayside, in part because the small amounts of gold that could be extracted from a large quantity of earth were irrelevant to the expanding early modern economy. Alchemy, more than any other natural practice, assumed that matter possessed a corpuscular structure and that by distillation it could be made purer, closer to what we would describe as a pure element. Alchemists had no need for the scholastic notion of forms, and among all the natural practitioners in early modern Europe they came closest to delivering useful remedies

for pain, fevers, infertility, infections, and potions to poison vermin (not to mention one's enemies). Their practices were suspect to church and state, yet they could be found everywhere in Western and Eastern Europe and the American colonies.

In early modern Europe, the practitioners of alchemy and astrology could also be mathematicians and astronomers, and the sharp distinction drawn today between magic and science—between the irrational and the rational—would not have made sense to many of the leading natural philosophers who lived in the sixteenth and seventeenth centuries.

The Renaissance revival of ancient learning contributed a new approach to nature, one that was simultaneously mathematical, experimental, and magical. Although the achievements of modern science depend on experimentation and mathematics, the impulse to search for nature's secrets presumes a degree of self-confidence best exemplified and symbolized by the seeker after gold or the elixir of life.

The Copernican Revolution

Nicolaus Copernicus was born in Poland in 1473. As a young man, he enrolled at the University of Kraków, where he may have come under the influence of Renaissance Platonism, which was spreading outward from the Italian city-states. Copernicus also journeyed to Italy, and in Bologna and Padua he might have encountered ancient Greek texts containing arguments for the sun being the center of the universe. We know very little about his early education.

Copernicus's interest in mathematics and astronomy was stimulated by contemporary discussions of the need for calendar reform, which required a thorough understanding of Ptolemaic astronomy. The mathematical complexity of the Ptolemaic system troubled Copernicus, who believed with the Neo-Platonists that truth was the product of elegance and simplicity. In addition, Copernicus knew that Ptolemy had predecessors among the ancients who philosophized about a heliocentric universe or who held Aristotle's cosmology and physics in little regard. Thus, a Renaissance education gave Copernicus not a body of new scientific truth, but rather an outlook that

COPERNICAN SYSTEM. In his *On Revolutions of the Heavenly Spheres*, Copernicus proposed a heliocentric model in which the planets orbit around the sun.

enabled him to break with traditional astronomical truth taught in the universities.

Copernicus became convinced that the sun was at the center of the universe. So he began a lifelong task to work out mathematical explanations of how a heliocentric universe operated. Unwilling to engage in controversy with the followers of Aristotle, Copernicus did not publish his findings until 1543, the year of his death, in a work titled *On the Revolutions of the Heavenly Spheres*. Legend says that his book, which in effect began the Scientific Revolution, was brought to him on his deathbed. Copernicus died as he lived, a Catholic priest, hoping only that his book would be read sympathetically.

The treatise retained some elements of the Aristotelian-Ptolemaic system; for example, Copernicus kept Aristotle's basic idea of the perfect circular motion of the planets and the existence of crystalline spheres within which the stars revolved. He also retained many of Ptolemy's epicycles—orbits within the circular orbits of the sun and planets. But Copernicus proposed a heliocentric model of the universe that was mathematically simpler than Ptolemy's earth-centered universe. His model eliminated some of Ptolemy's epicycles and cleared up various problems that had troubled geocentric astronomers.

Copernicus's genius lay in the pursuit of an idea—the concept of a sun-centered universe—and he pursued it with a lifelong dedication as well as considerable brilliance in mathematics. By removing the earth from its central position and by giving it motion—that is, by making the earth just another planet—Copernicus undermined the system of medieval cosmology and made possible the birth of modern astronomy.

Most thinkers of the time were committed to the Aristotelian-Ptolemaic system and to biblical statements that they thought supported it, and they rejected Copernicus's conclusions. They also raised specific objections. The earth, they said, is too heavy to move. How, some of Copernicus's colleagues asked, can an object falling from a high tower land directly below the point from which it was dropped if the earth is moving so rapidly?

The Laws of Planetary Motion: Tycho and Kepler

Copernicus laid the foundation for the intellectual revolution that gradually overturned the medieval conception of the universe and ushered in modern cosmology. But it fell to other observers to fill in the important details. Tycho Brahe (1546–1601) never accepted the Copernican system, but he saw it as a challenge to astronomers. Aided by the king of Denmark, Tycho built the finest observatory in Europe. In 1572, he observed a new star in the heavens. Its existence offered a direct and serious challenge to the Aristotelian and scholastic assumption of unalterable, fixed, and hence perfect heavens. To this discovery of what eventually proved to be an exploding star, Tycho added his observations on the comet of 1577. He demonstrated that it moved unimpeded through the areas between the planets and passed right through the crystalline spheres. This finding raised the question of whether such spheres existed, but Tycho himself remained an Aristotelian. Although his devotion to a literal reading of the Bible led Tycho to reject the Copernican sun-centered universe, he did propose an alternative system, in which the planets revolved around the sun but the sun moved about a motionless earth.

Ultimately, Tycho's fame rests on his skill as a practicing astronomer. He bequeathed to future generations precise calculations about the movements of heavenly bodies. These calculations proved invaluable. They were put to greatest use by Johannes Kepler (1571–1630), a German who collaborated with Tycho during the latter's final years. Tycho bequeathed his astronomical papers to Kepler, who brought to these data a scientific vision that was both experimental and mystical.

Kepler searched persistently for harmonious laws of planetary motion. He did so because he believed profoundly in the Platonic ideal. According to this ideal, a spiritual force infuses the physical order, beneath appearances are harmony and unity, and the human mind can begin to comprehend that unity only through *gnosis*—a direct and mystical realization of unity—and through mathematics. Kepler believed that both approaches were compatible, and he managed to combine them. He believed in and practiced astrology (as did Tycho) and throughout his lifetime tried to contact an ancient but lost and secret wisdom.

In the course of his observations of the heavens, Kepler discovered the three basic laws of planetary motion. First, the orbits of the planets are elliptical, not circular as Aristotle and Ptolemy had assumed, and the sun is one focus of the **ellipse**. Unlike Tycho, Kepler accepted Copernicus's theory and provided proof for it. Kepler's second law demonstrated that the velocity of a planet is not uniform, as had been believed, but increases as its distance from the sun decreases. Kepler's third law—that the squares of the times taken by any two planets in their revolutions around the sun are in the same ratio as the cubes of their average distances from the sun—brought the planets into a unified mathematical system.

Kepler's work possessed immense significance. He gave sound mathematical proof to Copernicus's theory; forever eliminated the use of epicycles, which had saved the appearance of circular motion; and demonstrated that mathematical relationships can describe the planetary system. But Kepler left a significant question unresolved: What kept the planets in their orbits? Why did they not fly out into space or crash into the sun? The answer would be supplied by Isaac Newton, who synthesized the astronomy of Copernicus and Kepler with the new physics developed by Galileo.

Galileo: Experimental Physics

At the same time that Kepler was developing a new astronomy, his contemporary, Galileo Galilei (1564–1642), was breaking with the older physics of Aristotle. A citizen of Pisa by birth, Galileo lived for many years in Padua, where he conducted some of his first experiments on the motion of bodies. Guided by the dominant philosophy of the Italian Renaissance—the revived doctrines of Plato—Galileo believed that beyond the visible

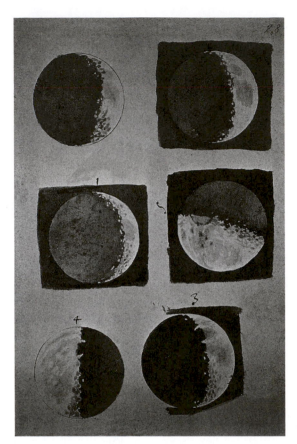

NOTEBOOK SKETCHES OF THE PHASES OF THE MOON, BY GALILEO GALILEI, 1609–1610. Galileo saw only shadows when he looked into his telescope. But because he was trained as an artist in the principles of light and dark coloring to emphasize or shorten distance, he knew that what he saw represented real objects, in this case mountains and valleys. Somewhat satirically, he compared the moon to Bohemia. (Scala/Art Resource, N.Y.)

world lay certain universal truths, subject to mathematical verification. Galileo insisted that the study of motion entails not only the use of logic (as Aristotle had believed) but also the application of mathematics. For this Late Renaissance natural philosopher, mathematics became the language of nature. Galileo also believed that only after experimenting with the operations of nature can the philosopher formulate harmonious laws and give

them mathematical expression. Moreover, Galileo was trained in the practices of Renaissance art, in using shades and shadows to represent the placing of bodies relative to one another. When he first looked at the moon through his telescope, that training became very important.

In his mechanical experiments, Galileo discovered that, all other things being equal, bodies of unequal weight will experience a uniform acceleration (due to gravity). He demonstrated that bodies fall with arithmetic regularity. Motion, therefore, obeys laws that can be expressed mathematically.

Galileo established a fundamental principle of modern science: the order and uniformity of nature. No distinctions in rank or quality exist between the heavens and earth; heavenly bodies are not perfect and changeless as Aristotle had believed. In 1609, Galileo built a telescope through which he viewed the surface of the moon. The next year, in a treatise called *The Starry Messenger*, he proclaimed to the world that the moon "is not smooth, uniform, and precisely spherical as a great number of philosophers believe it and the other heavenly bodies to be, but is uneven, rough, and full of cavities . . . being not unlike the face of the earth, relieved by chains of mountains and deep valleys."[2] In addition, Galileo noticed spots on the sun, providing further evidence that heavenly objects, like earthly objects, are physical bodies susceptible to change. Nature is the same throughout. When he saw shadows through his telescope, he assumed that actual bodies were casting them, just as they do on an earthly landscape. Galileo's art and science were of a piece. When contemporary moon expeditions cannot locate a single element unknown on earth, Galileo would probably give a wry smile.

Through his telescope, Galileo also observed moons around Jupiter—a discovery that supported the Copernican hypothesis. If Jupiter had moons, then all heavenly bodies did not orbit the earth. The moons of Jupiter removed a fundamental criticism of Copernicus and opened up the possibility that the earth, with its own moon, might be just like Jupiter, and that both might in turn revolve around a central point—the sun.

With Galileo, the science of Copernicus and the assault on Aristotle entered a new phase. Scholastic priests began to attack Galileo from their pulpits in Florence. In Galileo's public

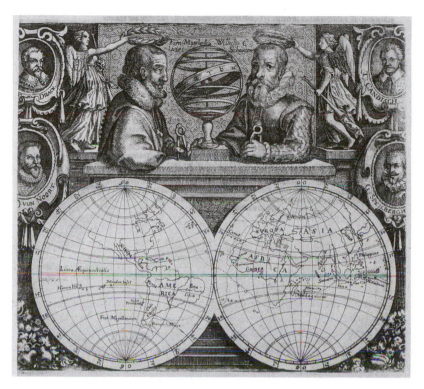

MAPPING THE HEAVENS AND THE EARTH. Contemporaries of Galileo knew that the discovery of the heavens was tied to the discovery of the New World, the exploration of the globe, and the mapping of the seas. Simultaneously, in the period from 1500 to 1700 Westerners found two new worlds, one in the heavens, the other very much on earth. (Hemera Technologies/© Getty Images.)

notoriety and his popularity among the laity, they saw a threat to their own power. A secret group of priests and academics, named the Liga, formed with the express purpose of silencing Galileo; they used Aristotle and the Bible to attack him. But Galileo was also a courtier with friends in high places, so he dared to challenge the clergy and to offer his science directly to the laity. He argued publicly with the theologians. In the early seventeenth century, the Catholic Church saw danger on every front: Protestants in Germany, Jews and Muslims in the East, and a laity demanding new schools that would provide practical education for their children. Now Galileo offered a view of the universe that conflicted with certain scriptural texts. He was in a bad place at a bad time.

The church attacked Galileo because he was a Copernican, that is, because he believed the sun to be at the center of the universe. There were other reasons. New evidence from the recently opened Vatican archives suggests that the church also may have worried about his corpuscular theory of matter and his abandonment of the scholastics' view of the relationship between matter and form. That view went to the heart of the doctrine of the Eucharist, and the church saw, rightly, that the new science threatened the philosophical foundations of certain key doctrines.

In 1632 and 1633, Galileo's teachings were condemned, and he was placed under house arrest. This act of repression cut short the open pursuit of science in many Catholic countries of the seventeenth century. Wherever the Inquisition was strong, the new science would be viewed as subversive. Censorship worked to stifle public intellectual inquiry. By midcentury, science had become an increasingly Protestant and northern European phenomenon.

THE NEWTONIAN SYNTHESIS: EXPERIMENT, MATHEMATICS, AND THEORY

By 1650, the works of Copernicus and especially of Galileo had dethroned the physics and astronomy of Aristotle and Ptolemy. A new philosophy of nature tied to empirical observation and Neo-Platonism had come into existence; its essence lay in the mathematical expression of physical laws that describe matter in motion. Yet no single overriding law had been articulated that would bring together the experimental successes of the new science, its mathematical sophistication, and its philosophical revolution. This law was supplied by Isaac Newton.

Newton was born in 1642, in Lincolnshire, England, the son of a modest yeoman. Because of his intellectual promise, he obtained a place at Trinity College, Cambridge, and there he devoted himself to natural philosophy and mathematics. Newton's student notebooks survive and show him mastering philosophical texts while also trying to understand the fundamental truths of Protestant Christianity as taught at Cambridge. Combining Christian Neo-Platonism with a genius for mathematics, Newton produced a coherent synthesis of the science of Kepler and Galileo, which eventually captured the imagination of European intellectuals.

In 1666, Newton formulated the mathematics for the universal law of gravitation, and in the same year, after rigorous experimentation, he determined the nature of light. The sciences of physics and optics were transformed. However, for many years, Newton did not publish his discoveries, perhaps because he feared controversy. Finally, another mathematician and friend, Edmund Halley, persuaded him to publish under the sponsorship of the Royal Society. The result was the *Principia Mathematica* of 1687. In 1704, Newton published his *Opticks* and revealed his theory that light was corpuscular or atomic in nature and

that it emanated from luminous bodies in a way that scientists later described as waves.

Of the two books, both monumental achievements in the history of science, the *Principia* made the greater impact on contemporaries. Newton offered universal mathematical laws, as well as a philosophy of nature that sought to explain the essential structure of the universe: matter is always the same; it is atomic in structure, in its essential nature it is dead or lifeless; and it is acted on by immaterial forces that are placed in the universe by God. Newton said that the motion of matter could be explained by three laws: inertia, that a body remains in a state of rest or continues its motion in a straight line unless impelled to change by forces impressed on it; acceleration, that the change in the motion of a body is proportional to the force acting on it; and that for every action there is an equal and opposite reaction.

Newton applied his laws to observable matter on earth and to the motion of planets in their orbits. He showed that planets remain in their orbits not because circular motion is natural or because crystalline spheres keep them in place. Rather, said Newton, planets keep to their orbits because every body in the universe exercises a force on every other body, a force that he called *universal gravitation*. Gravity is proportional to the product of the masses of two bodies and inversely proportional to the square of the distance between them. It is operative throughout the universe, whether on earth or in the heavens, and it is capable of mathematical expression. Newton built his theory on the work of other scientific giants, notably Kepler and Galileo. No one before him, however, had possessed the breadth of vision, mathematical genius, and dedication to rigorous observation to combine this knowledge into one grand synthesis.

The universe now became matter in motion; governed by invisible forces that operate everywhere, both on earth and in the heavens, and these forces could be expressed mathematically. The medieval picture of the universe as closed, earthbound, and earth centered was replaced by a universe seen to be infinite and governed by universal laws. The earth became simply another moving planet, and bodies in the heavens were seen to be uniform in composition.

Newtonian principles were taught by generations of Newton's followers as, in effect, applied mechanics. A revolution in thought had changed Western ideas about nature forever and also created a body of knowledge that could be practically applied to everyday bodies. But what was God's role in this new universe? Newton and his circle labored to create a mechanical worldview dependent on the will of God. At one time, Newton believed that gravity was simply the will of God operating on the universe. As he wrote in the *Opticks,* the physical order "can be the effect of nothing else than the wisdom and skill of a powerful ever-living agent."[3] Because of his strong religious convictions, Newton allowed his science to be used in the service of the established Anglican Church, and his followers argued for social stability anchored in an ordered universe and an established church. Newton, a scientific genius, was also a deeply religious thinker committed to the maintenance of Protestantism in England. Among his contemporaries, however, freethinkers such as John Toland (see "Skeptics, Freethinkers, and Deists" in Chapter 18) used his ideas to argue that nature can operate on its own, without the assistance of a providential God.

BIOLOGY, MEDICINE, AND CHEMISTRY

The spectacular advances in physics and astronomy in the sixteenth and seventeenth centuries were not matched in the biological sciences. Indeed, the day-to-day practice of medicine throughout Western Europe changed little in the period from 1600 to 1800, for much of medical practice relied, as it had since the Middle Ages, on astrology and on the necessity for bloodletting.

Doctors clung to the teachings of the ancient practitioners Galen and Hippocrates. In general, Galenic medicine paid little attention to the discovery of specific cures for particular diseases. As a follower of Aristotle, Galen emphasized the elements that make up the body; he called their manifestations *humors.* A person with an excess of blood was sanguine; a person with too much bile was choleric. Health consisted of a restoration of balances among these various elements, so Galenic doctors often prescribed purges of one sort or another. The most famous of these was

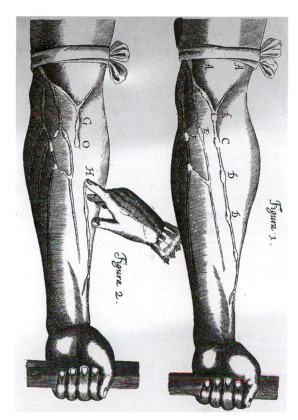

SCIENCE AND BLOOD. For centuries, it was believed that blood carried character traits as well as nobility. The English experimenter William Harvey viewed blood as simply a liquid that circulated in the body in a uniform way. Illustrations such as this one made the point graphically. (© Bettmann/Corbis.)

bloodletting, but sweating was also a favorite remedy. Taught devotedly in the medical schools of Europe, these methods were often as dangerous as the diseases they sought to cure.

Despite the tenacity of Galenic medicine, sixteenth- and seventeenth-century innovators and reformers challenged and eventually overturned medical orthodoxy. With an almost missionary zeal, Paracelsus (1493–1541), a Swiss-German physician and mystical Neo-Platonist, introduced the concept of diagnostic medicine and relied heavily on alchemy. He argued that particular diseases can be differentiated and are related to chemical, not humorial, imbalances. His treatments relied on chemicals and not on bloodletting or the positions of the stars (although he did not discount such influences), and he proclaimed an almost ecstatic vision of human vitality and longevity. In most universities, the faculties of medicine bitterly opposed his views, but by 1650 in England and later in that century in France, Paracelsian ideas had many advocates. Support for Paracelsian medicine, often combined with alchemy, invariably accompanied an attack on the traditional medical establishment and its professional monopoly, and it often signaled an interest in the new science. The struggle between Galenists and Paracelsians quickly took on a social dimension; the innovators saw themselves pitted against a medical elite, which, in their opinion, had lost its commitment to medical research and existed solely to perpetuate itself. In the eighteenth century, Paracelsian ideas, stripped of their alchemical associations, became commonplace.

The medical reforms of the eighteenth century did not rest solely on the Paracelsian approach; they also relied heavily on the experimental breakthroughs made in the science of anatomy. A pioneer in this field was the Belgian surgeon Andreas Vesalius (1515–1564), who published *The Structure of the Human Body* in 1543. Opposing Galenic practice, Vesalius argued for observation and anatomical dissection as the keys to knowing how the human body works. By the late seventeenth century, doctors had learned a great deal about the body, its structure, and its chemistry.

The study of anatomy yielded dramatic results. In 1628, William Harvey (1578–1657) announced that he had discovered the circulation of blood. Harvey compared the functioning of the heart to that of a mechanical pump, and once again the tendency to mechanize nature, so basic to the Scientific Revolution in physics, led to a significant discovery. Yet the acceptance of Harvey's work was very slow, and the practical uses of his discovery were not readily perceived.

The experimental method in medicine produced other innovations, among them systematic examination not only of corpses but also of patients. In the late 1600s, the finest doctor of the age, Herman Boerhaave, taught his students in Leiden, in the Dutch Republic, by taking them on house calls, arguing that nothing in medicine can be known without a careful and rigorous examination of the body. He proclaimed that he was trying to bring the methods and philosophy of the new science to medicine, and he pioneered hands-on medical techniques.

Just as Newton applied the theory and method of science to the heavens, his contemporaries on both sides of the English Channel sought to utilize science to illuminate every object we experience. Protestantism inspired them to be aggressive in their assault on scholasticism. Indeed, the most original experimenter of the age, who codified the experimental method as we know it, was a devout English Protestant. Robert Boyle (1627–1691) believed that Aristotle's physics and the philosophy that supported it promoted Catholic teachings and thus amounted to little more than magic. At a time when English Protestants feared a revival of Catholic and absolutist monarchy, Boyle wanted to abolish the invisible forces on which Catholic theology rested. He also wished to defeat the magic of what he called "the vulgar," that is, the beliefs of the populace, whose disorder and tendencies to rebellion he feared.

To accomplish these aims, Boyle urged scientists to adopt the zeal of the magicians and alchemists, but without their secretive practices and their conjuring with spirits. As an alternative to spirits or scholastic forms, Boyle advocated the atomic explanation of matter: it consists of small, hard, indestructible particles that behave with regularity. According to Boyle, the existence of these corpuscles explained the changes in gases, fluids, and solids.

Boyle pioneered the experimental method with such exciting and accurate results that by the time of his death no serious scientist could attempt chemical experiments without following his guidelines. Thus, the science of chemistry acquired its characteristic experimentalism; it was also based on an atomic theory of matter. But only late in the eighteenth century was chemistry applied to medical research, particularly in an effort to cure tuberculosis.

BACON AND DESCARTES: PROPHETS OF THE NEW SCIENCE

The new science needed prophets and social theorists to give it direction and to assess its implications. During the early modern period, two major

RENÉ DESCARTES
Né à La Haye en 1596.

PORTRAIT, FRANCIS BACON. Francis Bacon is seen as a prophet of the new science. Witness to the extraordinary scientific energy visible in Elizabethan England, Bacon wrote in order to urge Elizabeth's successor, James I, to embrace science and make it a state priority. Bacon also turned science into an activity of the pious; doing God's work with nature became as important as knowing God's biblical word. (Philip de Bay/© Historical Picture Archive/Corbis.)

PORTRAIT, RENÉ DESCARTES. If the Scientific Revolution had a revolutionary, it was Descartes. Trained by the Jesuits and a devout Christian, Descartes nevertheless turned his back on scholasticism and based learning on the power of the individual mind. "Cogito ergo sum"—"I think, therefore I am"—rallied generations of inquirers, as did Descartes's mechanical understanding of matter in motion. (© Chris Hellier/Corbis.)

reformers tried, in disparate ways, to channel science into the service of specific social programs: Francis Bacon (1561–1626) and René Descartes (1596–1650).

Bacon

The decidedly practical and empirical Francis Bacon stands as the most important English proponent of the new science, though not its most important practitioner. Bacon was lord chancellor of England under James I, and he wrote about the usefulness of science partly in an effort to convince the crown of its advantages. He wanted science to serve the interests of strong monarchy and also to improve the human condition through better medicine and application. Partly inspired by alchemy, Bacon brought notions of progress to the enterprise of science.

No philosopher of modern science has surpassed Bacon in elevating the study of nature to a humanistic discipline. In the *Advancement of Learning* (1605), Bacon argued that science must be open and that all ideas must be

FONTENELLE, PORTRAIT BY BERNARD PICART. Fontenelle understood the new science, but most important, he could make it understandable to those less learned than himself. He gave a eulogy on the death of Newton that was read throughout the century, and he also worked tirelessly for the French Academy of Sciences. (© Corbis.)

allowed a hearing. Science must have human goals: the improvement of humanity's material condition and the advancement of trade and industry. Bacon also saw the need for science to possess an inductive methodology grounded in experience; the scientist should first of all be a collector of facts.

Although Bacon was rather vague about how the scientist actually works, he knew that preconceived ideas imposed on nature seldom yield positive results. An opponent of Aristotle, Bacon argued that university education should be taken out of the hands of the scholastics and based upon the new learning. A powerful civil servant, he was not afraid to attack the guardians of tradition. The Baconian vision of progress in science leading to better lives and the security of the state inspired much scientific activity in the seventeenth century,

particularly in England. Bacon also benefited from the vibrancy of London's scientific community, one of the largest in Europe.

Descartes

René Descartes, a French philosopher, went to the best French schools run by the Jesuits, and he knew the mathematics and scholastic philosophy of his day. Yet in his early twenties, he experienced a crisis of confidence and came to the conclusion that everything he had been taught was irrelevant and meaningless.

Descartes began to search within himself for what he could be sure was clear and distinct knowledge. All he could know with certainty was the fact of his existence, and even that he knew only because he experienced, not his body, but his mind: "I think, therefore I am." From this point of certitude, Descartes deduced the existence of God and of nature. He argued that science should be grounded on the human mind's ability to arrive at clear and distinct ideas, to think for itself and not slavishly follow tradition or doctrine.

God exists because Descartes had in his mind an idea of a supreme, perfect being, and, Descartes reasoned, this idea could have been put there only by such a being, not by any ordinary mortal. Therefore, God's existence means that the physical world must be real, for no Creator would invent a vast hoax.

For Descartes, the new science meant confidence: in his own mind, in the knowability of the physical world, and in mathematics and reason. Scientific thought meant an alternative to everything he associated with the medieval: confusion, disorder, conflict between church and state, fear of the unknown, and magic. Turning his back on the centuries immediately preceding his own, Descartes, possibly as a result of knowing Bacon's ideas for practical science, proclaimed that "it is possible to attain knowledge which is very useful in life, and that, instead of that speculative philosophy which is taught in the schools [that is, scholasticism], we may find a practical philosophy by means of which . . . we can . . . render ourselves the masters and possessors of nature."[4] Descartes was among the first to dream about the capacity of science to control and dominate nature, though

René Descartes: *Discourse on Method* (1637)

René Descartes gave a meaning to the new science that validated human courage to think for one's self. He grounded everything that could be learned about nature on the individual's capacity to reason and to discover truth.

Part One

Good sense is, of all things among men, the most equally distributed; for everyone believes himself so well provided with it that even those who are the most difficult to please in everything else, do not usually desire a larger measure of this quality than they already have. It is not likely that they are deceived in this. It indicates rather that the power of judging well, and of distinguishing the true from the false, what is properly called good sense or reason, is by nature equal in all men. . . . For it is not enough to have a vigorous mind; but the main thing is to apply it well. . . .

I have been brought up on books from my childhood, and as I was persuaded that by their help a clear and certain knowledge of all that is useful in life might be acquired, I had an extreme desire to learn them. But as soon as I had finished the entire course of study, at the close of which one is normally admitted into the ranks of the learned, I completely changed my opinion. For I found myself so encumbered by doubts and errors that it seemed to me I had advanced no further in all my attempts at learning, than the discovery at every turn of my own ignorance. And yet I was studying at one of the most famous schools in Europe, where I thought that there must be learned men if there were any of them anywhere on earth. I had been taught all that others learned there; and not contented with the sciences actually taught us, in addition I read all the books I had been able to get my hands on . . . ones . . . most curious and most rare. . . .

I was especially pleased with mathematics, on account of the certitude and evidence of its reasoning; but I did not as yet notice its true use, and thinking that it only served the mechanical arts, I was astonished thereby that its foundations being so firm and so solid, that no one had built anything lofty upon them. On the other hand, I compared the writings of the ancient pagans that deal with morals and found them to be towering and magnificent palaces with no better foundation than sand and mud. They extol the virtues so highly, and make them appear more valuable than anything in the world. . . .

I revered our theology, and aspired, as much as anyone else, to reach heaven; but I came to understand that the way is not less open to the most ignorant than to the most learned, and that the revealed truths that guide us there are beyond our comprehension. I would not have dared to submit them to my feeble reasoning, and I thought that in order to undertake to examine them and to succeed in it, one would need to have some extraordinary help from heaven and need to be more than a mere man. . . . And finally, considering that all the same thought that we have when we are awake can also come to us when we are asleep, without there being any of them at that time that be true, I resolved to feign that all the things that had ever entered my mind were no more true than the illusions of my dreams. But, immediately afterward, I took note that, while I wanted thus to think that everything was false, it necessarily had to be that I, who was thinking this, were something. And, noticing that this truth—*I think, therefore I am*—was so firm and so assured that all the most extravagant suppositions of the skeptics were not capable of shaking it, I judged that I could accept it, without scruple, as the first principle of the philosophy that I was seeking.

Questions for Analysis

1. Why is Descartes so eager to find a new way of knowing?
2. What does the statement "I think, therefore I am" proclaim?

Margaret C. Jacob, *The Scientific Revolution: A Brief History with Documents* (Boston: Bedford/St. Martin's, 2009)

LA VÉRITÉ, BY BERNARD PICART. In the early eighteenth century, French critics of the existing order in church and state used Descartes as a symbol. Here he is pointing to the slaying of error and ignorance by truth. The engraver who created this picture was eventually forced to flee France and settle in the Dutch Republic. (Teylers Museum, Haarlem, The Netherlands.)

he never could have imagined its modern potential to destroy nature.

Affirming existence of anything other than the abstractions of mathematics required that Descartes proclaim the existence of God and the physical world. He radically separated matter from spirit and mind from nature, and in the process, he widened a gap in Western thought that would haunt philosophers for centuries. What if a thinker who understood the implications of Descartes's separation of matter from spirit was to argue that only matter existed? Within the mechanical understanding of nature lurked the possibility of materialism.

Benedict de Spinoza (1632–1677) brought that possibility out into the open. Born in Amsterdam of recently immigrated Jewish parents, he was trained in classical languages and Hebrew thought. His genius drew him to the new science, and he became an early explicator of Descartes's philosophy, in which he spied a central weakness: its inability to explain the linkage between matter and spirit or to connect God to nature in any meaningful way. Spinoza's solution was radical, logical, and thoroughly heretical to monotheistic

thinkers: he argued that God is, as it were, Nature, that matter and spirit in effect are one.

To this day, philosophers dispute Spinoza's purpose. Was he an atheist who wanted to do away with the monotheistic conception of God, or was he a mystic who wished to infuse God into Nature? His contemporaries of every religious persuasion (he was expelled from his Amsterdam synagogue) deemed him an atheist and thought that he had become one by reading too much science. Their condemnation made "spinozism" a byword for atheism and freethinking. In the Enlightenment, freethinkers and materialists would claim to have been inspired by Spinoza.

The thoughts and visions of Bacon, Descartes, and Spinoza revealed the power and importance of scientific knowledge. Science could promote human well-being, as Bacon insisted; it could make human beings and nature the foundation of all meaningful knowledge, as Descartes assumed; science could express pantheism or justify a belief in Nature as God, as Spinoza suggested. Whichever position educated westerners embraced by the late 1600s, science would be used to challenge the traditional authority of the clergy, whether Catholic or Protestant. Why believe in dogmas and texts when nature offered another kind of truth—universal and, just as important, applicable to human problems? For good or ill, the Scientific Revolution gave its followers a sense of power and self-confidence unimagined even by Renaissance proponents of individualism or by the theorists of absolute state power.

THE SOCIAL IMPLICATIONS OF THE SCIENTIFIC REVOLUTION

Among the critical factors in the success of the Scientific Revolution lay the acceptance and use of the new science by artisans as well as educated elites. Without such acceptance, the science of Galileo, Kepler, Descartes, Boyle, and Newton would have remained the specialized knowledge of the few—or, worse still, a suspect, even heretical, approach to nature. Galileo could not have succeeded as much as he did in disseminating his theories (despite the hostility of the church) without his large European reading public and his many aristocratic patrons, particularly in Florence.

Access to the printing press in Europe promoted the acceptance of the new mechanical understanding of nature. Descartes understood that fact when he left France, after the condemnation of Galileo, and published and lived in the Netherlands. Persecution and censorship meant that the new science made far less of an impact in Catholic than in Protestant Europe. It is not accidental that most of the leaders within the scientific movement wrote and published in their native languages, not in Latin.

Equally important, the new science offered the dream of power to both governments and early promoters of industry. In the seventeenth century, this dream enticed monarchs and statesmen to give their patronage to scientific academies and projects. The achievements of the new science were quickly institutionalized in academies dominated either by the state, as in France, or by the landed and commercial elite, as in England. Founded in the 1660s, scientific academies such as the Royal Society in England became centers for the dissemination of science at a time when many universities, still controlled by the clergy, were

BENEDICT SPINOZA. Spinoza lived most of his life in Amsterdam, but was cast off from his synagogue by an expulsion. We do not know why he was expelled, but it may very well have had something to do with his radical understanding of nature as the only substance in the world. His closest friends were a Dutch sect of devout Protestants who deeply believed in the freedom to think for one's self. (Archive Photos/Stringer/Getty Images.)

hostile to its attack on scholasticism. In Paris, the new French academy devoted its time to the study of mathematics, mechanics, and alchemy.

The new mechanical learning—not easily learned from Newton's *Principia*, which was far too technical for most people—required elementary handbooks and lectures in mechanics. This newly systematized science came to be applied in Britain and Scotland during the second half of the eighteenth century. Applied mechanics improved the steam engine and utilized it in coal mining and water engineering. The knowledge of mechanics stemmed from Newtonian lectures and books, which proliferated in Britain during the

1700s. The road from the Scientific Revolution leads more directly to the Industrial Revolution than is often realized. James Watt, who perfected the steam engine, had been tutored in Newtonian mechanics. His engine revolutionized the manufacturing of cotton and the draining of coal mines. In the same period, the scientific gentleman and woman became fashionable icons. Elite and mildly prosperous families brought microscopes and globes into their homes. Owning these objects caused the family's status to rise, even if no one in the family became an engineer or doctor. Science had captured the Western imagination, and in Birmingham, Leeds, and Manchester, the new industrial centers, applied science became all the rage.

THE MEANING OF THE SCIENTIFIC REVOLUTION

The Scientific Revolution decisively shaped the modern mentality; it shattered the medieval view of the universe and replaced it with a wholly different worldview. Gone was the belief that a motionless earth lay at the center of a universe that was finite and enclosed by a ring of stars. Gone, too, was the belief that the universe was divided into higher and lower worlds and that the laws of motion operating in the heavens were different from those working on earth. Nature became uniform and could be mastered conceptually and mathematically.

The experimental methodology of the new science played a crucial historical role in reorienting Western thought away from theology and metaphysics and toward the study of physical and human problems. In the Late Middle Ages, most men of learning were Aristotelians and theologians. By the mid-eighteenth century, knowledge of Newtonian science and the dissemination of useful learning had become the goal of the educated classes. All knowledge, it was believed, could emulate scientific knowledge: it could be based on observation, experimentation, or rational deduction and it could be systematic, verifiable, progressive, and useful. This new approach to learning used the scientists of the sixteenth and seventeenth centuries as proof that no institution or dogma had a monopoly on truth. The scientific approach would

JAMES WATT (1736–1819). This engraved portrait of James Watt was rendered in his successful years. His somewhat grim affect is consonant with the depression he often described in his letters.

yield knowledge that might, if properly applied for the good of all people, produce a new and better age. Such an outlook gave thinkers new confidence in the power of the human mind to master nature and led them to examine European institutions and traditions with an inquiring, critical, and skeptical spirit. Scientific societies and academies sprang up all over Europe. In the Dutch Republic in 1785, women founded a society where they received a scientific education. Most scientific academies, however, excluded women into the twentieth century.

The Scientific Revolution ultimately weakened traditional Christianity. God's role in a mechanical universe was not clear. Newton had argued that God not only set the universe in motion but still intervened in its operations, thus leaving room for miracles. Others retained a place for God as

Art of the Seventeenth and Eighteenth Centuries

1. Peter Paul Rubens, *The Betrothal of Saint Catherine*, sketch for a large altar painting, c. 1628.
(Staatliche Gemaldegalerie, Berlin, Germany/The Bridgeman Art Library.)

The influence of political, economic, and social change permeates the visual arts of the seventeenth and eighteenth centuries. Perhaps most significant to the artists who made their living by providing paintings with religious themes for churches, as well as for private patrons, were the religious conflicts that split apart European society. Catholics and Protestants quarreled and openly fought over doctrine and dogma; as a result of the struggles, artists had to decide how best to please patrons whose religious sympathies may have changed or developed in new directions. Politically, the seventeenth and eighteenth centuries are also marked by the emergence of new sovereign states and by a change in the nature of artistic patronage.

Although a number of terms are used to describe the seventeenth and eighteenth centuries, the one most commonly applied by art historians is *baroque*. The word literally means irregularly shaped, whimsical, grotesque, or odd. Its origin is French, but it is generally agreed that the baroque style of art originated in Rome.

Baroque art is hard to explain within the context of the social and political changes that were sweeping over Europe. Some historians see it as illustrative of the Counter-Reformation; others point out that the style was equally appealing to Catholics and Protestants. Nor was the baroque style favored only by the absolute rulers of France or other monarchs; it was also a style of the bourgeois.

2. Giovanne Benedetto Castiglione, *Melancholia*, Mid-Seventeenth Century. (Philadelphia Museum of Art, The Muriel and Philip Berman Gift, acquired from the Matthew Carey Lea Bequest of 1898 to The Pennsylvania Academy of Fine Arts.)

One of the most famous baroque painters was Peter Paul Rubens (1577–1640) of Flanders, which, prospering from its commercial connections, was home to many successful artists and patrons in this period. To study painting, Rubens traveled to Rome in 1600 and spent many years visiting other artistic centers in Italy. There he learned to paint on large-scale canvases and play with the size and weight of his subjects. Despite the influence of his southern contemporaries, however, his style remained essentially Flemish.

In his painting *The Betrothal of Saint Catherine* (Figure 1), we immediately sense the energy and fullness of the figures typical among Italian artists. But we also notice that Rubens's palette is much lighter than theirs, and consequently, the figures of Saint Catherine and the saints who surround her seem to move lightly as well.

Noteworthy, too, in this canvas is the depiction of the figures, whose hairstyles and mode of dress is contemporary rather than suggestive of biblical times. This juxtaposition of scenes from the Bible with the flavor of everyday life in the seventeenth century reveals much about the connection between the artist and his own surroundings.

The baroque style of highly finished, realistic works is very familiar to us. But we must also recall that baroque artists were skilled draftsmen. As an example, there is Giovanne Benedetto Castiglione's *Melancholia* (mid-seventeenth century) (Figure 2), a brush drawing in oil with added red chalk. Works on paper do not always survive as well as those on board or canvas. The drawings we do have attest to the artistic skill of seventeenth-century artists, who used line and shadow as well as did their Renaissance predecessors.

Melancholia is an allegory about the human dilemma of choosing among the worlds of art, religion, science, and learning. Symbols from each of these worlds—scientific tools, musical instruments, a globe, and the like—surround the figure of Genius, who sits in a contemplative pose.

Although by and large the artists of the baroque period were not well-rounded humanists like those of the Renaissance, some of them could work in a variety of art forms. For example, Gian Lorenzo Bernini (1598–1680) distinguished himself as a sculptor as well as an architect.

Bernini was responsible for the sculptural program of Saint Peter's Basilica in the Vatican. He also completed sculptures in other Roman churches, including the Cornaro Chapel in the Church of Santa Maria della Vittoria. His *The Ecstasy of Saint Teresa* (1644–1647) (Figure 3) is a remarkable work that tells a dramatic story. The heart of Saint Teresa of Avila was said to have been pierced by an angel's golden arrow; the pain was exquisite, for not only was it the pain of death but also the pleasure of everlasting life in the arms of God. Bernini skillfully portrays the exact moment of Saint Teresa's ecstasy, in a theatrical setting using not only sculpture but also the architectural elements of the chapel.

The saint and the angel are carved of white marble and seem to be floating on a cloud. The sculpted golden rays, which descend from a point above the figures, are bathed in light by a window hidden behind the frame that surrounds the two figures. Bernini decorated the entire chapel to follow the theme of Saint Teresa; ceiling frescoes show clouds of angels celebrating the event.

While Bernini was gaining fame in Italy, a French painter—one who spent almost his entire career in Rome—was winning an international reputation. Nicolas Poussin (1593/4–1665) relied strongly on the art of the classical and especially the Hellenistic periods for his inspiration. His *The Rape of the Sabine Women* (c. 1636–37) (Figure 4), a lavish and richly painted canvas, captures action like a carefully posed photograph. Indeed, if Bernini was theatrical in his portrayal of Saint Teresa, one could say that Poussin is cinematographic.

The story depicted in *The Rape of the Sabine Women* is derived from classical mythology; the

3. Gian Lorenzo Bernini, *The Ecstasy of Saint Teresa,* 1644–1647. (Scala/Art Resource, N.Y.)

poses of the figures hark back to the Hellenistic period. Compare the positioning of the arms of the women on the left of the canvas with the tortured stance of Laocoön in the sculpture shown in Figure 4 of the first art essay. Other groups in the Poussin canvas are also reminiscent of that sculpture. As another bow to the ancient past, Poussin paints in the background buildings that are faithful to Roman prototypes. Such reliance on archaeology and mythology are typical of his work.

While paintings depicting mythological, historical, or religious themes dominated the major art markets during the baroque era, patrons in Holland sought paintings that related more to their own experience. For that reason, the genre of the still life—paintings of flowers, fruit, dishes, food,

4. Nicolas Poussin, *The Rape of the Sabine Women*, c. 1636–1637. (Image copyright © The Metropolitan Museum of Art/Art Resource, N.Y.)

and other familiar objects—reached its zenith in that country.

Willem Kalf (1622–1693), among the most skilled of Dutch still-life masters, was able to take a collection of objects and turn it into an object of art. His *Still Life* (Figure 5) showcases his meticulous, almost photorealistic style. In particular, it focuses on the way in which glass reflects light and on the juxtaposition of different textures. Although modern art historians view some still lifes as merely ornamental displays of technical skill, there was a reason for them. The popularity of still lifes and of landscapes probably has to do with the human desire for reassurance that "things are as they should be," that the status quo is being maintained, regardless of the religious or political turmoil affecting other aspects of life. No matter what was going on politically, no matter what religious dispute was being negotiated, people could find a degree of comfort in being surrounded by familiar objects or scenes.

While Kalf distinguished himself as a still-life painter, another Dutch master, Rembrandt van Rijn (1606–1669) gained fame for his historical and religious canvases. Rembrandt was influenced in his early years by Italian painters, especially by their use of light. But that was not his only strength. His reputation as a portrait painter made him renowned and made his fortune in Amsterdam.

Even more impressive were his self-portraits, which he painted not for the commissions of patrons but entirely for himself in the pursuit of truth. For an artist to paint as many self-portraits as Rembrandt did in the seventeenth century was very unusual. Self-portraits are analogous to autobiographies: in both, the artist examines himself because he believes his own self is worthy of self-examination.

Rembrandt's quest for the meaning of the inner life is compatible with the growing introspectiveness of the seventeenth century, an age that also produced Descartes's dictum that to think is to be, the soliloquies of Shakespeare's Hamlet, and the hallucinations of Cervantes' Don Quixote.

Rembrandt produced a series of sixty-two self-portraits during the course of his lifetime, an exhaustive autobiography in pictures in which he seemed to engage in a dialogue with himself in a variety of attitudes and poses: vigorous, youthful, heroic, flamboyant, melodramatic, enigmatic, aging, distraught, struggling with despair, grimly resolved, disdainful, strong, weak. Rembrandt completed *Self-Portrait at Old Age*, 1669 (Figure 6), the fifty-fifth in a corpus of sixty-two self-portraits, in the last year of his life. It is among a cluster of self-portraits in which he appears to have "pulled himself together" and defined his identity. In it, we find Rembrandt staring back at us with the calm assurance of a man who has mastered his art and life, and surpassed his time and place.

The later part of the eighteenth century marks the beginning of the rococo and neoclassical periods in art history. Especially popular in France, the rococo and neoclassical movements owed much to political and social forces. The term *rococo* describes a style that is frothy and frivolous and compatible with the peripheral concerns of royalty. In 1698, King Louis XIV ordered the redecoration of his palace at Versailles with works that were lighthearted and youthful instead of stodgy and serious. His dabbling with artistic matters led to quarrels and esthetic disagreements in the artistic community.

An example of the rococo is François Boucher's (1703–1770) *The Toilet of Venus* (1751) (Figure 7). Although some art historians describe his work as slick and artificial, Boucher became the darling of the French court. In his *The Toilet of Venus,* the goddess is full figured and lush, surrounded by all the sensual accouterments that the

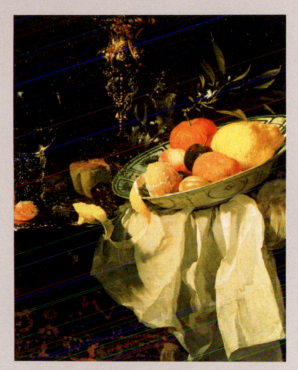

5. Willem Kalf, *Still Life,* c. 1660. (Scala/Art Resource, N.Y.)

goddess of love and erotic pleasure should have. Given her appearance and her surroundings, Boucher's Venus looks as though she would have been comfortable in period dress, supervising the decor of her boudoir at the palace at Versailles. Clearly, Boucher understood his audience well.

While Boucher exemplified the light and airy sentiment of the rococo style, Jacques Louis David (1748–1825) typified the neoclassical. The neoclassical style represents a return to the rationality and harmony of the classical past; many of the works from this period also reflect contemporary political events.

Justice, honor for one's country, and the need to portray inspirational themes were the guideposts of the neoclassical artists. Their training ground was Italy, primarily because it was the source of the classical prototypes from which they could learn. Jacques Louis David's *The Death of Marat* (1793) (Figure 8) captures the essence of that event in a manner that combines the best of Poussin and Rubens.

6. Rembrandt van Rijn, *Self-Portrait at Old Age*, 1669. (Erich Lessing/Art Resource, N.Y.)

The subject matter is important because it illuminates the neoclassical concept of virtue, represented by the martyrdom of Marat, a revolutionary. The style borrows from Poussin's ability to capture a scene with photographic stillness, rendering the figures in an almost sculptural way. But David has also appropriated Rembrandt's technique of skillfully juxtaposing light and shadow. While the neoclassicists sometimes paid homage to the distant past in their subject matter, they also showed their reverence for the revolutionary ideals of their own time.

7. François Boucher, *The Toilet of Venus*, 1751. (Image copyright © The Metropolitan Museum of Art/
Art Resource, N.Y.)

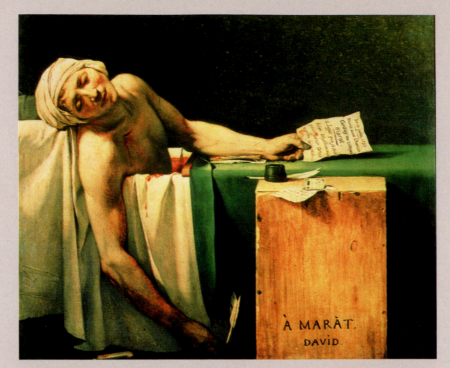

8. Jacques Louis David, *The Death of Marat*, 1793. (Bridgeman-Giraudon/Art Resource, N.Y.)

Sir Isaac Newton (1642–1727)

Today we know much more about Sir Isaac Newton, about his beliefs and life, than did his contemporaries. Newton was very private, even secretive. He wanted to appear to the world solely as a natural philosopher interested in local motion and the motions of the heavenly bodies. He said sternly, "I do not frame hypotheses," when asked to explain what universal gravitation actually is. In his heart, he believed it to be the will of God operating in the universe. This deeply religious man devoted as many hours of his work-week to theology and biblical prophecy as he did to experiments. Perhaps most surprising of all his labors are his alchemical pursuits. Like the magicians of old, he wanted to understand the secret workings of chemical action, and he believed that someday the truly pious natural philosopher would be able to transform ordinary metals into gold. Evidence of the private Newton sits amid his vast manuscript collections, which are now dispersed all over the world. On the Internet, the Newton Project has succeeded in putting many of these manuscripts online so that everyone can read them. Go to http://www.newtonproject.sussex.ac .uk/prism.php?id=1.

Creator but regarded miracles as limitations on nature's mechanical perfection. Applied to religious doctrines, Descartes's reliance on methodical doubt and clarity of thought and Bacon's insistence on careful observation led thinkers to question the validity of Christian teachings. Theology became a separate, and for some an irrelevant, area of intellectual inquiry, not fit for the interests of practical, well-informed people. Not only Christian doctrines but also various popular beliefs grew suspect. Magic, witchcraft, and astrology, still widespread among the European masses, were regarded with disdain by elite culture. Large numbers of people remained devoted to some form of traditional Christianity, and the uncertainty of a universe governed by devils, witches, or the stars continued to make sense to the poor and oppressed.

In Catholic countries, where the Scientific Revolution began, hostility toward scientific ideas gathered strength after the condemnation of Galileo. The mentality of the Counter-Reformation enabled lesser minds to exercise their fears against any idea they regarded as suspicious. Galileo was caught in this hostile environment, and the Copernican system was condemned by the church in 1616. In Spain and Poland, it was not officially taught until the 1770s.

Gradually, the science of Newton became the science of Western Europe: nature mechanized, analyzed, regulated, and mathematized. As a result of the Scientific Revolution, learned westerners came to believe more strongly than ever that nature could be mastered. Mechanical science—applied to canals, engines, pumps, and levers—became the science of industry. Thus, the Scientific Revolution, operating on both intellectual and commercial levels, laid the groundwork for two major developments of the modern West: the Age of Enlightenment and the Industrial Revolution.

❖   ❖   ❖

NOTES

1. Quoted in Jean D. Moss, *Novelties in the Heavens* (Chicago: University of Chicago Press, 1993), 33.

2. Excerpted in *Discoveries and Opinions of Galileo,* ed. Stillman Drake (Garden City, N.Y.: Doubleday, 1957), 28.

3. Excerpted in *Newton's Philosophy of Nature,* ed. H. S. Thayer (New York: Hafner, 1953), 177.

4. Excerpted in *Descartes' Philosophical Writings,* ed. Norman Kemp Smith (New York: Modern Library, 1958), 130–131.

SUGGESTED READING

Electronic resources: for Galileo, http://galileo.rice.edu/

For Boyle, http://campus.udayton.edu/~hume/Boyle/boyle.htm

For Harvey, http://www.fordham.edu/halsall/mod/1628harvey-blood.html

Gleick, James, *Isaac Newton* (2004). A great read.

Harkness, Deborah, *The Jewel House: Elizabethan London and the Scientific Revolution* (2007). This is a remarkable account of the depth of scientific practice in one of the largest cities in Europe and gives a wholly new understanding of the origins of the Scientific Revolution.

Jacob, Margaret C., and Larry Stewart, *Practical Matter: Newton's Science in the Service of Industry and Empire* (2004). A survey of the way Newton's science spread, first in Britain but then onto the Continent. The fruits of this new scientific culture were put on display at the Great Exhibition in London in 1851.

Ridley, Glynis, *The Discovery of Jeanne Baret. A Story of Science, the High Seas, the First Woman to Circumnavitate the Globe* (2010) A story of a woman desperate to go to sea, a search for new knowledge about nature never before explored, and the thrill and dangers of scientific discovery.

Newman, William R., *Atoms and Alchemy: Chymistry and the Experimental Origins of the Scientific Revolution* (2006). Argues for the central role of alchemy in the new science.

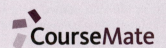

Chapter 18

The Age of Enlightenment: Reason and Reform

Engraving by William Hogarth. During the eighteenth century it became fashionable to make fun of the clergy and their privileges. Here William Hogarth, the most brilliant engraver of the period, has the congregation in a bedlam-like state while the preacher invokes hellfire and brimstone. (© Roger-Viollet/The Image Works)

Focus Questions

1. What does it mean to say that someone in the eighteenth century was "enlightened"?

2. Who were the Freemasons, and what role did they play in the eighteenth century?

3. What is a freethinker? A deist? An atheist? A pantheist?

4. With what economic doctrines do we associate Adam Smith?

5. To whom did Adam Smith's theories appeal? Why?

6. What is the enduring legacy of the Enlightenment? What were its political implications?

7. What do we mean by the Radical Enlightenment?

The eighteenth century's most exciting intellectual movement is called the Enlightenment. So powerful was its dedication to toleration and rational thought that until quite recently the era was sometimes characterized as the Age of Reason. It is more accurately described as an age of criticism, civility, and agitation for reform. What by 1750 came to be known as the Enlightenment began in the late seventeenth century. Three factors were critically important in this new intellectual ferment: revulsion against monarchical and clerical absolutism, especially as practiced by Louis XIV in France; a new freedom of publishing and with it the rise of a new public and a secular culture, especially in England and the Dutch Republic; and, not least, the impact of the Scientific Revolution, particularly the excitement generated by Newton's *Principia* (1687).

When Newton's great work appeared, censorship or imprisonment for ideas disliked by church or state was still commonplace. In France in 1685, the revocation of the Edict of Nantes left Protestants with few choices: they could either convert to Catholicism, go to prison, or try to find a way out of the country, an illegal act that often separated families. More than 150,000 French Protestants—many of them highly literate and all of them deeply angry—were forced to leave for the Dutch Republic, England, or Geneva or to journey to the American colonies. Others languished in French prisons. In the Dutch Republic, opponents of the Calvinist clergy who were deemed heretics could be detained indefinitely; one man died after three years in jail without a trial, probably a suicide. In England, Oxford University routinely expelled students whose ideas were seen to be heretical or unorthodox. In the papal territories, Jewish children were still forcibly baptized and then removed from their homes. By 1750, such extreme measures were rare anywhere north of the Alps or in the American colonies. A new set of values had come to prevail.

Rationality and order—imitative of the order found in Newton's universe—seemed to be gaining momentum. Proponents of enlightened values sought to impose an ordered freedom on social and political institutions. They were prepared to attack in print, though sometimes anonymously, the attitudes and beliefs that stood in the way of tolerance, freedom, and

Chronology 18.1 ❖ The Enlightenment

1685	Revocation of the Edict of Nantes; persecution of Protestants in France
1687	Publication of Newton's *Principia*
1688–1689	Revolution in England: the clergy's power is weakened and censorship loosened; James II, a king with absolutist ambitions, is sent into exile in France
1690	Publication of Locke's *Two Treatises of Government*
1695	Publication of Locke's *Reasonableness of Christianity*
1696	Toland's *Christianity Not Mysterious* makes the case for deism
1717	Founding of the Grand Lodge, London; the beginning of organized Freemasonry
1719	Anonymous publication of the *Treatise on the Three Impostors*, the most radical text of the period
1733	Voltaire publishes *Letters Concerning the English Nation*
1740	Frederick the Great invades Silesia; the War of the Austrian Succession ensues
1748	Hume publishes *An Enquiry Concerning Human Understanding*; Montesquieu publishes *The Spirit of the Laws*
1751	Publication of the first volumes of Diderot's *Encyclopedia* in Paris
1756–1763	Seven Years' War
1762	Rousseau publishes *Émile* and *The Social Contract*
1775	American Revolution begins
1776	Adam Smith publishes *The Wealth of Nations*
1785	Russian Charter of Nobility; the servitude of the peasants is guaranteed
1787	Dutch Revolution begins
1789	French Revolution begins

rationality. As combative intellectuals and pundits, they earned the name *philosophes*—simply the French word for "philosophers"—now used in many languages to describe the bold and witty satirists of clergymen, courtiers, and the pious in general. Thinkers as diverse as Voltaire in France, Benjamin Franklin and Thomas Jefferson in America, and Immanuel Kant (1724–1804), an abstract philosopher in Germany, may be labeled *philosophes*.

Late in the eighteenth century, Kant gave a succinct definition of *enlightenment*: bringing "light into the dark corners of mind," dispelling ignorance, prejudice, and superstition. Kant went to the heart of one aspect of the Enlightenment: its insistence that each individual should think independently, without recourse to the authority of schools, churches, or clergymen.[1]

Being a political moderate and living in authoritarian Prussia, Kant hoped that the call for self-education and critical thought would mean no disruption of the political order, at least at home. In his moderation, he was similar to most philosophes. Distrusting the uneducated people, these intellectual leaders sought a gradual transformation of the human condition.

Radicals could also be found amid the enlightened. Often publishing anonymously they advocated pantheism or materialism, railed against the power of the clergy, and attacked the power of monarchies. Such thinking was visible as early as the 1690s. During the late eighteenth century, there were radical thinkers, such as the American revolutionary Thomas Jefferson (1743–1826) and the feminist Mary Wollstonecraft (1759–1797), who were prepared to endorse an immediate political disruption of the traditional authority of monarchy, aristocracy, fathers, and churchmen. Whether radical or moderate, the philosophes were united by certain key ideas. They believed in the **new science**, were critical of clergy and all rigid dogma but tolerant of people's right to worship freely, and believed deeply in freedom of the press. They were also willing to entertain, though not necessarily accept, new heresies such as **pantheism**, which equated nature with God; or the belief that the earth had gradually evolved; or the view that the Bible was a series of wise stories but not the literal word of God.

Philosophes thrived in the major European cities, where they clubbed and socialized in literary and philosophical societies. By the 1770s, Paris was the center of the Enlightenment, but circles of philosophes could be found in Berlin, Moscow, Budapest, London, The Hague, and, across the Atlantic, in Philadelphia. Their writings spread far and wide because they adopted a new style for philosophical discussion: clear, direct, witty, satirical, even naughty and audacious. At times, they were more like journalists, propagandists, writers of fiction, even pornographers, who sought to live by their pens. Their success owed much to the growing literacy of urban men and women, a new prosperity that made books affordable and a fashionable sociability where new ideas could be discussed. The philosophes' readers, too, were fed up with all vestiges of medieval culture. They resented priestly and aristocratic privileges, monarchical decrees in place of deliberation in representative assemblies, and restrictions on who could manufacture what and where. It also helped that the printing presses were relatively free to publish what they pleased in both England and the Dutch Republic.

Appealing to the professional classes, literate merchants, and women with leisure to read, the philosophes opposed the old scholastic learning of the universities, mocked the clergy, and denied the Christian mysteries. They expressed confidence in science and reason, called for humanitarian treatment of slaves and criminals, and played a cat-and-mouse game with censors. Dedicated to freedom of thought and person, they combined these liberal values with a secular orientation and a belief in future progress. The philosophes helped shape, if not define, modern beliefs in tolerance, human rights, and free speech. They also put into print some of the most outrageous writings ever seen in the West; one of these, published in 1719, even labeled Jesus, Moses, and Muhammad as the three great impostors.

THE FORMATION OF A PUBLIC AND SECULAR CULTURE

In England and the Dutch Republic, by 1700 freedom of the press was a practical or a legal reality. During the same period, in 1685, Louis XIV outlawed Protestants from France. In exile, they set up journals and newspapers, formed new clubs, and began a vast international discussion—conducted in French, the language of all well-educated Europeans—aimed against the injustices of monarchical absolutism and the evils of religious persecution. In journals and newspapers, the reformers endorsed the need for political change, the end of clerical privileges, and the wisdom of Newtonian science.

At the same time, relative freedom of assembly in the cities of Western Europe (even in Paris, which was too big to police) gave rise to a new public and secular sphere: a zone for social life outside the family but not attached to churches or courts. The new public sphere, found in *salons* (gatherings in private homes), coffeehouses, and Masonic lodges, as well as in academies for scientific learning such as the Royal Society of London, provided the social space wherein the Enlightenment emerged.

All these autonomous and voluntary groups helped create a new secular and public culture. In this new and free mental space, what we now call *civil society*, people mingled with strangers, politeness and conviviality became norms of behavior, and informal learning flourished. Lecturers gave scientific demonstrations, ordinary men learned to vote for their leaders or to debate publicly, and women met outside the home to discuss novels or politics. Indeed, in some of the Parisian salons, women were often the key organizers. By the 1780s, throughout Western Europe, no town of any size was without a private association, club, and newspaper. In the Dutch Republic in 1785, the first scientific society founded by and for women met in the town of Middelburg (located in the province of Zeeland and no larger than about 17,000 souls).[2] The women chose a Freemason and follower of Voltaire to give scientific demonstrations, and they set about learning Newtonian mechanics with such dedication that their society lasted for more than a hundred years.

Men and women met at these sociable gatherings out of a common interest in politics, science, the new novels, or self-improvement. Members shared certain characteristics: they were highly literate; they possessed some surplus wealth and leisure time; and, if titled aristocrats, they were not opposed to mixing with bourgeois lawyers, doctors, civil servants, and merchants. Such cosmopolitan men and women made the theories of the philosophes come alive. The new societies thus became schools where the literate expanded their universe, learning about peoples of the East and the Americas and about the Newtonian heavens. In the words of Kant, they dared to think for themselves.

This training in self-governance, self-education, and social criticism helped prepare the way for the liberal revolutions that swept across America and Europe at the end of the eighteenth and during the first half of the nineteenth century. In the first years of the French Revolution, one of the earliest activities of the revolutionaries was to set up clubs based on equality and fraternity and modeled after the clubs and lodges of the Enlightenment.

Salons

Perhaps the most famous of the many new forms of secular culture were the salons, often run by women and mostly found in Paris. Intellectually ambitious women, such as Madame Necker and Madame Geoffrin, organized regular evening receptions in their drawing rooms. There philosophes graced the tables of aristocrats and discussed ideas in an atmosphere that was civilized and open. Originally, the salon was an institution found only in noble homes, where the room designated for leisure activities gave the gathering its name. The habits of luxurious feasting and gaming soon were challenged by serious, if somewhat formal, egalitarian conversation. Salons also developed an international correspondence; letters from all over Europe were read to the assembled guests, many of whom were aristocrats. A new republic of letters as well as cosmopolitanism were occasionally experienced in the salons. Some salons, however, excluded women, who were attacked as frivolous and gossipy.

Freemasons

As the search for a new religiosity during the Enlightenment came to mean a striving after alternatives to traditional beliefs, private groups with a ritual and ethical component began to flourish. The most famous of these were the Freemasons, a fraternity that evolved in the late seventeenth century in England and Scotland. Originally guilds of working stonemasons, the Masonic lodges evolved into fraternities of middle-class and aristocratic men (and some women). By the 1720s, they could be found in London and on the Continent. Keeping to the ideals of the older stonemasons, they said that all men should meet "upon the level." In practice, this meant calling one another "brother," holding elections for their leaders, and living under rules for correct behavior, all codified in a published book, *Constitutions* (1723). In Britain, after the Revolution of 1688–1689, lodges adhered to constitutional practices, religious toleration, charity, and self-education. The lodges sought to make their members virtuous, disciplined, and civilized. For some men, this experience came to rival that found in the churches. Philosophes such as Benjamin Franklin and, late in his life, Voltaire, joined lodges; in some cities, lodges became cultural centers. In Vienna, Mozart was a Freemason and wrote music for his lodge; in Berlin, Frederick the Great cultivated the lodges, which in turn became centers for the cult of enlightened monarchy. Both George Washington and Paul Revere were Freemasons.

FREEMASON INITIATION CEREMONY. By the time this engraving was made (1805), freemasonry had become an accepted part of Western social life. But also by that year, the freemasons had been blamed for the French Revolution. They, along with the French philosophes, were said to be responsible for it. That was purely a myth, but it became a part of ultraconservative thought into the twentieth century. Here a blindfolded novice is being led to an initiation ceremony. (*http://commons.wikimedia.org/wiki/File:Freimaurer_Initiation.jpg.*) Initiation of an apprentice Freemason around 1800. This engraving is based on that of Gabanon on the same subject dated 1745. The costumes of the participants are changed to the English fashion at the start of the 19th century and the engraving is colored, but otherwise is that of 1745. (© P. Rotger/Iberfoto/The Image Works.)

By the middle of the eighteenth century, perhaps as many as fifty thousand men belonged to lodges in just about every major European city. British constitutionalism, as well as the old fraternal ideals of equality and liberty, took on new meaning in these private gatherings. In France in the 1780s, the national Grand Lodge instituted a general assembly of elected representatives from the entire country, as well as a monthly payment of charity for impoverished brothers. The lodges for women became places where women and men actually talked about the meaning of liberty and equality for their own lives. Many lodges were dominated by the most elite elements in Old Regime society (see Chapter 19), who found themselves giving allegiance, and often considerable financial support, to a new system of belief and governance—a system that was ultimately incompatible with the principles of birth and inheritance on which their power rested. In 1738, the pope condemned membership in the lodges. At the time of the French Revolution, its opponents claimed that the lodges were responsible for the uprising. There was no truth to the claim, but it has often been repeated by right-wing opponents of modernity and reform. The subversive quality of the lodges lay not in any conspiracy but rather in the freedom they allowed for thought, self-governance, and discussion.

Scientific Academies

By midcentury, in capitals as well as in provincial cities, scientific academies flourished. The first scientific societies had formed in the 1660s in London and Paris. They were imitated in Turin, Budapest, Berlin, and small cities of the Dutch Republic, such as Haarlem and Middelburg. Members of these societies performed experiments of greater or lesser sophistication, listened to learned papers, and searched for natural samples. Each society kept a cabinet of "rarities" containing everything from rocks to deformed animal bones. Anyone who possessed what the age called curiosity could join one of these groups and try to become proficient in the new science. Gradually, women were admitted—not as members but as spectators. By the 1770s, these scientific societies served as models for groups specifically interested in the application of scientific knowledge or in useful learning. The new groups became centers for the reformers and critics of the age, who sought to turn the Enlightenment into a movement for reform.

In Germany and France, where the scientific academies were dominated by aristocratic leadership, new societies with a utilitarian purpose were founded and had to compete with the older societies. The applied and the utilitarian were more visible in England and Scotland. In France, the academies became centers for abstract and advanced science and mathematics—for important and original contributions with little practical application. During the French Revolution, however, the academies were purged, and emphasis was then placed on applications of mechanics and chemistry. In northern England during the 1790s, the Lunar Society provided a meeting place for some of the most important leaders of the new movement to apply power technology, like the steam engine, to industry. The application of scientific principles to technological innovation defined the industrial side of the British Enlightenment.

ALTERNATIVES TO ORTHODOXY

Christianity Under Attack

No single thread had united Western culture more powerfully than Christianity. Until the eighteenth century, educated people, especially rulers and state servants, had to give allegiance to one or another of the Christian churches—however un-Christian their political actions. The Enlightenment produced the first widely read, systematic assault on Christian doctrines launched from within the ranks of the educated. The philosophes argued that many Christian dogmas defied logic—for example, the conversion of the substance of bread and wine into the body and the blood of Christ during the Eucharist. They also ridiculed theologians for arguing about obscure issues that seemed irrelevant to the human condition and a hindrance to clear thinking. "Theology amuses me," wrote Voltaire. "That's where we find the madness of the human spirit in all its plenitude." In the same vein, the philosophes denounced the churches for inciting the fanaticism and intolerance that led to the horrors of the Crusades, the Inquisition, and the wars of the Reformation. They viewed Christianity's preoccupation with salvation and its belief in the depravity of human nature as barriers to social improvement and earthly happiness. Although liberal clerics led a moderate and religious Enlightenment, the secular-minded philosophes became far more famous and unorthodox.

Skeptics, Freethinkers, and Deists

An early attack on Christian dogma came from the skeptic and French Protestant refugee Pierre Bayle (1647–1706). He saw superstition as a social evil far more dangerous than atheism. Bayle had fled to the Dutch Republic as a result of Louis XIV's campaign against Protestants. Although a Calvinist in background, Bayle also ran into opposition from the strict Calvinist clergy, who regarded him as lax on doctrinal matters. He attacked his critics and persecutors in a new and brilliant form of journalism, his *Historical and Critical Dictionary* (1697), which was more an encyclopedia than a dictionary. Under alphabetically arranged subjects and in copious footnotes, Bayle discussed the most recent learning of the day and never missed an opportunity to ridicule the dogmatic, the superstitious, or the just plain arrogant. In Bayle's hands, the ancient philosophy of skepticism—the doubting of all dogma—was revived and turned into a tool; rigorous questioning of accepted ideas became a method for arriving at new truths. As Bayle noted in his *Dictionary* "It is therefore only religion that has anything to fear from Pyrrhonism [that is, skepticism]."[3] In this same critical spirit, Bayle, in his dictionary article entitled "David," compared Louis XIV to Goliath. The message was clear enough: great tyrants and the clergy who prop them up should beware of self-confident, independently minded citizens who are skeptical of the claims of authority made by kings and churches and are eager to use their own intellects to search for truth.

Bayle's *Dictionary* had an enormous impact throughout Europe. Its alphabetical format captured the imagination of the philosophes. Here was a way of simply, even scientifically, classifying and ordering knowledge. Partly through Bayle's writings, skepticism became an integral part of an enlightened approach to religion. It taught its readers to question the clerical claim that God's design governs human events—that God "ordains" certain human actions. Skepticism dealt a serious blow to revealed religion and seemed to point in the direction of "natural" religion, that is, toward a system of beliefs and ethics designed by rational people on the basis of their own needs.

The religious outlook among the enlightened drew heavily on the writings of late-seventeenth- and early-eighteenth-century English freethinkers. These early proponents of the unorthodox used the term *freethinking* to signal their hostility to established church dogmas and their ability to think for themselves. They looked back to the English Revolution of 1640–1660 for their ideas about government; many English freethinkers were republicans in the tradition established in the 1650s. Indeed, the freethinkers of the 1690s and beyond helped popularize English republican ideas at home and in the American colonies, where in 1776 these views would figure prominently among American revolutionaries. French Protestant refugees also translated their writings and made them accessible to all who could read French.

The freethinkers had little use for organized religion or even for Christianity itself. In 1696, the freethinker John Toland (1670–1722) published *Christianity Not Mysterious*. In it, he argued that most religious doctrines seemed to contradict reason or common sense and such beliefs as the resurrection of Jesus and the miracles of the Bible should be dropped. Toland also attacked the clergy's power; in his opinion, the Revolution of 1688–1689 had not gone far enough in undermining the power of the established church and the king. Toland and his freethinking associates wanted England to be a republic governed by "reasonable" people who worshiped, as Toland proposed, not a mysterious God but intelligible nature. For Toland, Newton's science made nature intelligible, and he used it as a stick with which to beat at the doctrines of revealed religion.

Combining science with skepticism, freethinking, and anticlericalism, critics found ample reason for abandoning all traditional authority. By 1700, the works of Bayle, the freethinkers, and philosophers such as Descartes provoked a general crisis of confidence in established authority. Once started in England and the Netherlands and broadcast via Dutch and French refugee printers, the Enlightenment quickly became international, with French as the language of choice.

Some of the early advocates of the Enlightenment were atheists. They often published clandestinely. A particularly early and outrageous example of their thinking appeared under the title *The Treatise of the Three Impostors* (1719). (See Primary Source box.) However, most of the philosophes were simply **deists**, who believed only those Christian doctrines that could meet the test of reason. For example, they considered it reasonable to believe in God, for only with a creator, they said, could such a superbly organized universe have come into being. However, after God set the universe in motion, he in effect disappeared. Thus, although deists retained a belief in God the Creator, they rejected clerical authority, revelation, original sin, and miracles. They held that biblical accounts of the resurrection and of Jesus walking on water or raising the dead could not be reconciled with natural law. Deists viewed Jesus as a great moral teacher, not as the Son of God, and they regarded ethics, not faith, as the essence of religion. Rational people, they said, served God

The Treatise of the Three Impostors

Never before in the Christian West had religion been attacked as forcefully as it was in the eighteenth century. Of course, there had been polemics among and between the various creeds, but the following document denounces all religion and even labels the founders of the three monotheistic religions as impostors. It is openly atheistic and advocates that people come out from under the influence of the clergy and simply worship Nature. To this day, we have only circumstantial evidence as to who wrote it, but we know the circle in the Dutch Republic where it originated. Predictably, it included book dealers (probably out to make some money) and angry French Protestants who had been persecuted and forced to flee their native country. Sometimes anger and persecution beget renunciation and denunciation, in this case of the very impulse that caused such grief—namely, religion in general.

. . . One should therefore not be astonished that the world is filled with vain & ridiculous opinions; nothing is better able to give them currency than ignorance; it is the only source of the false ideas which men have of the Divinity, the Soul, Spirits, & of almost all the other objects which compose Religion. . . .

. . . The partisans of these absurdities have succeed so well that it is dangerous to combat them. It matters too much to these impostors that the people be ignorant, to suffer that they be disabused.

If the people could understand into what an abyss ignorance throws them, they would soon shake off the yoke of unworthy leaders, for it is impossible to let reason act without its discovering the truth.

These impostors have sensed this so well, that to prevent the good effects which it [reason] would infallibly produce, they have had the idea of painting it to us as a monster . . . [and] they would nevertheless be much annoyed if the truth were listened to. . . .

Those who are ignorant of physical causes have a natural fear which proceeds from uneasiness & from the doubt they are in, if there exists a Being or a power which has the capacity to harm them or to preserve them. Thence the penchant which they have to feign [i.e., invent] invisible causes, which are only the Phantoms of their imagination, which they invoke in adversity & which they praise in prosperity. They make themselves Gods out of these in the end, & this chimerical fear of invisible powers is the source of the Religions. . . .

Questions for Analysis

1. What does the text say about the origin of the human impulse to have a religion? How does this text belong to the Radical Enlightenment?
2. Who are the imposters?

Margaret C. Jacob, *The Enlightenment: A Brief History with Documents* (Boston: Bedford/St. Martin's, 2009).

best by treating their fellow human beings justly. Early freethinkers, pantheists and deists in both England and the Dutch Republic constituted what historians now call the Radical Enlightenment.

David Hume (1711–1776), a Scottish skeptic, attacked both revealed religion and the deists' belief in order and design. He maintained that all religious ideas, including Christian teachings and even the idea of God, stemmed ultimately from human fears and superstitions. The universe, said Hume, might very well be eternal, and the seemingly universal order might simply be more in our heads than in reality. Hume laid great emphasis on social conventions, with which he associated religion. Reason should best be expressed through skepticism.

Voltaire the Philosophe

The French possessed a vital tradition of intellectual skepticism going back to the late sixteenth century, as well as a tradition of scientific rationalism exemplified by Descartes. In the early eighteenth century, however, French thinkers found it difficult to gain access to the new literature of the Enlightenment because Louis XIV controlled and censored the French printing presses. As a result, a brisk but risky traffic developed in clandestine books and manuscripts subversive of authority, and French-language journals poured from Dutch presses. *The Treatise of the Three Impostors*, written in French, was first circulated on this clandestine circuit.

As a poet and writer struggling for recognition in Paris, the young François Marie Arouet, known to the world as Voltaire (1694–1778), encountered some of the new ideas being discussed in Parisian salons. In the French capital, educated people interested in the new ideas, some hostile to the church or to the Sorbonne, the clerically controlled university, had to proceed with caution. Individuals had been imprisoned for writing, publishing, or owning books hostile to Catholic doctrine. Although Voltaire learned something of the new enlightened culture in Paris, it was in the early to mid 1720s, when he journeyed to the Dutch Republic and then to London, that Voltaire the poet became Voltaire the philosophe. Voltaire fled Paris after he was arbitrarily arrested when defending himself in a fight with a local aristocrat. His anger toward the French church came to resemble the hostility found among the exiled French Protestants.

In England, Voltaire became acquainted with the ideas of John Locke and Isaac Newton. From Newton, Voltaire learned the mathematical laws that govern the universe; he witnessed the power of human reason to establish general rules that seemed to explain the behavior of physical objects. From Locke, Voltaire learned that people should believe only the ideas received from the senses. Locke's theory of learning, his *epistemology*, impressed many of the philosophes. Again, the implications for religion were most serious: if people believed only what they experienced, they would not accept mysteries and doctrines simply because these concepts were taught by churches and clergy. Voltaire enjoyed considerable freedom of thought in England and witnessed social and religious toleration that was in sharp contrast with French absolutism and the power of the French clergy. He also witnessed a freer mixing of

VOLTAIRE AND KING FREDERICK. The roundtable was beloved by the aristocracy because it claimed every one of them as equals. Here Voltaire visits with Frederick the Great and perhaps imagined himself as an equal. (Bildarchiv Preussischer Kulturbesitz/Art Resource, N.Y.)

bourgeois and aristocratic social groups than was permitted in France at this time.

Throughout his life, Voltaire fiercely supported toleration and free inquiry. He criticized churches and the Roman Catholic Inquisition. His books were banned in France, but he probably did more there than any other philosophe to popularize the Enlightenment. In *Letters Concerning the English Nation* (1733), Voltaire offered constitutional monarchy, Newtonian science, and religious toleration as models to be followed by all of Europe. In the *Letters*, he praised English society for its encouragement of these ideals. As he put it, "This is the country of sects. An Englishman, as a free man, goes to Heaven by whatever road he pleases."[4] Voltaire never ceased to ridicule the purveyors of superstition and blind obedience to religious authority, and in such works as *Candide* (1759) and *Micromegas* (1752), he castigated the clergy.

Voltaire, a practical reformer, campaigned for the rule of law, a freer press, religious toleration, humane treatment of criminals, and a more effective system of government administration. His writings constituted a radical attack on several aspects of eighteenth-century French society. Yet, like so many philosophes, Voltaire feared the power of the people, especially if goaded by the clergy. He was happiest in the company of the rich and powerful, provided they tolerated his ideas and supported reform. Not surprisingly, Voltaire was frequently disappointed by eighteenth-century monarchs, such as Frederick the Great in Prussia, who promised enlightenment but sought mainly to increase their own power and that of their armies.

Perhaps the happiest decision of Voltaire's life was to team up with the scientist and philosophe Madame du Châtelet (1706–1749). Together they read Newton, although she became the more proficient mathematician. Before her death during the birth of their child, Madame du Châtelet made the only French translation of the *Principia*, explicated it, and trained scientists who took up Newtonian ideas and spread them throughout Western Europe.

POLITICAL THOUGHT

With the exception of Machiavelli in the Renaissance and Thomas Hobbes and the republicans during the English Revolution of 1640–1660, the Enlightenment produced the greatest originality in modern political thought witnessed in the West up to that time. Three major European thinkers and a host of minor ones wrote treatises on politics that remain relevant to this day: John Locke, *Two Treatises of Government* (1690); Baron de la Brède et de Montesquieu, *The Spirit of the Laws* (1748), and Jean Jacques Rousseau, *The Social Contract* (1762). All repudiated the divine right of kings and strove to check the power of monarchy; each offered different

formulas for achieving that goal. These major political theorists of the Enlightenment were also aware of the writings of Machiavelli and Hobbes and, though often disagreeing with them, borrowed some of their ideas. They also made use of Spinoza (d. 1677), who argued that God and his creation are one substance and who deeply influenced what the freethinker John Toland first called *pantheism*.

During the Renaissance, Machiavelli (d. 1527) analyzed politics in terms of power, fortune, and the ability of the individual ruler; he did not call in God to justify the power of princes or to explain their demise. Machiavelli also preferred a republican form of government to monarchy, and his republican vision did not lose its appeal during the Enlightenment. Very late in the eighteenth century, most liberal theorists recognized that the republican form of government, or at least the virtues practiced by citizens in a republic, offered the only alternative to the corruption and repression associated with absolute monarchy assisted by the church.

Political thinkers of the Enlightenment were ambivalent toward much of the writing of Thomas Hobbes (1588–1679). All, however, liked his belief that self-interest is a valid reason for engaging in political activity and his refusal to bring God into his system to justify the power of kings. Hobbes said that power did not rest on divine right but arose out of a contract made among men who agreed to elevate the state, and hence the monarch, to a position of power over them. That contract, once made, could not be broken. As a consequence, the power of the government, whether embodied in a king or a parliament, was absolute.

Hobbes published his major work, *Leviathan*, in 1651, when England had just emerged from civil war; thus, he was obsessed with the issue of political stability. He feared that, left to their own devices, men would kill one another; the "war of all against all"[5] would prevail without the firm hand of a sovereign to stop it. Hobbes's vision of human nature was dark and forbidding. In the state of nature, the original men had lived lives that could only have been "nasty, brutish, and short." Their sole recourse was to make a contract among themselves and establish a power over themselves that would restrain them. For Hobbes, the state was, as he put it, a "mortal god," the only guarantee of peace and stability. He was the first political thinker to realize the extraordinary power that had come into existence with the creation of strong centralized governments. Most Enlightenment theorists, however, beginning with John Locke, denied that governments possessed absolute power over their subjects, and to that extent they repudiated Hobbes. Many European thinkers of the eighteenth century, including Rousseau, also rejected Hobbes's gloomy view that human nature is greedy and warlike. Yet Hobbes lurks in the background of the Enlightenment. He is the first wholly secular political theorist, and he sounded the death knell for Christian political theology and the divine right of kings. The Enlightenment theorists started where he left off.

Locke

Probably the most widely read political philosopher during the first half of the eighteenth century was John Locke (1632–1704). Locke came to maturity in the late 1650s, and like so many of his contemporaries, he was drawn to science. Although he was a medical doctor, his major interest lay in politics and political theory. His *Two Treatises of Government* was seen as a justification for the English Revolution of 1688–1689 and the notion of government by consent of the people. (Although the treatises were published in 1690, Locke wrote them before the Glorious Revolution; that fact, however, was not known during the Enlightenment.)

Locke's theory, in its broad outlines, stated that the right to govern derived from the consent of the governed and was a form of contract. When people gave their consent to a government, they expected it to govern justly, protect their property, and ensure certain liberties for the propertied. If a government attempted to rule absolutely and arbitrarily—if it violated the natural rights of the individual—it reneged on its contract and forfeited the loyalty of its subjects. Such a government could legitimately be overthrown. Locke believed that a constitutional government that limited the power of rulers offered the best defense of property and individual rights. He also advocated religious toleration for religious

LOCKE ON THE CONTINENT. John Locke enjoyed an international reputation. This highly stylized portrait of him is adorned with French text. Locke had lived in the Dutch Republic, and his writings were promoted by French Huguenot refugees who hated the monarchy they left behind. (© Bettmann/Corbis.)

groups whose beliefs did not threaten the state. Locke denied toleration to Catholics because of their association with the Stuarts and to atheists because their oaths to God could not be trusted. He also promoted the necessity for education, particularly for those who saw themselves as the natural leaders of society. And not least, he advocated commerce and trade as one of the foundations of England's national strength.

Late in the eighteenth century, Locke's ideas were used to justify liberal revolutions in both Europe and America. His *Two Treatises of Government* had been translated into French early in the century by Huguenot refugees. These Protestant victims of French absolutism, persecuted for their religion, saw that the importance of Locke's political philosophy was not simply in his use of contract theory to justify constitutional government; he also asserted that the community could take up arms against its sovereign in the name of the natural rights of liberty and property. Locke's ideas about the foundation of government had greater impact on the European Continent and in America during the eighteenth century than in England. The Dutch and American revolutions found their justification from reprinted editions of Locke's *Second Treatise.*

Montesquieu

Baron de la Brède et de Montesquieu (1689–1755) was a French aristocrat who, like Voltaire, visited England late in the 1720s and knew the writings of Locke. Montesquieu had little sympathy for revolutions, but he did approve of constitutional monarchy. His primary concern was to check the unbridled authority of the French kings. In opposition to the Old Regime, Montesquieu proposed a balanced system of government, with an executive branch offset by a legislature whose members were drawn from the landed and educated elements in society. From his writings we derive our notion of government divided into branches. Montesquieu genuinely believed that the aristocracy possessed a natural and sacred obligation to rule and that their honor called them to serve the community. He also sought to fashion a government that channeled the interests and energies of its people, a government that was not bogged down in corruption and inefficiency.

In stressing the rule of law and the importance of nonmonarchical authority, Montesquieu became a source for legitimating the authority of representative institutions. Hardly an advocate of democracy, Montesquieu was nonetheless seen as a powerful critic of royal absolutism. His writings, particularly *The Spirit of the Laws,* established him both as a major philosophe who possessed republican tendencies and as a critic of the Old Regime in France. Once again, innovative political thinking highlighted the failures of absolutist government and pointed to the need for some kind of representative assembly in every European country. In addition, Montesquieu's ideas on a balanced system of government found favor in the new American republic.

Rousseau

Not until the 1760s did democracy find its champion: Jean Jacques Rousseau (1712–1778). Rousseau based his political philosophy on contract theory and his reading of Hobbes. For Rousseau, the people choose their government and, in so doing, effectively give birth to civil society. But he further demanded (in contrast to Hobbes) that the contract be constantly renewed and that government be made immediately and directly responsible to the will of the people. *The Social Contract* opened with this stirring cry for reform, "Man is born free; and everywhere he is in chains," and went on to ask how freedom could be attained. Freedom is in the very nature of man: "to renounce liberty is to renounce being a man, to surrender the rights of humanity and even its duties."[6] Human beings are born free and innocent in the state of nature; only society and government corrupt them.

Rousseau's political ideal was the city-state of ancient Greece, where men (but not women) participated actively and directly in politics and were willing to sacrifice self-interest to the community's needs. In the ancient republics, the state was a moral association that made people better and in which good citizenship was the highest form of excellence. In contrast, modern society was prey to many conflicting interests; Rousseau said that the rich and powerful used the state to preserve their advantages and power and that the poor and powerless viewed it as an oppressor. Consequently, obedience to law, devotion to the state, and freedom—the characteristics of the Greek city-state—had been lost.

In *The Social Contract,* Rousseau tried to resolve the conflict between individual freedom and the demands of the state. His solution was a small state, modeled after his native city of Geneva as well as after the Greek city-state. Such a state, said Rousseau, should be based on the *general will*: that which is best for the community and expresses its common interests. Rousseau wanted laws of the state to coincide with the general will. He believed in human beings' wisdom

ROUSSEAU. Rousseau sought innocence and a return to nature. Here children lead the way. (© Roger-Viollet/The Image Works.)

to arrive at laws that serve the common good, but to do so, they must set aside selfish interests for the good of the community. For Rousseau, freedom consisted of obeying laws prescribed by citizens inspired by the general will. The citizens themselves must constitute the lawmaking body; lawmaking cannot be entrusted to a single person or a small group.

In Rousseau's view, those who disobey laws—who act according to their private will rather than in accordance with the general will as expressed in law—degrade themselves and undermine the community. Therefore, government has the right to force citizens to be obedient, to compel them to exercise their individual wills in the proper way. He left the problem of minority rights unresolved.

No philosopher of the Enlightenment was more dangerous to the Old Regime than Rousseau. His ideas were perceived as truly revolutionary—a direct challenge to the power of kings, churches, and aristocrats. Although Rousseau thought that the philosophes had been corrupted by easy living and salons filled with aristocrats and dandies, he nevertheless earned an uneasy place in the ranks of the philosophes. The French revolutionaries invoked his name to justify democracy, and of all the philosophes, Rousseau probably would have been the least horrified by the early phase of that revolutionary upheaval.

SOCIAL THOUGHT

Rousseau looked on society as the corrupter of human beings, who, left to their own devices, were inherently virtuous and freedom loving. Many enlightened thinkers also viewed society, if not as corrupting, at least as needing constant reform. Some critics were prepared to work with those in power to bring about social reforms. Other philosophes believed that the key to reform lay not in social and political institutions but in changing the general mentality through education and knowledge. All developed new ideas about humankind as travelers told of new peoples and places where commonplace concepts, such as the Judeo-Christian God, had never existed. The societies of Native Americans fascinated Europeans, who vacillated between feeling superior and believing themselves mired in baroquely rigid customs. In general, the travel literature freed the European imagination to think about the complexity of human customs and to compare themselves with other peoples and their religions.

Epistemology and Education

Just as Locke's *Two Treatises of Government* helped shape the political thought of the Enlightenment, his *Essay Concerning Human Understanding* (1689) provided the theoretical foundations for an unprecedented interest in education. Locke's view that at birth the mind is blank—a clean slate, or **tabula rasa**—had two important implications. First, if human beings did not come into this world with innate ideas, then they were not, as Christianity taught, inherently sinful. Second, a person's environment was the

Mary Wollstonecraft

One of the founders of modern feminism and a deeply committed defender of liberty, human rights, and the French Revolution, Mary Wollstonecraft (1759–1797) came to maturity in a circle of English radicals. Her friends included the Unitarian ministers Richard Price and Joseph Priestley, and she knew the British-born American radical Thomas Paine. Although she received little formal education, she taught herself languages, made a living as a translator, read Rousseau critically, and began an intellectual odyssey that took her from liberal Protestantism to freethinking and possibly atheism. She went to France during its Revolution and wanted to raise her daughter there because she believed that in France she would be freer. By far her most famous book is *A Vindication of the Rights of Woman* (1792), a classic statement of women's rights and the causes of prejudice and inequality. Since the two hundredth anniversary of Wollstonecraft's famous book, her writings have been revived, and she has been placed at the center of the European Enlightenment as an embodiment of its belief in science and the possibility of human emancipation.

decisive force in shaping his or her character and intelligence. Nine of every ten men, wrote Locke, "are good or evil, useful or not, [because of] their education." Such a theory was eagerly received by the reform-minded philosophes, who preferred attributing wickedness to faulty institutions, improper rearing, and poor education rather than to a defective human nature.

In the Enlightenment view, the proper study of humanity addressed the process by which people can and do know. Locke had said that individuals take the information produced by their senses and reflect on it; in that way, they arrive at complex ideas. Aside from an environment promoting learning, education obviously requires the active participation of students. Merely receiving knowledge not tested by their own sense experience is inadequate.

More treatises were written on education during the eighteenth century than in all previous centuries combined. On the Continent, where the clergy controlled many schools and all the universities, the educated laity began to demand state regulation and inspection of educational facilities. This insistence revealed a growing discontent with the clergy and their independent authority. By the second half of the century, new schools and universities in Prussia, Belgium, Austria, Hungary, and Russia attempted to teach practical subjects suited to the interests of the laity. Predictably, science was given a special place. In France, for all the interest in education on the part of the philosophes, by 1789, probably only 50 percent of the men and about 20 percent of the women were literate.

The standards of education for girls and women were appalling. Only a few philosophes, mostly women, and the occasional clergyman who had seen firsthand the poor quality of female education called for reform. But reform did not come until after 1800, when industrialization put more women in the work force and required some literacy. As for higher education, women were excluded, with a few exceptions. Madame du Châtelet in France had studied mathematics with a private tutor; and in Italy, Laura Bassi became the first woman to teach in a European university, at Bologna. In the Netherlands, women founded a scientific academy in 1785. However, these were isolated waves in a sea of largely male and clerical indifference.

Generally, Protestant countries were better at ensuring basic literacy and numeracy for boys and probably also for girls. Lutheran Prussia and Presbyterian Scotland excelled in the field of education, but for very different reasons. In Prussia, Frederick the Great decreed universal public education for boys as part of his effort to surpass the level of technical expertise found in other countries. His educational policy was another example of his using the Enlightenment to increase the power of the central government. In Scotland, improvements in education were sponsored mainly by the established Presbyterian (Calvinist) church. The Protestant universities were by and large more progressive intellectually than their Catholic counterparts. The Jesuits, for instance, resisted teaching the new science. By contrast, medicine at the universities of Edinburgh—along with medicine at the University of Leiden in the Netherlands—became the most advanced of the century. But ironically, the universities were never at the forefront of the Enlightenment. For the latest ideas, one went to the salons and not the professors.

That fact fitted in very well with Locke's doctrine that knowledge comes primarily through experience. Rousseau took it up and brought it to its logical conclusion. In *Émile* (1762), he argued that individuals learn from nature, from people, or from things. Indeed, Rousseau wanted the early years of a child's education to be centered on developing the senses and not spent with the child chained to a schoolroom desk. Later, attention would be paid to intellectual pursuits, and then finally to morality. Rousseau grasped a fundamental principle of modern psychology: the child is not a small adult, and childhood is not merely preparation for adulthood but a particular stage in human development with its own distinguishing characteristics.

Rousseau appealed especially to women to be virtuous and to protect their children from social convention, that is, to teach their children about honesty and sentiment. There were problems with Rousseau's educational system. He would make the family the major educational force, and he wanted the products of such education to be cosmopolitan and enlightened individuals, singularly free from superstition and prejudice. However, women (whom Rousseau would confine to the home) were to bear the burden of instilling enlightenment, although they had little experience of the world beyond the family, and in France their education was entirely in the hands of nuns.

Rousseau's contradictions, particularly about women, sprang in large measure from his desperate search for an alternative to aristocratic mores

and clerical authority. He also shared in the gender bias of his age, although what may seem bias to us may also have reflected his belief that women sought the home as a solace and refuge. Certainly, many women read him critically, but essentially as an ally and defender.

Humanitarianism

Crime and Punishment.   No society founded on the principles of the Enlightenment may condone the torture of prisoners and the inhumanity of a corrupt legal system. On those points, all the philosophes were clear, and they had plenty of evidence from their own societies on which to base their condemnation of torture and the inhumanity of the criminal justice system.

Whether an individual was imprisoned for unpaid debts or for banditry or murder, prison conditions differed little. Prisoners were often starved or exposed to disease, or both. In many Continental countries, where torture was still legal, prisoners could be subjected to brutal interrogation or to random punishment. In 1777, English reformer John Howard published a report in England and Wales that documented how prisoners went without food or medical assistance.

It was the reformers of the Enlightenment who began to agitate against the prison conditions of the day. Even if torture was illegal, as was the case only in England, prison conditions were often as harmful as torture to the physical and mental health of inmates. Conditions still present in some prisons and detention centers today would have been intolerable to the philosophe-reformers.

Although there is something particularly reprehensible about the torturer, his skills were consciously applauded in many countries during the eighteenth century. Fittingly, the most powerful critique of the European system of punishment came from Italy, where the Inquisition and its torture chambers had reigned with little opposition for centuries. In Milan, during the early 1760s, the Enlightenment had made very gradual inroads, and in a small circle of reformers, the methods of torture employed by the Inquisition and the relationship between church and state in the matter of criminal justice were avidly discussed.

THE INQUISITION. In one of the first histories of all the world's religions (published in 1723), the engraver Bernard Picart depicted the Inquisition as cold and ruthlessly interrogating (top panel), then as barbarous in its use of torture; at the bottom center is the practice of waterboarding. (Bibliotheque des Arts Decoratifs, Paris, France/Archives Charmet/The Bridgeman Art Library International.)

Out of Milanese intellectual ferment came one of the most important books of the Enlightenment: *Of Crime and Punishment* (1764), by Cesare Beccaria (1738–1794). For centuries, sin and crime had been wedded in the eyes of the church; the function of the state was to punish crime because it was a manifestation of sin. Beccaria cut through that thicket of moralizing. He argued that the church should concern itself with sin and should abandon its prisons and courts. Instead, the state should concern itself with crimes against society, and the purpose of punishment should be to reintegrate the individual into society. Punishment should be swift but intended to rehabilitate.

Beccaria also inquired into the causes of crime. Abandoning the concept of sin, Beccaria—rather like Rousseau, who perceived injustice and corruption in the very fabric of society—regarded private property as the root of social injustice and hence the root of crime. Pointedly, he asked, "What are these laws I must respect, that they leave such a huge gap between me and the rich? Who made these laws? Rich and powerful men. . . . Let us break these fatal connections. . . . Let us attack injustice at its source."[7]

Beccaria's attackers labeled him a *socialist*—the first time (1765) that term was used—by which they meant that Beccaria paid attention only to people as social creatures and that he wanted a society of free and equal citizens. In contrast, the defenders of the use of torture and capital punishment, and of the necessity of social inequality, argued that Beccaria's teachings would lead to chaos and to the loss of all property rights and legitimate authority. These critics sensed the utopian aspect of Beccaria's thought. His humanitarianism was not directed toward the reform of the criminal justice system alone; he sought to restructure society in such a way as to render crime far less prevalent and, whenever possible, to reeducate its perpetrators.

When Beccaria's book and then the author himself turned up in Paris, the philosophes greeted them with universal acclaim. All the leaders of the period—Voltaire, Rousseau, Denis Diderot, and the atheist d'Holbach—embraced one or another of Beccaria's views. But if the criminal justice system and the schools were subject to scrutiny by enlightened critics, what did the philosophes have to say about slavery, the most pernicious of all Western institutions?

Slavery. On both sides of the Atlantic during the eighteenth century, criticism of slavery was growing. At first, it came from religious thinkers such as the Quakers, whose own religious version of the Enlightenment predated the Europe-wide phenomenon by several decades. The Quakers were born out of the turmoil of the English Revolution, and their strong adherence to democratic ideas grew out of their conviction that the light of God's truth works in every man and woman.

Many philosophes on both sides of the Atlantic knew Quaker thought, and Voltaire, who had mixed feelings about slavery, and Benjamin Franklin, who condemned it, admired the Quakers and their principles.

On the problem of slavery, some philosophes were strangely ambivalent. In an ideal world—just about all agreed—slavery would not exist. But the world was not ideal, and given human wickedness, greed, and lust for power, Voltaire thought that both slavery and exploitation might be inevitable. "The human race," Voltaire wrote in his *Philosophical Dictionary* (1764), "constituted as it is, cannot subsist unless there be an infinite number of useful individuals possessed of no property at all."[8] Diderot thought that slavery was probably immoral but concluded that, given the importance of slavery in the colonies and the fact that the French monarchy provided no leadership in changing the situation, there was no point in trying to abolish slavery at the time. Indeed, not until 1794, and only after agonized debate, did the French government, no longer a monarchy, finally abolish slavery in its colonies.

It must be remembered that political thinkers of the Enlightenment, among them Locke (who condoned slavery) and Montesquieu (whose ideas were used to condone it), rejected God-given political authority and argued for the rights of property holders and for social utility as the foundations of good government. Those criteria, property and utility, played right into the hands of the proslavery apologists. Montesquieu condemned slavery, but that did not stop its apologists from using his ideas about the relationship between hot climates and sloth to justify enslaving Africans. Even radicals inspired by the French Revolution, such as the British manufacturer Thomas Cooper, could emigrate to the Carolinas and become slave owners and apologists for the system.

Yet if the principle held, as so many philosophes argued, that human happiness was the greatest good, how could slavery be justified? In his short novel *Candide,* Voltaire has his title character confront the spectacle of a young African slave who has had his leg and arm cut off merely because it is the custom of a country. Candide's philosophical optimism is shattered as he reflects on the human price paid by this slave, who harvested the sugar that Europeans enjoyed so abundantly. Throughout the eighteenth century, the emphasis that the Enlightenment placed on moral sensibility produced a literature that used shock to emphasize over and over again, and with genuine revulsion, the inhumanity of slavery.

By the second half of the century, a new generation of philosophes launched bitter attacks on slavery. With Rousseau in the vanguard, they condemned slavery as a violation of the natural rights of man. The philosophes invented the concept of *human rights*. In a volume issued in 1755, the great *Encyclopedia* of the Enlightenment, edited by Diderot, condemned slavery in no uncertain terms: "There is not a single one of these hapless souls . . . who does not have the right to be declared free . . . since neither his ruler nor his father nor anyone else had the right to dispose of his freedom."[9] That statement appeared in thousands of copies and various editions of an encyclopedia that was probably the most influential publication resulting from the French Enlightenment. Indeed, French writers led the enlightened attacks on slavery. The Dutch novelist Betje Wolff had to translate French writers when, in 1790, she launched her attack on the Dutch slave trade.

These writers put the followers of the Enlightenment in the antislavery camp. But that victory was clouded by ambiguous language coming straight from the pens of some of Europe's supposedly most enlightened thinkers and by their prejudice against blacks as non-Europeans.

Social Equality. The humanitarian impulse inevitably entailed taking a cold, hard look at social inequalities, which were very obvious in a century when dress, speech, body gestures, and even smell told all. The poor were visibly underfed; workers wore the costumes of their trade; aristocrats, both men and women, dressed in elaborate wigs, shoes, silks, jewels, and lace. Devout Calvinist women often wore black, and only their rings or headpieces betrayed their social status. How could the ideal of human equality be conceptualized in such a society?

Voltaire despised the lower classes. Kant said that women should feel and not reason: "her philosophy is not to reason, but to sense."[10] Women had few property rights, and the poor had even fewer; the Lockean contract seemed irrelevant to their circumstances. Yet in the American and French revolutions, the leaders proclaimed human

A Dutch Jewish Family Preparing for a Feast. Nothing makes the religious toleration advocated by enlightened critics more real than this portrait of a Jewish family in Amsterdam preparing for a religious feast day. They are made to resemble the Dutch in dress and interior design. In short they are being humanized, in contrast to the many anti-Semitic images to be seen in Europe well into the eighteenth century and beyond. (The Art Archive/Galerie Saphir Paris/Gianni Dagli Orti.)

equality as an ideal. But even though France freed the slaves in the colonies, the Jacobins closed down women's political clubs. In the new American republic, women began to take a more active role in civil society; slavery, however, remained (in every northern state, though, it was abolished by 1804). Modern critics condemn the Enlightenment for being inconsistent, but historical reality can be understood only in relation to the backward alternatives offered by absolute monarchs and established churches.

More than any other previous historical movement, the Enlightenment put human equality on the mental agenda of Western societies. Men and women could meet as equals at social gatherings, the new novels could depict the suffering of women at the hands of brutal men or describe the wretched life of the poor, women could travel abroad as never before, and traveling scientific lecturers frequently sought their tuition. Leisure, literacy, public and secular culture, fiery journalism, local newspapers, travelers' reports, even the new and naughty pornography—all attacked the superstitions and contradictions that centuries of custom had enshrined. The new science pointed to a universe where matter was everywhere the same—atoms are all equal—and it universally obeyed impersonal and impartial laws. The struggle to achieve democratic equality—the dilemma of modern life—first came to the surface in countless acts of reading and conversing in the new enlightened and urban culture. It continues to this day.

ECONOMIC THOUGHT

The Enlightenment's emphasis on property as the foundation for individual rights and its search for uniform laws inspired by Newton's scientific achievement led to the development of the science of economics. Appropriately, that intellectual achievement occurred in the most advanced capitalistic nation in Europe, Great Britain. Not only were the British in the vanguard of capitalist expansion, but by the third quarter of the eighteenth century, that expansion had started the Industrial Revolution. Britain's new factories and markets for the manufacture and distribution of goods provided a natural laboratory where theorists schooled in the Enlightenment's insistence on observation and experimentation could watch the ebb and flow of capitalist production and distribution. In contrast to its harsh criticisms of existing institutions and old elites, the Enlightenment on the whole approved of the independent businessman—the entrepreneur. And there was no one more approving than Adam Smith (1732–1790), whose *Wealth of Nations* (1776) became a kind of bible for those who regarded capitalist activity as uniformly worthwhile and never to be inhibited by outside regulation.

Throughout the seventeenth century in England, there had been a long tradition of economic thought. The resulting ideology stressed independent initiative and the freedom of market forces to determine the value of money and the goods it can buy. By 1700, English economic thought was already well ahead of what could be found on the Continent, with the exception of some Dutch writings. That sophistication undoubtedly reflected the complexity of market life in cities such as London and Amsterdam.

One important element in seventeenth-century economic thought, as well as in the most advanced

thinking on ethics, was the role of self-interest. Far from being considered crude or socially dangerous, it was seen as a good thing to be cautiously accepted. In the mid-seventeenth century, Hobbes took the view that self-interest lay at the root of political action. By the end of the century, Locke argued that government, rather than primarily restraining the extremes of human greed and the search for power, should promote the interests of its citizens. By the middle of the eighteenth century, enlightened theorists all over Europe—especially in England, Scotland, and France—had decided that self-interest was the foundation of all human actions and that at every turn government should aid people in expressing their interests and thus in finding true happiness.

Of course, in the area of economic life, government had for centuries regulated most aspects of the market. The classic economic theory behind such regulation was mercantilism. Mercantilists believed that a constant shortage of riches—bullion, goods, whatever—existed and that governments must direct economic activity in their states so as to compete successfully with other nations for a share of the world's scarce resources.

It required faith in the inherent usefulness of self-interest to assert that government should cease regulating economic activity and that the market should be allowed to be free. The doctrine of **laissez faire**—leaving the market to its own devices—was the centerpiece of Adam Smith's massive economic study on the origins of the wealth of nations.

As a professor in Glasgow, Scotland, Smith actually went to factories to observe the work. He was one of the first theorists to see the importance of the division of labor in making possible the manufacture of more and cheaper consumer goods. Smith viewed labor as the critical factor in a capitalist economy: the value of money, or of an individual for that matter, rested on the ability to buy labor or the byproducts of labor, namely goods and services. According to *The Wealth of Nations*, "labor is the real measure of the exchangeable value of all commodities."[11] The value of labor is in turn determined by market forces, by supply and demand. Before the invention of money or capital, labor belonged to the laborer, but in the money and market society, which had evolved since the Middle Ages, labor belonged to the highest bidder.

Smith was not bothered by the apparent randomness of market forces, although he was distressed by signs of greed and exploitation. Beneath the superficial chaos of commerce, he saw order—the same order that he saw in physical nature through his understanding of the new science. He used the metaphor of "the invisible hand" to explain the source of this order; by that he probably meant Newton's regulatory God, made very distant by Smith, who was a deist. That hand would invisibly reconcile self-interest to the common or public interest. With the image of the invisible hand, Smith expressed his faith in the rationality of commercial society and laid the first principle for the modern science of capitalist economics. He did not mean to license the oppression of the poor and the laborer. Statements in *The Wealth of Nations* such as "Landlords, like all other men, love to reap where they never sowed" or "Whenever there is great property, there is great inequality"[12] reveal Smith to be a moralist. Yet he knew of no means to stop the exploitation of labor. He believed that its purchase at market value ensured the working of commercial society, and he assumed that the supply of cheap labor was inexhaustible.

For all their differences, Smith and the French physiocrats shared certain characteristics common to enlightened economic theorists. Smith wanted to find the laws that regulated economic life; in that search, these economic theorists imitated the successes of the new science. In addition, they believed that progress was possible and that wealth and well-being could be increased for all. Knowledge is progressive; hence, by implication, the human condition also yields to constant improvement. This vision sometimes made the advocates of laissez faire myopic when it came to poverty and the injustice of the market. What they bequeathed to the modern age was a belief in the inevitability of progress wedded to capitalism and free trade—a belief that remains powerful to this day.

THE HIGH ENLIGHTENMENT

More than any other political system in Western Europe, the Old Regime in France was directly threatened by the doctrines and reforming impulse of the Enlightenment. The Roman Catholic Church was deeply entrenched in every aspect of life: landownership, control over the universities and the presses, and access to both the court and, through the pulpit, the people. For decades, the church had brought its influence to bear against the philosophes, yet by 1750, the Enlightenment had penetrated learned circles and academies in Paris and the provinces. After 1750, censorship of the press was relaxed by a new censor deeply influenced by Enlightenment ideals. In fact, censorship had produced the opposite of the desired effect: the more irreligious and atheistic the book or manuscript, the more attractive and sought after it became.

By the 1740s, the fashion among proponents of the Enlightenment was to seek an encyclopedic format for presenting their ideas. After Bayle's *Dictionary,* the first successful encyclopedia was published in England by Ephraim Chambers in 1728, and before too long, a plan was under way for its translation into French. A leading Freemason in France, the chevalier Ramsay, advocated that all the Masonic lodges in Europe should make a financial contribution to this effort, but few, if any, responded to the call.

Four aggressive Parisian publishers took up the task of producing the encyclopedia. One of them had had some shady dealings in clandestine literature, which had acquainted him with the more irreligious and daring philosophes in Paris. Hence, he knew the young Denis Diderot (1713–1784), who had spent six months in jail for his philosophical and pornographic writings. Out of that consortium of publishers and philosophes came the most important book of the Enlightenment, Diderot's *Encyclopedia.* Published in 1751 and in succeeding years and editions, the *Encyclopedia* initiated a new stage in the history of Enlightenment publishing. In the process, it brought to the forefront heretical ideas, which, until that time, only the most radical freethinkers in England and the Netherlands had openly written about. The new era thus ushered in, called the *High Enlightenment,* was characterized by a violent attack on the church's privileges and the very foundations of Christian belief. From the 1750s to the 1780s, Paris shone as the capital of the Enlightenment. The philosophes were no longer a persecuted minority. Instead, they became cultural heroes.

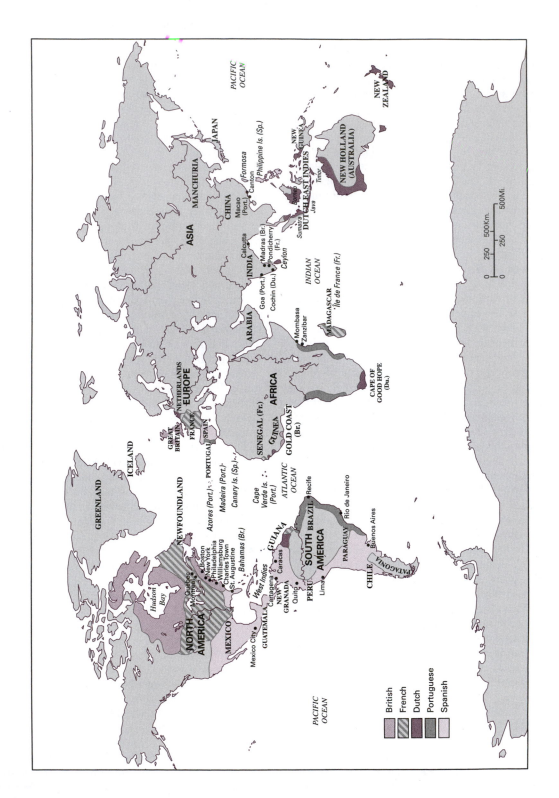

PACIFIC OCEAN

NEW ZEALAND

JAPAN

MANCHURIA

CHINA

ASIA

Formosa

Macao (Port.)
Canton

Philippine Is. (Sp.)

NEW GUINEA

DUTCH EAST INDIES

NEW HOLLAND (AUSTRALIA)

Borneo

Timor

Java

Sumatra

Calcutta

Madras (Br.)
Pondicherry (Fr.)

INDIA

Ceylon

Goa (Port.)

Cochin (Du.)

INDIAN OCEAN

île de France (Fr.)

ARABIA

MADAGASCAR

Mombasa

Zanzibar

CAPE OF GOOD HOPE (Du.)

NETHERLANDS

EUROPE

AFRICA

GREAT BRITAIN

FRANCE

SPAIN

PORTUGAL

SENEGAL (Fr.)

GUINEA

GOLD COAST (Br.)

ICELAND

GREENLAND

Azores (Port.)

Madeira (Port.)

Canary Is. (Sp.)

Cape Verde Is. (Port.)

ATLANTIC OCEAN

Recife

Rio de Janeiro

NEWFOUNDLAND

BRAZIL

SOUTH AMERICA

GUIANA

PARAGUAY

Buenos Aires

NORTH AMERICA

Hudson Bay

Quebec
Montreal
Boston
New York
Philadelphia
Williamsburg
Charles Town
St. Augustine

Bahamas (Br.)

West Indies

Cartagena

Caracas

NEW GRANADA

Quito

PERU

Lima

CHILE

PATAGONIA

MEXICO

GUATEMALA

Mexico City

PACIFIC OCEAN

500 Mi.

500 Km.

250

250

0

British

French

Dutch

Portuguese

Spanish

440

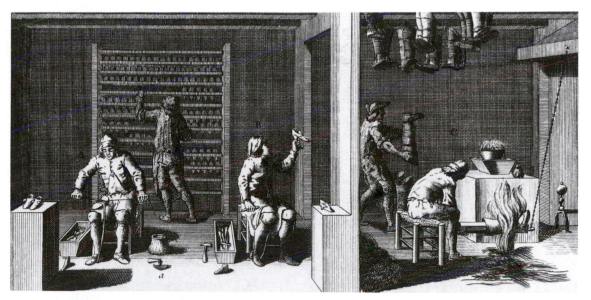

Diderot and Artisans. There are many extraordinary aspects of Diderot's great *Encyclopedia*. Among the most noted are the quality and precision of the engravings that depict workers at their crafts. To this day, the volumes remain important sources for knowledge about every craft of the age. (© Bettmann/Corbis.)

The *Encyclopedia* had to be read by anyone claiming to be educated.

In his preface to the *Encyclopedia*, Diderot's collaborator, Jean d'Alembert (c. 1717–1783), summed up the principles on which it had been compiled. In effect, he wrote a powerful summation of the Enlightenment's highest ideals. He also extolled Newton's science and gave a short description of its universal laws. The progress of geometry and mechanics in combination, d'Alembert wrote in his preface, "may be considered the most incontestable monument of the success to which the human mind can rise by its efforts."[13] In turn, he urged that revealed religion be reduced to a few precepts to be practiced; religion should, he implied, be made scientific and rational. The *Encyclopedia* itself explicitly followed Francis Bacon's admonition that the scientist should be first of all a collector of facts; in addition, it gave dozens of examples of useful new mechanical devices.

D'Alembert in the preface also praised the epistemology of Locke: all that is known is known through the senses. He declared that all learning should be catalogued and readily available, that the printing press should enlighten, and that literary societies should encourage men of talent. These societies, he added, "should banish all inequalities that might exclude or discourage men who are endowed with talents that will enlighten others."[14]

During the High Enlightenment, reformers dwelled increasingly on the Old Regime's inequalities, which seemed to stifle men of talent. The aristocracy and the clergy were not always talented, and seldom were they agitators for enlightenment and reform. Their privileges seemed increasingly less rational. By the 1780s, Paris had produced a new generation of philosophes, for whom Voltaire, Diderot, and Rousseau were aged or dead heroes. But these young authors found the life of the propagandist to be poor and solitary, and they looked at society's ills as victims rather than as

◀ *Map 18.1* **European Expansion, 1715**
Globalization as a process began in the eighteenth century with European trade, exploration, and colonization. (Copyright © 2013 Cengage Learning.)

reformers. They gained firsthand knowledge of the injustices catalogued so brilliantly by Rousseau in *The Social Contract*.

The High Enlightenment's systematic, sustained, and occasionally violent attacks on the clergy and the irrationality of privilege link that movement with the French Revolution. The link did not lie in the comfortable heresies of the great philosophes, ensconced as they were in the fashionable Parisian salons. Rather, it was to be found in the way those heresies were interpreted by a new generation of reformers—Marat and Robespierre among them—who in the early days of the Revolution used the Enlightenment as a mirror on which they reflected the evils of the old order.

EUROPEAN POLITICAL AND DIPLOMATIC DEVELOPMENTS

Warfare

The dreams of the philosophes seemed unable to forestall imperial developments in power politics, war, and diplomacy. The century was dominated by two areas of extreme conflict: Anglo-French rivalry over control of territory in the New World and hegemony in northern Europe; and intense rivalry between Austria and Prussia over control of Central Europe. These major powers, with their imperialistic ambitions, were led by cadres of aristocratic ministers or generals. The Enlightenment did little to displace the warmaking role that had belonged to the aristocracy since the Middle Ages. In Berlin, some philosophes enjoyed the brilliance of court life and turned a blind eye to Prussian militarism.

France and England were the great rivals in the New World, although colonization had been well under way since the early sixteenth century. Spain had been the first sovereign state to establish an empire in America; located principally in South America and Central America, this empire was based on mining gold and silver, trade, and slaves. The English and the Dutch had followed, first as settlers and then also as slave traders, but their colonies lay to the north—in Virginia, New Amsterdam (later to become New York), and New England. Farther north, the French explored and exploited Canada and the region now known as the midwestern United States.

Early in the eighteenth century, the Dutch and the Spanish had largely dropped out of the race for colonies in North America, leaving the field to the French and the English.

By the middle of the eighteenth century, the rivalry of these two powers for territory in the New World increased tension in the Old World. Earlier, the British had sought to contain the French colossus and to ensure their historic trading interests in the Low Countries and the Rhineland by allying themselves with the Dutch Republic and the Austrians, who controlled what is today called Belgium. The alliance of the Maritime Powers (Britain and the Netherlands) with Austria tilted the balance of power against France for the entire first half of the eighteenth century.

Meanwhile, Prussia under Frederick the Great was entering the ranks of the major powers. In 1740, Frederick launched an aggressive foreign policy against neighboring states and ruthlessly seized the Austrian province of Silesia. The forces of the new Austrian queen, Maria Theresa, were powerless to resist this kind of military onslaught. Silesia augmented the Prussian population by 50 percent. The Austrians never forgave his transgression.

In 1756, Maria Theresa formed an alliance with France against Prussia; the ensuing Seven Years' War (1756–1763) involved every major European power. Austria's alliance with France in 1756, which ended the historic rivalry between France and the House of Hapsburg, is known as the *diplomatic revolution*. The Austrians had grown to fear Prussia in the north more than they feared the French. From the Austrian point of view, Prussia had stolen Silesia in 1740, and regaining it was more important than preserving historic rivalries with France. On the French side, King Louis XV longed for an alliance with a Roman Catholic power and for peace in Europe so that France would be better able to wage war against Britain in the New World.

For their part, the British sought an ally in the newer, stronger Prussia and reneged on their traditional ally, Austria. Frederick the Great stood at the head of a new state that was highly belligerent yet insecure, for all the European powers had reasons to want to keep Prussia weak and small. The Seven Years' War—which seesawed between the opponents, with French, Austrian, and Russian forces ranged against Frederick's Prussians—changed things little in Europe but did reveal the extraordinary power of the Prussian war machine. Only gradually did Prussia join the ranks of the Great Powers, as did Russia.

Hostilities in North America tipped the balance of power there in favor of the English. From 1754 to 1763, the French and the English fought over their claims in the New World. England's victory in this conflict—which was also part of the Seven Years' War—led ultimately to the American Revolution. England secured its claim to control the colonies of the eastern seaboard, a market that would enrich its industrialists of the next generation enormously—though, from the colonists' point of view, unjustly. The French, having been pushed out of North America, tried without success to establish a colony in Guyana; thousands recruited by the French ministry died as a result of mismanagement and disease.

While the major Western European powers were growing stronger, some Eastern European countries were falling further under the domination of the Ottoman (Turkish) Empire as the result of warfare. Only Hungary decidedly benefited from the wars led by Austria against the Turks. With its new independence finally secured from the Turks in 1718, Hungary, now part of the Austrian Empire, entered an era of peace and enlightenment.

Empires and nation-states were the beneficiaries of eighteenth-century war and diplomacy. Only in the Dutch Republic did a little-noticed revolution in 1747 and 1748 provide any indication that the Great Powers or the merchant capitalists had anything to fear from their home populations. The Dutch Revolution was led by men who identified with the Enlightenment and who wanted to reform the institutions of government. Inspired by the restoration of the House of Orange, Amsterdam rose in a democratic rebellion headed by a coalition of small merchants and minor philosophes. In 1748, they failed to effect any meaningful changes, but the calls they made for reform and renewal would be heard again in Amsterdam in 1787 and in Paris in 1789. On the latter occasion, the world would listen. For most of the eighteenth century, however, warfare seemed only to confirm the internal security and stability of the ruling monarchs and elites controlling most European states.

Enlightened Despotism

Enlightened despotism, an apparent contradiction in terms, was a phrase used by the French philosophe Diderot as early as the 1760s. Wherever the philosophes used this term, it referred to an ideal shared by many of them: the strong monarch who would implement rational reforms, removing obstacles to freedom, ending book censorship, and allowing the laws of nature to work, particularly in trade and commerce. When historians use the term *enlightened despotism,* they generally are describing the reigns of specific European monarchs and their ministers: Frederick the Great in Prussia; Catherine the Great in Russia; Charles III in Spain; Maria Theresa and, to a greater extent, her son Joseph II in Austria; and Louis XV in France.

These eighteenth-century monarchs instituted specific reforms in education, trade, and commerce and against the clergy. This type of enlightened government must be understood in context: these countries developed late relative to the older states of Europe. Prussia, Austria, and Russia had to move very quickly if they were to catch up to the degree of centralization achieved in England and France. And when monarchies in France and Spain also occasionally adopted techniques associated with enlightened despotism, they generally did so to compete against a more advanced rival—for example, France against England or Spain against France.

Austria. In the course of the eighteenth century, Austria became a major centralized state through the administrative reforms of Charles VI and his successors. Though Catholic and devout at home, Charles allied himself abroad with Protestant Europe against France. In the newly acquired Austrian Netherlands, he supported the progressive and reforming elements in the nobility, which opposed the old aristocracy and clergy. His daughter Maria Theresa (1740–1780) continued this pattern, and the Austrian administration became one of the most innovative and progressive on the Continent. Many of its leading ministers—such as the Comte du Cobenzl in the Netherlands or Gerard van Swieten, Joseph II's great reforming minister—were Freemasons. This movement often attracted progressive Catholics (as well as Protestants and freethinkers), who despised what they regarded as the medieval outlook of the traditional clergy.

Dynastic consolidation and warfare did contribute decisively to the creation of the Austrian state. But in the eighteenth century, the intellectual and cultural forces of the Enlightenment enabled the state to establish an efficient system of government and a European breadth of vision. With these attributes, Austria came to rival (and, in regard to Spain, surpass) older, more established states in Europe. Frustrated in their German territories, the Austrian Hapsburgs concentrated their attention increasingly on their eastern states. Vienna gave them a natural power base, and Catholic religiosity gradually united the ruling elites in Bohemia and Hungary with their Hapsburg kings. Hapsburg power created a dynastic state in Austria, yet all efforts to consolidate the German part of the empire and to establish effective imperial rule met with failure. Also problematic were Joseph II's interventions in the southern Netherlands. He offended the clergy without winning liberal support. Revolution erupted in Brussels in 1787.

Prussia.   German unification proceeded very slowly, and even enlightened despotism could not achieve it. Under the most famous and enlightened Hohenzollerns of the eighteenth century, Prussian absolutism acquired some unique and resilient features. Frederick II, the Great (1740–1786), pursued a policy of religious toleration and, in so doing, attracted French Protestant refugees who had manufacturing and commercial skills. Intellectual dissidents such as Voltaire also were attracted to Prussia. Voltaire eventually went home disillusioned with this new Prussian "enlightened despotism," but not before Frederick had used him and in the process acquired a reputation for learning. By inviting various refugees from French clerical oppression, Frederick gave Berlin a minor reputation as a center for Enlightenment culture. But alongside Frederick's courtship of the French philosophes, with their enlightened ideals, there remained the reality of Prussia's militarism and the serfdom of its peasants.

Enlightened despotism was, in reality, the use of Enlightenment principles by monarchs to enhance the central government's power and thereby their own. These eighteenth-century monarchs knew, in ways their predecessors had not, that knowledge is power; they saw that application of learned theories to policy can produce useful results.

But did these enlightened despots try to create more humanitarian societies in which individual freedom would flourish on all levels? In this area, enlightened despotism must be pronounced a shallow deployment of Enlightenment ideals. For example, Frederick the Great decreed the abolition of serfdom in Prussia, but he had no means to force the aristocracy to conform because he desperately needed their support. In the 1780s, Joseph II instituted liberalized publishing laws in Austria; but when artisans began reading pamphlets about the French Revolution, the state quickly retreated and reimposed censorship. In the 1750s, Frederick the Great too had loosened the censorship laws, and writers were free to attack traditional religion; however, they were never allowed to criticize the army, the key to Frederick's aggressive foreign policy. Although Catherine the Great gave Diderot a pension, she would hear of nothing that compromised her political power, and her ministers were expected to give her unquestioning service.

Finally, if the Enlightenment means the endorsement of reason over force, and peace and cosmopolitan unity over ruthless competition, then the foreign policies of these enlightened despots were uniformly despotic. There were no major philosophes who did not grow disillusioned with enlightened monarchs on the rare occasions when their actions could be observed at close range.

THE ENLIGHTENMENT IN EASTERN EUROPE

The impact of the Enlightenment in the countries of Eastern Europe varied enormously. Where it made greatest inroads, we see the subsequent

Map 18.2 Europe, 1789 ▶
The Hapsburgs had vast holdings, and this situation did not make the other German states feel secure. This entire map would change after 1800 as Napoleon swept through Europe.
(Copyright © 2013 Cengage Learning.)

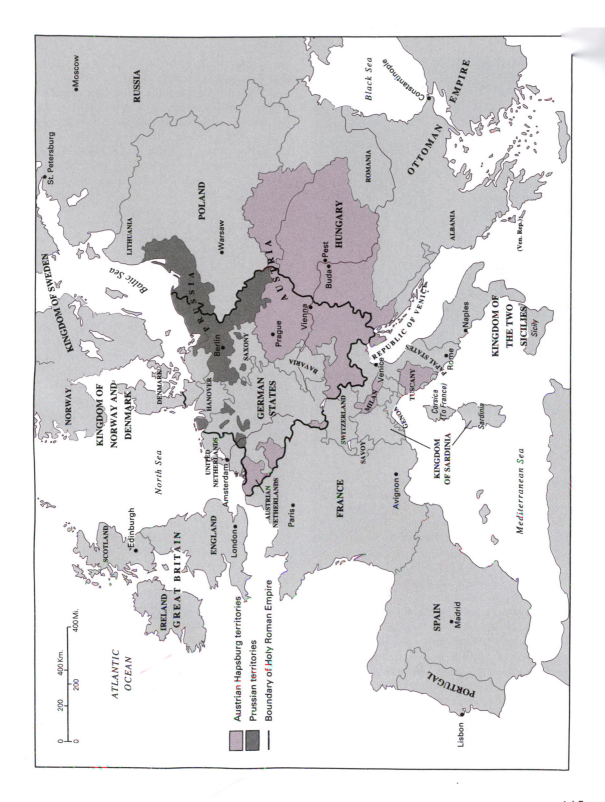

CATHERINE THE GREAT. Catherine the Great adorned herself to show her aristocracy that she was its superior. (Photo by Popperfoto/Getty Images.)

emergence of discernibly modern social and political ideas and aspirations. In Hungary, for example, independence from the Ottoman Empire in 1718 left a country that was still essentially feudal yet eager for reform and renewal. In the 1720s, peace brought regeneration. The population doubled in the course of the eighteenth century, agricultural techniques markedly improved, and by midcentury schools and universities had begun to teach the new science. Hungarian Protestants who had traveled and studied abroad came home with the ideas of the philosophes. A lay intelligentsia was created, and with it came new literature and drama, as well as Western-style civil society: lodges, salons, clubs, and societies. By 1790, the Enlightenment and the French Revolution had inspired a movement for Hungarian nationalism and against the control of the Austrians and Hapsburgs. Then, in 1795, its leaders were executed. However, their nationalistic ideals survived well into the nineteenth and twentieth centuries.

In Poland and Lithuania, the Jesuits remained strong even after they were expelled from other Eastern European countries, such as Hungary. In Poland, the Catholic clergy continued to control education, and the Enlightenment remained a deeply censored, almost underground movement. Yet it did exist and influence educational reform, especially after the expulsion of the Jesuits in 1773. Those who advocated the Enlightenment allied themselves with the monarchy, which they saw as the only force that might be strong enough to oppose the entrenched clergy and aristocracy. The power of the Polish nobility had dire historical consequences for the country. No central authority emerged in eighteenth-century Poland comparable in its unifying ability to the monarchs of Prussia, Austria, and Russia. Not once but three times, in 1772, 1793, and 1795, Poland was partitioned by these three potent neighbors, who took portions of it. Some Poles resisted; a Polish nobleman even appealed to Rousseau in 1771 to help draft a constitution for his beleaguered country. The document in which Rousseau expressed his thoughts on Polish government was cautious and judicious, giving power to all the various elements within Polish elite society. The last partition of Poland wiped it off the map of Europe for more than a hundred years.

The failure of the Enlightenment to take hold in parts of Eastern Europe had far-reaching consequences, with which the people of those countries continue to grapple. In the 1990s, those countries that had experienced the Enlightenment—such as Hungary and the Czech Republic—seemed to show the greatest cohesiveness in the struggle to create a unified, secular, tolerant, and independent state.

THE AMERICAN REVOLUTION

England's victory over France in the Seven Years' War set in motion a train of events that culminated in the American Revolution. The war drained the British treasury, and now Britain faced the additional expense of paying for troops to guard the new North American territories that it had gained in the war. Strapped British taxpayers could not shoulder

THE BOSTON TEA PARTY. The engraver chose to depict free blacks as well as whites applauding one of the early acts that led to the American Revolution. (akg-images.)

the whole burden, so the members of Parliament thought it quite appropriate that American colonists should help pay the bill; they reasoned that Britain had protected the colonists from the French and was still protecting them in their conflicts with Indians. Thus, new colonial taxes and import duties were imposed. Particularly galling to the colonists were the Stamp Act (which placed a tax on newspapers, playing cards, liquor licenses, and legal documents) and the Quartering Act (which required

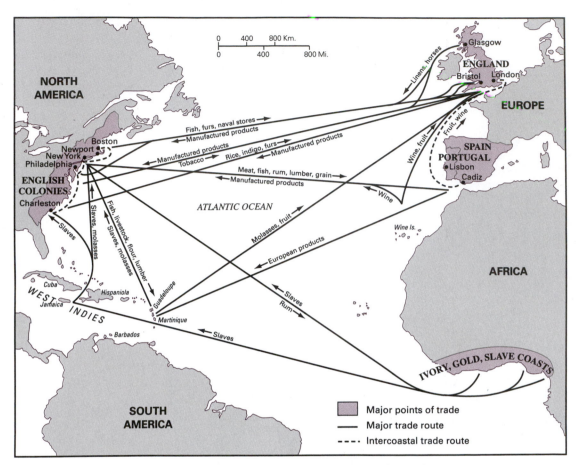

Map 18.3 TRADE ROUTES BETWEEN THE OLD AND NEW WORLDS The trade routes of the eighteenth century foreshadow the globalization of trade with which we are familiar. (Copyright © 2013 Cengage Learning.)

colonists to provide living quarters and supplies to English troops stationed in America).

Vigorous colonial protest against taxation for which no consent had been given compelled the British Parliament to repeal the Stamp Act, but new taxes were imposed, raising the price of many everyday articles, including tea. The stationing of British troops in Boston, the center of rebelliousness, worsened tensions. In March 1770, a crisis ensued after a squad of British soldiers fired into a crowd of Bostonians who had been taunting them and pelting them with rocks and snowballs. Five Bostonians died, and six were wounded. A greater crisis occurred in 1773, when Parliament granted the East India Company exclusive rights to sell tea in America. The colonists regarded this as yet another example of British tyranny. When a crowd of Bostonians dressed as Indians climbed aboard East India Company ships and dumped about ninety thousand pounds of tea overboard, the British responded with a series of repressive measures, which included suppressing self-government in Massachusetts and closing the port of Boston.

The quarrel turned to bloodshed in April and June 1775. On July 4, 1776, delegates from the thirteen colonies adopted the Declaration of Independence, written mainly by the philosophe Thomas Jefferson. Applying Locke's theory of natural rights, this document declared that government derives its power from the consent of the governed, that it is the duty of a government to protect the rights of its citizens, and that people have the right to "alter or abolish" a government that deprives them of their "unalienable rights."

Why were the American colonists so ready to revolt? For one thing, they had brought to North America a highly idealized understanding of English liberties. Long before 1776, they had extended representative institutions to include small property owners who probably could not have voted in England. The colonists had come to expect representative government, trial by jury, and protection from unlawful imprisonment. Each of the thirteen colonies had an elected assembly that acted like a miniature parliament; in these assemblies, Americans gained political experience and quickly learned self-government.

Familiarity with the thought of the Enlightenment and the republican writers of the English Revolution also contributed to the Americans' awareness of liberty. The ideas of the philosophes traversed the Atlantic and influenced educated Americans, particularly Jefferson and Benjamin Franklin. Like other philosophes, American thinkers expressed growing confidence in reason, valued freedom of religion and of thought, and championed the principle of natural rights.

Another source of hostility toward established authority among the American colonists was their religious traditions, particularly Puritanism, which viewed the Bible as infallible and its teachings as a higher law than the law of the state. Like their counterparts in England, American Puritans challenged political and religious authorities who, in their view, contravened God's law. Thus, Puritans acquired two habits that were crucial to the development of political liberty: dissent and resistance. When transferred to the realm of politics, these Puritan tendencies led Americans to resist authority that they considered unjust.

American victory came in 1783 as a result of several factors. George Washington proved to be a superior leader, able to organize and retain the loyalty of his troops. France, seeking to avenge its defeat in the Seven Years' War, helped the Americans with money and provisions, and then in 1778 entered the conflict. Britain had difficulty shipping supplies across three thousand miles of ocean, was fighting the French in the West Indies

and elsewhere at the same time, and ultimately lacked commitment to the struggle.

Reformers in other lands quickly interpreted the American victory as a successful struggle of liberty against tyranny. During the Revolution, the various former colonies drew up constitutions based on the principle of popular sovereignty and included bills of rights that protected individual liberty. They also managed, somewhat reluctantly, to forge a nation. Rejecting both monarchy and hereditary aristocracy, the Constitution of the United States created a republic in which power derived from the people. A system of separation of powers and checks and balances set safeguards against the abuse of power, and the Bill of Rights provided for protection of individual rights. To be sure, the ideals of liberty and equality were not extended to all people. Slaves knew nothing of the freedom that white Americans cherished, and women were denied the vote and equal opportunity; human equality remained an issue throughout the nineteenth and twentieth centuries, as it is today. To reform-minded Europeans, however, it seemed that Americans were fulfilling the promise of the Enlightenment. They were creating a freer and better society.

THE ENLIGHTENMENT AND THE MODERN WORLD

Enlightened thought culminated a trend begun by Renaissance humanists, who attacked medieval otherworldliness and gave value to individual achievement and the worldly life. It was a direct outgrowth of the Scientific Revolution, which provided a new method of inquiry and verification and demonstrated the power and self-sufficiency of the human intellect. If nature were autonomous—that is, if it operated according to natural laws without the need of divine intervention—then the human intellect also could be autonomous. Through its own powers, the mind could uncover the general principles that operate in the social world, as well as in nature.

The philosophes sought to analyze nature, government, religion, law, economics, and education by thinking for themselves, with little reference to Christian teachings, and they rejected completely the claims of clerics to a special wisdom. The philosophes broke decisively with the medieval view that the individual is naturally depraved, that heaven is the true end of life, and that human values and norms derive from a higher reality and are made known through revelation. Instead, they upheld the potential goodness of the individual, regarded the good life on earth as the true purpose of existence, and insisted that individuals could improve themselves and their society by the light of reason.

In addition, the political philosophies of Locke, Montesquieu, and Rousseau rested on an entirely new (and modern) concept of the relationship between the state and the individual: states should exist not simply to accumulate power but also to enhance human happiness. From that perspective, monarchy, and even oligarchy not based on merit, began to seem increasingly less useful. And if happiness is a goal, then it must be assumed that some sort of progress is possible in history.

When we observe societies that have never experienced their own version of enlightenment, oftentimes we see the oppression of women and authoritarian governments, sometimes run by clergymen. Religion can turn to intolerance or even the fanaticism of terrorists if unchecked by questions or doubt.

The philosophes wanted a freer, more humane, and more rational society, but they feared the people and their potential for revolutionary action. As an alternative to revolution, most philosophes offered science as the universal improver of the human condition. Faith in reform without the necessity of revolution proved to be a doctrine for the elite of the salons. In that sense, the French Revolution can be said to have repudiated the essential moderation of philosophes such as Voltaire, d'Alembert, and Kant.

However, the Enlightenment established a vision of humanity so independent of Christianity and so focused on the needs and abuses of the society of the time that no established institution, once grown corrupt and ineffectual, could long withstand its penetrating critique. To that extent, the writings of the philosophes point toward the democratic revolutions of the late eighteenth century. To a lesser extent, the writers of the Enlightenment also point toward ideals that remain strong in most democratic Western societies: human rights in general, religious toleration, freedom from torture, a disdain for prejudice and superstition, a fear of unchecked political authority, and, of course, a belief in the power of the human mind to recognize the irrational and attempt to correct it.

❖   ❖   ❖

NOTES

1. "An Answer to the Question: 'What Is Enlightenment?'" in *Kant's Political Writings*, ed. Hans Reiss (Cambridge: Cambridge University Press, 1970), 54–60.

2. *Wetten van het Natuurkundig Genootschap, door eenige Dames opgericht, binnen Middelburg den 6 August. 1785* (Rules for the Scientific Society established by women within Middelburg on 6 August 1785) (Middelburg, 1785), 29. The only known copy is to be found in the Provincial Library in Zeeland, the Netherlands.

3. Pierre Bayle, *Historical and Critical Dictionary*, ed. Richard H. Popkin (New York: Bobbs-Merrill, 1965), 195.

4. Voltaire, *Philosophical Letters* (New York: Bobbs-Merrill, 1961), 22.

5. Thomas Hobbes, *Leviathan*, ed. C. B. Macpherson (Harmondsworth, England: Penguin, 1977), 189.

6. Jean Jacques Rousseau, *The Social Contract and Discourses* (New York: Dutton, 1950), 3, 9.

7. Quoted in Franco Venturi, *Utopia and Reform in the Enlightenment* (Cambridge: Cambridge University Press, 1971), 101.

8. Voltaire, *Philosophical Dictionary,* ed. Theodore Besterman (Harmondsworth, England: Penguin, 1974), 183.

9. Quoted in David B. Davis, *The Problem of Slavery in Western Culture* (Harmondsworth, England: Penguin, 1970), 449.

10. Immanuel Kant, *Beobachtungen,* in *Kants Werke,* ed. W. Dilthey Wilhelm (1900–1919), 2:230.

11. Adam Smith, *The Wealth of Nations,* ed. George Stigler (New York: Appleton, 1957), 3.

12. Ibid., 98.

13. Jean Le Rond d'Alembert, *Preliminary Discourse to the Encyclopedia of Diderot,* trans. Richard N. Schwab (New York: Bobbs-Merrill, 1963), 22.

14. Ibid., 101–102.

SUGGESTED READING

Armitage, David, *The Declaration of Independence: A Global History* (2007). Discusses the enormous contribution of the Declaration to world history.

Hunt, Lynn, *Inventing Human Rights: A History* (2007). An examination of the contribution of enlightened practices to the invention of the doctrine of human rights.

Hunt, Lynn, Jacob, Margaret, Mijnhardt, Wijnand, *The Book that Changed Europe. Picart and Bernard's Religious Ceremonies of the World* (2010).

Jacob, Margaret, *Strangers Nowhere in the World: The Rise of Cosmopolitanism in Early Modern Europe* (2006). Not a history of an idea but a look at practices that gave rise to cosmopolitan behavior.

Sorkin, David, *The Religious Enlightenment* (2008). An attempt to highlight Christian and Jewish leaders who embraced a version of the Enlightenment not hostile to religious belief.

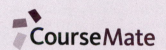

Go to the CourseMate website at **www.cengagebrain.com** for additional study tools and review materials—including audio and video clips—for this chapter.

Index

Note: Page numbers followed by *ph* refer to photographs. Page numbers followed by *m* refer to maps.